Crime and Justice

Crime and Justice

A CASEBOOK APPROACH

Carolyn Boyes-Watson

Suffolk University

Boston | New York | San Francisco
Mexico City | Montreal | Toronto | London | Madrid | Munich | Paris
Hong Kong | Singapore | Tokyo | Cape Town | Sydney

Series Editor: Jennifer Jacobson
Editorial Assistant: Elizabeth Lee
Marketing Manager: Krista Groshong
Production Editor: Anna Socrates
Editorial-Production Service: Omegatype Typography, Inc.
Composition and Prepress Buyer: Linda Cox
Manufacturing Buyer: Andrew Turso
Cover Administrator: Kristina Mose-Libon
Interior Design: Carol Somberg
Photo Researcher: Laurie Frankenthaler, F & F Associates
Electronic Composition: Omegatype Typography, Inc.

For related titles and support material, visit our online catalog at www.ablongman.com.

Between the time Website information is gathered and then published, it is not unusual for some sites to have closed. Also, the transcription of URLs can result in unintended typographical errors. The publisher would appreciate notification where these errors occur so that they may be corrected in subsequent editions.

Library of Congress Cataloging-in-Publication Data

Boyes-Watson, Carolyn.
    Crime and justice : a casebook approach / Carolyn Boyes-Watson.
        p. cm.
    Includes bibliographical references and index.
    ISBN 0-205-29213-5
    1. Criminal justice, Administration of—United States—Case studies.   2. Criminal law—United States—Cases.   I. Title.

HV9950 .B69 2003
364.973—dc21

                                                                    2002025551

Printed in the United States of America
10 9 8 7 6 5 4 3 2 1   07 06 05 04 03 02

This book is dedicated to my husband, Mark,
whose integrity, love, and support is my inspiration and my foundation;
and to my two wonderful children, Emily and Matthew,
who bring light and joy to my life every single day.

CONTENTS

PART ONE
Justice and the Criminal Justice System

CHAPTER 1

Crime, Law, and Justice   1

CASE 1: *A Seventeenth-Century Crime Wave:
The Salem Witch Trials   1*

In the late seventeenth century, twenty-four persons were tried, convicted, and executed for the crime of witchcraft in Salem, Massachusetts. Hundreds more were accused, and many confessed to the crime.

CHAPTER 2

The Struggle for Justice   21

CASE 2: *And Justice for All:
The Scottsboro Trials   21*

During the Depression, nine young black males were charged, tried, and convicted of raping two white women in the South. This case became a symbol of the injustice of the Southern legal system, in which the Constitutional rights of black citizens were routinely denied.

P A R T **TWO**

Enforcing the Law

C H A P T E R 7

Police and the Law   127

CASE 7: *Security or Dignity?*
                   Rosa at the Border   127

A Columbian women traveling by air to the United States,
as a suspected drug smuggler, is subject to a detention
and monitored bowel movement by Customs agents.
The Supreme Court upholds body cavity searches based
on "reasonable suspicion."

C H A P T E R 8

Beyond the Limits of the Law:
Police Culture and the Problem
of Violence   149

CASE 8: *The Thin Blue Line: Rodney King*
                   and the LAPD   149

Rodney King was apprehended after leading the
California Highway Patrol and the Los Angeles Police
Department on a high-speed chase through a section
of South Central Los Angeles. At the scene, a bystander
videotaped LAPD officers using batons, boots, and Tazers
to subdue Mr. King before his arrest. Four officers on
the scene were subsequently charged with the use
of excessive force.

CHAPTER 9

The Mission of Policing in the Twenty-First Century 174

CASE 9: *A Woman in Charge: The Case of Chief Paula Meara* 174

In 1988, Paula Meara won a historic sexual discrimination suit against the Springfield, Massachusetts Police Department in which the court found a workplace climate hostile to women in the nearly all-male police force. In 1994, she was selected as the first woman police chief in a city in New England.

PART**THREE**

The Judicial Process

CHAPTER 10

The Structure of the U.S. Judiciary 195

CASE 10: *The Poor Man in Court: The Case of Clarence Gideon* 195

In 1961, a convicted petty criminal successfully petitioned the U.S. Supreme Court to hear his claim that he had been denied due process of law because he was denied a court-appointed lawyer at his trial.

CHAPTER 11

Players and Plea Bargains in the Courtroom 214

CASE 11: *Bargaining for Justice: Bordenkircher v. Hayes* 214

Paul Hayes was charged with issuing a forged check in 1973. The prosecution offered him a deal in exchange for a guilty plea. When Hayes refused, the prosecutor filed new charges carrying life imprisonment. The case went to trial, and Hayes was convicted and sentenced to life imprisonment.

PART **FOUR**

Corrections and Punishment

C H A P T E R **15**

The Community and Corrections   310

CASE 15: *Circles of Hope: Community Justice in South St. Paul   310*

Darrol Bussler came home one evening to find that his home had been seriously vandalized and destroyed. In the aftermath, Darrol sought a victim–offender mediation with the offenders, which became the start of a community-based alternative sentencing project in the city of Minneapolis.

CASES

PREFACE

Crime and Justice: A Casebook Approach was developed over ten years of teaching introductory courses on criminal justice at a four-year institution. One of the great pleasures of teaching this course is the central importance of justice as a foundation to our lives as human beings. The study of crime and justice is inherently fascinating to students; few topics taught at university elicit such strong opinions rooted in passionate convictions about right and wrong. Because the topics studied in this course are so important, teachers have a powerful opportunity to engage students in critical thinking about the justice system and their own lives.

Teaching an introduction to the criminal justice system, however, poses unique challenges. Because students come to the material with many implicit assumptions, there is a need to stimulate thinking about such fundamental questions as "What is crime?" and "What is justice?" and to encourage students to draw connections between processes within the criminal justice system and structures in the wider society. At the same time, students need to be systematically exposed to an encyclopedic range and volume of information, using material drawn from criminal law, criminology, sociology, anthropology, psychology, forensics, education, philosophy, and political science.

The casebook approach evolved as a hugely successful means to achieve both these objectives in a format that is fun and accessible for the student. Ten years ago, I began to use cases to engage students in lively discussion and active learning, followed by informative lectures providing core knowledge about the system. Students enjoyed the rhythm of the class, warming to their own roles as active participants and appreciating the need to acquire a solid core of knowledge to be better informed about the criminal justice system. I sought a textbook that would combine in-depth case material with explanatory text, but found most casebooks oriented toward the law student. I decided to write a "casebook" to meet the unique pedagogic needs of instructors in the field of criminal justice.

The Structure of the Casebook

Each chapter begins with a case elaborated in five to ten pages, followed by a traditional text about twenty to thirty pages in length. Students read the case and respond to the critical thinking questions for class discussion and analysis. Students also read the accompanying text, which provides background, concepts, and core knowledge about the justice system. Review and study questions are designed to assist students in acquiring the core foundation required for an introductory course on the criminal justice system. Key terms and other resource materials are also provided to assist in acquisition of a comprehensive introduction to the criminal justice system.

The Case Method

I was introduced to the case method while an instructor in sociology at Harvard University in the mid-1980s. The method has long been applied successfully at Harvard Business School, and I was invited to participate in a workshop for teachers within the College of Arts and Sciences. My enthusiasm for this method owes much to the awesome power of the case to compel students to engage with their peers, teachers, and, most important, with their own ideas about the subject matter.

For the student, the case is the "hook." As students become engaged in the dramatic narrative, the critical thinking questions invite students to view the administration of justice through multiple lenses and to raise critical questions about the meaning of justice in a broad sense and in the events connected to their own lives. Abstract issues of law, criminology, political science, sociology, and criminal justice administration come alive as students grapple with the concrete dilemmas raised by each case.

The casebook approach also creates a lively interactive classroom environment based on discussion and dialogue among students and instructors. Students remain focused and interested in the drama of the cases, are better able to apply the concepts, become active participants in the learning process, and have a deeper understanding of the issues presented in lectures and the text. Students enjoy the class because this approach builds on what is of most direct interest to the student: the drama of actual people who are facing, reacting to, and "doing" justice.

The case method is ideal for teaching in the field of criminal justice. *Crime and Justice: A Casebook Approach* offers all the tools instructors need to apply the case method approach to a traditional classroom. Key questions provide the basis for critical analysis of the case. The Instructor's Manual provides detailed suggestions for in-class assignments and exercises such as mock trials, debates, role-plays, and individual and small-group exercises using the case material adaptable to different-size classrooms and pedagogic styles.

The Text

The traditional text portion of each chapter covers the core knowledge required for an overview of the criminal justice system, preparing students for higher-level courses on the justice system. Thematically, the text emphasizes the process of social change within the criminal justice system. Throughout the text, students are encouraged to see the justice system as a "work in progress": the meaning and administration of justice has evolved historically and is continuing to do so as it is influenced by forces within the broader society. Students are encouraged to consider their own roles in shaping the future of the criminal justice system.

All the chapters in the casebook focus on the ongoing struggle for equality before the law for all members of U.S. society. Issues of race, class, and gender inequality are raised through multiple cases emphasizing legal and policy developments that have resulted from various social movements. A second key focus is the evolving role of victims in the criminal justice system. The victim's perspective is highlighted in the explanatory text through several cases that raise the victim's perspective within the criminal justice system. Finally, the emerging field of restorative and community justice is viewed in the context of earlier reforms and public policy debate. The changing role of the criminal justice system in its relationship to the community is explored through multiple lenses within the context of policing, courts, and corrections. Throughout the casebook, students are asked to evaluate and reevaluate their own sense and understanding of justice and the role of the criminal justice system in the future.

An Overview of the Cases

The introductory sequence of the casebook is covered through examination of six cases. The first chapter introduces key ideas about crime, law, and due process. Case 1, A Seventeenth-Century Crime Wave: The Salem Witch Trials, invites students to think about the value of due process in the justice system today. Even though the social order and justice system of the seventeenth century have little in common with the justice system today, the concept of the "witch hunt" remains relevant to the modern context. In this case, students are encouraged to view the familiar rights guaranteed by the Constitution through fresh eyes. Case 2, And Justice for All: The Scottsboro Trials, illustrates the persistent gap between rights enjoyed de jure and the de facto practices of the justice system, given deep inequality within the wider society. The chapter examines the structure of the criminal justice system and illustrates the historical and ongoing political and social forces that seek to achieve equal justice for all citizens.

Chapter 3 looks at the overall justice process and emphasizes the importance of discretion within the system. Case 3, The Spectacle of Criminal Justice: The Case of Willie Horton, tells the complex story of a furloughed prisoner who committed terrible crimes in the midst of a presidential election campaign. This case demonstrates the reality of discretionary decision making in all parts of the criminal justice system, sometimes with disastrous outcomes. It also shows the intensely political nature of criminal justice policy making based on media attention to celebrated cases. Chapter 4 looks at types and measurement of crime. Case 4, The Fall of the Queen of Mean: The Case of Leona Helmsley, tells the story of the prosecution and conviction of Helmsley for tax fraud. Helmsley is hardly the typical criminal, and students rarely think of tax fraud when talking about crime. Using this case to introduce the variety of behaviors that constitute crime invites students to think about the stereotypes we unconsciously bring to the study of crime. This chapter introduces students to all kinds of crime, including those that are hard to measure and those we rarely think about as crime, such as state and political crimes.

Chapter 5 focuses on the principles of criminal law. The shooting death of a Japanese exchange student, Yoshi Hattori, demonstrates the principles of criminal law through a close analysis of the prosecution and defense of Rodney Peairs, who was acquitted at trial. In Case 5, Accident or Homicide? The Shooting of Yoshi Hattori, students are exposed to the nature of legal reasoning in criminal law. This case also raises questions about racism in the application of the law and its pervasive influence in the determination of "reasonableness" in the criminal law. Chapter 6 focuses on the perspective and role of the victim. Case 6, Facing the Demons: Making Amends for Drunk Driving, describes a victim–offender mediation between family members and an offender convicted of vehicular homicide. The case raises questions about the unique needs of victims and their role in the criminal justice process. The chapter examines the victims' rights movement, victimology, and the idea of restorative justice.

Part Two, Enforcing the Law, begins with the case of a Columbian drug mule subject to a body-cavity search in a U.S. airport. Case 7, Security or Dignity? Rosa at the Border, invites students to think about the importance of the Fourth Amendment and the delicate balance between the needs of security and civil liberties. Although Rosa is not a U.S. citizen, students are asked to think about the appropriate powers granted to law enforcement under the U.S. Constitution. The text for Chapter 7 provides an overview of the structure of U.S. law, describing the variety of law enforcement agencies and responsibilities. Chapter 7 also presents a detailed treatment of the impact of the Fourth and Fifth Amendments on policing.

Case 8, The Thin Blue Line: Rodney King and the LAPD, covers the beating of King, the response to the video, and the subsequent trials of the four LAPD officers. Although this case is extraordinary in some respects, it raises important questions about the relationship of police, particularly urban police, to the citizenry they are dedicated to serve and protect. In this case and the accompanying text, students are invited to think about the conditions in the culture and mission of policing that promote the abuse of authority by those sworn to uphold the law. Case 9, A Woman in Charge: The Case of Paula Meara, tells the story of an exceptional woman police officer who overcame substantial obstacles to rise to the rank of chief in a major city in New England. The case and accompanying chapter focus on the culture, mission, and strategy of modern policing. The chapter examines the historical origins of police, current issues in policing, and looks toward a vision of policing in the new century.

Part Three, The Judicial Process, opens with the famous case of *Gideon* v. *Wainwright.* Case 10, The Poor Man in Court: The Case of Clarence Gideon, tells the dramatic story of a poor prisoner who won the right to counsel for all poor defendants by appealing to the U.S. Supreme Court from inside his prison cell. This case illustrates the ongoing struggle to achieve equal justice for the disadvantaged and the persistent problem of the gap between rights that exist de jure and those that exist de facto in the day-to-day operations of the system. The text covers the overall structure of the state and federal court system and explores the impact of U.S. Supreme Court decisions on criminal justice policy and practice.

Case 11, Bargaining for Justice: *Bordenkircher* v. *Hayes*, explores the reality of adjudication through a close examination of a failed plea negotiation that resulted in life in prison for defendant Paul Lewis Hayes. The chapter looks at the players in the courtroom work group and the formal and informal roles played by each of the key players. The role of the prosecutor, defense attorney, and judge in "settling" justice raises questions about the fairness of plea negotiations and the continuing advantages of privileged defendants in the informal processes of adjudication. Case 12, Judging Justice: The Case of Reginald Denny, returns to the scene of the Los Angeles riots and looks at the trial and jury deliberations of the men accused of beating white truck driver Reginald Denny. Assessing the jury verdict and its relationship to the broader context of race relations in Los Angeles raises questions about the institution of the jury and its role in our justice system. The chapter also looks at the mechanics of the trial process and examines the history and functioning of the modern jury system.

Part Four, Corrections and Punishment, begins with the sentencing of Kemba Smith for drug trafficking in Case 13, The Crime of Punishment: The Case of Kemba Smith. Convicted of drug conspiracy for her minor role in the drug operation of her abusive boyfriend, Kemba was eventually pardoned by President Clinton after serving six years of a twenty-four-year sentence. The case raises questions about the purpose of sentencing and the goals of punishment. The chapter reviews the goals of punishment, the range of modern sentences, and the issue of capital punishment. Case 14, Surviving Time: The Case of Rubin "Hurricane" Carter, recounts the twenty-eight-year odyssey of Rubin Carter in the New Jersey prison system. This case reveals much about the internal world of the prison and raises many deep concerns about conditions of confinement, inmate subculture, race relations, issues in prison management, and the value of incarceration. The accompanying text reviews the historical origins of prisons, social dynamics inside prisons, and key issues in prison management today. Case 15, Circles of Hope: Community Justice in South St. Paul, tells the story of a unique community justice partnership in St. Paul, Minnesota, which was started by a victim who adopted a problem-solving approach to his own victimization. This final chapter examines the history of community-based corrections and investigates the role of the community and victims in the future of the justice system.

A Word about Selection

The cases in this book are not intended to be representative or "typical" of a particular crime or justice event. Cases serve as launching pads for the exploration of broader themes, concepts, or dilemmas. Through singular in its details, each case was chosen for its power to raise broad themes for analysis and discussion. Limits of space required a difficult winnowing of cases for selection; suggestions for future cases from instructors who have used the text or who have developed other cases will be highly appreciated in future revisions of this book.

Features

The casebook offers all the tools instructors need to apply the case method approach to the traditional classroom.

Comprehensive Instructor's Manual

A companion Instructor's Manual offers in-class exercises, Web-based resources, group projects, assignments, and video resources to facilitate expanded exploration of each case and related text material. For each chapter, the companion Instructor's Manual provides

- Chapter outline and summary
- Suggested lecture outline
- Critical thinking class assignments and project suggestions
- Web-based assignments and project suggestions
- Video-based assignments and project suggestions
- Test bank: multiple-choice/true–false/fill-in-the-blank/short answer
- Essay question and discussion questions

Thinking Critically about This Case

Following each case is a series of questions designed to engage students in an in-depth exploration of important themes raised by the case. Depending on the preference of the instructor and the size of the class, these questions may serve as the basis for large- or small-group discussions, debates, mock trials, in-class or out-of-class writing assignments, group projects, or Web explorations. Suggestions for how to utilize these critical thinking questions designed to fit a variety of classroom environments are included in the Instructor's Manual.

Check Out This Case

At the end of each case are suggestions for either Web resources or video resources to facilitate further exploration of the case and the issues it has raised. The Instructor's Manual provides suggestions for exercises, assignments, and projects using these resources.

Learning Objectives

At the start of the text of each chapter is a list of main learning objectives to assist students in reading the chapter and studying the material. Review and study questions focus students on achieving the learning objectives for the chapter.

Review and Study Questions

At the end of every chapter are ten questions designed to elicit thorough review of the explanatory text. Answers to these questions can be found in the text. If students are able to answer the Review and Study Questions, they will have achieved the learning objectives for the chapter.

Key Term Definitions in Margins

Within the chapter itself, key terms are highlighted in bold type, with the accompanying definition in the margin. This allows students easy access to precise definitions and facilitates studying for exams.

Check It Out

Each chapter concludes with a Check It Out section, which includes recommended Web sites for further exploration of the explanatory material. The address for each Web site is provided along with a brief description of the site and a particularly interesting or relevant reason to visit the site. The Instructor's Manual provides specific Web-based questions, assignments, and projects for instructors interested in extensive use of the Web for student work.

Check It Out also includes recommended video resources that contain material related to the explanatory text. Running time, a brief description of the video, and how to obtain it are provided. Both documentaries and fiction video resources are included. Some videos might be shown by the instructor in class; others are commercially available videos that students can be assigned to view outside class. The Instructor's Manual provides specific questions and assignments based on each video and suggestions on how to incorporate this material into the class material.

Acknowledgments

I consider myself fortunate to have many supportive colleagues, friends, and family to thank for assistance of all kinds in the completion of this project. First, I would like to thank Karen Hanson at Allyn and Bacon for recognizing the power of this approach and supporting the idea from the start. My great thanks go to my editor, Jennifer Jacobson of Allyn and Bacon, who has been a thoughtful, considerate editor throughout this process. Several of the reviewers for the casebook were enormously helpful, and I would like to thank them for their constructive and concrete suggestions for improvements: Kimberly Cook, University of Southern Maine; Vincent Del Castillo, John Jay College of Criminal Justice; William Head, Indiana University; James Jones, American University; Nelson Kofie, Goucher College; Michael Norman, Weber State University; Lee Ross, University of Wisconsin–Parkside; Sudipto Roy, Indiana State University; and Jeanette Sereno, California State University, Stanislaus.

I would also like to thank several colleagues, including Mary Waters, Alexandra Todd, and Maureen Norton Hawk, who read drafts of the casebook and encouraged me to pursue this project when my own commitment faltered. Without their enthusiasm, those chapters might have slipped back into the drawer and stayed there. I am indebted to Chief Paula Meara for her graciousness in giving her time for an interview, and to Kay Pranis for her friendship and valuable insights about restorative justice. A special debt of gratitude goes to Alison Bachi, who contributed enormously to the research for this book.

I would also like to express my heartfelt appreciation to those who allowed me to pursue this project free of the burdens of other obligations. Carolyn Edsell shouldered many of the responsibilities for the Center for Restorative Justice in the final months of the project. Alexandra Todd, the chair of the Sociology Department at Suffolk University, Don Morton, director of the Graduate Program in Criminal Justice, and Janice Fama of the Sociology Department made it possible for me to complete this project in the midst of a busy semester. Molly Baldwin and others at Roca Inc. provided support, encouragement, and understanding for my frequent and lengthy absences from our ongoing projects.

Last, but hardly least, I thank my wonderful family. My children and my husband sacrificed countless weekends and evenings of family time so that I could write this book. They did so without complaint, offering steadfast encouragement, excellent company, and cheerful good humor in times of need. I am blessed beyond measure to have such love in my life.

Crime and Justice

C A S E 1

A Seventeenth-Century Crime Wave: The Salem Witch Trials

The year is 1692; the place is a small farming village in Massachusetts. Inside the household of the Reverend Samuel Parris, a small group of young girls, 9-year-old Betty, her 12-year-old cousin Abigail, and a pair of friends have spent hours indoors, amusing themselves with secretive games of "fortune telling" and "little sorceries," predicting futures and performing magic on household objects. This obsession with the occult was inspired by tales told by a West Indian slave named Tituba, who worked as a cook in the Parris household. Before long, more girls from the village had joined in the mysterious club that met in the kitchen of the parsonage during the long dull afternoons.

The master of the household, Reverend Parris, was having troubles of his own during this difficult winter. He had recently been appointed minister of a new church in the village of Salem, a position of great importance and power in the colonial community. But this position was very shaky: only a handful of people within the community had elected to join the new church. Many more refused to worship at the village meetinghouse or to pay the taxes to support his salary, and at a recent annual election in October, a majority in the village had voted out of office those who had been responsible for his appointment. The future of Reverend Parris seemed very precarious in the winter of 1692 as the new Village Committee challenged his right to the position of minister and refused even to pay for firewood to warm his hearth.

As winter wore on, the "black magic" games of the young girls came to the attention of the adults in the Parris household and the wider village community. Rumors spread that the girls were meeting in the woods to perform the black magic Tituba had brought with her from her native Barbados. The youngest of the girls was the first to exhibit strange

and worrisome behaviors: sudden fits of screaming, convulsions, barking and scampering about on all fours like a dog. The adult women in the household fretted in muted tones that the afflictions of the child were a malady brought on by the dark forces of witchcraft.

Witchcraft was believed to be a particularly terrifying and horrible crime, not only because it was responsible for evil consequences such as murder, physical torture, or destruction of property, but also because it challenged the supremacy of God in the affairs of human beings. The crime of witchcraft was written into English statutes of law as early as the sixteenth century. The Massachusetts Law of Statutes, likewise, included the crime of witchcraft as a capital offense.

The belief in Satan and his role in affairs of humans and their evil doings was not confined to hysterical young girls or religious fanatics. On the contrary, the idea that the Devil was real and operated to do malicious things in the affairs of human beings was a widely accepted belief, common to most individuals of all social backgrounds and educational levels. It was believed that a person who entered into a convenant with the Devil by signing his book had the power to call Satan to enter his or her body to perform evil doings and deeds upon others. By deploying the power of the Devil, the witch was able to act out his or her own petty hates toward other human beings.

At the suggestion of Aunt Mary Silbey, who lived in the house, Tituba was asked to prepare the traditional "witches' cake," a recipe guaranteed to identify the source of the affliction. By baking a "witches' cake"— a recipe that involved combining rye meal with the child's urine and feeding the cake to a dog—it was thought that the dog would immediately identify its master, the witch. Before this method of investigation could be completed, however, Reverend Parris called in the town physician, a William Griggs, who examined the girls and proclaimed the chilling news. Malevolent witchcraft was the source of their malady, not any sickness responsive to the cures of medicine: the Devil had come to Salem Village.

The strange behaviors first seen in the Parris household now began to spread like wildfire among the group of girls who attended the secret meetings in the Parris's kitchen. Parris and another father, Thomas Putnam (one of Parris's key supporters and father of Ann Putnam, aged 12), urged the girls to reveal the names of the individuals responsible for their suffering. The girls hesitated at first, but then named three women: Sarah Good, a local beggar known throughout the Village for her nasty temper and bitter tongue; Sarah Osborne, an elderly women with a dubious reputation; and Tituba, the slave woman herself. On February 29, several men, including Putnam, traveled to Salem Town to swear out formal complaints charging witchcraft against the three women before the local magistrates. Warrants were issued for the arrest of the three women, and an interrogation or preliminary hearing was hurriedly scheduled for the following morning.

All three accused were typical of those found guilty of witchcraft throughout Europe and Colonial America. They were marginal, unrespectable, powerless, and deviant in their conduct and lifestyle. Although they lived within the community, they were, in a sense, outsiders, viewed with suspicion and dislike by the majority of the community. Sarah Good, at the time of accusation, was both homeless and des-

titute: she and her husband William had been reduced to begging for shelter and food from neighbors. In her requests for assistance, she had the effrontery to be aggressive and angry, cursing and muttering reprisals to those who refused to offer her charity. Few in the community stood to support her once she was accused; indeed, her husband was one of the first to proclaim that she was, in fact, "either a witch or would be one very quickly."

Sarah Osborne, too, was an "outsider." Although she possessed an estate from her first husband, she was old, had no children, and had suffered the gossip and disapproval of the community when several years earlier she had cohabited with her second husband for several months before becoming officially wed. The slave woman, Tituba, was, of course, a natural target of suspicion, and her involvement in the baking of the cake only hardened assumptions that it was she who was acting as an agent of the devil.

THE INVESTIGATIONS

The date for the first hearing to determine if there was sufficient evidence to hand down an indictment for the crime of witchcraft was scheduled to take place the next day at the inn in Salem Village, but on the morning of the hearing so many townspeople turned out to witness the proceedings that the venue was changed to the larger meetinghouse to accommodate the agitated and curious crowd. The accusers—the afflicted girls—were seated in the front row as, one by one, each of the women was brought before the magistrates for questioning. As each of the women came into view, the girls began to exhibit tortured and tormented behavior in a dramatic enactment of the charge itself. The behavior that had so frightened their parents astonished observers and convinced many skeptical witnesses that they were indeed suffering from an affliction of supernatural causes.

> These children were bitten and pinched by invisible agents; their arms, necks and backs turned this way and that way, and returned back again, so as it was impossible for them to do of themselves, and beyond the power of any epileptic fits, or natural disease to effect. Sometimes they were taken dumb, their mouths stopped, their throats choked, their limbs wracked and tormented so as might move a heart of stone, to sympathize with them. . . .[1]

During the proceedings, as the girls were contorting in dramatic displays of torture and physical agony, the magistrates pressed the women with questions: "How long have you been a witch?" "Why do you hurt these folk?"[2] The girls themselves continued to moan and plead for the women, especially Sarah Good, to put an end to their torments. Before long, Tituba confessed, named the other two as her accomplices, and announced that there were many others in the Colony engaged in the conspiracy against the community of God. While Osborne continued to maintain her innocence, Good eventually accused Osborne and by so doing implicated herself in the eyes of the magistrates. At the end of the interrogation and before a crowded and tightly packed audience composed of the entire village and many from neighboring communities as well, the magistrates ordered all three sent to jail on suspicion of witchcraft, to be held there until trial.

THE PROSECUTION

At the religious services the very next day, the fits and afflictions of the young girls continued, along with more accusations of witchcraft directed against other women in the community. During the service, 12-year-old Abigail Williams suddenly began to shout out that she saw an apparition of one of the townspeople in the rafters, a Martha Corey, who had publically expressed her own doubts over the whole affair. The next day, Goodwife Corey was arrested, to be examined in the presence of their accusers before the magistrate. Within a month, two more "witches" had been identified by the girls and were arrested: Rebecca Nurse and the 4-year-old daughter of Sarah Good.

As the snows melted, the intensity of the girls' affliction seemed to increase rather than wane. By the end of April, a total of twenty-eight more people had been accused and charged with the crime of witchcraft. The month of May saw an additional thirty-nine people accused. The town of Andover requested that the afflicted girls come to their village and identify suspected witches among the townspeople. Although the girls did not know personally any of the people accused, they managed to name more than forty persons as witches. By the time of the first trial on June 2, 1692, a total of 160 persons had been publically and legally accused, and many of them were languishing in the local jail awaiting trial. These included not only men and women who were marginal or poor but a large number of men and women of considerable wealth and power, including the former minister of the parish, George Burroughs, who was arrested in his new parish in Maine and transported back to Salem, charged with being the Master Wizard during the years he had served in Salem Village.

THE TRIALS

The royal governor of Massachusetts had just arrived from England when he was confronted with the epidemic of witchcraft accusations that had swept through the villages of New England in the preceding four months. Governor Phipps responded to the crisis with swift action, appointing a special judicial body known as the Court of Oyer and Terminer, which means literally to "hear and determine"; the Massachusetts attorney general was ordered to begin prosecutions; a jury was selected; and on Friday, June 2, 1692, the infamous Salem witchcraft trials began.

The first to appear for a formal trial was Bridget Bishop, an unpopular and widely despised woman who had been held in prison since her indictment on April 18. The evidence against Goodwife Bishop was considerable, and many people came forward to provide testimony supporting the charges against her. She was accused of causing the death of a child by visiting as an apparition and causing the child to cry out and decline in health from that moment onward. Several men and women testified that she had visited them and afterwards they had suffered from strange misfortune or peculiar experiences. The jury returned a verdict of guilty against Goodwife Bishop and she was sentenced to death by hanging. On June 10, 1692, Bridget Bishop was the first to be executed, in a public hanging on a rocky hillside forever after known as Witches' Hill.

At the second sitting of the court of Oyer and Terminer, the court tried and sentenced to death five more accused witches. A session on August 5 produced six more convictions and five executions, including that of the former parish minister, George Burroughs. In September the court sat two more times, passing death sentences on six more persons in one sitting and nine more in the final session of the court on September 17. The last executions were held on September 22, when eight persons, six women and two men, were hanged on the gallows. A total of thirty-seven persons accused of witchcraft died: nineteen by hanging, seventeen while in jail awaiting trial, and one by being crushed to death from heavy rocks piled on his prostrate body, an ancient form of execution reserved for those who refused to testify at all.

The evidence given in the trials was typical of that used to prove the crime of witchcraft but quite different from that used to provide evidence for ordinary murders, assaults, and thefts. The ordinary rules of trial procedures called for two eyewitnesses in a capital offense, but in the case of witchcraft the rule was altered because witchcraft was deemed a "habitual" offense. It was sufficient, therefore, that two or more witnesses come forth with testimony about different images or incidents to support the charge of witchcraft.

The most abundant form of evidence came in the form of spectral evidence. These were eyewitness accounts of seeing an image or apparition of the accused. This might occur in a dream or in their bedroom at night, or even in a crowded meetinghouse or courtroom. The unique difficulty with spectral evidence was that it was believed that the image might be visible only to those being tormented, while being completely invisible to others present in the very same room. As long as more than one person came forth with spectral evidence, it was not necessary for them to "see" the same image. The behavior of the girls at the trial provided the most convincing evidence to the jurors, since the accusers often described the image of the accused flying around the rafters, or exhibited signs of distress and torment as the accused witch moved her head or arms.

In addition to testimony by witnesses of spectral evidence, there were several other important forms of evidence. Because it was believed that the Devil would not permit a witch to proclaim the name of God or recite the Lord's Prayer without error, there was often a trial by test in which the accused was asked to perform these tasks. Errors, stumbles, or failures of memory were seen as proof that the accused were agents of the Devil. Evidence of "anger followed by misfortune" was another form of evidence. Because the crime of witchcraft was believed to be an instrumental one, in which the witch takes out her personal anger against others using the power of Satan, the testimony of those who gave examples of conflict, disputes, or angry outbursts followed by bad fortune was also seen as compelling evidence of the crime of malevolent witchcraft. In the case of Bridget Bishop, five townspeople came forth to accuse her of being responsible for "murdering" a family member. In each instance, evidence was presented of a display of anger on the part of the accused, followed some time afterward by an illness or accident befalling the one who had displeased her. A fourth form of evidence came in the search for physical marks on the bodies of the accused, such as moles, warts, or scars, which were believed to be "witches' teats" or places where the Devil and other evil creatures gained sustenance from the witch herself.

A final form of evidence, and ultimately one of the most compelling, was the freely given confession of the accused. Beginning with Tituba herself, as many as fifty of the accused eventually confessed to their status as witches and to their involvement in witchcraft, in some cases providing elaborate detail and accusing others in the process. During the hearings, as soon as an accused confessed to the crime, the agonized writhing of the girls suddenly and instantly ceased and the girls fell upon the confessed witches with kisses and tearful pledges of forgiveness. None who confessed was brought to trial or hanged: the intention of the court was to spare them in order to make use of them in testifying against others in future trials. Only those who continued to proclaim their innocence were made to suffer the spectacle of trial and the horror of public execution.

THE AFTERMATH

Between June 10 and September 22, 1692, twenty people were executed for the crime of witchcraft. As the New England fall began to cool the air, an additional 150 people remained waiting trial in local jails, and 200 more formal accusations had been made against others. However, there was a sudden sense of unease on the part of the judicial authorities about the quality of the evidence used to convict and hang those convicted. Anyone might fail to recite the Lord's Prayer with a slip of the tongue, particularly when standing before a packed courtroom charged with being a representative of Satan. And legal opinion was plagued by the question that it might be possible for the Devil to present himself in the image of innocent folk as well as those who had struck a covenant with him.

On October 3, Reverend Increase Mather, president of Harvard College, delivered an address in which he claimed that evil spirits might be impersonating innocent men and women and implied that it was possible the girls themselves were fabricating their afflictions. Mather went on to declare that "It were better that ten suspected witches should escape, than that one innocent person should be condemned."[3] Many more joined the chorus, objecting to the fallibility of the court to prove the crime, and the injustice of the proceedings in potentially condemning the innocent based on the unsubstantiated accusations of the inflamed. Within days, the governor disbanded the court of Oyer and Terminer and replaced it with a court that forbade the use of spectral evidence. The jury acquitted forty-nine of the fifty-two cases it heard; the other three accused had entered confessions, but they were given immediate reprieves by the governor. The remaining prisoners were all discharged, and a general pardon was issued for all who had been accused in the terrible and most infamous series of trials within our nation's history. Two years after the trials, the crime of witchcraft was no longer a legal offense in the colony of Massachusetts Bay.

Case adapted from Paul Boyer and Stephen Nissenbaum., Eds. *The Salem Witchcraft Papers: Verbatim Transcripts of the Legal Documents of the Salem Witchcraft Outbreak of 1692.* Vol. 1 (New York: Da Capo Press, 1977); Kai Erickson, *Wayward Puritans: A Study in the Sociology of Deviance* (New York: Wiley & Sons, 1966); Richard Weisman, *Witchcraft, Magic and Religion in 17th Century Massachusetts* (Boston: University of Massachusetts Press, 1984).

THINKING CRITICALLY ABOUT THIS CASE

1. Do you believe the accused in the seventeenth-century Salem received a "fair trial?" Why or why not?

2. Why did so many people confess to the crime of which they were accused? What forces might induce innocent people to confess to a crime they did not commit?

3. Consider the powerful statement made by Increase Mather: "It were better that ten witches should escape, than that one innocent person should be condemned." Do you agree with this statement? Why or why not? Would you still agree with this statement if we substituted the crime of murder, rape, or drug dealing for the crime of witchcraft? Why or why not?

4. Consider the spectacle of the public execution. How do you think you would feel if you were to witness such a event? Would you bring your children to an execution? Why or why not?

5. The term "witch hunt" has moved into our common everyday parlance. What does it mean to you? Give some examples of contemporary "witch hunts" in U.S. society.

CHECK OUT THIS CASE

On the Web

Salem Massachusetts Witch Trials, www.salemweb.com/witches.htm

Salem Witch Museum, www.salemwitchmuseum.com/
Visit these two Web sites to learn more about Salem in the seventeenth century.

Witchcraft in Salem Village, etect.lib.virginia.edu/salem/witchcraft/
Check this Web site for access to the detailed information about the victims and the accused. Search rare documents of current debates and dialogues on the crime of witchcraft. Explore historical sites and consult the experts with your questions!

Famous American Trials, jurist.law.pitt.edu/trials.htm
Click onto this Web site for access to the actual transcripts of the trials. Read the narratives of the "examinations" by the judges. Read individual biographies of those who were accused. Find out what happened to the accusers after the hysteria was over.

On Film

The Crucible (124 minutes)
This is a lavish film starring Winona Ryder and Daniel Day Lewis with a screenplay written by the original playwright, Arthur Miller. Miller fictionalizes the events of 1692 by inventing an affair between Abigail Williams and John Proctor but otherwise presents a historically accurate narrative of the climate and events of the time. The Crucible was written and produced in the 1950s originally to criticize the anticommunist "witch hunt" of Senator Joseph McCarthy, who accused hundreds of celebrities and politicians of being communists, forcing people to defend their innocence, confess and accuse others, or risk losing their careers and livelihoods.

Crime, Law, and Justice

WHAT IS CRIME?

Through contemporary eyes, it is tempting to dismiss the "crime" of witchcraft as religious superstition. Given our knowledge of science and technology, it is hard for us to believe those girls were really tormented by witches wielding the dark powers of the Devil. To people in the seventeenth century, however, the existence of God and Satan, and their active roles in the affairs of human beings, was common sense, a set of beliefs about the world shared by most members of society, rich and poor, educated and illiterate alike. Sociologists claim that all human ideas, from our basic beliefs about the nature of the physical world to the rules of social interaction, to our convictions about what is right and wrong, are a product of that human society. Is a rock inhabited by living spirits? Is it composed of tiny particles so infinitesimally small they can never be seen by the human eye? What you believe depends on the society in which you live. Beliefs about "reality" are embedded in the cultural beliefs of the entire society: most people (except, perhaps, those who are mentally ill) accept the **social construction of reality** defined by their culture. Members of every society collectively define and interpret the world around them. This set of shared understandings is what we call culture and is a product of human interaction.

Like all beliefs within society, we can also view **crime as social construction.** What we believe to be crime is a result of the beliefs, values, and institutions of our society. Although we may no longer believe in witchcraft as a source of harmful conduct, our own beliefs about crime are similarly rooted in our cultural world view. It is true that most societies have categories of behavior they refer to as "criminal," but it is not true that they identify the same kinds of behaviors as criminal. What is a crime in one culture is not necessarily a crime in another culture. Moreover, definitions of crime change over time: what is criminal today (e.g., the manufacture, sale, and distribution of cocaine) was not a crime a hundred years ago.

Crime and Deviance

People in our culture who believe in witchcraft or the idea that invisible powers can cause personal misfortune or illnesses among children

Deviant behaviors are not always considered criminal. This young man's hairstyle may look bizarre, but he is not violating any law in modern American society.

are not expressing the social construction of reality taught to most members of a modern industrial society. People who hold the view that illnesses are caused by spells cast by witches using the dark power of Satan are "deviant" in adhering to those beliefs. These ideas no longer form the basis of "common sense," as they did for the people of Salem Village. Those who follow these beliefs form a distinct minority by holding views that are not widely shared.

Sociologists use the term **deviance** to refer to conduct which is contrary to the norms of conduct or social expectations of the group. Not all forms of deviant conduct are considered crimes. We might think a person who believes in the Devil quite odd, and we might not want to associate with that person, hire him as a babysitter or fully believe his testimony in a court of law, but in our society, to believe in unusual ideas is not a crime. Many other forms of conduct are considered deviant but not criminal in our society, such as picking one's nose in public, piercing one's nostrils, dying one's hair green, or talking to oneself on the subway.

Sociologists have long argued that there is nothing inherently "deviant" about any form of conduct: a behavior is deviant if it is viewed and reacted to as such by others within the society. Kai Erikson, who wrote about the Salem witch trials, suggests: "The term deviance refers to conduct which the people of a group consider so dangerous or embarrassing or irritating that they bring special sanctions to bear against the persons who exhibit it."[4] We need to ask: Who makes the rules? Who identifies the rule breaker? Who proclaims the violation as a serious threat to the social well-being of the community? According to sociologists, what constitutes deviance is the labeling, identification, and successful application of that label to a particular person and his or her conduct.

Harold Becker coined the term **moral entrepreneurs** to refer to those people who seek to impose a particular view of morality on others within society. Moral entrepreneurs, he believed, are those people who identify certain forms of conduct as particularly

social construction of reality: process by which members of every society collectively define and interpret the world around them.

crime as social construction: behaviors defined as crimes are the result of the beliefs, values, and institutions of the society.

deviance: conduct that is contrary to the norms of conduct or social expectations of the group.

moral entrepreneurs: people who identify certain forms of conduct as dangerous to society and mobilize others to exert social control over those who engage in that conduct.

dangerous and in need of social control by others within the group. These moral entrepreneurs are often responsible for mobilizing the group against the behavior or for making sure that a law is written against a certain form of conduct. These activists are also able to construct a sense of **moral panic** about the threat of this behavior to the well-being of the entire society.

Crime as Legal Construction

As we noted above, not all forms of deviant behavior are crimes. It is also true that not all kinds of crime are really deviant. Some crimes are so commonplace that it would be hard to describe these behaviors as deviant at all. An estimated one-third of all Americans cheat on their income taxes despite the law. Probably more people violate the speed limits on our nation's highways than observe them, and having sex before marriage may still be illegal in several state criminal codes, but it can hardly be considered deviant according to national polls of attitudes toward premarital sex.

Both deviance and crime, therefore, are social constructions—that is, they are products of collective action by individuals within society. What distinguishes the rules of the criminal code from other types of social rules that govern our behavior in society, such as the rules that we should eat with a fork, or shake someone's hand when it is extended toward us in friendly greeting? In a sense, the answer is quite simple: crime is behavior that violates criminal law. Without criminal law there is, literally, no such thing as "crime." It is possible for any behavior to be made a crime by being written into the criminal code. In many U.S. states, it is a crime for a man to dress as a woman; in some countries there are criminal laws regulating the acceptable lengths of a woman's skirt; and in some Muslim states, women are prohibited from wearing any clothing other than a full-length robe and a veil that covers both their head and face.

What makes a law different from a social taboo, convention, habit, or custom? Sociologists refer to rules of society as norms. A **norm** is a societal expectation of "normal" or expected behavior for a member of that group within a specific set of circumstances. Human behavior is deeply rule-bound, yet many of these rules are never written down nor are they even necessarily verbalized. Yet human beings raised within a given society learn these rules as part of the normal process of growing up within that culture, a process known as **socialization.** Much of the rules we learn through the socialization process belong to the category of rules William Graham Sumner (1840–1910) identified as **folkways.**[5] Sumner studied a wide range of societies and argued that much of human behavior is governed by informal rules beyond the codified criminal code.

Folkways are unplanned but expected ways of behaving within a society. These include what to wear and what is appropriate attire for any given social setting. Take a quick look at your fellow students in class and observe the normative nature of the unwritten dress code. Has anyone chosen to come to school in pajamas? Or beach attire? Or evening dress? Considering the fact that most colleges do not have a written dress code, there is a remarkable degree of conformity because we are regulated by informal rules to an even greater extent than we are regulated by formal rules. Folkways include rules about appropriate foods to consume, rituals for making oneself attractive and presentable, manners, etiquette, and so forth. Failure to adhere to the standards of dress in your college classroom, for instance, would probably elicit some odd stares from your classmates, a disapproving comment or two, and a tendency for others to gossip about, or withdraw from, such an odd person. These minor sanctions operate quite effectively (and often unconsciously) to maintain the dress code. Because most human beings tend to avoid ridicule and desire social acceptance, these forms of "punishment" operate quite efficiently to enforce social norms.

Mores, according to Sumner, are far more important rules of conduct within any society. **Mores** are rules that define, not simply what is expected or appropriate, but

moral panic: shared belief that a particular behavior is a significant threat to the well-being of the entire society.

norm: expected behavior for a member of a group within a specific set of circumstances.

socialization: process of learning the norms, values, and beliefs of a given culture.

folkways: unplanned but expected ways of behaving within a given culture.

mores: important rules of conduct within a society that define what is right and wrong.

what is right or wrong. While failure to comply with a dress code may elicit some negative reactions, failure to conform with societal mores is taken far more seriously by others within that society. Wearing strange clothing in public may violate a folkway, but wearing no clothes in public violates mores, at least in our culture. The sanctions for failing to abide by social mores are far more substantial than our myriad responses to breaches of social etiquette, manners, or social custom.

How is law different from both mores and folkways? **Laws** are norms that are codified and enforced through the use of coercion backed by the authority of the state. The key element in defining law, according to Max Weber, is that laws are norms that are enforced by specialized institutions granted the power to use force to obtain compliance. In order to have law in a modern sense, it is necessary for a society to develop political institutions such as legislatures, governments, courts, law enforcement, and penal systems, which enact the formal laws of a society, enforce compliance with those laws, and punish those who fail to do so. The legal system endows certain individuals within society with the legal right to use physical coercion in order to ensure compliance with the law. These institutions are those agencies and organizations to which we refer collectively as the criminal justice system. The institutions of the criminal justice system include the legislature that creates the laws, the police who enforce the law, the courts that adjudicate and interpret the law, and the penal system that provides sanctions to those who are found to have violated the law.

Crime and Morality

Many people assume that crime and morality are two sides of the same coin: a behavior is crime because it is immoral, and all immoral behavior is criminal. It is natural to assume that all conduct we think immoral is included in the criminal code, and that the criminal law reflects the moral values of the majority of law-abiding citizens. However, the relationship between crime and morality is not as simple as it may seem. First, not all conduct that we would agree is immoral is necessarily criminal. For instance, we may think it wrong for a person to refuse to come to the aid of another who has collapsed on the street gasping for breath, but people who stand and stare or who turn away with a shrug are not committing a crime unless there is a specific legal rule that requires them to assist their fellow citizens, and many states do not have such laws in their criminal codes.

It is also possible for governments to write immoral laws. Nazi Germany passed many laws that legalized the theft and murder of innocent citizens because they were Jewish; South Africa and the United States both have had laws that sanctioned the cruel and even murderous treatment of other human beings because they were nonwhite. Not all immoral or harmful conduct is necessarily criminalized within our society, and not all laws are necessarily moral and just.

What is the relationship between crime and morality? If crime does not reflect our moral values, is it merely a set of legal rules established by the state to regulate conduct? If it is not grounded in our sense of right and wrong, must we obey the law? Do we obey the law simply because the state is powerful and we are afraid of legal sanctions? Are we morally obligated to follow the law even if we believe it is unjust?

Many people argue that law is grounded in a higher set of moral principles: what makes the law a system of justice is that it embraces ideals of right and wrong that are universally agreed upon. This is the idea of **natural law:** the belief that there are agreed-upon standards of right and wrong common to all human societies and that are ethically binding for all human societies.[6] For some, the precepts of the Ten Commandments, such as the prohibition against murder, theft, and the obligation to be faithful to one's spouse and to honor one's parents, are so fundamental to human societies that they believe them to be found in all moral and ethical codes. The idea of natural law says that there are sources of right and wrong above the particular human rules created by particular men and women in any given society.

laws: social norms that are codified and enforced through the authority of the state.

natural law: the belief that law is grounded in a higher set of moral principles that is universal to all human societies.

We find a powerful belief in the idea of a "natural law" across many different societies that believe in many different kinds of gods. In the case of Salem Village, this higher power was God. We find this belief too in our own Constitution. When our founding fathers wrote "And we find these principles to be self-evident," they were stating that the right of all persons to liberty, life, and the pursuit of happiness was a principle beyond the whims and preferences of human powers, reflecting a higher authority governing the affairs of human society. The Bill of Rights is based on the "natural law" concepts of John Locke (1632–1704), according to whom all men are, by nature, free, equal, and independent. Underlying our faith in the justice of our legal system is a foundation of belief in the natural law that protects the inalienable "natural rights" of all individuals. According to Thomas Jefferson, the purpose of government is to protect the natural rights retained by the people, and it is extremely important that the government itself not be permitted to transgress these rights.

Is there really such a thing as natural law? If there is, how do we explain the existence of the legal crime of witchcraft in the seventeenth century and its absence today? The people of the Massachusetts Bay Colony also believed in the idea of natural law and that the rules of human society were ultimately created by a higher authority. So which society is correct? Concepts of natural law have been used to support ideas to which we would no longer subscribe today, such as the "natural" inferiority of women, nonwhites, and Native Americans. Theories of "natural law" claiming that there are universal principles of right and wrong found in all societies are also hard to square with the different ways in which societies define criminal behavior. All societies condemn killing other human beings, but only under some circumstances and only in some types of relationships. In Comanche society, husbands were free to kill their wives, and this act was not considered murder. In our society, the taking of a life in defense of one's own self or one's own property may also not constitute murder. Before the Civil War, in the South, a slave owner could legally kill a slave if he or she was engaged in routine discipline. If there is such a thing as natural law, how can there be such variation between different social groups in how they define rights and wrongs of behavior that is as clearly wrong as murder?

Morality refers to beliefs about the rightness and wrongness of human conduct. Sociologists have long argued that there is no universal moral code to which all societies adhere. They point out that the belief that a certain behavior is wrong, immoral, or evil is a product of human collective definition making. Crime and morality are part of the cultural belief system. Like our beliefs about the physical world, moral beliefs are a collective human product.

Crime and Power

If the law does not reflect a natural or divinely inspired order of right and wrong common to all human societies, where does law come from and whose morality does it represent? There are two broad theories to explain the social forces that create the law: one based on forces of consensus and another focusing on conflict as a source of law. The **consensus model of law** holds that the law, especially the criminal law, reflects the widely shared values and beliefs of the society.

According to Emile Durkheim, all societies define some conduct as crime: "crime" and the broader category "deviance" are normal parts of any society. People collectively define some conduct as unacceptable, harmful, dangerous, or immoral. Even a "society of saints," according to Durkheim, would define some types of behavior as unacceptable or deviant or criminal. Durkheim stated that "An act is criminal when it offends strong and defined states of the collective conscience."[7] Defining certain conduct as deviant, in Durkheim's view, serves a kind of natural bonding function for any given group, drawing the community together in its mutual disgust at the deviant, affirming the identity of the community while simultaneously defining boundaries of acceptable conduct.

morality: beliefs about the rightness and wrongness of human conduct.

consensus model of law: law reflects the collective conscience or widely shared values and beliefs of a given society.

In the consensus model, law reflects the common morality of the social group and also serves a **latent function** of strengthening the social bonds of the group. Kai Erikson, following the consensus model, believed that the Salem witch trials tightened the bonds of a community undergoing substantial social change. The moral panic instigated by the witch trials was a barometer of the strength of those widely shared moral values. Just as communities today rally against the threat of illegal drugs to "just say no" to the dealers who threaten the safety of their children, the villagers of New England were taking the steps they believed necessary to protect themselves and their families from both physical and moral destruction.

The **conflict model of law** argues that law reflects the power hierarchy within a given society. Because societies are composed of diverse groups with different perspectives on moral values (based on race, class, age, gender, religion, ethnicity, region, etc.), laws will inevitably be shaped by the interests of those who have the most resources to influence the law. Powerful groups shape the law so as to ensure that it reflects their morality and preserves their position of power within society. The law may even be thought of as a tool that enables this group to maintain its position of power over others in the society. For example, laws declaring that black men were not really men at all upheld a social order of white supremacy over nonwhites. Nonwhites, obviously, were not involved in the making of those laws.

Jeffrey Reiman argues that the conflict perspective is relevant to interpreting public attitudes toward serious crimes of violence in our society.[8] Many forms of conduct that cause substantial harm in our society are not criminal according to our legal system. When we think of the crime of murder, our first mental image is of a vicious individual who has personally attacked, shot, or knifed another human being. However, the number of deaths each year resulting from criminal homicide is only a fraction of the number of deaths caused by willful neglect by corporations in the workplace. Reiman asks: "Is a person who kills another in a bar brawl a greater threat to society than a business executive who refuses to cut into his profits to make his plant a safe place to work?"[9] Yet because of the specific way that the law defines homicide, the business executive is not viewed as a criminal and is seen to be pursuing legitimate business goals despite the lethal consequences of his or her actions on others within society.

Social norms do not simply "become" crimes through some kind of divine, natural, or automatic process. Rather, there is a social process whereby someone or some group creates a law and ensures that it will be enforced. The social construction of criminal law, its application, interpretation, and enforcement by particular social agencies and actors within this society, is the business of the criminal justice system. To understand the criminal justice system, we must study the processes by which laws are made; why some forms of conduct are included in the criminal code and others are not; why some laws are enforced and others are ignored; and why some persons who violate the law are never suspected, arrested, prosecuted, or punished.

Social Control versus Crime Control

Law and the institutions of the criminal justice system are only one type of social control in modern society. Sociologists recognize that the power of formal social control exercised by the law and its agents, such as police and the courts, is trivial compared to the subtle and awesome power of other sources of social control within society. Law is simply one form of **social control** among many, and arguably, it is far from the most powerful form of social control.

Crime control, unlike social control, is a reactive form of societal control. For the most part, crime control enters the picture only after a criminal violation has occurred. Can the criminal justice system really "control" crime? As we will see in later chapters, criminal justice professionals such as the police or the correctional system cannot address the social conditions within the community that generate serious criminal

latent function of law: a by-product of law is to define the identity and strengthen social bonds among members of a group.

conflict model of law: law reflects the values, beliefs, and interests of powerful elites within a given society and serves to help those in power preserve their position within the society.

social control: formal and informal processes that maintain conformity with social norms.

crime control: formal and informal processes that respond to violations of legal norms.

behavior. Fair and just working of the major institutions within our society, such as the family, the economy, schools, and so forth, create peaceful communities. Conditions of injustice or unfairness within our communities—endemic poverty, homelessness, drug abuse, unemployment, alienation, boredom—are societal conditions that lead to high rates of crime within society. The criminal justice system itself is not designed to address these widespread societal problems.

Reiman believes that the criminal justice system cannot really "control" crime, and he goes further to state that the criminal justice system does not even really aim to control crime: the criminal justice system is one that depends on its own failures for its continued success in society. The more the system fails to reduce crime, the more resources we devote to crime control. Reiman (and many others) point out that if we were serious about controlling crime, we would focus on strengthening the forms of social control in society, such as work, family, and community, which enhance conformity for positive reasons.[10]

Van Ness and Strong[11] see a more positive role for the criminal justice system. It is the job of the justice system to maintain a just order. The criminal justice system is not simply about crime control, but about the creation of a just society. What do we mean by "justice"? What does a just order look like? What does justice mean to us as Americans? How do we define justice and how do our institutions deliver it to us? Let us return to the tragic summer of 1692 to ask: was this justice?

WHAT IS JUSTICE?

> Remove justice, and what are kingdoms, but gangs of criminals on a large scale? St. Augustine (354–430 A.D.)

The criminal justice system is not simply about catching criminals or "crime control," but about delivering "justice" in our society. When we talk about the modern criminal justice system, many people ask: justice for whom? Is the system's highest priority to obtain justice for the victims of crime within society? Or are we talking about justice for the person who has been accused? Are all citizens in this country equally subject to the justice process, or are minorities right when they complain that the criminal justice system is a "just us" system, which delivers harsh punishment only to those who are poor, young, and powerless. Do all defendants, rich and poor, get an equal chance at "justice for all"? Do all communities get equal protection from the police?

Along with the need to understand what "crime" is, sociologically, we need to understand what "justice" is, substantively and procedurally. Is a process just as long as it is legal? Is justice something different from the law, or is it attainable only through the rule of law? What do we mean when we talk about justice? Do all Americans agree on what justice means?

crime control model of justice: prioritizes the efficient and effective enforcement of the law as a basic precondition for a free society.

due process model of justice: prioritizes rules of due process that guarantee and protect individual civil liberty and fairness in the enforcement of the criminal law.

Crime Control versus Due Process Models of Justice

The first question to consider is the relationship between law and justice. When you read the events of those proceedings back in 1692, did you feel that the women and men accused of those crimes were treated justly? What makes a process just? Traditionally, the U.S. system of justice has sought a balance between the rights of individuals and the power of the state to respond to crime. The two poles of this delicate balance are referred to as the interests of **due process** and the interests of **crime control**.[12] According to many observers, the due process model of the system competes with the crime control agenda of the system in a more or less constant struggle over the defining notion of justice. Both sets of values are important to our system and are deeply incorporated in the structure of our justice system.

Crime control advocates point out that a society in which no one is free to walk within the streets of their community or dwell within their own home without constant fear of being robbed, mugged or assaulted by their fellow citizens, is not a free society. As President Clinton remarked in his 1994 State of the Union address, "Violent crime and the fear it provokes are crippling our society, limiting personal freedom and fraying the ties that bind us." Women argue that fear of rape forces many women to live according to a restricted "rape schedule," resulting in a substantial reduction in personal freedom for half of the American population.[13] Black Americans who lived in fear of lynching by angry white mobs were not really free to walk the streets of their own town or sit at a lunch counter and enjoy a quiet meal.[14] Parents in many urban communities today complain that they are not free in our society if they cannot let their children walk to school or ride a bicycle on the sidewalk without fear of gunfire from rival gangs fighting over drug turf.[15]

If violence is rampant in the streets, no one is free to enjoy the "life, liberty, and the pursuit of happiness" promised in the Constitution. Crime control advocates point out it is the responsibility of an effective government to prevent citizens from terrorizing one another. Efficient and effective enforcement of the law is a basic precondition for a free society.

A competing and equally important notion of freedom centers on the right of the individual to be free from governmental tyranny. The values of due process claim that no one is free in a society in which the state can knock on your door whenever it wants, search your house and arrest you without answering to a higher authority. This is the basic notion of individual liberty and individual rights. According to this view, no one is really free in a society if they must fear the unbridled power of the state to arrest, charge, convict, or punish, without adequate protections against the abuse of that power.

Recall that the definition of crime is a rule that is enforced by the legal power of the state. The important concept here is *legal power*: we grant the state the legal right to use force against us under certain circumstances, that is, when we violate the legitimate laws of the land. In our system, however, we do not give the state carte blanche in the use of force: that force is limited to certain circumstances. Every police officer on the street, every correctional officer, every judge, and every prosecutor must obey these laws; they are not free to use their powers in any way they please. These limits are what is known as the rules of due process.

From this perspective, the power of the state to control crime must be limited by due process protections for individuals accused of a crime. Without those protections, the unchecked power of the state would threaten the liberty and basic freedom of all citizens. The fundamental value at the heart of due process rules is fairness. Proponents of a due process model of the criminal justice system remind us that police states such as Nazi Germany enjoyed very low crime rates because citizens had no rights, and the police had the right to use force in any way they saw fit. Of course, although there was less crime, the citizens of Germany paid a terrible price in loss of individual liberty. Because we give the state the legal power to use force, we must have protections against the abuse of that power. We grant the power to control crime to the state because we value security as a basic ingredient of freedom, but we need the procedures of due process to protect us against the abuse of that legal right by the criminal justice system itself.

Due Process in the Seventeenth Century

Let us examine the procedures used in the Salem witch trials in order to understand our own system of due process better. Due process of law in criminal proceedings is generally understood to include the following basic elements: the principle of legality, which means that a law is written down that clearly states what the criminal conduct is and what the punishment will be; there is some impartial body who will hear the facts of the case; people who are accused are told what they are accused of and given an opportunity to defend themselves against the charge; at the trial, evidence is heard according to a set of rules and procedures that places the burden on the state to prove its case against the accused; and if people are legally found to be not guilty, they are free to return to a complete state of liberty, just like other free citizens.

Most of the rights of the accused are defined in the Bill of Rights, the first ten Amendments to the U.S. Constitution (see Figure 1.1). Yet the Salem trial took place almost a hundred years before the framing of the Constitution. The colonists brought with them from England, however, some important elements of the due process. What elements of due process were present, and which were not in the Salem witch trials?

The **rule of law** is a basic foundation for democratic society in which the exercise of governmental power is legitimated by the institutions of representative government. The crime of witchcraft was codified within the statute books of the Massachusetts Bay Colony as early as 1641.[16] The **substantive criminal law,** therefore, specifically defines those actions that are prohibited by the law (or, far less frequently, those that are required), as well as the penalty for violation of the criminal law. Basic to criminal process is the rule of *nullum crimen sine lege,* which means "No crime without a law." A fundamental element of fairness is the requirement that citizens should have advance warning of the behavior that is unlawful, and that these rules should be clearly spelled out so that citizens will know what they should not do or what they are required to do.

Procedural criminal law refers to the nature of the proceedings whereby someone is accused, arrested, investigated, tried, and possibly convicted of a crime. Whereas sub-

rule of law: the basic principle that the exercise of governmental power is regulated by laws formulated by legitimate institutions of representative government.

substantive criminal law: actions that are prohibited or prescribed by criminal law.

procedural criminal law: the lawful process for creating, enforcing, and implementing the criminal law.

A right to be assumed innocent until proven guilty
A right against unreasonable searches of person and place of residence
A right against arrest without probable cause
A right against unreasonable seizures of personal property
A right against self-incrimination
A right to protection from physical harm throughout the justice process
A right to an attorney
A right to a trial by jury
A right to know the charges
A right to cross-examine prosecution witnesses
A right to speak and present witnesses
A right not to be tried twice for the same crime
A right against cruel and unusual punishment
A right to due process
A right to a speedy trial
A right against excessive bail
A right against excessive fines
A right to be treated the same as others, regardless of race, sex, religious preference, and other personal attributes

FIGURE 1.1   Individual Rights Guaranteed by the Bill of Rights

stantive criminal law defines those actions or omissions that are unlawful, procedural criminal law defines the lawful process for creating, enforcing, and implementing the criminal law. Procedural law defines the rights of accused persons and the protections that exist within the law to guarantee that they will be tried according to legally established procedures.

The Magna Carta, or Great Charter, signed in 1215 by the English monarch guaranteed that "no freeman shall be . . . in any way imprisoned . . . unless by the lawful judgment of his peers, or by the law of the land."[18] Article 1, Section 9 of the U.S. Constitution offers the privilege of the **writ of habeas corpus** to citizens to challenge the legality of imprisonment by state or federal authorities within a court of law. No governmental authority may legally detain or confine an individual if he or she violates the rules of criminal procedure enshrined in the Constitution.

Adversarial versus Inquisitorial Systems

Most contemporary observers will notice immediately that those accused of witchcraft were not represented by a defense attorney during the trial. The absence of a defense attorney in these trials generally strikes us as fundamentally unfair. Without an opportunity to cross-examine witnesses and present evidence, there is little opportunity for accused persons to question the credibility of those testifying against them. In the seventeenth century, defendants were required to speak in response to the questions by the magistrate and by the prosecutors, but they were not permitted an attorney to speak, ask questions, or interview witnesses on their behalf. It is the one-sided nature of the trial itself that seems to make the Salem witch trials patently unfair.

The Sixth Amendment to the U.S. Constitution guarantees the accused the right to a defense. Although this right was enshrined in the Bill of Rights as of 1791, it was a privilege that was available only to those who could afford to pay for a lawyer in their own defense. As we will see in later chapters, it was not until the twentieth century that defense counsel became a right for rich and poor alike. In an **adversarial system,** the two sides must be equal if the battle is to be genuinely fair.

The Salem witch trials, however, did not follow a strictly adversarial model. Like our current crime control campaigns such as the War on Drugs, the fight against witchcraft was given highest priority by the members of the New England communities, who feared the loss of security from these dangerous individuals within their communities. The crime of witchcraft was viewed with the same sense of "moral panic" as is the crime of drug dealing today. Just as we are motivated to relax many procedural due process protections in order to fight the "war on drugs," the colonists opted to utilize specialized judicial procedures in order to stem the tide of this serious crime wave.

The specialized higher court that heard the witch trials was, in fact, not structured on an adversarial model but followed instead a more inquisitorial structure. The inquisitorial system places the judge in charge of the questioning or fact-finding process. It is the judge who calls forth witnesses and actively examines them. It is the judge who investigates and collects information by calling expert witnesses to the stand. Judges, in short, perform many functions that our system typically assigns to the two opposing attorneys. Notice that in the Salem trials, the judges ask the question of the witnesses, the victims, and the accused. In an **inquisitorial system,** the presentation of the facts is very one-sided: there is only one truth, and the judge is charged with uncovering that truth.

In the adversarial model, the business of presenting the truth is shared by the two opposing attorneys. The truth is achieved through a kind of contest between two competing and quite partial views of reality. Each side presents its own facts and interpretation of the facts before an impartial judge and jury, who declare one side the "winner" of the battle for truth and one side the "loser." Central to the adversarial system is the concept of advocacy: the job of the attorney is to allow each side to argue its case before a fair and impartial jury.

writ of habeas corpus: a petition to the court contesting the legality of imprisonment.

adversarial system: the state and the accused are represented by equal advocates before a neutral judge and jury.

inquisitorial system: the state is represented by a judge who has the power to investigate, interrogate, adjudicate, convict, and sanction the accused.

Before the adversarial method for determining the truth, there was a method known as trial by ordeal or trial by test. Belief in the truth-finding capacity of such processes rested on a belief in God. If the accused denied guilt, he or she would be required to undergo some ordeal such as walking over red hot coals, or plunging his or her hands into boiling water to retrieve a stone. Guilt was determined by the healing of the skin: it was believed that God would prevent the accused from being scalded if he or she was indeed innocent. Evidence of a burn was evidence of guilt. At the time of the witch trials, trial by test was still a legal method for determining truth: the accused were ordered to recite the Lord's Prayer, and any mistake or hesitation in their recitation was believed to be a signal from God.

The Confessions

The Fifth Amendment to the U.S. Constitution provides citizens various rights such as the right to a grand jury hearing before being formally indicted, the right to due process of law, and protection against double jeopardy. The most well known and important right articulated in the Fifth Amendment is the privilege against self-incrimination. No person accused of a crime can be forced to provide testimony against herself. The accused has the right to remain silent before the court: failure to answer questions cannot be used as evidence of one's guilt. At the time of the Salem witch trials, this right was not granted to those accused of a crime. Indeed, the worst punishment was reserved for the one man who refused to respond at all to the interrogations during the trial.

The importance of the right to remain silent, or the privilege against self-incrimination, can be seen in the willingness to confess of so many of those accused of witchcraft. The vast majority of those who confessed did so after the first wave of hangings. Upon hearing that the magistrates had decided to exempt those who admitted their guilt from execution, the accused acted to save their necks. In the words of one woman who tried to retract her confession in order to spare the lives of those she had implicated, "they told me if I would not confess, I should be put down into the dungeon and would be hanged, but if I would confess I should have my life."[18] Her retraction was ignored, and those she had implicated were summarily put to death even though she herself was spared.

The framers of our Bill of Rights recognized that the use of threats and torture to force people to confess to crimes makes a mockery of the justice system. Unless the accused is protected against coerced confessions, the rights of citizens to be free from the arbitrary power of the government simply does not exist.

The Punishments

Nineteen persons were hanged in Salem after they were legally convicted of witchcraft; three persons died while being held in jail awaiting trial or punishment; and one person was crushed to death beneath heavy stones for remaining mute during the trial itself. One of the most dramatic differences between the justice system of the colonial period and the justice system today lies in the area of punishment. Although there is much we share in common in the legal process of the courtroom, the legal and social norms around the punishment of criminal offenses are profoundly different between the two societies.

The Eighth Amendment to the U.S. Constitution guarantees to citizens protection against "cruel and unusual punishment." However, it is important to remember that what was cruel and unusual by the standards of the seventeenth century and by today's standards are quite different. The colonists brought with them from Europe many forms of the death penalty that we would find repugnant today. Few of us would advocate bringing children to witness the execution of an offender; and few would rest easy if the decaying body of the condemned were left hanging in the town square for days after the event. How do we decide what constitutes "cruel and unusual punishment"?

The U.S. Supreme Court has ruled that execution itself, for heinous and shocking crimes, does not violate standards of public decency. However, the court has also established that the infliction of unnecessary pain and suffering in the process of execution is a violation of the Eighth Amendment. By today's moral standards, we require the painless execution of those we condemn to die. To our forefathers in the seventeenth century, this would seem as strange as their use of torture and public humiliation does to us today.

THE VALUES OF CRIME CONTROL VERSUS DUE PROCESS

The witch trials in Salem marked the end of an era in our nation's history. Two years after the epidemic, the criminal statute on witchcraft was removed from Massachusetts law. After that fateful summer, no one was ever again prosecuted as a witch on U.S. soil. Why was there such a dramatic shift away from these prosecutions? What did people at the time feel about these events? What lasting impact did these trials have on the criminal justice system?

Today, we have adopted the phrase "witch hunt" to refer to a powerful conspiracy to prosecute individuals without due process and without protections of individual rights. The Salem experience made a lasting impression on the colonists, who recognized the awesome power of a judicial system that failed to preserve the rights of those accused of crimes. In the throes of a "moral panic," the citizenry of New England abandoned the values of the due process model in favor of an aggressive campaign of crime

In the Salem witch trials, defendants faced their accusers without the due process protections of defense counsel or the privilege against self-incrimination.

control. That delicate balance was severely tipped against those accused of this crime, and in their zeal to protect their community from a feared criminal conspiracy, the process of justice swept up many who appeared to have been unjustly accused, convicted, and executed. In the wake of that bloody summer, influential thinkers in New England realized the danger of abandoning the due process protections even when the threat seemed serious and overwhelming.

Increase Mather said in a speech in 1692, "It were better that ten suspected witches should escape, than that one innocent person should be condemned." This statement reflects the values of the due process model. For those who are concerned about the power of government to infringe on the rights and liberties of individual citizens, it is far more important that we ensure against wrongful convictions than that we guarantee that all guilty persons are caught and convicted. It is true that the crime of witchcraft was a serious threat to the communities of New England. They felt about witchcraft the same way that contemporary communities feel about drug dealing and child abuse. These are terrible and serious crimes, often hidden from view, often hard to prove in a court of law. We hate the thought that persons who are guilty of these crimes are able to use the rules of evidence and criminal procedure to "get off" on legal technicalities. In our zeal to protect our children and our communities, we may wish that these procedural rules could be relaxed when we are faced with a criminal defendant whom we believe to be guilty. At times such as these we are far more likely to adopt the values of the crime control model and prefer that the balance of power be tipped in favor of the state to put away those who are a danger to us all.

The values expressed by Mather's statement remain a central value of the due process model. Substitute the word "child molester" or "murderer" for the term "witches" and the difficult choice of adopting that position may be more meaningful to modern readers. Protecting the rights of those who may in fact be guilty is the only way to ensure the rights of those who are innocent. If we desire "perfect" crime control, we would have to relinquish certain rights such as the right to privacy, the right to a defense attorney, the right against self-incrimination, the right against unreasonable searches, and so forth. Without these protections, the state would have fewer obstacles in its pursuit of criminals. Yet it is also inevitable that among those who are accused and convicted, some will be innocent of the crime. Without the obstacles that place the burden on the state to be sure "beyond a reasonable doubt" that a person is guilty of a crime, many more innocent persons would be swept up in the powerful net of the criminal justice system.

The choice made by the framers of our Constitution is clear. They chose the protection of individual rights and liberties above the ability to limit and control crime. Today we continue to operate a system of crime control that is bound by the law of criminal procedure enshrined in the Bill of Rights. We have a system that pursues the control of crime regulated by due process procedures of the law. As a society, we continue to debate the relative balance of due process and crime control when we are faced with what we perceive as serious threats to our own communities.

KEY TERMS

social construction of reality p. 6
crime as social construction p. 6
deviance p. 7
moral entrepreneurs p. 7
moral panic p. 8
norm p. 8
socialization p. 8
folkways p. 8
mores p. 8

laws p. 9
natural law p. 9
morality p. 10
consensus model of law p. 10
latent function of law p. 11
conflict model of law p. 11
social control p. 11
crime control p. 11
crime control model of justice p. 12

due process model of
    justice p. 12
rule of law p. 14
substantive criminal law p. 14
procedural criminal law p. 14
writ of habeas corpus p. 15
adversarial system p. 15
inquisitorial system p. 15

REVIEW AND STUDY QUESTIONS

1. What does it mean to say that crime is a social construction?

2. What is the difference between crime and deviance? What does it mean to say that crime is a legal construction?

3. Explain the distinction between the concept of folkways, mores, and laws. What is the distinguishing feature of laws?

4. What is the role of the moral entrepreneur in the deviance process? Who was the moral entrepreneur in the Salem witch trials? What is the meaning of the concept of a moral panic?

5. What is the concept of natural law? How does this concept differ from the sociological view that morality is a social construction?

6. Explain the difference between a consensus model of law and a conflict model of law. Discuss the Salem witch trials from each of these theoretical perspectives.

7. Identify forms of social control, other than the law, which operate in society today. Explain the distinction between crime control and social control.

8. What are the greatest threats to individual freedom from the perspective of the crime control model? What are the greatest threats to individual freedom from the perspective of the due process model?

9. Explain the difference between the substantive criminal law and the procedural criminal law.

10. What is the adversarial system of justice and how does it differ from an inquisitorial system of justice?

CHECK IT OUT

On the Web

The Crucible, **www.sdroe.ca.us/score/cruc/cructg.html**
Check out this Web site for access to primary sources on Joseph McCarthy and the House Committee on Anti-American Activities, the hearings on anticommunism, and the hysteria of blacklisting in Hollywood in the 1950s.

Witch Hunt Information Center, **www.geocities.com/jgharris7/witchhunt.html**
Click here to find links to a series of modern day care abuse cases, which are being compared to the witch hunts of the earlier era.

On Film

Witch Hunt: The Wenatchee Sex-Ring Case
(23 minutes)
This documentary chronicles the largest child abuse case in U.S. history, in which forty-three adults were indicted on

more than 29,000 counts of rape and molestation of sixty children. Were these charges true, or was this a miscarriage of justice similar to the Salem witch trials? Available from Films for the Humanities and Sciences at **www.films.com.**

When Children Accuse: Sex Crimes (43 minutes)
*What happens when overzealous social workers and investigators coach young children as witnesses in cases concerning accusations of sexual molestation. Are there parallels to the Salem witch trials, in which nineteen people were executed based on the accusations of children? Available from Films for the Humanities and Sciences at **www.films.com.***

Frontline: Innocence Lost (120 minutes)
*This documentary is about the Little Rascals Day Care Center trial, and charges a gross miscarriage of justice based on the testimony of children coached by therapists and investigators. Available from PBS videos at **www.pbs.org.***

NOTES

1. Paul Boyer and Stephen Nissenbaum, Eds., *The Salem Witchcraft Papers: Verbatim Transcripts of the Legal Documents of the Salem Witchcraft Outbreak of 1692*, Vol. 1 (New York: Da Capo Press, 1977), p. 9.

2. Ibid., p. 113.

3. Ibid., p. 27.

4. Kai Erickson, *Wayward Puritans: A Study in the Sociology of Deviance* (New York: Wiley, 1966), p. 6.

5. William Graham Sumner, *On Liberty, Society and Politics: The Essential Essays of William Graham Sumner*, Robert C.

Bannister, Ed. (Indianapolis, IN: Liberty Fund, 1992), pp. 357–359.

6. Howard Abadinsky, *Law and Justice: An Introduction to the American Legal System* (Chicago: Nelson Hall, 1995), pp. 5–11.

7. Emile Durkheim, *Division of Labor in Society* (Glencoe, IL: The Free Press, 1960), pp. 73–80.

8. Jeffrey Reiman, *The Rich Get Rich and the Poor Get Prison: Ideology, Class and Criminal Justice* (Boston: Allyn & Bacon, 1998), pp. 51–91.

9. Ibid., p. 77.

10. Elliot Currie, *Confronting Crime: An American Challenge* (New York: Pantheon, 1985), pp. 226–229.

11. Daniel Van Ness and Karen Heetderks Strong, *Restoring Justice* (Cincinnati, OH: Anderson, 1997), p. 63.

12. Herbert Packer, *The Limits of the Criminal Sanction* (Stanford, CA: Stanford University Press, 1968). pp. 149–173.

13. Susan Brownmiller, *Against Our Will: Men, Women and Rape* (New York: Simon & Schuster, 1975).

14. Randall Kennedy, *Race, Crime and the Law* (New York: Vintage, 1998). p. 41.

15. John DiIulio, "The Question of Black Crime," *The Public Interest,* Fall 1992, pp. 3–32.

16. Richard Weisman, *Witchcraft, Magic and Religion in Seventeenth-Century Massachusetts* (Boston: University of Massachusetts Press, 1984), p. 12.

17. Theodore F. T. Plucknett, *A Concise History of the Common Law,* 5th edition, (London: Butterworth and Co., 1956), p. 24.

18. Ibid., p. 157.

CASE 2

And Justice for All: The Scottsboro Trials

The date was March 31, 1931, the first spring of the deepening economic crisis that came to be known as the Great Depression. The nation's railroads were magnets for drifters, young and old, men and women, black and white, roaming in search of work, shorter breadlines, or simply a place to sleep. A Southern Railroad tank car traveling west through northern Alabama was on its way to Memphis, Tennessee. A group of black youth met up with a band of white boys who challenged their right to be on the train. The argument led to rock throwing and a fistfight in which the losers, the white boys, were thrown from the train at one of its many stopping points. For the black youth still on the train, the departure of the angry boys was the end of the incident. The train chugged on for another forty miles and the boys soon forgot about the scuffle.

As the train rolled into the sleepy station of Paint Rock, a strangely large crowd was assembled at the tiny platform. The sheriff of Jackson County had deputized every male who owned a gun, with orders to capture all the Negroes on the incoming train. Dozens of white men armed with pistols, rifles, and shotguns were waiting to meet the train. Standing among them were the white boys who had been thrown from the train. As the black boys emerged from the train, they were immediately arrested by the posse. Nine boys ranging in age from 13 to 19 were bound together by a plow line and told they were being charged with assault and attempted murder. They were herded onto an open flatbed truck and transported to a jail in Scottsboro, Alabama, twenty-one miles away.

When they arrived at the jail, the boys were told that the charges were even more serious than as-sault and attempted murder. Two white women had been riding the train that day and as they got off at the Paint Rock station, they claimed that they had been raped by the boys after the fight. The two women were dressed in men's overalls and had been watching the scene from the sidelines. After the boys were bound and tied into the open truck, one of the women came forward and told the sheriff that she and her friend had been raped by the men. The sheriff took the women to the jail and there the two women, Victoria Price and Ruby Bates, identified each of the nine boys as the sheriff lined them up outside their cells in the jail.

For black men in the Deep South in the 1930s, the news that they had been accused of raping a white women was devastating. An accusation of rape by a white woman against a black man carried with it an almost certain death sentence. As one boy later acknowledged, "I knew if a white woman accused a black man of rape, he was as good as dead."[1] In the world of "he said, she said," the word of a white woman was always accepted before that of a black man, and the act of sexual relations between a black male and a white woman was almost always viewed as a form of rape because, in the words of one Mississippi editor, no white woman, no matter how depraved or destitute, would ever willingly "bestow her favors on a black man."[2]

As the boys huddled in the cells, they could hear the restless anger from the several hundred white men and boys gathered outside the jailhouse, clamoring for traditional Southern justice. Lynching was a potent and terrible tool of Southern-style "justice." In the decades following the Civil War, white Southerners resisted the idea of formal equality for blacks by exercising a form of terror whose primary tools were the rope and the burning cross. Most vulnerable to vigilantism were blacks who dared to be "familiar" with white woman. Although blacks were lynched for a variety of alleged offenses, the majority concerned accusations of rape against white women.

Lynching was perceived by many white Southerners, including members of law enforcement, governors, newspaper editors, and other respectable citizens, as a legitimate form of justice. They did not trust the State to exact justice and believed that honor demanded direct action on the part of the wronged family to exact revenge through lynching.

By the early 1930s, lynching had slowed to a trickle: fewer than ten black lynching victims were reported per year, compared to a horrifying rate of more than one hundred black victims per year in the post–Civil War years.[3] There were now many white citizens in the South who disapproved of lynching. They believed that the South should demonstrate its commitment to the rule of law and forbid this form of private justice from taking place. They believed that lynching simply generated more lawlessness and violence; even in the case of rape, they believed that lynching still undermined the rule of law and order.

Luckily for the nine boys held in the jail, those who opposed lynching as a response to violent crime included the county sheriff and the governor of the state of Alabama. By late afternoon a very large crowd had gathered outside the jail; by evening they had cut the wires on the deputies' cars to prevent them from removing the boys to a more secure jail. The sheriff called the governor, who ordered out the National Guard, which arrived at 11 p.m. with orders to disperse the crowd and guarantee that law, not vigilante justice, would have the final word in this case.

THE FIRST TRIALS

Justice by law came fast and furious. On March 30, all nine boys were indicted for rape by a Jackson County grand jury. One week later, a mere twelve days after their initial arrest, the boys went to trial. The boys were represented by an attorney who arrived in the courtroom at 9 a.m. stone drunk. Although he had been paid by black church leaders to represent the boys, the drunk white attorney told the judge he was not really their counsel but only there to offer advice. He admitted that he had not talked to the boys or prepared a case in their defense. The judge then appointed another attorney from the crowd assembled, a local attorney who reluctantly agreed to come forward. Together the two attorneys consulted briefly with the boys, and with no investigation or preparation, the trials began.

The four trials lasted only four days, and by April 9, four separate juries had convicted and sentenced eight of the boys to die by electrocution. A mistrial was declared in the trial of the ninth, Roy Wright, who was only 13 years old, because the jury divided over whether he should be sentenced to death or to life imprisonment. The prosecution had asked for a life sentence because of his age, but eleven of the jurors insisted on the electric chair for him, and the judge declared a mistrial.

The judge, prosecution, defense attorneys, and jury were all white males. No black man had ever served on an Alabama jury. No women or blacks were even permitted in the courtroom as observers. The packed courtroom consisted entirely of white men over the age of 21. When the verdict was announced, Haywood Patterson, one of the boys, described the courtroom as "one big white smiling face."[4] When the first verdict came down there were cheers and applause inside the courtroom, and a band struck up a tune to the joyous shouts of the enormous crowd of nearly 10,000 gathered outside.

During the trials, the main witnesses were the two women, Ruby Bates and Victoria Price, who described their ordeal in vivid detail. They pointed at the boys and told which one did what to whom and when. They claimed that the boys told them that they were going "to take us north and make us their women or kill us."[5] Others took the stand and testified to seeing the boys with the women on the train. Medical testimony confirmed that both women had had intercourse during the time in question, although there were no physical signs of beating or abuse. Called to the witness stand during these trials, some of the boys began to accuse one another of doing the crime, affirming widespread belief in their guilt. Six denied all knowledge of doing the crime or seeing others do it, but three of them, Norris, Patterson, and Wright, testified that they had seen others commit the alleged acts.

Years later, in an interview, Roy Wright, only 13 at the time of the trial, revealed what had taken place before he testified before the court.

> I was sitting in a chair in front of the judge and one of those girls was testifying. One of the deputy sheriffs leaned over to me and asked me if I was going to turn State's evidence, and I said no, because I didn't know anything about this case. Then the trial stopped awhile and the deputy sheriff beckoned to me to come out into another room—the room back of the place where the judge was sitting—and I went. They whipped me and it seemed like they were going to kill me. All the time they kept saying "Now will you tell?" and finally it seemed like I couldn't stand it no more and I said yes. Then I went back into the courtroom and they put me up on the chair in front of the judge and began asking a lot of questions and I said I had seen Charlie Weems and Clarence Norris with the white girls."[6]

Clarence Norris, too, had been beaten on the night of the first day of the trials. Not surprisingly, he turned state's evidence the very next day and testified against the others.

In less than two weeks after being charged with the crime, eight of the nine boys had been tried, convicted, and sentenced to die, with an execution date set for less than six months away. The newspapers were full of praise for the halls of justice in the South. They declared that "The people of Jackson County have shown to the world that they believe in Justice, regardless of color. . . . Our courts have shown the world that they believe in swift and undelayed justice being meted out." According to another newspaper, the defendants received "as fair a trial as they could have gotten in any court in the world."[7]

A LEGAL LYNCHING?

The boys had been spared a lynching by the angry mob, but in the eyes of many outside observers, particularly in the North, the trial itself and the death sentences that followed were merely lynching with a legal face. What was viewed in the South as a success for due process was perceived as a mockery of justice by the rest of the world. Far from an impartial examination of the evidence demanded by the Bill of Rights, Northern newspapers charged racism and abuse. In the wake of the trial, the governor of Alabama, the mayor of Scottsboro, and Southern newspapers were flooded with mail from around the world demanding the verdict be overturned on

appeal. Within days of the verdict, attorneys from the North paid for by the National Association for the Advancement of Colored People (NAACP), the American Civil Liberties Union (ACLU), and the International Communist Party were mobilized to come to the boys' assistance. For many in the North, this case symbolized the truth about Southern justice, which denied due process to its black citizens despite the nearly sixty years since the passage of the Fourteenth Amendment.

By late spring, these Northern attorneys had won a stay of execution for the boys pending appeal to the Alabama Supreme Court. The lawyers based their appeal on lack of adequate counsel for the boys, the exclusion of blacks from the jury in Alabama, and the hordes of spectators and press coverage of the case, which precluded the possibility of a fair trial. When the Alabama Supreme Court upheld the verdicts, claiming that the requirements of due process had been met and the boys had had a fair trial, protests were held as far away as Switzerland, France, Germany, and Spain. The attorneys filed and received a second stay of execution pending appeal to the U.S. Supreme Court. The highest court in the land agreed to hear the case in May 1932.

THE FIRST APPEAL: *POWELL* V. *ALABAMA*

On November 7, 1932, by a vote of seven to two, the U.S. Supreme Court overturned the conviction of the first four trials in the famous decision known as *Powell* v. *Alabama*, remanding the cases back to the lower courts for new trials. This was the first time in the nation's history that the Supreme Court set aside a state court's criminal conviction. The ruling was based on the argument that the boys had not been afforded adequate counsel and therefore had been denied due process under the Fourteenth Amendment.

Justice George Sutherland, in the majority opinion, wrote that a trial without a lawyer or real legal counsel could hardly be considered fair, and that the "failure of the trial court to give the defendants reasonable time and opportunity to secure counsel" was "a clear denial of due process."[8] The boys had been arraigned immediately after the return of the indictments, and at their arraignment the judge did not ask them if they had counsel or if they wished to have counsel appointed. They were given no opportunity to contact their parents or anyone else who might come to their aid. Nor did the presiding judge appoint a specific person to represent them. Instead the judge vaguely appointed the entire defense bar of the small town, seven defense attorneys. According to Sutherland, this was equivalent to assigning no one, because no one was obligated to prepare defense. In fact, it was only moments before the first trial began that the judge specifically appointed an individual attorney to represent the boys.

The majority of the Supreme Court concluded that to accept these guilty verdicts and execute these young men on the basis of this kind of legal process would be equivalent to a legal lynching. Execution without a retrial, according to the Supreme Court, would be judicial murder. The justices ordered a new trial for the boys.

THE SECOND TRIAL

Samuel Leibowitz was a famous criminal defense lawyer from New York City. He believed that his job was to defend anyone who claimed to be innocent, and it was the job of the jury and the judge to determine who was really guilty. His mission was to uphold the presumption of innocence by giving a spirited and zealous defense of his client in a court of law. He agreed to represent the boys *pro bono* (for free) in the new trial, which began March 27, 1933.

During the months leading up to the trial, Northern investigators came down and began asking questions, interviewing witnesses, and preparing evidence to defend the boys, a process that had not occurred before the first trial. Almost immediately, the story that came out began to look very different from the one told by the two women in the courtroom. Far from being the "flower of Southern womanhood," both of these young women were notorious prostitutes, who were raised in poor mill towns where blacks and whites intermingled freely. Both women resided in Chattanooga and had worked in a house of prostitution run by blacks. Both were known to solicit white and black men despite the laws that prohibited this conduct. Ruby Bates had even once been arrested on charges of hugging a black man in public.

Many in the North began to believe that the woman claimed to be "raped" to avoid humiliation or even prosecution when the train appeared in Paint Rock station. A witness came forward to testify that he had seen the women try to steal away from the posse when they first got off the train. They made their accusation twenty minutes after being apprehended by the posse; neither woman had torn clothing or seemed physically or emotionally distraught. White women who solicited sex from black men were subject to the worst kind of social condemnation and even criminal prosecution; as "poor white trash," Price and Bates knew they might be thrown in a jail cell, at the very least, for being hobos and vagrants. They were used to running from the For Price and Bates, the trials were the first time

they were treated as "virtuous" women in their entire lives.

Samuel Leibowitz began his defense with a pretrial motion that challenged the indictments because they had been handed down by a grand jury of Jackson County, and blacks were excluded from the rolls in Jackson County. If the indictments themselves were a violation of due process, the whole case might simply be dismissed. The prosecution countered by bringing officials from the election commission to testify that there were no specific laws or rules that excluded black citizens from serving on juries. Rather, blacks were not selected because they lacked the education, the character, and intelligence to serve on a jury. Despite the fact that there were lawyers, doctors, preachers, and school teachers among the possible black candidates within the county, white officials insisted that black citizens lacked sufficient qualifications to serve on a jury, testifying in court that no Negro in the county had the required sound judgment and "they will nearly all steal."[9] The motion to overturn the indictments was denied by Judge Horton. Jury selection took place and again there were no blacks on the jury, because there were no blacks in the jury pool in the county. This fact would serve as the basis for a later appeal to the U.S. Supreme Court.

The star witness for the prosecution, Victoria Price, took the stand to tell her story in a court of law for the fifth time. During the initial trials, the hapless defense attorneys had attempted to raise questions about the character of Victoria Price and Ruby Bates by asking them about their profession and about their previous liaisons with men. However, the prosecution objected to every question, and these objections were sustained by the judge every time. The court record also showed that the testimony of the doctor was vague and confused but that the defense was so inadequate no objections were raised at the time.

This time, star witness Price faced an experienced defense attorney ready and able to challenge the inconsistencies in her story. Like any good defense attorney, Leibowitz had entered the courtroom prepared with investigations into the facts, and had interviewed and subpoenaed witnesses who testified she had not been where she said she was. Witnesses testified that they had seen her the previous night with men in a hobo camp and that they had seen her board the train in the company of two white men. These two white men were found, and they testified that they had been with Price and Bates on the train the night before and had had sexual relations with the women that night.

Leibowitz also called many of the original witnesses and challenged their testimony as to what they had seen, forcing them to admit that they had not actually seen the boys with the two girls, that they might have been mistaken in what they saw or were not able to see fully what they claimed to have seen. Finally, he called the boys themselves and allowed them to testify. He pointed out to the jury that at least one of them had been so physically disabled that day that he could barely walk, let alone take part in a fight and ravage two women. Others testified that they had fought with the boys but that was all that had happened. None said they had even seen the women until they arrived at the train station swarming with the posse.

But the most amazing and shocking testimony came from the second victim, Ruby Bates. At the final moments of the trial, Leibowitz shocked the courtroom by calling her up as a witness for the defense. In an astounding fifteen minutes, Ruby Bates corroborated the testimony of the two white men and completely recanted her earlier testimony. The boys had not raped, touched, or even spoke to her or Victoria Price on that train ride. Victoria had told her to say that to avoid being arrested for vagrancy and crossing the state line with men. It had all been a big lie. To a stunned silence in the courtroom, the defense rested its case.

The prosecutor fought back. He claimed that Bates was lying. Ruby Bates had changed her story, so we knew she was a liar: she had lied before or she was lying now. Either way she was not to be believed. He said she had been bought with Northern "Jew" money, and Jews were telling her what to say. He claimed that Alabama justice was about to be sold with Jew money from New York. He accused Leibowitz of being a communist out to undermine the system of law and order in the United States.

The jury returned a guilty verdict, with death by electrocution for defendant Haywood Patterson. The jury chose to believe the testimony of Victoria Price over that of the witnesses for the defense. Charges of racism were countered with charges of Northern communist influence and Jewish subversion. The attention from around the world in this case was unprecedented. A march on Washington was organized in which thousands of people showed up to see Ruby Bates arm in arm with the mothers of the nine boys, demanding equal justice in the Southern courts. In the midst of all the tensions and protests, the courts put the other scheduled trials for the remaining boys on hold.

The defense attorneys made a motion for a new trial for Patterson, claiming that they had been denied due process because of the publicity surrounding the trial and the accusations of anti-Semitism made during the trial. The judge from the trial, Judge Horton, agreed to consider the motion on the grounds that the finding of the jury was contrary to the evidence presented in court. Judge Horton cited precedents when a trial judge had overturned the guilty verdict of a jury on the grounds that the jury had been swayed by bias, passion, and prejudice. On examining the testimony given in court, Horton declared a mistrial, overturned the judgment of the jury, and ordered yet a third trial for the defendant. Horton hoped that the prosecution would decide not to prosecute a third trial and the infamous Scottsboro case would end there. Judge Horton was defeated in the next election by an angry Southern public, who objected to his view that the boys had not received a fair trial. The prosecution re-filed an indictment against Patterson and the trials resumed under a new judge, William Callahan, who would preside over the remaining trials for all nine boys.

Judge Callahan made no secret of his opinion that this was a case of Northern outsiders interfering with the business of the Southern courts. He made no secret of his belief that the boys were guilty as charged. He denied all defense motions for a change of venue. He ruled that evidence presented by the defense to show that the jury rolls had been tampered with to show the presence of blacks on the list was not to be admitted into the courtroom because it would reflect badly on the jury board. He did not allow Leibowitz to ask questions during the trial about Victoria Price's character or her activities prior to boarding the train. He repeatedly cut off Leibowitz during questioning and ruled exclusively in favor of the prosecution.

Not surprisingly, the jury found Patterson guilty and for the third time sentenced him to die in the electric chair. The other boys were all scheduled for new trials to be presided over by the same judge. Those trials took place quickly, and with the same presiding judge came to the same harsh conclusion: guilty as charged, with the electric chair as punishment.

THE SECOND APPEAL: *NORRIS V. ALABAMA*

Again, Northern attorneys filed an appeal, this time on the basis of the conviction of Clarence Norris. The attorneys appealed to the U.S. Supreme Court, asking the court to review the record of the trial and claiming that Norris's Constitutional right to a fair trial had not been observed. This time the argument they focused on was the widespread and systematic exclusion of black citizens from the jury pool. Leibowitz argued before the court that even though the formal law of Alabama did not exclude blacks from the jury pool, those who were administering the law did.

The Supreme Court agreed that there was ample evidence that blacks had been systematically excluded from the jury rolls and that local officials had forged the jury rolls to conceal this fact. In a unanimous opinion, Chief Justice Charles Evans Hughes agreed with the defense position that Negroes had been systematically excluded from the jury rolls of the state of Alabama in violation of the equal protection clause of the Fourteenth Amendment. Even though there was no formal rule, it was evident that not one black man had ever been called to serve on a jury. The conviction of Norris was overturned, and his case was remanded back to Alabama for a new trial.

THE FINAL ROUND

A new round of trials began for the boys. Most people in the North believed that the state of Alabama would finally give up trying to prosecute these boys, especially because the Norris case required at least some representation by blacks on the grand jury and on the trial jury as well. But within seven months after the Supreme Court decision, the district attorney announced that he would seek new indictments to be handed down by a new grand jury that included one lone black juror, the first ever to serve in the history of the state of Alabama.

The date was now January 21, 1936, and the boys had been held in custody for five years. Haywood Patterson appeared for his fourth trial, with Victoria Price as the only witness against him. Again the jury found him guilty, sentencing him, this time, to seventy-five years in prison instead of the electric chair. Over the next year, four of the remaining boys were also tried, convicted, and sentenced to long prison terms ranging from twenty to ninety-nine years. Four of the boys who had served six-and-a-half years in jail were freed because they had been so young at the time of the crime, or because they were in such poor health that it seemed pointless to continue to charge them with serious rape and assault charges. They were released on the condition that they never return to the state of Alabama.

Eventually, the remaining imprisoned boys were given their freedom on parole after serving more than fifteen to twenty years on death row. Although the boys were tried and retried again, they never fully established their innocence; only two managed to receive official pardons twenty to forty-five years after the accusations were first made.

PILOGUE

e Scottsboro case was famous in its time as a symof Southern injustice toward African Americans. many, the repeated guilty verdicts, despite the whelming evidence that the accusations were ication, were confirmation of the racist real-he Southern legal system. For the rest of the

world, the trial was a contest between the Southern system of racial apartheid and the forces for equal rights. The lasting legacy of the case was the clear indication that the U.S. Supreme Court would seriously enforce the Fourteenth Amendment within the state courts. The Bill of Rights applies to all citizens in all proceedings at any level of government, and the Supreme Court gave clear notice that it would overturn convictions if the states did not respect the due process rights of its citizens, black or white.

Case adapted from James Goodman, *Stories of Scottsboro* (New York: Vintage Books, 1994); Lawrence Friedman, *Crime and Punishment in American History* (New York: Basic Books, 1993); Michael Maher, "The Case of the Scottsboro Boys," in Lloyd Chiasson, ed., *The Press on Trial: Crimes and Trials as Media Events* (Westport: Greenwood Press, 1997).

THINKING CRITICALLY ABOUT THIS CASE

1. What difference did the defense attorney make in the retrials of the Scottsboro boys? Were these "fair" in your view? Why or why not?
2. The Roman statue of Justicia, which often symbolizes the ideal of "justice for all," is a blindfolded goddess holding the scales of justice. Why is the goddess blindfolded? What is the blindfold intended to represent? Can our due process procedures create a system of "blindfolded" justice if the people who administer the laws are not blind to these differences?
3. Why, in your view, did the jury convict the Scottsboro defendants in the second trial despite the new evidence introduced by the defense?
4. Do you believe that the outcome of the trials would have been different if there had been substantial representation by black Alabaman citizens in the jury pool? Why or why not?
5. Should the judge have granted a change of venue for this trial? If so, where should the case have been tried? Should it have been tried in the North? Why or why not?
6. After the Supreme Court overturned the original convictions, the district attorney chose to pursue a second series of trials. After the dismissal of the charges at the second trial by Judge Horton, the district attorney elected to pursue a third series of trials. Following the second Supreme Court decision in *Norris* v. *Alabama*, the prosecutor's office chose to indict the boys for a fourth time. A prosecuting attorney has the discretion to dismiss charges against an accused or to continue to pursue them, guided by his or her own assessment of the "interests of justice." In your view, should the

district attorney have continued to prosecute the boys? Why or why not?

7. What about Ruby Bates and Virginia Price? As prostitutes, do you believe they would have received similar treatment if the accused had been white instead of black? Why or why not?

CHECK OUT THIS CASE

On the Web

Famous American Trials, jurist.law.pitt.edu
Learn more about the trial and events surrounding this case. Read transcripts of testimony made by key witnesses in each of the trials. Review the evidence and the judges' rulings. Read newspaper editorials of the time and check out an unpublished report written in 1931 by female reporter Hollace Ransdell about attitudes toward poor white women in Alabama

Greatest Trials of All Time, www.courttv.com/greatest trials/scottsboro/players.html
Go to this Web site for lots of detail about the players, interviews with historians, and an on-line video of the trials.

Scottsboro: An American Tragedy, www.pbs.org.wgbh/amex/scottsboro
Check out the PBS Web site that accompanies the PBS documentary about Scottsboro. See timelines, maps, and biographies of Victoria Price, Ruby Bates, Samuel Leibowitz, and others. Use this site to explore themes about race in the United States in the 1930s, lynching, and attitudes toward Jews, blacks, and women.

Langston Hughes on Scottsboro, www.pbs.org.wgbh/amex/scottsboro/filmore/ps_hughes.html
Langston Hughes was one of America's most respected black poets and writers. Read the four classic poems, "Justice," "The Town of Scottsboro," "Christ in Alabama," and "Scottsboro," penned by Langston Hughes in response to the trials in 1932.

On Film

Scottsboro: An American Tragedy (90 minutes)
*2000 Academy Award nominee for best documentary feature, this is a powerful documentary that uses archival footage to tell the complex story of one of the most controversial criminal justice trials of the century. Available from PBS at **www.pbs.org**.*

The Struggle for Justice

SOCIAL CHANGE IN THE CRIMINAL JUSTICE SYSTEM

The criminal justice system of the United States consists of federal, state, and local agencies involved in the control of crime. Together we refer to these agencies as the criminal justice system, although the term "system" suggests that there is more coordination among these agencies than there really is. The criminal justice system is a loosely connected network of agencies involved in the definition of, enforcement of, and response to criminal conduct. Decisions made in each of these agencies affect decisions in other agencies, but there is no single criminal justice system nor is there a single chief or administrator capable of coordinating or streamlining the overall process of crime control.

The criminal justice system is, also, not a static, unchanging system. In fact, the structure of the justice system has changed dramatically over time, is changing today in significant and important ways, and will look quite different in the future. Part of the goal of this text is for students to appreciate some of the important transformations in the criminal justice system and understand some of the forces that are creating change within the system today. The criminal justice system of the seventeenth century has some features in common with our system today but is profoundly different as well. The nineteenth century brought many innovations such as city and state police forces, penitentiaries and reformatories, systems of probation and parole, and the juvenile justice system. In recent decades we have seen important changes to the system such as community policing, community courts, community corrections, drug courts, boot camps, electronic monitoring, day reporting centers, substance abuse treatment centers, victim advocacy, restorative justice, and other types of innovations.

This chapter will examine one of the key forces for change in the administration of criminal justice: the struggle for equal justice for all members of our society. The Salem witch trials illustrate the fundamental importance of due process protections for individuals facing criminal prosecution by the state. The procedural elements of the criminal law, which govern how the law is made and enforced, are key to our understanding of justice in our society. We believe that all individuals should be treated fairly by the justice system and that neither the federal government nor the states "shall deprive any person of life, liberty or property without due process of law." The fair and equal treatment of all persons by the same set of rules is fundamental to our concept of justice based on equal rights for all.

The Scottsboro trials were hailed as a great achievement for equal justice in our society yet they took place almost one hundred and forty years after the Bill of Rights was written! Although rights may exist **de jure,** in law, they do not necessarily exist **de facto,** in practice. Many changes within the justice system were the result of political and social action on the part of those within our society who recognized a painful gap between the ideal of equal justice and the reality of the justice process. We refer to this as a "struggle" because it has involved a long and protracted effort to change aspects of the system that deny equal justice to certain segments of society. It is also important for students to recognize that it is a struggle that is ongoing, because the ideal of equal justice remains an elusive but worthy goal.

THE STRUCTURE OF THE CRIMINAL JUSTICE SYSTEM

To understand the social process whereby groups within U.S. society have fought for equal rights in the justice system, we must first have a clear picture of the architecture of the justice system. The U.S. form of government is uniquely complex by design. The founders of our government took seriously the warning issued by Lord Acton in the seventeenth century, that "Power corrupts and absolute power corrupts absolutely." The structure of the U.S. government divides power among three branches of government and further segments the power of government through the preservation of four separate levels of government: municipal, county, state, and federal. **Jurisdiction** refers to the legal authority within a given area of law or geographical boundary. In the U.S. system of government, legitimate power is divided into many different jurisdictions to create a very decentralized criminal justice system.

Federalism

The American Revolution instituted a major change in the administration of justice by creating a national system apart from the justice system operating within each state itself. The Tenth Amendment to the U.S. Constitution gives states jurisdiction over creating law in all matters not directly concerning the federal government. Violations of federal law are investigated by federal law enforcement personnel and prosecuted in federal courts, whereas violations of state law are handled by state criminal justice agencies. Federal crimes constitute a mere fraction of most criminal offenses; the vast majority of criminal behavior falls within the legal jurisdiction of the states.

The business of criminal justice is overwhelmingly a responsibility of local and state governments, with 60 percent of all justice personnel employed at the local level of government. Each state has its own criminal code and its own systems for administering those laws. The **supremacy clause** of the Constitution states that federal law supercedes or is supreme when federal and state law conflict. For many crimes there is a concurrent violation of both state law and federal law; which governmental agency has jurisdiction may depend on who originally arrested the offender or by local agreements worked out among the agencies. Although each state has a bill of rights in its own constitution, individual states cannot reduce citizens' rights below a minimum set by the federal Constitution. States are, however, free to raise the standard for individual rights above those set by the federal Constitution.

de jure: rights or practices that are established by law.

de facto: rights or practices that exist in fact.

jurisdiction: a sphere of legal authority.

federalism: a union of states agreeing to abide by the authority of the central government in areas of law specified by the U.S. Constitution.

supremacy clause: Article VI, Clause 2, of the U.S. Constitution declares federal law to be "the Supreme Law of the Land."

Separation of Powers

The separation of powers among the judiciary, legislature, and executive branches of government is enshrined in the Constitution, reflecting the political wisdom of the founding fathers, who sought to prevent the concentration of power in any one branch of government. To create a system of checks and balances, each stage of the criminal justice process comes under a different branch of governmental authority. The authority to make criminal laws is separated from the authority to interpret the law and adjudicate guilt or innocence, which is again separated from the authority to arrest, investigate, and sanction those who are convicted of criminal violations. At each level of government, different branches of government have jurisdiction over different parts of the process.

The power to make law rests principally with democratically elected representatives at all four levels of government: state and national legislatures, along with city and local governments. For the most part, misdemeanor and felony law are created by state and federal representatives whereas ordinances are created at the town, village, or city level of government. In the South before the Civil War, blacks were excluded from the process of political participation, as were nonwhites and women. The law of slavery that made it a capital offense for a black man to have consensual sex with a white woman but did not criminalize forcible sex by a white male with a black woman was written by legislatures composed exclusively of white males.

Whereas the power to make law rests with the legislature, the authority to administer and enforce the law is a responsibility of the executive branch of government. When the Scottsboro boys were initially arrested, they were apprehended by "deputies" of the Jackson County Sheriff's Department, the legal authority within county government that generally has jurisdiction over law enforcement within its geographical boundaries. The power to "deputize" ordinary citizens to use force legally to apprehend a fellow citizen is held by the legal agents of law enforcement. Their authority is to arrest suspects, gather evidence about their alleged crime, and assist the public prosecutor in presenting that evidence in a court of law.

Although law enforcement may use force to apprehend a citizen suspected of a crime, it is not the legitimate authority of law enforcement to determine if that citizen is guilty of that crime. The **presumption of innocence** is, in fact, a guiding principle for how law enforcement is, ideally, supposed to treat all citizens suspected of crimes.

The only branch of government with the judicial authority to determine legal guilt is the judiciary. It is the job of the judiciary to determine the facts of the case. The Scottsboro boys were accused of committing rape, but until they were tried in a court of law according to the rules of evidence and within the bounds of due process, they could not legally be convicted of the crime.

Once a sentence is ordered by a judge, the responsibility for carrying out the sentence falls to the correctional system, which is a part of the executive branch of government. The custodial responsibility for the boys during the many years they sat awaiting trial and during the time they served their sentences fell to the prison system, which may be run by municipal, county, state, or federal governments. Usually, individuals convicted of violating a municipal, county, state, or federal law come under the custodial supervision of that legal entity. The Scottboro boys were held in a county jail awaiting trial initially, but were later transferred to the state prison of Alabama. The conduct of their jailers and the conditions of their incarceration are an executive branch responsibility.

Power of Judicial Review

The judiciary is given a unique power to oversee the activities of the other two branches of government. For this reason, unlike the executive and the legislature, who are elected by the public and are responsive to public opinion, the judiciary, for the most part, is

---

separation of powers: the division of the government into three branches: executive, legislative, and judicial.

presumption of innocence: guiding principle of criminal procedure, which places the burden of proof on the state.

independent. The appointment of federal judges and U.S. Supreme Court justices for life is intended to protect the independence of this branch of government and preserve its capacity to enforce the rule of law on even the most powerful members of society, namely, those within the government itself.

At the pinnacle of the three equal branches of government sits the U.S. Supreme Court, which has the power to render acts and decisions of the other two branches null and void if the Supreme Court determines that their actions violate the Constitution. It is the inviolability of the Constitution and the ultimate power of the Supreme Court as the **court of last resort** to interpret the Constitution that creates a unique source of standardization on all fifty states and thousands of local jurisdictions across the United States.

The power of **judicial review** means that the courts are able to exercise control over the other two branches of government by insisting that they adhere to the rule of law. No president or governor may place him- or herself above the law; the courts are independent of the executive branch so they can act effectively as a check on possible abuses of power by individuals in public office. Courts may declare laws written by legislatures unconstitutional; they may declare practices of prisons and treatment of prisoners unconstitutional, they may overturn the decisions of lower courts, and they may declare police behavior to be crossing the boundaries of the legitimate and legal use of force. The legal right of the courts to act as a watchdog over the other branches of government has been crucial for the struggle by less powerful groups within our society—minorities, women, children, and poor people—to establish equal rights under the law.

The Constitution as Sleeping Beauty

The first ten Amendments to the U.S. Constitution, known as the Bill of Rights, were formulated to regulate the relationship between the citizen and the federal government. The Constitution was drafted at a time when the threat of tyranny by the distant king of England was paramount, and most colonists were concerned about the threat to their autonomy from a national government. As we have seen, most of the text of the Bill of Rights defines the meaning of due process for the administration of criminal justice.

The Constitution is a living document, interpreted anew and made relevant to the changing values and conditions of society. The judiciary is the ultimate interpreter of the Constitution, and no governmental authority may violate the Constitution, although the Constitution may itself be amended by Congressional majority ratified by two-thirds of the states. Amendments to the U.S. Constitution are extremely rare: between 1800 and 1992, it was amended only twenty-seven times.

Until the end of the nineteenth century, the Supreme Court interpreted the Bill of Rights as regulating only the relationship between citizens and the federal government. According to the interpretation of Supreme Court justices in 1833, the Constitution provided citizens no protection against state or local governmental action.[10] The Fourteenth Amendment, passed by Congress and state legislatures across the land, was a direct response to this narrow judicial interpretation: if the Supreme Court declared that there was nothing in the Bill of Rights that said it pertained to the states, then an amendment to the Constitution was needed to protect the civil rights of all citizens in this nation. The Fourteenth Amendment declares, in part, that:

> No State shall make or enforce any law which shall abridge the privileges or immunities of citizens of the United States; nor shall any State deprive any person of life, liberty or property, without due process of law; nor deny to any person within its jurisdiction the equal protection of the laws.

The Scottsboro case marked one of the first times that the federal judiciary enforced the due process requirement of the Fourteenth Amendment by overturning a state court

court of last resort: the power of the state supreme court to be the final interpreter of the state constitution and the power of the U.S. Supreme Court to be the final interpreter of the U.S. Constitution.

judicial review: the power of the judicial branch to declare acts of the executive or legislative branch unconstitutional.

conviction. Although the amendment had been passed more than sixty years earlier, the Fourteenth Amendment was "brought to life" by a new interpretation of its meaning by the Supreme Court beginning with the Scottsboro case. For the first time, the Supreme Court overturned a state court conviction on due process grounds.

The majority opinion in *Powell* v. *Alabama* stated that the trial in this case violated a sense of fundamental fairness that underlies all the rules of criminal procedure laid out in the Bill of Rights. These are immutable principles of justice that were clearly violated in the trials in Alabama even though they appeared to go through the motions of legal procedure. The **fundamental fairness doctrine** articulated by the Supreme Court in the Scottsboro case states that the U.S. Supreme Court will examine state court processes on a case-by-case basis to be sure that they are substantively "fair."

In the Powell case the Supreme Court also relied on a different legal doctrine in ruling the trial unconstitutional. The **incorporation doctrine** states that the due process clause in the Fourteenth Amendment includes or "incorporates" all the provisions of the Fourth, Fifth, Sixth, and Eighth Amendments. Because the Fourteenth Amendment says that states may not violate "due process," then it must mean that states may not violate all the safeguards in all of these amendments, because they define what due process is. While the full incorporation doctrine has never been accepted by the majority of the Supreme Court, over the years the Court has opted for a system of **selective incorporation,** identifying specific elements of each of these amendments that are seen as fundamental to a fair justice process. In *Powell* v. *Alabama,* the Court took the first step in selective incorporation by establishing that the Sixth Amendment right to counsel, at least in cases where defendants were facing execution, was "incorporated" within the meaning of the phrase, "due process of law."

Despite the rulings in the Scottsboro cases, the Supreme Court was reluctant to expand the rights "incorporated" in the Fourteenth Amendment and interfere with the state courts during most of the 1930s and 1940s. Beginning in the early 1960s, however, there was an avalanche of rulings by federal appellate courts and the Supreme Court that signaled the start of what has been termed the "due process" or "criminal law" revolution. The Supreme Court and other federal courts exercised their power of judicial review to "awaken" other provisions of the Bill of Rights and enforce those provisions on the states, relying on the selective incorporation doctrine to do so.

fundamental fairness doctrine: the definition of due process that focuses on substantive fairness in the application of the law.

incorporation doctrine: the legal principle that all the procedural protections of the Bill of Rights apply to state courts under the due process and equal protection clauses of the Fourteenth Amendment to the U.S. Constitution.

selective incorporation: the legal principle that only some of the protections in the Bill of Rights applies to state courts under the due process and equal protection clauses of the Fourteenth Amendment.

AND JUSTICE FOR ALL?

The Bill of Rights was added to the Constitution in 1791 to articulate the basic protections for citizens from the powers of the federal government. However, in 1791 the privilege of citizenship did not extend to nonwhites or to women. Although the Constitution is based on the "natural law" principle that all men are created equal, the status of personhood was reserved for white males only. Native Americans, blacks, women, and children were all seen as "nonpersons," ineligible for the "self-evident" rights afforded to all. From the start, the concept of equal rights was based on a form of injustice: the exclusion of whole categories of persons from the status of personhood.

The fundamental bias in the administration of justice can be seen clearly in the Dred Scott case in 1856, when the Supreme Court ruled that Scott could not be considered a citizen because he was a Negro. The justices of the Supreme Court conceded that individual states may choose to grant citizenship to nonwhites but that, as individuals, blacks had no right to claim citizenship because they did not have self-evident rights as persons. In the words of Chief Justice Roger Taney, at the time the Constitution was written, members of the black race were viewed as "altogether unfit to associate with the white race either in social or political relations; and so far inferior, that they had no rights which the white man was bound to respect."[11]

Women, too, were clearly seen as essentially "different" and "inferior" to men. In a case involving the request of a woman to practice law, the U.S. Supreme Court upheld the state law that prohibited women from admission to the bar, stating: "The paramount destiny and mission of woman are to fulfill the noble and benign offices of wife and mother. This is the law of the Creator."[12] Thus, despite the formal rights granted in the Bill of Rights, the interpretation of that doctrine tolerated and perpetuated profound inequalities between categories of persons within society.

Chief Justice Earl Warren, who some believe to have played the role of "Prince Charming" to the slumbering Bill of Rights, believed the Constitution should be seen as a living document to be interpreted and adapted to the "evolving standards of decency" within society. This has allowed the Constitution to serve as a tool for social change as disadvantaged groups have sought to use the power of the Constitution's words to bring the daily workings of the system in line with the lofty ideals expressed in those documents. It is the architecture of our system of government, which grants the power of judicial review to the courts, which serves as an enormously valuable avenue for those excluded and oppressed by the system to force some modicum of positive social change.

Not all movements to change the criminal justice system have relied on the Constitution and the Supreme Court to bring about different laws, policies, and practices. Other movements have changed the attitudes of lawmakers toward certain crimes or certain segments of society. The awareness of child abuse, drunk driving, violence against women, and victims rights are only a few areas where the efforts of citizens in our society to raise awareness has resulted in significant changes in the law and policies of the justice system.

Legacy of Racial Injustice for African Americans

Before the Civil War, the criminal law itself was part of the system of white supremacy and control. States were permitted to write unequal laws that made different crimes for whites and blacks. It was a crime for blacks to learn to read, to gather to worship without the presence of a white person, to neglect to step out of the way when a white person approached on a walkway, to smoke in public, to make loud noises, or defend themselves or their families from physical assault.[13] Even free Negroes in the slave states were subject to a different set of legal rules: every slave state in the south except Delaware, and several Northern states as well, prohibited free Negroes from testifying against whites in court, and many states had laws that prohibited free blacks from meeting with, talking to, or associating with slaves, on pain of whipping or worse.

For blacks, the law offered little or no protection from white violence. Actions that were considered criminal when the victim was white were not criminal if the victim was black. The law simply did not view rape of a slave woman as a crime, and the use of physical violence against slaves was permissible under the law. The use of the whip to punish errant slaves was the prerogative of the master and mistress—even if that whipping led to the death of the slave—so long as the violence was done in the service of discipline. The main check on white violence against black slaves was the economic interest of their owners: as valuable property, slave owners often prosecuted other whites who "damaged" their property with excessive use of violence.[14]

The end of the Civil War was marked by an extraordinary flurry of legislative activity and the passage of the Thirteenth, Fourteenth, and Fifteenth Amendments to the Constitution. The Thirteenth Amendment outlawed the institution of slavery. Almost immediately, many Southern legislatures passed discriminatory "Black Codes" that criminalized a wide range of conduct by black citizens only. In Mississippi, for example, it became a criminal offense for a black to make an insulting gesture toward a white. Whites beat or killed African American citizens for such "crimes" as failing to step off the sidewalk, to use deferential forms of address, or attempting to vote. The criminal justice system, for the most part, refused to protect blacks against the tidal wave of illegal violence by white citizens and, with the end of slavery, there was no longer any "property" interest by white owners to protect the lives of blacks.

The Civil Rights Act of 1866 was written by Congress to abolish these discriminatory criminal codes in the Southern states. This act stipulated that all citizens "of every race and color, without regards to any previous condition of slavery or involuntary servitude . . . shall be subject to like punishment, pains and penalties." To further ensure that every local law enforcement officer and court across the land would treat all citizens the same, in 1868, Congress passed the Fourteenth Amendment to the Constitution, which obligates the states to bestow upon all persons, "the equal protection of the law."[15] The Fifteenth Amendment of 1879 prohibits states from excluding persons from the vote on the basis of race. All of these amendments were designed to protect the civil rights of black men in the South.

During the period of Reconstruction, many blacks entered into political offices and participated in the justice system as never before. Blacks were able to serve as jurors, legislators, magistrates, sheriffs, police officers, and even state supreme court justices. Supported by the efforts of the federal government and the newly created U.S. Department of Justice, there were numerous efforts to end vigilante terror groups such as the Ku Klux Klan. But by 1877 the forces of Reconstruction fell to the dominance of Southern whites, who regained power in virtually all legislatures across the South. The end of Reconstruction ushered in fifty long years of segregation, discriminatory laws known as Jim Crow laws, and systematic illegal violence against black citizens.

Vigilantism flourished in the South. Although the South lost the Civil War, the attitudes of the people there did not change. Many in the South felt that the North was imposing laws on them through the federal government and its Constitutional amendments. The Klan organized to enforce the "true" law of the South, the unwritten law of white supremacy.

More than 2,500 blacks were murdered in the sixteen years before 1900. Lynching was a powerful tool of racial social control. Lynching was intended as a warning to other blacks to stay on their side of the color line. It was the violation of the unwritten codes of color etiquette that most often sparked this form of violence, and the most egregious crossing of the line concerned the sexual relations between black males and white women.

Underenforcement of the Law

The evidence clearly shows that the criminal justice system did not offer black citizens the type of security against victimization afforded to white citizens. For the most part, until the latter part of the twentieth century, the entire criminal justice system was "lily white": there were no black jurors, no minority police officers, few black lawyers, fewer black judges, no black correctional guards or probation or parole officers. As Patterson noted when he faced the courtroom, all he saw was "one big smiling white face." Crimes committed by whites against blacks were difficult to prosecute, because they depended on white witnesses, jurors, and prosecutors to enforce these laws.

However, the vast majority of criminal victimization, in the past as well as today, occurs within racial groups, and the criminal justice system also failed to respond to criminal victimization *within* black communities. The problem of underenforcement of the law of crimes committed by blacks against other black citizens was noted by Gunnar Myrdal in 1944 in his famous book on the problem of racism within American society. "Leniency toward Negro defendants in cases involving crimes against other Negroes is thus actually a form of discrimination."[16]

Absence of adequate police protection within the black community continues to be a concern among African Americans today. Some people believe that the current epidemic of drugs and violence in the inner cities is tolerated only because those most affected are predominantly minority residents of poor inner-city communities.[17] Media coverage of crimes continues to vary with the racial status of the victim, with the me-

vigilantism: illegal violence conducted by groups or individuals who believe they are enforcing justice despite the actual content of the law.

African Americans have endured high levels of violence at the hands of whites. Lynching was used by Southern whites to terrorize blacks and enforce compliance with the unwritten codes of white supremacy while the legal system refused to prosecute those who committed these terrible crimes.

dia showing relatively little interest in publicizing crimes that involve a black perpetrator and a black victim. When a young, affluent white woman was raped in New York's Central Park in 1989, the case was front-page news all over the country. That same week there were twenty-eight other cases of sexual assaults, some just as brutal, seventeen of which involved black women as victims, yet most of these cases barely made the back pages of the newspapers.[18] In Cases 3 and 4, we examine the stereotypes in the official crime statistics, news, and entertainment, which perpetuate the widely held assumptions that criminal danger emanates primarily from persons of color.[19]

Overenforcement of the Law   Even more controversial than the issue of underenforcement of black victimization is the belief that the justice system overly polices and punishes minority citizens. For many African Americans (and other minorities), there is a strong conviction that the justice system is a "just us" system bent on the racially selective pattern of enforcement of our nation's laws.[20] The attitudes of the American public on this subject are profoundly divided by race: the vast majority of blacks in 1995 believed that the police and courts discriminate against blacks, while an equally large majority of whites did not believe the system treats blacks unfairly.[21] Whatever may or may not be true about racism within the criminal justice system today, it is clear that attitudes among blacks and whites on this subject are divided by race.

The most disturbing evidence of racial discrimination can be found in the growing racial disparity in the numbers of nonwhite Americans under criminal justice supervision in this county: as of 1994, the United States imprisoned black males at a rate six times higher than white males; although African American males make up less than 7 percent of the U.S. population, they constitute more than half of the prison population.[22] By 1994, one out of every three African American males in the nation between the ages of 20 and 29 was under some form of criminal justice supervision.[23]

Other data show evidence of persistent forms of discrimination in the policing of minority communities, particularly for drug offenses,[24] incidents of police shootings[25] and police brutality,[26] jury selection,[27] and the application of the death penalty.[28] Scholars who study the criminal justice system today are divided on this issue, with some believing that the evidence of discriminatory patterns in arrest, conviction, and sentencing of black defendants is clear and convincing,[29] while others argue that apart from the existence of occasionally racist individuals, the evidence shows that the system treats blacks and whites alike, given the difference in the pattern of offending between the two groups.[30] Researchers differ on whether or not racial discrimination exists in the making of laws, such as the disparity in penalties for crack cocaine versus powder cocaine; in the activities of the police on the inner-city streets or the nation's highways through racial profiling; in the backroom prosecutorial discretion in plea bargaining; or in judicial sentencing and parole.

Race is also compounded by issues of class.[31] The experience of privileged criminal defendants who enjoy the advantages of skillful defense attorneys and other hidden advantages of class operate to influence the outcome of the justice process. The criminality of the streets rather than the criminality of the suites is the predominant target of the justice system. The legacy of black unemployment concentrated in heavily policed urban spaces has led to a spiraling cycle of criminality and social disorganization within many minority communities.[32]

In cases to follow we will examine the issue of racial profiling on our nation's streets, highways, and airports; the causes of police brutality and the history of relations between the police and the minority community; the issue of race and jury decision making; and the impact of mandatory sentencing on the overincarceration of minority youth and young adults in our nation's prisons.

Legacy of Gender Injustice

When Haywood Patterson looked out to see one big smiling white face in the courtroom, it was the smiling face of a man. Until 1870, women were barred from practicing law, and women did not have the right to vote until 1920. Nor were women a significant presence in policing or corrections until recent decades, and even now there remains considerable sexual discrimination in policing, corrections, and the legal profession. Historically the law has also failed to protect women from serious victimization by males in society, particularly in crimes of violence and sexual assault committed within the context of intimate relationships.

Criminalizing Male Violence against Women   The formal law, deriving from centuries of common law tradition, embodied a serious bias against women, especially in the marital relationship. Just as the law failed to criminalize routine violence by whites against blacks, so too was the criminal law silent on the use of violence by men against their lawful wives. Just as the master had the absolute legal authority to use violence to discipline his slaves, so too did the father have the right to use violence against his wife and children. The law did not recognize women as independent adults: according to the legal doctrine of *coverture*, the wife's legal status was subsumed under her husband's identity as a citizen. She did not have the right to own property or to control her own resources once she was legally joined to her husband in marriage.

The common law doctrine regulating the use of violence by husbands to discipline their wives was known as the **rule of thumb:** the use of physical force was not a form of criminal assault unless the husband made use of a stick that was thicker than a human thumb. In the United States the statutory law did not take wife beating seriously: a law in Maryland, for example, make it a only a misdemeanor for a man to "brutally assault and beat his wife."[33] Assaults that were not "brutal" were, of course, perfectly legal.

The *de facto* practice of underenforcement of male violence against women parallels the experience of blacks who suffered from a failure of the justice system to criminalize violence of whites against blacks. Even when the laws prohibited violence within the home, the informal attitude of the justice system prevented enforcement of those laws. In an infamous decision in 1874, a North Carolina judge acknowledged that it was barbaric for husbands to beat their wives but declared the courts were not interested in meddling in affairs that take place within the home. "In order to preserve

rule of thumb: common law doctrine regulating the use of physical force by husbands against their wives.

the sanctity of the domestic circle, the Courts will not listen to trivial complaints.... it is better to draw the curtain, shut out the public gaze, and leave the parties to forgive and forget."[34]

The courts and police failed to respond to violence against women unless it was an attack by a stranger; the violence that took place within the home was considered not the business of the justice system. Men were tacitly seen as exercising their right to discipline their wives or it was seen as a private matter, a domestic disturbance that should properly be settled by the parties themselves. Police who responded to a call in these cases were told to calm the parties down and mediate the disagreement.[35]

Sexual violence against women, the crime of rape, was also subject to a systematic pattern of selective enforcement throughout our nation's history. The degree of seriousness and even the criminality of the act depended far more on the status of the victim and the offender than on the crime itself. As we have seen, black women were never perceived as genuine "victims" of rape. But this "double standard" was also true of women who were divorced, sexually promiscuous, or whose dress, behavior, or occupation meant they were less than virtuous.[36] If the accused in the Scottsboro case had been white men, this case would never have gone to trial, because women like Bates and Price would hardly have been considered worthy victims, given their social status.

The law of rape demanded that a woman charging rape prove her virtue in the trial. It was often the woman's sexual history and character that was on trial when a charge of rape was prosecuted in a court of law. The law also required women to show evidence of actual resistance. Thus, when women failed to show signs of physical violence and struggle, they were seen as having consented to the act. The burden was on the victim to show that she had resisted the actions of the man.

Denied the vote until 1920, women had no voice in shaping the law of rape or domestic violence. Even after the passage of the Nineteenth Amendment, giving women the vote, women continued to be excluded from full participation in the justice system until recent decades. Major changes came as the feminist movement in the 1970s mobilized around the area of legal reform to fully criminalize male violence against women and to end the "blame the victim" attitude that excused men from full responsibility for their actions by focusing on the allegedly provocative actions of the victim. The two key areas of criminal justice reform started by the women's movement were sexual assault and domestic violence.

In the 1970s, **rape shield laws** were passed by most states, barring evidence of past sexual activity at trial and eliminating the requirement that victims show evidence of resistance. Until the 1970s, husbands were granted immunity in state legal codes from the crime of rape committed against their spouse. Rape was defined as forcible sexual act upon a woman "other than a wife." Husbands, simply, could not be prosecuted for raping their wives because these acts were not criminalized. Reformers fought for changes in the state criminal codes to remove this exemption for husbands, and by 1989 only nine states continued to maintain this discriminatory law on their books.[37]

Rape remains a highly underreported crime largely because of the shame of victims and continued social attitudes that blame women for male violence toward them. Ongoing areas of reform include the effort to raise awareness about other forms of intimate violence, such as date rape or acquaintance rape. Women activists have also fought to have rape crisis units within police forces so that police will not "revictimize" women who come forward to make the charge.

The area of domestic violence is another key focal point of social reform in the criminal justice system brought about by political action of women. Beginning with the battered women's shelter movement in the early 1970s, women began organizing to provide safe havens for women victimized by violent partners. By 1989 there were 1,200 shelters or safe homes across the nation.[38] Women activists also fought for state legislation authorizing judges to issue **domestic violence restraining orders** and "no contact" orders in response to the complaints of victims. Within the courtroom, women have advocated for reform of the law of self-defense to include criteria that fit the situation

rape shield laws: laws that bar the introduction of evidence about a victim's prior sexual conduct.

domestic violence restraining orders: legal remedies created for abused women, which can be sought at the discretion of the complaining party to prohibit or restrict contact with an abusing spouse or partner.

Violence against women has been routinely underenforced by the criminal justice system, which often fails to take domestic violence seriously and to aggressively prosecute men who use violence against their wives and intimate partners. Since the 1970s, activists have lobbied for reform in the system to protect women against male violence.

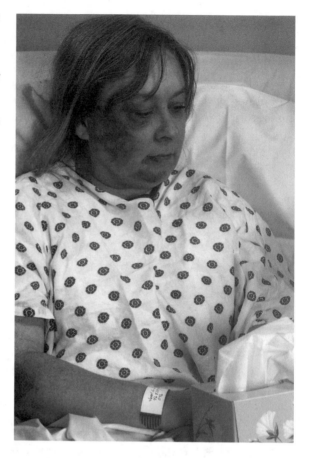

when women are being threatened by the men in their lives. The *battered woman's defense,* as it has come to be known, has been used in cases where women are prosecuted for killing or assaulting their intimate partner.[39]

One of the obstacles preventing justice for women as victims has been the exclusion of full female participation in the criminal justice system itself: as legislators, jurors, attorneys, judges, police officers, and correctional officers. As noted earlier, there were no woman lawyers before the 1870s, and women were barred from participation on juries until well into the twentieth century. Today the picture looks quite different. As of the year 2000, it is estimated that women make up nearly half of the nation's lawyers. The first woman to be appointed to the U.S. Supreme Court, Sandra Day O'Connor, has been joined by another female justice, Ruth Bader Ginsburg. Women have had a small presence on urban police forces since the early twentieth century: the first female police officer worked in Portland, Oregon, in 1905; by 1914, the Los Angeles police force had eight policewomen.[40] In the 1990s, women represented about 9 percent of the police forces, although this percentage was considerably higher in larger urban departments, where women make up as much as one-fifth of the workforce.[41]

Yet women continue to face substantial obstacles toward achieving equal status and participation within the predominantly male occupations of the criminal justice system. Women were not permitted to work as patrol officers until the 1960s, and there were no female sergeants in the entire nation until a successful lawsuit was won against the New York Police Department in 1965. In 1991, only 8 percent of all state judges and about 9 percent of all federal judges were women; and women are conspicuously absent in the higher ranks of both policing and corrections. Although there is far greater equality and diversity within the field of criminal justice today than in the past, women and minorities still find it necessary, at times, to use the laws against discrimination in order to struggle for equal participation in the administration of justice.

KEY TERMS

de jure p. 29
de facto p. 29
jurisdiction p. 29
federalism p. 29
supremacy clause p. 29
separation of powers p. 30

presumption of innocence p. 30
judicial review p. 31
court of last resort p. 31
fundamental fairness
    doctrine p. 32
incorporation doctrine p. 32

selective incorporation p. 32
vigilantism p. 34
rule of thumb p. 36
rape shield laws p. 37
domestic violence restraining
    orders p. 37

REVIEW AND STUDY QUESTIONS

1. Explain the difference between rights that exist de jure and those that exist de facto.
2. Define the concept of jurisdiction.
3. What is the meaning of separation of powers, and how does it operate to balance authority within the criminal justice system?
4. What is the power of judicial review? How was it used in the Scottsboro case?
5. Why have people referred to the Constitution as "Sleeping Beauty"?
6. What are the fundamental fairness doctrine and the incorporation doctrine? Explain how these legal theories have affected the struggle for justice in the United States.

7. Describe the pattern of underenforcement of the criminal law for African American citizens. Why is this a form of racial discrimination?
8. What does it mean to say that lynching was used as a tool of social control by whites over black citizens?
9. Describe the pattern of underenforcement of the criminal law in the area of male violence toward women. How is rape used as a tool of social control by men over women?
10. Identify two reforms that have increased prosecution of males who commit violence against women.

CHECK IT OUT

On the Web

Southern Poverty Law Center, **www.splcenter.org/**
Web site of an organization founded in 1971 to win equal rights for poor people and minorities.

VAWA: Violence against Women Office Homepage, **www. ojp.usdoj.gov/vawo/welcome.html**
Check out the VAWO home page to learn about the Violence against Women Act of 2000 and national strategies to criminalize and prosecute violence against women.

On Film

Lynching: Postcards from a Heinous Past (22 minutes)
A documentary featuring picture postcards from the period, which create a grim chronicle of the gross inhumanity

and public spectacle of lynching. Available from Filmakers Library, **www.filmakers.com.**

To Kill a Mockingbird (129 minutes)
This classic fictional film starring Academy-Award winner Gregory Peck is set in a Southern town and closely parallels the real-life events of the Scottsboro trials.

Mississippi Burning (128 minutes)
This contemporary film portrays the first successful civil rights convictions of white defendants accused of murdering black civil rights workers, won in a Southern court with an all-white jury in Mississippi.

NOTES

1. James Goodman, *Stories of Scottsboro* (New York: Vintage, 1994), p. 5.
2. Ibid., p. 21.
3. Lawrence Friedman, *Crime and Punishment in American History* (New York: Basic Books, 1993), p. 191.
4. Goodman, *Stories of Scottsboro*, p. 6.
5. Ibid., p. 14.
6. Ibid., p. 97.
7. Michael Maher, "The Case of the Scottsboro Boys," in Lloyd Chiasson, Ed., *The Press on Trial: Crimes and Trials as Media Events* (Westport, CT: Greenwood, 1997), p. 105.
8. *Powell* v. *Alabama*, 287 U.S. 45 (1932).

9. Ibid., p. 110.

10. *Barron* v. *Baltimore,* 32 U.S. (7 Pet.) 243 (1833), 70.

11. *Scott* v. *Sanford,* 19 How. 393, 410 (1857), 7,66,67,68.

12. *Bradwell* v. *Illinois,* 16 Wall. 130 (1873), 7.

13. Randall Kennedy, *Race, Crime and the Law* (New York: Vintage, 1997), p. 76.

14. Friedman, *Crime and Punishment in American History,* p. 86.

15. Ibid., p. 85.

16. Gunner Mrydal, *An American Dilemma: The Negro Problem and Modern Democracy,* Vol. 2 (New York: Harper Brothers, 1944), p. 551.

17. Robert Staples, "Black Male Genocide: A Final Solution to the Race Problem in America," in David Baker, Ed., *Reading Racism and the Criminal Justice System* (Toronto: Canadian Scholar Press, 1994), pp. 57–69.

18. Kennedy, *Race, Crime and the Law,* p. 72.

19. Coramae Richey Mann, *Unequal Justice: A Question of Color* (Bloomington: Indiana University Press, 1993), pp. 25–74.

20. Ibid., p. 115.

21. "Nation Seeing Simpson Case in Black and White," The Associated Press, October 1, 1995; Mark Whitaker, "Whites v. Blacks," *Newsweek,* October 16, 1995, p. 34; Michael C. Dawson, Riaz Khan, and John Baughman, "Black Discontent: Final Report on the 1993–94 National Black Politics Study," Center for the Study of Race Politics and Culture, University of Chicago Working Paper No. 1, 1996.

22. Marc Mauer, *Americans behind Bars: The International Use of Incarceration, 1992–3* (Washington, DC: The Sentencing Project, 1994).

23. Marc Mauer, *Young Black Americans and the Criminal Justice System: Five Years Later* (Washington, DC: The Sentencing Project, 1995).

24. Michael Tonry, *Malign Neglect: Race, Crime and Punishment in America* (New York: Oxford University Press, 1995).

25. Arnold Binder and Lorie Fridell, "Lethal Force as a Police Response," *Criminal Justice Abstracts 16.2* (1984), pp. 250–280; James Fyfe, "Blind Justice: Police Shootings in Memphis," *Journal of Criminal Law and Criminology 73* (1982), pp. 707–722; William A. Geller and Michael S. Scott, *Deadly Force: What We Know* (Washington, DC: Police Executive Research Forum, 1992).

26. Kenneth Adams, "Measuring the Prevalence of Police Abuse of Force," in William A. Geller and Hans Toch, Eds., *And Justice for All* (Washington, DC: Police Executive Research Forum, 1995); Anthony M. Pate and Lorie Fridell, *Police Use of Force,* 2 vols. (Washington, DC: Police Foundation, 1993); Albert Reiss, "Police Brutality—Answers to Key Questions," Transaction 5 (July–August 1968), pp. 10–19.

27. David Cole, *No Equal Justice: Race and Class in the American Criminal Justice System* (New York: The Free Press, 1999), pp. 101–131; Hiroshi Fukari, Edgar W. Butler, and Richard Krooth, "Where Did Black Jurors Go? A Theoretical Synthesis of Racial Disenfranchisement in the Jury System and Jury Selection," in David Baker, Ed., *Reading Racism and the Criminal Justice System* (Toronto: Canadian Scholars Press, 1994), pp. 87–97; Hiroshi Fukurai, Edgar W. Butler, and Richard Krooth, *Race and the Jury: Racial Disenfranchisement and the Search for Justice* (New York: Plenum, 1991).

28. David Baldus, George Woodworth, and Charles A. Pulaski, *Equal Justice and the Death Penalty: A Legal and Empirical Analysis* (Boston: Northeastern University Press, 1990); William Bowers, "The Pervasiveness of Arbitrariness and Discrimination under Post-*Furman* Capital Statutes," *The Journal of Criminal Law and Criminology 74* (1983), pp. 1067–1100.

29. Mann, *Unequal Justice;* Steven Donziger, Ed., *The Real War on Crime: The Report of the National Criminal Justice Commission* (Washington, DC: National Center on Institutions and Alternatives, 1996), pp. 99–129; Mauer, *Young Black Americans and the Criminal Justice System;* Jerome Miller, *Search and Destroy: African American Males in the Criminal Justice System* (New York: Cambridge University Press, 1996).

30. William Wilbanks, *The Myth of a Racist Criminal Justice System* (Monterey, CA: Brooks/Cole, 1987); Donald Black and Albert Reiss, "Police Control of Juveniles," *American Sociological Review 35* (1970), pp. 63–77; Donald Black, "The Social Organization of Arrest," *Stanford Law Review 23* (1971), pp. 63–77; Samuel Walker, Cassia Spohn, and Miriam DeLone, *The Color of Justice: Race, Ethnicity and Crime in America* (Belmont, CA: Wadsworth, 1996).

31. Darnell Hawkins, Ed. *Ethnicity, Race, and Crime* (Albany, NY: State University of New York Press, 1995); James W. Wilson, *The Truly Disadvantaged* (Chicago: University of Chicago Press, 1987).

32. Troy Duster, "Crime, Youth Unemployment and the Black Urban Underclass," *Crime and Delinquency 33.2* (1987), pp. 300–316.

33. Friedman, *Crime and Punishment in American History,* p. 429.

34. *State* v. *Oliver,* 70 N.C. 61, 62 (1874).

35. Eva Buzawa and Carl G. Buzawa, *Domestic Violence: The Criminal Justice Response,* 2nd ed. (Thousand Oaks, CA: Sage, 1996).

36. Susan Estrich, *Real Rape* (Cambridge, MA: Harvard University Press, 1987); Julie Horney and Cassia Spohn, "The Influence of Blame and Believability Factors on the Processing of Simple and Aggravated Rape Cases," *Criminology 34* (1996), pp. 135–162.

37. Friedman, *Crime and Punishment in American History,* p. 433.

38. Ptacek, *Battered Women in the Courtroom* (Boston: Northeastern University Press, 1999) p. 46.

39. Lenore Walker, *The Battered Woman* (New York: HarperCollins, 1980).

40. Friedman, *Crime and Punishment in American History,* p. 364.

41. Susan Martin, "Women in Policing: The Eighties and Beyond," in D. Kenny, Ed., *Police and Society* (New York: Praeger, 1989).

CASE 3

The Spectacle of Criminal Justice: The Case of Willie Horton

In early spring of 1988, the polls had good news for Governor Michael Dukakis of Massachusetts, front-runner Democratic candidate for U.S. President. Dukakis was leading Republican George Bush by a wide margin of 16 percentage points, and his overall favorability ratings with the general public far outweighed those of his opponent. By late July the figures looked even better for Dukakis as he headed into the final months of the election campaign. But by September, everything had changed: almost overnight, Dukakis's negative ratings soared to over 42 percent and were still climbing.

A political campaign ad appeared on cable TV channels early in September. The visual copy for the ad featured the disheveled mug shot of an African American man, his eyes half-closed and face sneering.[1] The voice-over for the ad proclaimed that this man had been given ten "weekend prison passes" by Governor Dukakis while serving a life sentence for stabbing a young boy nineteen times and then had raped and terrorized an innocent young couple in their home in Baltimore, Maryland, while on furlough. In the fall, a Times-Mirror poll showed that 61 percent of respondents planned to reject this candidate because of this issue.[2] Governor Michael Dukakis lost the 1988 Presidential election to George Bush, and all future political candidates learned a lesson they would never forget.

THE MAN BEHIND THE MUG SHOT

William Horton was born in 1952 and grew up in the small town of Chesterfield, South Carolina.[3] Young William was a poor student who began to skip many days of school by the time he reached seventh grade.

His first arrest came at age 12, when he was convicted for breaking and entering and sent to the state reformatory for six months. Rather than go back to school when he was released, William found some menial jobs and went to work for a living, but it wasn't long before he committed another burglary and was sent back to the state reformatory for a full year. In 1968 William Horton committed a more serious crime when he pulled a knife on a taxicab driver outside a nightclub in a dispute over the fare. In the struggle the driver was stabbed, and William was charged with assault with intent to kill. At age 17, he was sent to an adult penitentiary for two years.

When he came out in 1969, Horton headed north to live with his mother and brother, settling eventually in Lawrence, Massachusetts, with his brother and his wife in 1971. By 1973, William was making decent money at the Raytheon plant and later in construction. He moved in with his girlfriend, Catherine May, along with her two daughters, and their new baby girl was born in April 1974. At age 23, William Horton appeared to be settling down.

But appearances can be deceiving. Like his alcoholic father, William Horton had a strong preference for vodka, with occasional indulgences in pot, heroin, and cocaine. He took up dealing to make extra money and continued, according to friends, to participate in muggings and burglaries to support his boozing and drugging. His police record during these years confirms that he was skating on the edge of serious trouble. He was arrested in 1972, 1973, and again in 1974 for low-level crimes such as driving without a license, public drunkenness, fighting, and small-time drug dealing. Each of these charges resulted only in a fine. Meanwhile, Horton continued to hold down a job and meet his obligations as a father and a husband.

THE MURDER OF JOEY FOURNIER

On the night of October 26, 1974, Horton stepped out for a Saturday night of drinking and partying with his friends. As usual, Catherine stayed with the children, doing her grocery shopping and visiting her mother. Horton, along with friends Alvin Wideman and Roosevelt Pickett, piled into Pickett's blue-and-white Chevy and headed for a party in nearby Lowell, Massachusetts. They left the party around 9 p.m. in search of excitement, and decided to commit a quick robbery in order to fund the evening's festivities.

The Mobil station where 17-year-old Joey Fournier was working alone was near the off ramp from Interstate 495. His family worried about him working the night shift alone. Several of Joey's friends who also worked at the station visited him about 9:15, and they were the last to see him alive. When several other customers arrived at the gas station at around 10 p.m. they found no one there to pump the gas. Fournier's body was discovered when a friend went looking for him inside the office. Joey Fournier had been stabbed to death nineteen times for the rolled-up wad of $250 in his pocket.

THE INVESTIGATION, APPREHENSION, AND CONVICTION OF THREE KILLERS

The police were at a loss to find the killers. With the case on the front page of the local newspapers,

there was a lot of pressure to solve it but very few clues at the crime scene and no witnesses who had seen anything happen. Not much happened in the investigation for an agonizing eleven days. Detectives scoured the area asking questions, but turned up little that was useful.

Then J. J. Thomas, a landlord and long-time-friend of Alvin Wideman, who worked at the Raytheon plant, appeared troubled and distracted to his foreman at work. His boss asked if anything was troubling him. Thomas, a father of six said, yes, he was troubled and worried, because Wideman had told him and his wife on the night of the murder that he had killed a man whom Thomas believed was Fournier. Thomas didn't want to turn in his friend, but he was concerned that he might be considered an accomplice to the crime if he didn't come forward with the information.

The foreman promised to ask his cousin, who was a captain with the Lawrence police force, if Thomas could get in trouble for withholding the information. He came back to Thomas with the information that now both he and Thomas could be charged as accessories. Thomas was forced to cooperate with the police. Together with the police, Thomas concocted a little plan to get his wife to come forward voluntarily and tell the police what Wideman had said. The police pretended to arrest Thomas as a suspect, which motivated his wife to march down to the police station and repeat what Thomas had already told them, that Wideman had confessed the crime to them the night of the stabbing.

Horton, Pickering, and Wideman were immediately arrested and brought to the station for interrogation. All three admitted to robbing the gas station, but Horton and Pickering each claimed to have been waiting in the car while the other man accompanied Wideman inside the station to commit the actual robbery. Wideman said that he and Horton had gone inside but that he had left after the robbery was over, leaving Horton alone with young Fournier. Horton screamed that he was being framed and repeated his assertion that he had stayed in the car. One prosecution witness at the trial gave some confirmation to Horton's story when he testified that he had seen a tall man with an "afro" in the driver's seat of the car, a physical description that fit only Horton.

In the end it didn't matter which of the three men actually went inside and killed Joey Fournier, and the prosecution never even tried to prove which one actually committed the murder. Under the theory of "joint venture," Massachusetts law permitted the prosecution to treat the crime as a team effort, with each man fully criminally responsible for the crime no matter who did the actual deed. Even without this legal theory, under the felony murder law in Massachusetts, any of the persons involved in the commission of felony, in this case the robbery of the gas station, is equally responsible if one person kills another during the course of that robbery. A jury took only three hours to convict all three of armed robbery and first-degree murder. Immediately following the verdict, the judge announced the sentence: the maximum allowable under the criminal statute, life in prison with no chance of parole.

LIFERS ON FURLOUGH?

In 1972, then Governor Francis Sergeant, Republican governor of Massachusetts, signed into law the Correctional Reform Act, intended to respond to conditions of intense overcrowding and unrest within the state prison system. The theory behind these reforms was to create an effective tool for internal prison management and to ease the transition of incarcerated inmates back into society and reduce the likelihood they would return to the system in the future.

The furlough program was part of a community reintegration process that granted qualified inmates provisional short stays in the community while under supervision by the system. As a tool for prison management, the incentive to spend short stays outside the walls with family members was an enormous privilege, inducing cooperative behavior behind the wall. Inmates had to earn the privilege of being granted OUS, or outside-under-supervision status. It would serve as a goal toward which prisoners could work for years inside the prison system.

Before inmates were granted any external privileges, they first had to earn classification within a minimum security facility. The reward system instituted by the Correctional Reform Act included movement between different types of facilities with greater or lesser degrees of internal freedom for the inmates. Initially inmates would be classified to a maximum, medium, or minimum security facility based on their crime, but they could earn a transfer up or down the restrictive scale depending on their behavior: number of disciplinary reports, participation in programs, behavior at work details, and so forth.

Once prisoners had earned classification to a minimum security facility and had performed successfully there for at least a year or longer with no serious infractions, they could apply for OUS status. Prisoners would begin gradually, by leaving the prison for classes, to perform community service assignments, or to participate in job training. Eventually, once they had proven their reliability through shorter periods of time under close supervision by system personnel, they might be granted the coveted privilege of spending a weekend at home with their family under the supervision of an approved sponsor.

There were three main rationales for states to institute these types of programs, which became common across the United States in the 1970s and 1980s. Economically, the burden of caring for aging prisoners without the support of Medicare or Medicaid meant that few state prison systems wanted to continue to house elderly prisoners who posed little threat of offending again once released. Second, the vast majority of prisoners would eventually be released back into the community, and data clearly showed that those who were released first on short stays were less likely to offend again. The third reason to institute these programs was to induce good behavior inside the institution, especially among those who were serving long sentences. The prospect of earning access to outside visits was a powerful incentive, which could keep inmates performing well for many years as they slowly earned the privileges that would lead to OUS.

By 1975, forty-four states allowed an adult convict to be temporarily released on some kind of furlough.[4] Between 1972 and 1987, 117,786 furloughs were granted to 10,553 inmates. During this time, 426 escaped, a failure rate of about 1.9 percent. Among lifers who went out on furlough the escape rate was about 2.7 percent between 1981 and 1986. Proponents of the program, while not minimizing the problem of the escapes, argued that the advantages of preparing inmates for a successful transition back to the community resulted in a lower incidence of crime in society.

In Horton's case, it took him eleven years to earn the privilege. Horton began his prison career in 1975 at the maximum security state prison at Walpole. Horton understood the prison routine and immediately began to work in a metal shop and earn his high school diploma. For the most part, Horton was never a troublemaker for the prisoner managers. On the other hand, he was not a model prisoner either. Horton earned occasional disciplinary reports by exhibiting signs of defiance; several times he was disciplined for use of marijuana and once for the far more serious offense of hard drug use. All of these behaviors meant that his application for furlough was turned down repeatedly.

Slowly and steadily, however, Horton earned his way from the maximum security facility to a medium security facility. He was once reclassified back to maximum security when evidence of hard drug use turned up in his cell. But by 1981, seven years into his sentence, he was back in medium security. In 1984, he was reclassified to a minimum security facility, where he was granted OUS status and therefore became eligible to participate in an outside program, as a volunteer in a local hospital working with mentally ill patients. For almost a year, Horton worked in the hospital with considerable freedom, demonstrating that he could be trusted to work in the community and not escape.

William Horton was granted his first twelve-hour furlough in August 1985. The program required Horton to have a community sponsor and to be in the sponsor's home and under supervision during the entire twelve-hour period. Sponsors signed a contract outlining their responsibilities and were subjected to a background check by the institution. After his first successful furlough, Horton was granted a second and then a third furlough, this time for a twenty-four-hour stay beyond the prison walls.

Over the next year, Horton continued to behave strictly according to the rules and continued to be granted furloughs, on Thanksgiving, Christmas, and then New Year's Eve. He was even granted permission to leave his sponsor's home to visit his daughter and to take her out to a movie.

After six visits, however, Horton's sponsor refused to work with Horton any longer. Later she would explain that Horton was giving her trouble about following the exact itinerary agreed to in advance with the prison officials, and she no longer felt he was trustworthy. At the time, however, the sponsor failed to report this reason to the prison officials, and they never contacted her and asked why she was dropping out of the program. Horton invented an excuse and requested a shift to a new sponsor, this time his sister-in-law, with no mention of the real reason he was having trouble with his first sponsor.

Horton's sister-in-law had little ability to monitor Horton. She was intimidated by him and worked long hours at two jobs. Even worse, Horton was going back to his old neighborhood and his old circle of friends. On these furloughs Horton began to take advantage of his sister-in-law's absences at work to sneak out of the house in violation of the furlough rules.

Horton's tenth and last furlough was May 8, 1986. It began Friday evening and was supposed to last forty-eight hours. The itinerary required Horton to be at his sister-in-law's home except for a trip to the movies on Saturday with his daughter and a visit to church on Sunday morning. By 2 a.m. William had borrowed a car from a friend and was headed out of the house with a wad of cash in his pocket from his clandestine drug dealing inside the prison. Police stopped the car for running a red light that night,

but Horton roared away and successfully eluded the police after a brief chase. When he failed to report in as he was supposed to, William Horton had officially escaped. Horton simply disappeared, and no one knew of his whereabouts for ten months—until he surfaced in a suburb of Baltimore after spending time in New York, Washington, D.C., and Fort Lauderdale, Florida.

TWENTY-FOUR HOURS OF TERROR

On April 3, 1987, Cliff Barnes arrived home from work. As usual, he went into the bedroom and was pulling off his shirt and tie when a masked man burst in upon him and held a gun to his head. The man escorted Barnes to the basement, where he bound him with neckties and belts to the basement stairs. Hours later, when Angela Barnes came home, she too was confronted by a now-drunk masked intruder pointing her own gun at her. The man struck her with the weapon, clamped his hand around her throat, and ordered her into the bedroom. There he blindfolded her and tied her up on the bed. Angela begged him not to kill her or to rape her, and she pleaded to know where Cliff was and if he was even alive. Horton demanded cash and jewelry, and she willingly gave him everything he asked for. But Horton wanted more. After several hours of more drinking, he cut off her blouse and then her jeans and proceeded to rape her on her own bed.

Horton held the couple hostage for nearly twenty-four hours, during which time he raped Angela again and went down to the basement and tortured Cliff with partial strangulation and by carving light flesh wounds into his chest. Cliff was sure he was going to die. The ordeal went on and on, Horton's behavior becoming more bizarre and vicious.

Desperate and fearing that the man would eventually kill him and Angela, Cliff managed to slip his way out of the cords around his wrists, took off his shoes, and climbed out a basement window. Cliff stumbled to a neighbor's home and dialed 911. Minutes later, Angela too managed to escape out a bathroom window.

Just as Horton was driving away in the couple's red car, a police cruiser put on the chase. Police caught Horton at an intersection, surrounded him, and opened fire as he ran into a woods. Horton fell as a bullet struck him, got up and ran some more, was struck again and finally collapsed.

William Horton was convicted of rape, home invasion, robbery, and torture. He was sentenced to two life sentences on the charges of rape and sentences of ten, fifteen, or twenty years for the various other counts. In his final report to any future parole board, Judge Vincent Femia gave his opinion of Horton's ability to ever be furloughed again: "This man should never draw a breath of free air again. He's devoid of conscience and should die in prison."

THE VICTIMS' STRUGGLE FOR JUSTICE

After the trial and the sentencing, the pain and rage inside the hearts of Angela and Cliff Barnes continued to burn, especially when they learned that Horton had been out on furlough while serving a life sentence without possibility of parole. The outrage of this injustice consumed the couple in the aftermath of their trauma.

A reporter for a local newspaper, the Lawrence (MA) *Eagle-Tribune,* was only 13 years old when Joey Fournier was killed back in 1974. At the time, the tragic story never reached beyond the local area: the killers were caught quickly and the story ended there, as the news media moved on to the next day's crime. But a local police officer in Lawrence remembered Horton. He told the story to the reporter, and a front-page story about the crime in Maryland and the recapture of Horton ran in the newspaper the next day. For the family of Joey Fournier, the pain and horror of Joey's death eleven years earlier was reawakened, together with a new sense of profound injustice. Why had the system let this terrible person back out into the community?

The editor of the *Eagle-Tribune* decided to stay with the story and give it top priority.[5] What kind of correctional system released a cold-blooded killer back into the community? What kind of governor supported this policy? The newspaper made the furlough program itself the lead story and aimed its attack squarely at the liberal governor of Massachusetts, who was now running for president of the United States. Joey Fournier's sister, Donna Cuomo, was contacted by a state legislator to describe her family's feelings and to speak in favor of a bill to end the furlough program.

Most state correctional systems and the federal prison system had furlough programs, and compliance rates hovered around 98 percent in these programs. Like all criminal justice decisions, furlough programs were not risk-free: no one could be 100 percent certain about the future behavior of an inmate. Releasing an inmate on furlough was a calculated risk, and when an inmate escaped—especially when the inmate committed another crime—the system and the program came under heavy criticism. In the view of most correctional professionals, however, furloughs were a risk worth taking, given the benefit of prisoner reintegration and the ability to manage prisoners inside the system better.

This rationale was not persuasive to either Donna Cuomo or the Barneses. The Barneses contacted the *Eagle-Tribune* and agreed to tell their story to the press and to join the legislative fight in Massachusetts to end the granting of furloughs to lifers.[6] They also filed a lawsuit against the state of Massachusetts for, in their words, letting monsters out of the correctional system.

THE TALE GROWS TALL

As the issue heated up, the coverage in the Lawrence *Eagle-Tribune* began to manufacture a larger-than-life monster out of the man William Horton. Unsubstantiated rumors appeared in stories about both crimes, and these tall tales were picked up by national media and reported as facts.

From the start, Horton was portrayed as the person who stabbed Joey Fournier, even though it was never established who did the killing and most of the existing evidence did not point to William Horton. The reporting on what had been done to Fournier also grew like the proverbial fish, to include the hacking of his arms and legs, the mutilation of his genitals, and acts of cannibalism and necrophilia. No one ever corrected these errors, and they were repeated by media across the nation and in legislative hearings to end the furlough program.

A 1989 letter to the *Eagle-Tribune* written by William Horton's daughter, who was just an infant when he was sent to prison in 1974, begged the newspaper to "leave him alone."[7] Although he was clearly responsible for the evil deeds he had done, he was not the depraved monster they were making him out to be.

THE END OF THE FURLOUGH PROGRAM

In the Massachusetts statehouse, the issue of furloughs for lifers was emotionally debated. On one side were the correctional administrators, who argued that a person who commits a horrible murder in his teens or twenties can change. By the time he is 40, he may be a different person, no longer capable of such behavior. Not all people who commit a terrible deed are monsters; did it make sense to keep them locked away for their entire lives? They also argued that maintaining geriatric prisoners at age 50, 60, or 70 who committed a crime in their teens or twenties was a costly burden on the system. Who would pay for their medical care? And if we need to release these aging men, given the prison environment and its antisocial nature, offenders who can maintain relationships with their families are more likely not to offend again, compared with those who were simply turned out onto the street. According to the administrators, the furlough program was good policy to protect public safety.

To the victims the furlough program was a profound injustice. Their lives were frozen in time at the moment their loved one was taken away. The finality of that loss demanded the same finality of loss for the offender. They also argued that the only way to protect the public from a monster who killed another was to lock up the perpetrator forever. Victims felt betrayed by a system that claimed to do one thing, namely, sentence prisoners to life without parole, and then proceeded to release them back into the community. Either the sentence meant what it said, or it was a deep betrayal of their faith and trust in the justice system.

The hearings were the first time state legislators heard from victims. Victims felt that no one in the justice system really cared about them: the correctional system seemed to forget about the victims' pain, which continued long after the trial was over. All the system seemed to care about was the offenders and their need for rehabilitation. Victims were angry and hurt, and many came forward to add their voice and join the organization started by Donna Cuomo to lobby for this bill, "truth in sentencing," and victim's rights. After an emotional battle, the bill was passed into law on April 28, 1988, ending the furlough program for lifers in the Commonwealth of Massachusetts.

THE POLITICS OF CRIME

As important as it was to the people of Massachusetts, how did this issue become the single issue that cost Michael Dukakis the national election? Ironically, it was a Democratic primary opponent of Dukakis, Al Gore, who was the first to use the issue to accuse Dukakis of being "soft" on crime. The Bush campaign picked up on the idea and decided to make the furlough program and the Horton case a central issue in the campaign. Lee Atwater, the campaign strategist for Bush, boasted that he would make "Willie" Horton the running mate of Governor Dukakis. When people thought of the governor, he wanted them to conjure the image of a wild and dangerous black man threatening an innocent white couple in their own home. The infamous ad depicting the mug shot of William Horton played into the deep and often unspoken racial fears of the American people.[8]

In a now-famous exchange during the Presidential debates, mild-mannered Michael Dukakis was asked if he would favor the death penalty if it was his own wife, Kitty, who had been raped and murdered. Dukakis responded with a calm, rational answer, which lost him support from voters who saw him as a "wimp" unable to take a tough stance even when his own family was being threatened. His lack of emotion over the issue troubled voters more than anything else.

Cliff and Angela Barnes took their grief and rage onto the national stage as the campaign heated up, appearing on popular talk shows such as Oprah Winfrey's. As victims, they were furious that Dukakis never expressed any sympathy to them directly or reached out to meet with them personally. Dukakis was seen as cold and unfeeling by some, weak and too intellectual by others: it was a deadly combination that ended his Presidential hopes forever.

EPILOGUE

Donna Cuomo remained in the public spotlight and eventually became a state senator in Massachusetts to fight for programs for victims' rights in the name of her brother, Joey Fournier. Years later, Angela Barnes was still struggling to recover from the trauma of her violent rape. She began to drink heavily. A turning point came when she was arrested for drunk driving and was brought before the same judge who had sentenced William Horton. Although she had changed forever, Angela decided she needed to free herself from the pain of that night and stopped drinking. She and Cliff began a family.

The Lawrence *Eagle-Tribune* won a Pulitzer Prize for its coverage of the Horton story and all the changes that resulted from it, despite the inaccurate and one-sided coverage of the issue. Later, many in journalism would decry the awarding of this prize given the absence of objective reporting, but at the time, the dramatic and emotional intensity of the story carried the day.[9]

The fallout from the loss of the Presidential election had a substantial impact on criminal justice policies in the following decade. The lesson from the election was clear: the specter of Willie Horton hovered over every campaign.[10] States and the federal government curtailed their furlough programs.[11] The number of prisoners released on furloughs, work release, and other community-based programs across the nation dropped by almost two-thirds.

Case adapted from David Anderson, *Crime and the Politics of Hysteria: How the Willie Horton Story Changed American Justice.* (New York: Random House, 1995); Martin Schram, "The Making of Willie Horton," *The New Republic*, 202 (1990), p. 17; J. Conason, "Roger and He," *The New Republic*, 202 (1990); David Nyhan, "Two Men, Two Destinies,"*The Boston Globe*, October 13, 1988; Steve Burkholder, "The Lawrence Eagle-Tribune and the Willie Horton Story," *Washington Journalism 11* (July–August) (1989); Sally Jacobs, "Activists Target Furlough Policy: Citizens Channel Anger over Murderers' Escape," *The Boston Globe*, January 28, 1988; Jonathan Kaufman, "Bush Ad Draws Charges of Racism; Some Say its Just Politics," *Boston Globe*, October 23, 1988; Alexander Cockburn, "A Disgusting Award for a Disgusting Paper," *The Nation* 246(8) (1988); John A. Mac-Donald, "Specter of Willy Horton Hovers over Pennsylvania Race," *The Hartford Courant,* October 15, 1994; Andrew . Malcolm, "Administration Moves to Curb Prison Furloughs: Bush Made Inmate Leave Emotional Campaign Issue," *The New York Times,* August 27, 1989.

THINKING CRITICALLY ABOUT THIS CASE

1. Discretion in the criminal justice system requires judges, police officers, parole boards, and correctional administrators to make predictions about how a person who committed an offense in the past will behave in the future. Who exercised discretion in this case? Do you believe they exercised poor judgment in furloughing Horton? Why or why not?

2. Proponents for "truth in sentencing" believe that offenders should serve the sentence imposed by the judiciary, regardless of the offender's behavior in the prison system. Advocates for parole authority argue that correctional systems should have the discretion to release prisoners who have demonstrated that they have changed. What do you think?

3. Both the family of Joey Fournier and Cliff and Angela Barnes felt that the criminal justice system was callous and insensitive to the suffering they experienced. What is the responsibility of the justice system to victims? Should victims participate in the sentencing of offenders? Why or why not? Should correctional authorities and parole boards consider the preferences of victims in the release decision? Why or why not?

4. The furlough program was 97 percent successful: the vast majority of participants complied with the rules of the program. Is that rate of success "worth" the cost of the 3 percent who commit additional crimes? Why or why not? Who should decide if the "risk" is worth the benefit?

5. The rationale of the furlough program was to prepare inmates for reintegration and a constructive transition back into society. Should the prison system take steps to keep prisoners connected to their families and communities and to assist them in preparation for a return to society? Why or why not?

6. If furlough programs exist, what factors should guide the decision making of correctional administrators in determining eligibility for furlough release? Discuss possible criteria, including the seriousness of the offense, the offender's background, the offender's conduct in prison, expressions of remorse, the impact of the crime on the victim, preferences of the victims, and the financial needs of the prison system. Are there other criteria that should be included? Are all of these criteria legitimate? Why or why not?

7. Was it fair to use the furlough program and the policy to include lifers against Dukakis in the Presidential campaign? Why or why not? What does it mean to be "soft on crime"? What does it mean to be "tough on crime"?

CHECK OUT THIS CASE

On the Web

Willie Horton Revisited, www.pressroom.com/~afrimale/jamieson.htm
Read "Insinuation and Other Pitfalls in Political Ads and News," by Kathleen Hall Jamieson, Dean of the Annenberg School of Communication, University of Pennsylvania.

The Justice Process

THE CRIMINAL JUSTICE SYSTEM

To understand the relationships among formal agencies of the criminal justice system, we begin by examining the process of the justice system. Only in the game of Monopoly does a player "go directly to jail": cases generally must flow through the system in a particular order. When someone is charged with committing a criminal offense, he or she must be processed via a series of stages: police must first arrest the suspect, whose case is then turned over to the prosecutor for investigation and charging; the accused is adjudicated guilty or not guilty by the appropriate judicial authorities; if the result is a conviction, only then is the person turned over to the jurisdiction of correctional authorities.

William Horton and his associates were arrested by the police, who in turn brought their case to the prosecutors, who argued against criminal defense attorneys before a judge and a jury of citizens. The judge sentenced the men and then placed them under the authority of a correctional system, in which wardens, correctional staff, and parole board personnel made the decisions that released Horton on ten occasions. The policies of the correctional system are under the authority of the governor and his administrators, who set policies for parole boards and probation departments.

Beyond these formal agencies we can also see that legislatures create the laws that frame the system, and the media helps to shape the political climate that impacts the legislature. In the spectacle of the modern criminal justice system, forces well beyond the criminal justice system also influence the justice process.

DISCRETION IN THE FIVE STAGES OF THE JUSTICE PROCESS

There are **five stages of the criminal justice system:** entry into the system, pretrial and prosecution, adjudication, sentencing, and corrections.[12] Police and prosecutors are the key players in the first stage; prosecutors, defense attorneys, judges, and court staff play the dominant roles in the second, third, and fourth phases; and correctional staff in prisons, jails, halfway houses, community corrections, probation departments, parole boards, and treatment staff are the primary players in the fifth stage of the justice process.[13]

While this pattern suggests an orderly progression through each of these five stages, the reality is far more complex. At each point in the process, criminal justice personnel make critical decisions in a process known as **selective enforcement of the law.** The exercise of **discretion** is a fundamental reality of the system: from the police officers who first approach a suspect to the attorneys who decide whether and what charge, to the judge who may evaluate the evidence or determine the sentence, to the correctional authorities who decide where to classify a prisoner or when a person is ready to return to society. Each individual has a sphere of discretion in deciding how to handle the case.[14]

Does this mean that there are no "rules" or laws guiding the system? Of course not. But the sociological reality is that a human being must always decide whether or not to enforce the law and then decide which law applies to the given facts of the case. The law may state that only offenders who express remorse are eligible for a given program, but who decides if an offender is remorseful? Or the law may specify that a given sentence should be applied when a crime is particularly heinous, but who evaluates how horrific the offense is? There is always an element of human decision making that must take place in the application and enforcement of the law. Laws do not enforce themselves automatically.

Stage One: Entry into the System

The first stage in the criminal justice process is the detection and reporting of a crime. In order for the legal system to respond to a crime, it is not enough for a crime to have simply taken place: someone, most often the victim, needs to bring the violation to the attention of the authorities. Most crimes are brought to the attention of the justice system when somebody in the community dials 911 to ask for help or to report a crime. Citizens hold a large amount of discretion in the criminal justice process.

For many reasons, citizens frequently do not report crimes to the justice system.[15] It is estimated that only one-third to one-quarter of crimes are ever reported to the police. Victims may feel ashamed or may be afraid to report a crime, fearing ridicule or retaliation by the perpetrator or his friends. They may be fearful of how they will be treated by the system, whether they will be believed or treated with respect. Victims of sexual assault and domestic violence have historically been unwilling to come forward and undergo the traumatic and often degrading process of prosecution. All too often, victims are retraumatized by a justice system that is insensitive to victims.

Citizens may be reluctant to report a crime when the offender is a relative, friend, or neighbor, just as the Thomases were reluctant to turn in Alvin Wideman. This does not necessarily mean that they approve of the criminal conduct, but they may be unwilling to get that person in trouble with the law. Citizens who are themselves engaged in illegal activities such as drug dealing, prostitution, or illegal drug use are unlikely to turn to the system when they have been victimized or to cooperate with the police, preferring to settle matters themselves, often through violent means.

The belief that the system can or will do little in response to the crime also influences citizens' decisions to report a crime to the police. If a bike is stolen, it may never be reported because the victim thinks it unlikely the police will ever recover the property or catch the perpetrator. For some victims of domestic violence and sexual assault, especially when the perpetrators are intimate partners such as husbands or boyfriends, victims fear the system will not keep them safe or take their complaint seriously. Crimes may also go unreported because victims are not even aware they have been victimized. Many white-collar and corporate crimes go unreported because victims don't know they are being "ripped off" at the checkout counter or by illegal price-fixing schemes.

five stages of the criminal justice system: entry, pretrial services and prosecution, adjudication, sentencing and sanctions, and corrections.

selective enforcement of the law: criminal justice personnel may enforce some laws and not others or may enforce them in some situations and not in other situations.

discretion: the authority to choose among alternative actions.

Thus the first layer of discretion in the justice system resides in the public's willingness to report crimes to the police. Police actually rely on citizens to bring crimes to their attention. They also rely on citizens who have been victimized or who have knowledge and information about criminal conduct to serve in court as witnesses or to serve as informants. The murder of Joey Fournier would never have been solved at all if J. J. Thomas had not spoken of the confession to his boss. Thomas and his wife were both reluctant to come forward with the information, reflecting a long-standing mistrust of the justice system within the minority community. The dependence of the justice system on the trust and cooperation of the community is one of the motivations behind the rise of community policing. The greater the mutual respect and trust between the system and the community, the more citizens will work with the system in the prevention and detection of crime.

Police Discretion   When a citizen calls the police to report a crime or make a complaint, the police must decide whether or not to treat the incident as a crime. If police decide to treat a particular incident as a crime, the incident is founded; if they determine that it is not a crime, then it is unfounded. Citizens sometimes think that something is a crime when it is not, or the facts of the incident may fail to support the allegation. Even if the incident constitutes crime, the police may also consider the crime too trivial to pursue, or they may believe the victim is unreliable or unwilling to cooperate fully with a prosecution. The discretionary power of police in the founding decision is one of the key stages of the justice process, serving a key gatekeeping role in the entire sequence of the judicial process.

The phase of **arrest** and investigation is primarily the responsibility of law enforcement and prosecutors, who rely on citizens as complainants, witnesses, and informers. An arrest is the first step toward prosecution: under some specific conditions this requires a **warrant** or judicial order authorizing police officers to arrest a suspect or to search premises, but in the vast majority of cases the officers are authorized to exercise their own judgment about whether there is reasonable cause to believe that the person to be arrested has committed a crime.[16]

Police have a wide range of discretion in how they respond to a citizen whom they believe has violated the law.[17] They may walk away and do nothing,[18] they may issue a friendly or a firm warning; they may insist that the person move along and alter his or her conduct; they may investigate further by frisking or questioning the suspect; they may collect information such as phone numbers or addresses; they may look for a criminal record in the computer; search the suspect; transport the suspect to the police station and then release him or her; or they may formally arrest the suspect. Police do not and cannot arrest for all violations of the law: we expect police to exercise discretion in their enforcement of the law.

On television, police are often depicted as interrupting a crime in progress, but such events are relatively rare. In the case of drug offenses and other so-called consensual or victimless crimes such as prostitution, gambling, and drug trafficking, and some forms of white-collar crime such as bribery and corruption of public officials, law enforcement is required to take a proactive rather than a reactive stance toward the detection of crime. To detect those involved in these crimes and to gather evidence for a conviction, police engage in an array of undercover strategies.

Stage Two: Investigation and Pretrial Activities

The second stage of criminal justice processing concerns the charging of the suspect with a specific violation of the criminal law, bail hearings, and other pretrial hearings.[19] This stage is largely the responsibility of the public servant known as the **prosecutor.**[20] The district attorney's (DA's) office will review the police report, assessing the existing evidence to determine the appropriate charge.[21] The prosecution is also responsi-

founding decision: decision made by police that a particular incident should be treated as a crime (founded) or not treated as a crime (unfounded).

arrest: the action of taking a person into custody for the purpose of charging him or her with a crime.

warrant: a writ issued by a judicial officer ordering law enforcement to perform a specific action such as a search or an arrest.

prosecutor: a government attorney who instigates the prosecution of an accused and represents the state at trial.

Police have a wide range of choices in how to respond to a citizen who they believe has violated the law. Police are expected to use judgment and discretion in the enforcement of the law and make decisions about the appropriate use of the power of arrest.

ble for the gathering of evidence against a suspect and for arguing the government's case before a judge and jury.

Prosecutors are the key link between the police and the courts. Early in the process, a consultation may take place between the police and an assistant district attorney to decide if the person who has been booked will be released or if formal charges will be filed against the defendant. There may be a decision to offer a "deal" to a suspect in exchange for his or her willingness to testify. The police captain who initially investigated William Horton had offered, at first, to charge him only with robbery instead of murder if he testified against the other two accused men. In this case, a more experienced detective overruled his decision, given the ability of the district attorney to charge all three with murder under the "joint venture" law.

Just as the police do not arrest all those who may have violated the law, prosecutors do not automatically charge all suspects with a crime. Instead, they make decisions about how best to use the resources of their office, what best serves the interests of justice based on the expectation of bargaining with a defense attorney or the charge they feel they can legally prove in court. Prosecutors may decide not to charge an accused in exchange for cooperation and testimony in the case against another suspect; or they may decide that it is a case they cannot win; or they may decide that it is a case that should not be prosecuted. Like the police, prosecutors have wide discretion in the decision to charge a suspect and the precise nature of that charge.

At the **initial appearance,** the accused is brought before a judge and informed of the charges against him or her. This is also a point in the process when a judge may decide to dismiss the case, if the judge feels there is insufficient evidence to proceed. The burden of proof lies on the government to present enough evidence to continue to take actions against the accused. It is the responsibility of the judge to make an independent assessment of the evidence and determine if the state has "probable cause" to charge this citizen with a given crime.

In many states, for serious felony offenses, the prosecution must present evidence to a grand jury in order to obtain an **indictment,** a formal document of a criminal charge against an accused. A **grand jury** usually consists of sixteen to twenty-three citizens

initial appearance: the first court processing stage after arrest, in which the accused is brought before a judge or magistrate to hear the formal charges.

indictment: a formal document of a criminal charge against an accused, issued by a grand jury, based on evidence presented by the prosecutor.

grand jury: a group of citizens, between sixteen and twenty-three, assembled to determine whether sufficient evidence exists to support the prosecution of the accused.

arraignment: a hearing before the court in which the defendant is formally informed of the charges and is required to enter a plea.

bail: money or other security placed in custody of the court in order to ensure the return of a defendant to stand trial.

release on recognizance (ROR): a nonfinancial release in which the accused promises to appear in court on the required date.

adjudication: the process whereby the court arrives at a decision regarding a particular case.

jury trial: evidence is presented to a panel of citizens, who are required to determine the defendant's guilt or innocence of the charges.

bench trial: court proceedings in which a judge hears the evidence and determines the defendant's guilt or innocence.

sentence: the specific penalty for a specific crime.

conviction: the judgment of a court, based on the verdict of a jury or judicial officer, that the defendant is guilty of the offense charged.

who listen to the evidence against the accused that has been gathered by police and prosecutors. Along with the judge, the role of the grand jury is to evaluate the quality of the proof the state says it has that the accused is likely to have committed the crime. If the grand jury or the judge disagrees that the evidence suggests it is likely that this person committed this offense, then they may refuse to hand down an indictment or *true bill.* An **arraignment** is a hearing in which the defendant is informed of the charges and is required to enter a plea.

During this stage, also known as the *pretrial phase,* the prosecution and defense attorney also present arguments before a judge about a number of other important procedural decisions, such as whether to release the suspect on bail, what evidence will be permissible in the trial, and where the trial will be held. **Bail,** from the French *baillier,* meaning "to deliver or give," is a form of temporary release—it usually involves the posting of some financial security to ensure that the suspect will return to face further trial proceedings. The judge may, however, decide to release a defendant **ROR** or **release on recognizance,** in the belief that the accused may be trusted to return to court on the date of trial. Alternatively, defendants may be detained before trial and held without bail if the judge believes that they are likely to flee before trial or if the judge believes they pose a danger to others.

Stage Three: Determination of Guilt

The third stage of criminal justice processing is **adjudication** of guilt or innocence by a judge or jury. Although few cases actually go to trial, this is the most celebrated moment in the justice process, when each side is given its opportunity to present the facts and arguments that support their version of the truth. Along with the judge and jury, the principal players are the prosecutor and defense attorneys who each present arguments regarding the defendant's actions, motives, or culpability for the alleged crime. It is the responsibility of the judge to preside over the trial and to ensure that procedures are followed fairly by both sides. In a **jury trial,** it is the responsibility of the jury to review the facts, hear the evidence presented by both sides, weigh the credibility of the witnesses, and return a verdict of guilty or not guilty. If the trial is a **bench trial** with no jury present, the judge both presides over the trial and makes the determination of guilt or innocence.

Most convicted offenders are not found guilty by either a judge or a jury in a trial. The decision to enter a guilty plea may be preceded by an informal negotiation between the defense attorneys and the prosecution in which each side agrees to a charge or sentence for the accused. Generally, defendants are advised to plead guilty if their attorneys believe that they will then get a less severe punishment for their actions. No defendant has a right to plea bargaining; and any party, including the prosecution, defense, or judge, may refuse to agree to any particular plea bargain. It is the job of the judge to ensure that the defendant understands what he is doing and is entering the plea voluntarily.[22]

Stage Four: Sentencing

The sentencing phase is traditionally the responsibility of the trial court judge. Once a guilty plea is formally entered by the defendant, we rely on the discretion of the judge to determine the **sentence**—the specific penalty for the specific crime.[23] After a guilty **conviction** (either through a trial or through a guilty plea), both the defense and the prosecution may offer a recommended sanction to the judge. The judge is given the final responsibility to determine the specific sentence for this specific offender, bound by the legal range of penalties in the criminal statute. Legislatures set the basic parameters for sentencing in the passing of the laws themselves.[24] In some states, special commissions have established sentencing guidelines that specify the range of options open to judges for a given type of offense.[25]

Sentencing options generally include a suspended sentence, probation, or imprisonment, as well as other sanctions such as fines, community service, treatment, or restitution. To assist the judge in making sentencing decisions, the probation department usually prepares a presentencing report with relevant information about the offender's family, job history, education, substance abuse issues, and prior criminal involvement.[26] Information about previous convictions might have been excluded from the jury trial, but this information is nearly always factored into the sentencing decision.

Judges may take into consideration the individual circumstances of the case, the prior record of the offender, the particular circumstances of the offender, and the suffering of the victim in determining the actual sentence for the offender. Mandatory sentencing statutes severely limit the discretion of the judiciary in the sentencing phase. These laws give judges very little latitude in determining the sentences of convicted offenders. Sentencing guidelines also restrict the sentencing discretion of judges even in offenses not covered by mandatory statutes. Sentencing guidelines were designed to ensure uniformity and fairness in the punishment of similar offenses.[27]

Judicial discretion making is often open to heavy criticism, especially for perceived leniency in sentencing. At the sentencing hearing the day after the jury returned a guilty verdict for William Horton, lawyers for each side requested a particular sentence from the judge. William Horton asked that he be permitted to go back to Massachusetts to serve his sentence. The judge denied the request and coldly told Horton that he now "belongs to the state of Maryland." The judge sentenced Horton to two consecutive life sentences, making it impossible for him ever to become eligible for parole. Just to be on the safe side, the judge also included in his sentencing report to parole officials of the state: "This man should never draw a breath of free air again. He's devoid of conscience and should die in prison."[28]

Stage Five: Corrections and Release

Corrections and punishment is the fifth stage of the criminal justice process. The sentence handed down by the courts is carried out by the correctional system. Correctional facilities are run at the county, state, and federal level, and the jurisdiction of each of these facilities depends on the crime and legal status of the offender. In addition to incarceration, a variety of sanctions may be meted out to those who violate the law. For the most serious of crimes and the most serious of offenders, thirty-eight states and the federal government provide execution as sentence. The responsibility to carry out the judicial order of capital punishment falls on the correctional system.

The placement, management, treatment, and release of convicted offenders is the responsibility of the correctional staff.[29] The sentencing judge has no authority over how the sentence is carried out once the offender enters the correctional system. For much of this century, most states and the federal system gave substantial discretion to correction officials to determine the length of time a prisoner actually served within the system. Offenders were required to serve a minimum portion of their sentence and then it was up to decision making by wardens, treatment personnel, social workers, or parole boards to determine where they served and when they were released and under what kind of restrictions or conditions.[30]

William Horton's file with the Massachusetts Department of Corrections was over six hundred pages long, reflecting the many decisions regarding Horton made by correctional personnel based on his behavior within the system and its programs. The decision to **furlough** Horton was within the discretionary responsibility of the individuals responsible for administering the program. But the decision to grant eligibility for the

corrections: a term that encompasses all the government agencies with authority for the intake, supervision, confinement, transportation, treatment, and custody of convicted offenders.

furlough: an authorized absence from a correctional institution for a specified period of time.

program to inmates serving sentences for first-degree murder was set at a higher level of policy making, by the executive authority or the legislature.

For less serious offenders and for first-time offenders, correctional supervision often takes place within the community.[31] **Probation** involves the monitoring of offenders while they remain living within the community. Probation almost always carries with it an array of conditions or requirements that must be met by the offender. **Parole** authorities supervise offenders within the community after they have served a portion of their sentence in jail. Standard conditions for both probation and parole include refraining from further illegal conduct, refraining from associating with known criminals, refraining from the consumption of alcohol, and regular reporting to the probation officer. It is also common for the conditions of probation to include a requirement that the offender attend school, work, or treatment of some kind. It is increasingly common for drug screening to be a routine part of probation and parole supervision, to verify that offenders are not using illegal substances.

MODELS OF THE CRIMINAL JUSTICE SYSTEM

To gain a perspective on the nature of the criminal justice system, scholars make use of metaphors that capture and convey important qualities of the system. *A metaphor* is a figure of speech or an image that describes a phenomenon by analogy or comparison. Metaphors help us to grasp certain realities of the system that are often difficult to comprehend or to even notice. In the sections that follow we will look at four metaphors or models that illustrate different but equally significant truths about the system: the wedding cake model, the justice funnel, the assembly-line model, and the obstacle-course model.

The Wedding Cake Model

Scholars have used the metaphor of a wedding cake to illustrate an important feature of the criminal justice system.[32] Picture in your mind a glorious, multitiered confection tall enough to feed five hundred guests. The classic wedding cake comes in several tiers of differing proportions. At the bottom is the largest layer; and each layer after that is substantially smaller, with the smallest one crowned with a miniature bride and groom and with the most elaborate decorations at the top (see Figure 3.1).

The **wedding cake** metaphor reminds us that only a few cases in the criminal justice system are highly visible. Willie Horton became a household name and an infamous villain because of the media spectacle that transformed Horton into a political symbol. When he was just an ordinary felon, no one beyond the immediate family members and local community were aware of his crime or his first victim, Joey Fournier.

---

probation: a criminal sentence that allows offenders to reside within the community.

parole: conditional release and supervision within the community as part of a criminal sentence.

wedding cake: a model of the justice process that describes the public's and the media's focus on a few extraordinary and exceptional crimes.

FIGURE 3.1
The Wedding Cake Model

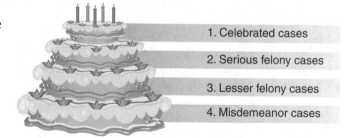

1. Celebrated cases
2. Serious felony cases
3. Lesser felony cases
4. Misdemeanor cases

Most cases we hear about on the evening news belong in this category: they are sensational, and that is what places them in the limelight. Often these involve celebrated trials with a great deal of media coverage; best-selling books are written about them, and the names of those involved are recorded in history. The Salem witch trials and the Scottsboro trials are two such important cases; today we continue to examine, study, and try to understand the processes of law and justice in those episodes of our nation's history. Serial murderers such as Jeffrey Dahmer, horrific murder cases involving children, or cases of rape or murder that implicate prominent individuals such as William Kennedy Smith or O. J. Simpson also made headlines. The processing of these cases is complicated, expensive, and drawn out, affairs that do not reflect the ordinary course of events in the criminal justice system. These cases sometimes have lasting effects on the law and on the conception of due process and equal justice.

However, we should take care to recognize that the Salem witch trials and the Scottsboro trials were not typical cases of their era. Willie Horton's vicious crime while out on furlough was profoundly atypical and quite different from the 97 percent of inmates who do not violate the conditions of their furloughs. The policy to roll back furlough programs in Massachusetts and across the country was based on a "top-of-the-wedding cake" exception, not the rule. The vast majority of prisoners participating in parole programs are not first-degree murderers, nor do they violate the rules while on furlough. However, the wedding cake model reminds us that the media, the public (and policy makers) rarely pay attention to less sensational cases.

Below the celebrated few are the still relatively rare serious felony cases such as rape, murder, and armed robbery. The term **felony** is defined broadly to encompass all offenses serious enough to be punishable by a period of time exceeding one year in state or federal prison. And far more numerous than murder and rape are "ordinary felonies," such as burglaries and auto thefts, in which no weapon is used and no one is threatened or injured. These crimes make up the third tier of the wedding cake.

Most numerous of all, however, are the thousands of misdemeanors—petty larcenies, public drunkenness, driving under the influence, vagrancy, and other minor crimes processed daily through the system—which make up the bottom layer of the wedding cake. The term **misdemeanor** refers to less serious offenses that are punishable by less than one year or by fines. These stories are rarely reported in the media for us to read about at all. For most members of the public, the lower layers of the criminal justice wedding cake are completely invisible.

The Justice Funnel

The image of the wedding cake is like a pyramid, with the smallest part at the top and the widest layer at the bottom. The image represents a reality about the system that is often forgotten by the public: namely, that the vast majority of criminal incidents are the least serious offenses, despite what we see depicted in the media. The image of a funnel illustrates another important reality about the criminal justice system and how it functions. Turn the wedding cake upside down and you have the shape of a funnel, with the widest layer at the top and the smallest at the bottom.

The **justice funnel** metaphor demonstrates a different but equally important reality about the criminal justice system: the impact of discretionary decision making by human beings inside and outside the system. The criminal justice system operates as a kind of filtering process: at every stage in the process, some defendants are processed out of the system while others are retained and sent forward to the next stage.

Picture a giant funnel (see Figure 3.2). At the wide opening of the funnel are the millions of crimes that are reported to the police. It is important to recall that only a portion of all the crime that occurs in society is ever reported to the system at all, and police only bring forward for prosecution a portion of those who are arrested. Once

felony: an offense punishable by more than one year in state or federal prison.

misdemeanor: a relatively minor offense punishable by a fine or up to one year in jail.

justice funnel: a model of the justice process that depicts the impact of discretionary decision making by criminal justice personnel as they sort and filter defendants through the five stages.

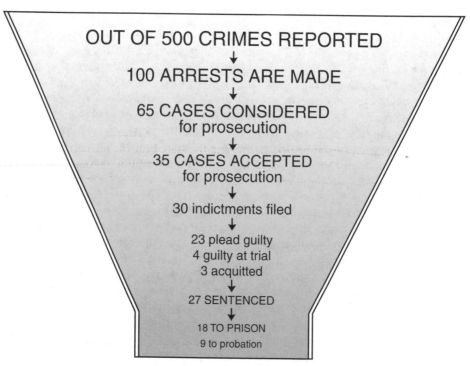

OUT OF 500 CRIMES REPORTED
↓
100 ARRESTS ARE MADE
↓
65 CASES CONSIDERED
for prosecution
↓
35 CASES ACCEPTED
for prosecution
↓
30 indictments filed
↓
23 plead guilty
4 guilty at trial
3 acquitted
↓
27 SENTENCED
↓
18 TO PRISON
9 to probation

FIGURE 3.2   The Criminal Justice Funnel

formal criminal justice processing begins, the process of attrition continues through later stages of justice decision making. In 1992, for every 100 felony arrests in large urban counties only 65 cases were carried forward for prosecution.[33] Of these 65 cases, most defendants were convicted through plea bargains, with only a tiny fraction of cases, about four, actually going to trial. The remaining defendants "dropped out" of the system, either at the prosecutorial screening stage or when they were dismissed by the courts. In the federal system, in 1999, a similar proportion of defendants dropped out of the system: for every 1,000 suspects, 600 were actually carried forward for adjudication.[34]

Assembly Line versus Obstacle Course

The next two metaphors, the image of the system as an assembly line processing criminal defendants the same way that a Ford plant manufactures shiny new cars and the counterimage of an obstacle course full of dead ends, false doors, high walls, and trap floors, offer us two different perspectives on the flow of people through the criminal justice system. Herbert Packer claims there are two competing models of the system, related to the values of crime control on the one hand, and the values of due process on the other.[35]

The crime control agenda wants the criminal justice system to operate as speedily as possible. The quicker the better: when cases are processed efficiently, the net result is more effective crime control, because criminals get the punishment they deserve. Criminals will be less likely to fall through the cracks or get off on technicalities, and the end result will be a better, more effective system of crime control. The image is of the production process in a modern industrial factory. The faster raw material moves along that conveyor belt, the better will be the system of justice. The ideal is to have defendants processed in as efficiently as possible. The **assembly-line model** of justice also implies

assembly-line model: a model of the justice process that depicts the system as processing cases as swiftly and efficiently as possible and in a standard manner.

standardization: each person is treated the same through routine processes that are applied regardless of individual circumstances.

The contrasting model of the system, which derives from the values of due process, imagines the justice process as more like the **obstacle course** designed by army boot camps to challenge raw recruits. At every point along the way, there are blind alleys that dead end, slippery high walls that must be scaled, and sudden chutes that whisk a person out of the system. In this model, processing a criminal defendant through the system requires enormous effort in order to surmount the obstacles intentionally designed to slow down the wheels of justice. By making the state bear the burden of proof and therefore need to struggle to prosecute a citizen, the end result is a system that protects the truly innocent of wrongful conviction. This model also implies **individualization** rather than standardization: each person is treated as unique, and the specific facts of the case are considered in the fullness of their complexity.

The four models we have discussed present different perspectives on the justice system. The wedding cake model reminds us that the general public is aware only of the "tip" of the process, and the everyday workings of the justice system may appear quite different than it really is if we carry only the image of the few celebrated "show trials" in our mind. The "cattle car" justice found in the lower courts would surprise many who imagine an impassioned Perry Mason debate for every legal conviction! The justice funnel metaphor tells us a great deal about the everyday working of the system: there are many pathways through the system and backstage decision making takes place at many junctures. Justice happens not only in the public display of the courtroom but also in the everyday decisions on the street, in the station house, in cramped offices, over lunch, in the hall, and even in the bathroom!

The assembly-line model and the obstacle-course model offer us two different ways to think about this process. Should the justice system operate quickly and impose standard procedures as much as possible? Should we strive to make the system look like an assembly line? Or is the image provided by the due process perspective a better ideal for the justice process? Do we want each case to be examined on its individual merits and unique qualities? Do we want the wheels of justice to turn slowly and with difficulty, so that we can ensure that we are protecting the rights of all our citizens?

THE DILEMMA OF DISCRETION

The *rule of law* expresses the ideal of the U.S. justice system that all citizens will be treated equally before the law. The fair and equal application of the criminal codes of our system is a foundational value of our system. But no law can enforce itself. The public is usually aware only of the awesome responsibility of the judge in determining sentences, but the reality is that all of the players in the system, including citizens, make choices in the process of "doing justice."

The police officer who witnesses a group of kids engaging in a minor act of vandalism must decide if he or she will arrest each of those teenagers or simply issue a warning to them and send them home to their parents. On a practical level, the state police cannot flag down every driver who violates the speed limits; instead, the police hope to deter speeding by selectively stopping those who are most flagrant and by occasionally flagging down random vehicles. It is simply impossible for law enforcement or the system as a whole to act with equal force toward all violations of the law.

Nor would that seem to be just. Most Americans want justice personnel to "sort" out those who are minor, first-time, or one-time offenders from those who are serious or chronic troublemakers. Americans value individualization by the assessment of each case on its own individual merits. There are significant differences even between

standardization: the concept that each case is treated according to the same rules, regardless of individual circumstances.

obstacle-course model: a model of the justice process which depicts the system as complex and convoluted, deliberately difficult to negotiate in order to protect due process rights of the accused.

individualization: the concept that each case be treated on the basis of its own unique and specific facts.

the dilemma of discretion: discretionary decision making is essential for justice but also creates possibilities for discrimination and bias in the justice process.

individuals who have committed the terrible crime of first-degree murder. Many people supported the ill-fated policy in Massachusetts that offered furloughs to people serving life sentences, because they believed that it was possible that some of these individuals might one day earn a commutation of their sentence from the governor and therefore should be eligible for programs that prepare prisoners to return to society as constructive citizens.

Often the public assumes that the funnel effect illustrates a flaw in the system that needs correcting. But many of the cases drop out of the system precisely because criminal justice personnel are doing their job ethically and correctly. Not every person arrested by the police is guilty of a crime. Not every person charged with a crime is guilty. Nor is it the case that every person who violates the law should be arrested and formally prosecuted by the system. The use of discretion—judgment and wisdom—is an essential element of justice. We expect criminal justice personnel to make discretionary judgements guided by the boundaries set by the law.

On the other hand, we also recognize that giving discretion to criminal justice personnel opens up the possibility of abuse when justice personnel look the other way or use their power to unfairly harass or wrongfully prosecute and convict innocent citizens. One of the greatest challenges in our system is the need to hold criminal justice system personnel accountable for their discretionary decisions and to institute oversight mechanisms to ensure that abuse of discretionary power does not take place.[36]

POLITICS AND CRIME: THE ISSUE OF EXPRESSIVE JUSTICE

The connection between crime and politics in the second half of the twentieth century suggests that being "tough on crime" is an important criterion for political success. We have seen politicians from all parts of the political spectrum compete with one another to support tough policies such as harsh mandatory sentencing to "express" their moral outrage at the injustice of crime. David Anderson refers to this as the **ideal of expressive justice,**[37] in which the use of punishment to express outrage is more important than the other ends of the justice system such as rehabilitation, cost, or even public safety. Expressive justice, according to Anderson, values the expression of vengeance over other goals of justice.

Much of the effort to "get tough" on crime has involved reducing judicial and parole discretion through laws that require offenders to serve long sentences for their crimes. Like the movement to end furloughs in Massachusetts, these efforts have often involved public activism by family members of victims.

In California, two highly publicized vicious violent crimes led to the passage of a state-wide "three strikes and you're out" law. The political battle was spearheaded by two grieving fathers who had lost daughters to violent offenders with long criminal histories for violent offenses. The abduction and murder of 12-year-old Polly Klaas from her own bedroom and the shooting death during a robbery of 18-year-old Kimber Reynolds outraged the citizens of California. The tough new sentencing law mandated twenty-five years to life for a third felony conviction following two prior serious or violent felony convictions. Voters responded to the emotional outrage of these fathers, politicians championed the cause, and the law was passed by a landslide in a general election.

Is this the best way to craft the laws and policies that will govern our criminal justice system? In California, the majority of offenders eligible to be prosecuted as "habitual offenders" do not fit the description of the violent men who murdered Polly and Kimber. They have committed robberies or drug crimes, both of which are serious

ideal of expressive justice: the use of harsh punishments to express moral outrage at the injustice of crime.

offenses, but hardly require life-long incarceration to protect the public. Is this the best policy for the people of California? Few politicians have been willing enough to risk the "Hortonization" of their political careers to even pose these questions for public debate.

The media play a key role in the demand for vengeance because the media do not provide an accurate image of crime in U.S. society. As we will see in the chapters ahead, the image of crime in our news and entertainment media is very different from the reality of crime. What the public fears is often shaped by a mythology of crime generated by the mass media looking to boost ratings. Many kinds of crime and many kinds of criminals are ignored by the media, and the public view of safety reflects a distorted understanding of the real risks of criminal conduct.

The tidal wave demanding "expressive justice" also reflects a long-standing neglect within the criminal justice system of the needs and interests of crime victims. The role of victims in the fight for tougher laws is the result of a system that has allocated resources to the needs of offenders while failing to attend to the needs of victims. In later chapters we will also look at the changing role of the victim in the justice process.

need for victims

KEY TERMS

five stages of the criminal justice
    system p. 48
selective enforcement of the
    law p. 49
discretion p. 49
founding decision p. 50
arrest p. 50
warrant p. 50
prosecutor p. 50
initial appearance p. 51
indictment p. 51
grand jury p. 51

arraignment p. 52
bail p. 52
release on recognizance p. 52
adjudication p. 52
jury trial p. 52
bench trial p. 52
sentence p. 52
conviction p. 52
corrections p. 53
furlough p. 53
probation p. 54
parole p. 54

wedding cake
    model p. 54
felony p. 55
misdemeanor p. 55
justice funnel p. 55
assembly-line model p. 56
standardization p. 57
obstacle-course model p. 57
individualization p. 57
the dilemma of discretion p. 57
ideal of expressive justice p. 58

REVIEW AND STUDY QUESTIONS

1. Identify the five stages of the criminal justice system.
2. Describe the discretionary decisions made by justice professionals at each stage of the justice process.
3. Describe the role of the citizen in the justice process.
4. Define the term "selective enforcement of the law". Why is selective enforcement of the law inevitable? Why is selective enforcement of the law desirable?
5. Describe the wedding cake model of the justice system. Identify a typical case for each tier of the wedding cake. What feature of the justice system is represented by this model?
6. Describe the justice funnel and how it operates. What key feature of the justice system is captured through the use of the funnel metaphor?

7. Contrast and compare the assembly-line model with the obstacle-course model. What values do each of these models represent?
8. What is the dilemma of discretion? What challenges does this dilemma pose for the justice system and for our wider society?
9. Explain the "Hortonization" effect. What is the role of the media in the justice process?
10. What is the ideal of expressive justice? How does it affect the politics of crime control?

CHECK IT OUT

On the Web

Justice Information Center, **www.ncrjs.org**
Visit this JIC site provided by the National Criminal Justice Reference Service to get information about all phases of the criminal justice system: victims, crime prevention, law enforcement, courts, corrections, and criminal justice statistics.

FSU Criminal Justice Links, **www.criminology.fsu.edu/cj.html**
Using the Criminal Justice Flowchart, check out sites for each phase of the justice process.

NOLO: Law for All, **www.nolo.com/index.cf**
Check out the Criminal Law Center and click on "Criminal Procedure: An Overview." Take "A Walk through Two Drunk Driving Cases: How the Criminal Justice System Works." See the process in two cases, from arrest through plea negotiations to conviction.

On Film

The Legacy: Murder and Media, Politics and Prisons (77 minutes)
*This documentary offers the story behind the passage of the California "Three Strikes Law," revealing the tragic story of two fathers' quest for justice and the complex and thorny process through which criminal justice policy is debated, promoted, and championed in the media-saturated world of high-stakes politics. Available from Films for the Humanities and Sciences, **www.films.com.***

Parole Problems: Crime and Punishment (43 minutes)
*ABC News anchor Ted Koppel examines the case of a convicted murderer eligible for parole, with little or no rehabilitation or preparation, from a maximum security lockup in Raleigh, North Carolina. Available at **www.films.com.***

NOTES

1. Martin Schram, "The Making of Willie Horton," *The New Republic 202* (1990), p. 17; J. Conason, "Roger and He," *The New Republic 202* (1990), p. 8.
2. David Anderson, *Crime and the Politics of Hysteria: How the Willie Horton Story Changed American Justice* (New York: Random House, 1995), p. 231.
3. Ibid., pp. 58–64; David Nyhan, "Two Men, Two Destinies," *The Boston Globe,* October 13, 1988, p.15.
4. Anderson, *Crime and the Politics of Hysteria,* p. 108.
5. Steve Burkholder, "The Lawrence Eagle-Tribune and the Willie Horton Story," *Washington Journalism 11* (July–August 1989), p. 14.
6. Sally Jacobs, "Activists Target Furlough Policy: Citizens Channel Anger over Murderers' Escape," *The Boston Globe,* January 28, 1988, p. B8.
7. Anderson, *Crime and the Politics of Hysteria,* p. 263.
8. Jonathan Kaufman, "Bush Ad Draws Charges of Racism; Some Say Its Just Politics," *Boston Globe,* October 23, 1988, p. 1.
9. Alexander Cockburn, "A Disgusting Award for a Disgusting Paper," *The Nation 246*(8) (1988), p. 632.
10. John A. MacDonald, "Specter of Willy Horton Hovers over Pennsylvania Race," *The Hartford Courant,* October 15, 1994, p. A2.
11. Andrew H. Malcolm, "Administration Moves to Curb Prison Furloughs: Bush Made Inmate Leave Emotional Campaign Issue," *The New York Times,* August 27, 1989, p. 11.
12. Bureau of Justice Statistics, *Report to the Nation on Crime and Justice,* 2d ed. (Washington, DC: U.S. Department of Justice, 1998), pp. 8–9.
13. Michael Gottfredson and Donald Gottfredson, *Decision Making in Criminal Justice: Toward the Rational Exercise of Discretion,* 2d ed. (New York: Plenum, 1988), pp. 1–13.
14. Lloyd E. Ohlin, "Surveying Discretion by Criminal Justice Decision-Makers" in Lloyd E. Ohlin and Frank J. Remington, Eds., *Discretion in Criminal Justice: The Tension between Individualization and Uniformity* (Albany: State University of New York Press, 1993), pp. 1–22.
15. M. Greenberg and R. Ruback, "Elements of Crime Victim Decision Making," *Victimology 10* (1984), pp. 600–616.
16. Lloyd E. Ohlin, "Surveying Discretion by Criminal Justice Decision Makers," pp. 11–12; Donald J. Black, *Manner and Customs of Police* (New York: Academic Press, 1980), pp. 85–108.
17. Laurie Weber Brooks, "Police Discretionary Behavior: A Study of Style," in Roger G. Dunham and Geoffrey P. Alport, Eds., *Critical Issues in Policing: Contemporary Readings,* 2d ed. (Prospect Heights, IL: Waveland, 1993), pp. 140–164.
18. Joseph Goldstein, "Police Discretion Not to Invoke the Criminal Process: Low-Visibility Decisions in the Administration of Justice," *Yale Law Journal 69* (1960), pp. 543–594.
19. George F. Cole, "The Decision to Prosecute," *Law and Society Review 4* (1970), pp. 331–343.
20. William McDonald, "The Prosecutor's Domain," in W. McDonald, Ed., *The Prosecutor* (Beverly Hills, CA: Sage, 1979), pp. 15–52.
21. Frank Miller, *Prosecution: The Decision to Charge a Suspect with a Crime* (Boston: Little, Brown, 1970).
22. Robert Satter, *Doing Justice: A Trial Judge at Work* (New York: Simon & Schuster, 1990), p. 144.
23. Huey Chen, "Dropping in and Dropping out: Judicial Decision-Making in the Disposition of Felony Arrests," *Journal of Criminal Justice 19* (1991), pp. 1–17; Robert O. Dawson, *Sentencing: The Decision as to Type, Length and Conditions of Sentence* (Boston: Little, Brown, 1969), pp. 193–210.

24. Andrew von Hirsch and Kathleen Hanrahan, "Determinate Penalty Systems in America: An Overview," *Crime and Delinquency 27* (1981), pp. 289–316.

25. Michael Tonry, "The Politics and Processes of Sentencing Commissions," *Crime and Delinquency 37* (1991), pp. 307–329.

26. Anthony Walsh, "The Role of the Probation Officer in the Sentencing Process: Independent Professional or Judicial Hack?," *Criminal Justice and Behavior 12* (1985), pp. 289–303.

27. Sandra Shane-DuBow, Alice P. Brown, and Erik Olsen, *Sentencing Reform in the United States: History, Content and Effect* (Washington, DC: National Institute of Justice, 1985).

28. Anderson, *Crime and the Politics of Hysteria,* p. 129.

29. Doris Layton MacKenzie and Robert A. Buchanan, "The Process of Classification in Prisons: A Descriptive Study of Staff Use of the System," *Journal of Crime and Justice 13* (1990), pp. 1–26.

30. Edna Erez, "Dangerous Men, Evil Women: Gender and Parole Decision-Making," *Justice Quarterly 9* (1992), pp. 105–126.

31. Harry E. Allen, Chris W. Eskridge, Edward J. Latessa, and Gennaro F. Vito, *Probation and Parole in America* (New York: The Free Press, 1985), pp. 81–94.

32. Samuel Walker, *Sense and Nonsense about Crime* (Monterey, CA: Brooks/Cole, 1985), pp. 30–31.

33. Brian Reeves and Phony Smith, *Felony Defendants in Large Urban Counties, 1992* (Washington, DC: U.S. Department of Justice, 1995).

34. U.S. Bureau of Justice Statistics, *Compendium of Federal Justice Statistics 1999* (Washington, DC: U.S. Department of Justice, 2001), p. 28.

35. Herbert Packer, *The Limits of the Criminal Sanction* (Palo Alto, CA: Stanford University Press, 1968), pp. 149–173.

36. Samuel Walker, *Taming the System: The Control of Discretion in Criminal Justice, 1950–1990* (New York: Oxford University Press, 1993), pp. 14–20.

37. Anderson, *Crime and the Politics of Hysteria,* p. 14.

CASE 4

The Fall of the Queen of Mean: The Case of Leona Helmsley

LONG LIVE QUEEN LEONA

Flip through the pages of any glossy magazine from the 1980s and you are likely to see a striking advertisement featuring the "Queen" of New York's Helmsley Palace, one of twenty-six luxury hotels owned by Harry and Leona Helmsley. Leona is wearing a gold lamé gown with a diamond tiara glittering on top of her immaculately coiffed jet-black hair. The advertisement declares the Helmsley hotel to be "the only Palace in the world where the Queen stands guard."

Leona and Harry Helmsley sat atop one of the most lucrative and extensive real estate empires in the world, which included ownership of the Empire State Building itself. Estimated at a net worth of about $6 billion, Harry Helmsley was listed as one of world's one hundred wealthiest men when he met Leona Mindy Rosenthal in 1970. Within two years, he had divorced his wife of thirty-three years, married Leona, and abandoned his former modest lifestyle to join Leona as Manhattan's premier socialite couple. The glossy ads declaring Leona to be the Queen of New York were more real than fictional: the two enjoyed a regal life, with a penthouse in Manhattan, a condo in Palm Beach, and a rambling mansion in Connecticut; they hosted elaborate parties and charity balls attended by all the right people during the heyday of the mad, rich 1980s. Like royalty, they hired hundreds of employees, who tended to their every need and wish. And too much like royalty, the Queen treated her staff with the arbitrary power of an au-

tocrat who believed the rules were made for everyone but her.

THE QUEEN STUMBLES...

Leona's fairytale began to crumble on December 2, 1987, when one of the New York newspapers ran headlines which claimed that the Helmsleys might have violated federal income tax laws by charging multimillion dollar renovations of their Connecticut mansion to their business properties in Manhattan. Leona and Harry had purchased the twenty-eight room mansion called Dunnellen Hall in 1983 for $8 million. Characterized as "cold, dreary, and horrible" by her interior designer, Leona embarked on a lengthy and elaborate renovation of the mansion, including an Italian marble pool enclosure with a dance floor on the roof; a walk-in silver vault; and a $130,000 indoor–outdoor sound system modeled after the one the couple admired in Disney World. In the fairyland created by Leona, sheep rambled through the meadows and music wafted from the flower beds and fountains.[1]

A sixteen-month state and federal investigation into the financial practices of the Helmsleys ended in a federal indictment for tax evasion. The federal government charged that the Helmsleys paid for their elaborate renovations by falsifying invoices and bills in order to claim them as deductible business expenses of nineteen different companies in the Helmsley enterprises. The million-dollar pool house became construction work on an apartment complex in Queens; the $210,000 jade water buffalo that stood in the hall of the mansion became an antique mahogany card table purchased for the Park Lane Hotel; the indoor–outdoor stereo system appeared as a security system for the Helmsley Building.

Among the hundreds of items falsely charged to various business accounts were such personal items as underwear, dry cleaning bills, and cosmetics. The Helmsleys claimed false tax deductions on these so-called business expenses, underreporting their own income to the federal government. In total, the government claimed that the Helmsleys knowingly and willfully underpaid their federal tax obligation by $1.2 million between 1983 and 1985.

In the sixteen months leading up to the trial, the New York press delighted in revealing the true nature of the Queen of New York, dubbed the "Queen of Mean" by the *New York Post*. Dozens of former employees came forward with stories of Leona's cheating, cruelty, viciousness, and spitefulness. She had once fired a worker for taking an apple from the hotel kitchen (even though the employee was working through her lunch hour); when she wasn't satisfied with a product or a service, she refused to pay the entire bill; she fired employees who had worked for the Helmsley companies for twenty, thirty, or even forty years on a whim. Contractors, attorneys, and retailers came forward with countless tales of unpaid bills ranging from under $10 to tens of thousands of dollars.[2]

Leona and Harry Helmsley could afford the best of everything, and they quickly assembled the finest legal defense team money could buy. The team immediately requested a change of venue, declaring that under the harsh glare of the media publicity about Leona, most of which did not concern the charges being leveled against her, an impartial jury would be impossible to find. According to her lawyers, Helmsley had already been tried and found guilty by the media, largely of being a penny-pinching "bitch." No jury drawn from Manhattan or the neighboring boroughs would be fair in judging Leona and Harry.

But the court refused to grant the change of venue. Now the lawyers filed a motion to drop Harry Helmsley from prosecution, declaring him "unfit" to stand trial. Harry Helmsley, twenty years older than Leona, suffered a series of strokes during the investigation, and his name was dropped from the indictments after a federal judge ruled that he was no longer mentally competent, stating that Harry was incapable of "cooperating in his own defense." Leona Helmsley alone would face the jury.

At the trial, the media soaked up the juicy testimony provided by forty-four prosecution witnesses. According to the hotel's comptroller, the accounting system at the Park Lane Hotel was the "Helmsley cheat-the-government-system."[3] Employees testified that Leona Helmsley specifically ordered them to sign falsified invoices and to write bills for items that did not exist. When they balked, she threatened to fire them. Among the most damaging testimony was the recollection by her former housekeeper that Leona had haughtily confided to her one of the cardinal secrets of the super-rich: "We don't pay taxes. Only the little people pay taxes."[4]

. . . AND FALLS

The trial took eight weeks and the jury deliberated for five days before finding Leona guilty. At her sentencing hearing, the federal judge sentenced the 71-year-old Leona to four years in prison and a $7.1 million fine for tax fraud in addition to paying the missing $1.2 million owed to the federal government. She also had to cover the costs of the government's prosecution of the case, as well as, of course, the costs of her own defense.

Given Leona's age, this was a stiff sentence. U.S. District Court Judge John Walker explained the reason for his lack of leniency: "I trust that the sentences today will make it clear that no person, no matter how wealthy or prominent, stands above the law. . . . unlike many defendants who come before the court, you were not driven to this crime by financial need. Rather your conduct was the product of naked greed. Throughout its course, you persisted in the arrogant belief that you were above the law."[5]

In addition to the prison term, Helmsley was ordered to perform 750 hours of community service during a three-year sentence of probation following her release from incarceration. Judge Walker recommended Helmsley serve her probation by doing community service at Hale House in Harlem, a treatment center for children born addicted to drugs or with AIDS.

Leona remained free on $25 million bail while her high-priced team of lawyers, including the famous Harvard Law School criminal defense attorney, Alan Dershowitz, as well as his brother Nathan Dershowitz and several others, appealed the conviction. The appeal failed: the U.S. Supreme Court declined to review the case.

On April 16, 1992, after exhausting all her possible appeals, Leona Helmsley flew in her private jet to the Federal Medical Center in Lexington, Kentucky, to begin her four-year sentence for income tax fraud. She was accompanied by her niece, personal physician, and bodyguard, but when she entered the facility, she walked in alone, no longer the Queen of Manhattan, now just a prisoner of the Federal Bureau of Prisons. At age 71, she was strip-searched and ordered to don the prison-issue blue shirt and pants. She would be eligible for parole on August 13, 1993, at the earliest.

WAS THIS FAIR?

The controversy surrounding Leona Helmsley's conviction and punishment continued long after she disappeared behind the walls of the federal prison system. Leona's punishment generated many conflicting opinions about government prosecution for tax evasion, the role of the media, the purpose of punishment, and the issue of justice for the rich and poor in our society. The overwhelming media coverage of this case was one of unmitigated celebration at the prosecution, guilty verdict, and stiff sentencing of Leona Helmsley. According to the federal prosecutors and judges, this trial and its outcome demonstrated loud and clear that the rich are treated the same as the poor in this country: no one is above the law, and this case proved this to all those who might be tempted to flout the tax laws of this nation. Once the spectacle of the trial was over, however, there were some who began to wonder if the image of Leona and Harry Helmsley portrayed in the media was a fair reflection of the truth.

LEONA AS SCAPEGOAT

In the aftermath, people began to point out that Leona and Harry were not the flagrant tax cheats they had been made out to be by the media. Putting the matter in more comprehensible terms, one columnist pointed out that had the Helmsleys earned $104,000 that year, they would have paid the equivalent of $54,000 in taxes. The underreporting of their income as business expenses would have amounted to the equivalent of an additional $1,700 on a tax bill of more than $54,000. In short, the Helmsley's paid almost half of their annual income in taxes that year, an amount totaling about $54 million; to argue that they were avoiding taxes, by focusing on the missing $1.2 million, greatly distorts the bigger picture.[6]

Is it possible that Leona had been used by the Internal Revenue Service to send a message to the nation's wealthy citizens? The IRS acknowledges there is no way that it can detect the vast majority of tax cheats among the American public.[7] Rather than hire many more tax examiners to detect the millions of "little fish" (Americans who cheat the government out of hundreds or thousands of dollars in each case), the most cost-effective method for the IRS is to target a few big fish, like Leona, whose minor "errors" are worth very big bucks. The IRS also knew that Leona would be a "hit" in the media and that they would get the maximum "deterrent" bang for their buck. Leona was served up as a scapegoat to send a message to the nearly one-third of Americans who commit this very common crime.

A common prosecutorial practice is to plea-bargain with a witness in exchange for testimony against a more serious criminal. One of the key attorneys to testify against Leona had been previously charged with fraud in another case. In exchange for his testimony, he was spared full prosecution for his crimes. And the infamous quotation that "Only the little people pay taxes," which condemned Leona in the court of public opinion, was supplied by a housekeeper who had been fired for incompetence only four months earlier.[8] The veracity of both these witnesses was never questioned by the media.

In addition to being unfairly prosecuted because she was rich, several observers felt that Leona had been targeted for prosecution because she was a woman.[9] Noting that charges against Harry Helmsley were dropped early on, people wondered why so few powerful males are ever targeted in such an aggressive and vicious prosecution by the IRS. What Leona did was certainly not uncommon among wealthy American citizens, particularly those who are self-employed, who often count personal expenses as business expenses or underreport their income. Could it be that the IRS and the media exploited widely held attitudes about "bitchy" women to drag Leona Helmsley through the mud of negative social stereotypes?

Lastly, the issue of her stiff punishment generated controversy as well. Some questioned the value to society of incarcerating a 71-year-old woman who was clearly not a danger to others or to herself. What benefit would such a punishment bring to those who had been harmed, namely, the public? Why not require Leona to use her enormous resources for good rather than waste our scarce public dollars on making her suffer?

According to some, Leona should go to prison because it's fair. Poor people go to prison when they break the law, so rich ones should, too. Unfortunately, sending Leona to prison won't help the poor. . . . Helmsley is in a position to serve society right now, but instead we are asking society to dip into its empty pockets and take care of her for four years. She could, with a wave of her hand, underwrite the establishment of six—who knows? maybe 12!—Head Start nurseries, endow and locate them in areas where children would not have to dodge bullets during recess.... Why do we let our appetite for retribution take from the common good? It is almost the 21st Century, yet here we are, still gathered in the market square, shouting and jeering and spitting while they strap a woman in the ducking stool.[10]

For others, Leona's punishment was absolutely fair and just: if she been a poor woman who shoplifted to put food on the table for her children, she still would have been subject to the harsh arm of the law if she had been caught. They felt no special sympathy for her plight. Indeed, as the judge remarked, they felt she deserved a lengthy sentence because she clearly was not motivated by need, but by "naked greed."

In the opinion of a jury of her peers (who heard the best defense money could buy), Helmsley committed a significant felony: She stole more than a million dollars in taxes from the government. It's indisputable that the money she stole wasn't needed for the bare necessities of life. If a man or woman steals to feed a family, pay a month's rent or attend to a child's needs (and, yes, in desperate economic times such things happen; everyone in prison is not a drug addict), and if that person, when caught, must go to prison (which happens daily, as a visit to the criminal courts on Centre Street will attest), how could we consider allowing a Leona Helmsley go scot free? Is it a good idea that we bestow freedom from prison on every convicted felon who's a millionaire and willing to fund day-care centers—or to house the homeless in her hotels, as Helmsley's lawyer proposed this week, just before Helmsley went to jail?

With more than a million men and women in prison nationwide and the vast majority of them dirt poor, and with cynicism already rampant among us about whom our government really serves, how could the concept of equal justice for all survive if the Helmsleys of this country could buy their way out of prison with a "charitable" contribution? And that's what it all comes down to.[11]

EPILOGUE

After serving twenty-one months in jail, Leona Helmsley was released on probation. Media coverage continued to dog her every move.

Case adapted from Gregg Krupa, "Two-Tiered Defense for the Hotel Queen," *Manhattan Lawyer*, July 25, 1989, p. 1; Andrew Blum, "A 'Queen's Defense': Countering Bad Press," *National Law Journal*, August 28, 1989, p. 8; Gregg Krupa, "Helmsley's Trials May Continue," *Manhattan Lawyer*, September 11, 1989, p, 3; Gregg Krupa, "If Convicted Helmsley Could Face 'Hard Time'," *Legal Times*, September 4, 1989, p. 4; Murray Kempton, "Leading the Royal Life: Real Kings and Queens Would Hardly Feel Deprived," *Newsday*, April 15, 1988; Murray Kempton, "Helmsley Degrees of Degradation," *Newsday*, July 6, 1989; Beth Holland, "Helmsley Accounts called 'Cheat System'," *Newsday*, July 20, 1989; Howard Kurtz, "Abuzz about the Hotel Queen: Ex-Employee's Stinging Testimony in Trial of Leona Helmsley," *Washington Post*, July 18, 1989; Paul Craig Roberts, "Leona Helmsley Is Being Persecuted," *The Atlanta Journal and Constitution*, April 3, 1992; Anthony Lewis, "A Little Helmsley in Many Americans," *St. Louis Dispatch*, September 8, 1989; Paul Craig Roberts, "Hotel Queen Deserves New Trial, Not Jail," *The Houston Chronicle*, April 4, 1992; Ellen Goodman, "We Could Have Given Leona a Break," *Newsday*, April 22, 1992; Jean Harris, "For Leona, Jail Is Not the Best Punishment," *Newsday*, April 9, 1992; Romy Franklin, "Leona's Just Deserts," *Newsday*, April 17, 1992.

THINKING CRITICALLY ABOUT THIS CASE

1. Was Leona sentenced for tax evasion because of "who she was" or because of "what she did"?

2. Should the justice system punish theft according to amount stolen or according to the percentage of a person's personal income? $1.2 million is a great deal of money, but not to Leona. Should there be higher penalties for wealthy people who violate the law for personal profit than for poor people who violate the law to help make "ends meet?" Why or why not?

3. The average sentence for burglary is 26 months, with an average of 15.6 months served; for larceny, the average sentence is 18.6 months with 15.9 months time served. The average sentence for a tax law violation is 22.2 months with 14.2 months actually served. Is this fair? Should the sentences for tax evasion and crimes of larceny (such as shoplifting) or house burglary be based on the dollar amount stolen or on some other criterion?

4. According to observers, Leona was being made an example by the Justice Department and the IRS to send a message to tax evaders across the country. Is this fair?

5. It is estimated that roughly one-third of all American citizens deliberately file inaccurate tax returns. If everyone is doing it, is it really fair to punish Leona?

6. The defense team offered the judge an alternative sentencing plan for Leona Helmsley that would have offered substantial benefit to the community. The defense argued that there was more value to society if her punishment involved restitution and community service than incarceration. Do you agree? Why or why not? If you were charged with devising an alternative sentencing plan, what would it consist of and why?

Understanding the Crime Picture

LEARNING OBJECTIVES

After reading this chapter, the student should be able to:

- Describe the three key methods used to gain an estimate of crime and identify the main limitations of each of these methods

- Explain why the incidence of white-collar crime is relatively invisible in our society and identify methods used to measure white-collar crime

- Identify main forms of violent crime and property crime, and identify the specific crimes that comprise the Total Crime Index

- Explain the term "victimless crime" and describe key methods for measuring these forms of behavior

- Explain the dramatic fallacy of violent crime

- Describe the image of crime depicted in our news media and popular entertainment

The Helmsley case is a classic "top of the wedding cake" case. It is exceptional in almost every respect: the defendants were super-rich, whereas the vast majority of criminal defendants are dirt-poor. The Helmsleys cheated on their income taxes and were caught, whereas an estimated one-third of Americans violate the IRS tax code without detection. Finally, this case is atypical because Leona, despite her enormous wealth and resources, was "processed" all the way through the system, actually serving substantial time in federal prison despite the best defense team in the country. This was a "show trial" for the Internal Revenue Service designed to send the message that no one, not even the super-rich, is above the laws of this land. The "top of the wedding cake" cases are the exceptions that prove the rule: this was not the typical crime to be processed by the justice system, and these were not the typical criminal defendants.

The commission of crime is a phenomenon that crosses boundaries of social class, age, race, and gender: it is not the speciality only of the poor and the young. But who becomes labeled a "criminal" by the justice system and which Americans end up inside the system subject to punishment is influenced by class, race, and gender. People like William Horton, not Leona Helmsley, are the typical offenders in the criminal justice system: young, male, not highly educated, working class or lower class, and, disproportionate to their numbers in the population, people of color.

This chapter gives an overview of how crime is categorized, measured, and studied, and offers a "snapshot" of different types of crime. Students will learn that we are better at studying and keeping official records of crimes of the street versus crimes of the boardroom. We are also better at policing and prosecuting certain segments of the American population than other segments. This systemic bias is reflected in the overall crime picture.

This chapter also takes a closer look at the images we as a society hold about the typical nature of crime. How does the "image" of crime in the news and entertainment media compare with the crime picture derived from official data and social science research? We contrast the picture of crime that comes into our living room every night with the picture produced by social science data. What is the relationship between the images we consume in the media and the reality of crime?

GETTING THE CRIME PICTURE

Crime is hard to measure. Like most forms of deviant behavior, the people who do it try to conceal their activities from others in order to avoid the negative response typically associated with all forms of deviant behavior. For a variety of reasons, a great deal of crime goes unreported to official sources, and much crime that is reported to the police is never entered into the official record. Despite all the ways we have to measure crime, there is one certainty agreed upon by all criminologists: we can only estimate the amount of crime that actually exists. Far more crime exists than we will ever be able to count or measure. The unknown amount of crime in society is referred to by criminologists as the **dark figure of crime.**

There are three key sources of information about crime: the official statistics of crimes known to the police and collected by the Federal Bureau of Investigation (FBI); victimization surveys, which collect information directly from citizens about their own victimization; and self-report studies, which ask citizens to report voluntarily about their own criminal conduct. Each of these measurement devices misses an element of the picture, but by examining all three for any given type of crime, we are able to fill in the gaps and piece together an approximation that is more reliable than if we used only a single source. Even so, certain types of crimes are still not likely to appear on the radar screen with these measurement tools, and we still recognize that the dark figure of crime remains a shadowy unknown.

The Uniform Crime Reports[12]

In 1920, the International Association of Chiefs of Police (IACP) realized the need for national statistics on crimes reported to the police. By 1930, Congress authorized the collection of this information and the task was delegated to the FBI, who adopted the format developed by the IACP.[13] Today, the **Uniform Crime Reports (UCR)** compile data from thousands of police agencies across the country.

The Uniform Crime Reports divide crime into two main categories, **Part I** and **Part II offenses.** Part I offenses are considered to be the more serious offenses and consist of eight crimes: murder and non-negligent manslaughter; forcible rape; robbery; aggravated assault; burglary; larceny theft; motor vehicle theft; and arson. These are "headline" crimes—those we conventionally think of when we think of crime, especially when we think of violent crime.

The **Total Crime Index** is the sum of all Part I offenses known to the police during a given period of time. The **Violent Crime Index** is the sum of all Part I violent offenses (homicide, forcible rape, arson, and robbery) or "crimes against persons"; burglary, auto theft, larceny, and arson constitute the **Property crime index.** Part II offenses include twenty-one other, less serious crimes, including *status offenses*, which are acts that violate the juvenile code but are not crimes if committed by an adult, such as violating curfew or running away from home. (See Table 4.1 for a list of Part I and Part II offenses.)

The FBI reports data in several different formats: arrest data, crimes reported, and clearance rates. The **crime rate** is calculated by dividing the number of crimes reported to the police by the total population and then multiplying by 100,000. **Clearance rates** for these eight offenses are also collected. Crimes cleared by arrest are those for which

---

dark figure of crime: crimes that do not become part of the official record.

Uniform Crime Reports (UCR): the collection and dissemination of national data on crimes known to the police and arrests, operated by the FBI.

Part I offenses: crimes designated by the FBI as most serious.

Part II offenses: crimes designated by the FBI as less serious.

Total Crime Index: the sum of Part I offenses reported in a given place for a given period of time.

Violent Crime Index: the sum of four Part I violent offenses (homicide, forcible rape, robbery, and aggravated assault) reported in a given place for a given period of time.

Property Crime Index: the sum of four Part I property offenses (burglary, larceny, auto theft, and arson) reported in a given place for a given period of time.

crime rate: the number of crimes known to the police for a given year divided by the population for that year and multiplied by 100,000.

clearance rate: the proportion of reported crimes that result in arrest.

TABLE 4.1

Uniform Crime Reports: Part I and Part II Offenses

Part I Crime Offenses	Part II Crime Offenses
Criminal homicide	Simple assaults
Forcible rape	Forgery and counterfeiting
Robbery	Embezzlement
Aggravated assault	Stolen property
Burglary—breaking or entering	Vandalism
Larceny-theft (except motor vehicle)	Weapons
Motor vehicle theft	Prostitution and commercialized vice
Arson	Sex offenses (except forcible rape and prostitution)
	Drug abuse violations
	Gambling
	Offenses against family and children
	Driving under the influence
	Liquor laws
	Drunkenness
	Disorderly conduct
	Vagrancy
	Curfew and loitering law violations
	Runaways

Source: "Appendix II: Offenses in Uniform Crime Reporting," in Federal Bureau of Investigation, *Crime in the United States, 1999* (Washington D.C.: U.S. Department of Justice, 2000), p. 407.

one or more persons are arrested for the offense. The proportion of crimes reported that are cleared by an arrest is the clearance rate. For Part II offenses, only the number of arrests for each category of crime are officially reported.

Criminologists have long criticized the focus on these eight crimes, which are overwhelmingly crimes committed by the poor.[14] Crime indexes, which serve as the official statistics for the rising or falling amount of crime in society, do not include the twenty-one offenses listed in Part II. Thus, a burglary committed by a young male is recorded in the official crime rate, whereas embezzlement committed by an older, middle-class employee is not. The crimes of the middle class and the well-to-do, such as insurance fraud, Medicaid fraud, filing inaccurate tax statements, insider trading, and price fixing, never appear in our official crime statistics.

Data on Part I offenses are also made available to the public in the form of **crime clocks**,[15] which show how often each of these crimes is committed if they were spread evenly over a twenty-four-hour period (see Figure 4.1). In 1999, there was one Crime Index offense every 3 seconds; one violent crime every 22 seconds, and one property crime every 3 seconds.

This graphic portrayal of crime in our society distorts our understanding of crime in our society. The crime clock seems to suggest that these terrible crimes are constantly occurring, random events happening to all Americans. If a homicide occurs every 34 minutes, one forcible rape every 6 minutes, and one robbery every 60 seconds, it is natural for citizens to fear predatory violence from strangers everywhere and at any time.

In reality, this picture is very far from the truth. Crimes are concentrated in certain neighborhoods, at certain times of the day and year, and among certain categories of

crime clock: a form of display used in the Uniform Crime Reports to illustrate the annual ratio of specific crimes to fixed time intervals.

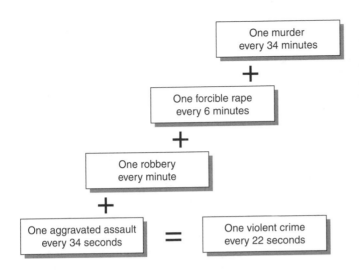

FIGURE 4.1 A Crime Clock from the Uniform Crime Reports

Source: Crime in the United States, 1999 Uniform Crime Reports, Federal Bureau of Investigation, U.S. Department of Justice, Washington, DC, Figure 2.1, p. 4.

victims. Most crime is not random but highly predictable. Violent crimes occur in certain kinds of social spaces, such as outside bars, at certain times of the day such as closing time, and most often, between people who know each other.

Limitations of the Uniform Crime Reports While the Uniform Crime Reports are a major source of statistics for crime in the United States, it is a serious error to suppose these data provide a perfect picture of crime. As we have noted, a large percentage of crime is not reported to the police. Furthermore, official crime statistics focus almost exclusively on the violent and property crimes of the poor. The vast majority of corporate crimes, such as price fixing, environmental crimes, and tax fraud, are committed almost exclusively by those from the upper echelons of society. Yet we do not broadcast a crime clock that measures how often and how costly such behavior is to the American public.

Another important drawback in this data is that the Uniform Crime Reports are a direct measure of the activity of the police and citizens and only an indirect measure of crime. In some cases, what appears to be a "crime wave," a dramatic increase in the rate of a particular crime, may be a change in the recording of crime by law enforcement. In 1973 citizens reported 861,000 aggravated assaults to the police, but only 421,000 appeared in the official police records; in 1988 citizens reported 940,000 aggravated assaults to the police and police recorded 910,000 of these incidents in the official reports. Changes in computer technology, police practices, or the willingness of victims to report crime affect crime data that appear in the UCR.[16]

The Uniform Crime Reports are also hampered by other sources of inaccuracy. The data are a summary entered monthly by each police department, and some jurisdictions do a better job than others in providing data in an accurate and timely fashion. Furthermore, statutory definitions of crime vary among the states: what constitutes larceny in one jurisdiction may not be counted as larceny in another. And the Uniform Crime Reports allow for the recording of only one crime, the most serious, per incident. Thus, if a robbery and rape were committed in a single incident, only the rape would appear in the official statistics; the robbery would not be recorded.

In 1987 the U.S. Department of Justice began implementation of a new system for recording criminal statistics to replace the Uniform Crime Reports and address some of its shortcomings. Known as the **National Incident-Based Reporting System (NIBRS),** the new system will record a standard complement of information on twenty-four different types of crime. The NIBS will be based directly on the reports officers make at the scene of the crime as well as other court reports, eliminating the monthly summaries, and it is designed to provide a much broader range of information than the UCR. For

National Incident-Based Reporting System (NIBRS): new system for recording criminal statistics to replace the Uniform Crime Reports, based on information about twenty-four types of crimes, with expanded data on victims and offenders.

each incident, specific details about the offense, such as whether it involved weapons or drugs and the type of losses sustained by the victim, and specific characteristics about the offender and the victim such as age, gender, and race, will be recorded. This new system is expected to be functional some time after the year 2000.[17]

Victimization Surveys

The second key source of information that we have on the extent of crime is the **National Crime Victimization Survey (NCVS),** conducted by the U.S. Bureau of the Census and published by the Bureau of Justice Statistics annually. Every year approximately 100,000 people are drawn from a nationally representative sample covering approximately 42,000 households. These same people are interviewed twice a year for three years. In addition to the household survey, the NCVS also conducts surveys in twenty-six of the nation's largest cities and surveys business victimizations. Statistics are published as research briefs called "Crime and the Nation's Households" and "Criminal Victimization," and annual reports entitled *Criminal Victimization in the United States.*

Victimization surveys ask individuals to report on their own victimization experiences within the previous six months. Individuals are asked about crime they or members of their household have experienced during this time period, and whether these events were reported to the police. The NCVS requests information about all index crimes except murder, kidnapping, arson, and victimless crimes. The survey also collects data about the age, race, sex, marital status, income, and educational level of victims, and minimal information about offenders such as age, race, sex, victim–offender relationship, the time and place of the crime, injuries or losses sustained, and weapons used. The NCVS has recently begun to include questions regarding victimization which takes place in the workplace as well as at home.

The interview process for the NCVS is designed to help respondents recall and report on experiences they may have forgotten, overlooked, or find difficult to talk about. Screening interviews conducted over the phone or face to face ask people to think about times when they have been threatened or attacked at home or school, even by people they know or members of their family. Often victims do not think of these incidents as "crimes" and would not think to report them if they were not asked explicitly by the interviewer.

The data obtained from victims clearly demonstrates that the UCR undercounts crime. The first survey, conducted in 1972, found the ratio between unreported crime and "crimes known to the police" to be as high as five to one in some U.S. cities.[18] Overall, victim surveys report two to three times the number of crimes as are reported to the police.[19]

Limitations of the NCVS   Just as the UCR has limitations, so too does the NCVS. First of all, victimization surveys do not measure all crimes. The NCVS also does not request information about victimless crimes such as prostitution, drug use, or pornography. Like the UCR, it does not collect data on the white-collar crimes of embezzlement, price fixing, or bribery. Furthermore, many victims of consumer fraud or corporate crime do not even realize that they have been victimized and so will not be able to reveal this information on the surveys even if they were asked.

Additionally, there is the problem of memory, accuracy, and honesty. Asking people about what happened to them in the past always raises questions about the quality of their memory, particularly with respect to the characteristics of the offenders. Since participation is voluntary, some people may be eager to talk, while others are unwilling to do so. It is not possible to know the extent to which people will underreport or exaggerate incidents that happen to them.[20] Victims of domestic violence may be afraid to report crimes committed by their spouses, especially because that person may be in the house or even present while the interview is being conducted. Finally, although the

victimization surveys: surveys that ask people whether they have been victims of crime during a given period of time.

National Crime Victimization Survey (NCVS): an annual survey of 100,000 people age 12 and older to determine the nature and extent of their victimization of crime, administered by the U.S. Bureau of the Census.

NCVS sample is quite accurate with respect to representing the U.S. population that resides in households, there are still significant categories of U.S. citizens who are not included in the survey, such as those who are homeless, in prison, or in the military.

Self-Report Surveys

The third and final method of measuring crime is voluntary reports by offenders themselves. These are known as **self-report surveys** because they ask individuals to reveal crimes they have committed and to report whether these crimes were brought to the attention of the police. Self-report surveys were originally developed in the 1960s, when criminologists began to interview prison inmates about the number of times they committed crime without getting caught. Researchers were astonished at the enormous amount of crime that is not detected by the justice system. The focus of much of this research was to assess if there were important differences between those individuals whose crimes were detected by the system and those who remained unknown to the justice system.

The first nationwide self-report survey was the **National Youth Survey,** which began by interviewing a group of 1,725 adolescents in 1977 about their delinquent activity. These youth were interviewed annually between 1978 and 1981 and four more times as adults until 1993. The survey asked respondents about their involvement in a wide range of activities, from misdemeanor offenses such as vandalism and minor assaults to drug offenses to serious felonies including arson, assault and battery, robbery, attempted rape, and assault with intent to kill. The data revealed that although most youth engaged in minor forms of delinquency, a relatively small group of highly active chronic offenders accounted for a large amount of the self-reported delinquent conduct.[21]

Self-report instruments remain a major source of data on the illegal use of drugs and other relatively minor forms of criminal conduct. The **High School Senior Survey,** sponsored by the National Institute of Drug Abuse, surveys a representative sample of high school seniors about drug and alcohol use and their attitudes toward these behaviors. These surveys help to track patterns in drug behavior and attitudes over time among adolescents and other specific populations.

Limitations of Self-Report Data   The limitations of these data are similar to those of victim surveys: are people accurate and truthful when they report the number of crimes they may have committed? Do some young people exaggerate the extent of their involvement in crime? Do others fail to report what is most serious? In the early years of self-report studies, the surveys tended to focus on lower-level crimes, on the assumption that respondents would not be likely to provide accurate information about more serious crimes. Critics argued that this underestimated the seriousness of juvenile crime, and later surveys were amended to include more questions about more serious criminal behavior.

Another important limitation of self-report data can be found in the samples themselves, which are often not representative of a wider population. Self-report data from incarcerated offenders may not reflect the activities of criminals who are smart or skillful enough to operate without detection. Only when samples are representative can we use the data to generalize with any degree of confidence. The National High School Senior Survey uses a representative national sample of high school seniors, making it possible to make reliable generalizations based on this data about the behavior of high school seniors across the country. Even this sample, however, fails to include adolescents who have dropped out of school or those who are chronically absent from school, both categories of youth likely to engage in heavy criminal and drug use activity. Thus, despite its extreme usefulness, it is important to bear in mind that the survey cannot be used to make accurate inferences about the behavior of all adolescents of this age group.

self-report surveys: surveys that ask people whether they have committed crimes during a given period of time.

National Youth Survey: A longitudinal survey of adolescents interviewed each year from 1978 to 1981 and then four more times as adults through 1993.

High School Senior Survey: an annual survey of a representative sample of high school seniors, which asks questions about use of drugs and alcohol and attitudes towards these behaviors, conducted by the National Institute of Drug Abuse.

Measurement of White-Collar Crime

The term **white-collar crime** was originally coined by criminologist Edwin Sutherland to refer to crimes of "respectable" persons. Sutherland defined a white-collar crime as one committed by "a person of respectability and high social status in the course of his occupation."[22] Not all white-collar crimes, however, are committed in the course of one's job: white-collar crimes include tax fraud, fraudulent claims for insurance or worker's compensation, check forgery, counterfeiting, and swindling through business schemes.

Today we consider crimes committed through one's occupation as **occupational crime,** which includes the crimes committed by the blue-collar employee wearing mechanic's overalls as well as the managerial employee in the starched white shirt. The common bond between these two is the use of one's job or occupation to commit crime for personal advantage. **Corporate crime** refers to the criminal conduct of employees of a firm carried out to benefit the corporation.[23] Both of these are forms of economic crime: illegal acts committed by nonphysical means involving concealment or guile to obtain money or property. As noted below, white-collar crime is not necessarily nonviolent; just as a robber's attempt to obtain property may result in violence, so too do many forms of white-collar crime result in death and injury, even though the goal was to obtain greater profits.

Organized crime[24] is essentially an illegal business that provides illegal goods or services to the public. The illegal business enterprise relies heavily on personal violence, fear, and corruption and is also known as syndicated crime. Although people often think of the Italian Mafia as synonymous with organized crime, almost every ethnic group and nationality has been represented by criminal syndicates at some point in time. Today, new ethnic gangs operate large-scale businesses that control the illegal drug market. Chinese, Dominican, Puerto Rican, Columbian, and African American are just a few of the ethnic groups who have formed syndicates that operate in these markets.

Unlike street crime, crimes of the boardroom are underexamined and undercounted in our society. There is no equivalent agency to the FBI's Uniform Crime Reports that collects and reports data on the frequency and extent of crimes such as price fixing, bribery, fraud, and violations of health, safety, and environmental regulations. There are virtually no government-sponsored official counts of the number of offenses known to the police or the number of white-collar offenders prosecuted every year.[25]

Partly, this absence reflects the fact that white-collar crimes are often undetected. Paper trails are hard to follow, and there are few mechanisms for policing illegal financial activities. Often, victims themselves are unaware they have been cheated or harmed. This is particularly common in crimes against consumers, who acknowledge a price hike but have no idea that it is the result of illegal collusion or other anticompetitive practices by corporations. And it is particularly true for the harm caused by exposure to dangerous toxins and carcinogens, which may cause death and disease in their victims over long periods of time.

Researchers, however, have used criminal and civil court records and the records of agencies such as the Securities and Exchange Commission, the Environmental Protection Agency, and the Internal Revenue Service to compile data on the extent of white-collar crime. The consistent result has found that criminal and administrative violations are quite common among many large corporations. Beginning in 1949 with Sutherland, researchers have found that many corporations are repeat offenders: that is, despite getting "caught" and paying fines, these corporations continue violating the law again and again.[26] A study of the nation's five hundred largest corporations found that 23 percent—almost one in four—had been subject to criminal or civil action for serious misconduct in the previous ten years.[27]

Victimization surveys for white-collar victims are relatively new. Recently this method has been used to ask a random sample of citizens about their own exposure to

white-collar crime:
a general term that encompasses crimes committed by "respectable" persons.

occupational crime:
offenses committed by persons acting in their legitimate occupational roles.

corporate crime:
criminal conduct of employees of an organization committed for the benefit of the organization.

organized crime:
an illegal business that provides illegal goods or services to the public.

fraudulent activities. One survey of more than 1,200 subjects reported that nearly one-third had been victims of attempted or successful fraud in the previous year.[28] The most typical forms of fraud were the use of "free prize" scams, which demand money in exchange for a nonexistent prize, and automobile repair ripoffs.

THE CRIME PICTURE

In this section we will attempt to provide a snapshot picture of the distribution of criminal conduct in the United States. There are many ways to categorize crime: violent, property, organized, sexual, white-collar, corporate, juvenile, domestic, organized, political, and more. What follows is a basic division of crime into four broad categories: crimes of violence, property crimes, victimless crimes, and state crimes.

The Violent Crime Picture

Most Americans fear violent crimes; in public opinion surveys, citizens report their concern about the threat of violent crime. Yet the vast majority of crime in U.S. society is not violent. As we will see even more clearly in the last section of this chapter, popular entertainment and our news media vastly overrepresent violent crime. Understanding the distinction between violent and nonviolent crime is critical for understanding the nature of crime and crime policy in U.S. society.[29]

The U.S. crime rate is not extraordinarily high compared to that of other nations; in fact, some countries such as Australia and Canada actually have higher rates of victimization for some types of crimes. Spain has a higher robbery rate than the United States, and the robbery rate in the United States is roughly equal to the rate in many European countries such as the United Kingdom and Italy. The crime of assault is roughly equivalent in the United States as it is in Australia and Canada and many European countries.[30]

The main area where the pattern in the United States differs from that in these other nations is **criminal homicide**: it is in the crime of lethal violence that the U.S. picture departs radically from that in other advanced industrial nations. Homicide is the killing of one human being by another; if it is not legally justifiable or excusable (see Chapter 5), it is a criminal homicide. Criminal homicide is usually divided into two categories, murder and manslaughter, and each of these is divided further by degrees of seriousness. At the close of the twentieth century, there were an average of 20,000 homicides each year in the United States.

The U.S. homicide rate far exceeds that of most advanced industrial democracies. For 1994, the U.S. rate, at 9.0/100,000, reveals our nation as a very violent place compared to other English-speaking developed countries such as England/Wales at 1.33/100,000, Australia at 1.9/100,000, and Canada at 2.3/100,000.[31] By 1999 there was a significant drop in the U.S. homicide rate to 6.3/100,000, which nonetheless remained high compared to other advanced societies.[32] If we change our point of reference and compare the United States to the poorer, developing world, particularly countries in Latin America and Africa, the United States appears to have similar or lower levels of violence than these nations. And there are a few countries, such as those with major drug trafficking economies such as Columbia (49/100,000) and Mexico (17.1/100,000), where the homicide rate greatly exceeds the U.S. homicide rate.[33]

For the whole of the U.S. population, homicide is the tenth leading cause of death, far below causes such as heart disease and cancer. However, the incidence of homicide is not distributed evenly across the population. Gender, race, and age are powerfully connected with both risk of offending and victimization. Most offenders

criminal homicide: unlawful killing of one human being by another.

and most victims of lethal homicide are males between the ages of 18 and 34. When we look at the impact of homicides on young males between the ages of 14 and 17, we see that intentional homicides kill more young men in this age group than any major disease.

One of the disturbing trends during the 1980s and 1990s was the rising number of young people killing and being killed. Between 1985 and 1993, the homicide rate among offenders aged 14 to 17 rose by 154 percent, surpassing the rate of offending among the group between 25 and 34. Victimization rates also rose dramatically among younger age groups: the homicide victimization rate for 14- to 17-year-olds increased almost 150 percent between 1985 and 1993.[34] During the 1980s and early 1990s, teenage boys in all racial and ethnic groups became more likely to die from firearms than from all natural causes combined. Among young male African Americans, the victimization rate is eight times higher than it is among white male youth.[35] Since 1993, homicide rates for all age groups have declined: in 1999, the victimization rate for people between the ages of 14 and 17 had fallen to 5.9/100,000, compared to a rate of 15.5/100,000 for those between the ages of 18 and 24 and 10/100,000 for those between the ages of 25 and 34.

The Dramatic Fallacy of Violent Crime   According to U.S. Department of Justice data, in 2000, 44.3 percent of murders were committed by offenders known to the victims.[36] The largest group were acquaintances, but this also included a substantial percentage who were connected by family ties. Violence erupts in the course of the relationship itself: an argument between brothers, an argument at a bar among acquaintances, a fight between a husband and a wife. Most lethal crimes are not the result of a robbery, rape, or mugging, but arise out of noncriminal contexts such as a personal argument, a clash of egos, or a perceived insult or slight. The not very dramatic truth is that "murder is in general the tragic result of a stupid little quarrel."[37] The two factors that contribute most to a lethal outcome are the closeness of a loaded gun and the distance of a well-equipped emergency room.

Forcible rape is generally defined as unlawful sexual intercourse with a female, forcibly and without her consent.[38] Traditional definitions of rape involve the following elements: (1) sexual intercourse (2) by a male with a female other than his wife, (3) against her will and without consent, and (4) by force or threat of force or while she is unconscious. Common law specified that the woman must be a person other than the individual's wife. Forty-nine states now have specific statutes that allow prosecution of a husband for raping his wife. Some states also now have specific statutes that criminalize the forcible rape of a male by a female, and other states have sexually neutral statutes that criminalize the forcible penetration of male victims.

Forcible rape is the least reported of all violent crimes, partly because of the tacit acceptance of male violence against women and partly because of the shame, stigma, and difficulty of successful prosecution of these crimes, which are rarely witnessed by others. Rape is a seasonal crime, with the highest incidence rates in the hot summer months from June through August. Most rapes are committed by an acquaintance, relative, friend, or partner of the victim, betraying a trust embedded in an ongoing relationship.

Since the 1970s, feminist activists have achieved substantial changes in the criminal justice response to victims of rape. Improved methods of responding to victims, through rape crisis centers, victim advocates, police sensitivity training, hospital emergency room rape counselors, and other kinds of innovations, have greatly increased the likelihood that women who are victims of rape will be willing to report the crime to the police.

The official data on the incidence of rape show an increase in the number of reported rapes even while some other forms of violent crimes have declined in recent decades. The first comparison between the UCR and the NCVS survey in the late 1960s

forcible rape: unlawful sexual intercourse with a female, without her consent and against her will.

found that only one-quarter of rapes were reported to police.[39] In 1992, data from the National Crime Survey suggested that women were more willing to report rape than thirty years ago: 53 percent of rapes that were reported in the victimization survey were also reported to the police.[40]

Robbery is the felonious taking of money or goods of another from his person or in his presence and against his will, through the threat of force and violence. Robbery, armed or not, is a crime against a person because of the direct face-to-face contact and threat to the victim. Purse-snatching and pickpocketing are not considered robberies but are classified as larceny-theft. Robbery is primarily an urban offense; after assault, robbery is the most common violent crime. Perpetrators arrested for robbery are overwhelmingly male (90 percent), under the age of 25 (63 percent),[41] and members of a minority (55 percent).[42] Second to individuals, typical victims of robberies are gas stations, convenience stores, and banks. In 1999, guns were used in 38 percent of all robberies and knives in 9 percent.[43] In one-fifth of the robberies in which a gun was used, the gun was actually discharged during the commission of the crime.

Assault refers to the intentional attempt or threat to injure another physically. **Aggravated assault** refers to the intent to inflict serious bodily injury, including murder, rape, or robbery; simple assault refers to the intent to do less serious harm. **Battery** refers to the actual culmination of the injury (provided it is not lethal, in which case it would constitute an act of homicide). Assault and battery therefore refers to the inflicted injury coupled with the intent to inflict that injury.

Aggravated assault is the largest category of crimes against persons or violent crimes. In 1999, 74.9 percent of violent crimes were aggravated assaults.[44] The vast majority of assaults do not result in serious harm or injury; these are incidents in which one person hits another or verbally threatens another person. Although it is considered a violent offense, only three of every hundred arrests for this crime result in any injury to the victim.[45]

Violence and White-Collar Crime

White-collar crime is often conceived as inherently nonviolent. This is a false characterization of the consequences of white-collar crime, which often has lethal effects on victims. Consider the Ford Pinto debacle of the 1970s:[46] a faulty design of the subcompact vehicle was detected well in advance by the designers at Ford. Recognizing that the fuel system was easily ruptured in a minor collision, the company elected to continue to market and sell the vehicle despite the fairly certain prediction that it would result in several hundreds deaths. The decision was made based on a cost–benefit analysis that showed the cost of recalling the vehicle to be greater than the projected cost of settling lawsuits with future victims. The company made a terrible miscalculation in its assessment of the cost of killing innocent consumers: in the lawsuits that followed the deaths of young people in the Pinto, judgments of fines against the company far exceeded the anticipated profits.

However, the criminal prosecution of the executives who willingly put profits ahead of consumers' lives is difficult to achieve under the current criminal statutes. The paradox of white-collar violence is that a human being who would never harm another person on a face-to-face basis may nonetheless make knowledgeable corporate decisions that may wound or kill. The Pinto case is not an exception. It is estimated that the annual death rate from white-collar crime, including faulty products, medical quackery, violations of safety and health codes, illegal toxic dumping, and other forms of environmental pollution far exceeds the annual death rate from person-to-person homicides. Much of this violence is what Ralph Nader referred to as "postponed violence."[47] The consequences of the illegal actions may not be experienced by victims immediately, but years and years (sometimes generations) after the fact. Illegal dumping of toxic materials may result in severe birth defects, cancers, and other illnesses for residents, detectable only decades after the events take place.

robbery: felonious taking of money or goods from another person through the threat of force and violence.

assault: intentional attempt or threat to injure another physically.

aggravated assault: intent to inflict serious bodily injury.

battery: the nonlethal culmination of an assault.

White-collar misconduct often has lethal consequences. Ford Motor Company chose not to make livesaving alterations in the Pinto model, based on the financial calculation that it would be more profitable to settle civil lawsuits for the 180 deaths Ford executives predicted would result from faulty fuel tanks.

The Property Crime Picture

The vast majority of felonies are not crimes against persons but crimes against property. Property crimes that constitute Index offenses include burglary, larceny-theft, motor vehicle theft, and arson. Part II property crimes include forgery and counterfeiting, fraud, embezzlement, buying and receiving stolen property or fencing of stolen property, and vandalism.

burglary: trespass through breaking and entering of a personal or commercial property with the intent to commit a crime.

larceny: taking and carrying away of personal property of another with intent to deprive them of the property permanently.

arson: willful or malicious burning or attempt to burn any dwelling, building, vehicle, or personal property.

Burglary most often involves the breaking and entering of a personal or commercial property, most often when no one is on the premises. Daytime burglary in residences is far more common than nighttime burglaries. Burglars, unlike those who commit assaults, are usually unknown to their victims, and the clearance rate for solving these crimes is quite low, only 14 percent in 1999. The average loss in a burglary is about $1,458.[48] **Larceny** is simply another name for theft. Some states distinguish between grand larceny and simply larceny involving losses below a set dollar amount such as $250. Larceny does not involve other kinds of thefts using forgery, fraud, or technology such as computers or the Internet. Larceny is the most frequently reported Index crime; the average value of items stolen in 1999 was about $678.[49] Bear in mind that most minor thefts are probably never reported to the police.

Arson and motor vehicle theft are the two remaining Index property crimes. Auto theft is a $7-billion-a-year crime that, like burglary, has a relatively low clearance rate, 15 percent in 1999.[50] Many cars are quickly sold on to "chop shops" to be disassembled and stripped of their parts. Arson data include only those fires that are known to have been willfully or intentionally set; those of unknown or suspicious origin are not included in the data. In 1999, the average dollar loss per instance of known arson was $10,882, and the total property damage nationwide was estimated to be over $1 billion.[51]

The Cost of Property Crime   The FBI Index offenses are designated as such because of their inherent seriousness. Yet if we compare the annual losses from those forms of property crime with the estimated losses from white-collar and corporate property crime, there is little doubt as to which form of criminal conduct has a greater economic impact on our nation's pocketbook.

From a purely financial perspective, the cost of white-collar and corporate crime far outstrips the costs from shoplifting, retail theft, home burglaries, personal robberies, and even bank robberies. According to the FBI, the loss from all bank robberies in the 1992 was $35 million; this total loss is equal to about 1 percent of the cost of just one fraudulent thrift institution, the Lincoln Savings and Loan, which cost the taxpayer $3.4 billion.[52] Consider the Helmsley swindle of $1.2 million in unpaid taxes. The cost of tax evasion alone has been estimated at between 5 and 7 percent of the Gross National Product, a figure that amounted to between $336 and 470 billion in 1994.[53] In 1995, the General Accounting Office of the U.S. government predicted that, based on patterns in the past year, fraudulent practices such as unnecessary tests, medications, and surgical procedures as well as other practices such as overbilling in the medical industry would cost the American public in excess of $100 billion.[54]

Victimless Crimes

Victimless crimes are often referred to as *consensual crimes* and are included in the statutes as crimes against public order, morality, or safety. Under English common law, such activities were not criminalized; instead, activities such as fornication outside marriage or adultery were handled by ecclesiastical courts, because the Church was the clear arbiter of sinful behavior. In the American colonies, however, the early settlers were successful in infusing the state with the legislative authority to enforce common morality.

Crimes against public order typically have no specific complaining victim who feels sufficiently injured to enter a complaint to the authorities. Consensual crimes are illegal acts in which the parties participate willingly and usually involve the sale or exchange of an illegal good such as a controlled substance, or services such as prostitution, gambling, or pornography. Most states in the United States continue to have statutes that prohibit and punish fornication, adultery, and illicit cohabitation.

It has long been debated whether these types of offenses can genuinely be considered "victimless crimes." Victims may be those community members who are forced to suffer the negative consequences of public drunkenness, wanton sexual conduct, illegal drug markets, and their associated violence. Victims are also those who suffer from the negligent behavior of those addicted to drugs or gambling, such as neglected children or impoverished families. These crimes are also seen as offensive to standards of public decency and morality, because such behavior undermines standards of conduct and promotes values that are contrary to the community norms. The "victims" of once called victimless crimes, therefore, also include those who experience a reduction in moral values in their community.

It was in the nineteenth century that states first began to outlaw the use of drugs, namely, alcohol in response to the many destructive habits associated with the rise of saloons—places of brawls and brothels, where many a paycheck disappeared in the froth of a brew and whiskey. Drunken husbands beat their wives and children, sprawled in the streets, and failed to show up at the factory on time for work. The alcohol problem became a clarion call for thousands and thousands of middle-class women and men attempting to save families and the nation from decay.

Many were skeptical about the beneficial effects of legislating against drunkenness. Like laws against adultery and fornication outside of marriage, it was predicted that such measures were doomed to fail. No amount of legal threat would stop people from

victimless crimes: illegal activities that involve willing participants, such as drug use, prostitution, and gambling.

engaging in these activities, and far greater harm would result from trying to use the law to stop them. Failure would lead to corruption in public life and erosion of civil rights as the justice system attempted in vain to enforce these unenforceable laws. Ironically, legal prohibition would lead to an increase in value of the commodity itself on the black market in the face of the persistent demand on the part of the public. The repeal of national prohibition in 1935 was fueled by these arguments.

Although President Nixon declared a "war on drugs" as early as the 1970s, the real growth in federal and state budgets to prosecute drug crimes began in the late 1980s, when media attention on the nation's "drug problem," particularly the use of crack cocaine, skyrocketed. President Reagan and his wife Nancy defined drug abuse as a major problem, and by 1992 the nation was spending $30 billion on the drug war.[55] By 2000 the federal drug control budget alone exceeded $18 billion.[56]

The data on the extent of illegal drug use principally comes from two key self-report surveys: the Monitoring the Future Project gathered by the University of Michigan's Institute for Social Research, which collects data on secondary school students' involvement in delinquent activities, and the household data collected by the National Institute of Drug Abuse, in its surveys of drug use among the U.S. household population aged 12 and over. The self-reports of high school seniors show a steady drop in reported use of marijuana, from a peak of about 51 percent of all high school seniors in 1979 down to 37.8 percent by 1999. Use of other drugs such as cocaine and heroin is much less prevalent, with 6.2 percent of students reporting use of cocaine and 1.1 percent reporting use of heroin in 1999.[57]

The sampling limitations of these two major self-report surveys help to explain a different pattern seen in two other sources of information about drug use. One is the **DAWN,** or **Drug Abuse Warning Network,** collected by the federal Substance Abuse and Mental Health Services Administration (SAMHSA), which relays information about drug overdoses and deaths in emergency rooms. These data show an increase of drug-related admissions in the same time period that we see a steady decline in the wider surveys. The second source is the **DUF** or **Drug Use Forecasting,** sponsored by the National Institute of Justice, data which report on routine urinalysis screens of people arrested under the criminal justice system. Like the DAWN data, the DUF shows patterns of heavy drug use by people arrested by the criminal justice system even for non-drug-related offenses. This pattern suggests a decline in drug use during the 1980s and 1990s by the high school population but an increase in the use of serious drugs by marginal populations on our nation's inner-city streets and prisons.

State and Political Crimes

The legal definition of crime defines these acts as "crimes against the state." But what about when crimes are committed *by* the state?[58] Like corporate crime and white-collar crime, the illegal acts of the government are not given much conscious attention when we talk about crime or crime control. Abusing legal authority has far-reaching effects on society by eroding public confidence in those institutions we have entrusted with power in our society. Crimes of corruption committed by police, correctional officials, judges, and other public authorities undermine the legitimacy of the law itself.

As a culture, we hear a great deal more about crimes of individual violence than we do about the crimes of mass violence. Ironically, people are more likely to be brought to "justice" if they kill one person than if they are responsible for the deaths of hundreds, thousands, or even millions of innocent people. Crimes of the powerful are generally far more destructive than the routine crimes committed by the powerless.

Genocide is not a crime in a legal sense, since it is not found in the codes of statutes and other legal doctrines. Typically, crimes waged against entire peoples by states—crimes such as civilian massacres, and other forms of mass killings are not criminal-

---

DAWN or Drug Abuse Warning Network: program that compiles data on drug overdoses and deaths reported by hospital emergency rooms, sponsored by the U.S. Department of Health and Human Services.

DUF or Drug Use Forecasting: U.S. Department of Justice program that compiles data on drug use by people arrested in selected cities.

state crimes: illegal acts committed by governments and other public authorities, in violation of domestic and international law.

genocide: an international crime consisting of specific acts of violence committed with intent to destroy, in whole or in part, a national, ethnic, racial, or religious group.

ized by a body of law. The history of European worldwide imperialism and colonialism is one of the most extreme cases of genocide, of both peoples and their culture and way of life. Before the seventeenth century, the presence of European soldiers on the continent of the Americas led to the death of between 60 and 80 million Native Americans, destroying the advanced civilizations and cultures of the Incas, Brazilians, and other sophisticated civilizations. From the perspective of the Europeans, the indigenous populations were seen as "subhuman" and therefore not true "victims" of unjust violence. In North America, the destruction of the native cultures and tribes continued well into the twentieth century. Africans were forcibly removed from their native lands and kidnapped into slavery and submission; again, these crimes were committed by governments that acted without any regard for the fundamental human rights of the victims.

Victims of these types of violence and injustice are often without recourse other than to appeal to international intervention based on principles of international law and declarations of human rights. Generally, citizens find it easier to see foreign governments as violating the law than to view their own government's action in this light. The mass beatings, murders, and arrests carried out by the Chinese government against student demonstrators in June 1989 were widely condemned within this country as illegal and in violation of international laws of **human rights.**

Yet U.S. history is full of examples of similar forms of illegal conduct carried out by the government against its own citizens engaged in legitimate political protests. As recently as the 1960s and 1970s, the FBI conducted illegal surveillance, burglary, and mail tampering to disrupt the activities of the Black Panthers and the American Indian Movement. American CIA agents have violated U.S. law and international law in their clandestine activities in Latin America and other parts of the world, destabilizing and even overthrowing democratically elected governments.

Also included in the category of state crime are criminal violations of the law by professionals in the criminal justice system. When police officers abuse their legal authority to use coercive force by beating an African American suspect, it is an example of state criminality, particularly when such conduct is widespread within a police force and tacitly condoned by the administration. When prison guards beat prisoners or deny them basic human needs such as adequate food or sanitation, agents of the state are engaged in an abuse of authority recognized as criminal conduct in violation of both U.S. and international law.

Still in its infancy, the concept of war crimes or the existence of human rights that are inviolable by any political entity speak to the need to hold individuals and nations accountable for crimes perpetrated by governments against their own citizens and the citizens of other nations.[59] Included in the conception of crimes against humanity are **crimes of omission,** when governments fail to provide decent opportunity for jobs, housing, education, and political rights for their citizenry.[60]

The crime of **terrorism** is a political crime defined by its motive to influence political policy or public opinion rather than for the purpose of financial gain or personal vengeance. The FBI defines terrorism as "the unlawful use of force or violence against persons or property to intimidate or coerce a government, the civilian population, or any segment thereof, in furtherance of political or social objectives."[61] Before 1993, most terrorist attacks committed against U.S. citizens occurred on foreign soil and were directed at military personnel, U.S. embassies, or international flights. The bombing of the World Trade Center by Islamic terrorists in 1993 marked the first major attempt at a domestic target. The car bomb planted in the parking garage of the Twin Towers left six people dead and injured a thousand people. In 1995, members of a right-wing extremist group in the United States set off a massive truck bomb at a federal building in Oklahoma City that killed 166 and injured hundreds more. Up until that time, this was the worst terrorist attack on U.S. soil. In response to the growing threat of domestic and international terrorism, the U.S. Congress passed the International

human rights: the concept that there are basic inalienable rights universal to all people by virtue of their humanity.

crimes of omission: failure of governments to provide decent opportunities for housing, education, jobs, and citizenship rights for their citizenry.

terrorism: use of violence against a target to create fear or coercion for the purpose of obtaining some political concession or reward or other goal.

The attack on September 11, 2001, was the most lethal terrorist attack in world history, killing more than three thousand innocent victims and creating an urgent need by law enforcement to increase security within the United States against politically motivated violence.

Crime Control Act of 1998, which vastly increased the authority of federal law enforcement to investigate, detect, prosecute, and punish international terrorism and other forms of transnational crimes.

On September 11, 2001, the world community was shocked by the coordinated hijacking and deliberate crashing of four U.S. airliners. Two of the planes were flown into the Twin Towers of New York City's World Trade Center, a third crashed into the Pentagon, and a fourth was headed for the White House or Congress before it was thwarted by passengers and forced to crash in a field in Pennsylvania. More than 3,000 U.S. and other nationals were killed as a result of these acts. In response, President George W. Bush created the Office of Homeland Security to coordinate federal, state, and local law enforcement on the actions of terrorism prevention within the borders of the United States.

UNDERSTANDING THE SYMBOLIC PICTURE OF CRIME

The final section of this chapter examines how Americans "imagine" and "talk" about crime in every day life. It is tempting to talk about the "crime" problem in the United States as if "crime" were a single form of behavior. Most Americans think of only certain types of crimes and certain "images" when they talk about "crime." Researchers believe that more than 90 percent of American adults have engaged in behavior that, if prosecuted, would result in a criminal conviction, but few of us look on our neighbors, teachers, and friends as "criminals." Usually we are not thinking about tax fraud when we refer to the "crime problem," nor are we imagining a 71-year-old socialite when we use the word "criminal." Leona Helmsley hardly fits most people's mental image of a convicted criminal because most of us operate with a stereotypical view of the "criminal" and "crime."

Although crime constitutes all of these diverse forms of conduct, when we refer to the "crime problem" we often are speaking in a kind of coded language to represent a particular type of crime and a particular type of offender. The concept of "crime" therefore takes on a symbolic meaning in our culture, representing our fear of "dangerous people, places, and classes." Sociologists refer to the transformation of a neutral term such as crime into a sacred symbol as the process of **reification.** Our culture has a tendency to "reify" the term "crime." When we speak about the "crime" problem as if it is a single type of behavior, we reify crime. We turn a legal category of behavior into a symbol with powerful but often unspoken meaning.

The Image of Crime in the Mass Media

The source for most Americans' mental pictures about crime derive from the images broadcast into our living rooms each evening and splashed across the headlines each morning. Crime has increasingly become a dominant theme both within the "news" media that purport to inform citizens about the important events of the current times and in the "entertainment" media that offer amusement and distraction. Both of these genres devote disproportionate attention to a very narrow definition of the "crime problem." News programming, popular television and film content, and a host of so-called reality programming offer the American media consumer a very distorted, one-sided, and racist picture of crime.

Crime in the News   The coverage of crime in the news media has been boosting sales since the advent of daily newspapers in the nineteenth century. By the turn of the century, reporters on major city newspapers began to specialize in the coverage of the crime beat, devoted to police reports and court cases. Once radio and then television entered the picture, the need to create a dramatic story of great interest to a fickle audience intensified, and heightened attention focused on the most sensational and gory of crimes.[62]

In recent decades, crime has continued to dominate our news media: on national television news, crime is the subject of 10 to 13 percent of all stories; on local television it constitutes 20 percent of all coverage. In the print media, between 22 and 28 percent of all news consists of crime or justice-related topics. Despite the decline in violent crime in the 1990s, the coverage of crime increased by more than 400 percent; between 1990 and 1995, while the murder rate declined by 13 percent, network news coverage of murder, even excluding coverage of the O.J. Simpson trial, increased by 336 percent. In the 1990s, crime was the leading television news topic.[63]

Although more than nine property crimes occur for every one violent crime, only 4 percent of crime news stories depicted instances of nonviolent crime. And those violent crimes that were reported were more likely to be ones that were committed by strangers than by acquaintances or intimates. Coverage of domestic violence and date rapes was also less likely than coverage of cases involving predatory strangers. Studies have shown that media coverage focuses most attention on crimes in which white females are victims and tend to ignore victimization of young men of color, who are most often the victims of violent crime. Although the Leona Helmsley case made headlines for nearly two years, usually there is little or no press coverage of tax fraud cases despite the prevalence of it in our society.

Crime as Entertainment   Most Americans form their opinion about the nature of crime and the crime problem not only from the news but also from entertainment media such as cop shows and movies. What is the image of crime that dominates our entertainment media? That is an easy question to answer. It is overwhelmingly crimes of

reification: the transformation of a neutral word or concept into a sacred and powerful symbol.

violence, particularly murder and rape. The world of television and movies is astonishingly more violent than the real world. Despite the fact that homicide is less than 1 percent of the major crime total, the National Coalition on TV Violence reports that the average U.S. child will view an average of approximately 500,000 murders on television by the age of 16. On prime-time television, the rate of homicide is 1,000 times greater than it is on our streets.[64]

One of the consequences of this distorted picture of crime and justice is to influence people's perceptions and fear of crime in their own lives. The more people watch television, the more they develop what George Gerbner calls the **mean world syndrome,** or the belief that the world is really full of predators lying in wait to assault total strangers for no reason other than pure malice.[65] The fear of crime often outweighs the actual risk of victimization, especially for the most violent crimes. Measures of public fear about the risk of crime indicate that people's perception of what is likely to happen to them is shaped more by how much and how often they watch television than by their own personal experience or that of their friends and neighbors. Watching about a terrible crime on the evening news makes people feel as if it happened in their own backyard, even if the crime took place halfway across the country. The more lurid the crime, the more likely it will be broadcast in communities across the nation.

As a consequence of media-driven fear, people often alter their behavior by staying off the streets at night and avoiding interaction with strangers. This may be good news for the private security industry, but it has the negative effect of undermining social life within public places. Abandonment of public spaces eventually may lead to an increase in street crime, because empty streets mean less chance of detection. To an extent, fear can become a self-fulfilling prophecy.

The Impact of Racial Stereotypes on Criminal Justice Policy

The typical criminal predator as depicted by the media is a person of color. Images of crime and typical criminals reinforce widespread stereotyping associated with excessive and heavy-handed criminal justice treatment of minority citizens. This constant imagery affects the beliefs of the public, and members of the justice system as well. For instance, these distorted images made it easier for the public and criminal justice professionals to believe that a strange black man shot white Charles Stuart and killed his pregnant wife Carol Stuart for a few dollars. It also was the unspoken imagery that helped the nation and the justice system believe Susan Smith's initial story, when she claimed that a strange black man abducted her two young boys and drove off with them in her car.

The symbolic use of black men as the image of evil predatory strangers protects the white middle-class male, such as Charles Stuart, who shot his own wife and unborn child for insurance money, and white mother Susan Smith, who drowned her own two children to make her more attractive to her lover, from our suspicions and fears. Both of these perpetrators of terrible crimes against their own family members fingered a black stranger for the crime, and both nearly succeeded with their racial hoaxes because of our preconceptions and our stereotypes of predatory criminals.

The disproportionate coverage of violent street crime and its racial bias shapes our crime policy. The "Hortonization" effect (see Chapter 3) is reinforced by media portrayal of minorities as dangerous criminals. A fearful public supports the building of more prisons and tougher sentencing laws. Despite a drop in the crime rate for seven consecutive years after 1990, the state prison population rose by 7 percent each year, along with heightened coverage of the worst kind of violent crime in the news and entertainment media.[66]

mean world syndrome: the belief that the world is full of predators waiting to assault innocent strangers.

KEY TERMS

dark figure of crime p. 67
Uniform Crime Reports p. 67
Part I offenses p. 67
Part II offenses p. 67
Total Crime Index p. 67
Violent Crime Index p. 67
Property Crime Index p. 67
crime rate p. 67
clearance rate p. 67
crime clock p. 68
National Incident-Based Reporting
    System (NIBRS) p. 69
victimization surveys p. 70
National Crime Victimization
    Survey p. 70

self-report surveys p. 71
National Youth Survey p. 71
High School Senior
    Survey p. 71
white-collar crime p. 72
occupational crime p. 72
corporate crime p. 72
organized crime p. 72
criminal homicide p. 73
forcible rape p. 74
robbery p. 75
assault p. 75
aggravated assault p. 75
battery p. 75
burglary p. 76

larceny p. 76
arson p. 76
victimless crimes p. 77
DAWN or Drug Abuse Warning
    Network p. 78
DUF or Drug Use
    Forecasting p. 78
state crimes p. 78
genocide p. 78
human rights p. 79
crimes of omission p. 79
terrorism p. 79
reification p. 81
mean world syndrome p. 82

REVIEW AND STUDY QUESTIONS

1. What is the dark figure of crime? Describe the three key methods used by criminologists to gain a reasonable estimate of this figure. Give examples of each method.
2. Describe the limitations of each of the methods of measurement.
3. Describe the methods to measure white-collar crime. Why is white-collar crime relatively invisible in our society?
4. What is a victimless crime? What are the rationales for prohibiting consensual activities such as prostitution, gambling, pornography, or drug use?
5. Describe the key difference between the crime picture in the United States and the crime picture in other major European and North American industrial de-

mocratic nations. How does the crime clock distort our understanding of crime?
6. What is the dramatic fallacy of violent crime? In what sense may corporate crime be violent crime?
7. What is state crime?
8. What is the process of reification? How does this process occur in the construction of the portrait of the "typical criminal" in U.S. society?
9. Describe the image of crime as depicted in our news and entertainment media.
10. What is a "racial hoax," and how are these false claims supported by the media portrayal of crime in our society?

CHECK IT OUT

On the Web
Federal Bureau of Investigation, **www.fbi.gov**
The FBI Web site will lead you to the Uniform Crime Reports; the Ten Most Wanted criminals; FBI case reports, major investigations, and more.

Sourcebook of Criminal Justice Statistics, Online, **www.albany.edu/sourcebook/**
This site provides data on all aspects of criminal justice in the United States. Check out the section on Statistics for the

Distribution of Known Offenses, which provides summary statistics from all the major sources for criminal data covered in this chapter.

Bureau of Justice Statistics: Key Crime & Justice Facts at a Glance, **www.ojp.usdoj.gov/bjs/glance.htm**

Criminal Offenders Statistics, **www.ojp.usdoj.gov/bjs/crimoff.htm**
Check out this site for information, statistics, and publications about criminal offenders in the United States.

Crimes of Persuasion and Other White Collar Crimes, **www.crimes-of-persuasion.com/**
Informative site that gives an overview of white-collar and organized crime involving telemarketing, investment, and other types of fraud. Has links to many sites on white-collar criminal investigation and prosecution.

Center for Victims of Crime, **www.ncvc.org/**
Check out this site for all kinds of information about victims.

World Crime Survey Data, **www.uncjin.org/**
United Nations surveys of crime trends around the world.

Human Rights Watch, **www.hrw.org**
Human Rights Watch is the largest human rights organization based in the United States. It provides a wealth of information on human rights abuses around the globe. Click on World Report 2002 to see details and check out the section on the United States, which includes information about overincarceration and race, prison conditions, police brutality, and the death penalty.

On Film

Violence: An American Tradition (55 minutes)
*From the violent repression of Native Americans through vigilantism and the contemporary epidemic of domestic violence, this documentary explores recurring patterns of violence in U.S. society. Available from Films for the Humanities and Social Sciences at **www.films.com.***

Crime in the Suites (24 minutes)
*This documentary examines the phenomenon of white-collar crime through profiling two notorious white-collar criminals and a victim of a scam, who lost his entire pension, to illustrate the harmful impact of these crimes and the absence of corporate ethics. Available from Films for the Humanities and Social Sciences at **www.films.com.***

Killing Screens: Media and the Culture of Violence (40 minutes)
*This video presents the research of George Gerbner, which demonstrates the negative effects of media violence through desensitization to real violence and encouragement of real violence. Available from Insight Media at **www.insight-media.com.***

Clockers (129 minutes)
A Spike Lee film that portrays young African American men and their chronic involvement in the drug trade and violence of street life.

Wall Street (126 minutes)
A classic Hollywood portrayal of a corrupt ethical culture that promotes and rationalizes illegal conduct among the highest echelons of the financial industry.

NOTES

1. Murray Kempton, "Leading the Royal Life: Real Kings and Queens Would Hardly Feel Deprived," *Newsday,* April 15, 1988, p. 15.

2. Murray Kempton, "Helmsley Degrees of Degradation," *Newsday,* July 6, 1989, p. 2.

3. Beth Holland, "Helmsley Accounts Called "Cheat System," *Newsday,* July 20, 1989, p. 4.

4. Howard Kurtz, "Abuzz about the Hotel Queen: Ex-employees Stinging Testimony in Trial of Leona Helmsley," *The Washington Post,* July, 18, 1989, p. D-1.

5. "Excerpt from Judge's Statement," *Newsday,* December 13, 1989, p. 3.

6. Paul Craig Roberts, "Leona Helmsley Is Being Persecuted," *The Atlanta Journal and Constitution,* April 3, 1992, p. A-11.

7. Anthony Lewis, "A Little Helmsley in Many Americans," *St. Louis Dispatch,* September 8, 1989, p. 2.

8. Paul Craig Roberts, "Hotel Queen Deserves New Trial, not Jail," *The Houston Chronicle,* April 4, 1992, p. C-12.

9. Ellen Goodman, "We Could Have Given Leona a Break," *Newsday,* April 22, 1992, p. 109.

10. Jean Harris, "For Leona, Jail Is Not the Best Punishment," *Newsday,* April 9, 1992, p. 109.

11. Romy Franklin, "Leona's Just Deserts," *Newsday,* April 17, 1992, p. 45.

12. Federal Bureau of Investigation, U.S. Department of Justice, *Crime in the United States—1999* (Washington, DC: U.S. Government Printing Office, 2000).

13. Albert Morris, *What Are the Sources of Knowledge about Crime in the U.S.A.?,* United Prison Association of Massachusetts, Bulletin No. 15, 1965.

14. Gregg Barak, *Integrating Criminologies* (Boston: Allyn & Bacon, 1998), p. 32.

15. Federal Bureau of Investigation, *Uniform Crime Reports, 1998* (Washington, DC: U.S. Department of Justice, 1999), p. 4.

16. Steven R. Donzinger, Ed., *The Real War on Crime: The Report of the National Criminal Justice Commission* (New York: HarperCollins, 1996), p. 4.

17. Federal Bureau of Investigation, *Structure and Implementation Plan for the Enhanced UCR Program* (Washington, DC: U.S. Department of Justice, 1989).

18. Law Enforcement Assistance Administration, *Criminal Victimization in the United States—1977* (Washington, DC: U.S. Government Printing Office, 1979).

19. Marianne W. Zawitz and U.S. Bureau of Justice Statistics, *Highlights from 20 Years of Surveying Crime Victims* (Washington, DC: Bureau of Justice Statistics, 1993).

20. J. Levine, "The Potential for Crime Overreporting in Criminal Victimization Surveys," *Criminology* 14(2) (1976), pp. 307–331.

21. Franklyn W. Dunford and Delbert S. Elliott, "Identifying Career Offenders Using Self-Reported Data," *Journal of Research in Crime and Delinquency 21* (1984), pp. 57–86.

22. Edwin H. Sutherland, *White-Collar Crime: The Uncut Version* (New York: Dryden Press, 1949), p. 9.

23. Marshall Clinard and Peter Yeager, *Corporate Crime* (New York: The Free Press, 1980), p. 18.

24. Jay Albanese, *Organized Crime in America,* 3d ed. (Cincinnati, OH: Anderson, 1996), pp. 4–6.

25. Stephen M. Rossoff, Henry N. Pontell, and Robert Tillman, *Profit without Honor: White Collar Crime and the Looting of America* (Englewood Cliffs, NJ: Prentice Hall, 1998), p. 12.

26. Sutherland, *White-Collar Crime,* p. 25.

27. Kelly Orr, "Corporate Crime: The Untold Story," *U.S. News & World Report,* September 6, 1982, pp. 25–29.

28. Richard Titus, Fred Heinzelmann, and John Boyle, "Victimization of Persons by Fraud," *Crime and Delinquency 41* (1995), p. 54.

29. Franklin E. Zimring and Gordon Hawkins, *Crime Is Not the Problem: Lethal Violence in America* (New York: Oxford University Press, 1997) pp. 3–6.

30. Donzinger, Ed., *The Real War on Crime,* p. 10.

31. "Comparative Homicide Rates in English-Speaking Developed Countries," February 2, 2002, http://www.worldpolicy.org/americas/usa/firearms-homicides.html.

32. Anne L. Pastore and Katherine Maguire, Eds., *Sourcebook on Criminal Justice Statistics, 1999* (Washington, DC: U.S. Government Printing Office, 2000), p. 267.

33. United Nations, "International Homicide Rates," in *Statistical Yearbook* (New York: United Nations, 1991), as cited in Zimring and Hawkins, *Crime Is Not the Problem,* p. 54.

34. Bureau of Justice Statistics, "Homicide Trends in the United States: Age Trends," http://www.ojp.usdoj.gov/bjs/homicide/talbes/vagetab.htm.

35. Donzinger, Ed., *The Real War on Crime,* p. 9.

36. Federal Bureau of Investigation, *Crime in the United States, 2000,* p. 21.

37. Marcus Felson, *Crime and Everyday Life,* 2d ed. (Thousand Oaks, CA: Pine Forge Press, 1998), p. 3.

38. American Law Institute, *Model Penal Code,* 1980, 213-213.6.

39. President's Commission on Law Enforcement and Administration of Justice, *Challenge to Crime in a Free Society* (Washington, DC: U.S. Government Printing Office, 1967), pp. 96–100.

40. Bureau of Justice Statistics Bulletin, *Criminal Victimization 1992* (Washington, DC: Bureau of Justice Statistics, 1994).

41. Pastore and Maguire, Eds., *Sourcebook on Criminal Justice Statistics, 1999,* p. 348.

42. Ibid., p. 352.

43. Ibid., p. 310.

44. Federal Bureau of Investigation, U.S. Department of Justice, *Crime in the United States—1999,* p. 210.

45. Donzinger, Ed., *The Real War on Crime,* p. 12.

46. Francis T. Cullen, William J. Maakaestad, and Gray Cavaender, *Corporate Crime under Attack: The Pinto Case and Beyond* (Cincinnati, OH: Anderson, 1987), pp. 145–188.

47. Quoted in Rossoff, et al., *Profit without Honor,* p. 81.

48. Federal Bureau of Investigation, U.S. Department of Justice, *Crime in the United States—1999,* p. 40.

49. Ibid., p. 45.

50. Ibid., p. 51.

51. Ibid., p. 55.

52. Ibid., p. 17.

53. Jeffrey Reiman, *The Rich Get Richer and the Poor Get Prison: Ideology, Class and Criminal Justice,* 5th ed. (Boston: Allyn & Bacon, 1998), p. 111.

54. Robert Sherrill, "Medicine and Madness of the Market," *The Nation,* January 9, 1995, pp. 45–72.

55. Jerome Miller, *Search and Destroy: The African American Male in the Criminal Justice System* (New York: Cambridge University Press, 1993), p. 81.

56. Pastore and Maguire, Eds., *Sourcebook on Criminal Justice Statistics, 1999* p. 15.

57. Ibid., p. 236.

58. Gregg Barak, "Toward a Criminology of State Criminality," in Gregg Barak, Ed., *Crimes by the Capitalist State: An Introduction to State Criminality* (Albany: State University of New York Press, 1991), pp. 3–18.

59. Stanley Cohen, "Human Rights and Crimes of the State: The Culture of Denial," *Australian and New Zealand Journal of Criminology 26* (1993), pp. 97–115.

60. Stuart Henry, "The Informal Economy: A Crime of Omission by the State," in Barak, Ed., *Crimes by the Capitalist State,* pp. 253–267.

61. Federal Bureau of Investigation, U.S. Department of Justice, *Terrorism in the United States, 1995* (Washington, DC: U.S. Government Printing Office, 1997), p. 2.

62. Katherine Beckett and Theodore Sasson, *The Politics of Injustice: Crime and Punishment in America* (Thousands Oaks, CA: Pine Forge Press, 2000), pp. 75–77.

63. Ibid., p. 77.

64. Ibid., p. 102.

65. George Gerbner, *Television and Its Viewers: What Social Science Sees* (Santa Monica, CA: Rand, 1976).

66. Beckett and Sasson, *The Politics of Injustice,* p. 20.

CASE 5

Accident or Homicide? The Shooting of Yoshi Hattori

It was Saturday night, October 17, 1992, six days before Halloween. In their modest brick ranch home in Baton Rouge, Louisiana, on a quiet street, Rodney Peairs, 30, and his wife, Bonnie, were just sitting down to a supper of grits and eggs with their two children when the doorbell rang. Not expecting visitors, Bonnie got up to peer through the curtains of the window. Unable to see clearly, she went to the side door of the house and opened the door a crack. Almost immediately, she slammed the door shut and with rising panic in her voice shouted, "Rodney, get your gun!" Rodney bolted to the bedroom closet to fetch his .44-caliber Magnum pistol fitted with a night hunting scope, which he kept fully loaded alongside his shotgun, rifle, and two pellet guns.

What frightened Bonnie Peairs was the sight of two 16-year-old boys, one a Japanese exchange student, the other a local boy, who had rung the doorbell expecting to be welcomed to a Halloween party actually taking place five doors down the street. Yoshi Hattori was dressed in a white tuxedo jacket in an attempt to imitate John Travolta; Webb was in ordinary clothing with bandages wrapped around his head to imitate an accident victim. Driving through an unfamiliar neighborhood to a classmate's Halloween party, the boys had mistakenly transposed the numbers of the address: instead of number 3131, they had arrived at number 1313. The house was festively decorated with a large Happy Halloween ban-

ner stretched across the front window, so they figured they had come to the right place. Walking up to the front door, they rang the doorbell expecting to be greeted by their friends. They saw someone peer out a curtain, and when Bonnie Peairs opened the carport door, Webb started to speak, saying, "Excuse me . . . ," only to be answered by Bonnie's slammed door.

Webb and Yoshi turned to leave and were walking back to their car when they heard the carport door reopen. This time it was Rodney, carrying a long-barreled and powerful gun pointed directly at the two boys. Yoshi turned and skipped back toward Rodney, arms out at his sides in a dancing motion, repeating a gleeful refrain, "We're here for the party!" Rodney assumed a crouch position and yelled "Freeze!" but Yoshi kept moving forward. Rodney shot him in the chest from about 5 feet away.

The entire sequence of events took less than two minutes. No words were exchanged other than the one sentence uttered by Yoshi, "We're here for the party," and the one word of warning uttered by Rodney Peairs, "Freeze!" Webb, standing only a few feet away, saw a man point a large gun at his friend, heard him shout "Freeze," then saw his friend collapse. Rodney shut the door and locked it while Webb screamed for help. Alarmed by the sound of the gunfire and the cries for help, a neighbor called the police. Twenty-five minutes later, Yoshi was declared dead from one fatal shot to his heart.

THE JUDICIAL PROCESS

The sheriff who arrived on the scene did not arrest Rodney Peairs or his wife Bonnie that night. Under Louisiana state law, a property owner has the right to use lethal force to defend his property from invaders or to compel someone to leave his property. In 1983, an amendment to the state code known as the "shoot-the-burglar" law permitted residents to justifiably kill someone they believed to be an intruder if they were within four walls of a residence.

Was Rodney Peairs acting in defense of his family, life, and property as permitted by law? Or did Rodney Peairs commit a crime when he shot and killed Yoshi Hattori? In the minds of the law enforcement officers who arrived on the scene that night, the answer was obvious. Rodney Peairs, a meatcutter at a local supermarket, was a family man protecting his property from what he believed was a lethal threat. They did not take him into custody that night, nor did they seek a warrant for his arrest in the following days.

But the district attorney's office took a different view of the matter. The district attorney convened a grand jury, seeking to indict Rodney Peairs on a criminal charge of negligent homicide. According to the district attorney, Rodney Peairs acted negligently when he fired his .44-caliber weapon point-blank at Yoshi Hattori. Owners of firearms have a special duty to use these weapons with care; although he did not believe that Rodney Peairs had the desire to kill Hattori and did believe he had been genuinely frightened by his wife's fear and by the unusual behavior and appearance of the two boys that night, he argued that, nonetheless, Peairs acted with a degree of carelessness that was criminal. The prosecutor believed that Rodney should be held criminally liable for the death of Yoshi Hattori because of his failure to use his firearm with sufficient care and diligence. The grand jury agreed, and Rodney Peairs was indicted for negligent homicide.

The case attracted enormous publicity, largely because of the interest taken in the case by the Japanese public.[1] While the killing of Americans by firearms is relatively commonplace, in Japan these events rarely happen even among the criminal underworld. With a population half the size of the United States densely crowded on a tiny series of islands, there are less than a hundred deaths from guns per year and most of these occur among organized crime gangs. Compare this to the 12,000 U.S. deaths each year from handguns alone to appreciate how shocking the death of Yoshi Hattori was to the Japanese public. Almost immediately, the case became a national issue in Japan.

In this kind of atmosphere, jury selection is always a delicate affair. Both sides presented potential jurors with elaborate questionnaires that asked the typical questions required of jurors. In addition, each attorney was permitted to ask questions specific to this case. The defense grilled potential jurors about their attitudes toward gun control and about the right of a person to defend his or her property against invasion by intruders. The questionnaire asked potential jurors if they were members of crime-watch groups, "What do you believe needs to be done to lower the crime rate?," how many owned guns, who potential jurors felt was their greatest hero, "Have you ever experienced unannounced visitors at your home, i.e., Girl Scouts selling cookies, charitable organizations, persons looking for directions, etc.?." From the answers to the questions, attorneys for each side argued that certain jurors were prejudiced against the case from the outset. Most of these arguments were made by the defense, because the law gives the defense a greater number of opportunities to strike potential jurors. In this case, the final jury that was seated consisted entirely of Louisiana citizens who believed in the right to gun ownership, the right to keep a gun at home, and the right to use a gun to protect one's family and property.

At the trial, there was little disagreement between the defense and the prosecution as to the "facts" during those fateful two minutes. The case hinged on the interpretation of those facts and what was in the mind of Rodney Peairs, and whether this was a reasonable state of mind for any citizen confronted by the same set of circumstances. The law of self-defense does not require an individual to be "correct" in the perception that he or she is facing a lethal threat. The law simply requires that the person act as any reasonable person would act faced with a similar set of circumstances. Would any "reasonable person" have come to the conclusion that he and his family were about to be subjected to an invasion of their home? Did Rodney Peairs act as any reasonable person would have done to defend his family from a lethal threat?

According to the argument presented by the defense, Rodney Peairs acted reasonably, justifiably shooting and killing Yoshi Hattori, given his perception in those seconds prior to the shooting. He was, in fact, wrong in those perceptions, and he is terribly sorry for the tragic mistake, but he acted legally and justifiably on the information he had at the time. Alarmed by his wife's cries and claiming never to have heard her so frightened, Rodney perceived Yoshi and Webb as invaders who were threatening his family. Rodney Peairs gave a verbal warning and Yoshi failed to heed his warning to stay back and "freeze." It was dark and Rodney thought the camera in his hand was a weapon. Yoshi was moving erratically, waving his arms about, and Rodney feared Yoshi might grab his own weapon from his hand. According to the defense attorney, Peairs acted as any reasonable person would have when he killed Hattori. He acted in self-defense. "I had no choice," Peairs testified on the stand. "I want the Hattoris to understand that I'm sorry for everything."[2]

The prosecution rejected the view that Peairs' reaction was a reasonable one under the circumstances. The prosecution argued that Peairs had many alternatives to the lethal use of his firearm. He was well armed when he peered out the carport window, and a phone stood at his elbow in the kitchen to call the police. The yard, carport, and street were brightly lit, so he could clearly see what the boys were doing. In fact, when he looked out the window, the boys had already turned and were leaving the house. They rang the doorbell just once. They did not loiter or linger about the house. They did not peer into the windows, ring the doorbell again, jiggle the doorknob of the house, try to open the door, or break into the carport door. There was no legitimate reason for Rodney Peairs to open his door and confront the boys with his gun. Even after issuing his warning, Rodney could have retreated into his house and locked the door rather than fire his gun. According to the prosecution, Peairs was guilty of the illegal discharge of a firearm. There was no justification for firing his weapon that night. Peairs made several bad decisions that night and deserved to be held responsible for them. "Otherwise," said the district attorney, "anyone who comes by your house, you could kill them. You don't need a reason."[3]

The jury deliberated for less than three hours. They returned a unanimous verdict of not guilty. The twelve-person, all-white jury found that Rodney Peairs had acted in self-defense when he killed Yoshi Hattori when he rang the wrong doorbell on a Saturday night at 8 p.m.

THE VICTIMS' PERSPECTIVE

Stories about crime rarely chronicle the experience of those who are most affected by crime itself, namely, the victims and their families. In the case of homicide, the survivors of the victim are often the last to be notified about almost every development in the criminal case. The parents of Yoshi Hattori were given the grim news of their son's death by the Haymakers, parents of Webb and Yoshi's "host" parents in the United States. Masaichi Hattori, an engineer with an auto parts manufacturer, and his wife, Mieko, a homemaker, flew to Louisiana, where the Haymakers tried to comfort and explain the incomprehensible to these parents and to their entire nation. Why was their son killed? What had he done to provoke such a lethal response? Why would someone shoot an unarmed young man? What were the Peairses thinking that they were so frightened by the mere presence of strangers outside their front door?

These were questions the Haymakers were at a loss to answer. Like many victims, the Hattoris sought answers to understand the reason for their son's death. They sought to understand the behavior and motives of their son's killer. But like all victims, they were prevented from asking any direct questions that would help answer these questions. During the months leading up to the trial, the Hattoris were denied any direct contact with the Peairs. No letter of regret, remorse, sympathy, or expression of sorrow ever came from Peairs or his wife directly to the Hattori family.

The Hattoris took their son home to be buried in Japan. The funeral was a major media event in Japan.[4] Thousands of mourners showed up to pay their respects to the Hattoris. There were flowers, bouquets, and messages from all over Japan, including expressions of sympathy from the U.S. government, Japan's major companies, and the Foreign Ministry. The Prime Minister of Japan called on Washington to change its gun ownership laws. There was, however, no sign of flowers or message sent from the man and woman directly responsible for the death of the 16-year-old boy.

The Hattoris returned to the United States several times over the next year as the criminal proceedings against Rodney Peairs churned forward. Like most victims, they felt compelled to be present, to hear and witness the proceedings, even though little new information or insight was offered to them. Hundreds of spectators showed up at the courtroom, and in the throng the parents of the victim were given little attention—finding it difficult even to find a seat among the crowd. At each hearing and for every day of the trial, Mr. Hattori sat impassively listening as the defense painted an unflattering portrait of his son's behavior that night. He described Yoshi as "erratic," "kinetic," and even "bizarre."

Illegal discharge of a firearm

Were these statements truthful? Is truth what takes place in a courtroom? Not necessarily. The job of the defense is to present the facts in a light most favorable to his or her client's interests. In this case, it was in the interest of Rodney Peairs that the actions of Yoshi Hattori be presented as menacing in order to convince the jury that Peairs was reasonable to be afraid of him and therefore acted legally in discharging his weapon. For the grieving members of the victim's family, such a zealous defense makes attending the trial a painful and difficult experience, in which they are made to feel as if their son, not the defendant, was to blame.

From the witness stand, Rodney Peairs testified that he felt deep regret over the incident. He stated in court that he was sorry but that he felt he had no choice but to shoot Yoshi. Beyond that testimony in the trial, the Peairs's made no attempt to contact the parents of the boy by letter, telephone, or face to face. In Japanese culture this failure to acknowledge personal responsibility to the victim's family is unthinkable. In Japan, an expression of sincere and deep apology is an expected response in the wake of such a violent act.

For the victims, the long silence from the Peairs was as incomprehensible and painful as the adversarial trial itself. Told that it would not be possible to interact with Peairs directly while criminal proceedings were in progress, the Hattoris believed that they were finally going to hear directly from the Peairses at a meeting scheduled after the acquittal. But it was not Rodney or his wife who showed up on that Monday morning for the meeting, but the lawyer who continued to speak for his client and defend his actions as "justifiable."

Even more painful for the Hattoris were the shouts of victory and the celebrations that erupted when the jury returned the verdict of "not guilty." For the Japanese the American-style adversarial system, which focuses all the attention on the "battle" of the trial and declares one side the "winner" and the other the "loser," was a mockery of their understanding of justice. Many were stunned by the conduct of the courtroom scene in which spectators cheered and made the V sign for victory even while the parents of Yoshi sat nearby watching the spectacle.

THE CIVIL TRIAL[5]

Shortly after the verdict in the criminal trial, the Hattoris announced that they were bringing a civil suit of wrongful death against Peairs. The money, they said, was of no interest to them. But they intended to bring this suit because "they wanted the U.S. judicial system to say their son's death was a wrongful death."[6] For the Hattoris, it was important for them to have the justice system confirm that a wrong had been done when their son was killed. According to their lawyer, Mr. Charles Moore, they filed a civil suit because they wanted "to show that what happened was not right."

The civil law differs from the criminal law in several important ways. In a civil trial, the state is represented only by the judge, who functions as the final decision maker. It is not necessary to have a jury in a civil case. A civil trial is subject to a lower standard of proof than a criminal trial, because the penalties are about making financial reparations rather than inflicting punishment on the defendant. A defendant who loses a civil case may be required to pay damages, but he or she cannot be punished by being sent to jail.

In the civil trial, a Baton Rouge trial court found Peairs guilty of wrongful death and ruled that he and his insurance company jointly owed the Hattoris $653,077. The state district court judge rejected the defense's argument that Peairs thought that Yoshi Hattori was a lunatic threatening to invade his home and harm his family, stating: "There was no justification whatsoever that the killing was necessary to save himself or his family.... There was absolutely no need to the resort of a dangerous weapon."[7] Peairs was ordered to pay $85,000—the maximum allowed under state law—for the youth's pain and suffering, $275,000 each to his parents for the wrongful death, and about $18,000 to cover funeral expenses.

Peairs appealed the decision, arguing that Hattori had been partially responsible for the incident so the amount should be reduced. This argument was rejected by the appeals court. Later the Louisiana Supreme Judicial Court denied a writ filed on behalf of Rodney Peairs, leaving the judgment against him to stand. The insurance company, Louisiana Farm Bureau Mutual, paid the $100,000 it was responsible for in Peairs's policy, and Peairs was technically responsible for paying the remaining $550,000.

The Hattoris knew from the outset that Peairs was unlikely ever to pay the money. The civil trial was not about the money. The Hattoris were seeking a symbolic statement from the justice system that what Peairs had done was neither reasonable nor right. The Hattoris offered a statement following the first civil verdict which stated that "We are satisfied to finally find out with whom the responsibility belongs." Mrs. Hattori also went on to say, "Although the verdict was in our favor, the hole in my heart will always be there forever.... Please decrease the number of handguns as much as possible."[8] After Peairs had exhausted all appeals, his lawyers argued that he was totally broke, having lost his job at the supermarket, his home, and was living in a trailer park working as an auto mechanic.

THE GUN CONTROL CAMPAIGN

The Hattoris announced that they would be willing to forgo the judgement against Peairs if he would give them the gun he had used to kill their son. Mieko Hattori said, "No matter how much financial compensation we are awarded, it is not equal to the loss of our son. Though the lawsuit has not yet been settled, we plan to negotiate with Peairs's representative. We hope to use the gun as a symbol of the gun control movement."[9] The money they received from the insurance company was already being used to sponsor a U.S. gun control award in memory of their son. The Hattoris have donated all that they received to a foundation established in their son's name for reform of U.S. gun control laws.

Like many survivors of murder, for the Hattoris the biggest question is *why*. Rodney Peairs was not a killer or a murderous criminal. The Hattoris, along with many of their fellow countrymen, struggled to comprehend the mindset of Peairs that led to the violent death of their son. Yoshi's mother wrote in an open letter to a major Japanese newspaper shortly after the acquittal, "When an innocent child is shot by mistake and the guilty party is let off scot-free, we can only conclude that such a society is sick."[10] The most obvious culprit in this terrible tragedy was the ubiquity of guns in U.S. households: to their mind, the true cause of their son's death was the overwhelming presence of guns in so many Americans homes.

Like many survivors, the Hattoris needed to do something constructive with their grief. Yoshi's mother explained that their son had always hoped to do something positive in the world, so in his place, they would speak out against the use of guns in American society. Within months of the shooting, by the time of the first pretrial hearing on the case, the Hattoris had begun a petition drive, signed by 800,000 Japanese citizens, urging the newly elected U.S. President Bill Clinton to push for more stringent gun control laws. In the petition written by the Hattorris, the parents clearly placed the blame for their son's death on U.S. laws that permit people to own guns. For this family, as for many survivors of murder, an outlet for grief is to turn their pain into activism that will prevent future tragedies. Few families can accept the idea that their loved one's death will be without some value or benefit to the world.

In the petition the Hattoris wrote: "The thing we must really despise, even more than the criminal, is the American law that permits people to own guns. We know many fine Americans, but we feel a fierce anger that these Americans have let their country become a place where people must walk the streets in fear."[11] Over the next year, the Hattoris collected more than 1.8 million signatures on that petition from Americans and from Japanese. They presented this petition to President Clinton at the White House on November 22, 1995, the day that would have been Yoshi's eighteenth birthday.

Case adapted from Adam Nossiter, "Student's Trust in People Proved Fatal," *The New York Times,* October 23, 1992; Peter Applebome, "Verdict in Death of Student Reverberates across Nation," *The New York Times,* May 26, 1992; Christopher Cooper, "Japan Tunes In as Trail in Teen's Slaying Begins," *The Times-Picayune,* May 18, 1993; T. R. Reid, "Japanese Media Disparage Acquittal in 'Freeze Case': Commentators See America as Sick Nation," *The Washington Post,* May 25, 1993; Christina Cheakalos, "Culture Clash Plays Out in Louisiana Hearing Set Today in Shooting Death," *The Atlanta Journal and Constitution,* January 7, 1993; T. R. Reid, "Angry Japan Lays to Rest Students Shot Dead in U.S.; Slaying Sparks Criticism of Gun Laws," *The Washington Post,* October 27, 1992; Christopher Cooper, "Slain Student's Father Hears Killer's Version," *The Times-Picayune,* May 23, 1993; Christopher Cooper, "Teen's Friend Recounts Shooting: Seeing the Gun Was Puzzling," *The Times-Picayune,* May 21, 1993; David E. Sanger, "After Gunman's Acquittal, Japan Struggles to Understand America," *The New York Times,* May 25, 1993; *M. Hattori and M. Hattori* v. *R. Peairs, B. Peairs and Louisiana Farm Bureau Mutual Insurance Company.* No. 95 CA 0144 (La.App. 1 Cir, 10/06/95); 662 So.2d 509; T. R. Reid, "Ruling Softens Japan's Image of Violent U.S.; After Monetary Award . . . 'There is a Sense of Justice in America After All,' " *The Washington Post,* September 18, 1994; "No Justification Whatsoever," *St. Louis Dispatch,* September 21, 1994; Adam Nossiter, "Judge Awards Damages in Japanese Youth's Death," *The New York Times,* September 16, 1994; *The Washington Post,* "Japanese Student's Parents Want Death Gun Destroyed," September 18, 1994; Joan Treadway. "Parents Turn Grief into Anti-Gun Effort," *The Times-Picayune,* October 6, 1996.

THINKING CRITICALLY ABOUT THIS CASE

1. Who are the members of the criminal justice system who had "discretion" in this case? How did the police, prosecution, and defense defend the interests of justice in their exercise of discretion?
2. If the job of the jury is to determine what is "reasonable," how important is the composition of the jury for making these decisions? Can we agree on a single standard for "reasonable" conduct?
3. Was this "justice" for the family of the victim? Why or why not?

4. Do you believe that race played a factor in this case? Did it influence the fear experienced by Bonnie and Rodney Peairs? Did you believe the issue of race influenced the decision of the jury?

5. Why was it important for the victims to meet with Rodney and Bonnie Peairs? Do you believe that such a face-to-face meeting should have been arranged? What about the adversarial process was disturbing to the victim's family?

6. Do you think Peairs should honor the request of the victims and hand over the gun used to kill their son, to serve as a symbol in the fight for gun control? Why or why not? Why was this important to the victims?

7. Even though he had been acquitted by the criminal system, Rodney Peairs was found liable by the civil law system. Which verdict do you believe is more just? Do you believe that Peairs "owes" restitution to the victims family? Why or why not?

CHECK OUT THIS CASE

On Film

The Shot Heard around the World (67 minutes)
*Documentary produced and directed by award-winning filmmaker Christine Choy about the shooting of Yoshi Hattori, the issue of guns, prejudice and the criminal justice system. Available from the Filmakers Library, **www.filmakers.com.***

Understanding Criminal Law

After reading this chapter, the student should be able to:

- Identify and define the five material elements of crime

- Explain the difference between murder, manslaughter, felony murder, and vehicular homicide

- Explain the principles of defense, including the idea of affirmative defenses, and know the difference between a defense of excuse and a defense of justification

- Identify and describe the five elements required to prove self-defense

- Explain the "reasonable person standard" and give an example in which the reasonable person standard introduces bias into the legal process

That Yoshi Hattori's death had been caused by the firing of a lethal weapon by Rodney Peairs is an undisputed fact in this case. No one denies that Peairs's act of firing his weapon was responsible for the death of Hattori. But did Peairs commit a crime? Although we know that Peairs was physically responsible for killing Hattori, the purpose of the trial was to determine if he was legally responsible. This is the important distinction between factual guilt and **legal guilt.** A person may be factually guilty of killing another person yet nonetheless be found legally "not guilty" for a variety of reasons. Legal guilt may only be determined through the legal proceedings of the criminal law.

Criminal liability[12] refers to the degree of blameworthiness assigned to a defendant as a result of the legal proceedings of adjudication. Once liability is established through the mechanisms of due process, the state can determine the appropriate sanctions. The purpose of the trial is to establish the degree of criminal liability, if any, of the defendant. Criminal liability or blameworthiness may be reduced or even entirely eliminated (as it was in this case) if the defendant had legal justification or excuse for his or her actions.

MATERIAL ELEMENTS OF THE CRIME

As we saw in Chapter 1, a foundation of due process in our system of criminal law is the presumption of innocence. Unless the state can prove that a person committed a specific crime, the citizen cannot be convicted of a crime. No one accused of a crime must "prove" his or her innocence before a court of law; the burden rests on the accusers to produce evidence to convict the defendant. What does the state have to prove? This depends on the specific crime as it is written in the specific statute or body of law. The substantive portion of the criminal code spells out the specific behaviors that are prohibited or, in rarer circumstances, the specific behaviors that are required.

There are five elements common to almost all criminal statutes: (1) the element of *actus reus,* which requires that there must have been an action or failure to act on the part of the defendant; (2) the guilty mind or *mens rea* element, which requires that there must have been a conscious mental decision to commit the act; (3) the concurrence requirement, which states that the harmful act and the guilty mind must occur simultaneously; (4) the requirement that these acts must have resulted in an identifiable harm to the victim and/or society; and finally, (5) the requirement to prove that the action was the genuine cause of the harm to the victim and/or society. Let us examine each of these elements in turn.

Actus Reus

The first requirement of criminal liability is known as the **human conduct rule.** The *actus reus* requirement states that a crime must be an act. In the Western tradition of law, we hold people accountable for their deeds, not their thoughts. We prohibit conduct, not ideas, fantasies, beliefs, or thoughts: no one can be punished for simply thinking about committing a crime—there must be behavior that puts thought into action.

Speech is a form of action. For example, talking to someone about hiring him to kill one's spouse may seem to be "merely speech." Yet the act of speaking satisfies the *actus reus* element, and the person who hires a killer is criminally liable for the crime of solicitation, and for the consequences of those words, that is, homicide. If a person yells "Fire" in a crowded theater and sparks a panicky stampede, she may be liable for any injuries that result. Similarly, threatening to harm someone may result in an arrest and criminal prosecution. Solicitation, conspiracy, and threat are all forms of criminal conduct that prohibit certain forms of speech that cause harm in society.

The human conduct rule distinguishes between "doing" and "being." The courts have interpreted the *actus reus* element to mean that criminal law may not penalize a person simply for "being" a prostitute, an addict, or a thief. The distinction between a state of being and a form of conduct was tested in the case of *Robinson* v. *California,*[13] in which a California statute declared it a criminal offense for a person "to be addicted to the use of narcotics." The Constitutional question was whether the statute violated the human conduct rule by punishing someone for a state of being rather than for a specific action. The U.S. Supreme Court reversed the ruling of the California court on the principle that although the state had the right to prohibit and impose criminal sanctions for the "acts" of manufacture, sale, possession, and use of narcotics, it could not punish an individual for "being" an addict.

The *actus reus* element also contains within it the requirement that an action be voluntary. A person who is forced to act by another or who acts by involuntary reflex caused by stimuli beyond the person's control may not be held criminally responsible. Actions undertaken during sleep or under hypnosis would also not be considered criminal even if they resulted in substantial harm to others and/or violated the criminal law.

The criminal code not only declares certain acts to be in violation of the law but also, in less frequent circumstances, makes criminal a failure to act in those instances where the law requires a person to act. In this case, it is the failure to act that is criminally liable. An obvious example is the requirement that all citizens file and pay taxes: failure to do so may be a criminal act. Parents and guardians, lifeguards, military personnel, doctors, and child care workers are some of the special categories of individuals who may be held criminally liable if they fail to take certain actions, such as providing for the well-being of their children, taking steps to save a drowning person's life, or reporting a suspected case of child abuse to the authorities. For example, a parent may be prosecuted for involuntary manslaughter for failing to obtain medical care for a child if the untreated illness results in that child's death.

In the case of Rodney Peairs, the law of Louisiana requires certain forms of action from gun owners similar to the kind of care required of people who operate motor vehicles.[14] Criminal negligence may exist when a person fails to exercise a reasonable standard of care. In Peairs's case, the district attorney argued that a reasonable person

legal guilt: proof of criminal liability beyond a reasonable doubt by admissible evidence within a court of law.

criminal liability: the degree of blameworthiness assigned to a defendant as a result of legal adjudication.

material elements of the crime: the five key elements common to almost all criminal statutes which must be proven within a court of law beyond a reasonable doubt according to the rules of criminal procedure and evidence to establish legal guilt.

actus reus: the physical element of the criminal act.

human conduct rule: the legal principle that a person must commit an act (performance, deed, or movement) or a failure to act (where the law specifies a duty to act) in order to be subject to criminal sanctions.

would have waited and observed Hattori's conduct from inside the house before shooting the gun; or would have phoned the police; or fired a warning shot into the air. Failing to take these cautionary steps made Peairs criminally liable for Hattori's death.

Mens Rea

The "state of mind" element is so fundamental to our concept of criminal responsibility that it is an essential element of criminal conduct. The term **mens rea** literally means "guilty mind" and refers to the mental state of the person when he or she committed the action. It is not enough simply to know who physically carried out a harmful action to satisfy our concept of criminal responsibility; we must also know if the person intended to do the harm. In the Western legal tradition, there is a fundamental notion that people should be held responsible for actions they voluntarily, willfully, and knowingly commit. We distinguish between actions that are purposeful, planned, or malicious and those that are unintentional, involuntary, or accidental. In justifying this distinction, U.S. Supreme Court Justice Oliver Wendell Holmes observed: "Even a dog distinguishes between being stumbled over and being kicked."[15] *Mens rea* does not refer to motive. **Motive** refers to the reasons a person commits a particular action, whereas *mens rea* refers to the conscious awareness of the outcome or consequences of one's conduct.

When people act with premeditated intent we consider their criminal liability or responsibility to be greater than when people act on the spur of the moment, out of fear or anger, or simply because of neglect. We punish more severely the mental state in which a person plans out a crime in advance and then implements that plan "in cold blood." This phrase refers to the deliberate and conscious intention on the part of an individual to carry out an act. This is the mental state most criminal codes refer to as *first* **degree,** and it is the most serious type of criminal conduct for which we reserve our most severe penalties.

Specific intent is the thoughtful and conscious intention to perform a specific act in order to achieve a particular result. If Rodney Peairs had seen Yoshi coming up the drive, told his wife and children he was "going to kill the bastard," and gone and fetched his gun in order to do so, his conduct would be clearly seen as intentional and purposeful. A specific intent crime means that the person consciously desired a particular outcome. Specific intent crimes are usually first-degree crimes, because in addition to the action itself, there is evidence that the person intended a specific outcome.

A less evil state of mind is referred to as **general intent.** General intent is often inferred from the behavior or conduct itself. When a person breaks into and enters a home, it is concluded from this conduct that he had the general intent to commit larceny. However, if the offender showed evidence of planning that crime in order to steal from the person there, he may be charged with first-degree larceny because he had a specific intent to deprive the owner of the property. The latter crime, in which the conduct is accompanied by strategic planning and preparatory actions, is seen as more serious than conduct in which intent is more or less formed on the spur of the moment.

Individuals are also held criminally responsible for their conduct when they do not have a particular intention to commit these acts. **Criminal negligence** refers to unconscious reckless conduct. In this case, the person may not have known that she was acting recklessly, but *she should have known.* Even if she did not intend the circumstances or the results and did not realize she was endangering others, it is her responsibility to be diligent, and if there are harmful consequences she may be held criminally responsible for those consequences. Thus, the mother who leaves a very young child unattended in the bathtub may be found criminally negligent if the child subsequently drowns.

The legal doctrine of **constructive intent** refers to cases in which actors did not intend harm but their conduct violated basic standards of responsible conduct. These are

mens rea: the mental element in crime, or criminal intent, or the guilty mind.

motive: reasons a person commits a particular action.

degree: the level of seriousness of the crime.

specific intent: the thoughtful and conscious intention to perform a specific act in order to achieve a particular outcome.

general intent: state of mind inferred from the behavior or conduct itself to commit the act.

criminal negligence: creation of high risk of harm without consciousness.

constructive intent: state of mind in which a person acts without intending harm but with a complete disregard for the rights and safety of others.

cases of either reckless conduct or negligent conduct. **Criminal recklessness** is knowingly creating a high risk of harm to others. The wrongdoer may not intend or desire to harm someone but nonetheless they know that they are acting in such as way as to place others at grave risk. For instance, leaving a loaded gun on a table is reckless conduct. The individual may not intend or want a child to pick up the gun and fire it at someone else, but if a child does, it is the gun owner who is criminally liable for the consequences. Although the gun owner did not mean to cause this outcome, he or she nonetheless knowingly acted recklessly by leaving a loaded gun where a child could pick it up.

Strict liability statutes[16] hold persons criminally liable for their actions regardless of whether they acted knowingly, recklessly, or negligently. There are relatively few of these types of statutes in U.S. criminal law. Traffic violations and crimes such as statutory rape are examples in which the mental state of the defendant is irrelevant to the criminal statute. Even if a person is unaware of the speed limit and does not at all willfully or even knowingly violate the speed limit, the law permits the conduct to constitute the offense regardless of the *mens rea* of the actor.

Legal Definitions of Criminal Homicide[17]

We can gain understanding into the importance of the *mens rea* of a crime when we examine the range of criminal statutes that prohibit the taking of human life. Depending on one's state of mind, a person factually guilty of killing another human being may be legally innocent or criminally responsible to varying degrees of seriousness.

Homicide is the killing of one human being by another. There are three basic types of homicide: **justifiable, excusable,** and **criminal.** As we will see later in this chapter, justifiable homicides are cases where the law permits killing, such as in the military, or as the defense successfully argued in the Peairs case, to protect one's self, family, and property. Excusable homicides are cases in which the act is not considered criminal because it was accidental or the person was not acting voluntarily or with full mental capacity. The remaining forms of killing fall within the category of criminal homicide.

Murder versus Manslaughter

There are two broad types of criminal homicide: murder and manslaughter. **Murder** is the unlawful killing of a human being with malice. There are two main categories: first degree and second degree. First-degree murder requires premeditation, which is defined, practically speaking, as a period of time for reflection between the time the intent was formed and the time the act was committed. If a person purchased some poison, for example, and later put it in someone's food, that period in between was time when she had the opportunity to reflect on her actions and sufficient evidence that she willfully chose to pursue the act of killing.

Second-degree murder is killing with malice but without premeditation. Malice does not necessarily refer to hatred of the victim or a particular state of viciousness. Rather, the concept refers to the state of mind in which the person intentionally acts to kill or harm another. In this sense it is similar to the idea of specific intent, in which a person purposefully and intentionally acts to harm another.

Felony murder is a specific subset of murder most often associated with second-degree murder. Felony murders are acts of killing that result from an intention to commit a different felony altogether. Thus, if a person is robbing a convenience store and kills someone in the course of committing that felony, she is guilty of murder regardless of whether the killing was intentional, reckless, negligent, or accidental. It is, in a sense, a form of strict liability in which the person is held fully responsible for her actions and the *mens rea* for the act is of no consequence legally. All the state must prove is that the defendant had the *mens rea* to commit a felony.

---

criminal recklessness: knowing creation of high risk of harm to others.

strict liability statutes: crimes for which one may incur liability without fault or intention.

homicide: the killing of a human being by the act, procurement, or omission of another human being.

justifiable homicide: homicide that is permitted under the law by reason of self-defense, necessity, or the execution of a public duty.

excusable homicide: homicide that is committed by persons without legal liability for their conduct or in a manner that the criminal law does not prohibit, e.g., accidentally.

criminal homicide: the purposeful, knowing, reckless, or negligent causing of the death of one human being by another.

murder: the killing of one human being by another with malice or premeditation.

felony murder: if a death occurs during the commission of a felony, the person committing the primary offense can also be charged with murder.

Manslaughter is a lesser form of criminal homicide. All forms of manslaughter are unlawful killings without malice. Generally there are two broad types: **voluntary manslaughter** and **involuntary manslaughter,** which also often includes forms of criminal negligence. Voluntary manslaughter is often a "crime of passion." This is because voluntary manslaughter is an intentional killing, usually in the context of an intense quarrel or sudden fit of rage or passion. Voluntary manslaughter rests on the notion that the killer was, to some extent, provoked by the circumstances, that he formed the intent to kill in response to that provocation (and not before, as in first-degree murder), that he acted in the heat of passion, and that he had no time to cool off to think more clearly about his actions.

Involuntary manslaughter encompasses acts of criminal homicide in which the *mens rea* of the defendant is one of recklessness or negligence. Unlike the other forms of criminal homicide, involuntary manslaughter generally does not entail the intentional desire to cause a person lethal harm. Rather, the individual acted with gross negligence, which involves a willful and conscious disregard of the safety of others and of one's duty to take care to protect the safety of others. **Vehicular homicide,** which is a separate count in many states, specifically prohibits the operation of a motor vehicle in a reckless manner.

In the Peairs case, there is no doubt as to the actions Rodney Peairs took that fateful evening in October. The key evidence in determining the issue of criminal liability concerned the mental state of Mr. Peairs during those two minutes when he fetched his gun, aimed it at Yoshi, and pulled the trigger. Did Mr. Peairs form a plan in his mind to kill Yoshi Hattori? Did he lure Yoshi to his house? Did he desire the death of this boy? Did he have an evil state of mind such that he wanted to kill any stranger or person who came to his front door? Was he terrified of his life and trying to protect his family? Was he acting on impulse with reckless and thoughtless regard for the safety of his fellow citizens?

The charge of negligent homicide required the district attorney to prove to the jury that Rodney Peairs failed to meet "the standard of care expected to be maintained by a reasonably careful person under like circumstances." Both the prosecution and defense relied on the **reasonable person standard** to convince the jury of their argument. The prosecution argued that Mr. Peairs failed to act prudently when he fired on Hattori. The defense claimed that any reasonable person in Peairs's shoes would have believed he was in imminent danger of home invasion by Hattori. The job of the jury was to decide which course of action was "reasonable" in these circumstances.

Concurrence

The element **concurrence** is the requirement that a given act and a given state of mind occur at the same time. In order for a crime to occur, there must be evidence that the act and the state of mind were happening together. If one preceded the other, the requirements of the criminal law have not been met. For example, if Billy threatens to kill his brother at one point in time, and two weeks later reconciles with him, goes on a hunting trip, and accidentally kills his brother, the earlier state of mind cannot be coupled with the later act. The relevant state of mind is that which is present at the time of the act itself. The act must be propelled forward by the state of mind.

Causation[18]

The fourth requirement for a crime to occur is that the *actus reus* or the action be the cause of a harm. To prove that a particular crime occurred, therefore, it is necessary to demonstrate not only that a harm occurred, but also that the actions of the defendant caused the harm itself. In the case of Rodney Peairs, this was not a difficult ele-

---

manslaughter: the unlawful killing of a human being without malice or premeditation.

voluntary manslaughter: the unlawful killing of a human being without malice but that is done intentionally upon a sudden quarrel or in the heat of passion.

involuntary manslaughter: an unintentional killing for which criminal liability is imposed.

vehicular homicide: the killing of a human being by the operation of a motor vehicle by another in a reckless manner likely to cause the death of, or great bodily harm to, another.

reasonable person standard: the circumstances as they appeared to the defendant would have created the same beliefs in the mind of an average, normal, sensible human being.

concurrence: the simultaneous coexistence of an act in violation of the law and a criminal intent.

ment to prove. Yoshi Hattori's death was clearly the result of the bullet that was fired from Peairs's gun.

In some cases, however, the element of **causation** can be very complex and difficult to establish. Consider the case of Gary Wall. Gary had been stabbed in the stomach by his roommate, Daniel. Gary was transported to the hospital, treated for the stab wound, and released. He died three days later from internal bleeding. Daniel was charged with second-degree murder, but the trial jury found him guilty only of assault. They did not find him criminally liable for Gary's death. Why? The defense argued that it was the failure of the surgeon who examined Gary but did not realize that the knife had penetrated his liver that actually caused the death. It was the doctor's criminal negligence that was the actual cause of death, not the initial stabbing by Daniel.

The element of causation uses a **"but for" standard** to determine criminal liability. Had Gary not been taken to the hospital, he surely would have died from those stab wounds and Daniel would have been fully responsible for his death. In that set of circumstances the charge of second-degree murder would have likely held against Daniel. In this case, however, there was an intervening cause, the treatment by the doctor. The actions (or failure to act in this case) by the doctor reduced Daniel's liability to a lesser offense. But for the mistreatment by the doctor, Gary Wall would have lived.

The principle behind the element of causation is whether it is fair to hold the accused accountable for a harm that occurred. Supposing Marty punches Sam in the nose with what would have been a nonlethal blow except for the fact that Sam is a hemophiliac who bleeds to death as a result. Is Marty liable for Sam's death under these circumstances, even though he didn't know about Sam's condition? The legal rules of causation would say "yes," applying the "but for" rule. But for Marty's blow, Sam would not have died. A preexisting condition, such as his illness, does not excuse Marty from criminal responsibility for the harm caused by his actions.

The guidelines for causation are that unless there is an unforeseeable intervening cause, criminal liability falls to the primary actions that set a chain of events in motion. If Sandy chases Bobby with a bat into the street, where Bobby is struck by a car and killed, the "but for" rule would hold Sandy responsible for that outcome, because Bobby getting hit by a car was reasonably foreseeable given his being chased into traffic by Bobby wielding a weapon. However, if Bobby was being chased in a field and was struck by lightening and killed, Sandy would not be liable for that outcome because he could not have reasonably foreseen that outcome or sequence of events.

Resulting Harm

A central principle of criminal law is that conduct that is criminalized is inherently harmful both to specific victims and to the wider society itself. For many crimes, this is relatively easy to see: murder, rape, robbery, fraud, and theft are clearly harmful to those who are directly victimized and clearly create a type of society that undermines everyone's ability to live with security and harmony. Understanding the impact on the quality of life in the community is one of the reasons we criminalize the "attempt" to commit crimes. Even though these are instances when an act is not carried out so no individual harm is suffered, it is understood that the purpose of the law is to discourage those forms of conduct among the wider public. Therefore, it is just as important to punish "attempts" as to punish actions that are successfully carried out.

It is important, however, to realize that the issue of criminalization, that is, whether or not a particular conduct ought to be prohibited or required by the criminal law, is a matter of social policy and legislative debate. The general issue of harm is not debated in a court of law, which is concerned with the application of existing law to a particular set of events. The criminalization of certain consensual activities such as drug use, prostitution, gambling, or pornography enters into law through political debates about the harmfulness of this conduct to the wider community.

causation: a causal link between an actor's conduct and a harm.

"but for" standard: a standard for determining causality which holds that "but for" the conduct of the accused, the harm in question would not have occurred.

harm: loss, disadvantage, or injury to a victim.

PRINCIPLES OF DEFENSE

Now let us turn to the job of the defense counsel in a court of law. Due process requirements of our legal system require that the prosecution's case be met by an equally vigorous case presented by an attorney for the accused. A criminal defense is the presentation of evidence and arguments in a court of law by an attorney representing the defendant, to show why the defendant is not criminally liable for the charges. The job of defense attorneys is to defend their clients to the utmost of their ability within the ethical boundaries set down by the legal profession.

Because of the basic presumption of innocence, the burden falls to the prosecution to prove affirmatively its case against the accused. One key defense strategy is to demonstrate that the prosecution has failed to provide evidence to convince a jury beyond a reasonable doubt. Is it possible there is an alternate explanation for the prosecution's conclusions? Is it possible a witness is not telling the truth? Is it possible a witness is mistaken in what he or she saw or recalls? A powerful role of the defense attorney is to test the strength of the prosecutor's evidence and to raise "reasonable doubt" in the mind of the jury or judge.

A second strategy for the defense is to challenge the due process requirements that should have been met by the state. Often referred to as "technicalities," these are key elements of the rights of the accused and fundamental to the protection of the rights of all citizens. Was the defendant read his rights by the arresting officer? Did the officers have a warrant when they searched the trunk of the car? Was the accused afforded competent counsel for his defense? Was jury selection fair and unbiased? One of the responsibilities of the defense attorney is to ensure that the laws of criminal procedure are not violated in any particular case.

Affirmative Defenses

affirmative defenses: defenses raised by the defendant's counsel that carry the burden of proof beyond a reasonable doubt.

defense of alibi: legal defense in which the defendant claims to have been in a different location when the crime was committed.

defenses of justification: a category of legal defense in which the defendant admits committing the act in question but claims that it was necessary to avoid some greater evil.

In both of these defense strategies, testing the prosecution's case and challenging the due process procedures followed by the state, there is no requirement on the part of the defense to prove their arguments beyond a reasonable doubt. Their job is to raise enough doubt to undermine the certainty needed for a conviction. Juries are instructed as to the meaning of the standard of "beyond a reasonable doubt" and are told that if they have "reasonable doubt," then they should allow the "benefit" of that doubt to go to the defendant.

When the defense chooses to argue self-defense, or claims an alibi or claims the defendant is mentally ill, the burden of proof switches from the prosecution to the defense in most jurisdictions. **Affirmative defenses** are subject to the same "reasonable doubt" standard as the prosecution's effort to convict. In the Peairs case, the defense counsel had to "prove" to the jury beyond a reasonable doubt that Peairs was acting in accordance with the legal requirements of justifiable homicide when he killed Yoshi Hattori.

There are three main categories of affirmative defenses. The first is known as the **defense of alibi.** This simply means that the accused is not guilty because she was somewhere else at the time the crime was committed and evidence of her whereabouts will be presented in court. Defenses of justification and defenses of excuse also are both known as affirmative defenses, because they require the defense to prove its version of events beyond a reasonable doubt.

Defenses of Justification   **Defenses of justification** make the claim that the defendant was morally justified in his choice of conduct because he thereby avoided a harm that was greater than the one he committed. In the Rodney Peairs case, when faced with a choice between two evils, permitting his home to be invaded by a dangerous stranger or killing Hattori, Peairs chose the lesser of two evils. The typical forms of justification are self-defense, including defense of others and property; execution of public duty; and necessity.

The execution of **public duty** permits the legal use of force in the service of a lawful arrest or apprehension. Thus law enforcement officers can claim the public duty defense if they are accused of assault and battery on a citizen during the course of an arrest. The use of force is lawful only if the person is resisting arrest and if the arrest itself is a lawful one. The **necessity justification** is generally used in the face of extreme threats from nature. If a person is stranded in a blizzard and therefore forced to break and enter a home for shelter, she may claim the defense of necessity.

The concept of **self-defense** is based on a widely recognized principle that every person has an inherent right to defend himself against an unlawful attack and that the person who harms or even kills an attacker does not so much as intend to take another's life as seeks to preserve his own. The use of force to defend oneself has been extended to include the protection and preservation of the lives of others who appear to be in imminent danger.

The use of lethal force is generally not permitted in the defense of property alone, although if the trespasser is armed, then the threat of force may justify a lethal response to protect property. In the Louisiana state code, the law permits the use of lethal force to remove a person from one's home regardless of whether that person is armed, in an amendment known as the "shoot the burglar" clause. In Louisiana, justifiable homicide includes an action taken against a person who is attempting to make an unlawful entry into a dwelling and is justified if it is necessary to compel the intruder to leave the premises.

The five main elements for a defense of self, others, or property are as follows. First there is a *reasonableness standard*. There has to be a reasonable perception such as that any "reasonable" man or women faced with the same circumstances would come to similar conclusions. Rodney Peairs claimed that he and his wife believed the boys were about to invade their home and that Hattori was going to grab his gun and kill him and his family. Peairs claimed these were reasonable inferences based on Hattori's appearance and behavior during those few minutes preceding the shooting.

The law also requires that one believe oneself to be in imminent danger. This requirement is designed to prevent the claim of self-defense in situations where someone is acting in retaliation or to forestall a future attack. Both of these cases, when a person might harm someone because "they deserve it" or "to get them before they get me" are not lawful and do not meet the requirements for self-defense. Thus, the law requires that only dangers that are likely to occur within a short period of time be considered as legitimate grounds for a claim of self-defense.

Third, it is necessary that the harm itself be unlawful. Defendants cannot claim self-defense when they are responding to the use of force by law enforcement. The fourth element in the classic self-defense argument is that the response is equal to the threat of force. The law does not generally permit a threat from fists to be met with a firearm. Peairs testified that he believed Hattori was armed, mistaking the camera that hung around his neck for a weapon.

The final requirement is that force is used as a last resort, although only a few state laws actually require a "retreat rule" for those who claim self-defense. Under these circumstances, if there is a retreat option, then the decision to use force is not seen as a form of defense but as a form of offensive action subject to criminal liability.

The one universal exception to the retreat rule is the "castle" exception. A man's home is his castle, according to the sixteenth-century jurist, Sir Edward Coke. No man must be forced to "retreat" from his home, business, or car. For this reason, special consideration is given to the protection of one's own property: under those circumstances, the individual need not flee from the home but may stand his ground and use force to get another to leave. This is the theory behind the "shoot the burglar" rule in Louisiana. The relevant clause in the statute for justifiable homicide in Louisiana reads: "A homicide is justifiable when . . . the person committing the homicide reasonably believes

public duty: a defense that claims the defendant was lawfully exercising authority at the time the act was committed.

necessity justification: a defense to a criminal charge that claims it was necessary to commit some unlawful act in order to prevent or avoid a greater harm.

self-defense: a defense to a criminal charge based on a person's inherent right to self-protection and to reasonably defend himself or herself from an unlawful attack.

that the use of deadly force is necessary to prevent the entry or to compel the intruder to leave the premises. . . . The homicide shall be justifiable even though the person committing the homicide does not retreat from the encounter."[19]

Defenses of Excuse   Excuses admit that the action committed by the defendant was wrong and violated the criminal law but argue that special circumstances absolve him of legal responsibility for his actions. There are a number of conditions or individual characteristics that excuse criminal liability. These include: mistake of law and fact; age; duress; entrapment; intoxication; insanity; diminished capacity; and mental and biological syndromes.

Ignorance of the law is generally not considered a valid legal defense, but under very rare circumstances, defendants may argue successfully that they made a reasonable effort to understand or learn what a law is and were honestly mistaken in their understanding of the law. **Mistake of fact** is a much more common excuse. In this circumstance, defendants have honestly misinterpreted the facts of the situation and therefore do not have the *mens rea* of the crime even though they may commit the criminal act. For instance, suppose you attend a party and pick up a coat that looks exactly like your own and go home with it. Although you have committed the act of larceny, you did not intend to steal the coat and your honest mistake is a valid defense against the charge. Of course, if your own coat was wool and the one you left with was mink, you would have a hard time convincing a jury or judge that you made a mistake.

The mistake of fact excuse was, in fact, a significant part of the defense of Rodney Peairs. Peairs claims that he mistook Yoshi Hattori for an intruder and he mistook the camera in Yoshi Hattori's hand for a weapon. In the dark and with all the confusion, Peairs argued that he believed Hattori to be armed and that he made a mistake of fact in assessing the danger to his home and family. No doubt this was an important part of the defense strategy in convincing the jury that Peairs's response was reasonable under the circumstances. Indeed, a crucial element of the mistake of fact defense is the reasonable standard: a reasonable mistake is one that would be made by any typically competent person faced with the same set of circumstances.

The **defense of duress** exists because we do not wish to punish people for actions they are forced to commit against their own free will. Recall the "human conduct rule," under which the criminal law punishes only actions that are voluntary. The defense of duress claims that defendants are not criminally responsible for their conduct if coerced to act by the use of or threat of unlawful force by another person. Thus, a bank teller who turns over money to a robber holding a gun is not guilty of embezzlement, nor is an airline pilot who veers off course in response to the commands of a terrorist guilty of the crime of hijacking. However, the defense of duress cannot be used if the person willingly placed himself in a situation in which he would be subject to pressure to act illegally. Thus, this defense is not available to a person who willingly joins a gang and then later claims that the gang forced him to commit crimes against his will.

Although being in an intoxicated state of mind diminishes the actor's capacity to form *mens rea*, a claim of intoxication is generally not regarded as an effective defense. At most, **voluntary intoxication** may lessen criminal liability by, for example, allowing the defense to argue that a charge of first-degree murder should be reduced to second-degree murder because the high level of intoxication undermined the defendant's capacity to form a specific intent to kill, the mental state required for a first-degree conviction. Otherwise, most states are wary about permitting intoxication to be used as a criminal defense. The exception is a claim of **involuntary intoxication.** Intoxication may be a legal defense if the substance was introduced into the person's body without his or her consent or without the knowledge that the substance would cause intoxication. Someone who has consumed punch spiked with LSD or taken an intoxicating drug upon medical advice may be excused from liability for his or her actions related directly to the intoxication, such as driving under the influence or illegal drug use.

defenses of excuse: a category of legal defense in which the defendant claims a personal condition at the time of the act that excuses him or her from criminal liability under the law.

ignorance of law: lack of knowledge of the law or the existence of the law.

mistake of fact: a defense claiming an error or misunderstanding of fact or circumstances resulting in an act that would otherwise not have been undertaken.

defense of duress: a defense to a criminal charge that the defendant was forced to act against his or her will.

voluntary intoxication: intoxication that is the result of willful personal choice.

involuntary intoxication: intoxication that is not willful.

Under English common law, the **defense of infancy**[20] held that children under the age of 7 were incapable of rational thought or planned action and therefore could not be held criminally responsible for their conduct. For centuries, the criminal liability for children between the ages of 7 and 14 was determined on a case-by-case basis, depending on the severity of the offense and the individual facts of the case. In the nineteenth century, most states wrote juvenile statutes that established a legal age of maturity somewhere between the ages of 16 and 21. Today most states continue to specify a blanket age of adulthood somewhere around 15 and 16, although all states have mechanisms whereby younger juveniles who commit serious crimes may be held fully responsible for their crimes in adult court. For the most part, children who commit crimes are subject to the authority of the juvenile courts, on the theory that they are not as fully capable as adults in recognizing the wrongfulness of their conduct and in making fully responsible choices between legal and illegal conduct.

Entrapment[21] refers to the inducement of a citizen into crime by law enforcement officers. The argument is that without the temptations set up by the "sting" operation, the citizen would have remained law-abiding because she did not seek out the illegal opportunity on her own. Entrapment most often occurs in the enforcement of laws against so-called victimless crimes. The standard used by the courts to determine entrapment is whether the person demonstrated a predisposition toward committing the crime before the government agent set him or her up for the "sting" operation.

The **defenses of insanity,**[22] diminished capacity and various "syndromes," all refer to the mental state of the accused at the time of the crime. This category of defenses is based on the widely accepted legal principle that only those who are of sound mind can be put on trial, held responsible for their actions, and punished for their actions. The insanity plea has a long history in Western criminal law but is rarely used and rarely successful as a defense. When defendants are successful in convincing the jury that they were, indeed, mentally ill at the time they committed their crime, they are likely to be confined to a mental hospital for the criminally insane. John Hinckley, for example, attempted to assassinate President Ronald Reagan in an attempt to gain the attention of actress Jodie Foster. At his trial, Hinckley was found not guilty by reason of insanity. He remains, however, confined to a maximum security hospital and is likely to remain there for the rest of his life.

The term *insanity* is a legal term, not a medical one. It is not synonymous with the term *mental illness*: it is entirely possible for a person to have a mental illness and still have sufficient *mens rea* to commit a crime. All jurisdictions in the United States require a defendant to be mentally competent in order to stand trial as a basic principle of due process. Defendants who are incapable of understanding the proceedings against them or in assisting in their own defense are legally incompetent to stand trial.

A related set of recent defenses also rests on the mental condition of the defendant at the time of the crime. Syndromes[23] such as the battered woman syndrome, urban survival syndrome, Vietnam vet syndrome,[24] child abuse syndrome, fetal alcohol syndrome, rape trauma syndrome,[25] and PMS[26] are all recognitions of specific pressures on individuals in particular circumstances that might influence their behavior to such an extent as to be a kind of compulsion on their behavior. The use of these syndromes as a defense of excuse is rarely successful and leaves many people uneasy, because they imply that people can point to harms done to them to "excuse" their own behavior. A legal excuse generally requires a force so powerful that it truly undermines the voluntariness of the act or the mental awareness of the actor. Despite the growing use of these syndromes, as in the Menendez trial in California, in which two brothers claimed to be victims of child abuse as the legal excuse for murdering their parents, these defenses are not convincing juries that these experiences absolve them of moral and legal responsibility for their own behavior.[27]

The **battered woman syndrome**[28] is an exception that has been used to augment a defense of justification, namely self-defense, rather than a defense of excuse. Battered woman's syndrome, or the more gender-neutral battered person syndrome, began with

defense of infancy: a defense that claims that individuals below a certain age should not be held criminally liable for their actions by virtue of their young age.

entrapment: the inducement of an individual to commit a crime not contemplated by him or her.

defenses of insanity: affirmative defenses seeking to prove a mental state that prevents an individual from comprehending the nature and consequences of actions or from distinguishing right from wrong.

battered woman (person) syndrome: a condition characterized by a history of repetitive abuse and learned helplessness.

the publication of Lenore Walker's book, *Battered Woman Syndrome* in 1984. Walker argued that women who had been victims of chronic abuse for years develop common psychological characteristics that she calls *learned helplessness*. This psychological understanding helps juries to believe that it may be "reasonable" for women to believe they are unable to leave their batterer to escape serious harm or eventual death. This syndrome has been used to assist in the argument of a self-defense in cases in which women have killed their husbands even though at the time of the killing he did not pose an imminent threat to them.[29] The killing may have occurred when the men are sleeping or not during an episode of violence or when they were unarmed, and it has been difficult for women to argue that they acted as a reasonable person would have done in those circumstances.

The battered woman syndrome asks the jury to judge the defendant's actions according to the criterion of a "reasonable battered woman."[30] This raises the question of whether a jury of men can adequately judge the reasonableness of the conduct of a woman who has been beaten, raped, tortured, humiliated, and threatened by the man in her life for years. What is "reasonable" conduct under those circumstances?

In the Peairs case, the defense argued that Peairs acted as any reasonable man would have done. Yet to many observers, it is inconceivable that shooting a young stranger within seconds of opening the front door is reasonable conduct. To many observers the perception that this was a potentially lethal home invasion was far from a reasonable belief based on the factual circumstances. Some believe, in fact, that Peairs's reactions were fundamentally racist, attributing danger to Yoshi Hattori because he was Asian. As in every case, however, the determination of the "reasonableness" standard was made by the twelve men and women sitting in the jury box. And in this case, the individuals in that jury box were peers of Rodney Peairs, men and women from Louisiana who believed in the right to gun ownership, in the right to use that gun to protect one's home, and who shared the same beliefs about those who appeared foreign. For them, Peairs's conduct that night was reasonable.

Is Racism "Reasonable"?

The jury's decision in the Peairs case raises thorny issues about the influence of racism on the criminal justice system.[31] Would the defense have been as successful at portraying young white Webb Haymaker as "crazy" or "bizarre" or been able to convince the jury that an unarmed 16-year-boy ringing a doorbell at 8 p.m. was a menace so "frightening" and "scary" that it put Rodney Peairs in desperate fear of a lethal home invasion? Would the jury have been as quick to see the couple's terror as "reasonable" and Peairs's split-second decision to fire point-blank as "reasonable" if the victim had been a local white teenager rather than a Japanese youth? Would the courtroom have erupted in applause at the verdict if the Haymakers had been the parents of the victim?

Americans have a long history of hatred, prejudice, and distrust of people of Asian ethnic background.[32] Since the late nineteenth century, there has been discrimination against various immigrants from Asian countries, beginning with the Chinese Exclusion Act of 1880. During World War II, Americans of Japanese descent were forcibly removed from their homes and interned in camps even though no similar actions were taken against citizens of German or Italian descent, whose status as Americans was never officially questioned. No matter how many generations Asian Americans have been citizens of this country, Asian Americans are still viewed through a racial lens that identifies them as "foreigners" and not true Americans.

Negative stereotypes of Asians as "Japs," "Chinks," the "yellow peril," or the "gooks" we fought in Vietnam are widely held by American citizens. In the Peairs trial, the defense attorney told the jury that Yoshi was acting in a menacing, aggressive fashion, "like a stranger invading someone's home turf." This tapped into perceptions of Asians as "the enemy" threatening American security and safety. For the Peairses, the "foreignness" of Yoshi Hattori was the quality they noticed above all else: when asked to describe

During World War II, thousands of American citizens of Japanese ethnic descent were forcibly removed from their homes and confined in camps under destitute conditions. Asian Americans have long been treated as foreigners within their own country.

what she saw that night, Mrs. Peairs responded during the trial, "I guess he appeared Oriental. He could have been Mexican or whatever." Mrs. Peairs screamed at her husband to get his gun because she saw someone who was foreign: Oriental or Mexican . . . it didn't really matter. She was terrified by his ethnic difference.

The law of self-defense requires that the belief and the action be reasonable. In this case, the jury shared the Peairses' view that Yoshi's foreign appearance was sufficient to generate such fear. They also agreed that the action Peairs took—firing his weapon point-blank at the young man's chest—was also "reasonable." Yet, as Judge Brown ruled in the civil trial, Peairs had many alternative courses of "reasonable" action that night: he could have stayed in the house and called the police; he could have simply let the boys leave; he could have fired a warning shot in the air from the doorway of his house.

In this case, we must ask ourselves the painful question of whether the loss of life of a "foreign boy" was easier for the jury to accept than if the loss had been of a young white boy. Research consistently shows that juries are more sympathetic when the victim is from the same racial, class, and social background. Research on prosecutors asking for the death penalty also indicates that more serious punishments are sought when the victim is white. Was Yoshi's life devalued because he was nonwhite?

The reality of racism presents a great dilemma for the legal system's reliance on the discretionary decision making of citizens, who carry with them all the biases and stereotypes of the society. Racial stereotypes affect all people, including prosecutors, judges, and jurors. Particularly troubling is the question of whether the "reasonableness" standard means that it is acceptable to act on irrational and emotional prejudices against people who look different. Rodney and Bonnie Peairs may be typical of the residents of Baton Rouge, Louisiana, in their perception that minorities, Asians or Mexicans or African Americans, are inherently dangerous. But the real question is whether this is "reasonable" according to the law. Should the law uphold these racist views simply because they are widespread? A typical belief is not necessarily a reasonable one even if it is shared by a large group of people. If this were true, then the view of German citizens that Jews were the source of all evil in their country and deserved to die should be deemed "reasonable" simply because it was shared by the majority of the citizenry.

In later chapters we will return to some of the questions about the composition of the jury and its capacity to make decisions that are fair and just. We can see here that the legal system cannot separate itself from the society in which it operates. Can we achieve "justice" in society where there is systemic injustice and racial bias? Are there reforms that we can institute that will help to achieve greater fairness for all, regardless of gender, race, or social class? Do we need to move beyond the adversarial system and examine alternative forms of justice in order to imagine a system that can deliver "justice for all"?

KEY TERMS

legal guilt p. 92
criminal liability p. 92
material elements of the crime p. 92
actus reus p. 92
human conduct rule p. 93
mens rea p. 94
motive p. 94
degree p. 94
specific intent p. 94
general intent p. 94
criminal negligence p. 94
constructive intent p. 94
criminal recklessness p. 95
strict liability statutes p. 95
homicide p. 95

justifiable homicide p. 95
excusable homicide p. 95
criminal homicide p. 95
murder p. 95
felony murder p. 95
manslaughter p. 96
voluntary manslaughter p. 96
involuntary manslaughter p. 96
vehicular homicide p. 96
reasonable person standard p. 96
concurrence p. 96
causation p. 97
"but for" standard p. 97
harm p. 97
affirmative defenses p. 98

defense of alibi p. 98
defenses of justification p. 98
public duty p. 99
necessity justification p. 99
self-defense p. 99
defenses of excuse p. 100
ignorance of law p. 100
mistake of fact p. 100
defense of duress p. 100
voluntary intoxication p. 100
involuntary intoxication p. 100
defense of infancy p. 101
entrapment p. 101
defenses of insanity p. 101
battered woman syndrome p. 101

REVIEW AND STUDY QUESTIONS

1. What is the human conduct rule, and why is it an important principle to prove in determining criminal liability?
2. What is *mens rea*? Explain how one's state of mind influences the seriousness of the crime.
3. Explain the differences between key types of criminal homicide: murder, manslaughter, felony murder, and vehicular homicide. How is the "intent" different in each form of criminal homicide?
4. What is the principle of causation? Explain the "but for" standard of causation.
5. Define the element of concurrence. Why is it an important principle for establishing criminal liability?
6. What is an affirmative defense? How do affirmative defenses differ from traditional defense strategies?
7. What is a defense of justification? What is a defense of excuse? How are these two defenses different from one another? Give examples of each type of defense.
8. Name the five elements required to prove self-defense.
9. What is battered woman syndrome, and how is it used in the defense of women prosecuted for killing their spouse or partner?
10. What is the "reasonable person" standard? How does this raise the possibility of bias in criminal justice decision making?

CHECK IT OUT

On the Web
Legal Information Institute at Cornell Law School, www.law.cornell.edu/
Type in "criminal law" in the search box and check out the criminal codes in each of the fifty states and the federal criminal code.

Nolo: Law for All, www.nolo.com/index.cf
Check out the Criminal Law Center for easy-to-use information about the criminal justice system, including a plain-English dictionary of legal terms and legal encyclopedia articles that offer full explanations of criminal law concepts and doctrines.

On Film

Who Killed Vincent Chin? (82 minutes)

Award-winning documentary by Christine Choy of the murder of a 27-year-old Chinese American man, Vincent Chin, in Detroit and the criminal trial of Ron Ebens, a Chrysler Motors foreman who was given a suspended sentence and a small fine for the brutally violent crime. Academy Award nominee for best documentary in 1989. Available from the Filmakers Library, www.filmakers.com.

When Women Kill (47 minutes)

Powerful award-winning documentary of three battered women and why they killed, confronting the issue of male violence and female self-defense. This film puts violence against women in legal and historical context, including a critique of the battered woman syndrome as a legal defense. Available from the Filmakers Library, www.filmakers.com.

Abused Women Who Fought Back: The Framingham Eight (44 minutes)

This documentary tells the dramatic story of eight women imprisoned for killing a spouse or partner. Each claimed battered woman syndrome as a defense. The program explores both sides of the issue, including prosecutors and family members of victims who believe the defense has gone too far. Available from Films for the Humanities and Social Sciences, www.films.com.

Guns: An American Way of Life and Death (22 minutes)

ABC News anchor Ted Koppel explores the love–hate relationship of U.S. society with firearms and contrasts U.S. attitudes, laws, and violence with our near neighbor Canada through interviews with police chiefs from both countries. Available from Films for the Humanities and Sciences, www.films.com.

NOTES

1. Christopher Cooper, "Japan Tunes in as Trial in Teen's Slaying Begins," *The Times-Picayune,* May 18, 1993, p. A1; T. R. Reid, "Japanese Media Disparage Acquittal in 'Freeze Case'; Commentators See America as Sick Nation," *The Washington Post,* May 25, 1993, p. A14; Christina Cheakalos, "Culture Clash Plays out in Louisiana Hearing Set Today in Shooting Death," *The Atlanta Journal and Constitution,* January 7, 1993, p. A–3; T. R. Reid, "Angry Japan Lays to Rest Student Shot Dead in U.S.; Slaying Sparks Criticism of Gun Laws," *The Washington Post,* October 27, 1992, p. A1.

2. Christopher Cooper, "Slain Student's Father Hears Killer's Version," *The Times-Picayune,* May 23, 1993, p. A1.

3. Christopher Cooper, "Teen's Friend Recounts Shooting: Seeing the Gun Was Puzzling," *The Times-Picayune,* May 21, 1993, p. A1.

4. David E. Sanger, "After Gunman's Acquittal, Japan Struggles to Understand America," *The New York Times,* May 25, 1993, p. A–1.

5. *M. Hattori and M. Hattori v. R. Peairs, B. Peairs and Louisiana Farm Bureau Mutual Insurance Company,* No. 95 CA 0144 (La.App. 1 Cir, 10/06/95); 662 So.2d 509.

6. T. R. Reid, "Ruling Softens Japan's Image of Violent U.S." *The Washington Post,* September 18, 1994, p. A29.

7. "No Justification Whatsoever," *St. Louis Dispatch,* September 21, 1994, p. 6–C; Adam Nossiter, "Judge Awards Damages in Japanese Youth's Death," *The New York Times,* September 16, 1994, p. A–12.

8. "Parents of Japanese Student Win $635,000 in Slaying Suit," *The Atlanta Journal and Constitution,* September 16, 1994, p. A–3.

9. "Japanese Student's Parents Want Death Gun Destroyed," *The Washington Post,* September 18, 1994, p. A20; Joan Treadway, "Parents Turn Grief into Anti-Gun Effort," *The Times-Picayune,* October 6, 1996, p. B1.

10. T. R. Reid, "Parents of Slain Japanese Student Mulling Civil Suit," *The Washington Post,* May 26, 1993, p. A22.

11. Reid, "Angry Japan Lays to Rest Student Shot Dead in U.S."

12. Paul H. Robinson, *Criminal Law* (New York: Aspen Law and Business, 1997), p. 5.

13. *Robinson v. California,* 82 S. Ct. 1417 (1962).

14. Criminal negligence exists when, although neither specific nor general criminal intent is present, there is such disregard of the interest of others that the offender's conduct amounts to a gross deviation below the standard of care expected to be maintained by a reasonably careful man under like circumstances. LA. R.S. 14:12 (2000).

15. Oliver Wendall Holmes, *The Common Law,* Vol. 3 (New York: Dover Publications, 1991).

16. Kenneth W. Simons, "When Is Strict Liability Just?," *Journal of Criminal Law and Criminology 87* (1997), pp. 1075–1137.

17. American Law Institute, *Model Penal Code: Official Draft and Explanatory Notes* (Philadelphia: The Institute, 1985).

18. H. L. A. Hart and A. M. Honore, "Causation in the Law," *Law Quarterly Review 72* (1956), pp. 58–90.

19. La. R.S. 14:20 (2000).

20. Sanford J. Fox, "Juvenile Justice Reform: A Historical Perspective," *Stanford Law Review 22* (1970), pp. 1187–1239.

21. Paul Marcus, "The Development of Entrapment Law," *Wayne Law Review 33* (1986), pp. 5–37.

22. Henry J. Steadman, Margaret A. McGreevy, and Joseph P. Morrisey, *Before and After Hinckley: Evaluating Insanity Defense Reform* (New York: Guildford, 1993), pp. 138–152.

23. Stephen J. Morse, The 'New Syndrome Excuse Syndrome,' *Criminal Justice Ethics,* Winter–Spring 1995, pp. 3–15.

24. John R. Ford, "In Defense of the Defenders: The Vietnam Vet Syndrome," *Criminal Law Bulletin 19* (1983), pp. 434–443.

25. A. Burgess and L. Holmstrom, "Rape Trauma Syndrome," *American Journal of Nursing 131* (1974), pp. 981–986; P. Giannelli, "Rape Trauma Syndrome," *Criminal Law Bulletin 33* (1997), pp. 270–279.

26. "Not Guilty Because of PMS?," *Newsweek,* November 8, 1982, p. 111.

27. Alan Dershowitz, *The Abuse Excuse* (Boston: Little, Brown, 1995), pp. 3–41.

28. Lenore Walker, *Battered Woman Syndrome* (New York: Springer, 1984), pp. 142–143.

29. P. Ewing, *Battered Women Who Kill: Psychological Self-defense as Legal Justification* (Lexington, MA: Heath, 1987), pp. 51–60.

30. C. Gillespie, *Battered Women, Self Defense and the Law* (Columbus, OH: Ohio State University Press, 1989), pp. 123–156.

31. Cynthia Kwei Yung Lee, "Race and Self-Defense: Toward a Normative Conception of Reasonableness," *Minnesota Law Review 81* (December 1996). pp. 367–426.

32. Pat K. Chew, "Asian Americans: The 'Reticent' Minority and Their Paradoxes," *William and Mary Law Review 36*(1) (1994), pp. 1–92.

CASE 6

Facing the Demons: Making Amends for Drunk Driving

Elaine Serrell Myers's routine was to drive home at night after her evening accounting class on the empty rural roads in the southwestern part of Washington state. The 57-mile trip usually took her about an hour, while at home her husband David Lee Myers often dozed off as he waited up for the sound of her car in the driveway. On April 27, 1993, he awoke with a start at 1 a.m. and knew immediately that something was wrong. The sound of footsteps on the porch brought him quickly to the front door, where a state trooper and two friends stood to break the terrible news. Two hours earlier, at approximately 11 p.m., his wife of 27 years had been killed instantly in a head-on collision on a deserted stretch of Ocean Beach Highway near Skamokawa, Washington. The driver of the vehicle, Susanna Kay Cooper, lay in critical condition in the hospital. Driving a 1991 Mazda, she had drifted across the center line and smashed into Elaine's 1984 Nissan. Both cars had been completely demolished, and the damage had been so great there was slim hope that Susanna, a single mother of two young children, would survive.

A GIRLS' NIGHT OUT

Susanna had spent the evening drinking peppermint schnapps at a friend's house. The friend persuaded her to stay for dinner to give the liquor time to wear off and later did not recall thinking Susanna was too drunk to drive when she left the house. Apparently Susanna herself thought she was too drunk to drive, because witnesses say she that when she stopped at a roadside tavern to use the bathroom, she tried to get a ride from someone to avoid getting back behind the wheel. In the end, Susanna made the fateful decision that would change the lives of so many. When the ambulance reached the emergency room Susanna's blood alcohol level measured twice the legal limit for the state of Washington.

THE DEVASTATION OF CRIME

In the wake of Elaine's death, despair enveloped the extended family of Elaine Serrell. Elaine had been a vibrant and vital person, central in the lives of many of her friends and family. She was known for her radio show on rainforest gardening, for the sweater vests made of wool that she dyed, spun, and knitted, and for her pottery. She was beloved by her parents, her three sisters and their husbands, and three young nieces. The day they planned her funeral would have been the 27th wedding anniversary of a couple who had been high school sweethearts. The funeral filled a local community hall with hundreds whose lives were touched by Elaine and her generous spirit.

In the weeks and months that followed, David was so crushed by his loss he was barely able to function. He recalls that at that time, if he were to have met the person who wrenched his beloved wife from him, he believed he was capable of killing her with his own hands. Elaine's parents were also deeply damaged by the violent loss of their daughter. Elaine's father became so profoundly withdrawn and depressed that Elaine's mother felt that at the moment she lost a daughter she lost her husband too. The nieces so close to Elaine struggled to return to normal but found they could not function: their school grades dropped and their nights were interrupted by bouts of crying and nightmares.

Like many other victims, Elaine's family suffered feelings of rage, grief, bitterness, and helplessness, common among survivors of violence and trauma. Elizabeth, Elaine's sister, began to attend Mothers Against Drunk Driving (MADD) meetings to connect with other victims in her situation.[1] She found that she was not alone in her feelings of bitterness and rage. And the anger grew stronger when she learned that the driver, Susanna Cooper, had been convicted of drunk driving once before, four years earlier.

At first it seemed likely that Susanna would die from the injuries she sustained in the crash. During those months of her hospitalization, Elizabeth found herself wishing that Susanna would live to feel the full horror of her actions and hoping that she would emerge blind, as a life-long punishment for the pain and suffering she had caused. When the family learned that the driver was going to survive the crash, they felt mixed emotions. But when they also learned that Susanna was considering pleading not guilty to the charge of vehicular homicide, their sorrow turned to acid rage. Elaine's mother referred to the driver as a "human weed that ought to be pulled up."[2]

It was Peter Serrell, Elaine's father, who remembered a lecture he had attended about victim–offender reconciliation. According to the speaker, mediator Marty Price, victims are able to come face to face with the people who have harmed them. Victims tell the truth about their loss and what was done to them, and then request some kind of restitution to be paid by the offender. These programs are designed to help offenders truly understand the suffering they have caused and to offer them some opportunity to right the wrong in a way that is meaningful to those who have been hurt.

Elaine's father was motivated to consider this type of process by an insight provided by Aileen, Elaine's 10-year-old niece, who visited the wreckage of the car only a day or so after the accident. It was Aileen who noticed that in the minivan driven by Susanna there were children's toys. Peter suddenly remembered Aileen's remark about there being toys in the car, and he realized that the monster who took his own child's life was herself a mother of two small children. This struck Peter deeply.

Like so many survivors of violence, it was crucial for Peter to see that Elaine's death served some positive purpose. Susanna had been convicted once before of drunk driving and even now, despite killing Elaine and nearly ending her own life, she was claiming that it was "just an accident." He saw that it was very possible, even if she was convicted of vehicular homicide, that she would do her time in jail, return home, and continue to drink and drive while raising children who would themselves follow in her footsteps. The ugly cycle of harm would churn on and the loss of his daughter would count for nothing in this world. That thought was more than the 80-year-old father could bear. He decided that although he himself would never forgive her for taking his child, he did not want to see two small children raised by a mother who continued to be an alcoholic in denial. Peter called the man he had heard lecture about mediation to ask about the possibilities for meeting with the person who was responsible for the death of his daughter, in the hopes that, at least, maybe something worthwhile would come of it.

Marty Price agreed to meet with Peter and the rest of his family to discuss the possibility of mediation. Unlike the majority of mediation cases, which involve crimes of theft and vandalism, mediation in cases of serious violence requires lengthy preparation for both victims and offenders before they are genuinely ready to meet each other face to face.[3] Marty Price knew that it was important for all of the family members to have the opportunity to reflect and think seriously about the idea of meeting the person responsible for killing Elaine. Peter had called with the intention that he alone would meet Susanna, but as an experienced mediator, Marty Price knew that such a meeting could tear apart even the closest of families. Peter agreed that he would not proceed with the mediation unless his wife Kathleen was prepared to join him.

THE START OF A HEALING JOURNEY

Most of the family members were skeptical about the idea. David, Elaine's widower, did not believe he would be able to contain his anger and hate in a meeting with the offender. Elizabeth, Elaine's sister, asked, "Why would I want to meet the woman who had taken away someone I loved?"[4] Both were willing to come to a family meeting to talk about the mediation, however. At the meeting the mediator asked the family to share their pain, discuss the impact of their loss, and brainstorm about what they wanted from the offender. During the emotional meeting, he asked them to think about the requests they might make of her, which would in some meaningful way address their loss. The meeting was the start of a healing journey for the family.

One commitment they all wanted from the driver was a promise that she would never drink and drive again and that she would use her terrible crime to prevent others from doing the same. Elizabeth realized when she attended the MADD meetings that if Susanna were simply sent to jail without undergoing some kind of treatment or rehabilitation for alcoholism, there was little to stop her from driving drunk again when she was released. The MADD meetings were full of tales of drunk drivers who had served jail time only to return to the same old patterns when they returned to society.

Second, the family realized that they wanted Susanna to take responsibility for being a good mother to her children: they wanted to know that the children would be cared for and raised to be positive members of society. They wanted this to be a turning point in her life and for Elaine's loss to be offset by a positive gain for those two young lives.

The more the family talked, the more various members of the family began to feel that they would like to participate in the mediation. Even David was moved to the point where he felt he could be present, and he even suggested that it was important for Susanna to have someone there to support her so she would not need to face all of them alone. After several months of these family meetings, it was David who proposed that if they were to meet Susanna, she should bring "someone who cares about her to sit next to her and hold her hand."[5]

Ultimately, Elaine's parents Peter and Kathleen, her husband David, two sisters, Elizabeth and Barbara, and their spouses, and Aileen, Elaine's favorite niece, were all present at the mediation meeting with Susanna. Another sister from out of state joined the meeting by speaker phone. Susanna herself was accompanied by her defense attorney and a close friend.

SUSANNA'S JOURNEY: DENIAL AND SELF-PITY

Susanna spent three months in intensive care. When she learned in the hospital that she had crossed the center line and caused the death of someone else, she simply wanted to die. But medical science saved her life, and as she slowly recovered physically, she came to the realization that she had to face up to what she had done.

When she was finally able to leave the hospital, Susanna was arraigned and charged with vehicular homicide. Elaine's family attended the arraignment and found themselves filled with anger and rage when her court-appointed attorney entered a plea of "not guilty" in response to the charges. The standard defense strategy to deny legal guilt was emotionally devastating for family members, who wanted Susanna to fully admit and acknowledge what she had done. In November 1993, Susanna herself decided to admit legal responsibility and entered a guilty plea to the charge of vehicular homicide. A date for the sentencing hearing was set and the family asked Marty Price to arrange for the mediation meeting to take place before the sentencing hearing, so the family could have input into Susanna's sentence.

The mediation team contacted Susanna's defense attorney and explained the desire of the victim's family to meet with Susanna. The defense attorney agreed to discuss the idea with Susanna. The next step was for the mediation team to meet with Susanna to prepare her for the mediation with Elaine's family.

At the first two-hour interview, Susanna acknowledged what she had done to this family but spent most of her time talking about her own physical suffering and her own concerns for her family and her future. Like many offenders, Susanna was shielded from the full impact of the pain she had caused Elaine's family. She had never met them, never knew Elaine, and had no concept of the full horror and suffering she had caused. Like so many offenders, her own pain and troubles were far more real to her. And quite naturally, her attention was focused on what lay in store for her.

Marty Price prepared Susanna by asking her to think about Elaine's family and how they had been affected; he asked her to think about what she could say to them or what she thought they might want from her. The purpose of these preparatory meetings was to assist Susanna in opening herself up to empathizing with the pain of her victims.

More troubling to the mediator, however, was Susanna's refusal to admit that she was an alcoholic. She explained that she was not a problem drinker and that what she drank that night was fairly normal among her friends and family. She admitted that her father drank too much, but she believed that she herself did not have a serious problem with alcohol.

The mediator explained that it was very important to Elaine's family that Susanna deal with her drinking problem, and the first step, in their view, was for her to get an alcohol abuse evaluation. If Susanna was to remain in denial about her drinking, the mediation could not proceed and nothing more could be achieved.

ACKNOWLEDGMENT AND RESPONSIBILITY

By the second meeting with Susanna, the mediation team felt that she had "changed." Somehow she had come to an understanding of what she was responsible for and had let go of the denial and defensiveness she had wrapped so tightly around herself in the first meeting.

Susanna had obtained the alcohol evaluation the family had asked for, and this had led her to some soul searching of her own. She learned from the evaluation that she was considered to be in the beginning to intermediate stages of alcoholism. She learned that the "normal" habits of her family and friends were both abusive and dangerous to others and to themselves. "It's normal to get drunk in my town. That's all there is to do. I thought it was normal to go out with my girlfriends and drink. We went out almost every weekend and some week nights. Now I know that it's not normal. I wish that what happened to me would wake up those people, but it hasn't. They don't think it can happen to them."[6]

During this period, Susanna had the opportunity to read the victim impact statements written by members of Elaine's family. The victim impact statements described what the loss of Elaine has meant in their lives, and Susanna had time to process the enormous consequences of her actions. Elizabeth's statement, in particular, was very powerful in its clear statement about what Elizabeth would need from Susanna if she were ever to forgive her for what had happened.

Elizabeth wrote:

Forgiveness is not something which I believe is my obligation to bestow unilaterally, but it can be earned. The perpetrator must show the five R's: recognition, remorse, repentance, restitution and reform. Recognition means admitting that what she did was wrong, and that she is responsible for the wrongdoing and all of the negative consequences that follow from it. (If she is in jail, she recognizes that it is because she drove drunk, not because the prosecutor or the judge was mean or unfair to her. If she is in pain, she recognizes it is because she drove drunk, not blaming it on the lack of pain medicine or lack of medical science's ability to fix her as good as new.) Remorse means that each time she thinks of the wrong she did, she regrets that she did not make a better choice. It is a repeated rehearsal of how she wishes she had done it differently, how she would do it differently if given another chance. Repentance is when a deep remorse leads to a firm resolve to do better in the future. Restitution cannot be direct in this case—there is no way that she can provide a wife for David or a sister for me. The only restitution she can make is a lifelong commitment to a daily effort toward making the world a better place for her having survived the crash. She is not required to complete the job of repairing the world, but she must not be excused from starting and continually working at the job. Reform means that she must create a new form of herself—to emerge as a sober person, a thoughtful and considerate person, a contributor. If she can do all these, I can forgive.[7]

THE MEDIATION

On January 17, 1994, eight months after the accident, Susanna and the Serrell family were ready to meet. Twelve people assembled in a small hotel conference room in Oregon. The Serrell family sat nervously awaiting the arrival of Susanna, her lawyer, and her best friend. When the family first laid eyes on Susanna, they saw a small, frail, gaunt young woman, clearly terrified of encountering the family of the person whose life she had ended.

The mediators allowed Susanna to speak first. She began to speak, only to be overwhelmed with sobs. Knowing her words were hopelessly inadequate, she nonetheless struggled to express her sorrow and apologies. She eventually controlled her emotions enough to state at least the start of what needed to be said.

Each of the family members was given an opportunity to talk about the crash and what the loss of Elaine meant to them. Susanna sat quietly and listened intently to it all, weeping silently as she heard the words of loss, knowing there was nothing she could do or say to make it right. She sat and listened as David described the loss of his lifelong partner, his companion and the love of his life. She sat and listened as he said, "In the end, my world will never again be right, and I will always have to live knowing the horror of Elaine's death."[8] She listened as Elaine's mother expressed her resentment and loss of not only her daughter but her husband as well.

The family was also given the opportunity to ask for answers to questions that were important to them. For instance, Elizabeth wanted to know about Susanna's thoughts the night she made the decision to drive drunk. Susanna explained that she had no memory of that night, or of the entire week before the crash. Aileen asked her to describe what she thought when she learned that someone had been killed in the crash. Again, Susanna dissolved in tears, communicating her genuine horror and remorse at what she had done.

The mediation lasted five hours. The agreement reached by everyone required Susanna to attend Alcoholics Anonymous (AA) meetings and victim impact panels while in prison; it required Susanna to write letters to her children weekly while in jail, and to write to Peter as well to provide updates on her progress; she also agreed to find ways to speak out against drunk driving in the community when she was released; and to complete her GED, take parenting classes, and give 10 percent of her income for the rest of her life to charity. The family agreed to present the mediation contract to the judge at the upcoming sentencing hearing.

A SHARED JOURNEY OF HEALING

At the mediation meeting, an extraordinary transition took place. The victims and the offender, in the words of Marty Price, "became allies in the healing of each other." The day after the mediation, David wrote in his journal, "What a wonderful effect of last night's mediation—I have regained my brightness and vigour."[9] He felt like a renewed man, able to walk with energy and to focus on the affairs of his life. Elizabeth reported feeling a great sense of relief: the tension that had been weighing on her had vanished, she let go of vengeance and felt ready to find enjoyment in life once more.

At the sentencing hearing, the parties shared with the judge the agreement reached during the mediation. The judge agreed that Susanna's willingness to meet with the family was evidence of her own rehabilitation. Nonetheless, because of her prior conviction, the judge felt compelled to order the maximum sentence under the state's mandatory sentencing guidelines. Susanna was sentenced to thirty-four months in state prison.

In the months that followed, the family petitioned the governor to reduce the sentence, but the petition for clemency was denied. After serving twenty-one months in jail, Susanna was paroled and began to speak out at MADD panels, telling her story; she also spoke at high school driver's education classes and agreed to have her real name and story published in the largest daily newspaper in Oregon. The story received national coverage. In the years that followed, Elaine's family and Susanna went public again and again with their story.

AFTERMATH

One year after her death, the family held a memorial service for Elaine at which they dedicated a headstone with an engraving that celebrated the way she led her life. With that ceremony, the Serrell fam-

ily felt a shift from mourning how Elaine died to celebrating how Elaine lived. Years later, the members of Elaine's family and Susanna remain in close contact with each other. The letters between Susanna and Peter Serrell began as progress reports but developed into a genuine ongoing correspondence. Aileen even exchanged letters with Susanna while she was in prison. The two families have appeared together on national television and at conferences to share their story of hope and healing. Susanna remains committed to keeping her promise to Elaine's family to remain sober, attend community college, and continue to openly and honestly tell her story to others in the hope that it will prevent the same tragedy from repeating itself in the lives of other human beings.

Case adapted from Marty Price, "The Mediation of a Drunk Driving Death: A Case Development Study," June 7, 1994, retrieved June 6, 2002, from Victim-Offender Reconciliation Program Information and Resource Center, **www. vorp.com/articles/lifeaft.html;** Spencer Heinz, "Coming Home: a Life Lost and a Life Saved," *The Sunday Oregonian,* December 31, 1995, retrieved June 6, 2002, from Victim-Offender Reconciliation Program Information and Resource Center, **www.vorp.com/articles/lifesave.html;** Florangela Davila, "Finding Peace Eye to Eye," *Seattle Times,* March 11, 1996, p. B1; Elizabeth S. Menkin, "Life After Death," *San Jose Mercury News, West Magazine,* 1994, retrieved June 6, 2002, from Victim-Offender Reconciliation Program Information and Resource Center, **www.vorp.com/articles/lifeaft. html;** Elizabeth S. Menkin with Lori K. Baker, "I Forgave My Sister's Killer," *Ladies Home Journal,* December 1995, retrieved June 6, 2002, from Victim-Offender Reconciliation Program Information and Resource Center, **www.vorp.com/articles/forgave.html.**

THINKING CRITICALLY ABOUT THIS CASE

1. How did a face-to-face meeting between Susanna and the victim's family change both of these parties' feelings about the crime that had taken place? Should such face-to-face meetings be encouraged by the criminal justice system? Why or why not?
2. Elaine's family wanted input into the sentencing. Do you feel this is appropriate? Should victims have a significant input into the sentencing process? Why or why not?
3. In your view, is healing victims an important part of "justice"? What is the responsibility of the justice system toward the healing process for victims?
4. Why was the future conduct of Susanna and the safety and well-being of her children important to Peter Serrell? Why would victims who have lost a loved one be concerned about the future of the person responsible?

5. Why was preparation important for the process of bringing the offender and the victims together in this case? What are the possible dangers if the two have not been prepared to meet one another face to face?

6. Consider the five "R's" that Elizabeth felt were necessary for forgiveness. Do you believe that Susanna Cooper would have achieved any of these goals without the experience of mediation? What was gained by Susanna through the mediation process?

CHECK OUT THIS CASE

On the Web

Victim-Offender Mediation Association, http://www.voma.org

Check out the website of the Victim-Offender Reconciliation Program Information and Resource Center

(VORP) *to learn more about these programs across the country. Read more articles by mediator Marty Price and check out the many resources and links available from this site.*

On Film

Restorative Justice Mediation Video (60 minutes)

This video includes the ABC news broadcast, "Restoring Justice," which tells the dramatic story of the Serrell/ Myers family and their meeting with Susanna Cooper, among other stories. Included also is a powerfully moving interview with Elizabeth Menkin, sister of Elaine Serrell Myers. To order, go to **www.vorp.com/video.html** *or send $25 to Victim-Offender Reconciliation Program, Information and Resource Center, 19813 N.E. 13th Street, Camas, Washington 98607.*

CHAPTER 6

Understanding Victims

LEARNING OBJECTIVES

After reading this chapter, the student should be able to:

- Describe the sense in which the criminal justice system is "offense focused" and "offender driven"

- Explain the process of "victim blaming" and the process of "secondary victimization"

- Identify key victim's rights that are currently guaranteed in most state and federal jurisdictions

- Identify the symptoms of post-traumatic stress disorder

- Define restorative justice and explain the difference between retributive and restorative justice

The institutions of the criminal justice system are designed to handle people who violate the law. Whether arresting, prosecuting, defending, punishing, or treating them, the primary focus of the agencies that make up the system are persons who commit crimes. The justice system as a whole is **offender focused.**[10] Until recently, virtually no justice personnel focused on protecting the rights, meeting the needs, or delivering "justice" directly to the people victimized by crime.

The criminal justice process focuses on the relationship between the defendant and the state. The defendant is accused of violating the law and the state makes its case against the accused. The adversarial process is well demonstrated by the justice process in the Peairs case (see Chapter 5). The prosecution's vigorous arguments were matched by equally zealous arguments on the part of the defense. The jury sat and listened to the two attorneys present quite different portraits of Peairs's behavior. The prosecution presented the picture of a man who was unnecessarily aggressive and reckless. The defense focused on the behavior of the victim, Yoshi Hattori, painting a picture of his behavior that night as weird, bizarre, and erratic. Each side had its supporters in the courtroom. When the jury returned a verdict of "not guilty," the friends and family of the Peairs's cheered and gave the V sign for victory.

But what about the victims? Was there any attempt to meet the needs of Yoshi Hattori's parents, who had lost their only child? Was this justice for them? What is the meaning of "justice" for victims of crime? What were the victim's needs in this case, and how did the system meet or fail to meet those needs? Should the criminal justice system attempt to meet the needs of victims? What is the role of the victim in the criminal justice system?

The Serrell family's involvement with Susanna Cooper is not typical of the criminal justice response to vehicular homicide. In the criminal justice system, the state is seen as the "victim" of the crime: the prosecutor acts in the name of the individual victim, in this case the deceased, and the wider public. Although the victims were clear in their preference for a kind of justice that involved restitution, remorse, repentance, and reform, the state sought a different kind of justice, which required imprisonment for Susanna.

This chapter looks at the experiences of victims, the changes in the criminal justice process that altered the role of victims over time, and current efforts to include the rights of victims in the justice process. We will also look at the different understandings of justice in the traditional system, which focus primarily on punishment and treatment of offenders, and other understandings of justice that focus on restoration and restitution of victims and communities. We examine alternative visions of justice rooted in pre-Western and non-Western societies and explore the rise of restorative justice in the contemporary justice system.

THE DECLINE OF THE VICTIM IN THE JUSTICE PROCESS

Prior to the modern era, victims played a leading role in the resolution of criminal matters.[11] Victims, and more frequently, their extended family or clan, used their own resources to extract reparations and avenge an aggressor. Early legal systems prioritized the need for offenders to settle directly with victims and their families. Many societies developed elaborate systems of compensation that were paid by the offender and the offender's family directly to the victim or the victim's family. The emphasis was on a direct obligation of the offender to the victim. The central goal of justice was to make victims whole.

State-centered justice began when centralized authorities, first the church and then the royal courts, defined crime as primarily an offense against the authority of these powerful institutions rather than a harm to individuals in the community.[12] In Europe, by the mid-thirteenth century, the concept of "crime" had been defined to refer to a violation of the "King's peace." The origin of the word *felony* comes from the Norman word for "breach of faith": a felony was a violation of a subject's loyalty to the king. To violate the "King's law" by committing theft against one's neighbor was now viewed as an act of treason against the king himself. By that reasoning, the offender now owed reparations to the monarch rather than the victim.

A system of fines paid to the King's court gradually replaced the system of compensation paid to victims: instead of restitution being paid directly to the victim whose horse was stolen or purse robbed, a fine was paid to the court. The king's magistrates and lawyers determined what law was violated and what fine was deserved. As early as the thirteenth century, revenues from criminal fines accounted for almost one-sixth of royal income. In medieval England, all the property owned by a person convicted as a "felon" became the property of the king and his lords. By "owning" crime, the monarch gained power and riches. If retribution was deemed necessary, the king's soldiers and executioners meted out physical punishment on the offender. In place of private vengeance, the public executioner staged a spectacle that punished an offender in the name of the king, usually in full view of the community.

By the modern era, people who had actually been harmed by criminal offenses gradually disappeared from the justice process except in their role in reporting the crime to the authorities and testifying in the case that the state brought against the offenders. Offenders lost all notion of direct accountability to victims for the harm inflicted and instead became embroiled in a defensive strategic battle against the state in a court of law. For victims, "justice" came to be served exclusively by the knowledge that offenders were being punished by the state.

offender focused: all the resources, policies, and personnel of the justice system are devoted to activities concerning the person who is accused of or has been convicted of violating the law.

This transformation from a victim-oriented system of justice based in the community to an offender-focused system of justice run by the government took place over a period of centuries. In colonial America at the time of the Salem witch trials, victims still conducted their own investigations, paid for warrants to have sheriffs make arrests, and hired private attorneys to indict and prosecute. If convicted of a crime, offenders were required to repay victims three times the amount they stole or damaged. The adoption of the Bill of Rights signaled a shift toward state-centered justice, and by the nineteenth century the role of the public prosecutor had expanded to include powers and responsibilities previously exercised by victims and the community.

THE FIELD OF VICTIMOLOGY

The field of criminology is generally considered to be over two hundred years old, originating with the work of European scholars who began the first serious scientific study of people who violate the criminal law. The field of victimology dates only as far back as the 1940s.[13] **Victimology** is now recognized as the scientific study of the physical, psychological, and financial harm people suffer because of crime and the handling of crime by the criminal justice system itself.[14]

Early victimologists focused on the victim–offender relationship, the vulnerability of different groups such as the elderly or women to crime, and the relative risk factors that contributed to the likelihood a person might become a victim of crime. Victimologists examined the victim–offender dynamic, the victim-proneness of different groups to crime, in order to identify preventative steps individuals and communities might take to reduce or avoid crime.[15] As we saw in Chapter 4, much of the information we have about the "dark figure of crime" comes from victimization surveys. Research also paid careful attention to analyzing the roles that victims themselves played in criminal events.[16] The concept of **victim precipitation**[17] refers to behavior such as walking alone at night, or frequenting certain types of bars, using drugs and alcohol, confrontational language, and so forth, which increases the likelihood of criminal victimization.

The research on victim precipitation has been criticized in recent decades as contributing to a widespread societal attitude of **victim blaming.**[18] "Blaming the victim" for being vulnerable to crime is a deep-seated American attitudinal response to crime. Victimization is an experience of weakness, and this is often perceived as a shameful experience within a culture that values power and control. Because all of us fear victimization, we psychologically look for ways to hold the victims personally responsible for what happened to them. We claim they were "stupid" to be out alone late at night, for carrying cash in their wallets, or for leaving windows open or wearing provocative clothing. This attitude helps us to feel more secure and falsely assures us that it won't happen to us as long as we are "careful." Being a victim of crime is a loss of control, and all of us seek to maintain the belief that we are in control of our fate.

As members of our culture, victims themselves often share these beliefs. Most of us consciously or unconsciously believe in a "just world," in which people deserve what happens to them: victims as well as offenders are on the receiving end of societal attitudes that blame individuals for the bad things that happen to them. One of the most common responses among victims is to blame themselves for being victimized. "If only I hadn't walked down that street . . . if only I had locked my windows. . . ." "If only" forms of thinking often torment victims long after a crime has taken place. Victims experience shame about being a victim and are often reluctant to talk about their experience with others. And when they do choose to talk about it, their response is often met with the judgmental response of those around them.

SECONDARY VICTIMIZATION BY THE CRIMINAL JUSTICE SYSTEM

Crimes that terrorize take many forms, from aggravated assault to petty thievery. But one crime goes largely unnoticed. It is a crime against which there is no protection. It is committed daily across our nation. It is the painful, wrongful insensitivity of the criminal justice system toward those who are the victims of crime. . . . The callousness with which the system again victimizes those who have already suffered at the hands of an assailant is tragic. (Senator John Heinz, sponsor of the Omnibus Victims Protection Act, passed by Congress in 1982.)[19]

victimology: the scientific study of the physical, psychological, and financial harm people suffer because of crime and the handling of crime by the criminal justice system itself.

victim precipitation: behavior of individuals that increases the likelihood of criminal victimization.

victim blaming: responsibility for the crime is shifted from the defendant to the victim.

secondary victimization: callous and insensitive treatment by the criminal justice system, which inflicts additional psychological harm and emotional trauma on victims.

Lighting a candle for victims is an important ritual for honoring loved ones lost to murder. The victims movement has called attention to the insensitive and callous treatment of crime victims by the justice system and lobbied for more resources and rights for victims of crime.

The anger and resentment of victims have been fueled by the neglect they experience in the criminal justice process itself. Victims, particularly those who have suffered serious crimes of violence, often find they experience a second victimization at the hands of an insensitive and callous justice system.[20] Police routinely question victims without any thought to their psychological or emotional state, often misinterpreting their anxiety and confusion as dishonesty or lack of credibility. Victims are told that if their injuries are not life threatening, their injuries are "not serious," and no support or assistance may be available to accompany a terrified victim back home or to assist with cleaning up a ransacked room or apartment. If victims are required to go to the hospital, no one in the justice system may offer them a ride, some extra clothing, a cup of coffee, or a sympathetic ear to help them through this stressful experience.

Rape victims, in particular, often have found themselves treated like the guilty party by male officers, who view them with suspicion and mistrust particularly when they do not fit the stereotype of the "worthy" victim. Prosecutors often refuse to charge a defendant if they feel the victim will not make a credible witness because of how she was dressed, where she worked, what she had drunk, or her relationship with the man accused of rape.

Although the prosecutor represents the interests of the victim, it is also the prosecutor's job to win the case for the state. Victims are only one of several constituencies that district attorneys seek to satisfy in making decisions about any particular case. In determining what to charge or whether to dismiss or reduce the charges, district attorneys must consider many factors beyond the victim's wishes, such as the limited resources of the office, the chances of winning a conviction, the credibility of the victim and witnesses, and the interests of the community and the system in prosecuting this crime. Prosecutors may be interested in using the defendant as an informant or key witness in other cases, or they may believe the defendant is a good candidate for diversion or other alternatives. Typically, prosecutors are neither trained nor organized to assist victims, explain the process to them, or meet their emotional, financial, or physical needs.

As a result, victims are routinely mistreated and misinformed by the system. They may be ordered to show up to testify at a hearing, forcing them to take time off from work (without pay), provide their own transportation and babysitting, only to find themselves sitting on a bench for hours waiting for a hearing that has been postponed until a later date. During this time they may even find themselves seated next to the defendant or surrounded by his family and friends. No one appears to inform them of the process, to offer them assistance or apologies for their time. This dismal and painful experience reoccurs repeatedly as the case grinds slowly and torturously through months of pretrial hearings.

At the trial itself, victims may find that truth is far from the genuine outcome. The story that is heard by the jury in the courtroom is shaped by the opposing attorneys, the rules of evidence, and what the judge will allow. Not all the evidence may be presented to the jury, because key evidence may be suppressed for due process reasons. Skillful defense attorneys will make use of cross-examination to raise reasonable doubt in the jury's mind and cast negative innuendo on the witnesses including the victim. In the courtroom, the rape victim, as often as not, finds herself placed on trial and her own sexual past used as evidence against her.[21]

Recall the defense's subtle portrayal in the Peairs case of young Yoshi as a kind of crazed bizarre freak. The defense sought to suggest that Yoshi himself was to blame for Rodney's decision to fire his gun. For Yoshi's parents, who were forced to sit in the back of the courtroom and who sometimes had trouble even finding a seat during the trial, this treatment is painful and terribly unjust. For people who have been injured by crime, this treatment is a second victimization.

The Victims' Rights Movement

In the 1970s and 1980s, several social movements contributed to a more politicized and empowering approach to victims and their role in the criminal justice system.[22] Victims began to form organizations to protest the poor treatment they received by the justice system and the wider society.[23] The organization formed by Donna Cuoma, sister of Joey Fournier, to advocate for the needs of victims, and the activities of two fathers of murdered daughters in California who fought for "three strikes" legislation for violent offenders, are examples of activist victims' groups that joined with law enforcement groups to lobby for tougher sentencing laws and other reforms.

The women's movement was a second social movement that contributed greatly to the resurgence of concern, respect, and attention paid to victims by the justice system. Feminists attacked the pervasive leniency toward men who victimized their wives and girlfriends. Victims of rape and domestic violence joined forces with feminists to make the justice system more sensitive to victims, to counter the powerful victim-blaming attitudes of justice personnel, and to provide institutional support, safety, and counseling for victims of male violence. The first rape crisis centers were established in 1972 in Berkeley, California, and Washington, D.C., and the first "safe" house for battered women followed shortly thereafter in 1974 in St. Paul, Minnesota.[24]

The women's movement fought against the tacit presumption that violence against wives was not "real" crime. Women who did not struggle against rapists were routinely depicted in court as consenting, even though they may have submitted in sheer terror, recognizing the likelihood of being killed by the rapist. Activists fought to change the legal criteria for rape, which required signs of resistance to prove the element of forcible rape. The feminist movement increased awareness of domestic and sexual violence against women and promoted a number of changes in the law and the justice

victims' rights movement: a social movement started in the 1970s to increase awareness of victims' issues and to advocate for the rights of victims in the criminal justice process.

system, including the placement of victims' advocates for rape victims, training for law enforcement, and "rape shield laws" to protect the past sexual history of the woman from being on trial.

Empowerment of Victims in the Criminal Justice System[25]

Before the victims' rights movement, victims had little or no input into the sentencing process. Unless the victim was called as a material witness, there was no right of the victim to be heard in the courtroom. Victims and their families were often not even permitted in the courtroom, out of fear their presence would prejudice the jury against the accused and provoke a mistrial. Sometimes judges warned victims that they should display no outward signs of emotion or they would be immediately removed from the courtroom, despite the fact that defendants' families often prominently displayed emotion in support of their loved ones. Even more disturbing was the denial of a direct voice to articulate the impact of the crime and how it had affected them. Victims had to rely on prosecutors to describe how they had been harmed.

The establishment of a right to make a **victim impact statement** to the court was an important gain for the victims' rights movement. Victims demanded the opportunity to be heard in the courtroom at the time of sentencing. While defendants had the opportunity to present information about themselves and to humanize themselves for the jury, victims felt that they were unfairly silenced and excluded from the process, which did not allow them to talk about how they had been harmed. Victims groups lobbied hard for victims to have the right to make victim impact statements to the judge.[26] Some states now require such a statement before sentencing can take place, while others offer victims the right to make a statement if they so choose. The victim impact statement provides an account of the loss sustained—financial, emotional, and physical—in the victim's own words. In some jurisdictions, this statement is incorporated into the presentence report prepared by probation; in others, the victim is permitted to read the statement directly to the judge at the time of sentencing.

Victims' rights groups also fought for the establishment of **victim witness and advocacy programs**[27] to assist victims in a host of ways in the criminal justice system. These programs, in some states as part of the district attorneys' office, provide an advocate for victims to accompany them to hearings and trial, to monitor the court process and provide them updates and information about the proceedings, and to assist them in preparing victim impact statements. Victims' advocates may also set up separate waiting spaces for victims so they are isolated from defendants and the general public, and offer basic useful information about the location of the court and other practical issues. Finally, they may provide assistance in the application for victim compensation and other forms of restitution available for victims.

Victims have also fought for the **right to be notified** by the system when an offender is being considered for parole and for the right to attend the parole hearing and to make a formal statement before the parole board. During the 1970s and 1980s, many victims' groups, along with other law enforcement interests, lobbied against parole as an unwarranted form of leniency for offenders, and many states and the federal government responded by reducing the use of parole release. Currently, about 35 percent of all prisoners are released under the supervision of a parole board, down about half from the late 1970s, when almost 72 percent of prisoners were released from jail on parole. Legislation in most states now grants victims the right to be present at parole hearings and to submit written or oral opinions on whether it should be granted to the offender. In some states, restitution to victims is a mandatory requirement for parolees.

victim impact statement: a report to the sentencing judge listing the effects of the crime on the victim.

victim witness and advocacy programs: an organized program with specialized personnel housed in district attorneys' offices or victims' assistance agencies, who assist victims throughout the justice process.

notification rights: the right of victims to be informed of key decisions and hearings related to their cases, such as plea agreements, parole hearings, or early-release decisions.

Another significant achievement of the victims' rights movement has been the establishment of state-funded **victim compensation funds** in all fifty states. These funds offer repayment to victims of serious crime for medical expenses, mental health services, and lost wages. Although some are funded out of general revenues or tax receipts, increasingly these programs are funded from fines and surcharges levied on persons convicted of misdemeanors or felony offenses. It is not necessary for an assailant to be caught and convicted for a victim to be repaid, but the victim must report the crime to the police and cooperate fully with the authorities in the investigation in order to be eligible for compensation.[28]

Finally, victims' groups also organized themselves into support groups for each other to overcome the "wall of silence" surrounding victims and to reduce some of the shame and blame that falls to victims of crime in our society. Work with victims has increased our understanding of the long-term psychological impact of crime and of the healing process for victims to restore them to equilibrium.

UNDERSTANDING THE PSYCHOLOGICAL TRAUMA OF CRIME

The impact of crime on victims extends far beyond the financial and physical losses inflicted by the offender. Even in the case of property crimes, research demonstrates that there is often a chronic and long-term psychological impact on crime victims. Crime undermines the basic sense of security in the world. It undermines the sense that the world is a "safe place." Mistrust, anxiety, fear, loneliness, and anger are lasting emotional states, often compounded by a sense of anxiety that the offender had acted deliberately against them, is watching them, and might be planning to return.

In person-to-person crime, such as rape or assault, the psychological trauma is even more severe. The research on the experience of rape victims as well as victims of domestic violence has contributed to our broader understanding of the psychological trauma of all types of victimization. Psychologists have found that many victims of serious crime suffer from **posttraumatic stress disorder (PTSD),** which has profound impact on their lives long after the crime has taken place.[29] Judith Herman[30] has studied victims of sexual violence, who suffer similar psychological symptoms as war veterans and other people who are exposed to violence during war. Herman argues that what earlier physicians termed "shell shock" can be understood to be PTSD brought on by exposure to the violence of war.

In the short term, exposure to severe violence leads to a physiological response of hyperarousal. The body reacts with shortness of breath, increased respiration, extreme anxiety, and feelings of terror and helplessness. For many victims of rape, the immediate response may appear to be cooperation but is in fact a psychological state of profound terror. This psychological state may be retriggered in the victim days, months, or even years after the crime occurred, by stimuli that remind the victim of the original incident such as a particular time of day, or a spatial cue or sound or smell. Many victims also experience physical symptoms of sleep disorders, stomach problems, muscle spasms, and other dysfunctions. Negative effects often last for months and may persist for years as victims continue to experience depression, anxiety, anger, guilt, and shame.

For family members of murder victims, the psychological harms are profound and lasting. Losing a loved one to a violent killing is not the same experience as losing a loved one to an accidental death. Family members of murder victims are often completely neglected by the system, especially when they have little to offer as witnesses in the case.

victim compensation funds: money collected by the state from criminal fines and awarded to victims to pay for medical bills, counseling, and to compensate for financial losses.

posttraumatic stress disorder (PTSD): a set of psychological symptoms suffered by some victims in response to the trauma of the crime.

The psychological impact of the crime often destroys marriages and creates a lasting psychological pain that is hidden from the wider society. Family members of murder victims suffer from the intense shame, loneliness, social isolation, anger, guilt, and frustration that is so common among all victims.

Healing and Justice

The study of victims has only begun to offer insight into the emotional and psychological healing process for victims of crime. Judith Herman has studied the healing process for victims of sexual violence. The first requirement for healing is safety: victims need to feel safe and in control of their own immediate environment. Too often, well-meaning family and friends are tempted to tell a victim what he or she "needs" to do. This has the unintended consequence of further undermining the victims' sense of their own autonomy and retards the healing process.

As part of the process of dealing with the pain of crime, victims often have many questions about the crime and the person who committed it. There is a need to "relive" the event, to reconstruct it in an attempt to understand it. Elaine's family responded to her death in a number of ways that are quite common among many survivors of violence. First of all they felt a need to understand why this crime occurred. It was important to the family to ask Susanna why she drove that night, to try and understand what she was thinking and what caused her to take the actions she did.

The Hattori family also sought answers to these same questions in trying to understand why Rodney Peairs owned several firearms and why he was so quick to use them against their unarmed and innocent son. One of the key needs for victims in the wake of crime is answers to the question of why: why me, why my house, why were you carrying a gun, what was going on in your head at the time, and so forth. Victims often feel a need to understand the motives of the offender and what about his or her life would help them make sense of this terrible injury.

By seeking answers to questions, victims are seeking the *meaning* of the injury. This is an attempt to restore some sense of moral order in the wake of actions that undermine their previous beliefs in morality and justice. The need for understanding is related to our need for control: unless we can make sense of what happens, we are powerless to steer our own course in the world. Humans require understanding in order to feel we can exercise meaningful control in our lives. Victims of burglaries, assaults, robberies, and rapes express the same basic need to understand why: why were they chosen, what was in the mind of the offender, who is this person who would do such a thing, what motivated them to do it? Often there are many very specific and painful questions that victims feel a need to ask, such as what the last few minutes of their loved one's life was like, if they suffered, if they uttered any last words.

Survivors' Missions

survivors' missions: sustained efforts by victims to bring about positive legislative or social change that will prevent the crime from happening to others or will assist victims in dealing with the trauma of crime.

Members of Elaine Serrell Myer's family gained enormous healing and solace from the knowledge that Susanna Cooper was not out on the streets drinking and driving again. The idea that she would return to the nation's highways unchanged and possibly inflict future tragedies on other families, or bring harm to her own young children, was more than Elaine's family could bear to contemplate. In the aftermath of the crime, victims often seek to take some kind of action that will make a positive difference in the future. Victims may become active in lobbying for new laws, for resources to study crime, for harsher punishment for offenders, or for assistance for other crime victims. Victims find solace in **survivors' missions,** which seek to help others who may be in the same position or to prevent others from going through what they experienced.[31] It is important to them to feel that their loved one did not die in vain.

Survivors of rape and sexual assault have joined forces with feminist organizations to fight for greater awareness of the prevalence of rape and violence against women. They demand more effective responses from law enforcement.

Victims need to regain control over their lives in the wake of crime. Because crime represents a profound loss of control, it is extremely important for victims to be active in the response to the crime. As we will see below, the criminal justice system excludes victims and makes them passive bystanders in the justice process itself. They are not decision makers, they do not take action, and they are generally not consulted by the professionals who take action against the offender. Thus, many victims channel their energies into "justice" through social action such as lobbying for tougher sentencing laws, or gun control, or the death penalty. This type of action gives meaning to their loved one's death and gives the victims an outlet for participation that is not possible in the current justice system.

In the mid-1980s, Candy Lightner, the mother of a teenage girl killed in an automobile crash by a drunk driver with numerous previous drunk-driving convictions, founded the organization Mothers Against Drunk Driving. MADD became a powerful lobbying organization that changed both the laws on "driving under the influence" (DUI) and public attitudes toward this crime.[32] MADD established drunk-driving awareness programs and pioneered a form of restitution in which victims tell their story to offenders and offenders go public with their stories to help prevent future tragedies. MADD has also helped promote increased penalties for drunk driving, including laws such as the automatic loss of a driver's license and mandatory prison sentences such as the one served by Susanna Cooper in the state of Washington.

The efforts by the Hattoris to pass gun control laws is one example of a survivor mission, as is the activity of Cliff Barnes to lobby against Michael Dukakis in the 1988 Presidential election, the lobbying of Polly Klaas's father for "three strikes" legislation in California, and efforts by the Serrell family to see that some good came from Elaine's death. In each of these cases, the victims and survivors of crime become involved in social movements to prevent others from becoming victims in the future. Although these victims may not all agree on the strategy of prevention, with some lobbying for harsher punishment and others lobbying against it, all became active as a result of their victimization.

AN ALTERNATIVE VISION OF JUSTICE: RESTORATIVE JUSTICE

Elaine's family sought a very different kind of justice than the one the state offered by sentencing Susanna Cooper to jail for thirty-six months. What the family wanted has been termed **restorative justice**.[33] The type of justice meted out by the criminal justice system by inflicting punishment on the convicted offender is referred to as **retributive justice.** These two understandings of justice are beginning to compete with one another in the contemporary justice system as more and more victims seek alternatives to the traditional justice response:

RETRIBUTIVE JUSTICE ASKS THESE QUESTIONS	RESTORATIVE JUSTICE ASKS THESE QUESTIONS
1. What law was broken?	1. What was harmed?
2. Who did it?	2. What is needed to repair the harm?
3. What punishment do they deserve?	3. Whose responsibility is to provide repair?

According to Howard Zehr, the retributive model of justice focuses on three key questions: What law was broken? Who broke it? And what punishment do they deserve? Much of the time and energy of the traditional justice system involves obtaining an accurate and fair answer to these three questions through arrest, investigations, collection of evidence, the trial process, and the imposition of sentencing. In the retributive model, most of the "work" of the justice process is done by professionals. Justice professionals protect the legal rights of the accused, determine legal guilt within the boundaries of due process, and ensure public safety and justice for victims and the community through the imposition of fair punishment and opportunity for appropriate rehabilitation. As we have noted before, the traditional response to crime focuses overwhelmingly on the offender.

A restorative response to crime focuses on three very different questions: Who has been harmed by the crime? What is needed to repair the harm? Whose responsibility and obligation is it to offer this repair? In this vision of justice, the victim and the losses sustained by the crime are the primary focus and victims themselves are put back into a role of central importance. The first question focuses on the direct and indirect victims of the crime. Often crime harms not only the direct victim of the crime; the victim's spouse or children may also suffer psychological trauma from the crime. The community may also be affected by a crime, as neighbors fear walking down the street or choose to withdraw or move in order to feel safe in their neighborhood. In the case we explored here, the family themselves were afforded the opportunity at the victim–offender mediation to articulate exactly what had been lost to them by the death of Elaine.[34]

The second question in a restorative response seeks to figure out what is needed to help restore or repair the harm. As Elizabeth stated, in the case of a homicide, it is just not possible to provide wholeness. Elizabeth acknowledges that Susanna cannot "provide a wife for David or a sister for myself." But the family did articulate what, in their view, would provide restoration. In this case, the family wanted Susanna to change her ways and devote her life to preventing drunk driving by having the courage to share her

restorative justice: a response to crime that seeks to restore the well-being of victims and the larger community while promoting responsible and productive behavior in offenders.

retributive justice: a response to crime that seeks to inflict punishment on offenders in just proportion to the seriousness of the offense.

story truthfully and in public. Repair is often not an exact return to a prior state but rather an understanding of what can be done to make amends for a past injury.

Who is responsible for doing this repair is the third key concern in a restorative response. Here the role of the offender is also quite different in restorative justice than it is in a retributive system. In the traditional system, punishment is imposed on offenders, who must passively be made to suffer for their crimes. The offenders are acted upon rather than taking actions themselves. In a restorative system, offenders, like victims, are more directly involved. Susanna was asked to meet directly with the people she harmed, an encounter that was as difficult for offenders as it is for victims. Susanna had to listen to the real and painful consequences of her criminal negligence and she has to live with the full knowledge of what she took from this family. Susanna is also charged with taking positive action for the rest of her life to make up for this loss. Unlike the traditional system, which asks only that an offender sit in jail for a period of time, the restorative system asks what an offender can do to make the victim and the community whole again.

The Hattoris's painful experience with the U.S. justice system derives in part from the contrast to the Japanese system, which operates on more restorative principles. The use of apology and direct acknowledgement of wrongdoing is highly prevalent in the Japanese system. For many victims, one of the deepest injuries of the traditional system comes from the absence of any expression of remorse, regret, or moral responsibility on the part of the offender. The insight of the restorative justice movement is that the traditional adversarial system discourages those who are accused of crimes from stepping forward and fully admitting their guilt. Conscientious defense attorneys advise their clients to remain silent, to allow the attorneys to negotiate the legal charge, and to let the matter be handled by the legal professionals. The unintended consequence is often that victims and offenders are denied an opportunity for honest accountability, remorse, and future reconciliation.

The restorative justice movement emerged within modern Western societies beginning in the 1970s, and a variety of restorative justice programs and practices are beginning to be implemented within traditional justice systems. Beginning in the 1970s, there was a rediscovery of the victim and the use of **restitution** as a means to compensate victims for their loss.[35] The first **victim–offender reconciliation programs**[36] also emerged in the 1970s, bringing the two together as a basis for genuine healing and reconciliation. Several states have embraced a return to the goal of restitution, accountability to communities through community service, and the use of restorative principles in the traditional system, particularly for juveniles and for less serious offenses.[37]

Practices in restorative justice have also been influenced by non-Western justice traditions that are being incorporated into the Western system. In New Zealand, the traditional practices of the Maori natives use a model of family group conferencing to bring victims, offenders, and their families together instead of the adversarial court process dominated by legal professionals. In 1989, the juvenile system in New Zealand adopted the **family group conferencing model** for all juvenile cases except those involving first-degree murder and sexual assault.

The restorative justice movement is still quite small, but it is affecting all parts of the criminal justice system.[38] In some communities, police are involved in experiments using the family group conferencing model to deal with young, first-time offenders. In other jurisdictions, offenders can be referred to community panels for restorative probation. These panels bring victims and offenders together, seek to show offenders whom they have harmed—victims and the community—and develop ways to make amends to those they have harmed. There are also experiments making use of the Native American peacemaking circles in the sentencing and disposition of cases in Canada and the United States.[39] In later chapters we will examine some of the possibilities and pitfalls associated with the growing use of restorative justice and its complex relationship to a traditional system of justice.

restitution: a criminal sanction in which offenders repay victims for their crime or provide work service to the community or the victim.

victim–offender reconciliation programs: programs that bring victims and offenders together in a face-to-face dialogue to discuss the impact of the harm and to negotiate restitution by the offender to the victim.

family group conferencing model: a form of restorative justice that originated in New Zealand, in which offenders, victims, and their respective families meet under the authority of the justice system to discuss the impact of the harm and negotiate accountability by the offender to the victim and the community.

KEY TERMS

offender focused p. 113
victimology p. 115
victim precipitation p. 115
victim blaming p. 115
secondary victimization p. 115
victims' rights movement p. 117
victim impact statement p. 118

victim witness and advocacy
    programs p. 118
notification rights p. 118
victim compensation funds p. 119
posttraumatic stress disorder
    (PTSD) p. 119
survivors' mission p. 120

restorative justice p. 122
retributive justice p. 122
restitution p. 123
victim–offender reconciliation
    programs p. 123
family group conferencing
    model p. 123

REVIEW AND STUDY QUESTIONS

1. Define the field of victimology. In what sense is the criminal justice system offense focused and offender driven?

2. What is the process of victim blaming? Why is this a common psychological reaction to victimization in our culture?

3. What is secondary victimization? Give examples of where this might take place in the criminal justice system.

4. What are victims' rights in the criminal justice process? Why are these important to victims? How do victims' rights address the problem of secondary victimization?

5. How do victims' rights differ from offenders' rights to due process? Are victims' and offenders' rights in competition with one another? Why or why not?

6. What are the symptoms of posttraumatic stress disorder? How can the criminal justice system respond effectively to the needs of victims with PTSD?

7. What is a survivors' mission? Why is such a mission important for victims?

8. Define retributive justice. What are the three questions Howard Zehr believes are central to retributive justice?

9. Define restorative justice. What are the three questions Howard Zehr believes are central to restorative justice?

10. Contrast a restorative justice response to crime with a retributive justice response to crime. Compare the role of the victim in restorative justice and retributive justice.

CHECK IT OUT

On the Web

Office for Victims of Crime, **www.ojp.usdoj.gov/ovc**
U.S. Department of Justice site with information about crime victims and resources for crime victims. Check out the Victims Assistance and Compensation programs in your state.

Parents of Murdered Children (PMOC), **www.pomc.com/**
This organization is dedicated to providing support and services for families and friends of those who have died by violence. The organization provides emotional support for parents, family members, and friends dealing with acute grief, and assistance in dealing with the criminal justice system as well.

Restorative Justice Online, **www.restorativejustice.org**
A service of the Center for Justice and Reconciliation of the Prison Fellowship International. Check the online tutorial about restorative justice, the interviews and annotated bibliographies of material
on restorative justice, and the links to action sites around the world.

Center for Restorative Justice and Peacemaking, **ssw.che. umn.edu/rj/**
Excellent Web site with tons of information about victim–offender mediation, conferencing, and the use of restorative justice in the United States.

Victim Offender Reconciliation Programs (VORP) Information and Research Center, **www.vorp.com**
Click here to learn more about the VORPS and how they are being used extensively in the criminal justice system and the community.

On Film

From Victim to Survivor (29 minutes)
The slow and painful restoration of emotional and spiritual recovery for three victims of rape, two women and one man, is explored in this excellent film about survival

and support. Available from Filmakers Library, www. filmakers.com.

Healing the Heart: Forgive and Remember
(30 minutes)
Survivors of homicide, including Bud Welch, whose daughter died in the Oklahoma City bombing, share their journey from shock through anger through grief to an attitude of forgiveness. Available from Films for the Humanities and Sciences, www.films.com.

Facing the Demons (57 minutes)
An extraordinary chronicle of a restorative justice using family group conferencing in Sydney, Australia. A senior police sergeant mediates the conference between two of the convicted murderers and the parents, friends, and co-workers of 18-year-old victim Michael Marslew five years after his death in an armed robbery. Available from First Run/Icarus Films, www.frif.com.

NOTES

1. Elizabeth S. Menkin with Lori K. Baker, "I Forgave My Sister's Killer," *Ladies Home Journal,* December 1995, retrieved June 6, 2002, from Victim-Offender Reconciliation Program Information and Resource Center, **www.vorp.com/articles/forgave.html.**
2. Ibid.
3. Marty Price, "The Mediation of a Drunk Driving Death: A Case Development Study," June 7, 1994, retrieved June 6, 2002, from Victim-Offender Reconciliation Program Information and Resource Center, **www.vorp.com/articles/lifeaft.html.**
4. Elizabeth S. Menkin with Lori Baker, "I Forgave My Sister's Killer."
5. Elizabeth S. Menkin, "Life after Death," *San Jose Mercury News, West Magazine,* 1994, retrieved June 6, 2002, from Victim-Offender Reconciliation Program Information and Resource Center, **www.vorp.com/articles/lifeaft.html.**
6. Marty Price, "The mediation of a Drunk Driving Death."
7. Ibid.
8. Elizabeth S. Menkin with Lori Baker, "I Forgave My Sister's Killer."
9. Elizabeth S. Menkin, "Life after Death."
10. Robert B. Coates, Boris Kalanj, and Mark S. Umbreit, *Victim Meets Offender: The Impact of Restorative Justice and Mediation* (Monsey, NY: Willow Tree Press, 1994), pp. 1–5.
11. Stephen Schafer, *Victimology: The Victim and His Criminal* (Reston, VA: Reston Publishing, 1977), pp. 5–32.
12. Daniel Van Ness, *Crime and Its Victims,* (Downers Grove, IL: Intervarsity Press, 1986), pp. 61–83.
13. H. Von Hentig, "Remarks on the Interaction of Perpetrator and Victim," *Journal of Criminal Law, Criminology and Police Science* 31 (March–April 1941), pp. 303–309; B. Mendelsohn, "The Victimology," *Etudes Internationales de PsychoSociologies Criminelle,* July 1956, pp. 23–26.
14. Andrew Karmen, *Crime Victims: An Introduction to Victimology* (Pacific Grove, CA: Brooks/Cole, 1990), pp. 23–24.
15. R. Block, "Victim-Offender Dynamics in Violent Crime," *Journal of Criminal Law and Criminology* 72 (1981), pp. 743–761; R. Black and Wesley Skogan, "Resistance and Nonfatal Outcomes in Stranger-to-Stranger Predatory Crime," *Violence and Victims* 1(4) (Winter 1986), pp. 241–254.
16. M. Wolfgang, "Suicide by Means of Victim Precipitated Homicide," *Journal of Clinical and Experimental Psychopathology and Quarterly Review of Psychiatry and Neurology* 20 (1959), pp. 335–349; Andrew Karmen, "Victim Facilitation: The Case of Auto Theft," *Victimology* 4 (1980), pp. 361–370; Susan Estrich, *Real Rape* (Cambridge, MA: Cambridge University Press, 1986).
17. R. Silverman, "Victim Precipitation: An Examination of the Concept," in I. Drapkin and E. Viano, Eds., *Victimology: A New Focus* (Lexington, MA: Heath, 1974), pp. 99–110.
18. Ryan William, *Blaming the Victim* (New York: Vintage, 1971), pp. 3–6.
19. J. Heinz, "On Justice to Victims," *The New York Times,* July 7, 1982, p. A19.
20. M. Symonds, "The 'Second Injury' to Victims," *Evaluation and Change* 7 (1980), pp. 36–38.
21. G. Hackett and G. Cerio, "When the Victim Goes on Trial," *Newsweek,* January 18, 1988, p. 31.
22. Robert Elias, *The Politics of Victimization: Victims, Victimology and Human Rights* (New York: Oxford University Press, 1986), pp. 9–25.
23. L. Friedman, "The Crime Victim Movement at Its First Decade," *Public Administration Review* 45 (November 1985), pp. 790–794.
24. Karmen, *Crime Victims,* p. 5.
25. National Institute of Justice, *New Directions from the Field: Victims Rights and Services for the 21st Century* (Washington, DC: U.S. Department of Justice, 1998), pp. 45–145.
26. D. Hellerstein, "The Victim-Impact Statement: Reform or Reprisal?" *American Criminal Law Review* 27 (1989), pp. 390–434.
27. Andrew Karmen, "Towards the Institutionalization of a New Kind of Justice Professional: The Victim Advocate," *The Justice Professional* 9 (1995), pp. 1–16.
28. T. Miller, M. Cohen, and B. Wiersema, *Victim Costs and Consequences: A New Look* (Washington, DC: U.S. Department of Justice, 1996), pp. 1–28.
29. T. Williams, "Post-traumatic Stress Disorder: Recognizing It, Treating It," *NOVA Newsletter,* February 1–7, 1987.
30. Judith Herman, *Trauma and Recovery* (New York: Basic Books, 1992), p. 207.
31. Ibid., pp. 207–211.
32. M. Thompson, "MADD Curbs Drunk Drivers," *Victimology* 9 (1) (1984), pp. 191–192.
33. Howard Zehr, *Changing Lenses* (Scottsdale, Pennsylvania: Herald Press, 1990, p. 181); Daniel Van Ness and K. Strong, *Restoring Justice* (Cincinnati: Anderson, 1997). p. 31.

34. M. Wright, "The Impact of Victim-Offender Mediation on the Victim," *Victimology* 10(1) (1985), pp. 630–646.

35. Charles Abel and F. Marsh, *Punishment and Restitution: A Restitutionary Approach to Crime and the Criminal* (Westport, CT: Greenwood Press, 1984, pp. 135–172); R. Barnett, "Restitution: A New Paradigm of Criminal Justice," in R. Barnett and J. Haagel, Eds., *Assessing the Criminal: Restitution, Retribution and the Criminal Process* (Cambridge, MA: Ballinger, 1977), pp. 1–35.

36. Robert Coates, "Victim-Offender Reconciliation Programs in North America: An Assessment," in Burt Galaway and J. Hudson, Eds., *Criminal Justice, Restitution and Reconciliation* (Monsey, NY: Willow Tree Press, 1990), pp. 125–134; Mark Umbreit and D. Greenwood, *National Survey of Victim-Offender Mediation Programs in the United States* (Washington, DC: Office of Victims of Crime, 1998).

37. Office of Juvenile Justice and Delinquency Prevention, *National Directory of Restitution and Community Service Programs* (Washington, DC: U.S. Department of Justice, 1998).

38. Office of Victims of Crime, National Institute of Justice, *Restorative Justice Fact Sheet* (Washington, DC: U.S. Department of Justice, 1997).

39. Kay Pranis, "Victims in the Peacemaking Circle Process," *The Crime Victims Report* 3(4) (September 1999), p. 51.

CASE 7

Security or Dignity: Rosa at the Border

A SUSPICIOUS PASSENGER

On her arrival at Los Angeles International Airport, a groggy Rosa Elvira Montoya de Hernandez walked stiffly down the airport corridor after the 10-hour flight from her home in Bogota, Colombia. It was after midnight and her high-heeled shoes pinched her swollen feet. She waited in the long line for Immigration Control to show her passport to the officer behind the glass booth and then proceeded to a customs line. Rosa didn't realize it, but several pieces of information about her had already raised the suspicions of the Customs inspector.

Probably the biggest strike against Rosa was her arrival on Avianca Flight 080, a direct flight from the largest source city for the worldwide cocaine drug trade. All passengers who arrive on international "high-risk flights," from places such as Bogota, Peru, Bolivia, Mexico, Jamaica, or Nigeria, are subject to greater scrutiny than the roughly 70 million international passengers who pass through U.S. Customs annually. Customs officers receive information from specialized investigative units called passenger analytical units (PAUs), which analyze the passenger lists of flights to identify known drug traffickers or terrorists. Inspectors also access the Advanced Passenger Information System, which provides information on passengers about to arrive in the United States and tracks any connecting flights a passenger may have made from another destination. The passenger list may be processed through the Interagency Border Inspection System, which includes the combined databases of U.S. Customs, the Immigration and Naturalization Service, the State Department, the FBI's National Crime Information Center (NCIC), and twenty-one other federal agencies. "People would be surprised how much we know about them and where they have been even before they step off the plane," says Robert Kelly, commissioner of U.S. Customs.[1]

In Rosa's case it was not high-tech information from the NCIC or the PAU that raised the inspectors' alarm: it was her passport, showing she had made at least eight trips between Bogota and either Los Angeles or Miami in the previous two years. It was also her response to the routine questions posed by Customs Inspector Serrato about the reason for her visit. In broken English, Rosa explained that she had come to Los Angeles to do some "shopping," was visiting no one in particular but vaguely planned to find a room at "a Holiday Inn," and would travel around by taxi. Her pattern of behavior fit the classic profile of a drug smuggler, probably carrying drugs somewhere inside her body.

Serrato signaled to Rosa to come to a "secondary" Customs desk for further questioning by an agent who spoke Spanish and for a search of her luggage and belongings. Rosa said she had come to Los Angeles to purchase goods for her husband's clothing store back in Bogota. That was the reason for the $5,000 in cash in $50 bills in her purse. She planned to go to J. C. Penney and KMart to buy goods, and she produced some old receipts and fabric swatches displayed in a photo album to confirm her story. But Rosa had no hotel reservations, no scheduled appointments, no credit cards, and no checks with her name or the name of her husband's business. Inside her small suitcase were several changes of clothing, odd because they were heavyweight and not suitable for a stay in sunny Los Angeles. Apart from the high-heeled shoes on her feet, there were no additional pairs of shoes in the suitcase. When asked how and where she had purchased her ticket, Rosa could not remember.

The inspectors believed that Rosa was a "balloon swallower": a drug courier who swallows balloons, usually condoms, filled with narcotics and transports them for a fee. After allowing the drugs to pass through her system, Rosa would deliver them to a contact and return home on the next available flight. The anonymous contact would hand her a ticket, just as the inspectors suspected someone had done for this flight.

Body-cavity smuggling is a very risky and desperate business: people have died from choking on a balloon, or from a massive overdose when a balloon leaked or burst internally, flooding their system with a lethal quantity of narcotics. Then, of course, there is the risk of being apprehended by the law: the penalty for drug smuggling is often 10 to 25 years in prison or more. This kind of smuggling is done by people with few choices in life: they are desperate to escape the misery of poverty or they are doing it to protect a loved one from violence from drug traffickers back home.

THE STRIP SEARCH

A terrified Rosa was escorted to a private area, and two female customs inspectors were called in to perform a pat down and strip search in a back room in the airport. A pat down or frisk is a physical inspection of a person's external body: a female agent runs her hands all over the suspect's body, including her breasts, abdomen, crotch, and buttocks. The strip search requires the suspected smuggler to remove all her clothing, bend over, and spread her buttock cheeks for visual inspection. A suspect is also required to open her legs and let an inspector examine her vaginal area visually. These so-called personal searches are done at the discretion of the Customs officers, based on a "reasonable suspicion"

that the person is carrying concealed drugs on or in his or her body. In Rosa's case, the pat down revealed what the inspector reported as a "firm" abdomen. The strip search revealed that Rosa was wearing two pairs of elastic pants with paper towels lining the crotch area. No actual contraband was discovered by the personal search.

At this point in the investigation, the U.S. Customs inspectors were uncertain about how to proceed with Rosa. They strongly suspected that she was a drug smuggler but they had not found any drugs. The next level of search involves either the examination of the suspect's body cavities by medical personnel, the taking of an X-ray at a hospital, or a monitored bowel movement, in which the person is required to defecate in the presence of one or more Customs inspectors. Customs inspector Jose Talamantes informed Rosa that he suspected she was carrying drugs inside her alimentary canal and asked her consent to be X-rayed at a local hospital. Rosa shook her head, claiming she was pregnant. The inspector offered to conduct a pregnancy test before administering the X-ray. At first Rosa consented, but when officers walked into the room and started to handcuff her in order to transport her to the hospital, she crossed her arms in front of her chest and shook her head. "You are not going to put those on me. That is an insult to my character." The Customs inspector asked his supervisor to request a court order forcing her to go to the hospital, but the supervisor decided that there was not sufficient evidence to convince a judge to sign such an order.

At this point, the inspector offered Rosa two choices: either she would to be sent back to Bogota on the next available flight, or she would have to remain in detention until she had produced a bowel movement—thus proving that she was not carrying drugs in her abdomen. They would not permit her to enter the country suspecting that she was carrying drugs inside her body. Rosa chose to leave on the next flight. But another flight was not available for many hours, and the inspectors told her she must remain in the detention room and could not leave until she had excreted by squatting over a wastebasket under the supervision of the two female officers in the room. De Hernandez responded, "I will not submit to your degradation. I'd rather die."[2]

AN ILLEGAL DETENTION?

Rosa remained locked in the room for almost 24 hours under the watchful supervision of three different sets of female officers while customs officials supposedly tried to find her a flight out of the country. They tried to place her on a flight via Mexico City, but since she lacked a Mexican visa, the request was refused. As she sat and waited, Rosa refused to drink or eat. She sat in the chair clutching her purse and weeping, repeatedly asking permission "to call my husband and tell him what you are doing to me."[3] Every time someone entered the room, Rosa took out two small photographs of her children and begged them to let her contact her husband or call an attorney. After about 12 hours, Rosa was strip searched again, "to ensure the safety of the surveilling officers." The search revealed no new information.

A change of shift brought a new inspector on duty, who immediately sought a court order to force Rosa to have a pregnancy test, X-ray, and body-cavity examination. The warrant summarized all the suspicious circumstances of Rosa's visit to Los Angeles: the absence of plans, her frequent trips, the cash in her purse, lack of clothing for a visit, the firmness of her abdomen, and the extra pair of underwear she was wearing. In addition, the warrant included the fact that Rosa had refrained from going to the bathroom during all these hours of detention, refused any drink or food, and had shown signs of extreme abdominal discomfort during that time.

A federal magistrate issued the order just before midnight of the next evening. A hysterical Rosa was handcuffed and transported to the hospital, where a rectal examination indicated the presence of a cocaine-filled balloon. At about 3:15 a.m., Rosa was formally placed under arrest and advised of her Miranda rights. During the course of the next four days, Rosa excreted a total of 88 balloons containing 528 grams of 80 percent pure cocaine hydrochloride.

A VIOLATION OF THE CONSTITUTION?

In federal district court, Rosa's attorney requested a suppression hearing, arguing that the evidence resulting from the rectal examination, namely, the 88 balloons filled with cocaine, had been obtained illegally and therefore was inadmissible as evidence. The argument centered on the length of Rosa's detention and the failure to seek a court order early in her detention. They believed that once the pat down and strip search failed to produce demonstrable evidence of drug smuggling, Rosa should have been released or deported. If the inspectors wished to detain her further and/or submit her to a more intrusive investigation of an X-ray or rectal examination, they would need to obtain a search warrant by convincing a judge that the evidence against her—namely, the firmness of her abdomen, her clothing, and the peculiarities of her travel plans—constituted probable cause that she was an alimentary-canal smuggler. According to defense attorneys, U.S. Customs investigators illegally detained Rosa in order to gather incriminatory information against her.

The district court judge disagreed and denied the motion to suppress. The evidence was submitted against Rosa and she was convicted of various narcotics charges in a bench trial. On appeal, however, a majority of the Ninth Circuit Court of Appeals took a different view of the legality of the evidence.[4] In the opinion of the Court of Appeals, the Customs inspectors, at the time they detained Rosa, did not have a "clear indication" that she was an alimentary-canal smuggler. They clearly had a reasonable suspicion that she was carrying drugs in her body and that suspicion gave them the grounds to pat down, strip search, and detain her for the length of time it took to complete that investigation. After the strip search revealed no drugs or hard evidence of drugs, however, the inspectors were in violation of the Fourth Amendment when they continued to detain her in order to collect more evidence against her.

Acknowledging that it is a difficult job to secure our borders and recognizing the tough choice facing U.S. Customs officers, who clearly believed Rosa would be conveying drugs into the country if they released her, the Ninth Circuit judges nevertheless felt that it was the job of the judiciary to make that tough decision. "These cases suggest that when in doubt the customs officers should present their information to a magistrate and permit that judicial officer to exercise judicial discretion in striking the delicate balance between human rights and the practical necessities of border security."[5] The Ninth Circuit Court of Appeals overturned the conviction of Rosa Montoya de Hernandez.

A REASONABLE BALANCE IN FAVOR OF SECURITY?

The U.S. Supreme Court, however, took yet another view of the matter, agreeing with district court and reinstating Rosa's original conviction. In a 7–2 decision, the majority of the Supreme Court argued that no one disputed that the original strip search was perfectly legal, based as it was on the grounds of "reasonable suspicion." A U.S. Customs officer, using his or her training and experience, reviews the totality of the circumstances and has a strong hunch that a person may be engaged in drug smuggling. On the basis of that hunch, he or she has the legal power, at the border, to pat down an individual or force that person to remove his or her clothes for visual inspection. The inspector does not need to be right in his or her suspicion, just reasonable.

Alimentary-canal smuggling presents a still greater challenge to law enforcement officers charged with policing our borders. The strip search is usually a sufficient method to detect drugs concealed in the body cavities of the rectum or vagina, but the use of the digestive tract to conceal drugs cannot be detected without the use of X-rays, forced bowel movements, or invasive examinations. Officers are caught in a "Catch-22": they cannot obtain a court order without some evidence beyond "reasonable suspicion," and they cannot obtain this evidence without a court order. In the view of the Supreme Court justices, it is necessary to lower the standard of evidence necessary to justify searches in order to detect this particular form of smuggling.

That it is humiliating to endure a monitored bowel movement is also not the fault of law enforcement but is a direct result of the chosen method of smuggling. The only logical solution, according to the majority opinion, is to permit inspectors to act based on reasonable suspicion and permit them to "search" those spaces, that is, body cavities, via X-ray, forced excretions, or rectal and vaginal examinations. Given the high public priority of preventing drugs from entering the country, the balance between private and public interests favored this intrusion on the individual based on reasonable suspicion.

"A DISGUSTING AND SADDENING EPISODE"?

Justice Brennan and Justice Marshall strongly dissented from the majority opinion of the Supreme Court, calling this case a "disgusting and saddening episode" at our nation's borders.[6] They said that to grant to all Customs officials patrolling our borders the right to determine if people should be forced to submit to the most intrusive searches of their most private and intimate parts of the body is a flagrant violation of the intent and the spirit of the Fourth Amendment. That these intrusions were described as "limited" struck these justices as outrageous. Being forced to defecate in front of strangers in order to "prove" your innocence is a profoundly degrading and humiliating experience.

According to the dissenting justices, the issue is this: "Does the Fourth Amendment permit an international traveler, citizen or alien, to be subjected to the sort of treatment that occurred in this case without the sanction of a judicial officer and based on nothing more than the 'reasonable suspicion' of low-ranking investigative officers that something might be amiss?"[7] The majority opinion had answered this question in the affirmative, stating that it was necessary to allow law enforcement officers the flexibility to conduct investigations based on experienced hunches. This is, in fact, the only way to uphold the

government's interest in protecting the borders from this kind of drug smuggling.

However, the dissent pointed out that the vast majority of those who are detained and subjected to these kinds of searches are totally innocent. Most of the time, "reasonable suspicions" turn out to be wrong. In theory, the intrusions based on low-level suspicions are relatively harmless, so the trade-off is worthwhile; weighed against the benefit of finding people carrying concealed weapons in the street or conveying drugs into the country, this "inconvenience" is easily worth the cost of stopping innocent citizens for brief questioning or pat downs.

To Justices Brennan and Marshall, however, there is nothing "harmless" or "trivial" about being brought to a back room of an airport for a strip search or being forced to defecate in a wastepaper basket in front of strangers. And it was hard to imagine anything more degrading and humiliating than being handcuffed and taken to a hospital for a forced X-ray or rectal exam.

The dissenting justices expressed concern that this degree of power in the hands of U.S. Customs agents would lead to the harassment of innocent people by unscrupulous or incompetent Customs officers. Would this power be abused, intentionally or unintentionally? Would some people be subject to these humiliating searches based on their skin color, dress, ethnicity, class, or age?

> I do not imagine that decent and law-abiding international travelers have yet reached the point where they "expect" to be thrown into locked rooms and ordered to excrete into wastebaskets, held incommunicado until they cooperate, or led away in handcuffs to the nearest hospital for exposure to various medical procedures—all on nothing more than the "reasonable" suspicions of low-ranking enforcement agents. In fact, many people from around the world travel to our borders precisely to escape such unchecked executive investigatory discretion. What a curious first lesson in American liberty awaits them on their arrival.[8]

Four years after Rosa's case was decided, a story broke on the front pages of a major newspaper describing the thousands of innocent travelers, most of them U.S. citizens, who are strip searched at our nation's airports and customs stations.[9] In 1997 and 1998, a U.S. General Accounting Office (GAO) study reported that U.S. Customs had conducted searches of approximately 93,764 international travelers ranging from pat downs to strip searches to forced ingestion of laxatives.[10] Out of all those pat-down searches, only 3 percent had revealed the presence of drugs. Of the almost 3,000 individuals who were strip searched,

77 percent were innocent. And for the almost 1,000 during those two years who were forced to be X-rayed, 69 percent were found to be innocent travelers who happened to fit the criteria of "reasonable suspicion" for alimentary-canal smuggling.

The GAO study was ordered in the wake of a broader public discussion and outrage over the widespread police practice of racial profiling and the use of the police power to stop, question, and search minority Americans on the nation's streets, highways, and airports. President Clinton ordered U.S. Customs to keep track of airport searches in order to document the race and gender of people who were stopped. The GAO study confirmed a racial bias in who was likely to be subject to a search by a U.S. Customs agent: black women were nine times more likely than white women to be X-rayed and 73 percent more likely than white women to be strip searched. The term "***flying while black***" was coined by the media to describe what critics claimed was widespread targeting of minorities as objects of "reasonable suspicion" based on the color of their skin.[11]

Case adapted from *Montoya De Hernandez* v. *United States* 473 U.S. 531; 105 S. Ct. 3304 (1986); 731 F2d 1369 (1984); Nelson Erik-Lars, "Changing the Profile at Customs," *Daily News,* October 15, 2000; U.S. General Accounting Office, *U.S. Customs Service: Better Targeting of Airline Passengers for Personal Searches Could Produce Better Results,* GAO/GGD-00-38, March 2000; Cathy Harris, *Flying While Black: A Whistleblower's Story,* (Los Angeles: Milligan Books, 2001); Lisa Bekin, "Airport Drug Efforts Snaring Innocents Who Fit Profiles," *New York Times,* March 20, 1990.

THINKING CRITICALLY ABOUT THIS CASE

1. In your view, was the detention and body-cavity search of Rosa a "reasonable balance" between liberty and crime control, or a "disgusting and saddening episode"? Explain why you agree with the majority or the dissenting opinion in this case.
2. Rosa Montoya de Hernandez is not a U.S. citizen. Yet the Supreme Court has held that the "aliens" on U.S. soil are nevertheless guaranteed due process by the Fourteenth Amendment to the U.S. Constitution. Do you believe that noncitizens should be entitled to equal protection under the Constitution? Why or why not? If aliens must obey our laws when they are in the country, should they not also be entitled to protections afforded by the law? Why or why not?
3. How does this case illustrate the trade-off between liberty and crime control? Why is the "protection of the innocent" in conflict with the "pursuit of the guilty"?
4. In striking a balance between individual liberty and crime control, the judiciary makes a determination about the potential threat of the crime weighed against the level of intrusion on individual liberty. In your view, did the Supreme Court strike an appropriate balance given the threat of alimentary-canal drug smuggling? Why or why not?
5. What are the trade-offs between civil liberties and threats posed by terrorism? Would you support a reduction in civil liberties in order to detect and apprehend terrorists? Why or why not?
6. The search of a passenger's luggage and person is considered to be a "trivial" loss of liberty. Is this true in your opinion? Do you consider a strip search a minor intrusion on liberty? Why or why not? Is any loss of liberty "trivial"? Why or why not?
7. Should law enforcement be permitted to use travelers' ethnic or racial identities as a factor supporting reasonable suspicion? Why or why not?

CHECK OUT THIS CASE

On the Web

U.S. Customs Service, www.customs.ustreas.gove/trave/travel.htm
Download the GAO Report on Personal Searches by the U.S. Customs Service, which shows data on race/gender of airport traffic searches. Learn more about the U.S. Customs and its antidrug, smuggling, and many other law enforcement responsibilities.

CHAPTER 7

Police and the Law

LEARNING OBJECTIVES

After reading this chapter, the student should be able to:

■ Explain the difference between the concepts of authority and power, and describe their relevance for the use of force by police in our society

■ Describe the structure of U.S. law enforcement

■ Understand the application of the Fourth and Fifth Amendments to police work

■ Identify the forms of proof associated with stop and frisk, arrest, and searches

■ Explain the exclusionary rule, and describe its intended purpose in our justice system

■ Recite the Miranda rights and explain why these rights are an important protection of the Fifth Amendment

The case of Rosa Montoya de Hernandez illustrates the dilemma of policing in a free society.[12] As the dissenting Supreme Court justices noted, one of the reasons people come to the United States is to be free from governments that can act against citizens and noncitizens without justification or restriction. In Nazi Germany there was very little crime, but there was also very little civil liberty: police could knock on people's doors at any hour, for any reason, search the premises, and arrest whomever they suspected of wrongdoing. In many countries around the world, noncitizens suspected of illegal activity may be detained without access to counsel or the guarantee of a right to a fair trial. American values embedded in the Constitution uphold the principle of individual liberties and high standards of fairness for citizens and noncitizens alike.

Yet it is also true that Americans rely on the powers of law enforcement to protect our right to live in an orderly society. Freedom depends on a degree of order. If U.S. Customs agents permit Rosa to enter the country to sell drugs, our freedom is impaired by the lawlessness and disorder created by the drug trade. Citizens forced to huddle behind closed doors to avoid a volley of bullets between rival drug gangs are hardly living in a free society. Most Americans find detention without trial and unexplained "disappearances" behind the closed doors of the authorities without access to counsel or contact with the outside world to be repugnant. But most Americans also recognize the need to weigh this evil against the magnitude of threat stemming from the illegal conduct, whether it be the smuggling of illegal drugs or the intention to commit violent acts of terrorism.

The question for the U.S. justice system is: How do we strike the balance between liberty and order? Where do we draw the line? The jurisprudence of the U.S. criminal law is constantly reevaluating the latitude law enforcement needs to ensure the safety and security of U.S. society. Should U.S. Customs be permitted to conduct body-cavity searches on the basis of reasonable suspicion in order to interdict illegal drugs? Is the threat of international terrorism worth the suspension of habeas corpus rights for those who are detained for questioning? Should law enforcement be legally able to use a person's racial or ethnic appearance as grounds for legitimate suspicion? In the pursuit of international terrorists, should the police be permitted to question Arab Americans on the basis of their ethnicity alone? In order to reduce street crime, should young African American males be subject to higher levels of suspicion on our city streets or nation's highways than other citizens?

This chapter looks at the overall structure of U.S. law enforcement and the legal boundaries that regulate the relationship between these officers of the law and the citizens they "protect and serve." Unlike countries such as Japan, China, and many Western European nations, the United States does not have a single national police force or a centralized structure of law enforcement.[13] Instead, there are there are over 17,000 different agencies, employing more than 800,000 people, responsible for the enforcement of the laws of this nation. The five major types of law enforcement agencies are municipal police departments, sheriff's departments, state police, federal law enforcement agencies, and special police forces limited to particular localities such as schools, parks, or airports. Some of these agencies are tiny, with fewer than ten officers; others are huge, complex bureaucratic organizations employing tens of thousands of police and civilian workers. Some are highly specialized, focusing only on a specific area of law enforcement, whereas others have a broad mandate to perform a wide array of functions for a particular community.

The dilemma of policing in a free society varies for different segments of the law enforcement community. At our borders, U.S. Customs agents have a narrow responsibility to protect our nation's borders and are granted greater powers to detain and search people and goods entering our borders to fulfill that responsibility. Within our borders, "calling the cops" is usually motivated by a desire for the someone with authority to solve a problem that a citizen cannot: a drunk who won't leave the restaurant, a husband who is threatening his wife, a loud party that refuses to quiet down.[14] Under appropriate circumstances police can lawfully stop citizens, ask them questions, physically restrain them, forcibly remove them, transport them against their will, deprive them of liberty, deliberately inflict pain, and even take their life. Public police have broad discretion about how to use their legal authority to respond to the myriad of problems they must deal with every day.

In all cases, however, the power held by law enforcement is not without limits, and these limits are defined by the law. A basic principle of a democratic society is that the police are accountable to use their power and perform their job within the bounds of the law. Law enforcement officers possess an awesome degree of legitimate authority to use coercive force. The distinction between *power* and *authority* is an important one. Possession of a gun gives the user "power" over others. In the exercise of power, "might makes right." **Authority** is a specific form of power characterized by a shared sense that the use of power is legitimate. In the exercise of authority, "right makes might." In a democratic society, only when police power is exercised lawfully is the use of force legitimate.[15]

THE STRUCTURE OF U.S. LAW ENFORCEMENT

The United States has the most complex law enforcement structure in the world. Most people do not think of U.S. Customs inspectors as members of law enforcement, but Inspector Talmante is one of 9,700 U.S. Customs agents, among 86,000 federal law enforcement employees who are a small subset of the approximately 920,000 employees across the land who can be found in municipal police departments, state police forces, highway patrols, county sheriff's departments, campus security, special police forces, or federal law enforcement agencies[16] (see Table 7.1).[17]

Although each agency may have its own sphere of law enforcement responsibilities, there are also overlapping responsibilities, with rivalries, competition, and territorial disputes between agencies. Different segments of policing emerged historically at different

authority: a specific form of power that is seen as legitimate by those subject to it.

TABLE 7.1

Structure of U.S. Public Law Enforcement

Federal	State	County	Local

TREASURY DEPARTMENT
Alcohol Tobacco & Firearms
Internal Revenue Service
United States Customs Service
United States Secret Service
United States Mint, Police
Federal Law Enforcement
   Training Center
	Highway patrol
	Fish and wildlife
	   agencies
	State police
	State park services
	State university police
	State bureaus
	   of investigation
	Weigh station
	   operations
	Port authorities
		County coroners
		Marine patrol agencies
		Sheriff's departments
			Municipal police
			   departments
			Campus police
			Transit police
			Coroner or medical
			   examiner
			Housing authority
			   agents

DEPARTMENT OF JUSTICE Federal Bureau of Prisons Drug Enforcement Agency Federal Bureau of Investigation United States Marshal's Office Immigration and Naturalization Service			
DEPARTMENT OF TRANSPORTATION United States Coast Guard			
U.S. POSTAL SERVICES Postal Inspections Service			

DEPARTMENT OF THE INTERIOR
United States Park Police
National Park Service
Bureau of Indian Affairs,
   Office of Law Enforcement
United States Fish and Wildlife Service,
   Division of Law Enforcement			

WASHINGTON, D.C. Metropolitan Police Department			

Source: Adapted from William A. Geller and Norval Morris, "Federal and Local Police," in Carl Klockars and Steven Mastrofski, eds., *Thinking about Police,* 2d ed. (New York: McGraw-Hill, 1992); Brian Reeves, *Federal Law Enforcement Officers* (Washington, DC: Bureau of Justice Statistics, 1997).

points in time and for different reasons. In addition to the complex structure of public law enforcement, there is also a burgeoning private security industry, which provides policing services to corporations and private individuals as a for-profit service. The number of personnel employed in the private policing industry in the year 2000 was more than double the number employed in public policing.

Local Law Enforcement

City police departments are, in a sense, the most important component of U.S. law enforcement. In 1996, the United States spent approximately $200 per capita on public policing.[18] Of those dollars spent on police protection, 72.1 percent came from local governmental coffers.[19] In 1995, over 80 percent of public police were employed by local police departments.[20] Municipalities may be large cities, small towns, or villages that are authorized to organize, hire, train, fund, and operate their own police forces. These can range vastly in size and scope: some 10,000 police departments across the country employ fewer than 10 officers; the average number of employees in a police agency was 39 in 1997.[21] At the other end of the spectrum are the large city police departments such as those of New York City, Houston, Chicago, Detroit, and Los Angeles, who employ 20,000 or 30,000 officers and a small army of civilian employees to perform such functions as crime analysis, record keeping, computer operations, communications, personnel, public relations, and legal support. Cities spend more than any other state or local unit of government for police protection.

Of all levels of law enforcement, municipal agencies have the broadest scope of authority to maintain public order within the community. The duties of the municipal police officer range from dealing with the ordinary nuisances of everyday life such as traffic control, medical emergencies, public drunkenness, and lost animals, to responding to extraordinary events of homicide, public catastrophes, and private traumas within citizens' homes. More than any other officer of the law, the police officer performs a sweeping service function for the community and therefore confronts the myriad of social problems that plague modern society. As we will see in later chapters, police officers interact closely with the life of the community and must balance often conflicting functions of crime control, service, and peacekeeping.

County Law Enforcement

The office of the sheriff is the oldest law enforcement position in the United States, brought to the colonies from England as the person appointed by the king to collect taxes, administer justice, and enforce the king's laws. Today, sheriffs are elected public officials whose agencies are responsible for law enforcement in the counties in which they function. Sheriff's departments run county jails, serve civil papers such as court-ordered liens or eviction notices, transport prisoners to and from courts,

Sheriff's departments, particularly in the South and West, are the primary law enforcement agency within the county responsible for investigation, apprehension, and enforcement of state law within the jurisdiction.

serve as the officers of the county court, and are responsible for housing detainees awaiting trial.

As an elected official (only Hawaii and Rhode Island do not hold elections for the position of sheriff), the sheriff is more politician than law enforcement professional. Sheriff's departments are also independent of civil service control and executive branch accountability. The jurisdiction of the sheriff's department is established by state law and generally circumscribed by the municipal boundaries of the cities within the county. About 90 percent of sheriff's departments have primary responsibility for criminal investigation within their jurisdiction, although in densely populated Eastern cities, they stay out of the affairs of the municipalities. In Southern and Western states, sheriff's departments are much more powerful and serve as the chief law enforcement agencies in the county.

State Police and Highway Patrols

State police departments employ about 10 percent of all public police officers.[22] The first statewide law enforcement agency was the Texas Rangers, formed in 1835. Most state police were formed in the early twentieth century in response to charges of corruption, inefficiency, and political partisanship on the part of municipal and county police. The first state to institute a modern state police force was Pennsylvania in 1905, in response to the massive coal strike of 1902. The advent of the automobile and the building of the nation's first highway in 1921 necessitated the development of a statewide police force on the nation's highways.

Today there are twenty-three state police agencies and twenty-six highway patrols in the United States. State police departments maintain law and order throughout the state, especially in regions with sparse population that are unable to afford their own police forces. State police departments generally also operate highway patrols, which regulate the state's highways but may also maintain helicopter fleets for traffic, criminal, and medical matters, and maintain forensic laboratories, narcotics divisions, fire investigation units, and auto theft divisions. California has the largest state police force, with about 11,000 full-time employees, followed by Pennsylvania with over 6,000 and New York with about 5,500 employees in 1995.[23] Highway patrols have more limited authority, focusing primarily on the regulation of traffic and limiting their activity to the patrol of state and federal highways.

Federal Law Enforcement

About 9.3 percent or 86,087 full-time sworn officers work for one of 141 federal agencies charged with enforcing more than 4,100 federal laws.[24] Federal agencies can only enforce federal laws, although they routinely assist and cooperate with state and local law enforcement. Congress has historically been reluctant to create a "superforce" or national police; most federal law enforcement agencies are highly specialized units designed to enforce particular bodies of law passed by Congress. Although there have been repeated attempts, in 1977 by President Carter and again in the late 1990s by President Clinton, to consolidate federal law enforcement, these mergers have been stymied by powerful interests seeking to maintain the autonomy and independence of each of the agencies.

The largest federal police agencies are the Immigration and Naturalization Service with 12,400 employees, the Federal Bureau of Investigation with 10,400 employees, followed by U.S. Customs with 9,700 employees and the Internal Revenue Service with 3,800 employees. The U.S. Customs and U.S. Marshals Service are the oldest, both established in 1789. See Figure 7.1 for an organization chart of the U.S. Department of Justice, showing the many agencies it includes.

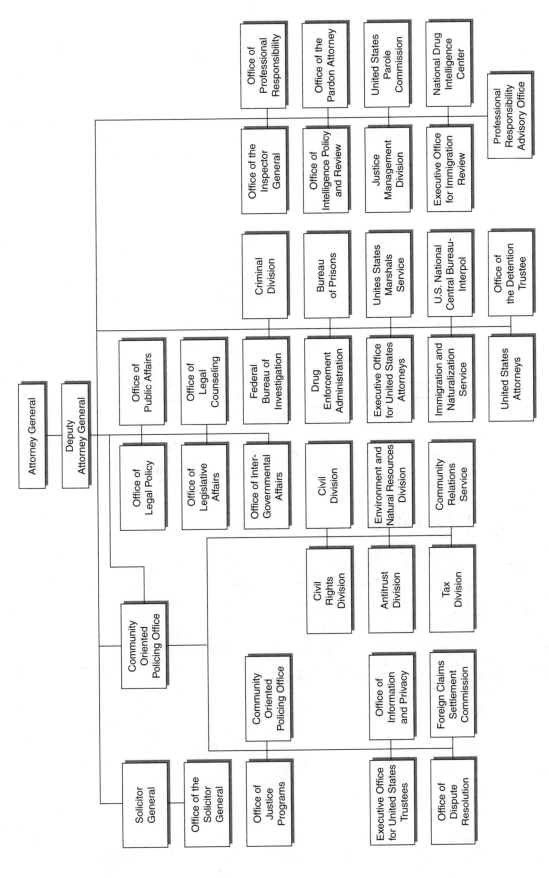

FIGURE 7.1 Organization Chart for the U.S. Department of Justice

Source: U.S. Department of Justice, www.usdoj.gov/dojorg.htm.

The Federal Bureau of Investigation (FBI) under the U.S. Department of Justice (DOJ) is probably the best-known law enforcement agency in the country and possibly in the world. It originated in 1870 as the investigative arm of the Department of Justice. In the early days, the agency hired private agents from the Pinkerton Agency or borrowed men from the Secret Service rather than hire its own agents. President Theodore Roosevelt wanted the agency to hire its own agents to enable the DOJ to enforce antitrust laws against big business, but Congress refused to authorize the President's request for a separate police force because it was fearful of creating a "secret police" that might be used to investigate members of Congress. In 1908, Congress reluctantly authorized a modest beginning when it established the Bureau of Investigation with thirty-five agents focused primarily on business and bankruptcy fraud.

The agency expanded over the years primarily by identifying "public enemies," which generated a sense of urgency that in turn pressured lawmakers to authorize growth in the agency. In 1924, J. Edgar Hoover was appointed to head the agency, a post he held until his death in 1972 at age 77. By 1935, when the name of the agency was changed to the Federal Bureau of Investigation, Hoover had transformed the agency into an elite general crime-fighting agency. He established a national fingerprint identification file, a crime laboratory, the Uniform Crime Reports, and the FBI National Academy. Hoover also created the "image" of the FBI agent as the heroic "G-man" fighting underworld mobsters, kidnappers, and bank robbers.

By the time of Hoover's death, however, the image of the FBI had been tarnished by public exposure of the surveillance activities of the FBI against lawful U.S. citizens and legitimate U.S. organizations, including members of Congress.[25] FBI harassment, infiltration, wiretapping, mail tampering, and other forms of illegal surveillance sullied the image of the elite crime-fighting unit.

Today, FBI employees staff fifty-nine field offices across the country.[26] The activities of the bureau are concentrated on white-collar crime, drug offenses, arson, civil rights violations, and violent serial offenders. The FBI operates the UCR and the National Crime Information Center, which supports law enforcement investigations across the country and around the world.

The Private Security Industry

Private police have long coexisted with public police. The first private security company was founded by Allan Pinkerton in 1850 to protect the property of the railroads and to fight on the side of businesses during a period of major industrial labor conflicts. For the most part, private security as a for-profit industry has grown to meet the needs of businesses. Major private corporations, such as Pinkerton, Wells Fargo, and Wackenhut, provide equipment and technology such as alarm systems, closed-circuit television, video cameras, electronic gates, armed couriers, bodyguards, undercover investigators, and security personnel.

Private security guards are not granted the same degree of authority as publicly sworn officers: in most states, guards cannot detain suspects or conduct searches without consent. Some states require special licenses, and some states grant security personnel the authority to make felony arrests. One key trend is the "moonlighting" of sworn public officers as private security personnel during off-duty hours, although some departments have regulations to limit the kind of employment that officers can accept.

In recent decades, the growth of the private security industry has included the provision of security for upper-income residential areas through gated communities and upscale apartment and condominium security services. Spending for private security now outstrips spending for public law enforcement by 73 percent.[27] Even the government spends more on the hiring of private labor to perform police-related functions than it does on public police.[28] The result is a privatization of security and public space as gated communities, shopping malls, and other retail spaces are closely regulated by private security, leaving public spaces more vulnerable and less secure.[29]

POLICING AND THE LAW

The right of the people to be secure in their persons, houses, papers, and effects, against unreasonable searches and seizures, shall not be violated, and no warrants shall issue, but upon probable cause, supported by oath or affirmation, and particularly describing the place to be searched and the persons or things to be seized.

The Fourth Amendment to the U.S. Constitution states that all coercive action on the part of the government against the lives, property, liberty, and privacy of individuals requires some "reasonable" grounds or evidence to justify that action. The amount of factual information depends on how coercive the action is, but the principle remains the same: to infringe on a citizen's right to be let alone, officers must have some kind of evidence that a crime has occurred or is about to occur. When officers operate outside the boundaries of the law in their efforts to enforce the law, they undermine the wider societal belief in the legitimacy of the law itself.

The **rule of thumb** for standards of proof states simply that the greater the intrusion into the individual's liberty, the greater the degree of proof required.[30] (See Table 7.2.) The Bill of Rights presumes that each citizen essentially has a basic and fundamental right to be let alone. In order to intrude upon that sphere of liberty, the state must have some kind of justification or proof.

The Pendulum Swing between Liberty and Order

Until the 1960s, the courts took a "hands-off" attitude toward enforcing the Bill of Rights in state and local law enforcement. As we saw in the Scottsboro case (see Chapter 2), despite the existence of formal rights in the Constitution, in practice, there was little attempt to enforce those rights in the daily operations of the thousands of police agencies across the land. Led by a former California prosecutor, Chief Justice Earl Warren, judicial decisions during the 1960s and 1970s established specific criteria regarding the delicate balance between liberty and order, with a tendency to place limits on the lawful power of law enforcement.[31]

In the 1980s and 1990s the Burger Court, followed by the Rehnquist Court, have shifted the balance toward the legitimate power of law enforcement to intrude upon the liberties of citizens. As we see with the decision in Rosa's case, the rationale for the expansion of police power has been based on the need to aggressively enforce the nation's drug laws. The tactics and strategies used by law enforcement to fight the war on drugs has led to a rollback in the civil liberties of the U.S. citizen. The burden of this rollback of civil liberties has fallen, as we will see later in the chapter, disproportionately on minority citizens, who are subject to routine searches and stops in their homes, on our city streets, on highways, and in airports.[32]

rule of thumb: the greater the intrusion into the liberty of an individual citizen, the greater the degree of proof required to justify that intrusion.

preponderance of the evidence: the standard for determining legal liability in civil trials, requiring a certainty of more than 50 percent of the defendant's guilt.

reasonable doubt standard: the standard of proof necessary for a conviction in criminal trials; the highest possible standard.

TABLE 7.2

Standards of Proof

Intrusion on Liberty	Level of Proof Required
Stop and frisk	Reasonable suspicion
Arrest	Probable cause
Search	Judicial affirmation of probable cause
Felony indictment	Grand jury affirmation of probable cause
Civil penalty imposed	Preponderance of the evidence
Criminal penalty imposed	Beyond a reasonable doubt

Police possess the authority to stop, question, and frisk citizens they reasonably suspect are engaged in criminal activity. Many in the minority inner-city communities believe some officers abuse this authority through selectively targeting young men of color for Terry stops.

Stop and Frisk

Where does the power of the police to intrude upon citizens' liberty begin? When citizens are walking along a city street—window shopping, for example, or simply walking down the street—can police officers stop them and ask them questions about where they are going and what they are doing? Can police legally frisk them for weapons or illegal drugs?

The ruling case regulating this aspect of police authority is *Terry* v. *Ohio*,[33] decided in 1968. In Cleveland, Ohio, Detective Martin McFadden observed two men conversing on a street corner and periodically peering into a particular store window. Convinced that they were casing the store in order to rob it, McFadden approached the men, identified himself as a police officer, asked for their names, and spun one of them, Terry, for a pat down on the outside of his clothing. The search revealed concealed weapons and the men were arrested. Both were convicted, and Terry was sentenced to one to three years in a state penitentiary. Terry appealed the conviction, arguing that Detective McFadden did not have probable cause for the arrest because the guns had been found in an illegal search. There was no reason to conduct the search in the first place, and the guns that were found should be suppressed as illegal evidence.

The U.S. Supreme Court agreed to hear the case and ruled that the detective was acting lawfully. In *Terry* v. *Ohio,* the Supreme Court established the principle that, even for a frisk, police must have some level of legitimate suspicion, which the court defined as "reasonable suspicion that a crime is afoot." The liberal Warren Court asserted that police could not simply decide to frisk a citizen arbitrarily: the Fourth Amendment applies even to the questioning and pat-down process, regardless of whether it leads to an arrest or not. Such an intrusion interferes with the basic dignity of the citizen, and like all intrusions it requires a standard of proof—albeit, a new, lower standard known as **reasonable suspicion.**

The reasonable suspicion standard, which is the basis for strip searches at our nation's airports, is an extremely open-ended standard. The courts have upheld a wide ar-

stop and frisk: technique used by police to "pat down" a person suspected of being armed or in possession of instruments of crime.

reasonable suspicion: reliable evidence that a person has been or is about to commit a crime.

ray of behaviors, such as being in a high-crime neighborhood, acting evasively toward the police, being a known gang member or drug user, or associating with a known gang member or drug user, as sufficient to justify a "Terry" stop. Although not originally intended to be used for evidentiary searches, if drugs and other forms of illegal contraband are found on a person in the course of these searches, that evidence has been ruled as acceptable to the courts.

The Basic Law of Arrest

The power to **arrest** is the power to "seize" citizens, transport them against their will, and detain them overnight. Technically, an arrest occurs whenever a person's freedom to leave is curtailed by a law enforcement officer. If a reasonable person believes that he is "not free to leave," then he has been arrested. Because Rosa was at the border, she could legally be detained without being arrested.

According to the Fourth Amendment, **probable cause** is needed to back up an arrest: probable cause are facts that would lead a reasonable officer to believe the person arrested has committed, is committing, or is about to commit a crime. If we think of proof as a continuum from a baseless suspicion at one end ("I don't like his face") to absolute certainty at the other ("I saw him do it"), probable cause is located somewhere in the middle. It is more than a mere hunch, more than "reasonable suspicion," but far less than the certainty of "beyond a reasonable doubt."

Most arrests are **warrantless arrests:** that is, they are based on the police officer's assessment that the facts are sufficient to provide probable cause that the person committed or is about to commit a crime. Information that satisfies probable cause is quite broad. Obviously, if a police officer actually sees a person committing a crime, there is sufficient probable cause. Otherwise the requirement usually allows for an overall assessment of the totality of the circumstances. Although each piece of information alone might not satisfy probable cause, when put together, they create a reasonable set of facts to justify an arrest. Facts that contribute to probable cause include physical flight by a suspect upon being approached, suspicious conduct, a tip from a reliable informant, the previous criminal record of the suspect, and physical clues such as footprints or fingerprints.

Entering a private home to arrest a person is another matter altogether and generally requires an **arrest warrant** that has been authorized by a judge or magistrate. Unless there is an emergency and the officer follows a suspect into a private residence while in "hot pursuit," the law requires officers to obtain a warrant before entering private homes to arrest suspects. Because of a long-standing tradition that protects the sanctity of the home against intrusions by the law, **judicial affirmation of probable cause** is required to knock on a person's door and place him or her under arrest.

Searches

Until 1967, the courts traditionally viewed the Fourth Amendment as protecting certain places, such as private property owned by the suspect. The right to be secure in one's own home has deep roots in Anglo-American law, harkening back to the sixteenth century when a man's home was seen as his "castle." In *Katz* v. *United States*,[34] the FBI placed a wiretap on the outside of a public telephone booth, from which Katz, a bookmaker, was conducting his illegal gambling business. The U.S. Supreme Court ruled in this case that the Fourth Amendment protects people, not places: what a person knowingly exposes in public is not protected by the Fourth Amendment, but what he seeks to keep private is. Katz's personal telephone calls, even if he was using a public phone, were protected by the Fourth Amendment, and the government should have obtained a search warrant before placing a wiretap on a public phone booth.

A **search warrant** is authorized based on the facts and circumstances that would lead a reasonable officer to believe that the places or persons searched will yield the

arrest: when a person is physically detained by an agent of the state and is not free to leave.

probable cause: facts that are reliable and generate a reasonable belief that a person has committed, is committing, or is about to commit a crime.

warrantless arrest: an arrest made without first seeking a warrant, based on probable cause and permissible under specified circumstances.

arrest warrant: a written order, based on probable cause and issued by a judge or magistrate, commanding that the person named on the warrant be arrested by the police.

judicial affirmation of probable cause: judicial review and agreement with the facts establishing probable cause for an arrest or search.

search: any governmental intrusion upon a person's reasonable expectation of privacy.

search warrant: an order issued by a judge and signed by a police officer, indicating where the search will take place and what is expected to be found in the search.

things or persons to be seized. The Fourth Amendment requires a search warrant be specific as to exactly what place is going to be searched and what is being looked for. A search warrant is not intended to give law enforcement the right to go searching for whatever illegal evidence they may find: the warrant must describe the places to be searched and state what is expected to be found there.

The warrant is generally accompanied by an affidavit or sworn statement by the officer about the facts and circumstances that make up probable cause. When the magistrate or judges issues the warrant, he or she has "affirmed" the officer's belief that there is probable cause. This was precisely what the U.S. Customs officers failed to obtain in the early stages of the search of Rosa Montoya de Hernandez, because they feared that a judge would not agree there was probable cause to do a body-cavity search and they would be required to release Rosa.

Warrantless Searches   There are a variety of circumstances in which searches are permitted without a judicial warrant. In fact, the vast majority of searches conducted by law enforcement every day are more likely to fall within these "exceptions" than those that require judicial approval.

When police arrest a suspect, they are permitted to conduct a limited search for concealed weapons or to prevent evidence from being destroyed. **Searches incident to a lawful arrest** are probably the most common kinds of police searches. The purpose of this search is to protect the safety of the arresting officers.

A **consent search** is simply one in which law enforcement asks permission and the citizen willingly agrees to allow the police to conduct the search of the citizen's person, home, or personal effects. People can, and do, voluntarily do give up their right against unreasonable searches and seizures and cooperate with a search. With consent, there is no issue of a violation of the Fourth Amendment unless the courts find that the consent was not truly voluntary. Unlike the so-called Miranda rights, police are not required to inform citizens that they have the right to withhold their consent, although it is the policy of some law enforcement agencies such as the FBI to inform suspects that they have the right to withhold their consent.

The issue of voluntariness is a critical one: do citizens really understand that they are free to say no when they are asked for their consent? Should the police be required to inform citizens that they have the right to withhold their consent, as we do in the process of informing them of their right to remain silent when they are arrested? In an airport detention, if the authorities are refusing to allow a person to leave, can we really say that their consent to an X-ray or some other procedure is "voluntary"?

We have already seen the **border exception** to the warrant requirement. In 1977 the Supreme Court ruled that all persons entering the country are subject to routine searches without probable cause.[35] Travelers entering into the country may have their luggage and persons searched by law enforcement without the need to meet a probable cause standard. Ironically, had Rosa been legally arrested, she would have been entitled to far more rights, including the right to an attorney and the right to make a phone call. The dissenting justices argued that people who are detained at the border are extraordinarily isolated and at the mercy of the law enforcement officers, who have the legal power to detain them on the barest of suspicions until they prove that they are innocent of any crime.

The **plain-view exception** states that police may lawfully seize items—weapons, stolen property, drugs—that are in plain sight, plain hearing, plain smell, or plain touch. Provided that the officers are where they have a legal right to be—for example, standing on a public sidewalk—if they can smell, hear, or see evidence of illegal material with their ordinary senses, even inside a building, the plain-view exception permits them to enter and legally seize those items. If they are using high-powered telescopes or mechanical hearing devices, this exception would not apply.

warrantless search: a search based on reasonable suspicion, made without first seeking a warrant, and permissible under specified circumstances.

searches incident to a lawful arrest: searches of persons immediately after an arrest, specifically for the purpose of seizing weapons or evidence.

consent search: warrantless search conducted when the party to the search provides voluntary and intelligent consent to law enforcement.

border exception: all persons entering the United States; citizens and noncitizens, may have their luggage and persons searched by law enforcement without probable cause.

plain-view exception: the rule that any evidence police can see or hear in plain view, when they are where they have a legal right to be, is admissible in court even without a legal warrant or probable cause.

The Fifth Amendment and the Law of Interrogation

No persons shall be held to answer for a capital or otherwise infamous crime, unless on a presentment or indictment of a Grand Jury, except in cases arising in the land or naval forces, or in the Militia, when in actual service in time of War or public danger; nor shall any person be subject for the same offence to be twice put in jeopardy of life or limb; nor shall be compelled in any criminal case to be a witness against himself, nor be deprived of life, liberty, or property, without due process of law; nor shall private property be taken for public use, without just compensation.

Interrogation has been defined by the U.S. Supreme Court as any behavior by the police "that the police should know are reasonably likely to elicit an incriminating response from the suspect." One of the central purposes of law enforcement is to gather information about the guilt of the suspect. At the same time, the Fifth Amendment states that "no person shall be compelled to be a witness against himself" in any criminal case. Freely given confessions on the part of criminal suspects are legitimate evidence in any court of law, but coerced confessions are not. Remember the suspects in the Salem witch trials (Chapter 1)? Most of them confessed to being guilty even though they were innocent, to avoid being hanged or burned at the stake. The purpose of the Fifth Amendment is to protect citizens from being intimidated into making false confessions.[36]

The first significant case to impact police interrogations was *Brown* v. *Mississippi,*[37] decided in 1936. In the investigation of the murder of a white man, the "confessions" of three black suspects were extracted by a series of physical beatings, whippings, and hangings by a rope by police interrogators. When the three finally "confessed," they were all duly convicted of murder. The convictions, which included a full disclosure of the beatings, were upheld by the Mississippi Supreme Court. The U.S. Supreme Court, however, overturned the conviction, stating that it was difficult to imagine a process of interrogation more "revolting" to a sense of justice than physical torture, terror, and beatings.

In addition to physical coercion, the U.S. Supreme court has also prohibited methods of psychological coercion used by law enforcement to induce suspects to confess. The Supreme Court ruled that defendants cannot be tricked into making a confession. If an officer tells a suspect that he will arrest the suspect's family, or the suspect will lose his job or his family will be kicked out of their apartment, the use of threat and deception renders the confession illegal.

These standards are difficult to enforce because interrogations are carried out behind closed doors, usually only with the police and suspect present. Only Minnesota and Alaska require that police record all interrogations. Otherwise, no one really knows what goes on in interrogation rooms.

The 1965 ruling in *Miranda* v. *Arizona*[38] attempted to solve this dilemma by ensuring that defendants are "read their rights" and given the opportunity to demand the presence of an attorney *before* going into the interrogation room. Ernesto Miranda was arrested on charges of suspected rape and abduction. He was positively identified by the victim and signed a confession stating that he had committed the crime. The U.S. Supreme Court overturned his conviction because he was never advised of his right to an attorney during his interrogation. In their ruling the court outlined the procedural safeguards that law enforcement must take to ensure a legal confession.

These procedures are what are now known as **Miranda rights.** As soon as law enforcement has taken a particular individual into custody, typically at the moment of the arrest, the defendant must be informed of his or her Fifth and Sixth Amendment rights. Specifically, the Miranda ruling requires that suspects be informed: (1) of their right to remain silent, (2) that anything they say can and will be used again them by the government, (3) that they have the right to have an attorney present during interrogations, and (4) if they cannot afford an attorney, the government will appoint one on their behalf.

interrogation: explicit questioning or actions by law enforcement that may elicit an incriminating statement from a suspect.

Miranda rights: Warnings that explain the rights of an arrestee, which police are required to recite at the time of arrest or before interrogation begins.

In addition, the Court has ruled that if the suspect states the desire to remain silent, the interrogation must cease at that point. If no attorney is present, the government must prove that a suspect voluntarily waived this right and the prosecution may not use the defendant's decision to remain silent as evidence against him or her at trial. Finally, any evidence obtained in interrogation that violates these procedural rules will be deemed inadmissible at trial.

The Miranda decision angered and concerned the law enforcement community, who felt that the balance had tipped way too far in favor of the rights of suspects. Law enforcement feared that in a post-Miranda world there would be few confessions and police hands would be seriously tied in obtaining voluntary confessions. Almost forty years of experience has shown, however, that Miranda has had little impact on the power of police. Miranda has not been as effective in protecting the rights of suspects as people had hoped it might be. Data show that the number of voluntary confessions is about the same today as before the Miranda ruling. The vast majority of suspects waive their rights, and many people have serious doubts that most suspects understand the significance of these rights.

The experience of Rosa Montoya de Hernandez in the backroom of an airport demonstrates the terror of being detained by the police without anyone to advocate on one's behalf. The Supreme Court recognized the profound imbalance of power when a suspect sits alone in an airless interrogation room disconnected from the outside world. Recalling the nation's experience with coerced confessions, they sought to provide protection for suspects by asserting their right to have someone present who would balance and protect the rights of the lone individual against the awesome power of the state.

The Exclusionary Rule: Putting Teeth in the Fourth and Fifth Amendments

exclusionary rule: the Constitutional prohibition of the use of illegally obtained evidence in court.

fruit of a poisonous tree doctrine: evidence obtained through other illegally obtained evidence is inadmissible because it is tainted by the illegality of the initial search, arrest, or confession.

good faith exception: exception to the exclusionary rule in which evidence obtained by police acting in good faith with a search warrant issued by a judge is admissible even though the warrant is ultimately found to be invalid.

In Chapter 1 we referred to the Constitution as a "sleeping beauty," whose power was "awakened" hundreds of years later by the interpretation of Supreme Court justices. The impact of court rulings on the day-to-day conduct of the police requires some kind of enforcement mechanism. That mechanism is the **exclusionary rule,** which bars the use of illegally seized evidence in court proceedings. The **fruit of a poisoned tree doctrine** states that any evidence derived from an illegal search should also be excluded as evidence. Once one step in the process is determined to be an illegal violation of due process rights, all subsequent parts of the investigation are also "tainted" by the violation and are inadmissable in court.

Mapp v. *Ohio*[39] made the exclusionary principle applicable to criminal prosecution at the state level. In Cleveland, Ohio, Dolree Mapp was suspected of harboring a fugitive wanted in a bombing. When Ohio police officers arrived, Mapp demanded to see their search warrant and refused them entry. They waved a piece of paper at her which was not a warrant and proceeded to force their way in to search her apartment. They found pornographic materials and charged and convicted Mapp with possession of obscene materials. In 1961 the U.S. Supreme Court overturned her conviction under the Fourteenth Amendment principle that no state shall "deprive any person of life, liberty, or property, without due process of law; nor deny to any person within its jurisdiction the equal protection of the laws."

The point of the exclusionary rule is to force police to obey the laws of the Constitution in the investigation, searches, and interrogations. In theory, the threat that evidence will be excluded and cases will fall apart should make police more concerned and careful about following legal procedure in how they conduct their investigations.

Recent decades have relaxed the impact of the exclusionary rule by creating what is called the **good faith exception** for cases in which police conduct illegal searches through honest error rather than intentional action. In *Leon* v. *United States,*[40] the

Supreme Court conceded that the magistrate had been wrong to issue the search warrant, but they reasoned that the police were acting in good faith in conducting the subsequent search and whatever was found at that time was admissible in court. The good faith exception to the exclusionary rule has emerged as a major avenue for police to continue to submit evidence even when significant errors are made, as long as it can be shown that these errors were not intentional.[41]

Debating the Issue of Racial Profiling

The practice of **racial profiling** refers to the use of race or other group characteristics, such as ethnicity or gender, as part of the criteria which make up "reasonable suspicion that crime is afoot." Group characteristics such as race, ethnicity, or gender are often empirically associated with the commission of crime. In theory, the use of race as part of a profile is a "neutral" practice, since any ethnicity or racial group may be part of a particular empirical pattern of criminal behavior. When U.S. Customs identified Rosa as a potential suspect for more careful investigation because she was a Colombian woman, they were using her ethnicity and gender as part of a pattern that indicated reasonable suspicion.

In a society that values equal rights for all its citizens, basic fairness requires that restrictions of liberty be equally distributed among all citizens. The equal protection clause of the Fourteenth Amendment states that no one should be deprived of equal protection of the law based on race, gender, religion, or ethnicity: the trade-off between liberty and crime control should be the same for all groups in U.S. society. The dilemma raised by racial profiling is the question of equality: Are some segments of U.S. society (minority citizens, but especially young African American males) subject to significantly fewer civil liberties than those enjoyed by other Americans and guaranteed by the Constitution?

Defenders of racial profiling believe that group characteristics such as race and ethnicity, when used properly, are legitimate and effective tools of law enforcement. Los Angeles Police Department Chief Bernard Parks, himself an African American, gives the following example in support of the use of profiling as a legitimate tool for law enforcement.[42] In the city of Los Angeles, there is a problem in some neighborhoods of violent crime against jewelry salespeople. The predominant suspects in these crimes are Colombians. Police have not found Mexican Americans, African Americans, or Anglos to be involved in the commission of this particular pattern of criminal activity in this local area. Parks believes that if police officers see six Colombians milling about in front of the Jewelry Mart, the officers should have reasonable suspicion to stop and question them.

Using this logic, the courts have ruled that law enforcement may use race and ethnicity as legitimate criteria as part of a criminal profile, as long as race or ethnicity are not the sole criteria used. In the decision to subject Rosa to a strip search, her ethnicity as a Colombian woman was only one element of suspicion, along with her travel plans, her method of purchasing her ticket, her past travel pattern, and so forth. Used in concert with other factors, the courts claim that race is a legitimate tool in the detection of crime. According to the courts, the fact that crime is committed disproportionately by specific racial or ethnic groups within society is simply an unpleasant fact that cannot be ignored. "We wish it were otherwise, but we take the facts as they are presented to us, not as we would like them to be."[43]

Critics of racial profiling argue that racial profiling unfairly targets the vast majority of minorities who are innocent, law-abiding citizens and subjects them to unfair and excessive police scrutiny. They argue that the courts underestimate the harm that results when our legal system says it is legal for police to be suspicious of citizens merely because they are black, Mexican American, or Colombian. The courts

racial profiling: the use of a group characteristic such as race, gender, or ethnicity as part of the evidence constituting reasonable suspicion that a crime has occurred.

claim that stopping and questioning a person on the highway or briefly detaining a traveler entering the country for questioning is "quite limited" in its intrusiveness. But, according to critics, to put someone under a cloud of generalized suspicion from law enforcement simply on the basis of race or ethnicity is a profound intrusion on a person's civil liberties.

When racial profiling is widely used, being stopped and questioned by the police is not a one-time event for minority citizens as it may be for a white citizen.[44] And it won't matter if they are innocent of any wrongdoing when they are stopped and questioned by the police, because the next time they are driving down the highway or walking down the street, a different police officer may stop them and question them, not because of what they are doing or not doing but because of their race. Critics argue that even if race and ethnicity are useful as tools of law enforcement, profiling comes at the cost of alienating the minority community, who come to resent and distrust the justice system.

After the terrorist attacks of September 11, 2001, the debate about racial profiling shifted from African Americans to the targeting of Arab Americans for police investigation and suspicion. Despite the earlier bombing beneath the World Trade Center in 1993, the Oklahoma City bombing in 1995, and the pipe bomb at the Olympic Games in Atlanta in 1996, the threat of violent terrorism on U.S. soil was not on the forefront of most citizens' minds until the catastrophic strikes on the World Trade Center and Pentagon, which caused the death of more than three thousand people. In the aftermath of the crisis, fear of violent terrorism led to the erosion of Constitutional protections of civil liberties for more than 20 million alien residents living in the United States and for thousands of Arab Americans who fit the physical profile of a terrorist. For some, the use of ethnicity as part of a profile of reasonable suspicion is sensible given the magnitude of the threat and what is known about previous terrorist profiles. For others, reliance on ethnic and racial characteristics by law enforcement undermines the values of U.S. society and threatens the foundation of U.S. justice as a system of equality for all.

KEY TERMS

authority p. 133
rule of thumb p. 139
preponderance of the
   evidence p. 139
reasonable doubt
   standard p. 139
stop and frisk p. 140
reasonable suspicion p. 140
arrest p. 141
probable cause p. 141

warrantless arrest p. 141
arrest warrant p. 141
judicial affirmation of probable
   cause p. 141
search p. 141
search warrant p. 141
warrantless search p. 142
searches incident to a lawful
   arrest p. 142
consent search p. 142

border exception p. 142
plain-view exception p. 142
interrogation p. 143
Miranda rights p. 143
exclusionary rule p. 144
fruit of a poisonous tree
   doctrine p. 144
good faith exception p. 144
racial profiling p. 145

REVIEW AND STUDY QUESTIONS

1. Describe the "dilemma" of policing in our society? Why is this a dilemma for societies that value the individual's right to be let alone?
2. Define the concept of authority. How is it different from power? Explain the difference between the exercise of authority and the use of power by police.

3. Describe the structure of U.S. law enforcement. Where are most police personnel employed?
4. What is the rule of thumb that guides police use of coercive force?
5. What is the proof needed to stop and frisk? What is the proof required for an arrest?

6. What is a warrantless search? Describe those circumstances when a warrantless search is legally permissible.

7. What is the ruling that established the exclusionary rule? What is the exclusionary rule, and what is its intended purpose in our legal system?

8. What are the Miranda rights? Describe the ruling that established the Miranda rules. Explain the purpose of the Miranda ruling. Explain the purpose of the Fifth Amendment and why Miranda is an important protection for the privilege against self-incrimination.

9. What is racial profiling? Give examples of racial profiling in contemporary law enforcement.

10. Outline the arguments for and against racial profiling. In your view, is racial profiling a legitimate law enforcement tool? Why or why not?

CHECK IT OUT

On the Web

Landmark Supreme Court Cases, **www.landmarkcases.org**
Go to this Web site and click on Mapp v. Ohio *and* Miranda v. Arizona *to read summaries of the cases and the majority and minority Supreme Court opinions.*

Directory of Law Enforcement Agencies, **www.officer.com**
Calling itself the most popular law enforcement Web site, this site offers an on-line directory for links to federal, state, and local agencies. Click on your state and city to view the Web page for your local law enforcement agency. Check out the Web sites for the federal law enforcement agencies too.

FBI Home Page, **www.fbi.gov**
The official Web site of the FBI, with links to crime information, data, and other law enforcement agencies.

Drug Enforcement Administration (DEA), **www.usdoj. gov/dea/index.htm**
Click onto this Web site to learn more about drugs, drug policy, and strategies of federal drug law enforcement.

Traffic Stop Data Collection Policies for State Police, 2001, **www.ojp.usdoj.gov/bjs/abstract/ tsdcp01.htm**
This report presents findings from the 2001 State Police Traffic Stop Data Collection Procedures. State police agencies were asked to report on their policies and procedures for collecting race and ethnicity data regarding motorists involved in traffic stops.

On Film

Racial Profiling and Law Enforcement: America in Black and White (41 minutes)
ABC news anchor Ted Koppel and correspondent Michel McQueen look at the issue of "driving while black" from the victims' viewpoint and then from the viewpoint of the law enforcement authorities. Available from Films for the Humanities and Sciences, **www.films.com.**

NOTES

1. Nelson Erik-Lars, "Changing the Profile at Customs," *Daily News* (New York), October 15, 2000, p. 43.
2. *Montoya de Hernandez* v. *United States,* 473 U.S. 531; 105 St. Ct. 3304 (1986) 546.
3. Ibid, p. 547.
4. *Montoya de Hernandez* v. *United States,* 731 F2d 1369 (1984) U.S. App. LEXIS 23221.
5. Ibid.
6. *Montoya de Hernandez* v. *United States,* 473 U.S. 531; 105 St. Ct. 3304 (1986) 549.
7. Ibid.
8. Ibid.
9. Lisa Bekin, "Airport Drug Efforts Snaring Innocents Who Fit 'Profiles'," *New York Times,* March 20, 1990, p. A-1.
10. U.S. General Accounting Office, "U.S. Customs Service: Better Targeting of Airline Passengers for Personal Searches Could Produce Better Results," GAO/GGD-00-38, March 2000.
11. Harris Cathy, *Flying While Black: A Whistleblower's Story* (Los Angeles: Milligan, 2001).
12. Herman Goldstein, *Policing in a Free Society* (Cambridge, MA: Ballinger, 1977).
13. Obi N. Ignatius Ebbe, *Comparative and International Criminal Justice Systems: Policing, Judiciary and Corrections* (Boston: Butterworth Heinemann, 1996); David H. Bayley, *Forces of Order: Police Behavior in Japan and the United States* (Berkeley, CA: University of California Press, 1976).
14. Egon Bittner, *The Functions of the Police in Modern Society: A Review of Background Factors, Current Practices and Possible Role Models* (Chevy Chase, MD: National Institute of Mental Health, 1970).
15. Jerome H. Skolnick and Jame J. Fyfe, *Above the Law: Police and the Excessive Use of Force* (New York: Free Press, 1993).
16. Ann L. Pastore and Katherine Maguire, *Sourcebook of Criminal Justice Statistics, 1999* (Washington, DC: U.S. Government Printing Office, 2000), p. 25.
17. William Cunningham, J. Strauchs, and Clifford W. Van-Meter, *The Hallcrest Report II: Private Security Trends 1990–2000* (Boston: Butterworth-Heinemann, 1990).

18. Pastore and Maguire, eds., *Sourcebook of Criminal Justice Statistics, 1999*, p. 10.
19. Ibid., p. 4.
20. Ibid., p. 18.
21. Ibid., p. 38.
22. Ibid.
23. Ibid., pp. 26–30.
24. Ibid., p. 25.
25. Tony Poveda, *Lawlessness and Reform: The FBI in Transition* (Pacific Grove, CA: Brooks/Cole, 1990).
26. William A. Geller and Norval Morris, "Federal and Local Police," in Michael Tonry and Norval Morris, eds., *Modern Policing* (Chicago: University of Chicago Press, 1992), pp. 231–348.
27. Bureau of Justice Statistics, *Private Security: Patterns and Trends* (Washington, DC: National Institute of Justice, 1991).
28. Marcia Chaiken and Jan Chaiken, *Public Policing—Privately Provided* (Washington, DC: National Institute of Justice, 1987).
29. Clifford D. Shearing and Philip C. Stenning, eds., *Private Policing* (Newbury Park, CA: Sage, 1987).
30. Wayne R. LaFave and Jerold H. Israel, *Criminal Procedure* (St Paul, MN: West, 1985).
31. Criminal Law Reporter, eds. *The Criminal Law Revolution and Its Aftermath (1960–1977)* (Washington, DC: Bureau of National Affairs, 1972).
32. David Cole, *No Equal Justice: Race and Class in the American Criminal Justice System* (New York: New Press, 1999), p. 218.
33. *Terry* v. *Ohio*, 392 U.S. 1 (1968).
34. *Katz* v. *United States*, 389 U.S. 347 (1967).
35. *Ramsey* v. *United States*, 431 U.S. 606 (1977).
36. Leonard W. Levy, *Origins of the Fifth Amendment: The Right against Self-incrimination* (New York: Oxford University Press, 1968).
37. *Brown* v. *Mississippi*, 297 U.S. 278 (1936).
38. *Miranda* v. *Arizona*, 384 U.S. 436 (1966).
39. *Mapp* v. *Ohio*, 367 U.S. 643 (1961).
40. *Leon* v. *United States,* 468 U.S. (1984) 104 St. Ct. 3405.
41. William J. Mertens and Silas Wasserstrom, "The Good Faith Exception to the Exclusionary Rule: Deregulating the Police and Derailing the Law," *Georgetown Law Journal 70*, pp. 365–466 (1981).
42. Randall Kennedy, "Racial Profiling Usually Isn't Racist: It Can Help Stop Crime and It Should Be Abolished," *The New Republic*, September 13, 1999, p. 30.
43. *Weaver* v. *United States,* 960 F2d 391 (CA8, 1992).
44. Kennedy, "Racial Profiling." p. 33.

C A S E

150

midnight
for a
his

CASE 8

The Thin Blue Line: Rodney King and the LAPD

From George Holliday 3 1991

THE VIDEOTAPE THAT STARTED IT ALL

Most people today recognize the name Rodney King and know that the acquittal of the four Los Angeles Police Department (LAPD) officers who were videotaped beating him sparked four days of some of the worst rioting in our nation's history. Most people also recall King's eloquent plea, "People . . . can we all get along?,"[1] broadcast over the nation's airwaves in an attempt to stop the violence. But no one would have heard of Rodney King or even known of his beating if it had not been for George Holliday, who captured the incident on video and supplied his tape to the local news station the following Monday morning. The video was aired for the first time that night on the local evening news, picked up by CNN, and broadcast nationwide by early Tuesday morning. By Wednesday, the videotape had become an international news sensation broadcasting the "truth" about police brutality against African Americans.

On March 3, 1991, George Holliday was awakened by the sound of police sirens and the whirr of a police helicopter hovering above his apartment. Holliday stood out on his second-floor balcony and saw a ring of police cars surrounding a large black man with his hands on the roof of a white Hyundai. He grabbed his new camcorder, which was fully loaded and ready to be used the next morning at the LA marathon, and began to tape the next nine minutes and twenty seconds of action in the street below.

The first thirteen seconds of the tape were somewhat blurry as Holliday shifted his position to get a better view. Later, these crucial seconds would be edited out of the version aired on the local television news station, only to reappear when the tape was shown as evidence in the trial of the four police officers. Those thirteen seconds, along with the full nine minutes and twenty seconds of the entire tape, would be painstakingly analyzed and viewed by the jury. Widely seen as the best evidence for the prosecution of the officers, the tape would come to serve as a key piece of evidence for the defense as well.[2]

WHAT HAPPENED THAT NIGHT[3]

The incident actually began far from the corner outside the Lake View Terrace apartments. On the evening of March 2, Rodney King was watching basketball and drinking malt liquor in the home of his childhood friend, Bryant Allen, and Allen's friend Freddie Helms. No one can remember why the three decided to go out for a drive, but a little past they got into King's Hyundai and headed park where King used to go night fishing with father. King sped along Interstate 210 singing to loud music on the radio while Helms fell asleep in the front seat. Allen, alone in the back seat, saw the headlights of a California Highway Patrol car and heard its sirens as it clocked the speeding vehicle at 80 miles per hour. Later Allen would testify that King seemed just to get "stuck" on driving and ignored the sirens and his pleas to stop. King testified at the federal trial in 1993 that he knew a DUI conviction would automatically revoke his parole. "I was scared of going back to prison and I just kind of thought the problem would just go away."[4]

Melanie and Tim Singer, both California Highway Patrol officers, were partners in work and marriage. At 12:30 a.m. on March 3, Melanie Singer began a high-speed, 7.8-mile pursuit of King's speeding vehicle. Ignoring the flashing lights and sirens of the patrol car, King went faster, reaching speeds of nearly 115 miles per hour on the freeway and continuing at speeds of 80 to 85 miles per hour on the residential streets. Tim Singer radioed for help, and they were soon joined by a car from the Los Angeles Unified School District and several LAPD patrol cars. King ran a red light at the intersection of Van Nuys and Foothill Boulevard and came to a halt near the entrance to Hansen Dam Park, blocked by a pickup truck that had pulled over when the driver heard the approaching sirens. The Hyundai was now surrounded by five patrol cars including three LAPD cars, while an LAPD helicopter hovered overhead shining a spotlight down on the scene.

One LAPD car held Officers Lawrence Powell and Timothy Wind; the other, Officers Theodore Briseno and Rolando Solano. Seargent Stacy Koon arrived in the third car alone. The LAPD officers drew their guns and took cover behind the car doors. More cars arrived, and by the end of the incident there were twenty-five law enforcement officers on the scene, including fourteen LAPD officers. These officers became known as "bystander" officers: none assisted in the arrest, and none took any action to stop or interfere with the arrest.

Using a hand-held microphone, Tim Singer ordered the occupants of the car to get out and surrender. Realizing they could not hear him over the din of the helicopter and other noise, Singer left his car and verbally shouted commands to the car occupants. Allen and Helms complied, but King remained in the driver's seat. Tim Singer began to handcuff the two on the ground while Melanie Singer continued to order King verbally to get out the car.

King slowly began to emerge, struggling with his seatbelt, smiling at the officers, waving at the heli-copter overhead. King did a little dance, talked gibberish, and went down on his hands and knees patting the ground. Sergeant Koon was in his car preparing an electric stun gun known as a Tazer to subdue King, who appeared to be drunk or on drugs and was clearly not cooperating. Melanie Singer continued to shout at King to put his hands where she could see them and lie down on the ground. King made another strange gesture, putting his hands on his buttocks and shaking them in the officer's direction. Singer continued to repeat her orders and King finally complied by placing his hands on the roof of the car. At this point, Singer drew her gun and began to approach King, gun in hand, in order to cuff him. When she was 5 or 6 feet away, she heard Sergeant Stacy Koon order her to "Stand back. Stand back. We'll handle this." Looking back, Singer saw the stripes on his uniform and, respecting rank, relinquished the arrest to the LAPD.

According to Koon, LAPD training teaches officers never to approach a suspect resisting arrest with a drawn gun, a dangerous move that gives the suspect a chance to wrestle the gun away from the officer. Koon ordered all his officers to return their guns to their holsters and then ordered Powell, Briseno, Wind, and Solano to "swarm" King by jumping on his back while trying to cuff King at the same time, but King pushed them off his back with a powerful gesture that allegedly frightened the officers. The officers later testified that King was an extremely large and powerful man, clearly "buffed out," most likely from a stay in prison, whom they believed to be high on PCP, a drug that made him "immune" to pain and "like a monster."

Koon shot the Tazer at King twice, hitting him first in the chest and then in the back. King groaned and collapsed but once more rose to his feet. Facing Powell with his arms outstretched, in Powell's recollection, King "charged him." King would later testify that because he was in tremendous pain from the Tazer shots, he had it in his mind to "run toward the hills, the park area," and he ran in the direction of Powell with his hands up in the air so the officers could see he did not have a gun and would not shoot him. From down on the ground, a man's voice, probably Allen's, can be heard on the tape saying, "You're gonna get shot, you're gonna get shot."[5]

It was exactly at the point that King rushed toward Powell with his arms in the air that George Holliday began shooting with his video camera. The first three seconds captured that precise movement, but the next ten seconds were blurry as Holliday jostled the camera to get into a good position. The remaining tape captured the next eighty seconds, during which Rodney King was hit in the face with a metal baton, collapsed on the ground, and was beaten by batons and kicks until he cried out "Please stop" and was handcuffed by Officer Powell. What the tape shows, and what the public saw over and over again, was three officers kicking and beating a man clearly on the ground surrounded by almost twenty-five law enforcement officers including a helicopter hovering overhead, who stood by and watched.

King passed out from the beating and awoke in the ambulance on the way to the hospital. Holliday's videotape showed the LAPD had double-handcuffed him and hogtied him by fastening the cords from his feet to his hands. They dragged the unconscious King to the car with his face on the ground. King suffered a broken cheekbone, multiple fractures on the right side of his face, lacerations on his forehead, a fracture of his right leg, and multiple bruises and abrasions on his torso and legs. King recalled feeling like a "crushed can."[6] Although no one can say with absolute certainty, it is estimated that in less than a minute and a half King was hit with the metal batons more than thirty-one times.

THE IMPACT OF THE VIDEOTAPE

Holliday's first response on Sunday morning was to call the Foothills Police Station and tell them about the videotape, but they were not interested in the tape. Next, Holliday phoned CNN's Los Angeles bureau, but no one was there to take his call. On Monday morning, Holliday took the tape down to the local news station, which immediately viewed the tape and then edited it for the evening news. Out of courtesy, the news station sent a copy to LAPD headquarters and gave them notice it would be aired on the evening news.

The fallout from the showing of the videotape was immediate and explosive. On March 5, the FBI opened an investigation, Chief Daryl Gates, head of the LAPD, pledged an inquiry, and Los Angeles Mayor Tom Bradley announced that appropriate action would be taken against the officers. On March 6 Rodney King was released from jail, with district attorney Ira Reiner stating that there was insufficient evidence to prosecute him. On March 7 Gates informed the public that the officers involved would be prosecuted. By March 8, fifteen officers who were on the scene were suspended and the DA convened a grand jury to seek indictments against several officers. The American Civil Liberties Union (ACLU) took out a full-page ad in the LA *Times* targeting Daryl Gates and demanding that he be fired. The ad blazoned the question: "Who do you call when the gang wears a blue uniform?" The mayor of Los Angeles immediately ordered a high-level independent investigation of the LAPD, to be headed by Warren Christopher, which swiftly echoed the mayor's demand for Gates's resignation.[8]

THE CRIMINAL PROSECUTION

Four LAPD officers were indicted by a grand jury on a total of eleven felony charges. Sergeant Koon, Officers Lawrence Powell, Timothy Wind, and Theodore Briseno were all accused of assault with a deadly weapon and assault under the color of authority. Koon and Powell were also charged with filing false police reports, because in the subsequent reports there had been no mention of the blows to Rodney King's head nor that he was lying on the ground for most of the time he was being beaten.

Lawrence Powell was in the most serious trouble: he was shown on the tape hitting Rodney King more than twenty times. There was also evidence that afterward he had gloated about the incident and evidence that he openly expressed racist opinions about blacks. Sergeant Koon never touched King except to fire the Tazer, but as the supervising officer he was responsible for the actions of the officers and had accepted responsibility, claiming the incident was a "controlled and managed use of force" within the bounds of LAPD policy and the law.[9] Officer Theodore Briseno was shown on the tape taking only one action that was potentially criminal: at one point, Briseno stomped King in the neck area. Briseno claimed he did this in order to protect King from blows coming from Powell's baton. Briseno believed that Powell was out of control, and his actions were designed to get King to stay down so that Powell would stop hitting him with the metal baton. Finally, Timothy Wind, a new recruit to the LAPD, was the least criminally liable as shown on the tape: he had used his baton to hit King, but only on his legs and torso.

THE CHANGE OF VENUE

In retrospect, many observers believe the crucial battle between the prosecution and the defense occurred long before the spectacle of the trial. The Fifth Amendment gives criminal defendants the right to be "tried by a jury of their peers and in the place where the crime was committed." Defendants, however, have the right to request moving the location of the trial if they can demonstrate they will not receive a fair trial in the place where the crime was committed because the jury, selected from that location, will not be fair minded. Defense attorneys claimed that constant airing of the videotapes and the publicity concerning the findings of the Christopher Commission made it impossible for their clients to receive a fair trial in any courtroom in Los Angeles County.

Requests for a *change of venue* are rarely honored in the California courts: only two had been granted in the previous twenty-five years. The judge refused the defense motion, agreeing with the prosecution that the King beating was so well known that there was nowhere it could be moved where it would be insulated from the worldwide publicity given the infamous videotape. The appellate court panel disagreed, however, citing the intense political nature of the case and in a decision that shocked the prosecution, ordered the change, with the precise location of the trial to be selected by the trial judge.

It was the precise location chosen by the trial judge, Stanley Weisburg, that most likely affected the outcome of the trial. For reasons no one quite understands (although many suspect it had to do with proximity to his own home), Weisburg chose a brand-new courtroom in the sunny city of Simi Valley, located 60 miles northwest of downtown LA, and home to thousands of LAPD officers who commute each day from the safe streets of quiet suburbia to work the gritty streets of central Los Angeles. The selection shocked prosecutors and delighted the defense. Weisburg could not have selected a more favorable location for finding jurors likely to be sympathetic to the defense. In 1991, only 1.5 percent of the population of Simi Valley was African American.[10]

Of the seven men and five women chosen to serve on the jury all were white except for one Latino and one Asian; all were middle class; all had law enforcement backgrounds or connections; they were an average age of 55; and all shared very positive attitudes about the police in general and the LAPD in particular. The jury was seated on March 2, 1992, just one day before the anniversary of the beating of Rodney King.

THE TRIAL

The most critical piece of evidence in the trial was clearly the videotape. If it were not for that objective record, it is likely that no one would ever have known about what happened to Rodney King. He might have filed a civil suit, but he was too drunk to remember, and in most of these kinds of cases, pitting the word of LAPD officers against that of complaining citizens, especially those with a criminal record, is a lost cause. The videotape provided an objective and permanent record. Most people believed the trial would be an open-and-shut case. The images spoke for themselves: this was the use of excessive force by white officers against a defenseless black man cowering and lying on the ground.

But the most powerful piece of evidence for the prosecution turned out to be the most powerful piece of evidence for the defense. One of the reasons was the missing thirteen seconds, which had been edited out of the original media version aired by station KVTA on its first showing the evening of March 3. The first three seconds show Rodney King upright and moving toward Lawrence Powell. The defense claimed that King was "charging" Powell, which justified self-defensive force on his part. Unlike the version that began with King on the ground, the jury was shown the full eighty-three seconds of tape to support the defense argument that the officers were responding to aggressive actions by King himself.

THE PROSECUTION'S CASE: OUT OF CONTROL AND EXCESSIVE

The prosecution's case centered upon urging the jury to "trust your eyes" and believe what you see on the videotape. The lead prosecutor, Terry White, did not deny that King had led the officers on a high-speed chase, or that he was drunk, or that he did, at first, resist arrest. White hammered home the point that what we see on the videotape is the excessive use of force. Powell, in particular, was "out of control," hitting Rodney King in the face and head, continuing to beat him even after he was on the ground and lying still. White presented eyewitness testimony from Melanie and Tim Singer, the only two law enforcement officers on the scene that night who testified for the prosecution, who saw Powell hit King in the face, in their opinion an unauthorized and excessive use of force. The prosecution presented evidence of the reports filed by Koon and Powell, which failed to portray what happened accurately, claiming that King was upright and resisting arrest, that they successfully "swarmed" him to cuff him rather than beat him incessantly while he was lying on the ground.

The prosecution's case included testimony from emergency room doctors and nurses about the extent of King's injuries and the taunting attitude displayed by Powell and other officers in the emergency room. In addition, there were computer messages and other LAPD communications from Powell boasting about the incident. Less than twenty minutes after the beating, Powell radioed a partner, claiming, "I haven't beaten anybody this bad in a long time." And short bursts of laughter erupt on the tape from an excited Powell as he calls for an ambulance to come to the scene.

The prosecution rested its case without calling Rodney King himself to the stand. The decision was hard for the team to make: they knew the jury would want to hear from King himself and that the jury needed to see him as a human being rather than the huge monster portrayed by the defense. But they feared King would lose his temper on the stand and appear unsympathetic to an all-white, middle-class jury. They were also concerned that King's recollection of the facts that night kept shifting and that he was not always truthful about what happened. At first King did not recall any racial slurs and then he did; at first he said he was not speeding and then he admitted that he was. Worried that King could do more damage than good, the prosecution announced it would not call Rodney King. Many in the media interpreted this decision as a signal of the confidence of the prosecutorial team in the quality of the evidence presented thus far. Most people outside the courtroom assumed that the videotape was so damning it was not necessary to put King on the stand.

THE DEFENSE'S CASE: THE "REASONABLE OFFICER" AND THE THIN BLUE LINE

There were four separate defense attorneys representing each of the four defendants. Requests for separate trials had been denied early in the process. The key defense strategy shared by three of the four defendants was simple: the officers had acted based on the "reasonable" perception that King was a dangerous felony suspect; on the "reasonable" perception that he was on PCP and therefore extremely aggressive and immune to pain; and on the "reasonable" perception that he was potentially dangerous because he had not been searched and might be armed.

According to the defense, it was Rodney King who was "in control" of events that night. The officers were reacting professionally and responsibly to his conduct: it was his choice to get drunk, to lead law enforcement on a high-speed chase, to refuse to pull over, to resist the lawful attempt by officers to cuff him and arrest him. If he had simply obeyed commands as Allen and Hymes did, there would have been no need for the use of force. The force that was used was reasonable, necessary, and in compliance with their training and LAPD policy.

Koon, as supervising officer, testified that he was completely in control of his officers that night and that their conduct was consistent with LAPD policy on how to subdue a combative and aggressive suspect. Koon openly acknowledged that the incident was brutal and violent but admitted that, at times, police work is brutal and violent. He reiterated his position that his main motive that night was to place King under arrest without the use of lethal violence. He followed his training, ordering his officers to holster their weapons, to use the "swarm"

technique, to use the Tazer and their metal batons. All of these actions were executed in a "managed and controlled" manner with the goal of subduing King. As soon as King went into "compliance mode," the violence stopped.

Lawrence Powell was the defendant with the most physical brutality and unprofessional conduct to explain and justify. He testified in his own defense about his state of mind that night. Like the other officers, he believed King was on PCP and therefore immune to pain, oblivious to instruction, and capable of extreme violence. He had also experienced King's great physical strength and observed his strange behavior. Powell claimed he was "terrified" and "in fear of his life," believing that King might rush him, overpower him, and grab his weapon.

It was with that state of mind that Powell, acting in self-defense, struck King above the neck. According to LAPD policy and the law, the only time that baton blows to the head are permissible is for the purpose of self-defense. Powell's attorney, Michael Stone, also argued that the injuries on Rodney King's face were caused by a fall to the pavement rather than by blows from Powell's baton. As part of his defense, Stone presented medical testimony that asserted it was possible that the fall caused Kings injuries, and upon cross-examination of the prosecution medical experts, Stone got them to admit that they could not be absolutely certain the injuries were caused by Powell rather than the fall.

POLICE SOLIDARITY FOR THE DEFENSE

A central part of the defense strategy was to use LAPD experts to analyze the videotape frame by frame and show that actions of the officers were in accordance with the policies of the LAPD. The jury saw the videotape dissected over and over. The defense put on three expert witnesses, all of whom testified that in their expert opinion this was a controlled and managed use of force. The star witness for the defense was LAPD use of force expert Charles Duke, who explained that it was LAPD policy to have officers use batons to subdue a suspect resisting arrest. He confirmed Koon's testimony that Koon had appropriately chosen to use the Tazer and ordered his officers to use batons rather than point a gun at King. The defense claimed that Koon's professional police work most likely saved Rodney King's life (or, possibly, the life of another officer on the scene), who was at extreme risk of being shot and killed if guns had been used.

The prosecution, too, put a use of force expert on the stand to argue that this was not a legitimate use of force, but his credentials and testimony were weak compared to the experts who testified for the defense. The prosecution had tremendous difficulty finding a use of force expert who would testify against the LAPD officers, despite the fact that many experts agreed that the use of force on the videotape was excessive. In the months leading up to the trial, the prosecution searched in vain for someone from the LAPD willing to testify. Even nationally recognized experts from other police departments or in the private sector refused to testify in this case. Three experts finally agreed, but all three backed out before the trial. Although each privately believed this was excessive force, none was willing to say so at the most notorious police trial of the century. Even Chief Daryl Gates, fearing personal liability, refused to testify at the trial despite his forthright statements in the media.

The prosecution tried to recruit an LAPD sergeant, Fred Nichols, who was in charge of the physical training and self-defense section of the LAPD Police Academy at the time of the incident.[11] Nichols had testified before the Christopher Commission that he believed the officers had used excessive force. He told this to Internal Affairs officers and to the grand jury that indicted the four officers. But by the time of the trial, Nichols had lost his job at the Police Academy and had been reassigned to a desk job. Out on "stress leave," he wanted nothing to do with the King case. The DA's office subpoenaed him but he fought the subpoena, claiming he was suffering from a stress-related disability. In a hearing before the judge, the prosecution claimed that Nichols was lying to get out of testifying. The judge ruled that the prosecution could not prove this and excused him. Later Nichols explained that he knew it looked like he was inventing a story to avoid testifying but said, "To be honest with you, I'm not concerned about appearance. I'm concerned about my well-being."[12]

Fourteen officers who were "bystanders" that night all testified for the defense. The only eye witnesses to testify for the prosecution were the California Highway Patrol officers, Melanie and Tim Singer. Each and every one of the officers who witnessed the scene testified that, in their opinion, the actions of the officers that night were "reasonable" under the circumstances. None of the officers would "break ranks" and condemn the actions of their fellow officers that night.

BENEDICT BRISENO

Only one officer crossed the line of solidarity and many believed he did so only to protect himself from criminal prosecution. Officer Theodore Briseno, a thirteen-year veteran, was charged with excessive use of force for a single stomp to King's neck with his boot. On the night of the incident, Briseno had complained to his partner Rolando Solano as they left the scene that Powell had been totally "out of control" and that Koon had badly mismanaged the arrest. Solano repeated these statements to the Internal Affairs investigators, and the damning statements made by Briseno that night were on record. At the trial, Briseno testified that Powell had struck a blow to King's face that he believed was accidental, but once he was down on the ground, Powell continued to swing and beat King with blows directed at his head. Briseno testified that he believed it was possible that Powell was going to beat King to death, and he put his foot on King's left shoulder to try get King to stay down so Powell would stop.

In the eyes of the LAPD, Briseno was a traitor. Indeed, they labeled him Benedict Briseno. Officers who refused to provide any information to prosecutors or the media about the past conduct of the other three officers on trial were eager to come forward with details about Briseno, including rumors about domestic problems and physical abuse of his spouse, and details concerning a previous discipline for use of excessive force. Two LAPD officers testified in the trial that Briseno was lying, hoping to absolve himself by putting the blame on Powell and Koon.

CLOSING ARGUMENTS

In his closing argument, Terry White urged the jury to look again at the tape. No one is above the law, he said, not even the LAPD. And it is up to you, the jury, to say, enough is enough. The defense pushed another line. They urged the jury to put themselves in the shoes of the police officers out there every day protecting the good citizens of Simi Valley from dangerous criminals like Rodney King. They are the "thin blue line" that keeps our children and homes safe, but they are humans, with fears and hopes. They do a tough job to keep good citizens safe from the bad elements; they deserve our gratitude and respect. They were just doing their job.

THE VERDICTS

The jury deliberated for seven days, a total of thirty-two hours of deliberation. In their deliberations, the jury decided quickly to acquit Wind, Briseno, and Koon and focused most of their deliberations on Powell. Ultimately, the minority, who held out to convict Powell of assault under the color of authority, caved in and voted with the majority. To a shocked and hushed courtroom, the foreman announced not-guilty verdicts on all counts for all four defendants.

Prosecutor Terry White had told the jury to "trust their eyes" and believe what they saw. But it appears the jury relied on the interpretation of the LAPD experts about what they were seeing on the tape. The jury clearly had been heavily influenced by the unity of opinion of the LAPD witnesses at the incident and use of force experts. As one juror commented, "In my opinion, it's not right or morally acceptable to beat any human being, but if LAPD policy has determined its right in certain circumstances, we had to go with that and we did."[13]

THE RIOTS

In the immediate wake of the verdicts, the political climate in LA was tense but calm. Nobody knew it at the time, but it was the kind of calm that precedes a terrible storm.[14] Nobody expected the storm because nobody expected the not-guilty verdicts. And nobody quite imagined the rage stored up in the derelict and impoverished neighborhoods of South Central LA, least of all the LAPD, whose mission it was to "protect" that city, its people, and its property.[15]

On Wednesday morning, April 29, the day the verdicts were to be announced, the police station at 77th Street, right in the heart of the worst poverty zone of South Central LA, received the first of a series of anonymous phone calls threatening violence in the streets. Mostly these phone calls were ignored. But when Lieutenant Michael Moulin, the watch commander, heard the verdicts announced on television at 2 p.m., he began to get worried. A twenty-year veteran of the LAPD, he personally believed the officers were guilty of excessive force. In his view, the criminal justice system had let down the people of LA, and now he was scared that they were going to burn the city down. Little did he know how nearly right he was.

By 3:20 p.m., five minutes after the verdict was announced, angry crowds had gathered outside the station. Crowds also gathered where King had been beaten and outside the Parker Center, headquarters for the LAPD. At 3:43 p.m. the first emergency call to the LAPD came when a man threw a brick at a passing truck and missed. Shortly after 4 p.m., five young black men bought some malt beer from a Korean-owned store and began to hurl the bottles at the glass door, shattering it. Another was aimed at the store owner's son, hitting him in the head. "This is for Rodney King," one of them yelled. The riot, one of the deadliest in the nation's history, had begun.

By now police cars in all parts of the city had become targets for rocks and bottles. By 5:43 p.m. Lt. Moulin, fearing for his officers' safety, ordered all police officers to retreat from the area and return to the station house. The LAPD headquarters was surrounded by a crowd throwing rocks, bottles, up-rooted plants, and chunks of concrete from broken roadways. An unoccupied guard shack and several vehicles were set on fire; City Hall, the LA *Times,* and the criminal courts buildings were broken into and attacked by rioters. By 10 p.m. forty-seven major fires blazed in the city. Firefighters were attacked trying to respond, while the LAPD was nowhere to be found.

The riot lasted from Wednesday to the following Monday.[16] On Thursday, the worst day of the rioting, more than twenty people died; another ten were killed on Friday, nine more over the weekend, and six more on Monday. As the world watched in horror, whites, Asians, and Latinos were dragged out of their vehicles and beaten, attacked, and murdered, on the streets, in broad daylight, filmed by television helicopters hovering overhead. In all, 862 structures were destroyed by fire. Almost 2,000 Korean American–owned businesses were looted and destroyed. On Friday, May 1, the governor of California requested federal assistance, and 3,500 troops and Marines were sent to LA. By Sunday a combined force of 13,000, including National Guard, military, and federal, state, and local agencies had been mobilized to bring order to the city.

THE FEDERAL TRIAL

After the acquittals in the state prosecution of the defendants, it was the federal government's turn to argue that what had happened to Rodney King was not within the bounds of the law. The federal trial began on February 25, 1993, only ten months after the riots. In *Stacey C. Koon* v. *United States,* the four officers were accused of the federal crime of violating the civil rights of Rodney King.[17]

In this trial, the prosecution learned from the mistakes of Terry White and his team.[18] The venue remained in downtown Los Angeles, a location as unfavorable to the defense as Simi Valley had been for the prosecution. There were two black jurors. The prosecution put King on the stand so the jury could see him as a human being rather than a PCP-crazed monster. And this time, the federal government had the benefit of an LAPD use of force expert who testified that the actions of Officer Powell were in violation of LAPD policy.

The verdicts were announced at 7 a.m. on Saturday, April 17, just two weeks short of the anniversary of the other announcement that had set LA ablaze. When the convictions of Koon and Powell were announced, celebration and joy erupted in the streets of South Central LA.

AND JUSTICE FOR NONE

Prosecutors requested the maximum sentence for Koon of nine to ten years and the maximum for

Powell of seven to nine years. The defense, too, submitted a sentencing recommendation, requesting probation or prison terms of less than one year for each of the defendants. They also asked that no fines be levied because both men had lost their jobs and were financially devastated by the costs of their legal defense. Judge John G. Davies wrote a fifty-four-page memo to explain his reasons for sentencing both defendants to only thirty months in prison. He also refused to levy fines, stating that both officers could hardly afford to pay and that both had suffered the loss of their livelihoods and reputations as a result of their convictions.

The reaction to the sentences was divided along racial lines: among African Americans the sentence was another "travesty of justice" and yet another example of the "just us" system of punishment, which treats whites with leniency when their victims are black. Among LAPD police officers and their supporters, the imposition of prison time was an outrage: from the point of view of the police, Koon and Powell were trying to do their job as best they could. The last thing they deserved was to be put in prison with the very criminals they were sworn to fight every day.[19]

Case adapted from Lou Cannon, *Official Negligence: How Rodney King and the Riots Changed Los Angeles and the LAPD* (New York: Random House, 1997); Gibbs Jewell Taylor, *Race and Justice: Rodney King and O. J. Simpson in a House Divided* (Jossey-Bass, 1996); Robert Deitz, *Willful Injustice: A Post-O. J. Look at Rodney King, American Justice and Trial by Race,* (Washington, DC: Regnery, 1996); Carl E. Pope and Lee E. Ross, "Race, Crime and Justice: The Aftermath of Rodney King," *The Criminologist 17* (1992); Jerry Gray, "In Police Brutality Case, One Videotape but Two Ways to View It," *The New York Times,* December 13, 1991; Mike Sager, "Damn! They Gonna Lynch Us," *Gentlemen's Quarterly,* October 1991; "Los Angeles Chief Assailed by Mayor," *The New York Times,* April 3, 1991; "Violence and Racism are Routine in Los Angeles Police, Study Says," *The New York Times,* July 10, 1991; Warren Christopher et al., *Report of the Independent Commission on the Los Angeles Police Department,* July 9, 1991; "Simi Valley Journal: Town Too Feels Eyes of Nation for Trial," *The New York Times,* February 22, 1992; "Los Angeles Policemen Acquitted in Taped Beating: Storm of Anger Erupts," *The New York Times,* April 30, 1992; "Riots in LA: The Blue Line Surprised, Police React Slowly as Violence Spreads," *The New York Times,* May 1, 1992; Nancy Abelmann and John Lie, *Blue Dreams: Korean Americans and the Los Angeles Riots* (Cambridge, MA: Harvard University Press, 1995); William Robert Gooding, ed., *Reading Rodney King: Reading Urban Uprising* (New York: Routledge, 1993); D. M. Osborne, "A Defense Turned Inside Out," *American Lawyer Media,* April 20, 1993; Courtroom Television Network, *The Rodney King*

Case: What the Jury Saw in California v. Powell, (MPI Home Video, 1992).

THINKING CRITICALLY ABOUT THIS CASE

1. In the immediate aftermath of the beating, the head of the LAPD police union said, "I don't think Rodney King was beaten because of his race. But I also don't think what happened to King would have happened to a white man." Do you agree with this statement? Why or why not?

2. Should the videotape have been aired by the media? Why or why not? What is the role of the media in monitoring the actions of law enforcement?

3. Should the officers have been tried in South Central LA, or in Simi Valley, or in some other location? In a case such as this, is it possible to obtain a fair jury? Why or why not?

4. What should Daryl Gates have done to respond to the King beating when the videotape was first aired on national television? What steps should he have taken in response to the videotape?

5. The riots were sparked by the verdict in the first King trial. What other factors accounted for the violence of those four days? What steps can the LAPD take to ensure that riots like these will not happen in the future? What steps can the city take to ensure that riots like these will not happen in the future?

6. The LAPD officers felt they had been unfairly punished for trying to "do their job." They lost their livelihoods, reputations, and life savings in the subsequent trials and publicity. Having to serve jail time as well seemed unjust in the eyes of LAPD personnel. On the other hand, minority citizens of South Central LA felt that the officers were given exceptionally lenient sentences. Thirty months in prison is well below the recommended sentence for their crime. What do you think? What would have been a just punishment for Koon and Powell?

CHECK OUT THIS CASE

On the Web

Shielded from Justice: Police Brutality and Accountability in the U.S., www.hrw.org/reports98/police/ *Report by Human Rights Watch on police brutality in fourteen major U.S. cities including Los Angeles, New York, Chicago, Detroit, and Boston. Read the Christopher Commission Report and the Furman Report on brutality and racism in the LAPD, and the St. Clair Commission Report on the Boston police department. See data and reports from each major city.*

On Film

The Rodney King Incident: Race and Justice in America (57 minutes)

*A documentary that interviews all the key participants, including Rodney King, the police officers, former chief Daryl Gates, and trial prosecutors, demonstrating complex divergent views of this case. Available from Films for the Humanities and Sciences, **www.films.com.***

The Rodney King Case: What the Jury Saw in *California* v. *Powell* (120 minutes)

*This program presents the prosecution and defense arguments in the Simi Valley trial of the four LAPD officers accused of the use of excessive force in the arrest of Rodney King. It includes eyewitness testimony and a frame-by-frame reply of the Holliday videotape. Available from Insight Media, **www.insight-media.com.***

CHAPTER 8

Beyond the Limits of the Law: Police Culture and the Problem of Violence

LEARNING OBJECTIVES

After reading this chapter, the student should be able to:

- Identify the various forms of police misconduct

- Describe the rules that regulate the use of lethal force by police

- Explain why a code of silence exists within policing and why a "blue curtain" separates police from civilians

- Explain the concept of the "working personality" in police and describe what features of police work contribute to this working personality

- Illustrate the war model of policing and discuss the impact of the war model on the incidence of police brutality

- Explain the paradox of coercive force and the "Dirty Harry" problem in policing

Stacey Koon testified in the Simi Valley trial that sometimes "police work is brutal and violent."[20] Like the military or prison, law enforcement is an institution that authorizes the use of violence by its agents in the pursuit of legitimate organizational goals. Police are society's agent of coercion; therefore, the use of force is an inevitable part of the police function. Yet, as we pointed out in Chapter 7, the use of force is legitimate only when it operates within the constraints of the law. Why do police step outside those boundaries and engage in extralegal violence?

This chapter examines the institutional and organizational features of policing that shape encounters between police and citizens, especially minority citizens. The pattern of conduct that leads to brutal and violent treatment of citizens, even by the few, permeates the entire organization of U.S. policing, not just one particular department or one isolated group of individuals. The sociological causes of this behavior are found in the characteristics of police work, the organization of policing, and the mission police defines for itself rather than in any of the individual personality characteristics of police officers themselves.

FORMS OF POLICE MISCONDUCT

Police brutality is one form of police misconduct, which also includes corruption, crime, and other abuses of power.[21] **Police corruption** has been an endemic problem in policing since the start of modern policing in the nineteenth century.[22] The temptation toward illegal conduct ranges from accepting free doughnuts and coffee from a local shopkeeper to the systemic operation of organized crime rings under the shield of the police badge. Beginning in the 1930s with the Wickersham Commission[23] investigation of the LAPD, periodic investigations have revealed pervasive and wide-ranging illegal conduct among police officers. In New York City, the 1993 Mollen Commission unearthed evidence of extensive drug dealing by New York's police. This criminal conduct is routinely protected by the infamous code of silence among police.

The lowest level of police corruption involves the acceptance of small favors such as free meals or coffee from local establishments. This is often related to patterns of selective law enforcement in which wrongdoing is routinely overlooked or ignored. Police officers are also often in a position to engage in opportunistic theft: in the course of a search they may pick up and pocket stolen jewelry or money; or they may confiscate and keep cash or drugs they find.

On a wider scale, police have operated protection rackets and organized systems of bribe taking to withhold law enforcement or to use it selectively at the request of a paying customer. The Knapp Commission, investigating the New York Police Department (NYPD) in 1973, distinguished between **"grass eaters,"** police who occasionally accepted bribes, and those who were **"meat eaters"** and systematically engaged in bribery and intimidation for financial gain.[24] Police association with the criminal underworld creates an enormous opportunity for officers to take part in illegal profit making. This is particularly true in the enforcement of laws against alcohol, drugs, and other kinds of vice. The huge flow of cash involved in this business and the multitude of opportunities to cash in on the profits result in the widespread participation of police officers in illegal businesses.

Finally, in addition to these forms of crime for profit are the abuses of police power through the systematic denial of due process, harassment, perjury in court, and tampering with evidence. Included in abuses of power is abuse of the use of force: the illegal use of police violence, including illegal violence toward suspects and other citizens, torture, and unjustifiable homicide. Often referred to as "curbside" justice, police use illegal violence as a form of social control, teaching those they think deserve it a "lesson" through the abuse of power.

REGULATING THE USE OF FORCE

Police training involves instruction in decision making around the use of appropriate levels of coercion. These are, of course, merely guidelines. The ultimate decision lies in the police officer's own "intuitive grasp of situational exigencies."[25] In other words, the officer must read the dynamics of a rapidly changing and unpredictable set of circumstances and make a split-second decision about appropriate conduct.[26] Nevertheless, police departments generate policies and train officers in the levels of force appropriate to different types of situations.[27]

The first "show of force" in an encounter between the police and citizens is the mere presence of the police officer on the street. By possessing the right to use force, police *threaten* that use of force by their very presence. Beyond mere presence is the use of verbal commands by police officers to order citizens to slow down, move along, or in some way change their conduct. Police officers may approach citizens or use their siren to pull them over, politely request to see their driver's licence, or respectfully ask them questions about their purpose in the neighborhood. While the request may be in a polite tone, the underlying reality is that the exchange is a command that citizens are not free to refuse. Police officers may also use a command tone of voice and more overtly order citizens to show their license or raise their arms.

Beyond verbal commands, the first level of physical force is a series of techniques called *firm grips*. Officers are trained in the use of various forms of body holds, such as

police brutality: the unlawful use of physical force by officers in the performance of their duties.

police corruption: misconduct by police officers through illegal activities for economic gain, including the acceptance of payments for services, nonenforcement of the law in exchange for payment, and active participation in criminal activities.

grass eaters: police officers who accept payoffs for rendering police services or who look the other way when police action is called for, in exchange for goods or services.

meat eaters: police officers who actively and systematically solicit bribes or conspire with criminals in criminal activity.

gripping the elbow of suspects or bending their head as they are placed in the patrol car under arrest. These firm grips are techniques for controlling the body of the subject without causing pain or injury. At a higher level are various techniques for inflicting pain in order to compel a citizen to comply with an officer's order. These *come-along*, or pain compliance, holds, such as hammerlocks, wristlocks, and finger grips, are methods for subduing a suspect who is resisting arrest. *Swarming* a suspect falls within this level of force.

One of the departmentally approved upper-body holds taught to LAPD officers is the carotid choke hold.[28] The carotid choke hold cuts off the flow of blood to the brain for the purpose of inducing unconsciousness. This technique had been classified by the LAPD as a low-level use of force similar to the hammerlock or wrist grips. Officers were authorized to use the choke hold to control unruly motorists in traffic accidents and other minor incidents. But fourteen citizens died in incidents involving the choke hold, the majority of them African American, leading to major lawsuits against the LAPD. Just prior to the Rodney King beating, the carotid choke hold had been upgraded to deadly force status by the department. In defense testimony at the trial of the officers, LAPD use-of-force expert Charles Duke testified that the recent ban on the choke hold forced officers to rely on the use of metal batons to subdue King. In his opinion, this created a more dangerous situation by forcing officers to use more aggressive and harmful levels of force.[29]

Impact techniques include the use of kicks, batons, chemical sprays, or electronic stunning weapons. The point of these techniques is to subdue a combative suspect without resorting to life-threatening means such as guns. This was the key defense offered by Stacey Koon and supported by the LAPD defense experts: the use of batons and the Tazer was departmentally approved use of force at a level below the use of lethal force. Koon testified that he himself would have administered the carotid choke hold and was prepared to do so if King had not finally submitted to the blows of the baton. As a form of lethal force, Koon was following appropriate procedure by relying first on the use of impact techniques such as the baton and the Tazer before moving to a higher level.

In testimony at the trial, Charles Duke analyzed the videotape frame by frame to show that each action by the officers was in response to a continued aggressive response on the part of Rodney King. Melanie Singer, Koon, Powell, and others issued verbal commands ordering King to lie down on the ground. When he ignored their orders, they used baton swings and the Tazer to force King to comply (see Figure 8.1). Duke testified that as long as King resisted being handcuffed, the officers were required to use their batons in appropriate ways to inflict pain and injury to compel King to comply.

When Is Lethal Force Justified?

impact techniques: techniques of coercive force designed to subdue a combative suspect without resorting to lethal force.

lethal force: force likely to cause death or great bodily harm; also known as deadly force.

fleeing felon doctrine: a now-defunct law enforcement rule that permitted officers to shoot a suspected felon attempting to flee from a lawful arrest.

Until about 1960, most U.S. states relied on the common-law doctrine commonly known as the **fleeing felon doctrine:** if a person suspected of committing a felony fled, then an officer was permitted to use deadly force to stop the person. The fleeing felon doctrine originated in English common law when all felony offenses were punishable by death. The use of lethal force to apprehend misdemeanor suspects was not permissible under common law. This rule was adopted in the United States even though few felonies in the U.S. legal code are capital crimes and even though the distinction between the severity of felonies and misdemeanor offenses has hugely diminished. By the 1960s, many states and big city police departments had adopted statutes and regulations that permitted officers to use lethal force only if the suspect was armed or dangerous.

A survey in 1980 found that thirty-two states relied on the fleeing felon doctrine, permitting police to shoot any suspect who fled, including those who were unarmed and had committed nonviolent offenses. This survey showed that eight states allowed deadly force only in defense of life, while ten states permitted deadly force against individuals suspected of committing violent crimes.[30]

Second-by-Second Account:

0:00	King begins to get up from his hands and knees.
0:02	King is up and charges in the direction of Powell.
0:03	Powell hits King in the shoulder area with his baton and King falls on his face.
0:04–0:14	Video out of focus. King hit by numerous blows from Powell to various parts of his body—probably including one blow to the head.
0:14–0:17	Video clears. King is on his stomach. No blows are struck.
0:17	Powell has baton raised and appears ready to strike King. Briseno puts his hand in front of Powell.
0:20	King is rising. Powell strikes King in arms and chest.
0:21	Wind strikes King near buttocks.
0:23	After Powell strikes King in upper chest, King topples over and turns.
0:25–0:26	Powell strikes King in arm and shoulder area.
0:27–0:28	Powell strikes King in back while King attempts to rise.
0:30	Powell hits King in left arm as King rises from his knees.
0:31	Wind swings at King as King begins to fall.
0:32	King falls. His face appears to hit asphalt.
0:33	Powell strikes King on knee, while Wind hits King in shoulder.
0:34–0:40	King's head is up. Powell and Wind deliver hard blows to King's back, buttocks, and thighs.
0:41	King rolls to left and cocks right leg.
0:43	After two-second break, officers resume force, striking King's legs.
0:44	King lifts his upper torso.
0:45–0:47	Powell strikes King's ankle while Wind strikes his back.
0:51	King rolls on ground while Koon puts arms in form of cross, showing the position he wants King to assume.
0:54	King, on his back, cocks his left leg.
0:56–0:58	King rolls as Powell strikes his hand.
1:02–1:04	Powell reaches for his handcuffs.
1:04–1:06	King raises his torso. Briseno stomps on King's shoulder and King's head hits asphalt.
1:08–1:09	Briseno points to King. Powell and Wind strike King's right arm.
1:10	King is on his hands and knees.
1:12–1:13	Wind strikes King's back three times.
1:16	Powell strikes King's left arm.
1:17–1:21	Wind delivers three kicks to King's shoulder and back area.
1:21	Video back in focus. Powell swings at King.
1:25	King is sitting on his calfs. Koon is pointing at King.
1:30	King puts his hands on his head.
1:35	Briseno begins handcuffing King.
1:43	King is put in handcuffs after officers.

FIGURE 8.1   The Holliday Videotape

Source: www.law.umkc.edu/faculty/projects/ftrials/lapd/kingvideo.html.

In 1985, the fleeing felon doctrine was declared unconstitutional in the Supreme Court case of *Tennessee* v. *Garner*.[31] In this case, a 15-year-old unarmed boy was chased by officers as he ran from a house. As he tried to escape by climbing over a chain-link fence, the pursuing officers shot him in the back. The Supreme Court ruled that the use of deadly force against a fleeing felon is justified only when it is necessary to prevent the escape of a suspect for whom there is probable cause to believe he or she poses a significant physical threat to the officer or to others.

Police jurisdictions have varying rules regarding the appropriate use of lethal force to apprehend a suspect. The use of lethal or deadly force by police officers is authorized in all jurisdictions for the purposes of self-defense. If police perceive themselves to be in lethal danger, they are not required to meet the force with equal force but are permitted to use whatever level of force is necessary to protect their own lives. In 1977, the LAPD revised its liberal fleeing felon policy to confine the use of deadly force only to apprehending a felon when the crime involved serious bodily injury or when there was substantial risk that the suspect would cause death or serious bodily injury to others if apprehension was delayed.

While Koon was attempting to make use of lethal force a last resort, Lawrence Powell was shown on the tape striking King in the face and head. The use of the baton above the neck is authorized by LAPD regulations only under those circumstances that justify the use of lethal force. Powell testified at the trial that he was in "fear of his life," believing that King was sufficiently strong to take his weapon from him and use it against him. In fact, about one-quarter of all police officers who are shot each year in the line of duty are wounded or killed by people who have disarmed them and turned their own weapons against them.[32] Powell testified that he was acting in self-defense when he struck King in the face as King charged him.

One burning question is whether or not minority suspects are more subject to the use of lethal force by police than nonminority suspects. The evidence shows that minority citizens are disproportionately subject to police killings: Milton et al. found that 70 percent of the suspects shot by the police in seven major cities were black, even though blacks made up only 39 percent of the population.[33] In some jurisdictions, black suspects were between five and thirteen times more likely than white suspects to be killed by police.[34] In Memphis, Tennessee, where Edward Garner was shot under the fleeing felon rule, research found that police had shot and killed thirteen unarmed African American suspects as compared to one white suspect who was unarmed and not assaultive.[35] Researchers have posed the question of whether this may be attributed to the reality of racial discrimination and the fact that police have "two trigger fingers"—one for whites and one for African Americans and Hispanics.[36]

An alternative explanation to racism for the racial disparity in victims of police shootings can be found in the disproportionate involvement of minority suspects in violent crime and in the prevalence of the use of guns by minority suspects.[37] When situational circumstances such as the nature of the crime, a high-crime area, and the use of guns are controlled for, then the disparity between white and black victims disappears in several studies.[38] Research has also found that the race of the police officer does not influence the likelihood of using lethal force: white, African American, and Hispanic officers are equally likely to fire weapons when assigned to certain high-crime precincts.[39]

Evidence also suggests that the use of lethal force toward suspects from all racial groups declines significantly when more restrictive polices regulating the use of force are adopted by the police department. Analysis of the racial disparity in police shootings under more restrictive policies suggests that these rules reduce the number of African Americans shot by police, suggesting that more permissive policies open the door for racial discrimination in the split-second decisions by police, at least in some cities.[40] The racial disparity between black and white victims of racial shootings has declined substantially, from 7:1 in 1970 to 2.8:1 in 1979 under the more restrictive policies of the post-Garner era.[41] One conclusion that can be drawn from this research is that the effect of racial discrimination has been substantially diminished under departmental policies that limit officer discretion in the use of lethal force. The remaining racial disparity that still exists may be explained by the disparate involvement of minorities in more serious violent crimes.[42]

EXPLAINING POLICE VIOLENCE

The most simple explanation for police violence points to the excesses of a few "aberrant" individuals. These "rotten apples" spoil the reputation of the vast majority of law enforcement officers, who are not violent and who conduct themselves within the bounds of the law in their encounters with citizens. According to the **rotten apple theory**, the key to understanding what happened outside Van Dam Park that night lies in the personality and character of Lawrence Powell.

Indeed, there is much evidence to support this idea. Many who knew Powell described him as "immature," "cocky," and "unprofessional." Son of a lieutenant in the U.S. Marshal's Service, Powell followed in his father's footsteps to become a law enforcement officer. In his first years as a police officer, Powell earned a reputation among his peers that was less than flattering. According to one black LAPD officer, "He treated everybody like crap. He always had his hand on his gun. We could be ordering a soda, talking to the lady at the register, and he would have his hand on his gun. We call it badge-heavy."[43]

By the time of the King incident, Powell had accumulated a record of incidents in which he was accused of improper conduct or excessive force in his interactions with citizens. Only five months earlier, Powell had been reprimanded for striking a handcuffed prisoner, Danny Ramos, with a flashlight. In an earlier incident, Powell had struck a suspect repeatedly with his baton breaking the suspect's elbow. The victim filed an excessive force lawsuit that had been settled out of court for $70,000. And only two weeks before the King arrest, three African American students from San Fernando Valley College filed a complaint against Powell, alleging that he forced them to lie on the ground and handcuffed them while he made racially derogatory remarks.

When Daryl Gates declared publically that this incident was an "aberration," he implied that this conduct was not the fault of the policies, practices, management, or structure of the LAPD as a whole, but acts of isolated individuals who should be punished and removed from the force.[44]

But does this explanation really fit the pattern of facts regarding the LAPD and its relationship with the minority community? In 1990, the year before the King beating, the city paid out more than $11.3 million in lawsuits and settlements in LAPD-related litigation. In 1989, the city paid out $9.1 million to settle lawsuits alleging police misconduct.[45] These payments were more than those of any other large urban city in the nation except for the city of Detroit, where the police department shared a similar poor reputation for its treatment of minority citizens. Considering that most cases of police misconduct never result in the filing of actual lawsuits, these figures represent the mere tip of the iceberg of LAPD misconduct. The cold reality is that this behavior is far too widespread and far too common to attribute to a few "bad apples."

The Working Personality of the Police Officer

Another possible explanation for the pervasiveness of police brutality is that police officers are more likely than ordinary citizens to be aggressive, cynical, or authoritarian in personality and temperament.[46] One theory is that policing attracts individuals with a tendency toward pessimistic views about human nature and a predisposition toward

rotten apple theory: the theory that extralegal violence by police is perpetrated by a few excessively aggressive individuals, or "rotten apples," who spoil the reputation of the police as a whole.

authoritarian attitudes. Yet research studies on the personality characteristics of recruits to police academies reveal that the typical police recruit does not differ from the average person in terms of these personality traits.[47] While the typical recruit may be the type of person who is more likely to be idealistic and more of an "adrenaline" junkie than an office type, people attracted to policing are not otherwise particularly aggressive, suspicious, or authoritarian. Indeed, many police departments use personality tests to screen out aberrant personalities.[48]

What researchers have found, however, is that a **working personality** among police officers emerges while being on the job itself. Over time, police develop more cynical, suspicious, and authoritarian personality traits. Police have one of the strongest vocational subcultures of any occupational group. Occupations such as doctors, clergy, and the military also tend to be "24-hour-a-day" identities: people in these occupational roles see their job as a defining identity for "who they are," even when they are not at work. Jerome Skolnick argues that the working personality of the police officer develops through the shared experience of being a cop on the street.[49]

The experience of being a patrol officer is shared by all levels of the police hierarchy. This common experience shapes the outlook of all police officers, simultaneously creating a strong bond between officers and opening an enormous gulf between police and civilians. In the King trial, the most important credentials of expert witnesses were their experience as streetwise police officers. The prosecution witness was easily discredited by his lack of experience as an officer on the street. Even the lawyers defending the police had experience as cops before they went to law school. More than any other credentials, the ability to empathize with the uniquely demanding position of police officers on the street generates respect and trust from other police officers. This attitude even infected the jury, who found the testimony of experienced officers more credible than that of those who lacked street experience.

Police Subculture: Danger and Authority

The source of the working personality therefore lies in certain features of police work itself.[50] The element of danger in policing means that police are trained to be suspicious of civilians in society. Most of us operate with certain stereotypes regarding who might be a threat to us on the street: we notice certain aspects of people's appearance and behavior that signal to us a potential threat. Many people in our culture, for example, see young black males as more likely to be a danger to them than an elderly white woman: we might cross the street to avoid passing the black male or avoid going down a street where a group of people who fit this description are gathered.

While citizens pay attention to **symbolic assailants** in order to avoid danger (i.e., cross to the other side of the street or leave the party), the police officer is expected to pay attention in order to face and suppress the danger. Police develop a list of subtle signals to identify symbolic assailants or people who pose a potential threat.[51] The identification of Rodney King as a "duster" (someone on PCP) and an ex-con were inferences officers made based on his appearance and his behavior. Both these cues communicated to the officers an inference about how King might behave and the potential threat he represented to the officers. To civilians, jumping to these conclusions seems fundamentally unfair, but for police, failing to make such inferences can be both dangerous and unprofessional.

The second key element of police work that affects the personality of the police officer is the possession of authority over others within society.[52] Police protect citizens against danger, but they are also charged with the responsibility of enforcing many laws of public order that most citizens violate at some point in their lives even if in relatively minor ways. Citizens resent police who stop them for speeding, or who come to their house at the request of a neighbor to ask them to turn down the music at a party. Police officers often feel a sense of social rejection by civilians even when they are off duty.

working personality: the effect of daily police work on officers' view of the world, characterized by cynicism and suspicion. The key features of police work generating this view are the response to danger and the obligation to exercise authority.

symbolic assailants: working stereotypes of citizens likely to pose a potential threat to someone's safety, used informally by police in their interactions with citizens on the street.

Police work requires officers to be suspicious of citizens to anticipate situations of potential danger. The possession of legal authority over citizens generates mutual hostility between police and the community, particularly within urban neighborhoods, where citizens accuse police of being too aggressive toward young men of color. Police feel they are misunderstood and underappreciated by citizens who do not understand the difficulties associated with the job of urban policing.

Police officers come to feel most at home in the company of other police officers, particularly when their own conduct may be in less than perfect accordance with the law.

The Blue Curtain: *Us* v. *Them* Mentality

The sense of danger and authority associated with police work leads police officers to isolate themselves from civilians and to develop an *us* v. *them* mentality. Police generally feel that the public resents their authority, does not understand how difficult their job is or what it entails, and is fickle in their support for police. Older officers often teach younger officers that is best to avoid socializing with civilians. As a result, police often come from "police families," marry into police families, choose to live near and socialize with other people in law enforcement. In a sense, police officers construct an invisible **blue curtain** between themselves, their families, and the rest of society.[53]

It is this peculiar reality of policing that helps to explain the enormous consequence of moving the King trial to a community like Simi Valley. The members of the jury were very likely to be predisposed to the belief that the media and politicians were unfair to the police and did not really understand what is it like to be an officer out there on the streets. Police often feel that citizens, especially minority citizens, view them as the enemy. The conviction that the public is ungrateful and uncaring about the risks police endure every day shows in the closing arguments of defense attorney Michael Stone. According to Stone, these people put their lives on the line every day so that ordinary civilians may enjoy peaceful lives. Chasing Rodney King and placing him under arrest is a difficult and dirty job: it is easy to condemn the action of the police officers from the safety of your living room while watching the videotape on the television. For police

blue curtain: social isolation of police and their families from civilians in society.

families, however, it is a different matter to be in the moment, facing a potential assailant whose behavior and conduct suggest you may be facing grave danger.

The Code of Silence

The working personality of the police officer leads to a sense of distrust of civilians, a pattern of social isolation from other civilians, and an intense reliance on connections to fellow police officers. The norms of the police subculture of loyalty, obedience, and solidarity then provide the foundation for the **code of silence** that prevents officers from criticizing their fellow officers to civilian outsiders. The code of silence is a powerful feature of all police subcultures and one that makes it very difficult to regulate police misconduct. On May 12, 1991, a guest editorial appeared in the LA *Times* demanding the resignation of Chief Daryl Gates for denouncing the beating as an "aberration."[54] The piece was written by Sergeant Stacey Koon. The unwritten code of the LAPD requires senior personnel to support their officers to the outside world and to be loyal to their version of the truth. Senior officers who fail to "back up their street cops" are seen as traitors to the norms of solidarity and loyalty.

The code of silence is rigorously enforced by other police officers in their treatment of those who violate the code and betray fellow officers. The treatment of Briseno and Nichols illustrates the kind of shunning treatment, demotion from jobs, and willingness to slander those who break the silence. While no officer came forward to talk about Powell's past record of misconduct, many were willing to talk about Briseno, and it appears that many were willing to commit perjury to punish his treachery. On a more fundamental level, police officers fear that if they violate the code, fellow officers will fail to "watch their backs" out on the street.

These features of police work help us to understand why police forces are so tolerant of the "rotten apples" in their midst. Valuing solidarity above all else and operating with the strong belief that civilians do not understand or appreciate the realities of police work, police departments routinely fail to correct misconduct that takes place within their ranks. The "thin blue line" serves as a thick blue curtain between the police and rest of society. The bystanders at the King incident may very well have had private feelings about the actions of Lawrence Powell, but they also very likely believed in the importance of protecting their fellow officers from the world of citizens who do not understand the difficult line police are forced to walk every day.

Deference and Demeanor

One of the key reasons Rodney King may have been beaten that night was because he symbolically challenged the authority of the police by his behavior. Rodney King was grinning, waving at the helicopter, jiggling his buttocks, and talking gibberish during this period. Even though King was on the ground and may not have represented an actual physical threat to the safety of the officers, research shows that police officers are more likely to beat an individual—even one who is handcuffed—if the suspect is still demonstrating a degree of symbolic resistance to the authority of the police.[55]

Respect for authority is crucial for police out on the street. Because police are suspicious of symbolic assailants, they maintain their authority by demanding that citizens display signs of respect. For the police, a show of disrespect is a danger sign signifying an individual who may be willing to use force against them. Research shows that police often use unnecessary force when they believe their authority is being challenged.

The sensitivity of police to signs of disrespect is exacerbated in minority communities, where relations between police and the community are extremely tense and mutually suspicious. From the police perspective, police believe that they are among people who do not accept the legitimacy of their authority. This heightens the tendency for some officers to be especially aggressive in their use of force in order to maintain that

code of silence: the unwritten norm to support fellow officers by not revealing problems and illegal conduct to outsiders.

authority. Being tough and using violent tactics against symbolic assailants such as young black males hanging out on a corner is one strategy for forcing respect. Constantly displaying their ability to use force is one method to command respect on the streets. The LAPD even had a name for it, "badge heavy." Officers like Lawrence Powell were quick to exercise their legal right to use force: Powell "always had his hand on his gun."

The Paradox of Coercive Power[56]

Yet there is a profound irony in this approach to maintaining authority. Respect and fear are two different attitudes toward people in power. The paradox of authority is that the more you use your power, the more you lose your authority. Police authority depends on careful use of force within the bounds of the law. While at times it is necessary to use force to maintain authority, excessive use of force by police undermines their legitimate authority on the street to use force. The more police behave in a heavy-handed fashion in their encounters with citizens on the street, the more they sow seeds that undermine their authority in the long run.

The distinction between power and authority is an important one for understanding the very delicate relationship between citizens and the police as they encounter one another on the street. If citizens do not accept the legitimate right of police to tell them what to do, for example, when approaching an intersection, then the job of the police standing there in the middle of the street is both extremely dangerous and fundamentally impossible. If every citizen resisted the authority of the police, then all the police would have to draw upon would be whatever power they possess, which is no match for the greater power of citizens to oppose them. This is the situation the LAPD found themselves in during those first hours and days of the riot, out there on the streets among thousands of citizens who were refusing to obey their authority. Under these circumstances, the police retreated for their own safety.

The more police rely on the use of force on the street, the more they are resented, hated, and seen as "just another gang out on the street." Hated cops are not safe cops.[57] And because police are not seen as individuals, officers like Lawrence Powell, who choose to instill fear rather than respect, create unsafe streets for all police. When people begin to resist the authority of the police on a large scale, as happened when the riots began, the power of the police is overwhelmed by the much greater power of the citizens in the community. The police no longer held the upper hand in terms of power and were forced to retreat for their own safety until the arrival of reinforcements from the military.

THE WAR MODEL OF POLICING

From its inception in the nineteenth century, municipal police organizations have adopted a quasi-military style of organization, with chains of command, ranks, divisions, platoons, squads, and details. Military language and metaphors pervade the culture and function of public policing. Waging a "war on crime" is the central metaphor governing the crime control function and the mission of the police. Yet the military model and mission may be profoundly dysfunctional for the real work of public policing, and it may seriously contribute to the incidence of extralegal violence on the part of police.

Probably more than any other police department in the nation, the LAPD had embraced a "war model" of policing since the early 1950s. William Henry Parker, chief of the LAPD for over twenty years, promoted an image of the LAPD as an elite commando force fighting the forces of evil in the city.[58] It was Parker who came up with the concept that the LAPD were the "thin blue line" protecting the "good" citizens of Los Angeles, mostly white, from the bad criminals, mostly Mexican, Asian, or African American.

paradox of coercive power: the more a person in authority uses power, the more they lose authority to use power.

war model of policing: the use of the military metaphor for the structure and mission of policing.

Specialized units or SWAT teams use military tactics and weaponry to handle rare incidents involving hostages, snipers, or armed suspects. Most large urban police departments have specially trained units to perform these jobs.

Daryl Gates rose through the ranks of the LAPD under William Parker. Gates, too, was steeped in the military model of policing. He had earned promotions for developing the Special Weapons and Tactics, or SWAT team, a heavily armed tactical unit designed to respond to street militants and hostage situations. The SWAT team was deployed in conflicts with the militant Black Panthers in the late 1960s and early 1970s. Lawrence Powell had served in the prestigious CRASH (Community Resources Against Street Hoodlums) unit that suppressed gangs using aggressive military-style tactics.

The military model of policing, however, lends itself to excessive use of force. In a war situation, violence against the enemy is normative: acting with restraint in the face of the enemy is foolish, and soldiers are trained to use whatever means are necessary to destroy the enemy. In public policing, force is supposed to be used only as a last resort and only to bring suspects to justice, not to vanquish them or eliminate them. The military use of force and the public police use of force are fundamentally different from one another.[59]

Cops as Soldiers

In his autobiography, Patrick V. Murphy, former police chief of Syracuse, Washington, DC, Detroit, and New York City, argues that the primary role of police in society is to "keep the peace and maintain order in a sophisticated, humane and Constitutional way."[60] This is very different from the job of the soldier in wartime, which is to destroy the enemy as efficiently as possible. Soldiers are expected to follow orders, not to exercise individual professional judgment to resolve a situation with the minimum of violence possible.[61] The military is a top-down hierarchy in which all the important decisions are made at the top of the organization. The commander in chief decides whether to go to war, where to wage battle, how many troops should be deployed, and what tactics to use. Down the line, discretion is increasingly diminished, until we reach the privates who are told their job is "not to reason why" but to "do or die."

In contrast, line police officers actually hold the decision-making authority to use force or not in countless discretionary and fluid decisions in encounters with citizens on the street. Should they arrest a person or warn them? Talk to drunks or wrestle them into the patrol car? Defuse the angry argument between two males by arresting them or by joking with them? Frisk suspicious-looking teenagers or let them walk on by? In policing, it is the person at the bottom of the chain of command who holds the "non-negotiable discretion" to decide if force should be used, when, and how much.

In the riots that erupted in the wake of the King verdicts, the disorder on the street required a command and control response characteristic of a military organization. The LAPD failed miserably to deliver this kind of response. Police are used to working in small teams of two or three to deal with isolated situations as they arise. It took genuine military operations of the National Guard and the Marines, trained to follow orders from command and control chiefs, to deal with this kind of mass violence.

Citizens as Enemies

> Look, folks, policing is done this way. You may like to live in Santa Monica and have your little wine party in the backyard and drive your Jaguar and do your little bar-beque. . . . Know that the reason you are allowed to do that in the safety of your community is because police officers go out and they clean up the streets and deal with all the scum that you don't want to know about. (Stacey Koon).[62]

In a war, the enemy is clearly defined. In the context of policing, the enemy is often claimed to be the "criminal" or, in Koon's vocabulary, "scum." But criminals are not easily distinguishable from ordinary citizens. Remember, most U.S. citizens violate the law at some point in their lives. How can police tell the "bad guys" from the "good guys"?

The war mentality makes it extremely easy for police to use the outward signs of race and class to identify the so-called enemy. Police rely on stereotypes, profiles, and typifications to decide who is "friend" and who is "scum." This means that black people become targets of police surveillance and investigation and harassment, because they are seen as part of the "enemy class."

Furthermore, people who violate the law are not "enemies" devoid of civil rights. By law, criminal suspects remain entitled to full protection of the Constitution until they are duly convicted in a court of law. It is not the job of the police to act as vigilantes delivering street justice to people they deem to be guilty. Even once they are convicted, criminals are still citizens with limited rights, nor should they be seen as "enemies." They may be criminals, they may be violent, but they are not enemies to be destroyed. The "enemies" mentality, which is functional in a war context, is highly dysfunctional for professionals in the criminal justice system, who must never treat suspects or convicted criminals as "enemies" to be destroyed. They remain their fellow citizens, guilty or not guilty.

But for officers who are operating as "soldiers" in a "war on crime," the civil rights of citizens and other Constitutional protections are seen as unfair advantages afforded to the enemy. Police are continually tempted to violate the law in order to enforce it. Carl Klockars referred to this temptation as the **"Dirty Harry Problem."**[63] In the 1971 film, *Dirty Harry*, Clint Eastwood is a detective on the trail of a vicious kidnapper of a 14-year-old girl. Dirty Harry uses violence and torture, all of it completely illegal, to force information from the kidnapper. Not only is he too late to save the victim's life, but Dirty Harry also finds that he has freed the kidnapper from legal punishment by his abuse of force: the evidence against him is ruled inadmissible in court because of the illegal use of force to obtain the confession.

Dirty Harry Problem: the temptation to violate the law by using illegal means in order to enforce the law and apprehend criminals.

Klockars believes that the attitude on the part of the police that they are the "forces of good" fighting the "forces of evil" encourages police to violate the law in order to "get the job done." The so-called Dirty Harry dilemma is faced by all cops who want to use extralegal violence to get the "bad guy." According to the U.S. Supreme Court, however, police may not violate the law in order to enforce it, because the ends do not justify the means. But in squad cars and locker rooms there is a different set of beliefs based on a military understanding of the war. No one wants to fight a battle with "one hand tied behind his back." Police resent the distinction between legal guilt and factual guilt and are tempted to use perjury, deceit, and other illegal means to "get the job done."

To the minority citizens of South Central LA, the LAPD had for decades paraded itself through their communities in the style of an occupying army rather than as public servants. Through quasi-military operations such Operation Hammer and Operation Rock, the LAPD used terrifying tactics of intimidation to round up citizens in massive police sweeps modeled after Vietnam-style "search and destroy" missions. To the citizens of South Central LA, the LAPD behaved like a hated army of occupation.

Getting the Job Done?

The ultimate flaw in the military model of policing is that crime is not a "battle" or "war" that police can "win." The source of crime lies within the dynamics of the wider society: in the structure of opportunity, in the lines between legal and illegal ways of making money, and in the moral values and norms of the entire culture. Police enter into the picture late in the game, only once the law has been violated. Police may be able to catch individual criminals, but the police cannot solve the problems of inner-city violence driven by poverty, structural unemployment, teenage pregnancy, systemic racism, and other societal forces.[64] Police can no more control crime than they can control the movement of the tides.

Telling police officers that they should fight a war on crime or a war on drugs is putting police in a no-win situation that can breed cynicism and frustration. Out on the street, day after day, many realize their efforts at arresting an endless stream of offenders is essentially futile. One person behind walls is replaced by another on the street in a matter of minutes. When asked how effective the police are in controlling the drug trade, an experienced narcotics officer answered, "We are like a gnat biting on a horse's ass."[65]

RETHINKING THE MISSION OF THE POLICE

A great deal of unnecessary violence and illegal violence therefore can be linked to our failure to understand the job of policing in our society. The war model of policing establishes unrealistic expectations for police, which breeds cynicism, corruption, violence, and mistrust between the police and the community. It also drives an ever-deeper wedge between those who are the victims of police abuse, namely, poor minority communities, and those who are insulated from such treatment. It is hard for white citizens in suburban communities to comprehend the resentment toward the police simmering within black America. As we saw in Chapter 7, privileges of class do not shield even middle-class and upper-class minorities from the "criminalization of blackness" by the police. Whether driving, flying, or walking while black (or Latino or Asian, depending on where you live), police target "visible" enemies in trying to fight crime. This treatment by police alienates law-abiding citizens and undermines their willingness to cooperate with the criminal justice system in the detection and prosecution of criminal behavior.

However, the heaviest burden falls on those who bear the disadvantages of both race and class. Poor minority communities like that in South Central LA suffer from the social conditions that breed crime. They are both the victims of crime within their own neighborhoods and the victims of ineffective and brutalizing military tactics by a police force that too often does more harm than good for the community it is paid to protect and serve.

The next and final chapter on policing takes a closer examination of the historical role of police so that we may look to the future and reassess the form that mission may take in the twenty-first century. Of great significance are signs of change in the culture and organization of policing, away from the military model and toward a more community-based model. It is also important to look at forces that may be changing the demographics of policing, as more women and minority officers enter police forces and struggle to achieve equality and opportunity.

Change in culture

KEY TERMS

police brutality p. 159
police corruption p. 159
grass eaters p. 159
meat eaters p. 159
impact techniques p. 160

lethal force p. 160
fleeing felon doctrine p. 160
rotten apple theory p. 163
working personality p. 164
symbolic assailants p. 164

blue curtain p. 165
code of silence p. 166
paradox of coercive power p. 167
war model of policing p. 167
Dirty Harry Problem p. 169

REVIEW AND STUDY QUESTIONS

1. What are forms of police misconduct? How widespread is this behavior in policing?
2. What is the fleeing felon doctrine? Why was it declared unconstitutional in *Tennessee* v. *Garner*?
3. Describe the evidence concerning the disproportionate shootings of minority citizens. How has the pattern changed since the 1970s? What does the evidence suggest about the role of racism in the use of lethal force against minority suspects?
4. What is the code of silence and the concept of the blue curtain? Why do researchers believe these develop as features of police subculture? How does the

culture of policing contribute to the problem of police brutality?
5. What is the working personality of police officers? What are the origins of this set of attitudes and values?
6. Describe how the war model of policing may contribute to the prevalence of police brutality.
7. In what way is the metaphor of cops as soldiers inaccurate for modern policing?
8. What is the paradox of coercive force? How does the use of force undermine police authority to use force?
9. What is the "Dirty Harry Problem"? How does this mentality undermine the authority of the police?

CHECK IT OUT

On the Web

Police Foundation, **policefoundation.org/**
Click on the National Center for the Study of Police and Civil Disorder, founded after the LA riots. Check out reports on police use of force, civil disorders, and community policing. The Police Foundation is a major think-tank on innovative ideas in policing, hoping to serve as a catalyst for new developments in policing.

Gallup Police Poll, **www.pollingreport.com/crim. htm#Police**
Check out the latest public opinion polls on citizens' attitudes toward police and beliefs about issues of

race and the use of excessive force. Note the consistent differences between blacks and whites in their attitudes toward the police.

On Film

Behind the Blue Wall: Police Brutality (50 minutes)
*The documentary details the killing of Amadou Diallo and the brutal assault on Abner Louima by the NYPD. It covers commentary by police leaders and community and civil rights advocates on the issue of police violence. Available from Insight Media, **www. insight-media.com.***

The Tarnished Shield: When Cops Go Bad (52 minutes)
Barbara Walters interviews Frank Serpico, who led a one-man campaign to rid the NYPD of corruption, and one of the key officers who was arrested for drug dealing in 1993, to explore the environment in which cops go bad and the code of silence that protects them and punishes those who blow the whistle. Available from Films for the Humanities and Sciences, www.films.com.

Serpico (129 minutes)
Starring Al Pacino in the true story of Frank Serpico, this film portrays the powerful subculture of the NYPD and its treatment of whistle blowers from within its own ranks. Pacino was nominated for an Academy Award for his performance in this drama.

NOTES

1. Cannon, *Official Negligences: How Rodney King and the Riots Changed Los Angeles and the LAPD* (New York: Random House), p. 346.
2. Jerry Gray, "In Police Brutality Case, One Videotape but Two Ways to View It," *The New York Times*, December 13, 1991, p. B7.
3. Mike Sager, "Damn! They Gonna Lynch Us," *Gentlemen's Quarterly*, October 1991; Jerome Skolnick and James Fyfe, *Above the Law: Police and the Excessive Use of Force* (New York: Free Press, 1993), pp. 1–22; Cannon, *Official Negligence*, pp. 20–43.
4. Cannon, *Official Negligence*, p. 43.
5. Ibid., p. 44.
6. Cannon, *Official Negligence*, p. 45.
7. "Los Angeles Chief Assailed by Mayor," *The New York Times*, April 3, 1991, p. A–17.
8. Warren Christopher et al., *Report of the Independent Commission on the Los Angeles Police Department*, (July 1991), p. 9–12.
9. Cannon, *Official Negligence*, p. 214.
10. "Simi Valley Journal: Town Too Feels Eyes of Nation for Trial," *The New York Times*, February 22, 1992, p. 6.
11. Cannon, *Official Negligence*, pp. 237–239.
12. Ibid., p. 238.
13. Ibid., p. 256.
14. Seth Mydans, "Los Angeles Policemen Acquitted in Taped Beating: Storm of Anger Erupts," *The New York Times*, April 30, 1992, p. 1.
15. Robert Reinhold, "Riots in LA: The Blue Line Surprised, Police React Slowly as Violence Spreads," *The New York Times*, May 1, 1992, p. A1.
16. Nancy Abelmann and John Lie, *Blue Dreams: Korean Americans and the Los Angeles Riots* (Cambridge, MA: Harvard University Press, 1995); William Robert Gooding, ed., *Reading Rodney King: Reading Urban Uprising* (New York: Routledge, 1993).
17. *Koon versus United States* 18 U.S.C. D.C. No CR-92, 606 (1993).
18. D. M. Osborne, "A Defense Turned Inside Out," *American Lawyer 20*, April 1993, p. 1.
19. Cannon, *Official Negligence*, p. 86.
20. Courtroom Television Network, *The Rodney Case: What the Jury Saw in California v. Powell*, MPI Home Video, 1992.
21. Herman Goldstein, *Police Corruption: A Perspective on Its Nature and Control* (Washington, DC: Police Foundation, 1975).
22. Samuel Walker, *Popular Justice: A History of Criminal Justice* (New York: Oxford University Press, 1980), pp. 161–183; Lawrence Friedman, *Crime and Punishment in American History* (New York: Basic Books, 1993) pp. 360–362.
23. National Commission on Law Observance and Enforcement, *Report on Lawlessness in Law Enforcement*, No. 11 (Washington, DC: U.S. Government Printing Office, 1931).
24. "Grass-Eaters and Meat-Eaters: Police Corruption in New York City," reprinted in Norman Johnston and Leonard D. Savitz, eds., *Legal Process and Corrections* (New York: Wiley, 1982), pp. 26–34.
25. Egon Bittner, *The Functions of the Police in Modern Society* (Chevy Chase, MD: National Institute of Mental Health, 1970).
26. William A. Geller and Kevin J. Karales, *Split-Second Decisions* (Chicago: Chicago Law Enforcement Study Group, 1981); James J. Fyfe, "The Split-Second Syndrome and Other Determinants of Police Violence," in Anne Campbell and John Gibbs, eds., *Violent Transactions* (New York: Basil Blackwell, 1986), pp. 207–224.
27. Jerome Skolnick and James J. Fyfe, *Above the Law*, pp. 37–43.
28. *City of Los Angeles v. Lyons*, 461 U.S. 95, 105 1983; David Cole, *No Equal Justice: Race and Class in the American Criminal Justice System* (New York: New Press, 1999), pp. 161–165.
29. Cannon, *Official Negligence*, pp. 100–105.
30. Lawrence Sherman, "Execution without Trial: Police Homicide and the Constitution," *Vanderbilt Law Review*, January 1980, pp. 71–100.
31. *Tennessee v. Garner*, 471 U.S. 1 (1985).
32. Skolnick and Fyfe, *Above the Law*, p. 42.
33. Catherine Milton, J. W. Halleck, J. Lardner, and G. L. Albrecht, *Police Use of Deadly Force* (Washington, DC: Police Foundation, 1977).
34. Paul Takagi, "Death by Police Intervention," in R. N. Brenner and M. Kravitz, eds., *A Community Concern: Police Use of Deadly Force* (Washington, DC: U.S. Government Printing Office, 1979).
35. James J. Fyfe, "Blind Justice: Police Shootings in Memphis," *Journal of Criminal Law and Criminology*, 73(2) (1982), pp. 707–722.
36. James J. Fyfe, "Reducing the Use of Deadly Force: The New York Experience," in Catherine H. Milton, ed., *Police Use of Deadly Force* (Washington, DC: U.S. Government Printing Office, 1978), p. 29.

37. John S. Goldkamp, "Minorities as Victims of Police Shootings: Dis-proportionality and Police Use of Deadly Force," *Justice System Journal 2* (1976), pp. 169–183.

38. Arnold Binder and Peter Scharf, "Deadly Force in Law Enforcement," *Crime and Delinquency, 28* (1982), pp. 1–23; Mark Blumberg, "Race and Police Shootings: An Analysis in Two Cities," in J. Fyfe, ed., *Contemporary Issues in Law Enforcement* (Beverly Hills, CA: Sage, 1981), pp. 152–167; Jerry Sprager and David J. Giacopassi, "Memphis Re-visited: A Reexamination of Police Shootings after the Garner Decision," *Justice Quarterly 9* (1992), pp. 211–225.

39. James Fyfe, "Who Shoots? A look at Officer Race and Police Shooting," *Journal of Police Science and Administration 9*(4) (1981), pp. 367–382.

40. Sprager and Giacopassi, "Memphis Re-visited."

41. William A. Geller and Michael S. Scott, *Deadly Force: What We Know* (Washington, DC: Police Executive Research Forum, 1992); Lawrence W. Sherman and Ellen G. Cohn, *Citizens Killed by Big City Police, 1970–1984* (Washington, DC: Crime Control Institute, 1986).

42. Samuel Walker, Cassia Spohn, and Miriam DeLone, *The Color of Justice: Race, Ethnicity and Crime in America* (Belmont, CA: Wadsworth, 1996), p. 95.

43. Cannon, *Official Negligence*, p. 81.

44. Daryl F. Gates (with Diane K. Shah), *Chief: My Life in the LAPD* (New York: Bantam, 1993).

45. Cannon, *Official Negligence*, p. 87.

46. Arthur Niederhoffer, *Behind the Shield: The Police in Urban Society* (Garden City, NY: Anchor, 1967).

47. Richard S. Bennett and Theodore Greenstein, "The Police Personality: A Test of the Predispositional Model," *Journal of Police Science and Administration 3* (1975), pp. 439–445; Raymond Cochrane and Anthony J. P. Butler, "The Values of Police Officers, Recruits and Civilians in England," *Journal of Police Science and Administration 8* (1980), pp. 205–11; Bruce N. Carpenter and Susan M. Raza, "Personality Characteristics of Police Applicants: Comparisons across Subgroups and with Other Populations," *Journal of Police Science and Administration 15* (1987), pp. 10–17.

48. George Pugh, "The California Psychological Inventory and Police Selection," *Journal of Police Science and Administration 13* (1985), pp. 172–177; Robert D. Meier, Richard E. Farmer, and David Mazwell, "Psychological Screening of Police Candidates: Current Perspectives," *Journal of Police Science and Administration 15* (1987), pp. 210–215.

49. Jerome Skolnick, *Justice without Trial: Law Enforcement in a Democratic Society* (New York: Wiley, 1975), pp. 42–70.

50. Ibid., p. 54.

51. John Van Maanen, "The Asshole," in Peter K. Manning and John Van Maanen, eds., *Policing: A View from the Street* (Santa Monica, CA: Goodyear, 1978), pp. 221–238.

52. Skolnick, *Justice without Trial*, p. 44.

53. William Westley, *Violence and the Police: A Sociological Study of Law, Custom and Morality* (Cambridge, MA: MIT Press, 1970), p. 226.

54. Stacey C. Koon, "It's Time for Gates to Step Down," *Los Angeles Times,* May 12, 1991, p. 5.

55. Albert J. Reiss, Jr., "Police Brutality: Answers to Key Questions," *Transaction,* July-August 1968.

56. William Muir, Jr., *Police: Streetcorner Politicians* (Chicago: University of Chicago Press, 1977), pp. 59–100.

57. Skolnick and Fyfe, *Above the Law,* p. 96.

58. Samuel Walker, *Popular Justice: A History of Criminal Justice* (New York: Oxford University Press, 1980), pp. 211–212.

59. Egon Bittner, *Aspects of Police Work* (Boston: Northeastern University Press, 1990).

60. Patrick V. Murphy and Thomas Plate, *Commissioner: A View from the Top of American Law Enforcement* (New York: Simon and Schuster, 1977), p. 270.

61. Bittner, *Aspects of Police Work,* p. 47.

62. Cannon, *Official Negligence,* p. 140.

63. Carl Klockars, "The Dirty Harry Problem," *Annals of the American Academy of Social and Political Science 452* (1980), pp. 33–47.

64. William Julius Wilson, *The Truly Disadvantaged: The Inner City, the Underclass and Public Policy* (Chicago: University of Chicago Press, 1987); L. J. D. Wacquant and William J. Wilson, "The Cost of Racial and Class Exclusion in the Inner City," *Annals of the American Academy of Political and Social Science 501* (1989), pp. 8–25.

65. Skolnick and Fyfe, *Above the Law,* p. 132.

CASE 9

A Woman in Charge:
The Case of Paula Meara

BREAKING IN

When Paula Meara graduated from high school in 1962, women were barred from jobs as police officers by such entry requirements as a 5-foot 7-inch height requirement and other physical tests. The recruitment officer for the Springfield, Massachusetts, Police Department informed Paula that, to qualify for a position as "policewoman," she would need at least two years of college credits in social work or a related field. For nine years, Paula took college courses at night to earn her bachelor's degree while she worked toward her goal of becoming a police officer.

Title VI of the Civil Rights Acts of 1964 prohibits discrimination for employment in the federal government based on race, creed, religion, or sex; in 1972, this law was extended to state and local government employers and the courts ruled that criteria such as the height requirement was discriminatory toward female applicants. Paula Meara was informed that there were no longer jobs for just "policewoman," and she would need to go to the back of the line to apply for a position as a "police officer." Paula Meara filed an employment lawsuit and won a regular appointment as a police officer. She joined the Springfield Police Department in 1974 as one of two female police officers in a force of four hundred. A single parent, Meara found herself assigned to the "dogwatch" from midnight to 8 a.m. with the unit dealing with child abuse, sexual assault, and domestic violence.

STAYING IN

In policing, promotions are based on scores on civil service examinations, superior recommendations, and oral interviews. Like many city departments,

Springfield police hiring, firing, and promotions are supervised by a police commission appointed by the mayor. Springfield Police Commissioner Edward Keating, Jr., had been appointed by his former business partner, Mayor Charlie Sullivan. Personal friends and political connections heavily influenced who was promoted in the Springfield police force.

Officer Paula Meara, smart and ambitious, took the civil service examination for promotion to the rank of sergeant in 1983. She scored third out of 143 applicants, but it was two years before she was promoted. At age 40, she finally reached the rank of sergeant, but she was still assigned to the midnight shift. In 1987 she took the test for lieutenant and made the top score. In the oral interview for the promotion, most of the forty minute interview concerned her use of sick days for the delivery of her three children. She was passed over for promotion four times in favor of male officers with lower test scores.

In 1988 Paula Meara hired a lawyer and sued on gender discrimination. She also filed a suit with the federal Equal Opportunity Employment Commission (EEOC) and the Massachusetts Commission against Discrimination. The state's civil service commission overturned the local commission's actions and ordered the police department to appoint her a lieutenant in 1989. At her swearing-in ceremony, her senior officers refused to shake her hand. Having reached the rank of lieutenant, Meara found herself, nevertheless, back on "dogwatch" again.

Once she was promoted, the department asked Meara to drop the discrimination suit in federal court, but she refused.[1] In early 1989 a federal judge urged the police department to settle, warning that the evidence appeared strongly in Meara's favor. In 1992 the city offered a settlement, acknowledging that the police department had been guilty of gender discrimination against Meara. That same year, Meara took the captain's exam and earned the second-highest score. Over the strenuous objection of the police chief, the commission appointed Meara the first female captain in the history of the Springfield Police Department.

DWELLING IN THE HOUSE OF HATE[2]

In the 1980s, female officers on the Springfield police force were experiencing intense gender discrimination on the job. There are two legally recognized forms of sexual harassment. The first is known as *quid pro quo harassment*, in which a superior or peer at work demands access to a women's sexual favors in exchange for a job or promotion. Darlene C. Dean, an aspiring female Springfield officer, rejected the persistent sexual advances from her superior officer during her first year as a rookie officer. Shortly thereafter she received a poor performance evaluation and was fired the day before her one-year probationary period would have ended.

A second form of sexual harassment refers to a *hostile and demeaning work environment* created by sexual references, jokes, innuendos, comments, pictures, and so on. The law states that employees have the right to work in an atmosphere free of threat, intimidation, or ridicule. In the Springfield Police Department, female police officers were exposed to a steady diet of sexually based commentary intended to belittle and undermine their ability to serve as professional police officers.

Women found tampons, artificial genitals, and other sexual devices placed in their desks; sanitary napkins taped to their lockers; cockroaches in their drawers; sexually demeaning cartoons with the names of female officers written on the characters taped to the walls in public places; nude photos of women prominently displayed in common areas; porn magazines widely circulating in the department; and constant sexual jokes and comments. Men would look at magazines and say to a female colleague, "I wish you looked like that." In another instance, a trio of male officers, nicknamed the "gruesome threesome," kept charts to score how much money was offered for each female cop posing as a prostitute.

Sometimes the harassment was physically threatening. In one case, a male officer repeatedly told a female police officer that he would like to put her in a Girl Scout uniform and rape her. Woman officers repeatedly found slashed tires on their cars. Coffee was spilled on their reports; keys were constantly missing. Women officers reported that they were afraid someone might plant drugs in their cars.

The message was clear: the nearly all-male work force did not want women on the police force, and they certainly did not want women to climb the ranks. More than half of the women who joined the Springfield Police Department during the 1970s and 1980s left the force "voluntarily." In the mid-1990s, out of a force of more than five hundred officers, only twenty-three were women. One woman officer who left her job, but refused to be identified, told a reporter, "It wasn't the work that was stressful, it was the treatment, the internal treatment. That is not the way things should be. If you do your job, then why should someone torture your life because you are not one of them?"[3] Most tragic of all was the fate of one female police officer, who committed suicide with her service revolver after being repeatedly passed over for promotion and being transferred from plainclothes division to a uniformed one.

THE SHEEP BITES BACK

In 1992, Meara decided enough was enough. All along the way the old-boy network had opposed her, and with every advance Meara made new enemies. Still she persevered. According to one of her supporters in the department, "Throw a sheep to the wolves and pretty soon the sheep gets big teeth and learns how to bite back."[4] Although the discrimination lawsuit had been settled in her favor, she felt a need to speak out for all the women on the force, especially those who had quietly left the department. The settlement of her lawsuit and the rules of her job prohibited her from speaking directly to the press, but when Paula heard that Senator John

Glenn was holding hearings in Washington, D.C., about sexual harassment in the workplace, she offered to testify before Congress about her experiences. Meara went public with the painful and shameful tales about a pervasive world of sexual harassment and discrimination so many women had endured in silence.

In the eyes of the targets of sexual harassment, there is nothing innocent or harmless about the jokes, pranks, or comments: the harassment is designed to intimidate. Women officers understood them as deliberate efforts to force women to leave. Detective Judy Glenn, 42, observed, "I'm more afraid of people in here than people on the street. On the street, I usually know where they're coming from."[5] During her detailed testimony to the U.S. Senate Governmental Affairs Committee in 1992, Meara testified that she recognized symptoms of battered women in her fellow female officers. Isolated, ashamed, frightened of retaliation, and demoralized, many of the women blamed themselves for the conduct of the men around them.

Meara's bravery began to pay off as the negative publicity undermined the old-boy network in the department. In 1992, for the first time in nearly twenty years, the mayor of Springfield declined to reappoint Edward J. Keating and his vice-chairman, Peter Carando, Jr., to the five-member police commission. Police Chief Fenton decided to retire, and newly appointed Chief Ernest Seltzer recognized the need to institute major changes in the face of all the negative press and fresh lawsuits. The pinups and cartoons were taken down, and new policies requiring supervisors to give female officers fair and equitable assignments were instituted.

CHALLENGING THE BOYS AT THE TOP

Ernest Seltzer died suddenly in 1994. The position of acting chief went temporarily to second-in-command Daniel Spellacy, a firmly entrenched member of the old-boy network. The rank-and-file expected Spellacy or one of other deputy chiefs to take their turn at the reins of power. But the selection of the permanent police chief lay in the hands of the five-member police commission, and this was a new era in the city of Springfield. Springfield was no longer the white, Irish American working-class city of the 1950s and 1960s: by 1990, the city was more than one-third black or Latino. With the minority community expanding, city politics were no longer controlled by the white Irish power base. Mayor Neal moved on to a seat in Congress, and the Irish Catholic candidate for mayor, Charlie Ryan, was up against a Hispanic city councilman named Michael Albano. When Ryan lost the election to Albano it was the first defeat of a traditional Irish politician in the city of Springfield in more than a century.

One thing that helped Albano in the close election against Ryan was the growing anger in the minority community toward the Springfield police force.[6] Hostilities between the predominantly white police force and the growing minority population in the city mirrored the tensions found in all major inner cities. The core of the problem was the same in Springfield as it was in Los Angeles, Detroit, Newark, or New Orleans: the community felt that police consistently used undue force against young men of color.

Thanks to the minority vote, Albano won a narrow victory over Ryan to become the first Hispanic mayor in the city's history. In his acceptance speech, newly elected mayor Albano vowed to shake up the police department and hire an outsider to be chief, using a professional independent consultant to evaluate the candidates. The police union balked. In negotiations with the mayor, they agreed to the outside professional evaluation, provided the candidates were drawn from the ranks of the department. The mayor agreed.

FAIR COMPETITION OR REVERSE DISCRIMINATION?

Captain Paula Meara decided to apply for the job. Ten candidates, including Meara, came forward to apply for the job as Springfield police chief.[7] The city hired the Massachusetts Municipal Association Consulting Group of Boston to rank the candidates and send the three top candidates to the police commission for final interviews. The assessment required candidates to react to scenarios they might encounter as chief. One scenario involved handling a meeting with a disgruntled community group. Another asked the candidates to describe how they would spend a $50,000 grant for "policing the disadvantaged."

Of the ten candidates, Captain Paula Meara received the highest score from the professional consultants: She finished first, with a score of 90.88. Her old boss, Deputy Chief William Fitchet, came in second with a score of 86.13, and Captain Peter Dillion was third with a score of 81.88. Both these men had their scores boosted by points awarded for length of service and for veteran's status, following civil service rules. Meara received no extra points and clearly outperformed the other two on the exam.[8]

A legal challenge to the selection process was mounted by several of the other candidates who did not make the "short list" for the chief's job. Five of the ten officers who took the assessment exam, including the acting Chief of Police Spellacy, requested a hearing of the civil service commission to investigate allegations that the selection process was being politically hijacked. Their attorneys argued that the process was rigged to favor the selection of Meara because the commission wanted a woman to serve as chief.

Understanding the public tensions around this appointment and wanting the process to be as fair and public as possible, the police commission decided to broadcast the interviews on cable television. The final interviews conducted by the commission were aired on a local cable television network so the public could see the process and judge its fairness for themselves. On February 2, 1996, Paula Meara became the first woman to head a police department in New England.

WELCOME TO THE TOP

Across the entire nation, there are fewer than one hundred female police chiefs.[9] Most of these are found on college campuses or in quiet small towns with only a handful of officers. Only two cities of any size, Austin, Texas, and Portland, Oregon, have ever hired a female to head their force. In traditional New England cities, there has never been a female police chief. From day one, Meara's tenure as chief did not sit well with the male officers, especially the deputy chiefs, who firmly believed Meara had stolen the job from the inner circle of men traditionally in line to inherit the position.[10]

Deputy Chief William Fitchet, Meara's former boss and runner-up in the selection process, fit the perfect portrait of a traditional Springfield cop. Known as one of Springfield's finest, Fitchet's style of policing was to "bust 'em or break 'em in two".[11] As head of the narcotics squad, Fitchet had a reputation of being a top-down, command-and-control, "in your face, get your back" kind of leader. An ex-Marine sharpshooter who had served in Vietnam, he valued discipline, loyalty, toughness, and order. If it was up to Fichet, all subordinates would salute their commanding officers.

Billy Fitchet had been Meara's direct superior for ten years while she served in the crime prevention bureau. At first he had been chivalrous toward her — he had even helped her string her Christmas lights one year when she was a single mother living alone. But as Meara rose in the ranks, winning her promotions through legal and political battles, Fitchet became one of the key figures of the old guard who opposed Meara. Fitchet was the ringleader of the notorious "gruesome threesome," who schemed to launch practical jokes at the expense of all the women on the force but especially Meara.

Deputy Chief Daniel W. Spellacy served as acting chief in the two years between Seltzer's death and Meara's appointment as chief. More than anyone else, he believed he had been denied a promotion he had legitimately earned. In his position of power, as deputy and acting chief, Spellacy had a reputation for maintaining his authority through the careful and skillful manipulation of rumors, leaked information, and strategically placed disinformation. Many on the force believed Spellacy held the levers that controlled the all-powerful rumor mill in the force.

In the world of policing, everyone on the force is vulnerable to a host of charges of misconduct, error, personal difficulties, or professional mistakes. While proof of these charges is often nonexistent, the damage from the rumors themselves operates as a powerful form of social control. Mere suggestion that a person is "on the take," has "trouble at home," is "leaving to take another job," "drinks too much," "caves under pressure," or "is a snitch" is damaging enough to undermine the trust and authority to do one's job. As one veteran officer described it, "At any given moment, any kind of rumor can be started about you. It is one of those things — you either sink or swim. If there is an inkling that it's true, you're done."[12]

Most officers on the force knew and understood the power of rumors; many knew it was a device to punish enemies, eliminate outsiders, settle scores, and protect friends, but most stayed quiet for fear the rumor machine would be turned against them. "Everybody is scared, you're always looking over your shoulder. Not on the streets, where you expect violence. It's from within. People talking bad about you. If I make a mistake, what will they do to me now?" said one veteran patrol officer.[13]

Once Meara was appointed chief, the rumors began to fly fast and furiously: there were reports that she was leaving to take another job, that she was quitting or was going to resign. Within one week of stepping into her new position, Fitchet and Spellacy came to Meara with a "rumor" that several officers, including one of Meara's key supporters, had stolen money confiscated in a drug raid. Although the allegations were more than six years old, Meara understood the game. The objective was to undermine her authority in the eyes of the rank-and-file. These allegations, no matter how baseless, would provide grist for the rumor mill, breeding disloyalty and discontent. If Meara ignored the allegation, she would be accused of a cover-up. If she acted on it publically, she was violating the code of silence. Either way, Meara stood to lose credibility with the rank-and-file at a time she especially needed to establish her authority.

Spellacy and Fitchet brought the report to her desk, telling her that they were "doing her a favor" by passing on useful intelligence about cops who might be dirty. Meara reviewed the allegations and quietly referred the case to the district attorney's office, which investigated and announced publically that the charges were baseless. Within two weeks the case was closed. The ploy by Spellacy and Fitchet had backfired. The press, the mayor's office, the district attorney's office, and the rank-and-file all saw it for what it was: an old rumor revived to unseat an unwelcome chief.

APPOINTED AGAIN

Two years after she was appointed chief in 1996, the state civil service commission submitted its final ruling on March 24, 1998.[14] In a victory for Spellacy and Fitchet, the ruling invalidated the appointment of Paula Meara as chief of police of Springfield, stating that the city erred when it did not include a written test as part of its selection process.[15] The commission ordered the city to administer a new written test for police chief and combine the score of this test with that from the previous assessment to select the top pick.

The police commission acted quickly to appoint Meara as provisional chief until the date of the written test seven months away. On October 20, six people took the fifty-question multiple-choice exam, which focused on local law and departmental policy.

When the results of the civil service written examination came in, no one was surprised that Paula Meara again achieved the top score. Before a crowd of 250 cheering supporters, the woman who has been the first to head a big-city police department in New England formally accepted the appointment for a second time.[16] Attorneys for the challengers still claimed the process was unfair and filed yet another lawsuit in Superior Court claiming discrimination.

POLICING WITH BRAINS INSTEAD OF BRAWN

Despite all the tension going on behind the scenes, Chief Paula Meara did indeed bring major changes to the Springfield Police Department in her first three years.[17] The nine male candidates were correct in their belief that Meara embraced a different style of policing from the traditional style favored by the previous leadership. Meara had been a longtime proponent of community policing. This new style of policing not only changed the organization and its approaches, it also challenged the basic identity of police, redefining its relationship to the community the police are hired to protect and to serve.

Meara reorganized the department from a top-down centralized command-and-control structure to a more decentralized structure that divided the department into nine policing districts. Within each district, captains were given the authority to direct foot and patrol officers whose primary focus was to be accessible and accountable to the residents in the neighborhoods in their district. "My mission is to get police officers as directly as I can in touch with the people they serve. To give them the vision and the goals of integrity and service," said Meara.[18] She ordered police captains to no longer sit behind a desk or hide inside a patrol car. Instead they were to go out on bikes or foot into the community. Departments were to find creative ways to connect with the community and to get to know the folks in the neighborhood, not just the criminals who preyed on them. One district came up with the idea of issuing mock baseball cards for local kids, with pictures and profiles of the careers of the district officers. Whatever it would take, Meara wanted her new police force to form closer ties with the community.

This philosophy and style lay at the opposite end of the spectrum from the approach favored by traditional cops like Fitchet and Spellacy. According to Fitchet, "You can't have every officer out there holding hands. When trouble happens you need to have tough officers who know how to fight and win."[19] Fitchet is, in a sense, a classic "wartime cop," relying most on the skills he learned in the Marines to function as a soldier in the war against crime.

Two incidents illustrate the differing approaches of Meara and Fitchet to policing. When a 22-year-old man holed up in a house and fired thirteen rounds at police in an eleven-hour standoff Fitchet conducted an effective SWAT team operation. He strategically dispensed officers around the perimeter of the house, deployed tear gas, and brought the man into custody without any harm to the officers or the suspect. It was masterful and professional: incident erupted and incident solved.

Meara's use of community policing techniques, by contrast, depends on building relationships with the community day after day. The basis for community policing is a genuine collaboration between the community and the police to make neighborhoods safer and to improve the quality of life for the residents. Police partner with the community to solve its problems, including crime. The old model reacts to each incident as if it were isolated, without a history or a future: the focus is on the law breaker to be identified, subdued, and apprehended. In the community model, the focus in on the neighborhood and on a full understanding of the history of the problem. The belief is that if police deal with issues such as broken windows or graffiti, this will pay off when serious crime occurs and police need information from the community to apprehend the suspect.

When five women were murdered in Springfield, Meara's months of investment in community relations made all the difference. Meara and homicide detectives immediately began meeting with neighborhood residents to discuss the crime. Though not as dramatic as a SWAT team intervention, these meetings resulted in information that led to the arrest of a suspect. The prosecution too could count on these same community members as witnesses for a successful conviction.

In addition to expanding community policing and reorganizing into nine decentralized districts, Meara also instituted a new youth assessment center, which combined the efforts of police, social workers, and psychologists to screen teenagers on the verge of serious trouble. She created a domestic violence unit in the police force, and she appointed a new head instructor of the police academy, who revised the curriculum to focus on civil rights, sensitivity to community, diversity training, and tolerance. One hundred new rookies, forty of whom are either African American or Latino, have undergone this new form of recruit training. Meara hopes that this new approach will heal some of the wounds of past police brutality and mistreatment of African Americans and Hispanics.

Case based on Paula Meara interview, August 22, 2001, Boston, Massachusetts; Susannah Pugh, "City, Police Captain Settle Sex Discrimination Lawsuit," *Union News*, March 13, 1993; Susannah Pugh and Jo Ann Moriarty, "Dial 911 for 'House of Hate'," *Union News*, January 26, 1992; Tom Vannah and Maureen Turner, "Against the Wall: Unanswered Questions and Unkept Promises Are Pushing Springfield's Police-Community Relations to Breaking Point," *The Springfield Advocate* (1997); Kevin Cullen, "Breaking the Thin Blue Line of Bias: Policewoman Is Likely Next Chief in Springfield," *The Boston Globe*, January 16, 1996; Kevin Cullen, "Springfield Selection Process Faces a 'Merit' challenge," *The Boston Globe*, January 17, 1996, p. B21; "Officers Try to Halt Naming of Chief," *The Boston Globe*, January 30, 1996; Rhonda Swan, "Policewomen Face Uphill Struggle for Equality," *Union News*, April 19, 1998; Jo Ann Moriarty, " 'True Blue' Cops Maneuver as Female Chief Hangs Tough," *Union-News*, October 12, 1998; Jo Ann Moriarty, "Chief Meara: Lone Woman in a Brutish, Macho World," *Union-News*, October 11, 1998; Rhonda Swan, "Policewomen Face Uphill Struggle for Equality," *Union News*, April 19, 1998; William F. Doherty, "Civil Service Voids Police Chief Choice," *The Boston Globe*, March 26, 1998; "After Battle, Springfield Police Chief Regains Title," *Boston Globe*, January 15, 1999; Jo Ann Moriarty, "Chief, Challengers Represent Past, Future of Department," *Union-News*, October 13, 1998.

THINKING CRITICALLY ABOUT THIS CASE

1. A reporter remarked that if Paula Meara were Paul Meara, her title of police chief would never have been stripped away. Do you agree? Why or why not?

2. Would you support a city council resolution requiring the police department to be 50 percent women within a ten- or twenty-year time frame? Why or why not? Should police forces reflect the racial diversity of the communities they serve? Why or why not? Given that most of crime is committed by males, should police be predominantly male? Why or why not?

3. Do you agree with Meara that community relationships are key to effective policing? Why or why not? Should police take a problem-solving approach to the job? Why or why not? Do you agree with Lt. Fitchet that professional police must know how to "fight and win"? Why or why not? Develop your own metaphor for the role of police officer in modern society.

4. Meara's appointment was challenged on the grounds that the use of scenarios and interviews was not as objective as the traditional civil service examination, which focuses on questions of law. What are important elements of a selection process for a police chief? What are the important qualities you would look for in hiring a police chief?

5. Alvin Toffler said that "Effective police work in the emerging society will depend less on the holster and more on the head." How does Meara's approach to policing illustrate Toffler's prediction about the future of policing?

6. What changes would you suggest to address the negative culture in the Springfield Police Department?

CHECK OUT THIS CASE

On the Web

Springfield Police Department, www.spfldpd.org/
Go to the Springfield Police Department Web site and read more about Chief Meara and the community policing strategy of the Springfield Police Department.

National Center for Women and Policing, www.feminist.org/police/
The National Center for Women and Policing is the only organization that annually tracks the number of women in policing. Read the latest figures and see if your own local police agency is included in the survey. Download the most recent report: "Equality Denied: The Status of Women in Policing."

CHAPTER 9

The Mission of Policing in the Twenty-First Century

LEARNING OBJECTIVES

After reading this chapter, the student should be able to:

- Explain why the modern police was invented in the cities of the nineteenth century

- Describe the problem of patronage and corruption in nineteenth-century policing

- Identify the current status of women and minorities in the profession of policing

- Discuss the key elements of professionalism in policing and the impact of technology on police–community relations

- Describe the three key functions of policing

- Explain the findings and significance of the Kansas City police preventative patrol experiment

- Explain the "broken windows" theory of crime and discuss its implications for police

L ike many urban police departments, Springfield, Massachusetts, faces the twenty-first century at a crossroads. The governing metaphor of police as "soldiers" in a "war on crime" is understood to be a deeply flawed model for policing in a democratic society. Treating citizens as the "enemy" under a war mentality encourages violence, illegal abuses of power, and the targeting of racial minorities and poor citizens for suspicious treatment. The war model also conceals the reality that crime cannot be vanquished in the same sense that a foreign enemy can be destroyed. Police become discouraged as they find themselves engaged in a never-ending battle that cannot be won.

What is an alternative model for the job of policing? One of the officers in Springfield asked his superiors, "Are we social workers then?"[20] For some, police officers must choose between profoundly different images of their job: one as all-purpose helper for people who are in need and the other as armed protector shielding the community from predators. Perhaps neither of these images accurately captures the complex and, at times, unrealistic responsibilities placed on modern police officers.

This chapter examines the role and mission of the public police within our society. We begin by looking backward at the development of city policing and its changing relationships to other institutions in our society. Why was urban policing first developed? What is the relationship of police to politics and to the community? Whom do police serve, and to whom are they accountable? We also examine the changing composition of policing and consider the importance of shifting demographics on the profession and its role in society.

We end the chapter by examining the community policing movement. For some observers, community policing is a passing fad that will end when the dollars that support it are used up. For others, community policing represents the most creative force for change in contemporary policing.[21] It is both a return to the past and a step into the future. We consider the strengths and weaknesses of community policing and evaluate its value in providing a model for policing a diverse society in the future.

ORIGINS OF POLICING

Before the nineteenth century, there were no police forces in the modern sense.[22] Traditional village communities, in England and in colonial America, relied on regular citizens to assist in maintaining order and peace in the community. In England, a community system known as the **frankpledge** required every male above the age of 12 to join the **tything,** a group of ten able-bodied men sworn to deliver to court any neighbor who committed a crime. Ten tythings were under the supervision of a constable appointed by the local nobleman. A hundred of these were grouped into shires under the leadership of a "shire reeve" or sheriff, who was appointed by the local landowner as a representative of the king.

Over time this system evolved into a structure consisting of a sheriff, constable, and watchman. The sheriff's duties included collecting taxes, apprehending criminals, serving subpoenas, and appearing in court. The sheriff was paid a fee for each task. Both the constable and the watch were unpaid positions served on a rotating basis by able-bodied male citizens. The main purpose of these jobs were to maintain order and protect the peace of the community. Their tasks included reporting fires, arresting or detaining suspicious persons, walking rounds at night, and raising the **hue and cry** if there was a serious threat to the community.

The investigation of crime was largely up to the victim or to a private system of **thief takers,** who provided this service for a fee.[23] A bounty hunter, the thief taker would recover stolen property or find the culprit and deliver him or her to a magistrate for a price. In the 1700s, one of England's most notorious criminals ran a "thief-taking" operation, stealing from victims and then taking a fee to "return" their property to them!

Sir Robert Peel and the London Bobbies[24]

By the nineteenth century, this community-based system of policing had collapsed. The rise of capitalism and the effects of the Industrial Revolution had dramatically altered economic and social conditions. The traditional system of policing was inadequate to deal with the chaos of rapid social change.[25] Between 1750 and 1820, the population of London doubled in size. Along with this growth came enormous civil disorder in the streets, as newly arriving migrants from the countryside flooded the cities in search of work, living in cramped squalor of the city's poor districts. Food riots, wage protests, street fighting, and crime became intolerable for the city's wealthy residents. The city's streets and highways became increasingly unsafe from robbers, muggers, pickpockets, thieves, and burglars.

Home Secretary Sir Robert Peel developed the concept of a modern police force that would patrol the streets to prevent crime and reduce public disorder in the street. Convincing Parliament that he was not proposing the creation of a new kind of army that would give the government power over its own people proved to be a difficult task. For decades, members of Parliament opposed Peel's proposal to create such a force. In the end, however, crime and disorder forced residents of the city of London to agree to try Peel's proposal. In 1829, the London Metropolitan Police Act created the world's first full-time uniformed police force.

The primary purpose of the police force was to be a preventative presence on the city streets. To have a deterrent effect, policemen were supposed to be visible and omnipresent. Peel chose an extremely noticeable hat for police and purposefully selected men to serve who were exceptionally tall. The idea of **preventative patrol** was that, through continuous patrolling of a fixed beat, the **bobbies** would ensure that city streets would be safe for law-abiding citizens to walk about without fear of being mugged or assaulted.

Peel was very sensitive to the concerns of citizens that the police might resemble the king's army with its power targeted at the citizens themselves. Although Peel chose to

frankpledge: a system of law enforcement in medieval societies, by which every male member of the community over the age of 12 was bound by a pledge to keep peace and assist in delivering offenders to court.

tything: In Anglo-Saxon law, an association of ten families bound together by a frankpledge.

hue and cry: an old English call for assistance in the pursuit of felons.

thief takers: eighteenth century mercenaries who offered to pursue felons for a fee.

preventative patrol: continuous and visible walking of public streets by police in order to deter crime.

bobbies: nickname for the first formal municipal police officers in London, named after Sir Robert Peel, the founder of the Metropolitan Police Force.

The London Bobbies were the first modern police force in the world created to perform the job of protecting citizens from crime within the streets of the city. The distinctive uniform and hat were designed to create a visible presence by the police in order to deter crime.

design his new organization in a quasi-military style, with rank designations and hierarchical forms of command and control, Peel was careful to distinguish the "bobbies" from the soldiers of the king's army. He clothed the men in blue instead of the military red, he did not allow them to carry guns, and he insisted that they act in a polite and restrained manner. Peel understood that the legitimacy of the newly created institution of public law enforcement depended on the principle that police act to uphold the law by remaining within the bounds of the law. To establish their authority, police would need to behave in a lawful manner, reassuring the citizenry that they were there to protect them from crime, not to control or dominate them.

Early American Police

Cities in the United States were experiencing the same problems of rapid growth, rampant street crime, and civil disorder as London.[26] The population of New York City, for example, mushroomed from 33,000 in 1790 to 150,000 in 1830. Much of the disorder arose from conflicts between rival ethnic groups, as new arrivals came in search of employment and housing and clashed with already established groups. Violence often erupted in fights between Irish, German, and native-born citizens of different ethnic backgrounds as the population of immigrants grew in size. Conflict and violence also erupted in U.S. cities, especially in the North, along racial lines. As the antislavery movement grew in prominence, hostility from whites toward blacks grew in the streets. Abolitionists were attacked as they spoke out against slavery, and black citizens were often the target of mob violence fueled by racism and competition for jobs and housing.

Even more than the British, Americans did not like the idea of a public police force with the power to use force against its own citizenry. Uniformed officers dispersed throughout the public streets brought to mind the hated British army. The American Revolution had been fought against the power of the king's army to enter into citizens' houses at will, garnish their property, and seize and search for weapons and other contraband. Americans were extremely suspicious of giving government that kind of power over its citizens. Many were afraid that a police force would act like a private army to do the bidding of rival politicians, and many resisted the idea of paying taxes to provide the salaries for this force.

Ultimately, however, the growing disorder in the streets, even more than the problem of crime, pressed the need to create some kind of force to maintain civil peace. The first police force emerged with the establishment of a day watch in Boston in 1838 comprising six officers. By the start of the Civil War in 1861, a number of U.S. cities, including Boston, New York, Baltimore, Philadelphia, New Orleans, and Chicago, consolidated a day watch and night watch under a single police chief modeled after the Metropolitan Police of London.[27]

Patronage and Corruption

Just as people feared, police of the nineteenth century were very much under the control of local politicians.[28] Police were a part of the political machinery, with police officers selected primarily on the basis of their political loyalty to the ward boss. Political parties controlled the mayor's office, which in turn controlled access to jobs in city services such as the fire department, schools, courts, and, of course, police. These well-paid jobs were handed out as rewards for political loyalty to party activists. In some places, a job as a police officer or a promotion within the force could be bought and sold for a fee paid to the party. On election day, a whole police force might be dismissed and replaced with new officers. Training was nonexistent: police were handed a baton and a a badge and sent out on patrol duty.

The function of the nineteenth century police department was quite broad and less focused on crime or controlling civil disorder than on being an all-purpose service agency for the city.[29] Police drove ambulances, handled licensing of businesses, provided services for the poor, took in lost children or the homeless. Patrol was the heart of police work, but there was little professionalism or supervision of the patrol officer on the streets. This set the stage for systemic corruption, as police on the street profited from the selective enforcement of laws against gambling, saloons, prostitution, illegal prize fighting, and other activities. Police ran protection rackets, demanding fees from businesses; police also looked the other way for pickpockets and thieves in exchange for a share in the proceeds.

Citizens were highly ambivalent about the police. Police were viewed as political hacks rather than public servants, and people who were arrested often fought back. Police were a part of the ethnic conflicts, not above them. Whichever group had control of political power in the city had control of the police. Clashes between the police and citizen groups led to the adoption and use of firearms by the police.

By the end of the nineteenth century, there was a movement to clean up police forces to create a truly professional police force independent of local political control.[30] The Progressive movement, largely middle-class reformers, sought to take the corruption out of city government and its institutions such as the police. Reformers believed that policing should be centralized on a citywide basis, police officers should be trained and selected on the basis of ability, discipline and procedure should be implemented, and the function of the police should focus on apprehending criminals and enforcing the law. The reformers argued that the broad service functions of the police should be handled by other professional agencies and that the police function should be narrowed to deal with crime alone.

The Progressives had little success in actually transforming police. In particular, the big cities of the industrial Northeast and Midwest continued to be bastions of patronage and profit-driven corruption. In 1929, President Herbert Hoover appointed the first national commission to report on the state of the U.S. criminal justice system.

patronage: a form of corruption in which the political party in power awards jobs and promotions as return for loyalty and favors to politicians.

Headed by former Attorney General George Wickersham, the National Commission on Law Observance and Enforcement, popularly known as the **Wickersham Commission,** published fourteen volumes on the criminal justice system in 1931.[31] The eleventh volume, entitled *Lawlessness in Law Enforcement,* garnered the most attention from the public with its systematic and thorough documentation of police brutality and abuses of authority across the country. Near the end of Prohibition, in 1931, the level of corruption was so great in the Chicago Police Department that a blue ribbon citizens' commissions seriously suggested that the only way to clean up the force was to fire all 4,000 officers and start from scratch to build a new tradition of professionalism and ethical policing.[32]

George Kelling and Mark Moore characterize the early period of policing until about 1930 as the political era of policing in which patronage and political considerations dominated big-city police organizations. The police performed a wide range of services for the local community, but they primarily served the political interests of the local bosses. Systemic corruption and brutality flourished largely unchecked within a highly decentralized police structure.

PROFESSIONALISM: A MASTER TREND

From 1910 to 1960, another, more successful movement to adopt a professional model for police was led by a series of influential police chiefs such as Richard Sylvester in Washington D.C., O. W. Wilson in Wichita, Kansas, and August Vollmer of the Los Angeles Police Department. The central goal of **professionalism** was to separate policing from politics.

August Vollmer[33] was chief of the Berkeley Police Force from 1905 to 1932, in Berkeley, California. Vollmer believed that police officers should be experts in their field; that police departments should be independent from political influences; and that they should use technology, science, and efficient administrative practices in their work.[34] Vollmer was the first police chief to recruit college students and the first to create college-level police education. From 1932 to 1937, Vollmer served as professor of police administration at the University of California at Berkeley. O. W. Wilson was a student of Vollmer. Wilson went on to become police chief in Wichita, Kansas, professor of police administration at Berkeley, and finally superintendent of the Chicago Police Department in 1960. Wilson was brought to Chicago to bring professionalism to a department heavily tied to urban politics and steeped in corruption and scandal.

The master trend toward professionalism and independence from politics is one that is uneven within U.S. policing.[35] Given its highly decentralized structure, change happens slowly and over time, as some departments move ahead in a particular direction while others remain entrenched or committed to an earlier style or structure of policing.

The Impact of Technology

By the 1960s, the ubiquitous patrol car, two-way radio, and telephone had profoundly altered urban policing and relationships between the police and the community.[36] Most city police departments had traditionally assigned officers to walk up and down specific streets, keeping the officers on the same beat to ensure familiarity with the residents. The use of patrol cars for preventative patrol removed officers from direct contact with citizens and placed them behind the glass of the rolling vehicle. Even driving slowly down the street distanced the officers from the people on the streets. Isolated in their cars with the windows rolled up, police no longer developed face-to-face relationships with residents and business owners.

Wickerham Commission: a panel of national experts convened in 1929 to conduct the first comprehensive national study of the criminal justice system. Evidence of systematic corruption and abuses in policing in the Wickersham Report generated public support for reform.

professionalism: the master trend in twentieth-century policing, which sought to separate policing from politics through civil service examination, education, training, and bureaucratization.

The two-way radio, telephones, and institutionalization of the rapid response system of 911 put the patrol car at the beck and call of citizens who demanded an urgent response from the police. With mobile command and control units, supervisors could more carefully monitor the movements of the officers via the two-way radio and mobilized them at different locations of the city. Success became measured by the speed of the arriving patrol car rather than the personal contacts made by the cop on the street corner.

The Paramilitarization of Policing

The 1960s were an era of huge social unrest and conflict. John F. Kennedy was assassinated in 1963, Malcolm X in 1965, Martin Luther King, Jr., and Robert F. Kennedy both died in 1968. It was a decade of mass protests, urban riots, campus demonstrations, and street revolts, a time of material prosperity and social discontent. The civil rights movement, the antiwar movement, the women's movement, the black power movement, and the gay rights movement all demanded greater equality within society. The courts reflected this liberal climate with many "due process" rulings that constrained the power of the police vis à vis citizens. By the late 1960s and the 1970s, radical student groups and other organizations talked openly about the need for armed resistance to the power of the state.

Crime rose dramatically during these two decades: the violent and property crime indexes climbed steadily during these years to peak in 1979. In 1965 President Lyndon Johnson created the President's Commission on Law Enforcement and Administration of Justice, which appointed several task forces to study crime, the administration of justice, and the riots that had erupted in so many of the inner cities between 1964 and 1968.[37] These commissions identified the underlying causes of the riots to be the rampant racism, inequality, poverty, and discrimination in the nation's black communities. Unemployment, discrimination in jobs and housing, inadequate social services, and unequal justice were the primary factors to blame for both rising crime and social unrest.

While recognizing the need to address the root causes of crime and social unrest, however, the President's Commission also promoted the concept of waging a federally funded "war on crime," using technology paid for by federal dollars. The Omnibus Crime Control and Safe Streets Act of 1968[38] created the Law Enforcement Assistance Administration (LEAA), a federal bureaucracy to develop new devices, techniques, and approaches in law enforcement and then provide funds and assistance to states in adopting these technologies and strategies.

The LEAA became an agency within the federal government to promote the new war on crime.[39] LEAA money supplied many police departments with the basic physical infrastructure of car radios, high-tech dispatch systems, and mobile command and control centers. LEAA grants also funded more sophisticated **paramilitarization** of policing in specialized SWAT units, technologically advanced helicopters, infrared technology for night viewing, and computer communications technology.[40]

To black innercity residents of neighborhoods in Los Angeles, Detroit, New York, Boston, Chicago, and other major cities, the patrol cars moving slowly around their city streets resembled the rolling fortresses of an occupying army, generating tremendous conflict between the minority community and the police. This conflict erupted into full-scale urban riots sparked by police behavior in almost every major city between 1964 and 1968.

George L. Kelling and Mark H. Moore refer to the era of U.S. policing between 1930 and 1980 as the Reform Era, when the strategic goal of crime control through rapid response, patrol, and centralized command and control systems were dominant strategies in major police departments.[41] Higher levels of professionalization and independence from political control was achieved through formalization and bureaucratization. The main drawbacks of these reforms were pervasive alienation between the police and the community, particularly those living in urban minority neighborhoods, and growing levels of distrust between minority communities and the police.

paramilitarization: use of military equipment, tactics, and weapons in policing.

Women and Minorities in Policing

Until the 1970s, most U.S. police forces were almost entirely all male and all white, even in communities such as Los Angeles and New York, which had large Hispanic or African American populations. Title VII of the federal 1964 Civil Rights Act prohibits discrimination on the basis of race, creed, color, sex, or national origin with regard to compensation, terms, conditions, or privileges of employment. In 1972, Title VII was amended to apply to state and local government employees including police officers, motivating many minorities and women to attempt to enter occupations previously closed to them.

As we see from the case of Paula Meara, minorities and women who did join police forces faced substantial discrimination and blocked opportunities for advancement. Tom Bradley, the first African American mayor of Los Angeles, began his career as an LAPD officer in 1940.[42] At that time, black patrol officers were required to have black partners; whites refused to work with blacks. Black officers were forced to serve in a segregated unit known as the Black Watch. Even though Vollmer and Parker had instituted civil service examinations for promotion, black officers experienced the same discrimination as Meara did. Even when they did well on the written portion of the exam, they were invariably rated low on the oral interviews by their white supervisors. With little hope for promotion in a racist institution, many ambitious black police officers like Mayor Bradley left policing to seek other opportunities as lawyers, judges, or politicians.

In the twenty years from 1972 to 1992, black representation in policing has come to almost equal the percentage of African Americans in the U.S. population as a whole. As of 1997, African Americans accounted for 11.7 percent of the nation's full-time local law enforcement personnel, while Hispanics accounted for about 7.8 percent.[43] This proportion of minority police is much higher in large cities than it is in small police departments. But percentages do not tell a full story. African Americans still remain underrepresented in the upper ranks of police administrations, despite some notable achievements in individual police departments such as the appointment of Willie Brown in Los Angeles in the wake of the Rodney King incident (see Chapter 8). In 1992, African Americans were 11.5 percent of all sworn officers in New York City, but only 6.6 percent held the rank of sergeant or above.[44]

The situation for women in policing is even less encouraging than that for male racial and ethnic minorities.[45] In 1990, the Police Foundation found that women made up 10.1 percent of the total number of officers in departments functioning under court orders to increase their proportion of women officers.[46] In agencies with voluntary affirmative action programs, women constituted 8.3 percent of officers; and where no affirmative action programs existed at all, only 6.1 percent of officers were women. Madison, Wisconsin, a highly progressive city, has the highest percentage of women, 25 percent, of any department in the country. Even under the leadership of Paula Meara, the police department in Springfield in 2000 had only 6 percent women officers.[47] Women remain underrepresented in command and supervisory positions.[48]

REIMAGINING THE ROLE OF THE POLICE

In the mythology of policing, officers are valiant or heroic "crime fighters," who risk their lives every day to get dangerous criminals off the streets. The language of policing is the language of the battlefield. The "thin blue line" imagery suggests that police serve as a protective shield against the forces of evil. Television depicts police chasing fugitives over fences, breaking in doors, screeching their car brakes in a dramatic shootout with the bad guys. On television, we see hard-boiled detectives at gritty crime scenes, solving violent crime with a handful of clues.

The reality of policing is far from this dramatic and exciting fiction we enjoy so much on our television screens and in detective novels. Policing is not nearly as dangerous an occupation as it appears to be in popular fiction. In 1998, sixty-one law enforcement officers, including federal, state, and local officers, were feloniously killed in the line of duty.[49] This rate is only slightly higher than the homicide rate for the entire population: the chance that an officer will be killed by a criminal is about the same as it is for everyone else. Other occupations, such as farming, construction, and mining, are far more lethal than policing. Police officers rarely discharge or fire their weapons; in New York City, guns are fired in only one out of every 352 encounters with criminal suspects.[50]

Although fiction portrays police as solving crime, the simple truth is that most crimes are not reported to the police, and police are not hugely successful in solving even the small percentage of crimes that are reported. Because most crime suspects cannot be identified, most crimes go unsolved. In the United States only about 21 percent of reported crimes are ever solved. This is higher for homicides, where the rate is about 67 percent, and very low for crimes such as auto theft, where the clearance rate is less than 15 percent.[51]

The Police Role: Image versus Reality

Although the image of police as foot soldiers in a never-ending battle against crime is our dominant image of police, less than one-third of all police work is spent in criminal law enforcement. The typical law enforcement officer rarely makes a felony arrest. In 1990, police officers made an average of 19 arrests per year: this is about two per month, and most of these are for minor incidents such as public drunkenness or disorderly conduct; Egon Bittner found that patrol officers make, on average, one felony arrest per month.[52]

Patrol is the heart of modern police work. Sixty-five percent of all police officers in the United States are assigned to patrol work.[53] Police officers drive around slowly in cars, essentially waiting for the radio dispatcher to send them on a call for service. Contrary to the view on television, patrol work is quite boring: most of the time is spent waiting for something to happen. More than 90 percent of police work is a reactive response to a call for service or assistance. Probably the most self-generated police work involves the stopping of motor vehicle operators who violate traffic laws.

James Q. Wilson has identified three key functions of the police.[54] The first is the peacekeeping or **order maintenance function,** which is achieved through patrolling the streets and keeping things under control. The second is the **service function.** This type of police work involves dealing with problems and people in society that no one else wants to deal with, such as the homeless or mentally ill, and a host of other concerns. The **crime control function,** the detection and apprehension of those who violate the law, is the third distinct function of modern police work.

Empirical data reveal that the bulk of police work involves performing either the order maintenance or human service function. Studies repeatedly find that somewhere between 15 and 25 percent of calls to police concern criminal matters.[55] Police most often deal with situations in which there has been no violation of criminal law but there is a need for some kind of assistance or intervention, such as loud parties or radios, drunken or lost individuals, rowdy teenagers, kids turning on a fire hydrant, a truck illegally parked and blocking a driveway, a car alarm that is stuck, traffic accidents, medical emergencies, suicides, animals that are out of control, barking dogs, people who are stuck, or the mentally ill. The list goes on and on. Citizens call upon the police for help in all sorts of situations, most of them noncriminal in nature. The police seem to function as a kind of all-purpose, 24-hour-a-day social service agency.

Preventative Patrol and Rapid Response

The concept of the modern police force is built on the notion of preventative patrol. The assumption is that if we increase police patrol, crime will go down; if we take officers off the street, crime will go up. Periodically, researchers have tested this theory to see if

order maintenance function: to maintain peace and order, handle disputes, deal with troublemakers, and keep public spaces free from disorder.

service function: to provide assistance with a wide array of social problems.

crime control function: detection and apprehension of law violators.

rapid response: urgent response system of policing based on citizen use of 911, two-way radios, and mobile command and control units.

it actually works. In one study, conducted in the mid-1950s by the New York City police department, many more foot patrols were added in one precinct. During the four months of the experiment, mugging, burglaries, and auto thefts fell. The data were used to justify an enormous increase in the number of police officers in New York City over the next twenty years.

However, along with the rise in the number of police officers out on the street, there was a steady increase in the crime rate during the next twenty years. This raised many questions about the relationship between patrol and crime commission. Another study of the New York City subway system, conducted in the 1970s, found that increasing patrols between the hours of 8 p.m. and 4 a.m. reduced the amount of crime. But researchers found a corresponding increase in the amount of crime taking place after 4 a.m. Crime was simply displaced to another time or place, when patrols were less heavy.

The most ambitious study to look at the preventative power of patrol was conducted in 1973 and is called the **Kansas City experiment.**[56] The goal was to test the proposition that preventative patrol has a deterrent effect on crime and makes citizens feel safer. Fifteen police beats were divided into three matched groups. The first group, chosen randomly, was the control group, in which patrol patterns stayed as before. The second group was the "proactive patrol" beats. The number of cruising cars was increased to two to three times the normal volume. In the third beat, the **"reactive patrol"** group, there was no preventative patrol at all. Police cars went out into the community only in response to calls for help from citizens. Researchers interviewed businesses and individuals before and after the experiment for their perception and fear of crime; and reviewed victimization reports and official statistics on crime before and after the experiment.

The results were startling to everyone. After a whole year, it was found that there were no difference at all among the three areas in the official crime rate, rate of victimization, level of citizen fear, or degree of satisfaction with the police. The only slight difference was that citizens in the proactive beats perceived that crime had gone up, largely because they saw many more police cars in the community and assumed the reason was that crime had gotten worse. The results from this study, and other work on policing, has led many to question the value of traditional-style patrol, particularly when it is done in police cars.

Responding to the studies of the 1970s showing that regular motor patrols have little impact on crime, police departments have experimented with other models of patrol. **Saturation patrolling** (or **problem-oriented patrolling**) targets particular locations or "hot spots" where crime is known to take place.[57] The aim is to enormously increase the police presence in very specific locations. Like the subway experiment, these strategies are quite effective but only in the short run, because they cannot be maintained indefinitely.

Another strategy is to disrupt markets for criminal activity through an active police presence without trying to arrest the criminals themselves. This is used most often to regulate prostitution and drug dealing in a specific public location.[58] Police may combine enforcement crackdowns with a pattern of surveillance designed to make business impossible, by scaring away customers for the illegal business. Uniformed officers may be stationed to conspicuously write down license plates of customers looking to purchase sex or drugs. This has the positive benefit of making the neighborhood much safer for the law-abiding residents, although the activity will resume as soon as the police presence is withdrawn.

Research conducted in the 1970s and 1980s also questioned the effectiveness of the "rapid response" approach to police calls for service.[59] The 911 system emphasized the ability of police to arrive on the scene in a short time, but the evidence shows that reducing the time it takes police to get to a crime scene has no impact at all on improving the likelihood that the criminal will be apprehended. Citizens tend to measure police responsiveness by the speed with which they arrive on the scene after placing a call, yet in cases of theft, at least, by the time the victim has discovered the loss, the offender is long gone. Arriving quickly may make a victim feel better, but it does not make much difference to the investigation of the crime. Even when there is a confrontation between a victim and suspect, victims generally take as long as twenty minutes before they phone the

Kansas City experiment: 1973 experiment that compared the deterrent effect of three different modes of police patrol.

reactive patrol: a police patrol model in which police respond only when there is a call for assistance.

saturation patrolling: increased police presence in "hot spots" known to have high amounts of criminal activity. Also known as problem-oriented patrolling.

police. Even with the quickest possible response, by the time police have arrived, the offender can no longer be followed or caught by law enforcement.

The really critical ingredient in successful criminal investigation is the quality of the information provided by victims and witnesses, which identify the offender and provide the evidence needed to make a successful legal prosecution.[60] Police need a description, name, address, or a license plate number. Most successful criminal investigations depend on the identification of a likely suspect by citizens; rarely do police identify a suspect based on an investigation. Typically, police investigate and collect evidence about a suspect identified for them by a member of the community.

Private Security as an Alternative to Police Patrol

By world standards, the United States is a heavily policed society: the United States has more police per capita than Australia, Britain, Canada, and Japan. In 1999, the United States had one police officer for every two hundred citizens, yet Americans are increasingly relying on the private security industry to keep them "safe" from crime. The number of private police hugely outnumbers the number of public police.

Have Americans lost faith in the police to keep us safe by choosing private companies to deliver that service instead of public police? Gated communities, shopping malls, and corporate businesses are all protected by paid security staff. Alarm systems and video cameras keep these kinds of spaces free of "vagabonds" and "organized gangs of thieves." More money is spent and more people are employed by private police operations than by all public police agencies combined. The annual spending on private police first exceeded spending on public police in 1977. Today, the private security industry employs close to 2 million people, with a budget well over $80 billion a year.[61] But poor people, who are overwhelmingly victims of crime, cannot afford this kind of protection. The private security industry provides safety only for people who can pay for it.

Community Policing

For its many supporters, the concept of **community policing** holds the most promise for reinventing public policing and reforming the institution to better serve the needs of the community as we enter the twenty-first century. The key concept of community policing is that, by building partnerships with the community and addressing the conditions that give rise to crime, police have an opportunity to abandon the futile and dangerous "war-making" approach to crime in favor of a peace-making model that relies on cooperation, trust, and mutual respect between police and the community. Chief Meara is a proponent of community policing and has high hopes that it will prove to be a solution to long-standing tensions between police and the community, especially minority citizens. Community policing, in some respects, is a move "back to the future," making a conscious effort to put police back out onto the street corner in direct contact with the citizens they serve.

The widespread and growing movement to institute community policing represents a third wave of reform, which is similar to the advent of professionalism partly because it is so diverse. There is no single theory or model of community policing. Rather, it is loose set of concepts and a host of strategies and approaches. Some departments have adopted community policing strategies under a comprehensive plan, while others are implementing only pieces of the strategy. Like the move toward professionalism, it is more accurate to say that there is a long, slow trend of change in this direction rather than a sudden or complete revolution in policing.

There are many in policing and in the wider community who are skeptical about community policing or who are professionally opposed to it as a crime control strategy. Traditionalists in policing believe that community policing is nothing more than the current fad, which will fade when the federal dollars that support it are gone. These officers do not support community policing because they are firm believers in the classical approach to policing. There are also those in the minority community who believe

community policing: pro-active policing strategy which relies upon problem-solving in close collaboration with the citizens within the community.

Only a third of police work involves traditional crime fighting. Police routinely perform an array of service functions for the community. Advocates of community policing urge police to form strong relationships with citizens in the community to reduce hostility and increase the capacity of the police to genuinely reduce crime.

that the so-called strategy of community policing is nothing more than a wolf dressed in sheep's clothing. The continuation of military-style tactics, undercover surveillance, and so-called quality-of-life policing amounts to an all-around war-like assault on the young men of the minority community. Community policing, in this view, is merely a public relations campaign by a more sophisticated police organization trying to control the public outcry when its aggressive tactics "get out of hand."

Quality-of-Life Policing   The **"broken windows" theory of crime** was developed by James Q. Wilson and George Kelling in an influential article that appeared in the the *Atlantic Monthly* in 1982.[62] Wilson and Kelling argued that mere police presence in radio cars or even on the street is not sufficient to make citizens feel safer. It is necessary for police to take a more proactive approach in dealing with minor crime, vandalism, and other negative "quality-of-life" issues within poor neighborhoods. Police should take the lead in cleaning up graffiti, broken windows, burnt-out cars, piles of garbage, broken street lights, or abandoned vacant lots because these signs of neglect signify an "unsafe" neighborhood. These seemingly trivial physical signs, along with the public disorders of teens hanging out, loud swearing, panhandling, or loud music, are signs of a neighborhood that is beginning to decay. When these problems are ubiquitous, law-abiding citizens feel unsafe and they abandon the neighborhood, by moving away if they are able or by staying indoors if they are not. Before long, the neighborhood has attracted far more serious criminal activity and has become a high-crime location. As one officer put it, "If you see garbage all around you, you begin to act like garbage."

New York City under the leadership of Police Commissioner William Bratton embraced the strategies of quality-of-life policing with a vengeance. Mayor Rudy Guiliani vowed to implement a "zero-tolerance policy" for minor "quality-of-life" violations such as jumping turnstiles in the subway, panhandling, kids who were truant from school, homeless people sleeping under bridges or in doorways, and the "squeegee operators," who frighten suburban drivers stopped at a traffic light by wiping their windscreens and asking for payments in return. Police were instructed to take these crimes seriously and arrest those who engaged in them. As often as not, an arrest would turn up an outstanding warrant or parole violation, which would lead to a stint in jail. Between 1994 and 1997, misdemeanor arrests in New York City rose by 73 percent.[63]

At the same time, the rate of serious crime fell dramatically in New York City. According to the broken windows theory, attention to trivial crimes will impact more serious crime. During these same years, the rate of serious crime also fell dramatically in New York: by 1998 the city had its lowest murder rate in thirty-eight years. Guilani and Bratton were quick to take credit for the decline and even fought over which of them

quality-of-life policing: aggressive enforcement of public nuisance laws.

"broken windows" theory of crime: minor crimes such as vandalism and graffiti are early signs of a neighborhood in decline, which lead to more serious criminal conduct in that location.

was really responsible for it. In truth, the decline in serious crime is a widespread pattern that predates the rise of quality-of-life policing and is linked to an array of factors.[64] According to most criminologists, no single police intervention can significantly impact the commission of crime.

Community–Police Partnerships   The community policing movement identifies two key reasons police need stronger bonds with the community. The first is that police need the community in order to successfully apprehend and prosecute people who commit crime. Paula Meara was effective in identifying the serial killer who was terrorizing the city. Her strategy was based on a long-term goal of cultivating ties with members of the community. Eventually, contacts within the community led to a positive identification. Without information, cooperation, trust, and support from the community, the police are nothing more than the rolling fortresses of an occupying army, cut off from access to any quality information about crime.

The second reason police need to develop close ties with the community is even more important. According to David Bayly, policing is based on a big untruth: police work, *even at its most effective,* cannot control crime. The power to genuinely prevent, and therefore reduce, crime does not lie with the police. The riots in the wake of the Rodney King beating were only sparked by police brutality. The fuel that fed these outbreaks of disorder were decades of poverty, unemployment, structural racism, rampant drug abuse and alcoholism, teen pregnancies, and other symptoms of social inequality. The solution to these problems is not to be found in the "band-aid" of reactive policing. The police respond to crime after it has already occurred. They have been shutting the barn door after the horse has escaped.

This fundamental reality puts police in a difficult situation: they are being asked to "fix" something without being given the tools to do the job. One option, according to proponents of community policing, is for the police to be more proactive in partnering with the community to deal with the problems that generate crime. Police cannot do the work alone, but they can collaborate with schools, human services, politicians, businesses, and other agencies to create solutions that correct the underlying problems. This is the reason Chief Meara set up an assessment center to work with other professionals and the community to identify kids before they get into serious trouble. Much crime is highly predictable: kids who are out of school and unsupervised by responsible adults will be committing serious crime before too long. Police can either wait for it to happen and then arrest them, or they can decide to run midnight basketball leagues or other sports programs to keep kids off the streets and out of trouble. This is the difference between a proactive and a reactive approach to policing.

Community policing is a response to the dilemma of policing in a free society. As we have seen, the modern police force was, to a significant extent, the creation of a state-run armed force to keep peace in the public streets. The key threat came from collective unrest due to ethnic and social inequality. In the twentieth century, the institution of policing found itself increasingly under attack from the public in its role as a coercive force. The requirements of a democratic society demand that police do not conduct a "war" against citizens or behave like an occupying army in enemy territory. White middle-class America is largely shielded from this source of tension: private security offers reduce social disorder for a hefty profit, while minority communities suffer from the twin evils of rampant crime and ineffective military-style policing strategies that isolate police from the very communities they are supposed to protect and serve.

As community police officers, police can take the lead in partnering with the community and other social services to assess the needs of the community, diagnose and understand the causes of crime and other forms of social disorder, and develop strategies to address those causes. They may not be the ones to implement all of those strategies, since many of them involve services and interventions that should be provided by other agencies and groups, but police can advocate for these interventions and help the community understand the link between negative conduct and these problems.

KEY TERMS

frankpledge p. 181
tything p. 181
hue and cry p. 181
thief takers p. 181
bobbies p. 181
preventative patrol p. 181
patronage p. 183

Wickersham Commission p. 184
professionalism p. 184
paramilitarization p. 185
order maintenance function p. 187
service function p. 187
crime control function p. 187
rapid response p. 187

Kansas City experiment p. 188
reactive patrol p. 188
saturation patrolling p. 188
community policing p. 189
quality-of-life policing p. 190
"broken windows" theory of
   crime p. 190

REVIEW AND STUDY QUESTIONS

1. Why was the modern police force "invented" in the first part of the nineteenth century? How did the concept of the police force differ from that of a military force?

2. Describe the problems of patronage and corruption in nineteenth-century police forces. In what ways do professionalism reforms reduce these kinds of problems in policing?

3. Describe the impact of technology on the methods of policing, on the effectiveness of patrol, and on relationships between the police and the community.

4. What is the purpose of preventative patrol? What evidence do we have today that patrol "works" to prevent crime? Describe the Kansas City experiment. What does this research suggest about the most effective use of police personnel? Describe the different strategies of patrol and discuss the relative advantages of each type of patrol.

5. What do police really do, and how does this contrast with the "image" of policing? What are the three functions of policing? Which is most important in your view, and why?

6. What is rapid response? What are the criticisms of rapid response as a measure of police effectiveness in solving crime?

7. Explain the "broken windows" theory of crime. What are the implications of this theory for police strategy?

8. What is community policing? Do you support the image of police as "problem solvers"? Why or why not? In your view, is community policing the latest fad or an important and lasting trend in police reform?

9. What is the status of minorities and women in modern policing? What steps, if any, would you advocate to increase the diversity of police?

CHECK IT OUT

On the Web
Community Policing Consortium, **www.community policing.org/index.html**
Check out this Web site founded by the federal Community-Oriented Police Services (COPS), which offers descriptions of community policing across the nation.

COPS Office, **www.usdoj.gov/cops**
Check out the federal Office of Community Oriented Police Services (COPS), which provides grant money to local police departments to implement community partnerships. See "Promising Practices in the Fields" and click on "Community Projects and Programs" for descriptions of community policing across the nation. Download the great bibliography on community policing.

Broken Windows, **www.theatlantic.com/politics/crime/windows.htm**
Read the original classic by James Q. Wilson and George L. Kelling outlining the philosophy of community policing.

Making Neighborhoods Safe, **www.theatlantic.com/politics/crime/safehood.htm**
In this follow-up to the 1982 article, Wilson and Kelling make the argument that fixing broken windows does more to reduce crime than conventional policing tactics.

Zero Tolerance v. Broken Windows, **www.thenewrepublic.com/041000/rosen041000.html**
Read this interesting contrast between the zero-tolerance approach to policing adopted by the New York Police Department and the community policing approach

adopted by other communities. Find out why some people believe these are two very different approaches to quality-of-life policing.

On Film

Memphis PD: War on the Streets (48 minutes)
This Emmy Award-winning documentary reveals the enormous stress experienced by police officers who fight crime on inner-city streets across the nation. Depression, alcoholism, and suicide are common: twice as many police officers commit suicide as are killed in the line of duty. The program chronicles the daily experience of several male and female police officers who fight a war on crime and reveal the impact of the job on their personal lives. Available from Films for the Humanities and Sciences, www.films.com.

Beyond the Blue: Life as a Female Police Officer
(25 minutes)
This film chronicles the balancing act of a SWAT team sniper who is also a wife and a mother.

The Limits of Justice (58 minutes)
When gang members stormed the funeral of a member of a rival gang, local community members decided to partner with law enforcement to reduce youth violence in the city of Boston. Through aggressive patrol combined with mentoring, job training, and other programs, this extraordinary alliance, which took a problem-solving approach, resulted in the near elimination of juvenile homicide in the city for two years. Available from Films for the Humanities and Sciences, www.films.com.

NOTES

1. Susannah Pugh, "City, Police Captain Settle Sex Discrimination Lawsuit," *Springfield Union News,* March 13, 1993, pp. 1–2.
2. Susannah Pugh and Jo Ann Moriarty, "Dial 911 for 'House of Hate,'" *Springfield Union News,* January 26, 1992, pp. 1–7.
3. Ibid., p. 5.
4. Jo Ann Moriarty, "True Blue' Cops Maneuver as Female Chief Hangs Tough," *Springfield Union-News,* April 19, 1998, p. 5.
5. Susannah Pugh and Jo Ann Moriarty, "Dial 911 for 'House of Hate,'" p. 3.
6. Tom Vannah and Maureen Turner, "Against the Wall: Unanswered Questions and Unkept Promises are Pushing Springfield's Police-Community Relations to Breaking Point," *The Springfield Advocate,* June 5, 1997.
7. Kevin Cullen, "Breaking the Thin Blue Line of Bias: Policewoman is Likely Next Chief in Springfield," *The Boston Globe,* January 16, 1996, p. 15.
8. Kevin Cullen, "Springfield Selection Process Faces a 'Merit' Challenge," *The Boston Globe,* January 17, 1996, p. B21; "Officers Try to Halt Naming of Chief," *The Boston Globe,* January 30, 1996, p. B18.
9. Rhonda Swan, "Policewomen Face Uphill Struggle for Equality," *Union News,* April 19, 1998, pp. 1–3.
10. Jo Ann Moriarty, "'True Blue' Cops Maneuver as Female Chief Hangs Tough," *Union News,* October 12, 1998, p. 1.
11. Ibid.
12. Jo Ann Moriarty, "Chief Meara: Lone Woman in a Brutish, Macho World," *Springfield Union News,* October 11, 1998, p. 4.
13. Ibid., pp. 1–5.
14. Rhonda Swan, "Policewomen Face Uphill Struggle for Equality."
15. William F. Doherty, "Civil Service Voids Police Chief Choice," *The Boston Globe,* March 26, 1998, p. A30.
16. Kevin Cullen, "After Battle, Springfield Police Chief Regains Title," *The Boston Globe,* January 15, 1999, p. B4.
17. Jo Ann Moriarty, "Chief, Challengers Represent Past, Future of Department," *Union News,* October 13, 1998, pp. 1–5.
18. Ibid.
19. Ibid.
20. Ibid.
21. Jerome H. Skolnick and David H. Bayley, *The New Blue Line* (New York: Free Press, 1986).
22. Harold T. Amidon, "Law Enforcement: From 'The Beginning' to the English Bobby," *Journal of Police Science and Administration 5* (1977), pp. 355–367; Wilbur Miller, "Police Authority in London and New York City, 1830–1870," *Journal of Social History 8*(2) 1975, pp. 81–101.
23. Andrew T. Scull and S. Spitzer, "Social Control in Historical Perspective: From Private to Public Responses to Crime," in David F. Greenberg, ed., *Corrections and Punishment* (Beverly Hills, CA: Sage, 1977), pp. 265–286.
24. Thomas A. Critchley, *A History of Police in England and Wales, 900–1966* (London: Constable, 1967).
25. Allan Silver, "The Demand for Order in Civil Society: A Review of Some Themes in the History of Urban Crime, Police and Riots," in David Bordua, ed., *The Police: Six Sociological Essays* (New York: Wiley, 1967), pp. 1–24.
26. Roger Lane, "Urban Police and Crime in Nineteenth Century America," in Michael Tonry and Norval Morris, eds., *Crime and Justice: A Review of Research, Vol. 13* (Chicago: University of Chicago Press, 1992), pp. 1–50.
27. Lawrence Friedman, *Crime and Punishment in American History* (New York: Basic Books, 1993), pp. 69–71.
28. Samuel Walker, *Popular Justice: A History of Criminal Justice* (New York: Oxford University Press, 1980), pp. 61–65; Miller, "Cops and Bobbies, 1830–1870." pp. 81–101.
29. Eric H. Monkkonen, *Police in Urban America, 1860–1920* (New York: Cambridge University Press, 1981).

30. Walker, *Popular Justice,* pp. 127–145.

31. Ibid., pp. 173–174.

32. Jerome H. Skolnick and James Fyfe, *Above the Law: Police and the Excessive Use of Force* (New York: Free Press, 1993), p. 129.

33. Nathan Douthit, "August Vollmer, Berkeley's First Chief of Police and the Emergence of Police Professionalism," *California Historical Quarterly 54* (1975), pp. 101–124.

34. A. Vollmer and A. Parker, *The Police and Modern Society* (San Francisco: University of California Press, 1936).

35. Robert M. Fogelson, *Big City Police* (Cambridge, MA: Harvard University Press, 1977).

36. Walker, *Popular Justice,* pp. 189–190.

37. The President's Commission on Law Enforcement and Justice Administration, *The Challenge of Crime in a Free Society* (Washington, DC: U.S. Government Printing Office, 1967).

38. The Omnibus Crime Control and Safe Streets Act of 1968, Public Law 90–351, 90th Congress, June 1968, 18 U.S.C., Sec. 2518.

39. U.S. Department of Justice, *The LEAA: A Partnership for Crime Control* (Washington, DC: U.S. Government Printing Office, 1976).

40. Christian Parenti, *Lockdown America: Police and Prisons in the Age of Crisis* (New York: Verso, 1999), pp. 21–23.

41. George L. Kelling and Mark H. Moore, "From Political to Reform to Community: The Evolving Strategy of Police," in Jack Green and Stephen D. Mastrofski, eds., *Community Policing: Rhetoric or Reality* (New York: Praeger, 1991).

42. Lou Cannon, *Official Negligence: How Rodney King and the Riots Changed Los Angeles and the LAPD* (New York: Westview, 1999), pp. 70–72.

43. Ann L. Pastore and Katherine Maguire, eds., *Sourcebook of Criminal Justice Statistics, 1999* (Washington, DC: U.S. Government Printing Office, 2000), p. 39.

44. Samuel Walker, Cassia Spohn, and Miriam DeLone, *The Color of Justice: Race, Ethnicity and Crime in America* (Belmont, CA: Wadsworth, 1996), p. 114.

45. Donna C. Hale and C. Lee Bennet, "Realities of Women in Policing: An Organizational and Cultural Perspective," in Alida V. Merlo and Joycelyn M. Pollock, eds., *Women, Law and Social Control* (Boston: Allyn & Bacon, 1995), pp. 41–54.

46. Susan Martin, *On the Move: The Status of Women in Policing* (Washington, DC: Police Foundation, 1990).

47. Paula Meara, personal interview, Boston MA, August 22, 2001.

48. National Center for Women and Policing, *Equality Denied: The Status of Women in Policing: 1999* (Washington, DC: National Center for Women and Policing, 2000).

49. Pastore and Maguire, eds., *Sourcebook of Criminal Justice Statistics, 1999,* p. 319.

50. William A. Geller and Michael S. Scott, *Deadly Force* (Washington, DC: Police Executive Research Forum, 1992).

51. Federal Bureau of Investigation, *Crime in the United States— 1999* (Washington, DC: U.S. Government Printing Office, 2000), p. 6.

52. Egon Bittner, *The Functions of Police in Modern Society* (New York: Jason Aaronsen, 1975).

53. David Bayley, *Policing for the Future* (New York: Oxford University Press, 1994), p. 16.

54. James Q. Wilson, *Varieties of Police Behavior* (Cambridge, MA: Harvard University Press, 1968).

55. Bayley, *Policing for the Future,* p. 17.

56. George Kelling, Tony Pate, Duane Dieckman, and Charles E. Brown, *The Kansas City Preventative Patrol Experiment: A Summary Report* (Washington, DC: The Police Foundation, 1974).

57. Lawrence W. Sherman and David Weisburd, "General Deterrent Effects of Police Patrol in Crime 'Hot Spots': A Randomized Controlled Trial," *Justice Quarterly 12* (1995), pp. 625–648; Christopher Koper, "Just Enough Police Presence: Reducing Crime and Disorderly Behavior by Optimizing Patrol Time in Crime Hot Spots," *Justice Quarterly 12* (1995), pp. 649–672.

58. David Weisburd and Lorraine Green, "Policing Drug Hot Spots: The Jersey City Drug Market Analysis," *Justice Quarterly 12* (1995), pp. 711–735.

59. U.S. Department of Justice, Response Time Analysis: Executive Summary (Washington, DC: U.S. Government Printing Office, 1978); George L. Kelling and David Fogel, "Police Patrol—Some Future Directions," in Alvin W. Cohn, ed., *The Future of Policing,* (Beverly Hills, CA: Sage, 1978), pp. 166–167; Bayley, *Policing for the Future,* p. 6.

60. Peter Greenwood, Jan Chaiken, and Joan R. Petersilia, *The Criminal Investigation* (Lexington, MA: Heath, 1977); John Eck, *Solving Crimes: The Investigation of Burglary and Robbery,* (Washington, DC: Police Executive Research Forum, 1982).

61. William J. Cunningham, J. Strauchs, and Clifford W. VanMeter, *The Hallcrest Report II: Private Security Trends 1990–2000* (Boston: Butterworth Heinemann, 1990).

62. James Q. Wilson and George Kelling, "Broken Windows," The Atlantic Monthly, March 1982, pp. 29–38; George Kelling and Catherine M. Coles, *Fixing Broken Windows* (New York: Martin Kessler, 1996).

63. Parenti, *Lockdown America,* p. 38.

64. Gordon Witkin, "The Crime Bust," *U.S. News & World Report,* May 25, 1998, pp. 28–33.

CASE 10

The Poor Man in Court: The Case of Clarence Gideon

It was the kind of case that would hardly make the back pages of the local newspaper, even in the sleepy town of Panama City, Florida. In 1961, Clarence Earl Gideon was accused of breaking and entering the Bay Harbor Poolroom to steal $25 in coins from the cigarette machine, a bottle of wine, and twelve cans of beer. When the judge called the case and inquired, according to standard procedure, if the State and the defendant were ready to go to trial, the assistant district attorney (ADA) answered with the routine, "The State is ready, your Honor."[1] But when the question was put to the defendant, he replied, "I am not ready, your Honor." "Why aren't you ready?" asked the judge. "I have no counsel," replied Clarence. "Why do you have no counsel? Did you not know that your case was set for trial today?" "Yes, sir, I knew that it was set for trial today." "Why then did you not secure counsel and be prepared to go to trial?" asked the judge.

At this question, the accused fumbled and mumbled inaudibly. The judge asked him to come closer and speak up. "Now tell us what you said again, so we can understand you, please." Clarence Earl Gideon, a small white man, 52 years old, with four previous felony convictions, stood before the judge and jury of six men and finally said in a clear voice, "Your Honor, I said: I request this Court to appoint counsel to represent me in this trial. . . . The United States Supreme Court says I am entitled to be represented by counsel." The judge corrected Gideon by explaining that

only in capital cases does the law require the court to appoint counsel for poor defendants. Following procedure, the judge said, "Let the record show that the defendant has asked the court to appoint counsel to represent him in this trial and the court denied the request."[2]

A POOR MAN'S DEFENSE

The trial of Clarence Earl Gideon went ahead that day on August 4, 1961, with Gideon acting in his own defense. The trial transcript showed that Judge Robert McCray assisted the defendant throughout the trial, giving him advice, explaining various points of law, and reminding him of his rights. At the outset of the trial, the judge informed Gideon that he had the right to remove any of the sitting jurors if he thought they might be biased against him. "You don't have to have a reason, just look them over and if you don't like their looks, that is all it takes to get them excused." Gideon shrugged, "They suit me all right, Your Honor."[3]

The principal witness for the prosecution was Henry Cook, a local young man who testified that he had seen Gideon inside the closed poolroom at 5 a.m., saw him leave the building with a pint of wine in his hand, go to a phone booth, call for a taxi, and leave in the taxi. Cook testified that he entered the poolroom and saw that it had been broken into and the cigarette machine money box was lying on a pool table. The next witness, a local police officer, testified that he discovered the break-in while on routine patrol. The taxi driver who picked up Gideon that morning from the phone booth was called by the prosecution, and he testified that he had picked up Gideon that morning. Gideon had paid his fare in small change and told him not to tell anyone he had seen him.

As counsel for his own defense, Gideon was given the opportunity to cross-examine the witnesses called by the prosecution. He asked Cook a string of questions, some potentially relevant to the case, others that were not. For instance, he asked if he had ever been arrested for a crime; Cook answered, no. He asked Cook if he was friends with Gideon, to which Cook answered, yes. More important is what Gideon did not ask Cook. He did not ask why Cook did not phone the police when he first discovered the break-in. Nor did he ask Cook what he was doing in front of the Bay Harbor Poolroom at 5 a.m. After closing statements by both the prosecution and Gideon, the jury was instructed by the judge, and sent out to decide the verdict. They returned swiftly with a guilty verdict, and in a sentencing hearing three weeks later the judge imposed the maximum sentence of five years in the Florida state penitentiary at Raiford.

NO STRANGER TO TROUBLE

This was not the first time that Clarence Earl Gideon had served time.[4] Born in Hannibal, Missouri, in 1910, Gideon ran away from home at 14, only to be placed in a juvenile reformatory for three years. Later in life, he would describe that reformatory as the "worst" of all the prisons he had ever known. Paroled at age 16, he went to work at a shoe factory, married at age 18, but shortly thereafter was sentenced to state prison for ten years on charges of robbery, burglary, and larceny. Paroled again at 22, Gideon found himself in the middle of the Depression in 1932. He managed to find some work again in a shoe factory but soon was arrested for stealing government property and sentenced to the federal penitentiary at Leavenworth, Kansas, for three years.

Gideon continued the same pattern for the next decade and a half: released from jail, he worked for a while, drifted, and then committed another burglary or robbery. For a while during World War II, he falsified a legitimate personnel record and draft card and found steady work on the railway as a brakeman. But that ended in 1944 when the deception was discovered and he was sent back to prison for six more years. When he was released in 1950, he was 40 years old, and had spent at least half of his adult life locked up.

Gideon married again, separated, served a short sentence in a Texas state prison, and then married another women who eventually bore him three children. During the 1950s, Gideon managed to stay out of prison. He had a series of arrests and dismissals, short sentences in jail for public drunkenness, but otherwise tried hard to support his wife and children, despite developing tuberculosis and being a chronic gambler and an alcoholic. When he was arrested in 1961 for this crime, Gideon was trying to get his children out of foster care, where they had been placed by the public welfare department while he was in the hospital having a lung removed. Gideon's wife, also an alcoholic, had been reported to the authorities for being negligent in caring for her children.

THE RIGHT TO COUNSEL

Clarence Earl Gideon acknowledged that he had made a lot of mistakes in his life, but this time he believed it was the state of Florida that was making a mistake in its refusal to appoint him a defense counsel. The Sixth Amendment to the Constitution reads:

In all criminal prosecutions, the accused shall enjoy the right to a speedy and public trial, by an impartial jury of the State and district wherein the crime shall have been committed; which district shall have been previously ascertained by law, and to be informed of the nature and cause of the accusation; to be confronted with the witnesses against him; to have compulsory process for obtaining witnesses in his favor, and to have the assistance of counsel for his defence.

Gideon was determined to assert his rights and to fight for a fair trial under the rules of the Constitution. While he admitted to offenses committed in the past, this time he claimed he was not guilty and had been denied his constitutionally mandated due process rights by the judge and the state of Florida. Gideon had spent half his life inside the prisons of Missouri, Texas, and Florida and knew first hand the hard truth that poor men and women do not receive a fair shake in a courtroom. In the tattered lives of his fellow inmates, he saw the outcome of trials for poor people, and he was determined to take a stand even if it meant taking the fight all the way to the Supreme Court of the United States.

> I always believed that the primary reason of trial in a court of law was to reach the truth. My trial was far from the truth. One day when I was being arraigned I seen two trials of two different men tried without attorneys. One hour from the time they started they had two juries out and fifteen minutes later they were found guilty and sentenced. Is this a fair trial? This is common practice through most of the state. This penitentiary is full of men who are here with five years for petty larceny, drunk and minor sex crimes . . . one of my fellow workers has two years for being drunk and resisting arrest. Most city police courts would give a citizen a twenty-five dollar fine for the same charge but he was tried without a attorney and convicted."[5]

On January 8, 1962, the clerks of the U.S. Supreme Court in Washington, D.C., received a large envelope from prisoner No. 003826. A federal statute and Rule 53 of the Supreme Court permits special procedures for poor people who want to appeal their cases to the Supreme Court. People who file as paupers are waived the requirement to pay fees and relieved of the burden of numerous procedural and technical requirements. For instance, instead of the usual forty copies of the petitions required, just one is acceptable and it need not even be typed. Gideon's petition was handwritten in pencil on ordinary lined paper provided by the prison. Gideon had submitted a petition once before, but it had been sent back along with a copy of the rules for how to file a case as a pauper. The second time around, Gideon followed those rules and submitted a "motion for leave to proceed in forma pauperis" (to file as a poor person) and filed a writ of habeas corpus claiming he was being illegally imprisoned by the state of Florida.

THE CONSTITUTIONAL ISSUE

The Supreme Court of the United States is the court of last resort, with jurisdiction over federal matters and Constitutional matters. As a matter of current law, Judge Robert McCray was right when he claimed that the Constitution did not require the State of Florida to appoint counsel for indigent defendants in cases that did not concern capital offenses. The only iron-clad requirement on state criminal procedure was that the court provide an attorney in cases where the defendant faced the prospect of death. The Sixth Amendment in the Bill of Rights, of course, states that defendants have the right to counsel but it does not explicitly state that defendants *must* have counsel. Indeed, the framers of the Constitution were

reacting to English common law, which forbade a man charged with a felony to be represented by counsel.[6] The Sixth Amendment secured the right to retain counsel in one's own defense; it did not say anything about the necessity of a defense attorney for a fair trial.

In 1962, the issue that troubled the courts was exactly this issue: were there absolute elements of fairness that should be present in all criminal proceedings, whether federal or state? Was defense counsel one of these absolute elements of fairness? In 1928, the courts had ruled that the Sixth Amendment required counsel in all federal criminal cases,[7] but the Supreme Court was reluctant to impose that federal requirement upon the states. Not until 1932, in *Powell* v. *Alabama*, did the Supreme Court impose any requirements or standards on state criminal procedure.

Further, the *Powell* decision was limited only to the "compelling circumstances" of facing a death sentence. A subsequent Supreme Court ruling on this question, *Betts* v. *Brady* in 1942,[8] followed this line of reasoning and stated that in all noncapital trials, the necessity of appointed defense counsel depended on special circumstances of the case, such as age, illiteracy, mental illness, capital sentence, or unusual complexity of the evidence. According to this decision, the right of a poor person to a state-appointed defense attorney was to be determined on a case-by-case basis by the Supreme Court and depended on these "special circumstances" that necessitated a lawyer.

When Gideon petitioned the Supreme Court to review his case, he was not claiming any special circumstances. He was asking the Court to overturn its previous decision in *Betts* v. *Brady*, and overturning decisions is not something the Supreme Court does lightly or with any great frequency. In 1961, the Court had overruled a prior decision only one hundred times in its entire history.[9]

The other issue that posed an obstacle for Gideon's claim was the issue of federalism. If the Supreme Court backed up Gideon's request for the right to a state-appointed defense attorney, the federal court would be imposing a single uniform national standard on all fifty states. As late as 1922, the Supreme Court was refusing to rule that First Amendment rights—freedom of press, religion, and assembly—applied to the states, and the court was even more unwilling to interfere in the realm of state criminal procedure. The tide began to turn with the landmark decision of *Powell* v. *Alabama* in 1932, and then *Mississippi* v. *Brown* in 1936 and the most recent decision, *Mapp* v. *Ohio*, decided in 1961, just a year before the Supreme Court granted Gideon's petition for review.

In addition to the obstacles of precedent and federalism, there was also the practical matter of the impact of a new ruling on the thousands of convicted felons serving time in the nation's prisons and jails. In Florida alone, at the time of the Supreme Court hearing, 4,500 of the state's 8,000 prisoners had been convicted without benefit of counsel. While many of these had pleaded guilty, others had gone to trial and lost. One major concern was that if the new decision was in favor of the Constitutional right to counsel for all felony charges, more than half of the state's inmates would have to be released and retried or, even worse, released without retrial.[10]

However, the timing of Gideon's petition was right: several justices of the Court, as well as members of the bar, law school professors, and state attorneys, felt that the *Betts* decision was a poor one that needed to be reconsidered. Many people felt that the criteria for special circumstances were vague and subjective, and others felt that it was fundamentally unfair to allow some criminal defendants the right to a court-appointed attorney and not others. The Supreme Court read the twelve-page handwritten petition submitted by Clarence Gideon and issued a writ of certiorari, agreeing to hear the case. To the attorney general of the State of Florida, it came as a shock to receive a notice from the Supreme Court requesting a brief from his office to discuss the following question: "Should this Court's holding in *Betts* v. *Brady*, 316 U.S. 455, be reconsidered?"[11]

THE SUPREME COURT HEARING

Although poor people may file a petition for themselves to the Supreme Court, if their petitions are accepted for review by the Court, no one expects that individual to come before the nine Supreme Court justices to argue the case. The Supreme Court itself appoints an able and talented lawyer to take on the case. The lawyer is not compensated for his or her time nor for the huge expenses that such a case represents. Other than paying for transportation costs to Washington, D.C., and the cost of printing the actual brief, the lawyer foots the bill for the whole process. Despite the enormous personal cost, the honor and privilege of arguing a case before the Supreme Court is one that few lawyers refuse.

Abe Fortas, 51, a talented partner in a large law firm and a future Supreme Court justice himself, eagerly took the case. Fortas had been a member of the *Yale Law Journal*, personal attorney to future President Lyndon Johnson, and was a founding partner of the prestigious law firm of Arnold, Fortas and Porter. As a high-powered Washington lawyer, Fortas had a

lot of legal talent and resources at his disposal, and he immediately put them into gear to try and win this case. He had the top legal apprentice minds in the nation work on background case investigation over the entire summer; then he assembled a team of the brightest young attorneys in his law firm to help prepare the argument itself. He contacted law professors, state attorneys general, and other prestigious organizations for their legal support in this case. This was relatively easy, because there was broad sentiment in the legal profession in favor of overturning *Betts* v. *Brady*.

Fortas's opponent was far from an equal match. The job of defending the state decision fell to the state attorney general's office and to a particular assistant state attorney general, Bruce Jacob, 26 years old and not long out of law school himself.[12] Jacob worked in the Criminal Appeals Division of the attorney general's office where four assistant attorneys general handled the appeals and habeas petitions for the state. Unlike Fortas, who could draw on the resources of a large and wealthy Washington law firm, Jacob had primarily himself to rely on. He even had to depend on his wife to type his brief, and the couple spent their weekends traveling to law libraries to do research.[13]

The more Jacob researched the matter, the more he discovered that he did not have much support even from among the state attorneys general. He wrote a letter to each of the attorneys general, requesting them to submit an *amicus curiae*, or "friend of the court," brief, in support of his argument that criminal procedure is ultimately a state's right and not subject to federal interference. Jacob found that the state attorneys were not the allies he thought they would be. His plan backfired in that the attorney general of Massachusetts decided to submit a brief in favor of the petition, and ultimately twenty-three state attorneys general signed that petition in support of Fortas's position. Only two states, Alabama and North Carolina, ultimately supported Jacob's position.[14]

The situation did not look good for Jacob when he appeared, nervous and serious, before the Supreme Court on the morning of Monday, January 14, 1963. Despite all the preparation of lengthy legal briefs submitted by both sides, the heart of a Supreme Court case takes place in oral argument before the nine sitting justices. Unlike a trial, no witnesses are called nor is evidence presented. The presentation is an argument of law. Further, the nine justices do not listen passively to the presenting attorneys. Instead, the justices pepper the attorneys with questions, interrupt them, inquire and probe to test the legal implications, the strength of their arguments, and their knowledge of the relevant case law. Each side is given either a half-hour or an hour and not a minute more. In this case, the justices granted each side one hour and an additional half-hour for one "friend of the court."

When Bruce Jacob entered the august chamber, he had been practicing law for only three years, the bare minimum required for an attorney to argue a case before the Supreme Court. He sat and watched as more experienced attorneys argued their cases, many of them wearing formal coats and tails. He worried that he was inappropriately dressed in a simple blue suit. He sat for a whole day without his case being called. The next day, it was not until just one hour before the lunch that the case was called.

It is a terrifying experience for any lawyer, much less one fresh out of law school, to argue before the most powerful court in the world. The presenting attorney stands at a podium surrounded by the nine justices sitting in a semicircle. Years later, Jacob would describe feeling as if he were in a "pit" with justices to his far left and far right. The podium was equipped with three lights: one green, one yellow, and one red, to tell the speaker when to speak and when his or her time was up. Oral arguments in the Supreme Court are unlike those in any other courtroom. Justices jump right in and fire questions at the attorneys, ranging from the minute to the global. They pose hypothetical questions, ask for implications, request facts, case law, and broad principles, and explore concepts in no standard or predictable order. Much of the time, they are using the questions to make points against one another and to underscore a particular concept or idea to their fellow justices. For the presenting attorney, it can be brutal, terrifying, and humiliating.

The first to present an argument was Abe Fortas, appearing in a brown suit, distinguished and self-assured. Fortas, as everyone expected, was relaxed and brilliant in his performance before the Court. Although he had his argument perfectly prepared, he was less than one or two sentences into his presentation when the justices began firing questions at him. Fortas answered the barrage of questions with calm equanimity, always sticking to his main point that "no man, however intelligent, can conduct his own defense adequately."[15]

When it was his turn, Jacob did his best, stumbling quite a bit, apologizing for the "stupidity" of some of his answers when the justices asked tough questions. The minute he began, the barrage of questions from the members of the Court began as well, and they did not let up until the red light signaled the end of the hour. Altogether, the justices asked him more than forty questions, many of which he was unable to answer. Still, Jacob did his best to argue the case on the grounds of federalism and for protecting states' rights in the sphere of criminal justice. He argued that *Betts* v. *Brady* already provided sufficient protection in individual cases when a defense attorney is really necessary, and that states should be left alone to create a system that works for them. Finally, he pointed out that if this case was applied retroactively, it would have major implications for the state prison population, requiring states to release or retry thousands upon thousands of inmates who had been convicted at trials without benefit of defense counsel.[16]

When the case was over and Jacob walked out into the hall, it was hard for him not to feel that he had done a poor job with this case. Jacob felt responsible for the defeat, although timing was in favor of Gideon and it was hardly an even match in legal skill and experience. Years later, as dean of Emory Law School, Jacob would recall that Abe Fortas, twice his age, shook his hand in the hall immediately after the case and praised him saying, "You know, you have a wonderful way before the Court," a comment that comforted him immeasurably and remained with him for the rest of his life.[17]

Only a few days later, the decision in *Gideon* v. *Wainwright* was publically announced by the Supreme Court. By unanimous decision, the Court overturned the decision in *Betts* v. *Brady* decided twenty-one years previously. With a single stroke of the pen, the nine sitting justices put forth the Constitutional requirement that each and every state provide adequate legal representation for each and every poor criminal defendant facing a felony conviction.

In the now famous opinion written by Justice Hugo Black, the Court gave its reasoning for overturning precedent:

> This seems to us an obvious truth. Governments, both state and federal, quite properly spend vast sums of money to establish machinery to try defendants accused of crime. Lawyers to prosecute are everywhere deemed essential to protect the public's interest in an orderly society. Similarly there are few defendants charged with crime, few indeed, who fail to hire the best lawyers they can get to prepare and present their defenses. That government hires lawyers to prosecute and defendants who have the money hire lawyers to defend are the strongest indication of the widespread belief that lawyers in the criminal courts are necessities, not luxuries. The right of one charged with crime to counsel may not be deemed fundamental and essential to fair trials in some countries, but it is in ours."[18]

GIDEON GETS HIS DAY IN COURT

For Gideon, still in Raiford penitentiary far from the marble halls of the Supreme Court, the wheels of justice were turning very slowly. It had been two years since the petition had been accepted for review. Now his case had been overturned and it was remanded back to the Florida courts for action consistent with the new interpretation of the Constitution. The Supreme Court decision did not free Gideon; it entitled him to a new trial, this time with defense counsel on his behalf paid for by the State of Florida. On May 15, 1963, the Florida Supreme Court issued an order entitling Gideon to a new trial; the date was set for July 5th in circuit court.

The prosecutors in Gideon's retrial were confident they would win again. Because this case had now attracted so much attention, the prosecutorial team was composed of the top prosecutors in the office. They firmly believed Gideon was guilty of the original charge and that if Gideon had been properly represented by defense counsel, he would have been advised to plead guilty in the first place.[19] But Clarence Gideon stuck with his plea of not guilty and the state called the same witnesses who had appeared in the first trial, including, of course, their star eyewitness, Henry Cook.

On the stand for the second time, Cook told the same story under questioning by the prosecution as he had in the first trial. He had seen Gideon inside the pool hall. But this time, on cross-examination, Cook faced Fred Turner, an experienced criminal lawyer with a great deal of local knowledge. Turner knew Cook quite well, having defended him in this very same courtroom on other criminal charges.

Turner began his cross-examination by asking Cook why he was outside the poolroom at 5 a.m.[20] Cook repeated that he had just returned from an all-night party in a neighboring town and had been dropped off by friends. But Turner pointed out that Cook lived only two blocks away—why had his friends not dropped him off right at his own house after driving him 60 miles? What was the real reason he was outside that poolroom in the wee hours of the morning?

Besides, Turner pointed out, how could Cook have seen Gideon inside the poolroom when the windows were covered with posters and very high up in the building, making it difficult to see inside? And where were his alleged friends who had driven him that night? Why aren't they here to testify? Wasn't it more likely that Cook and his friends had been the ones to break into the poolroom and Gideon was fingered to take the blame when the police officer discovered the break-in on routine pa-

trol? Cook denied these accusations, but the jury was listening closely.

For a final question, Turner asked Cook if he had ever been convicted of a felony offense, a question Gideon had asked the first time, and this time Cook answered truthfully. When the jury was shown the record of the previous trial, in which Cook had lied about his criminal record, the jury understood that this was an eyewitness whose testimony was not to be believed.

The defense continued to cross-examine many of the same witnesses who had appeared in the original trial. The taxi driver, for example, had been called by the prosecution and had given the same damaging testimony as in the first trial, that Gideon had asked him not to tell anybody about this ride. But this time, it was followed by a simple question from the defense attorney that put the testimony in a very different light: "Had he ever said that to you before?" "Oh yes," said the taxi driver, "He said that to me every time I picked him up." "Why?" asked Turner. "I understand it was his wife—he had trouble with his wife," replied the driver.[21]

And this time the defense called a new witness to the stand. A local grocer had seen Cook that morning, and Cook had told him that he himself had been taken in for questioning in the break-in by the local police. It was only after being questioned by the police that Cook had reported that he had seen "someone" inside the poolroom, although he confided to the grocer that he wasn't sure who it might be and only thought it might be Mr. Gideon.

Finally, Turner called Gideon to the stand to explain for himself what he was doing that morning. In his first trial, Gideon had declined to take the stand and offer testimony. He did not think anyone would believe anything he had to say. This time, under the guidance of a defense attorney, he felt able to offer testimony. Turner began by asking him if he drank beer or wine, to which Gideon replied, no, he only drank whiskey. For a man who loves whiskey, wine and beer are not very appealing. Why were his pockets bulging with coins? After an all-night game of poker, his pockets were full with about a hundred dollars in coins from the game. Another witness testified that Gideon often paid in coins, since his main source of income was from gambling and he always carried his winnings in coins.

In closing argument, Turner focused the jury's attention back on Henry Cook. Perhaps Cook was the one who broke into the pool hall. Perhaps, after being out all night drinking with his pals, Cook broke in for more beer and wine, saw Gideon at the phone booth, and conveniently fingered him when Cook was questioned by the police. Gideon may be a gambler, an alcoholic, and a convicted felon, Turner told the jury, but he did not break into the Bay Harbor Poolroom on August 25, 1961.

The jury left to deliberate after receiving the judge's instructions that they must find Gideon guilty beyond a reasonable doubt. After one hour, the jury came back with the verdict that Clarence Earl Gideon was "not guilty": Clarence Earl Gideon was free.

The Supreme Court opinion, of course, affected not only the fate of one man, but that of all felons convicted without benefit of counsel, in the past and in the future. Because the opinion was retroactive, the State of Florida was obliged to release about 4,300 inmates as a result of this decision.[22] The historical record and subsequent studies show that astonishingly few of these inmates committed any further crimes.

For future defendants in the State of Florida and every state in the nation, the U.S. Supreme Court had now ruled that the state must provide counsel for those who who need it.

GIDEON'S FATE

Gideon had displayed remarkable persistence: against all odds, he had insisted on his right to a fair trial. When asked why he was so adamant that he must have a lawyer in order to receive a fair trial, Gideon gave an answer based on bitter experience: "I knew that was my only chance. I don't know if you've ever been in one of these courtrooms, but the prejudice is obvious. In this state . . . they just run over people who have nothing. . . . Without a lawyer, with the criminal record I had, what I'd have said they'd never have paid any attention to."[23]

The legacy of Gideon continues to affect the world of criminal justice to this day. The name is famous and known to all who enter the legal profession. But whatever became of the man himself? Few have bothered to find out. One person who was curious, not surprisingly, was Anthony Lewis, who wrote a best-selling book about the case in 1964 and years later found out how Gideon had fared in the years after his case.[24]

After the trial, Gideon went back to the drifter's lifestyle he had known his whole life: gambling, drinking, and wandering from place to place. He went to the Kentucky Derby and lost. Crossing the Ohio River to a nearby town, Gideon was picked up by the local police on a charge of vagrancy. At this hearing, Gideon handed the magistrate a copy of Lewis's book about his famous trial and the magistrate recognized his now-famous name. He offered to put Gideon in jail long enough for him to write a

petition to the Supreme Court requesting the right to an attorney in petty misdemeanors as well as serious felonies, but Gideon declined the opportunity to make legal history twice in his lifetime. Instead, Gideon chose to plead guilty, pay the fine, and simply walk away. Nine years later, Gideon died, alone, poor, and unknown, at the age of 61 in Fort Lauderdale, Florida.

Case adapted from Anthony Lewis, *Gideon's Trumpet* (New York: Vintage Books, 1964). See also " Proceedings of Conference on the 30th Anniversary of the United States Supreme Court Decision in Gideon v. Wainwright: Gideon and the Public Service Role of Lawyers in Advancing Equal Justice," *American University Law Review 43* (Fall 1993), pp. 1–49.

THINKING CRITICALLY ABOUT THIS CASE

1. Do you agree with the Supreme Court majority that lawyers are "necessities, not luxuries" in a court of law? Why or why not?

2. Do you believe that rich people and poor people are treated equally in the U.S. criminal courts? Why or why not?

3. Should the state be required to fund a poor person's lawyer with the same amount of money spent on the prosecution? Why or why not? Should poor defendants be able to choose their own attorney? Why or why not?

4. Celebrity defendants such as O. J. Simpson or Leona Helmsley (see Chapter 4) typically outspend government resources for prosecution. These well-funded defense teams can afford to hire expert witnesses, jury consultants, and an entire cadre of attorneys to devise strategy. Is this fair? Should we limit the amount of money spent on private defense? Why or why not?

5. Do you agree with Gideon's perception that the testimony of poor defendants with prior criminal records is rarely believed by judges and juries? If you agree, what are the implications of this attitude for poor people accused of crimes?

6. Do you agree with Gideon's perception that poor defendants receive harsher sentences than wealthy defendants? Why or why not? How does representation by a lawyer influence the sentencing of a criminal defendant?

7. Justice Black stated, "There can be no equal justice where the kind of trial a man gets depends on the amount of money he has." In your view, did *Gideon v. Wainwright* solve this problem? What other measures could be taken to create equal justice for rich and poor alike?

CHECK OUT THIS CASE

On the Web

Landmark Cases, **www.landmarkcases.org/**
Click on Gideon v. Wainwright to get linked to the Supreme Court decision and to other information about this case.

On Film

Gideon's Trumpet (105 minutes)
A 1979 film starring Henry Fonda as Clarence Earl Gideon and John Houseman as Chief Justice Earl Warren. Written, directed, and produced by David Rintels.

Gideon's Trumpet: The Poor Man and the Law (51 minutes)
This 1964 documentary includes interviews with Clarence Earl Gideon, attorney Abe Fortas, state and federal prosecutors, and judges about the impact of this case on the court. Available from Films for the Humanities and Sciences, **www.films.com.**

CHAPTER 10

The Structure of the U.S. Judiciary

LEARNING OBJECTIVES

After reading this chapter, the student should be able to:

- Describe the basic structure of the courts and explain the key differences between the lower courts, trial courts, and appellate courts

- Explain why it is important to have a record of court proceedings, and explain the right of appeal

- Describe the unique function of the U.S. Supreme Court and describe how its proceedings are different from trial court and state appellate court proceedings

- Describe the composition of the U.S. Supreme Court in terms of race and gender

Over the doors of any courthouse one finds inspirational words carved in stone or marble that proclaim the awesome responsibility of the institution to deliver justice. Courthouses are usually elaborate public buildings with fancy facades, graceful columns, and intricate marble. The splendor of the outside of the building is meant to reflect the importance of what takes place inside the building. It is in these hallowed spaces that the mysterious and majestic process of "justice" unfolds before the public.

Trials are public ceremonies bound by ritual and solemn dignity. Where else in modern society do public officials sit on a high platform and wear long black robes? Where else does an audience "all rise" to mark the hushed entrance of the main speaker? And where else, in modern society, do we still use such words as "hear ye, hear ye," "to wit," or address a public official as "your honor"? If you are thinking that the courthouse reminds you of the ceremony one might find in church on Sunday, then you are right in seeing that courts, like religious institutions, are places where ritual and ceremony symbolize an important social function in our society. For better or worse, courts are where people most often look to "see" how the U.S. justice system works.

Historically, in the American colonies, each colony had its own court system, both criminal and civil, for resolving disputes. These formed the basis for the state court system we have today. As the nation grew, the local courthouse emerged as an integral and central public space in the community. It was there that local disputes were solved, public announcements were made, and people gathered to meet in times of crisis or celebrate in times of joy. The courthouse stood at the center of the town and, like the church, was a place where news and gossip were exchanged.[25]

Indeed, before the rise of a professional body of trained lawyers at the end of the nineteenth century, local justices of the peace settled many matters of civil disputes and minor criminal matters in an informal way. Once a month, on "court day," a traveling judge would appear to hear more serious criminal cases. The more serious the crime, the more likely that on the day of the trial the courthouse would be packed with spectators eager to "see" justice done. And as we have seen in the case of the Salem witch trials (Chapter 1), before the rise of prisons as the main form of criminal sanction, the meting out of physical punishment was also a public ceremony attended by young and old alike.

Tremendous changes in the state court system took place in the nineteenth and twentieth centuries as society became more complex. In addition to local and county courts run by magistrates and justices of the peace and higher courts for more serious matters, there developed police courts, mayor's courts, municipal courts, night courts, probate courts, juvenile courts, family courts, traffic courts, and drug courts. Each state devised its own system for naming and organizing the courts and assigning them different forms of **jurisdiction** or authority over various facets of the law. In addition, of course, the federal court system evolved, operating in a parallel track with its own complex system of administrative, specialized, lower and higher courts. By the end of the nineteenth century, a growing army of trained lawyers was needed simply to understand which court held jurisdiction for a given legal matter. The trained practitioner increasingly became a "necessity" to navigate the complex system of procedures and processes for bringing a case to court for adjudication.

THE STRUCTURE OF THE COURTS

jurisdiction: the geographical district or subject matter over which the authority of a court extends.

courts of limited jurisdiction: also called inferior or lower courts, these courts are restricted to processing of misdemeanor trials and arraignments, preliminary hearings, and other pretrial proceedings for serious felony trials.

courts of general jurisdiction: also called trial courts, these courts are authorized to handle all criminal and civil proceedings.

courts of appellate jurisdiction: the jurisdiction of these courts is restricted to matters of appeal and review.

Many countries have a single national court system, but the United States has a highly decentralized, complex, and diverse system of many different types of courts with jurisdiction over different types of legal issues. Courts have jurisdiction based on a number of different criteria: political boundaries, geography, subject matter, or function. Court jurisdiction is defined by geography because certain courts have jurisdiction to hear cases for crimes that took place within a particular city, county, or state. Courts may also be authorized to hear only certain types of cases: there may be a traffic court to deal with violations of the traffic laws; a family court to deal with divorce and custody proceedings; or a probate court to settle the handling of wills and estates.

Courts are always differentiated according to their specific procedural function within the hierarchy of the court system itself: courts may have **limited, general,** or **appellate jurisdiction.** Courts of limited jurisdiction do not try felony cases, are restricted in scope, and do not have appellate authority. Courts with general jurisdiction are the principal trial courts. These courts have the power and authority to try and decide many cases, including appeals from lower courts. Trial courts have the power to hear a case from the start, examine the evidence, and apply the law to those facts, whereas courts with appellate jurisdiction have the specific function of hearing cases on appeal only, and of settling matters of legal procedure.

Broadly speaking, there are two types of courts in the U.S. criminal justice system: the state court system and the federal court system. The U.S. Constitution, Article III, Section 1, created the federal system by establishing "one supreme Court, and . . . such inferior courts as the Congress may from time to time ordain and establish," with jurisdiction over Constitutional issues, federal laws, disputes between states, and treaties. State courts in each individual state have jurisdiction over state law. For every criminal case filed in federal court, nearly three hundred are filed in state courts, since most crimes are defined by state laws.[26] Table 10.1 outlines the structure of the U.S. court system.

Three- or Four-Tier System

Each state has organized its court system in a unique structure that reflects the particular history and politics of that state. Some have specialized lower courts for different areas of the law, whereas others do not; some have three levels whereas others have four

TABLE 10.1

Structure of Courts in the United States

State Courts	Jurisdiction	Federal Courts
Courts of last resort	Appellate	U.S. Supreme Court
Intermediate appellate	Appellate	U.S. Court of Appeals
General trial courts	General	U.S. District Courts
Lower or inferior courts	Limited	U.S. Magistrate's Courts

or even five distinct levels of courts. Not only are no two state court systems exactly the same, even more confusing is the fact that the various states use different terminology to label the different courts. For example, all states have general trial courts, but in Massachusetts these are called "superior courts," in New York they are labeled "supreme courts," and in Florida they are called "district courts."

Despite the labels, all state court systems and the federal system share in common a fundamental structure that consists of three or four basic tiers: courts with limited jurisdiction at the bottom, courts of general jurisdiction at the next level, and then the appellate courts at the top, usually divided into intermediate appellate courts and final appellate courts.[27]

LOWER COURTS: COURTS OF LIMITED JURISDICTION

Courts with limited jurisdiction, often referred to as lower courts or inferior courts, have limited authority over the criminal justice process. There are more than 13,000 lower courts across the nation. Generally speaking, they do not try felony cases and cannot hear appeals. Most civil cases are heard in lower courts.

In urban areas, the lower courts are often called municipal, magistrate's, or police courts. These courtrooms are the busiest of all courts because the number of cases they handle is most numerous. They hear thousands of misdemeanor and petty offenses such as prostitution, drunkenness, disorderly conduct, petty larceny, and traffic offenses. Television programs like *Judge Judy* depict some of the flavor of lower courts, where the offenses are minor, juries are rare, and the atmosphere of the court is relatively informal. Judges generally dispense "justice" in quick fashion, leading many to characterize these courts as a form of inferior or **"rough" justice.**[28]

Lower courts are also the point of entry into the courts for more serious felony offenses. For defendants charged with felonies, lower courts have the authority to hold initial appearances, preliminary hearings, and make bail decisions. In rural areas, justice of the peace courts handle an array of criminal and civil matters, most commonly, performing marriage ceremonies. In many remote jurisdictions, justices of the peace are not attorneys and may have no legal training at all.

Ultimately the lower courts actually process about 90 percent of all criminal cases: they are noisy, crowded places with little trappings of pomp and ceremony. Some refer to these courts as "assembly-line justice" because cases are decided in matters of minutes or even seconds, with quick consultations between attorneys and judges. It is not unusual for a public defender to meet a client for the first time, examine the file, advise the client, and argue the case before the judge, all in a space of five minutes or less. Then it is on to the next client and the next case. The courtroom, particularly in the busy urban courts, is jam-packed with defendants, victims, mothers, fathers, spouses, children, attorneys, police officers, probation officers, parole officers, and other social service workers. No one is listening to the activity taking place at the bench, and even if someone

"rough" justice: informal proceedings within the lower courts which do not conform to formal due process.

wanted to listen, most of the discussion takes place quietly between the attorneys and the judge.[29] Crowded dockets mean that many cases scheduled for that day will not be heard, so all the people standing around will be expected to come back the next day and often the day after that as well. Cases are frequently postponed because one or the other party is not present.

TRIAL COURTS: COURTS OF GENERAL JURISDICTION

Courts with general jurisdiction are the major trial courts authorized to try civil and criminal cases. These courts may be referred to as high courts, circuit courts, superior courts, courts of common pleas, or supreme courts. They have original jurisdiction to try any case, including those that involve less serious offenses, and they have authority to hear cases on appeal from the lower courts. About 10 percent of the defendants originally brought into the lower courts have cases tried in the higher court. These are also known as **courts of record** because a court recorder makes a transcript of the trial proceedings, which forms the legal basis for further proceedings and appeals.

In most states a defendant tried in the lower court system has an automatic right to a new trial in the trial court system. At the lower level a detailed record of the proceedings is not kept: case files include information on the charge, the plea, the finding of the court, and the sentence. Lower courts are often criticized for being loose with a defendant's rights, and a safeguard has been the **trial *de novo* system,** which affords defendants an automatic right to a new trial in the general court system if they are convicted in the lower courts. For many critics, however, the *de novo* system has been a perfect example of unnecessary duplication in the system and some states, such as Massachusetts, have eliminated the *de novo* system as part of court unification and reform.

APPELLATE COURTS AND THE RIGHT OF APPEAL

All jurisdictions give defendants the right to have the proceedings of lower courts and trial courts reviewed by a higher court. In most states, the right of **appeal** is exclusively a defendant's right. The prosecution is not able to appeal a verdict or a judgment of acquittal. Appellate courts, which include intermediate appellate courts in thirty-eight states and the courts of last resort in every state, are distinct from trial courts because they have jurisdiction only to review the record of cases on appeal from the lower and trial courts. An appeal by a convicted defendant asks a higher court to review the proceedings that took place in the lower court. Generally, appellants claim that there was an error in procedure.

These courts examine the written transcript of the lower court proceedings and may hear brief oral arguments from the attorneys. There is no jury in the appellate process. The appellate court does not conduct a new trial or reexamine the facts of the case. The focus is on the legality of the proceedings. If the appellate court finds no legal error or if it finds that the legal error was "harmless" and did not affect the verdict, the court will affirm the conviction; alternatively, the court may reverse the decision and remand it back to the lower court for some modified legal proceeding. A **remand** ruling directs the lower court to rehear a case with a new set of proceedings.

An **intermediate court of appeal** (the third tier) exists to reduce the burden for the highest state court. Usually, it consists of a panel of judges who review all cases that are appealed in a legal manner. The vast majority of these are civil cases involving child custody, property disputes, alimony, and child support.

At the highest level is the **court of last resort,** which operates as the final word in that particular hierarchy of courts. We have seen the extraordinary impact of the U.S.

courts of record: courts in which a full transcript of the proceedings is made for all cases.

trial *de novo* system: statutory right of a defendant to a new trial in the general court system if convicted in a lower court.

appeal: a request by a convicted defendant to have a higher court review the proceedings, claiming an error in due process proceedings that significantly affected the outcome of the case.

remand: ruling of a higher court directing a lower court to rehear the case with a new set of proceedings.

intermediate court of appeal: a court charged with automatic review of all appeals by defendants, whose decisions are subject to review by a court of last resort.

court of last resort: court whose ruling has final authority in a given jurisdiction.

Supreme Court, with its ultimate power to be the final arbiter of the interpretation of Constitutional law. Each state has its own court of last resort, referred to by various names, such as the Supreme Court, Supreme Court of Appeals, Court of Appeals, or Supreme Judicial Court. The highest court in the state is not required to review all cases that are appealed after an unfavorable decision in the intermediate appellate court. Like the U.S. Supreme Court, the justices sitting on the state court of last resort are given the power to choose which cases it will hear except in cases involving capital punishment.

The push for states to reform and unify their court systems has been a major effort across the nation in the last thirty years. Reformers have called on states to reduce the number of courts, standardize their names, and clarify their respective jurisdictions. Eliminating the *de novo* system has been a major push of court reform. As caseloads have multiplied and backlogs mushroomed, the inefficiency, duplication, and sheer waste of time of the courts has been sharply criticized by those in state government. Yet the pace of change has been very slow. Political interests, power struggles, control, and funding issues favor the status quo and resist the overhaul of a system that the public often does not really understand.

THE FEDERAL COURT SYSTEM

The federal court system is structured into the same basic four-tier system. At the lowest level are the U.S. Magistrate's Courts, with very limited powers to try lesser misdemeanors, setting bail in more serious cases, issuing search and arrest warrants, and other legal matters. The courts of general jurisdiction in the federal system are the U.S. District Courts created by the federal Judiciary Act passed by Congress on September 24, 1789. U.S. district courts have original jurisdiction over all cases involving alleged violations of federal statutes. Cases heard in U.S. District Courts generally involve violations of federal law, including bank robbery, civil rights abuses, mail fraud, counterfeiting, smuggling, kidnaping, drug trafficking, national security issues such as treason, sedition, and espionage, violations of the many federal regulatory codes such as the SEC and the IRS, and so forth.

The next tier in the federal judicial hierarchy is the intermediate appellate level called the U.S. Court of Appeals. There are thirteen of these courts, each covering a defined geographic portion of the United States. For example, the U.S. Court of Appeals for the Sixth Circuit handles federal appeals that arise from district court cases in Michigan, Ohio, Kentucky, and Tennessee. The Courts of Appeals have mandatory jurisdiction for cases heard in federal District Courts: defendants who are disappointed in their conviction in federal District Court have the right to have their appeal heard by the circuit Court of Appeals.

The U.S. Supreme Court

At the pinnacle of the federal and state court system sits the ultimate court of last resort, the U.S. Supreme Court. The jurisdiction of the Supreme Court is spelled out in Article III, Section 2, of the Constitution. The highest court of the land has original jurisdiction over suits between states, constitutionality of state laws, and matters relating to ambassadors. For these matters, the Supreme Court may function like a trial court.[30]

The Supreme Court has appellate jurisdiction over all federal issues that primarily concern the constitutionality of a lower court ruling or procedure. As we saw with the Gideon case, defendants do not have the right to have their cases heard in the ultimate court of last resort, and of the thousands of cases filed each year, only a tiny percentage are granted a review or *writ of certiorari*. The Supreme Court does not concern itself with protecting the rights of individual defendants: a case that showed such a violation

The current Supreme Court is the most diverse in U.S. history. The nine justices of the U.S. Supreme Court: Back row (left to right) Ginsburg, Souter, Thomas, Breyer. Front Row (left to right) Scalia, Stevens, Rehnquist, O'Connor, Kennedy.

would not be heard before the Supreme Court. The highest court of the land agrees only to hear cases that will settle ambiguous areas of the law that need clarification.

Procedurally, a request for review is made by petitioning for a **writ of certiorari,** and granting of review is signaled by the Court's issuance of the writ. The phrase comes from the Latin *certiorari volumus,* which means "we wish to be certified" or "we wish to be heard."[31] Of over 8,000 cases on the docket in 1998, Supreme Court justices granted review in only 81 cases.[32]

The selection of which cases are heard by the supreme court in each individual state and in the U.S. Supreme Court, known as its **certiorari power,** is a matter of judicial discretion and utmost importance. Unlike the intermediate appellate division, which must hear all appeals regardless of their merits, the court of last resort is highly selective about which cases it will hear. Since the mission of the lower appellate court is to protect the rights of individual defendants, it must hear all cases, since every defendant has the right to appeal a criminal conviction or civil judgment. If an error has been made in the trial court, it is the function of the appellate court to correct that error by ordering a new trial or procedure.

The purpose of Supreme Court deliberations, however, is not to protect rights of individuals: indeed, the Supreme Court will not grant a writ even in cases where there has been an error because, in the words of Chief Justice Charles Evan Hughes, "Review by the Supreme Court is in the interest of the law ... not in the mere interest of the litigants."[33] The **Rule of Four** is the requirement that at least four of the Supreme Court justices approve a case for consideration by the full Court. Cases that are selected for review, therefore, are of major significance in settling serious confusion about the correct interpretation of the law.

The U.S. Supreme Court does not have jurisdiction over the all the decisions made in civil and criminal matters in the state court system, but only when a federal statute has been interpreted or a Constitutional right is at issue. In Gideon's case, his claim that he was entitled to an attorney under the Sixth Amendment was a Constitutional claim, which made the rulings of the Florida state circuit judge, appeals judge, and supreme

writ of certiorari: document issued by a higher court directing a lower court to prepare the record of a case and send it to the higher court for review.

certiorari power: judicial discretion of a supreme court to select cases for review.

Rule of Four: the requirement that a minimum of four U.S. Supreme Court justices must consent to issue a writ of certiorari.

court subject to review by the U.S. Supreme Court *if* the justices decided the matter warranted review.

Twenty years of the existing interpretation of the right-to-counsel rule in the Sixth Amendment under *Betts* v. *Brady* was a bone of contention across the nation. Many states' attorneys disagreed with the standard that only under "special circumstances" was a person entitled to an attorney; and many felt that the guidelines for setting those standards were unfair and arbitrary. Gideon had no such "special circumstances" to claim, yet his petition said that the correct interpretation of the Sixth Amendment entitled him to a court-appointed defense attorney. The time was ripe for reopening this question to settle the matter.

When the Supreme Court decides a case, there are several possible outcomes of the review. The Court may **affirm** the lower court decision, which means that the conviction remains in force. It may **reverse** the decision or overturn the conviction and remand the case back to the original jurisdiction, which in the Gideon case was Panama City, Florida, for a new trial under the new set of legal standards. When an appellate court issues a reverse and remand ruling, the state prosecutor faces several options. In some cases, the state's attorney may decide not to try the defendant again, for any of a variety of reasons. Or it may, as in Gideon's case, retry the case under the new guidelines by appointing defense counsel for the defendant. In some cases, the Supreme Court may order a reversal of the original decision *with prejudice,* specifically requiring a trial court judge to resentence a defendant, or ordering prison conditions found to be unconstitutional to be corrected.

THE IMPACT OF THE SUPREME COURT ON CRIMINAL JUSTICE POLICY

The Supreme Court is composed of nine justices, one Chief Justice and eight associates. Each justice is nominated by the President of the United States, confirmed by the Senate, and appointed for life. For most of our nation's history, the composition of the highest court has been exclusively white, wealthy, male, and Protestant.[34] It was not until the mid-nineteenth century that the court broke with religious tradition to include a Roman Catholic, and not until the early twentieth century that a Jew, Justice Louis Brandeis, was appointed to the court. The inclusion of minorities and women has come more recently: the first African American justice was Thurgood Marshall, appointed by President Lyndon B. Johnson in 1967, and the first woman justice, Justice Sandra Day O'Connor, was appointed by Ronald Reagan in 1981. Of 108 Supreme Court justices in our nation's history, two have been women and two have been African Americans.

Today the court is more diverse than it ever has been in the past. As we enter the twenty-first century, there are two women, Sandra Day O'Conner and Ruth Bader Ginsburg, one African American, Clarence Thomas, two Jewish justices, Ruth Bader Ginsburg and Stephen Breyer, and two Catholics, Antonin Scalia and Anthony M. Kennedy. In other respects, however, the Supreme Court is very homogenous. Most Supreme Court justices spent years working in the federal judiciary and at other top-level governmental jobs.[35] Most are graduates of elite law schools, predominantly Harvard, Yale, Stanford, Columbia, or Northwestern. Most are substantially wealthy before they are appointed to the court and hail from upper- or upper-middle-class social backgrounds. The one exception to this homogenous social background was former Justice Thurgood Marshall, who graduated from Howard University and whose father was a steward on a passenger train. Marshall achieved prominence as a civil rights lawyer, serving as chief counsel to the NAACP, then as a federal judge and solicitor general of the United States, before being appointed to the Supreme Court.

affirm: ruling by an appellate court to uphold the decision of a lower court.

reverse: ruling by an appellate court to overturn the decision of a lower court.

Before the 1960s, it would have been extremely unusual for the Supreme Court to grant a writ to rule on state criminal procedure. Except in extreme cases, the Supreme Court preferred to leave states to operate their own criminal justice systems as they saw fit. In previous decades, Bruce Jacobs's arguments would have been very persuasive to the court. Greater Supreme Court involvement in state criminal justice systems began with the Mapp decision in 1961 under the leadership of Chief Justice Earl Warren, a former prosecutor. By 1969, most of the provisions of the Bill of Rights related to criminal violations had been "incorporated" into the due process clause of the Fourteenth Amendment.

During the 1970s and 1980s, under the leadership of Chief Justice Warren Burger, the Supreme Court moved more toward the crime control model of the criminal justice system. The 1980s saw the "good faith" exception to the Mapp rule, which gave police the opportunity to violate a citizen's civil liberties as long as they could show that they had made a good faith effort to respect the citizen's civil liberties. Exceptions to the Miranda ruling also loosened the court's interference with police interrogation practices. The public safety exception and the inevitable discovery exception both allow police to ignore Miranda when there is an overriding concern with public safety or when it is likely they would have uncovered the information from sources other than the suspect's confession. In the 1990s, under the leadership of another conservative, Chief Justice William Rehnquist, the court has continued to value the crime control philosophy. As we saw in the Montoya de Hernandez case in Chapter 7, the majority opinion favors the preservation and expansion of the prerogative of law enforcement to fight the war on crime.

Despite the so-called political leanings of individual justices at the time of their appointment, however, the history of the court tells us that Supreme Court justices often surprise observers by their rulings. The lifetime appointment of justices to the bench is designed to offer the justices independence from the pressures of political affiliations. It appears that the future direction of the Court on criminal justice matters will follow the conservative emphasis on crime control, but that is by no means a certain outcome.

DID *GIDEON* "WORK"?

Four Supreme Court cases form the cornerstone of the **right to counsel.** In 1928, the Supreme court ruled in *Johnson* v. *Zerbst* that a poor defendant is entitled to counsel in federal criminal prosecution; in 1932, *Powell* v. *Alabama*[36] ruled that the state must provide "competent counsel" for indigent defendants accused of capital offenses; *Gideon* v. *Wainwright* in 1963 ruled that all indigent defendants accused of felonies are entitled to counsel at state expense; and in 1972, in *Argerslinger* v. *Hamlin*,[37] extended that right to poor defendants accused of misdemeanors if the penalty includes loss of liberty. The result of the these decisions, particularly *Gideon*, was to require all of the states and counties across the nation to provide defense counsel for indigent defendants.

The vision of justice implied in Gideon's case was that all Americans, regardless of their station in life, are equal before the law. Every person, rich or poor, has the right to be presumed innocent unless proven guilty beyond a reasonable doubt through a fair and public trial. Providing poor people with publically paid-for lawyers is an important milestone and monumental achievement in the struggle to establish a criminal justice system that treats all defendants alike. More than 80 percent of criminal defendants in our nation's courts are poor; therefore, the vast majority of criminal defendants today are represented by publicly appointed counsel.[38]

Despite the massive infrastructure in legal aid, assigned counsel, and public defenders, do poor people receive equal justice in the courts? In 1990, federal, state, and local governments spent $1.3 billion to provide legal representation for criminal defen-

right to counsel: a defendant's Constitutional right to the assistance of an attorney during prosecution.

dants, but that same year, federal, state, and local governments spent about $5.5 billion to prosecute criminal defendants.[39] According to the director of the Public Defender Service in Washington, D.C., the answer is not what many had hoped in the heady and idealistic days of 1963:

> Imagine practicing law in the basement of an old, dilapidated building with peeling paint, asbestos, broken toilets. Imagine sharing a small office cluttered with broken furniture with one, maybe two other lawyers. Envision having to consult with your office mates before you meet with your client just to get some privacy. Imagine sharing a secretary with seven or eight other lawyers. And imagine working in these conditions sixty to seventy hours per week making one-half, perhaps one-third of what other lawyers with your same experience are making."[40]

This description by Angela Davis is of the working conditions in her own office, known as the top public defender's office in the entire nation. There are few resources with which to hire investigators, social workers, or expert witnesses to help their clients win a case. Some offices cannot afford to pay for collect calls, so attorneys are forced to refuse calls from their own clients. In Kentucky, public defenders carry caseloads of 120 felony cases per defense attorney, and the attorneys are so poorly paid that in one jurisdiction, public defenders were found to be moonlighting in another county to pay their bills.[41] The quality and quantity of resources devoted to supporting competent legal services for the poor suggest that we continue to have a two-tiered system of justice in this country.

Frequently, public defenders feel the best they can do for their clients is to convince them to plead guilty. Some systems even have financial incentives that favor guilty pleas. For example, some jurisdictions pay the same flat fee to court-appointed attorneys or public defenders whether they enter a guilty plea, which requires about a half-hour's worth of work, or if they take the case to trial, which may require a hundred or more hours of work. Whether their client pleads guilty or they work to defend their client's presumption of innocence at trial, either way, the fee is a set amount: $300 for a misdemeanor offense and $750 for a felony.[42]

As we will see in later chapters, the absence of adequate defense counsel is most egregious in capital cases. Defendants facing the death penalty too often have publically appointed defense counsel who are drunk, who fall asleep, who never meet with them, who are completely unprepared, or who may be grossly inexperienced in the legal complexities of capital defense. Although incompetent counsel is technically a basis for an appeal, the burden of proof rests on defendants to "prove" the incompetence of their counsel on appeal. Anthony Lewis describes the difficulty of this burden by sarcastically calling the legal standard of competence the "spoon test": "if you hold a spoon up to a defense lawyer's mouth and it shows he is breathing, he is competent."[43]

The simple reality of the court system is that only a tiny fraction of criminal cases ever go to trial. The dramatic presentation of evidence and the cross-examination of witnesses that relies so heavily on the skill and preparation of talented advocates almost never happens in criminal convictions. In more than 90 percent of cases, defendants plead guilty to the charge. The practice of plea bargaining is an alternative and routine judicial proceeding that is far more common than the public trial. It involves the same cast of characters: the judge, prosecutor, and defense attorney, all of whom play major roles in a complex process of give and take to produce a criminal conviction. Although it is less public and dramatic, the process of plea negotiations affects the fate of most criminal defendants, especially those who are poor, to a far greater extent than the adversarial trial process.

We turn in the next chapter to the role of the various courtroom players and the way the business of the court is conducted every day. We will see that in the process of plea bargaining, advantages and disadvantages of wealth and privilege continue to affect the legal process and generate very different outcomes for the poor and the rich in the criminal justice system.

KEY TERMS

jurisdiction p. 204
courts of limited jurisdiction p. 204
courts of general jurisdiction p. 204
courts of appellate
    jurisdiction p. 204
"rough" justice p. 205

courts of record p. 206
trial *de novo* system p. 206
appeal p. 206
remand p. 206
intermediate court of appeal p. 206
court of last resort p. 206

writ of certiorari p. 208
certiorari power p. 208
Rule of Four p. 208
affirm p. 209
reverse p. 209
right to counsel p. 210

REVIEW AND STUDY QUESTIONS

1. What is jurisdiction? Explain the difference between limited, general, and appellate jurisdiction.
2. Describe the basic tiers that make up the structure of the state and federal court systems.
3. What is a court of record? Why is it important to have a recording of the proceedings?
4. To what does the term "rough" justice refer? How are the proceedings in the lower courts different from those in the trial courts?
5. What is the role of the appellate court in the court system? How is the court different from a trial court?

6. What is the trial *de novo* system?
7. What is the function of the U.S. Supreme Court? How are the proceedings of the U.S. Supreme Court different from those in a trial court?
8. What is a writ of certiorari? Explain the Rule of Four.
9. Explain what it means when the Supreme Court affirms, reverses, or remands a lower court decision.
10. Did Gideon "work"? Why or why not?

CHECK IT OUT

On the Web

The Supreme Court, **www.supremecourtus.gov/**
Go to the Web site of the U.S. Supreme Court and click on "About the Court" to learn more about the Supreme Court justices, past and present, a history of the court, and to check out cases on the docket of the court today. To hear oral arguments (in RealAudio) of cases that have gone before the Supreme Court, go to **http://oyez.nwu.edu.**

Federal Courts, **www.uscourts.gov**
Go to this Web site to learn more about the federal courts.

Courts.net, **http://www.courts.net**
Click on your own state to find out about the structure of the judiciary in your state.

National Center for State Courts, **www.ncsc.org/**
Check out this Web site for links to federal, state, and international court and court-related Web sites around the world.

Center for Court Innovation, **www.courtinnovation.org/**
Check out this Web site which gives you access to a unique private–public partnership presenting innovations of problem-solving courts dealing with domestic violence, addiction, and child abuse, designed to better serve the community and its problems.

On Film

And Justice for All? (60 minutes)
Bill Moyers looks at a crisis in the U.S. court system, in which a shortage of public defenders and other legal aid workers leaves the poor without adequate or timely representation. A panel of judges discusses some possible remedies to the crisis. Available from Films for the Humanities and Sciences, **www.films.com.**

NOTES

1. Anthony Lewis, *Gideon's Trumpet* (New York: Vintage Books, 1964) pp. 9–10.
2. Ibid., p. 11.
3. Ibid., p. 160.
4. Ibid., pp. 67–81.
5. Ibid., p. 79.
6. Ibid., p. 109.
7. *Johnson* v. *Zerbst*, 304 U.S. 358 (1928).

8. *Betts* v. *Brady,* 316 U.S. 455, 462 (1942).

9. Lewis, *Gideon's Trumpet,* p. 89.

10. Bruce R. Jacob, "Remarks," Conference on 30th Anniversary of the U.S. Supreme Court's Decision in Gideon v. Wainwright, pp. 32–43.

11. Lewis, *Gideon's Trumpet,* p. 45.

12. Ibid., pp. 146–148.

13. Jacob, "Remarks," p. 36.

14. Lewis, *Gideon's Trumpet,* p. 160.

15. Ibid., p. 179.

16. Jacob, "Remarks," pp. 36–37.

17. Ibid.

18. *Gideon* v. *Wainwright,* 372 U.S. 335 (1963).

19. Lewis, *Gideon's Trumpet,* p. 240.

20. Ibid., pp. 243–243.

21. Ibid., p. 245.

22. Ibid., p. 215.

23. Ibid., p. 104.

24. Anthony Lewis, "Keynote Address," Conference on 30th Anniversary of the U.S. Supreme Court's Decision in Gideon v. Wainwright, pp. 15–22.

25. Samuel Walker, *Popular Justice: A History of Criminal Justice* (New York: Oxford University Press, 1980), pp. 21–22; Howard Abadinsky, *Law and Justice: An Introduction to the American Legal System* (Chicago: Nelson Hall, 1995), p. 55.

26. Administrative Office of the U.S. Courts, *Judicial Business of the U.S. Courts, 1994* (Washington, DC: Administrative Office of the U.S. Courts, 1995), pp. 7–9.

27. Henry R. Glick, *Courts, Politics and Justice* (New York: McGraw-Hill, 1993), pp. 24–27.

28. Malcolm Feeley, *The Process Is Punishment: Handling Cases in a Lower Court* (New York: Russell Sage Foundation, 1979).

29. John A. Jenkins, "The Lobster Shift: One Night in the Nation's Busiest Court," *ABA Journal 56* (1986), p. 76.

30. Robert G. McCloskey, *The American Supreme Court* (Chicago: University of Chicago Press, 1960).

31. Lewis, *Gideon's Trumpet,* p. 26.

32. Ann L. Pastore and Kathleen Maguire, eds., *Sourcebook of Criminal Justice Statistics 1999* (Washington, DC: U.S. Government Printing Office, 2000), p. 467, 468.

33. Lewis, *Gideon's Trumpet,* p. 26.

34. Glick, Courts, Politics and Justice, p. 149.

35. Ibid., p. 151.

36. *Powell* v. *Alabama,* 287 U.S. 45 (1932).

37. *Argerslinger* v. *Hamlin,* 407 U.S. 25 (1972).

38. Bureau of Justice Statistics, "Indigent Defense," in *BJS Selected Findings* (Washington, DC: National Institute of Justice, 1996), pp. 1–4.

39. Steven K. Smith and Carol J. Defrancis, *Indigent Defense* (Washington, DC: U.S. Department of Justice, 1996).

40. Angela Jordan Davis, "Remarks," Conference on 30th Anniversary of the U.S. Supreme Court's Decision in Gideon v. Wainwright, pp. 43–49.

41. Ibid.

42. Ibid.

43. Anthony Lewis, "Keynote Address," Conference on 30th Anniversary of the U.S. Supreme Court's Decision in Gideon v. Wainwright, p. 18.

CASE 11

Bargaining for Justice:
Bordenkircher v. Hayes

THE CRIME

On a cool day late in November 1973, Paul Lewis Hayes and his friend, Larry Frazier, entered the Pic Pac Grocery store on South Upper Street in Lexington, Kentucky.[1] The pair roamed the store, picking up a few items—some dog food, a carton of cigarettes—and placed them on the counter along with a check from the Brown Machine Shop several blocks away on West Street. Clerk Robin Grey eyed Paul Lewis suspiciously and picked up the check to examine it. Later Paul would claim that the check belonged to Larry, who had headed away from the counter to collect more groceries, but at that moment Hayes stood at the counter offering the check as payment to the clerk. Robin said she needed to talk to the manager before she could cash the check.

The store manager, Gayle Bourne, came forward from the back room. Only last Sunday another man had come into the store with a check stolen from the Brown Machine Shop. Bourne recognized the check and phoned the police to come as quickly as they could. A nearby patrol car arrived within minutes and Paul Lewis Hayes, still standing at the counter, found himself staring down the barrel of a .38 revolver. His companion Larry disappeared out the back door. The officers informed Hayes that he was being arrested for breaking and entering the Brown Machine Shop. Hayes protested, "But it's not my check. You got the wrong guy!"[2] Later, Larry Frazier would be arrested and charged with the break-in. Paul Lewis Hayes, age 29, was arrested, booked, and ultimately charged with issuing a forged check in the amount of $88.30.

A GOOD DEAL?

The state of Kentucky had been providing counsel for its poor citizens even before the Supreme Court

ruling in *Gideon* v. *Wainwright*. Paul Hayes certainly qualified as indigent. The sixth child in a family of sixteen, Hayes had made it only to the ninth grade before being sent to reform school.[3] His father, an alcoholic, died from heavy drinking. His mother, diabetic and sickly, raised the family and was the only person in the world Hayes thought cared whether he lived or died. He had briefly married, only six or seven weeks; he had a child by another woman, but she lived in Florida with his son. At age 29, Hayes lived with his mother, two sisters, and two brothers and earned a meager living working as a horse groom at the Koto Horse Transport Company. Hayes's small salary, together with a welfare check from the local office of public assistance, supported his mother and siblings. When the judge set bail at $1,000, Hayes was unable to meet the bond and began a long wait in jail to go to trial.

Five weeks later, on January 8, Assistant District Attorney Glen Bagby asked the grand jury to return an indictment against Hayes on the charge of check forgery.[4] After arraignment, at a pretrial conference held between Hayes, his publically appointed defense attorney, the state prosecutor, and the clerk of the court on February 2, Bagby offered Hayes what he believed to be a very good deal, because forgery in Kentucky carries a penalty of two to ten years. Bagby put on the table an offer of five years in state prison in exchange for an immediate guilty plea.

RAISING THE STAKES

For an $88.30 forgery, five years in prison does not sound like much of a bargain. But the real deal here was not the sentence for the forgery charge. Paul Lewis Hayes had been in trouble before. When he was still a juvenile, he had pleaded guilty to "detaining a female against her will with intent to have carnal knowledge."[5] As a minor, he had served five years in a state reformatory while his co-defendant, an adult, got a life sentence. In his early 20s, Hayes pleaded guilty to a robbery, for which he was given a five-year suspended sentence. Paul was still on probation for that offense three years later when he was charged with the check forgery. Now he faced his third felony conviction, the third strike. On his record were the two prior felony convictions, and under the Kentucky Habitual Criminal Act,[6] a person convicted of a third felony was subject to prosecution as a habitual offender. If convicted as a Habitual Criminal, the penalty was much more than five years. In fact, the mandatory punishment was life imprisonment. The real deal being offered to Hayes was the prosecutor's offer not to charge Hayes under the Habitual Criminal statute.

A DEVASTATING GAMBLE

Hayes listened as his defense attorney, Anthony Todd, explained the situation. Given his record of offenses, it was in the district attorney's power to go back before the grand jury and seek a second indictment under Kentucky's Habitual Criminal statute, which carried a mandatory life sentence. If Hayes was going to make the state go to all the trouble, expense, and inconvenience of a trial, the prosecutor was going to raise the stakes. If Hayes lost, he would lose big: on the line was his freedom for the rest of his natural life. The choice is yours, said the state prosecutor, save the state the time and inconvenience of a trial by pleading guilty to this offense or risk spending the rest of your life locked away in Kentucky state prison. The choice was laid out for Paul Hayes in plain language.

Kentucky law requires all defendants charged under the Habitual Criminal Act to undergo psychiatric evaluation. Dr. German Gutierrez interviewed Hayes on February 7, 1973,[7] and found no intellectual impairment or emotional disorder that would interfere with his ability to understand the legal charges or to make responsible decisions for himself. In the view of the psychiatrist, Paul Hayes was intellectually competent, but emotionally he was consumed with anger and hostility over a sense of injustice toward his treatment in life. As a poor black man, he felt he had been subjected to negative treatment all his life. Once before, he felt he had been pressured by the advice of his defense attorney and his mother to admit guilt to avoid going to jail. In his mind, he had once before admitted to guilt when he believed he was innocent.

No one knows what went through Paul's mind in making the decision to ignore the advice of his defense counsel and his mother this time. Maybe those five years in the reformatory had something to do with his choice. Going inside prison for any length of time might have been just too hard to face. If he took his chances at trial, there was still a possibility he could go free. The hope that he might avoid prison may have blinded him to the risk of being stuck there forever. Maybe Hayes was truly innocent of the charge and wanted to go to trial to prove it. Or maybe Hayes was too angry or upset to understand the magnitude of the choice he was making.

Whatever the rationale, Paul Lewis Hayes turned down the bargain and entered a plea of "not guilty." The district attorney did as he said he would: he returned to the grand jury and obtained a second indictment against Mr. Hayes, charging him on two counts: first of issuing a forged instrument and second, for being a habitual criminal.[8] Bail was set at $1,000, again, much too high for Lewis to pay. Paul Lewis Hayes remained locked up in the Kentucky county jail until trial, which was set for April 19, 1973.

LOSING BIG TIME

On Thursday, April 19, twelve jurors listened to testimony from the owner of the machine shop, the store manager, the store clerk, Paul Hayes, and Larry Frazier, who was now serving time at the Kentucky state reformatory for theft of the stolen checks. Despite his protestation of innocence, the jury firmly believed that Paul Hayes "did willfully, unlawfully, fraudulently, knowingly and feloniously utter and publish to Robin Gray of the Pic-Pac Food Store, as true, the check of the Brown Machine Works in the amount of $88.30."[9]

The jury also was charged with finding Hayes guilty or not guilty on the second charge of being a habitual criminal. According to the judge's instructions, if the jury found, beyond a reasonable doubt, that Hayes had been convicted of a felony in 1962 and again of a felony in 1971 and finally of the third charge of uttering a forged instrument, "then you shall fix the defendant's punishment at imprisonment in the penitentiary during his life."[10] If the jury had reasonable doubt about either of the two previous charges, then they were charged with fixing his punishment at ten to fourteen years. If they found reasonable doubt about whether he had been convicted of both of the prior felony charges, then they were charged with fixing a sentence between two and ten years.

But there was no reasonable doubt in the two prior convictions: Paul Lewis Hayes had pleaded guilty to both prior felony convictions. And the jury had just found him guilty on the third count. The jury decision was inevitable. The jury returned a verdict exactly one sentence in length: "We, the jury, fix the defendant's punishment at imprisonment in the state penitentiary for life."

CRUEL AND UNUSUAL PUNISHMENT?

Appellate attorneys from the public defender's office filed a writ of habeas corpus on behalf of Paul Lewis Hayes to the U.S. District Court, claiming his imprisonment by the state of Kentucky was a violation of his Constitutional rights.[11] A writ of habeas corpus is a request to the courts to review the reasons the state is imprisoning a citizen. In essence, the writ claims to the courts that the individual is being held illegally and asks the courts to order the citizen's release from prison.

Hayes's attorneys claimed that the penalty of life in imprisonment for a writing a bad check for $88.30 was so disproportionate to the crime as to constitute "cruel and unusual punishment," which is prohibited by the Eighth Amendment. The Habitual Criminal act was repealed two years after Lewis was convicted and replaced by a new statute that imposed life only if the defendant had been over 18 when he committed each offense and only if he had actually served time for the subsequent offenses. Under the terms of the new statute enacted in 1975, Paul Lewis Hayes would not have been given a life sentence. Keeping Hayes locked up for the rest of his life would be out of keeping with the punishments meted out to other Kentuckians for similar crimes.

THE RIGHT TO TRIAL OR THE RIGHT TO DEAL?

Hayes also raised another Constitutional issue in his habeas corpus petition to U.S. District Court. The Fourteenth Amendment states that no state may abridge a citizen's right to due process as specified in the Bill of Rights. It was Hayes's contention that prosecutors had robbed him of his right to a trial by threatening him with the Habitual Criminal statute. The prosecutor brought that second indictment against Hayes for the sole purpose of dissuading him from exercising his Constitutional right to a fair trial before a jury of his peers.

Plea bargaining has a long and not very noble history in the U.S. court system.[12] Despite the fact that attorneys and judges have been negotiating deals in the courts since the nineteenth century, for most of our nation's history there was no official recognition by the courts that the practice was taking place. Attorneys and their clients would broker deals in quiet back rooms, while no one ever admitted that such conversations and agreements had taken place. Plea bargaining came out of the closet, so to speak, in the 1970s, when many influential groups began to argue that the practice should be abolished. In one state, Alaska, the state's chief prosecutor banned the practice of plea bargaining for all state district attorneys, effectively ending the process.[13]

However, the U.S. Supreme Court affirmed plea bargaining, ruling in 1970 that plea bargains were an acceptable and pragmatic process for the efficient administration of justice—provided the defendant voluntarily and knowingly agreed to the bargain.[14] The Supreme Court qualified its approval of plea bargaining by stating that certain conditions must be met to ensure that the process complies with the Constitution.[15] First, defendants must never be coerced or tricked or deceived into agreements. They must fully understand and agree to the terms on a voluntary basis. Second, prosecutors and judges must hold up their end of the bargain: the state cannot promise one sentence and then impose another once the defendant has entered a guilty plea. Third, and most relevant for this case, it is unconstitutional for judges or prosecutors to use their power to punish someone for choosing not to plea bargain. The charge of either judicial or prosecutorial vindictiveness refers to the abuse of power in cases where defendants opt to exercise their rights to due process.

VINDICTIVE PROSECUTION? CHALLENGING THE MOTIVES OF THE PROSECUTION

The issue in the Hayes case focused on whether the decision to seek the second indictment under the Habitual Criminal act was an act of prosecutorial vindictiveness, and on whether life imprisonment for his crimes was "cruel and unusual punishment." The U.S. District Court flatly rejected both of these arguments. Hayes's mandatory life imprisonment was neither cruel nor unusual in their view. Nor did the U.S. District Court agree that the prosecutor had acted unconstitutionally by choosing to raise the more serious charge once Lewis insisted upon his right to trial. The right to choose which charge to bring against a defendant is well within the discretionary power of the prosecutor. The prosecutor was merely exercising his power to make a deal: the law gave the state certain advantages, and he used them.

The U.S. Sixth Circuit Court of Appeals, however, saw the matter very differently.[16] They believed Hayes was right to claim that his due process rights had been violated. In their assessment, the sole reason Hayes was charged under the Habitual Criminal act was because he was choosing to exercise his right to a jury trial. The prosecutor openly admitted that the only reason he sought the second indictment was to induce Hayes to plead guilty. During the trial, on cross-examination of the defendant, he reminded the accused, ". . . isn't it a fact that I told you if you did not intend to save the court the inconvenience and necessity of a trial and taking up this time that I intended to return to the grand jury and ask them to indict you based upon these prior felony convictions?"[17]

For the court it was significant that the state attorney chose to file the Habitual Criminal charges after Hayes insisted upon a trial. Without a doubt, the sole purpose of the more serious charge was to dissuade him from exercising his due process rights. Since the prosecutor did not opt to charge Hayes as a habitual offender on the first indictment, the state prosecutor must have decided that the interests of justice were not served by a habitual offender charge for this defendant. If this was true, then it was clear to the judges that the prosecutors were using their power only to prevent Hayes from claiming his right to a trial. If there were no other purposes for the second indictment than to prevent Hayes from going to trial, then he was being denied his due process rights under the Fourteenth Amendment. The Court of Appeals decided that this case was a clear-cut example of prosecutorial vindictiveness.

> When a prosecutor obtains an indictment less severe than the facts known to him at the time might permit, he makes a discretionary determination that the interests of the state are served by not seeking more serious charges. Accordingly, if after plea negotiations fail, he then procures an indictment charging a more

serious crime, a strong inference is created that the only reason for the more serious charges is vindictiveness. Under these circumstances, the prosecutor should be required to justify his action. In this case, a vindictive motive need not be inferred. The prosecutor has admitted it.[18]

The court reversed the district court decision and remanded the case back to the Circuit Court with instructions that the petitioner (Hayes) should serve only a lawful sentence for the crime of forgery, which may range from two to ten years. It would be up to the judge to set the terms of that sentence.

HOPE AND FRUSTRATION FOR HAYES

Like many prisoners locked away and forgotten by society, Hayes's entire existence revolved around his "case" and the hope that he would someday persuade the court to reduce his sentence and set him free. Hayes wrote again and again from behind the prison walls to the judge, defense attorneys, clerks, anyone who might have the power to issue an order for his release. In July 1973, Hayes filed a motion on his own behalf requesting the court to suspend further execution of his sentence. Hayes petitioned the court to show him and his family some mercy: he promised to abide by the rules and violate no further laws; his employer was willing to have him back, and his income was crucial for the welfare of his siblings and ailing mother. His motions for suspension were denied; most of his letters went unanswered.

On February 9, 1977, the Fayette Circuit Court issued an order to move Hayes from the state penitentiary to the custody of the county jail to await a new hearing ordered for 9 a.m. on March 8, 1977. Hayes must have been filled with hope, believing the transfer was bringing him one step closer to freedom, but the news he received at the hearing on March 8 was not good. The attorney general of the state of Kentucky told the court that he had filed a motion to stay the release of Hayes pending appeal of the decision to the U.S. Supreme Court.

Hayes's attorney requested a bond that would release Hayes while the case went before the nation's highest court. Everyone doubted that the Supreme Court would agree to review the case. Hayes had already served three-and-a-half years of hard time, and his attorneys asked that he at least be freed on bond until the Supreme Court ruled on whether it would hear the case. The motion to release Hayes pending the appeal to the Supreme Court was denied, and in what must have been a crushing defeat for Hayes, he was transported back to the Kentucky state penitentiary on May 16, 1977.

LAWFUL DISCRETION OR PROSECUTORIAL VINDICTIVENESS?

In 1978, the question of when and how plea bargaining was consistent with the Constitution and the rules of due process was a powerful and important issue in the courts. The Supreme Court had stated that it is better that plea bargaining be recognized and regulated than that it be driven "back into the shadows from which it had so recently emerged." The justices recognized the need to clarify and define more precisely the boundaries of permissible conduct on the part of prosecutors, judges, and defense attorneys during the plea bargaining process. Just as the timing favored the issue brought forward by Gideon about the right to counsel, the luckless Paul Hayes was pushed into the spotlight to serve the "higher interests of the law." Much to the surprise of the local attorneys, the U.S. Supreme Court granted certiorari in what was now the U.S. Supreme Court case, *Bordenkircher v. Hayes*.[19]

PLEA BARGAINS ARE DIFFERENT FROM TRIALS

By a slim 5–4 majority, the U.S. Supreme Court reversed the ruling of the Sixth Circuit Court of Appeals, extinguishing the last glimmer of hope for prisoner #28862. According to the majority, Hayes had been fully informed at the pretrial conference of the intention of the prosecutor to charge him under the more serious statute if he chose to plead not guilty. In fact, the justices argued, this case is no different than if the state attorney had first indicted Hayes under the habitual offender statute and then offered at the negotiations to drop the charges. Either way, this kind of "give and take" is the nature of plea negotiations, and it is in the very nature of plea negotiations that each side use whatever it legally can to make the other side give in.

Justice Potter Stewart wrote the opinion for the majority, stating that "as long as the accused is free to accept or reject the prosecutor's offer," this does not constitute an instance of punishment or retribution. Furthermore, it is Constitutionally legitimate for the prosecutor to have as his or her main goal at the bargaining table to dissuade the defendant from pleading not guilty. Realistically, the justices said, that is precisely what plea bargaining is about: inducing defendants to cooperate in order to save the state the time and money of a formal trial. Prosecutors are free to use whatever legitimate sentencing options are at their disposal in order to achieve this end, including the habitual offender statute.

In two previous cases, *North Carolina* v. *Pearce*,[20] and *Blackledge* v. *Perry*,[21] the Supreme Court had found evidence of vindictiveness in the plea bargaining process.[22] In both those cases, the defendant had been subject to additional and more serious charges or sentences in retaliation for exercising due process rights. In *North Carolina* v. *Pearce*, the defendant had been granted a new trial after a successful appeal on Constitutional grounds. At that second trial, however, he received a more serious sentence than he had in the original trial. In this case, the Supreme Court reasoned that the sole reason for the longer sentence was judicial vindictiveness or punishment of the defendant for exercising his right to appeal.

In *Blackledge* v. *Perry*, Perry had been given a six-month sentence on a misdemeanor charge in lower court. After he appealed the case and sought his right to a second trial *de novo* in the Superior Court, the prosecutor filed felony charges rather than misdemeanor charges. These charges carried a much higher penalty, and in the second trial the defendant was convicted and sentenced for a much longer period of time, five to seven years. The Supreme Court concluded in both these cases that the defendants had been maliciously punished by the state for having "done what the law plainly allows" them to do.

But in Hayes's case, the justices argued that the plea bargaining situation was different from the trial process. In plea bargaining, the defendant still has the option of accepting or rejecting the prosecution's offer. Hayes could have accepted the deal and served the five years. Prosecutors always have a wide range of legitimate charging alternatives, "so long as the prosecutor has probable cause to believe that the accused committed an offense defined by statute, the decision whether or not to prosecute, and what charge to file or bring before a grand jury, generally rests entirely in his discretion."[23] Sure the motive was to dissuade him from going to trial, but that is always the motive for the prosecution when it comes to plea bargaining. Whether the state is offering a defendant a more lenient charge or threatening the defendant with one that is more severe, the overall goal is to influence the decision of the defendant to plead guilty to the charge.

PUTTING JUSTICE ABOVE EFFICIENCY: THE DISSENTING OPINION

Four Supreme Court justices strongly dissented from the majority opinion. In their view, the interests of efficiency, the central reasoning behind the practice of plea bargaining, was a distant second to the paramount interests of justice. In their view the Sixth Circuit was totally correct. Prosecutorial vindictiveness is defined as those actions where the state seeks to discourage a citizen from the exercise of his right to trial. To use one's discretionary power as a state prosecutor to file excessively harsh charges or to use one's power as a judge to sentence a defendant harshly because a defendant is protesting innocence constitutes an abuse of that power. "Prosecutorial vindictiveness in any context is still prosecutorial vindictiveness," whether it takes place at the bargaining table or in the courtroom.

The justices acknowledged that in the real world of the courtroom, boosting the charges for the purposes of bargaining, a practice known as overcharging, is common among prosecutors. But just because it is common does not mean that it is fair, Constitutional, or legitimate. When charging a defendant, prosecutors should make their decision based solely on the interests of justice, encompassing such considerations as public safety, seriousness of the offense, and prior criminal conduct of the individual. The decision of what to charge should not be based on whether they are trying "win" a deal from the defendant. Prosecutors should reach their own decisions about what to charge, independent of defendants' willingness to plead guilty; otherwise, defendants who believe themselves to be innocent will be forced to take "devastating gambles" to maintain their innocence.

WHATEVER HAPPENED TO HAYES?

Paul Lewis Hayes tried to appeal his life sentence one last time. He and his attorneys filed for a writ of habeas corpus in the U.S. District Court, again on the grounds that his sentence constituted "cruel and unusual" punishment for the crime committed. The U.S. District Court rejected his claim, and when the matter went to the U.S. Court of Appeals, they too rejected the argument that life imprisonment for the offense of forgery was a violation of the Eighth Amendment. A previous Supreme Court ruling, *Rummel* v. *Estelle*,[24] had ruled that U.S. citizens do not have an Eighth Amendment Constitutional right to have punishment proportionate to the severity of the crime. What constitutes "unusual" punishment for any given crime is totally up to the state legislatures to decide. When the Hayes case was appealed to the Supreme Court, a writ of certiorari was denied. Paul Lewis Hayes remains serving a life sentence in a Kentucky state prison.

Case based on primary documents in *Bordenkircher* v. *Hayes* 434 U.S. 357, 363 (1978); *Paul Lewis Hayes* v. *Henry Cowan*, United States District Court, Eastern District of Kentucky, No. 75-61, October 9, 1975; *Commonwealth of Kentucky* v. *Paul Lewis Hayes* 73-C-29, April 19, 1973.

THINKING CRITICALLY ABOUT THIS CASE

1. Do you agree with the majority opinion or the dissenting opinion in this case? Was this a case of prosecutorial vindictiveness, or fair and lawful exercise of prosecutorial discretion?

2. When Paul Lewis Hayes was asked to choose between taking the prosecutor's offer or going to trial under the Habitual Criminal act, was this a fair choice for Hayes to make? Why or why not?

3. If you were a defendant facing the choice of pleading guilty to a crime you did not commit or going to trial under a habitual offender statute, what choice would you make? What factors would you consider? How would you feel about the justice system?

4. If Hayes had been offered a suspended sentence for the charge, do you believe he would have been willing to plead guilty? Would you plead guilty to an offense you know you did not commit if you were offered probation, or would you maintain your innocence and risk conviction at trial and a prison sentence?

5. Mandatory sentencing statutes increase the power of prosecutors in the plea bargaining process. Explain how this case illustrates that enhanced prosecutorial power. In your opinion, does this advance the interests of justice? Why or why not?

6. Most convictions are the result of guilty pleas entered by defendants. Is it possible that innocent defendants enter guilty pleas in order to receive lenient treatment? What are the implications of this reality for the "three strikes" statutes, which seek to punish repeat offenders severely?

7. Does plea bargaining undermine the legitimacy of the legal system? Why or why not? Is there a viable alternative? What safeguards do you think need to be put in place to ensure that plea bargaining does not undermine the interests of justice?

CHECK OUT THIS CASE

On Film

Plea Bargains: Dealing for Justice (26 minutes)
This film deals with the vast majority of criminal cases and takes a hard "behind the scenes" look at who gets out of jail, who doesn't, and who decides what kind of deal to make. Emmy Award Nominee. Available from Films for the Humanities and Sciences, www.films.com.

CHAPTER 11

Players and Plea Bargains in the Courtroom

LEARNING OBJECTIVES

After reading this chapter, the student should be able to:

- Define the courtroom work group and describe the primary functions of the judge, prosecutor, and defense attorney

- Understand the unique role of the prosecutor in the U.S. justice system

- Describe the role of the defense attorney and describe the different segments of the defense bar

- Define the process of plea negotiations and define the different forms of plea bargaining

- Understand the advantages and disadvantages of plea bargaining

Clarence Gideon and Paul Lewis Hayes have a lot in common. Both are poor men with a long and troubled history with the criminal justice system. Both found themselves locked up as young teens, followed by a life spent in and out of prison. Clarence Gideon knew from bitter experience that the rules, customs, and procedures of the court were confusing, strange, and incomprehensible to ordinary folk like himself. Because of his determination, the Supreme Court acknowledged that even highly intelligent and educated persons, if they are unfamiliar with the culture and norms of the law, may be lost and bewildered inside a courtroom. Gideon's triumph in securing the right to an attorney for all poor criminal defendants benefited those who came after him like Paul Hayes, who was afforded legal representation in all of the proceedings against him.

But Hayes's case illustrates a different reality about the halls of justice in U.S. society. Despite the symbolic importance of the trial, where Americans can see "justice" happen, few criminal convictions are the result of these types of proceedings. Over 90 percent of all felony convictions are the result of guilty pleas.[25] In one study conducted by the U.S. Department of Justice, the data revealed that for every 100 felony arrests, fifty-six resulted in convictions. Of those fifty-six convictions, fifty-four were the result of guilty pleas.[26] Clearly, other types of proceedings, such as pretrial conferences, informal negotiations, and other forms of "deal making" are far more important to the justice process than the formal trial.

The chapter takes a close look at the "players" of the courtroom and what they do in the array of proceedings that constitute the adjudication phase of the criminal justice system. Lawyers dominate the proceedings in the courthouse, but there is a cast of "supporting" roles played by nonlawyers. Clerks, secretaries, guards, bailiffs, stenographers, victim advocates, probation officers, social workers, and mediators form a growing army of nonlegal personnel who are engaged in the "business of the court." We will look at the roles of these different occupational groups, both in the formal process of the trial and in the less visible but more significant process of negotiation commonly referred to as plea bargaining.

At the close of the chapter, we return to the question raised in the last chapter: do poor and rich defendants receive "equal" justice in our courtrooms? *Gideon* v. *Wainwright* attempted to ensure equal justice before the law by providing funds for poor people's defense. At the start of the second trial of Clarence Gideon, the state attorneys observed that had Clarence been represented by defense counsel from the start, there would probably never have been a trial. A competent defense attorney would probably have advised Gideon to plead guilty in exchange for a "deal."

This observation refers to the fact that, most of the time, criminal defense attorneys mount no formal defense: their main contribution is negotiating on behalf of their client with the prosecutor and the judge. Had Gideon had a defense attorney and had he pleaded guilty, it is likely that his sentence would have been far less than five years. In plea negotiations, it is the job of the defense attorney to get the best deal for his or her client. Clarence Gideon realized that poor defendants without the benefit of counsel were not only more likely to be convicted but were also likely to serve long sentences for relatively minor crimes. In this chapter we look at the informal reality of plea bargaining, the prospects of poor defendants in the informal process of plea negotiations, and the impact of these proceedings on the goal of "justice for all."

THE COURTROOM WORK GROUP

The **courtroom work group** refers to the professional occupational roles whose primary mission is the administration of criminal justice. It includes judges, prosecuting attorneys, defense attorneys, public defenders, and others who earn their living serving the court. In a sense, defendants, victims, witnesses, and members of the jury are all "outsiders" to the world of the courthouse. When a criminal prosecution proceeds to adjudication, ordinary citizens temporarily penetrate the boundaries of the strange world of the court, which has its own language, customs, and rules. Typically, victims, offenders, witnesses, and their families feel completely lost in this world without the assistance and representation of "insiders"—the criminal justice personnel who earn their living by serving the court and administering the judicial process.

The **adversarial system** formally pits one side against the other in the battle for truth and justice. Formally, the prosecuting and defense attorney fight vigorously in accordance with the rules of due process to win the case for their client. As we have seen in the case of Clarence Gideon, a very different version of the facts may emerge when testimony and evidence is tested in the presence of a skilled and experienced advocate. For a trial to be genuinely fair, both sides must be evenly matched, with skilled advocates to prosecute and to defend in a formal contest of opposing sides. As Justice Brennan noted in Gideon, "Lawyers are necessities not luxuries."

Informally, however, the defense attorney, prosecutor, and judge are all part of a single system.[27] They are colleagues who work together day in and day out, disposing of thousands of cases over the course of long careers. While they may act out adversarial roles in front of the public, behind the scenes they share coffee in the judge's chambers, eat lunch together, play squash, have attended the same schools, live in similar neighborhoods, and belong to the same clubs and associations. Many judges are former prosecutors or defense attorneys, many public prosecutors go on to become private defense attorneys, public defenders join the judiciary, and so forth. The members of the courthouse work group generally have more in common with each other, both professionally and personally, than they do with the defendants and victims whom they represent.

Despite the importance of the adversarial system, most cases processed by the criminal justice system are not resolved by a formal trial.[28] What appears to be an adversarial

courtroom work group: criminal justice professionals who conduct the daily business of the criminal courts.

adversarial system: a system in which the prosecution and the defense are each on opposing sides seeking to persuade the judge and the jury to accept its version of the truth.

process is often more a cooperative process. The informal reality is that courtroom work groups arrange settlements on cases through plea bargaining and other forms of negotiation in the vast majority of cases.[29] In a purely adversarial system, one side is the winner and the other is the loser; but in the real world of criminal justice, justice is most often a compromise between the two sides, negotiated in the judge's chambers, in the hall, on the phone, over lunch, even in the restroom. In the view of Abraham Blumberg, the reality of the criminal law is that the adversarial system operates only a facade or "con game," concealing a kind of conspiracy to induce defendants to plead guilty in order to meet the organizational needs of the courtroom work group.[30]

THE LEGAL PROFESSION

Harvard University established the first law school in the United States in 1817, but attendance at law school through most of the century was rare.[31] Until the late nineteenth century, most lawyers gained their knowledge and skill simply by apprenticing to practicing attorneys. The American Bar Association was formed in 1878 to regulate standards for law schools and help establish state-wide bar examinations to control the standards of the profession and who was permitted to practice it.

The profession of lawyering has historically been segregated by class, race, and gender. In England, the occupation divided into two segments: barristers of high noble birth wore white wigs and black robes to argue the case before the court, while solicitors, from more modest middle-class backgrounds, prepared briefs and advised clients outside of court. In the United States, the occupation of lawyer functioned like a "gentlemen's club," dominated by white Protestant males from wealthy classes.[32] Law schools were costly and refused to admit worthy candidates from less privileged backgrounds. Catholics, Jews, blacks, women, and others were barred from access to the elite institutions of legal education such as Harvard, Yale, and Columbia.

The first female to be admitted to the bar was Arabella A. Mansfield in 1869, the same year that the first female law student, Ada Kepley, graduated from the University of Chicago Law School.[33] Despite her degree, however, Ada Kepley was denied admission to the Illinois Bar because of her status as a woman. In *Bradwell* v. *Illinois*[34] in 1873, the Supreme Court ruled that women did not have a Constitutional right to engage in all of the professional occupations in civic society.

For many in the nineteenth century, the courtroom and the profession of law were deemed "unsuitable" for the feminine character. According to the chief justice of the Wisconsin Supreme Court that rejected the application of women to the bar in 1876: "The peculiar qualities of womanhood, its gentle graces, its quick sensibility, its tender susceptibility, its purity, its delicacy, its emotional impulses, its subordination of hard reasoning to sympathetic feeling, are surely no qualifications for forensic strife."[35] In the 1880s there were only about two hundred women attorneys practicing in the United States. By 1900 thirty-four states permitted women to practice law, and by 1920 all states had admitted women to the bar. Yale Law School accepted women in 1918, Columbia Law School in 1927, but Harvard Law School refused to admit women until 1950. As late as 1971 only 5 percent of all the students involved in law were female.

The 1970s and 1980s saw a dramatic influx of women into the profession. By the mid-1990s, half of all law school students were women. By 2000, women constituted about 29.6 percent of all practicing attorneys.[36] But women lawyers still earn significantly less than male lawyers and are more likely to work in less lucrative public agencies, or in solo practice. Women are still greatly underrepresented on the faculties of law schools, in partnerships, in leadership positions in bar associations, and on the bench. In 1990, only 6 to 8 percent of state judges and 9 percent of federal judges were women.[37]

The status of racial and ethnic minorities in the practice of law is considerably bleaker than it is for women. In 1983, African Americans made up less than 3 percent of U.S. lawyers, while Hispanics accounted for less than 1 percent of practicing attorneys. More than fifteen years later, in 1997, Hispanic representation had grown to about 3.8 percent while the number of African American lawyers remained about the same at only about 4 percent.[38] Of the more than 30,000 judges nationwide, fewer than 1,000 are African American, and in 1992 African Americans constituted only about 4 percent of the nation's prosecutors.[39] In 1995, of a total of 8,432 state court judges, only 293, less than 4 percent, were African American.[40] Despite the fact that Hispanic and African American citizens are disproportionately the target of criminal justice prosecution and punishment, few of these groups are represented in the occupational roles of the courthouse work group.

The Role of the Judge

Judges are public officials who preside over courts of law. The judge is umpire, referee, coach, advisor, and teacher all rolled into one. The judge is responsible for the legal conduct in the courtroom and the administrative flow of cases through the courtroom. The role of the judge is to uphold the rights of the accused and to ensure that the laws of criminal procedure are upheld in all proceedings. Gideon asked the judge to appoint him an attorney because it is a judicial obligation to see that defendants' rights are duly protected. Administratively, especially in the lower courts, the job of the judge expands to include management of the court itself, evaluation of court personnel, the budget, and even responsibilities for the physical building of the courthouse itself.

Before the trial, the judge rules on all motions concerning the venue of the trial, the granting of bail, jury selection, submission of evidence, and the like. During the trial, it is the responsibility of the judge to manage the conduct of the attorneys and to guarantee that what the jury hears and sees during the proceedings is in accordance with the law. It is also the duty of the judge to explain the relevant law to the jury and to give the jury legal guidance as they begin their deliberations. Any judicial decision during a felony proceeding in a trial court may be the basis for an appeal by a defendant arguing that he or she was denied a fair trial according to the law. Judge McCray's decision that Gideon was not legally entitled to an attorney formed the basis for Gideon's appeal to the federal courts to review that ruling.

From pretrial proceedings through sentencing, the judge is also charged with assessing the strength of the prosecution's case against the accused. The judge retains the power to dismiss the charges against the defendant at any point in the judicial process if he or she believes sufficient evidence to convict is lacking. Substantively, the judicial role is to protect the accused against frivolous or malicious prosecution. In superior court proceedings, defendants may waive their right to a jury trial and choose a **bench trial,** in which the judge is both neutral arbiter of the process and the person who decides if witnesses are telling the truth, what the evidence really means, and whether the defendant is guilty as charged beyond a reasonable doubt.

In the lower court proceedings where juries are rare, judges are the ultimate decision makers, interpreting the evidence and evaluating the credibility of witnesses.[41] In these busy courts, most cases are dispensed with through guilty pleas negotiated on the spot in routine exchanges between the courtroom work groups. Here the job of judge is closer to that of a kind of justice broker, helping sides come to agreement, offering quick deals one after the other in routine cases that repeat themselves in mind-numbing succession.

The Manhattan Criminal Court is one of the busiest courts in the nation and the only one in the country that actually operates 24 hours a day, 365 days a year.[42] Prostitutes, addicts, drug dealers, car thieves, angry spouses, and drunks parade in front of the judicial bench in a steady stream of human misery and confusion. This is "assembly-line

judges: public officials who preside over courts of law.

bench trial: a trial in which the judge hears the facts and issues a verdict on the guilt or innocence of the defendants.

justice," where juries are nonexistent. Police officers round up defendants, who are signed over to court officers and taken to holding cells just off the courtroom. There each prisoner, most of whom are indigent, is briefly interviewed by a Legal Aid lawyer in preparation for arraignment. Standing in front of the bench, the Legal Aid lawyer, the assistant defense attorney, and the judge quickly negotiate the deal to be offered to the defendant waiting in the pen. Judges settle most cases at the time of arraignment, entering charges, hearing the facts, and delivering the sentence in a matter of minutes.[43] The majority of defendants charged with misdemeanor offenses appear before the judge without an attorney.

Appellate judges play a very different role from either lower court or trial court judges. Appellate judges neither examine evidence nor hear from witnesses, they don't assess credibility or make inferences from the facts of the case; rather, the job of the appellate judge is to analyze the legality of the proceedings, review legal briefs written by the opposing attorneys, listen to oral arguments made by both sides, and determine if the law has been properly executed. If there has been an error in procedure, the appellate court may order a new trial or order a sentence to be revoked. But an appellate judge will never second-guess a lower court judge's assessment of the evidence or credibility of the witnesses; the appellate court monitors the legality of the proceedings rather than the veracity of the evidence.

One of the most important judicial functions is sentencing of criminal defendants. In most criminal statues, there is a wide range of sentencing alternatives for a given charge. Historically, the discretion of judges in making this important decision has been very broad. Judges are assisted in this decision by presentence reports written by probation officers and by recommendations from defense attorneys and prosecuting attorneys. Criminal statutes such as the Kentucky Habitual Criminal act, which specify a mandatory sentence, remove the judge from the key role in sentencing. Under this form of sentencing, far less discretionary decision making is required of the judge.

Judicial Selection   Judges are either appointed, selected, or elected.[44] Federal judges are nominated by the President and then confirmed by the Senate. Most appointments are confirmed unanimously, but occasionally there are heated disputes over a presidential nomination, particularly for Supreme Court justices. For lower court federal judges, senators have tremendous influence in promoting or resisting particular candidates to the U.S. District and Appeals Courts in their state. All federal judges hold their offices for life, and an appointment to the Supreme Court, as we have seen, can be highly influential in shaping the law of the nation. Indeed, the issue of appointments to the U.S. Supreme Court is a significant factor in the political election of the President of the United States, since the influence of the Supreme Court lasts far beyond the term of any individual President.

At the state level, the selection of judges is determined by state law. One method of selection is via regular party politics: judges campaign for election just like any other politician, by securing a party nomination and running on the party ticket. The major concern about judicial elections is that politics may erode the impartiality of those on the bench, who must think about reelection and returning political favors rather than upholding the law. States where judges are simply appointed by the governor of the state are also subject to the criticism that such a method of selection fosters favoritism and corruption in the courts, which should be above political influence and bias.

In an effort to overcome the drawbacks of both elections and appointments, the **Missouri merit selection plan** was devised in 1940. This is a hybrid system that relies on an independent commission of lawyers to draw up a list of qualified nominees for the bench. The governor then selects a nominee from this list, who is then provisionally appointed for a probationary term subject to voter approval. By the 1990s, twenty-three states had some version of merit selection for judges in operation.[45]

Missouri merit selection plan: judicial selection plan devised in 1940 that relies on an independent commission of lawyers to nominate candidates for final appointment by the governor of the state subject to voter approval.

The Prosecuting Attorney

The **prosecutor** has become the most powerful figure in the criminal justice system, exercising enormous discretion and power in the decision to prosecute. The prosecutor is a government lawyer charged with the responsibility of enforcing the law by investigating the accused and representing the state at trial. As an advocate in the adversarial process, the prosecutor pursues conviction of the accused in accordance with the rules of due process and champions the state in courtroom combat.

The functions of the prosecutor are extremely broad and span the entire criminal justice process. They begin with the investigation of criminal suspects: prosecutors work with police to prepare search and arrest warrants. In some cases, prosecutors may initiate investigations on their own. Following arrests, prosecutors screen cases at the intake phase to assess the evidence and to determine the charge. The prosecutor is also responsible for preparing the information report that establishes probable cause and, in jurisdictions that require it, bringing the evidence before the grand jury to obtain an indictment.

The prosecutor participates in all pretrial proceedings as the state's attorney and is responsible for giving formal notice of the charges to the defendant. If the case should go to trial, the prosecutor is the state advocate who prepares and presents the evidence, arguing the case for the state. The prosecutor also makes recommendations for sentencing, responds to appeals made by the defendant, and participates in parole hearings by making recommendations for or against early release of the inmate.

Federal prosecutors, known as U.S. attorneys, are appointed by the President and confirmed by the Senate. There are federal prosecutors in each of the ninety-four U.S. judicial districts. They work hand in hand with the Federal Bureau of Investigation to investigate and prosecute federal crimes. The attorney general of the Department of Justice formally supervises the U.S. attorneys and their assistants, but in practice each U.S. attorney is relatively independent and free to decide which cases will be investigated and prosecuted. The position of U.S. attorney is very prestigious and public; frequently, it is a stepping stone to political office or appointment to a federal judgeship.

The office of state prosecutor is also a highly public role and integrally connected to the political arena. State prosecutors (referred to as district attorneys, county attorneys, commonwealth attorneys, or state's attorneys) are almost all elected officials answerable to the electorate. The office of state prosecutor is very often a first step on the ladder of a career in state politics. As political figures, state attorneys are frequently in the media, and these professionals typically have close ties with political parties and political circles.

Across the United States, about 2,300 state prosecutors employ approximately 21,000 assistant district attorneys (ADAs), who carry out the actual duties of the prosecutor.[46] The elected prosecutor acts as an office administrator, setting policy within the office for the disposition of cases. The average state prosecutor's office has a staff of only eight employees, but in urban districts with populations exceeding half a million, the staff may number in the thousands. Los Angeles County is the largest state prosecutor's office in the nation, with a staff of 2,700.[47]

The typical assistant prosecutor is a recent law school graduate seeking to gain some trial experience for three or four years before moving into private legal practice. Turnover is high, pay is low, and the hours are long. Like public defenders, public prosecutors often experience "burnout" from the grueling, endless processing of human misery, incompetence, failure, anger, and pain. Some assistant prosecutors stay on to become career prosecutors, and a few seek the office of state chief prosecutor as a stepping stone to higher public office in the judiciary, legislature, or executive branch.

The Interests of Justice   The question before the U.S. Supreme Court in the Hayes case concerned the motives and ethical conduct of the prosecutor. Prosecutor Glenn

prosecutor: a government attorney who instigates the prosecution of an accused and represents the interests of the state at trial.

Elected official Gil Garcetti, serving as District Attorney of Los Angeles County, oversaw hundreds of state prosecutors. The job of the prosecutor is to enforce the law and to uphold the interests of justice for the entire community.

Bagby diligently interviewed witnesses and victims in the Hayes case. He reviewed the police report, decided on a charge, and presented evidence of probable cause to the grand jury. He made a pretrial offer to the defendant and his attorney for a plea agreement, with a sentence he felt was just. Once the defendant decided to go to trial, Bagby sought and won a new indictment against Hayes and then successfully argued and won the case before a jury, who found Hayes guilty as charged. There is little doubt that Bagby fulfilled his duties as an advocate for the state of Kentucky.

But the job of the prosecutor is broader and more ambiguous than simply representing one side in an adversarial battle. As a public servant and chief law enforcement officer of the state, the prosecutor is also charged with the responsibility of upholding the **interests of justice** in the name of the whole community. As an elected official, the prosecutor is ethically sworn to administer justice for all. On taking office, prosecutors take an oath that requires them to "seek justice."

According to the American Bar Association General Standards: "A prosecutor should not institute, cause to be instituted, or permit the continued pendency of criminal charges in the absence of sufficient evidence to support a conviction."[48] A prosecutor is ethically barred from advocating for any fact or position that he or she knows is untrue, and prosecutors should only pursue cases when they believe the evidence is sufficient "beyond reasonable doubt." The ABA Standard for Criminal Justice 3-1.1 describes the prosecutor's duty this way: "The duty of the prosecutor is to seek justice, not merely to convict." Prosecutorial discretion is ideally guided by a commitment to justice rather than a desire to win a conviction at all costs.

interests of justice: ethical duty of the prosecutor to administer justice for all rather than seek conviction.

Prosecutorial Discretion   According to Supreme Court Justice Robert H. Jackson, "The prosecutor has more control over life, liberty, and reputation than any other person in America."[49] The police may act as gatekeepers to the criminal justice system by bringing most suspects in through the power of arrest, but it is the prosecutor who has the power to reopen that gate and allow them to leave the system. It is the prosecutor, more than any other player, who has a highly influential role in determining the pathway through the system that particular defendants must take: are they charged with a misdemeanor or a felony? Is it a serious felony or not? How many counts? These decisions affect how long individuals will be in the system, where they will be in the system, and how they will be treated. Like the selective pattern of law enforcement operated by the police, **selective prosecution** is the unrestricted discretion to choose who is prosecuted and who is not.

The sphere of prosecutorial discretion over the justice system has expanded largely at the expense of the judiciary.[50] In a largely administrative system of justice in which jury trials are a rarity, it is the prosecutor who makes most of the decisions about the fate of a given defendant. Discretion begins with the decision to investigate. Commonly, prosecutors face the decision to investigate and prosecute suspects who have been arrested by the police, although prosecutors can, and do, initiate investigations. Like the decision to investigate, the decision to file charges is entirely in the realm of prosecutorial judgment. The policy decision by the district attorney's office to prosecute aggressively certain kinds of crime, such as drug offenses, while devoting less resources to other types of crime, such as gambling or prostitution, has a significant impact on other parts of the system. The screening prosecutor may decide to divert the individual to a social service agency or specific program or dismiss the case for a variety of reasons.

Once the case has been formally entered in the court record through arraignment, the prosecutor still has the power to terminate the proceedings. The entry of a *nolle prosequi,* also known as *nol. pros.* or simply *nolle,* is a formal entry of record that simply declares an unwillingness to prosecute a case. The prosecutor may do this without explaining the reasons for this decision to any other party in the criminal justice system.[51]

The most common reasons for dismissing cases are witness problems and other evidentiary difficulties.[52] Witnesses may be reluctant to testify, lack credibility, or be unavailable, errors may have been made by the police in the arrest or search phase, or the lab may have damaged crucial forensic evidence needed to try the case successfully. Other reasons for dismissal include conserving resources for more serious cases, dropping charges in exchange for information and cooperation on a more serious offense, the petty nature of the crime, or the fact that it is a first offense of an otherwise well-behaved individual.

Dismissals from prosecution are also often based on the prosecutor's quick judgments and stereotypes about the credibility of the victim. Young black males, young women who are engaged in questionable occupations such as exotic dancing or prostitution, and victims who are in intimate relationships with the suspect all are seen by prosecutors as risky foundations on which to build an effective case. Prosecutors often exercise a double standard depending on the status, background, and behavior of the victim rather than the evidence and actions of the perpetrator. Many victims of crime, especially in cases of domestic violence, rape, and sexual assault, find that cases are dismissed by prosecutors despite the victim's willingness to testify.[53]

In addition to deciding whether to prosecute, it is also within the realm of prosecutorial discretion to determine what to charge a defendant with. When Hayes was indicted the first time, the prosecutor had the power to charge Hayes as a habitual offender based on his prior felony convictions or charge him only for the forgery that brought him into the system this time. For most criminal acts, there is a range of possible statutes that may be applied to the facts. Prosecutors may prefer to seek multiple charges in order to increase their chances of conviction if the case goes to trial or to gain leverage in plea negotiations. The power to drop or reduce the charges at any point in the process gives the prosecutor enormous leverage in the negotiation process of plea bargaining.

selective prosecution: the authority held by prosecutors to use discretion in choosing whom to prosecute.

nolle prosequi: a formal entry in the record by which a prosecutor declares he or she will not prosecute the case.

The Defense Attorney

The highest priority of the **defense counsel** in a criminal case is to advocate for the interests of the accused. In the adversarial system of justice, counsel for the defense has a singular purpose: acquittal or the least punitive sanctions possible for the client. Unlike the prosecutor, who is sworn to uphold "justice" for all parties, the job of the defense attorney is to represent zealously and advocate for the defendant, regardless of innocence or guilt. It is only the government's lawyer who is sworn to be pursue the truth. According to the ABA General Standards: "The basic duty the lawyer for the accused owes to the administration of justice is to serve as the accused's counselor and advocate with courage, devotion, and to the utmost of his or her learning and ability and according to the law."

According to Alan Dershowitz, one of the most famous private criminal defense attorneys, "The zealous defense attorney is the last bastion of liberty—the final barrier between an overreaching government and its citizens."[54] It is not the responsibility of the defense to assess the guilt of the accused; to do that would be to usurp the function of the judge or the jury. The function of the defense is to challenge the government at every turn, in order to act as a check on the power of the state to prosecute its citizens. Justice Jackson acknowledged the awesome power of the prosecution to use the resources of the state to proceed against an individual citizen. To protect the right of all citizens, it is essential for the defense attorney to advocate zealously for the accused regardless of guilt or innocence.

The responsibility of the defense attorney includes representing the interests of the accused as soon as possible after arrest. *Miranda* v. *Arizona*[55] established the right of the accused to be represented by counsel as soon as he or she is identified as a formal suspect by the state. Defense counsel may be present at interrogations to ensure that the defendant's civil rights are observed by the police and courts as the accused is processed by the system. The defense files pretrial motions on behalf of the accused, represents him or her at all bail hearings, reviews police reports, interviews the witnesses, examines evidence collected by the state in the discovery process, and collects additional evidence and witnesses on behalf of the accused. If the case goes to trial, the defense prepares the case for trial, represents the accused, and provides assistance and advice in sentencing and appeal. Defense counsel pursue appropriate bases for appeals and prepare briefs and oral arguments at appeal.

The criminal defense bar can be divided into three general types: elite private defense attorneys, ordinary private criminal lawyers, and indigent counsel systems. The practice of each of these defense attorneys is quite different from the others, along with the outcome. Despite the implementation of the public defender systems and the noble and famous *Gideon* ruling, the quality of the criminal defense and the outcome of a criminal prosecution is often predicated on the size of the defendant's bank account.

defense counsel: an attorney whose ethical duty is to zealously represent the interests of the defendant before the court.

elite private defense attorneys: a small percentage of criminal defense attorneys who have lucrative practices that specialize in representation of the rich and famous.

Private Defense Counsel   The practice of criminal law is the least prestigious and least lucrative of all the types of legal practice.[56] Of approximately 820,000 licensed attorneys in 1994, only 30,000 to 40,000 practiced criminal law on a regular basis.[57] Most of these are either solo practitioners or operate in small two- or three-person firms in big cities, where the numbers of criminal arrests and prosecutions are high. The typical low status of the average criminal defendant parallels the relatively low status of the criminal attorney in the hierarchy of law.

Elite private defense attorneys such as Alan Dershowitz, F. Lee Bailey, Johnny Cochran, and Harvey Silvergate form the famous "dream teams" retained in celebrated "wedding cake" cases of the rich and famous. Counsel for defense in these cases spares no expense in advocating for their clients: pretrial motions are filed, one at a time to slow down the judicial process; large sums are spent on investigations, finding witnesses and preparing them, scientific jury selection, hiring specialized consultants, DNA analysis, and expert testimony. In these celebrity trials the amount of money spent on the defense can easily outweigh the state's budget to prosecute.

But few defense attorneys ever perform this full range of advocate functions. Typical private defense attorneys perform their job far from the spotlight and glamor of the celebrated trials.[58] Most practice criminal law by necessity rather than choice: usually, criminal cases are part of a larger general practice of civil law. Some attorneys pick up criminal cases by hanging around the courthouse and finding clients who are desperate and need a lawyer immediately. There is little prestige or glory in the gritty world of the criminal defense attorney, who spends a large amount of time in jails, prisons, and station houses meeting with defendants. The typical defense attorney's clients are not the rich and famous but society's misfits and unfortunates, who have hurt and damaged others as they may have been hurt and damaged themselves.

The private criminal attorney must also face the challenge of getting paid by clients who may refuse to pay once a case is over, especially if the case is lost. It is common practice for criminal attorneys to require an up-front retainer for at least part of the fee in advance. By necessity, quantity takes precedence over quality—criminal attorneys spend small amounts of time on many cases to eke out a living wage. Since court appearances often result in continuances or waiting for witnesses or defendants or police officers who do not appear, defense attorneys typically overbook their own schedules. The result is even more delays when the defense attorney fails to appear in the courtroom. Most of the members of the courtroom work group understand that when a defense attorney appears before a judge to ask for a continuance because the client has not yet appeared, the attorney is really saying that the client has not yet paid his fee.[59]

Indigent Defense   The vast majority of criminal defendants are poor and cannot afford even the modest fees of ordinary private counsel. In 1996, 80 percent of criminal defendants relied on public defenders or court-appointed attorneys whose legal fees are paid by the court or by the state.[60] There are three main systems for delivering indigent defense: assigned counsel, voluntary defender systems, and public defenders.

Assigned counsel systems are the oldest and most widely used ways of providing defense counsel for the poor. Judges appoint counsel from a list of volunteers or from a list of all available attorneys; attorneys are paid by the court on a fixed-fee basis. About 60 percent of the counties, mostly rural counties, in the United States use court-appointed private attorneys to represent the poor. Fees paid to assigned counsel are considerably lower than those of private defense attorneys, although they do have the advantage that they are guaranteed to be paid by the court. In New York City, for example, attorneys hired by the courts are paid $40 an hour for in-court work and $25 an hour for out-of-court work, fees much lower than the typical $100 to $200 an hour charged by private attorneys.[61]

Voluntary defender programs are staffed by full-time attorneys who work for legal aid offices that provide a wide array of legal services to the poor, including criminal defense services, although most concentrate primarily on civil and family issues. During the mid-1960s, federal funds supported legal services within poor communities as part of Lyndon Johnson's war on poverty. The Legal Services Corporation was established in 1974 and federal funding for legal aid services continued into the 1980s, when their budgets were slashed by the Reagan administration. A more recent method of delivering these services is the contract system, in which individual attorneys or law firms contract with the court to provide legal services to poor defendants for a specified dollar amount.

The major system of indigent defense is the **public defender office.** Public defender offices are funded by the county, state, or federal government; public defenders are government employees who earn a fixed salary and specialize in criminal defense.[62] When Gideon filed his case in 1961, only 3 percent of the nation's counties, serving only a quarter of the U.S. population, had public defender systems in place. Most counties and

indigent defense: state-funded systems for providing defense counsel for the poor.

assigned counsel systems: Appointment of private defense counsel by the trial judge compensated on a fixed fee basis by the court.

voluntary defender programs: full-time attorneys who work for legal aid officers funded by federal or state governments who provide a full range of civil and criminal legal aid for poor citizens.

public defender offices: full-time attorneys funded by state or federal governments who specialize in criminal defense for the poor.

states relied on private counsel who were appointed and compensated by the court. The Gideon decision came as a "wake-up call," galvanizing the states to provide legal counsel to low-income Americans, not only in criminal but also civil cases. Public defender systems are concentrated in urban centers with dense populations; in 1993, public defender systems represented 80 percent of all criminal defendants.[63]

Like the job of assistant state prosecutor, the job of public defender is typically a stepping stone in the legal career of a young graduate from law school. Most are paid quite low salaries and carry heavy caseloads. The people they represent are drug dealers, muggers, thieves, pimps, prostitutes, rapists, murderers, and swindlers. While some defendants are innocent of the charges, many more are guilty of harming other people. Public defenders must present an ethical defense regardless of the guilt or innocence of their clients. Although most realize that public defenders are performing an important social function, they are tainted by their association with those who are at the bottom of society's heap.

Furthermore, defendants often take a dim view of the quality of legal representation offered by public defenders.[64] A common streetwise quip is "Did you have a lawyer when you went to court? No, I had a public defender." There are good reasons for many criminal defendants to feel this way. Most meet their lawyers for the first time in the court hallway or jail lockup, for five or ten minutes. The public defender rifles through the stack of files and quickly gets to the point, stating what deal they think they can get if they plead guilty. For many defendants, it appears that the public defender is part of the system itself, working as an agent for the prosecution with a strong interest in closing the deal as quickly as possible. Many defendants do not realize the enormous burdens on the individual attorneys, nor may they realize the futility of taking their particular case to court.

Hayes's insistence that he was innocent angered the courtroom work group. In the business of processing hundreds of these cases, the situation of Paul Lewis Hayes was a **dead bang case,** in which the evidence against him was solid. Although we do not have a record of what took place in the pretrial conference between the attorneys, it is likely that the public defender agreed with the prosecution and urged Hayes to "cop a plea." A competent defense attorney would have advised Hayes that the risk of going to trial was too high given his prior record and the evidence against him in this case. Hayes's refusal to plead guilty was probably against the advice of counsel, who, as a member of the courtroom work group, was more apt to agree with the prosecutor than the defendant about how justice should happen.

THE PROCESS OF PLEA NEGOTIATION

The hidden secret of the U.S. justice system is that the adjudication process is rarely the celebrated adversarial trial. Plea negotiation or **plea bargaining** has operated in the U.S. court system for more than a hundred years.[65] It was not until the late 1960s that the practice came out into the open and launched a heated political debate in scholarly and judicial circles. In 1972, the National Advisory Commission on Criminal Justice Standards and Goals recommended that plea bargaining be abolished by 1978.[66] Alaska initiated a no-plea-bargaining policy to force the criminal justice system to conduct itself professionally without reliance on "deals" and "shortcuts."[67] During the same period, however, Supreme Court decisions ruled that plea bargaining was both Constitutional and necessary for an efficient system of justice.[68]

There are three major kinds of plea bargaining: implicit expectations of leniency in sentencing, or straight pleas; explicit sentence bargaining; and explicit charge bargaining. Bargains may also be made by exchanging a guilty plea for release on bail or for the benefit of dropping a charge in another jurisdiction for a different offense. The preferred system of bargaining and an implicit understanding of the **going rate** for guilty

dead bang case: case in which the evidence to convict is strong.

plea bargaining: the negotiation of an agreement among the prosecutor, judge, and the defense counsel as to the charge or sentence to be imposed if the defendant enters a guilty plea.

going rate: local informal norms concerning the typical sentence for a given crime within a particular court or jurisdiction.

pleas is determined largely by the local norms of the particular court or jurisdiction.[69] Although not all the details of the agreement are ever made explicit, most states now require the final agreement to be in writing and signed by all parties involved. By signing an agreement, in theory, defendants are acknowledging that they are voluntarily and knowingly entering into the agreement.

The first form of plea negotiations, known as the **straight plea,** is probably the most common and does not really involve overt bargaining at all. Because so many defendants are guilty and there is ample evidence to support a conviction against them, some kind of "reward" is implied to criminal defendants who do not contest their guilt and thereby make the justice process more efficient for everyone. Without any explicit offer or deal, a defendant pleads guilty with the informal or tacit understanding that his or her sentence will be far more lenient than if he or she were to be convicted at trial.

Fulfilling this expectation is entirely within the realm of judicial discretion—judges exercise the latitude they have in sentencing to "reward" the guilty defendant who enters a plea and saves the state the expense and time of criminal prosecution. Although the Supreme Court has ruled that judges who sentence defendants at trial too severely are engaging in judicial vindictiveness, empirical studies show that judges consistently dispense harsher sentences to people convicted through jury trials than to those who opt for a bench trial or those who negotiate plea agreements.[70] A recent national study confirmed that felons who are convicted at jury trial received an average sentence of twelve years, versus the five years for those who pleaded guilty.[71]

Explicit **sentence bargaining** involves more overt exchange agreements between the parties to arrive at an agreeable sentence. This is precisely what Prosecutor Bagly did in the first round of negotiations with Hayes: the statute had a range of two to ten years and he made an offer of five. Sentence bargaining may be initiated by the judge, the prosecution, or the defense, although all sides have to come to an agreement.

Charge bargaining is exclusively within the control of the prosecution. An initial charge may be reduced to a lower offense, or some of the counts on a multiple charge may be dropped. If one man beats up another on the street, the prosecutor may charge the first with anything from assault to attempted murder. **Vertical overcharging** refers to charging a single offense at the most serious level possible in order to maximize the advantage at the bargaining table. This is the strategy the district attorney adopted the second time he charged defendant Hayes; Bagby expected this serious charge to bring Hayes to the table.

Prosecutors also routinely overcharge by bringing the defendant up on as many charges as possible, a process known as **horizontal overcharging.** These "multiple count" indictments include the major offense as well as any additional crimes, often known as "lesser and included offenses" committed in association with the offense. This gives the prosecutor the option to drop some of the lesser charges, which will reduce the amount of punishment the defendant must face upon conviction.

With the rise of habitual offender laws and mandatory sentencing laws, charge bargaining gives prosecutors far more leverage than other players in the courtroom work group. Once convicted, the judge must sentence according to the statutory prescription for the charge chosen by the prosecutor. Under these types of sentencing laws, the charging decision is synonymous with the sentencing decision.

The Courtroom Work Group and Plea Bargaining

There are strong organizational pressures to forego the formal adversarial system in favor of this system of informal exchanges among the courtroom players who process case after case, day after day.[72] Members of the courtroom work group share a common and strong interest in seeing cases disposed of, efficiently and swiftly. Attorneys are often pressured to cooperate in order to preserve informal standing as a team player in the courtroom work group. Failure to cooperate often leads to retaliation and lack of cooperation from others in future cases.

straight pleas: defendant's formal entries of a guilty plea without explicit negotiation by the courthouse work group.

sentencing bargaining: plea negotiations that agree on the type of sentence to be imposed in exchange for a guilty plea on a given charge.

charge bargaining: plea negotiations that agree on the charges to be filed in exchange for a guilty plea by the defendant.

vertical overcharging: charging a single offense at the most serious level possible to maximize the state's advantage in plea negotiations.

horizontal overcharging: charging multiple count indictments to maximize the state's advantage in plea negotiations.

Just as police cannot arrest every person they find violating the law, prosecutors must be selective about which cases to prosecute. The sheer volume of cases leads prosecutors to seek to plea bargain rather than go to trial. Court calenders are full and trials may be set months or years in advance. Rather than engage in a lengthy process or simply dismiss a case, prosecutors prefer to strike a deal that gets them a speedy conviction and avoids both dismissal and acquittal. When a case is weak, prosecutors are also more willing to come to the table with a reduced charge or sentence. This is particularly true in the types of serious cases such as sexual assault or child abuse, which rely on the word of the victim and are hard to win at trial. Rather than lose the case at trial, prosecutors may reduce the charges to get some kind of conviction. The agreement enables them to at least get the person whom they may believe is guilty, on some charge, even if it is not the one they believe most accurately fits the offense.

Prosecutors are also operating under organizational and career pressures to demonstrate high conviction rates.[73] Successfully negotiated guilty pleas add to their tally of convictions, which boosts the efficiency of their office and their personal reputations as prosecutors. Plea bargaining can be a very efficient means to a high conviction record. Bringing weak cases to trial and losing is a black mark for a prosecutor and is discouraged by judges and their superiors in the district attorney's office.

Defense attorneys also have reasons to negotiate rather than go to trial. The goal of defense attorneys is to act in the best interests of their clients. The prevalence of plea bargaining means that the most valuable skill of the defense attorney is not necessarily about what happens in the courtroom, but what happens at the negotiating table. Experienced defense attorneys are trusted by the judges and prosecutors to make reasonable assessments about their clients' options, to advise their clients well, and to be shrewd, realistic, and efficient bargainers at the table. If a defense attorney insists on going to trial despite what the judge and prosecutors want, he or she is likely to lose the cooperation of these colleagues in future cases. For most private defense attorneys, fees are earned by the ability to strike quiet deals behind the scenes, rather than the ability to win the hearts of juries through showy speeches at contentious trials. Through plea negotiations, many more cases can be efficiently handled, and for the defense attorney this also means that many more fees can be collected.

Judges too want to see cases negotiated, and increasingly judges are taking a major role in the process. Judges may even order the prosecutor and defense counsel to meet and see if they can work out an agreement prior to trial. In the interest of efficient administration, the judge is trying to avoid the time and expense of a trial. The courtroom work group prefers a predictable and efficient outcome to the case.[74] What may happen when a case comes before a jury is relatively uncertain and unpredictable. The everyday workers in the courtroom have a shared interest in routinizing the administration of justice.

Inequality and Plea Bargaining

Gideon v. *Wainwright* was a triumph for the struggle for justice—a real accomplishment in bringing equal justice to the forefront. The theory of the U.S. justice system rests on the zealous advocacy of opposing sides playing under fair rules of evidence before a neutral judge and a jury of the defendant's peers. The process of plea bargaining contradicts that mythology, replacing it with a process that bears little resemblance to the formal process. Much of this reality may be hidden from the public by various kinds of impression management.

The process of plea bargaining, like all forms of exchange, depends on the amount of resources each side brings to the table. In such a process, those who have more resources get more, while those with less can expect to receive less. Not surprisingly, then, plea bargaining heightens the advantages that wealthy defendants with competent counsel have in the justice process, at the same time that it compounds the disadvantages of those represented by public counsel.

Plea bargaining, particularly for wealthy white-collar offenses, is routine but requires tremendous skill on the part of defense and the prosecution. In these cases, the private defense attorney advises the client through a complex series of negotiations calibrated to undermine the prosecution's case and serve the best interests of the client. White-collar criminals and others such as those involved in organized crime or drug trafficking operations often have information that can be exchanged in the plea negotiation process. In exchange for dropped or reduced charges, a defendant may agree to cooperate with the prosecution of a partner or accomplice.

Asset forfeiture laws also enhance the bargaining power of some criminal defendants and provide another incentive for the prosecution to engage in plea bargaining. Asset forfeiture laws allow the confiscation of cash and other property used in the commission of crime or purchased with criminal profits. The practice of seizing the assets of criminal suspects occurs principally in the prosecution of drug cases. Through a **contingent plea agreement,** prosecutors can stipulate that defendants forfeit or surrender specific financial assets before a deal can be struck. The possession of these assets is another bargaining tool for the defense attorney and another incentive to prosecutors to strike a favorable deal in exchange for the forfeiture of the property.

For a defendant like Paul Lewis Hayes, too poor to afford a private defense attorney, the negative impact of being socially disadvantaged begins early in the process. Poor defendants like Hayes can rarely even make bail. The prospect of going to jail for three to six months just to await trial is often enough to encourage a poor defendant to trade a guilty plea in exchange for a suspended sentence. The conviction goes on record as a guilty plea, but the immediate advantage of going home often is more attractive than the future costs of a conviction on their criminal record.

Defense attorneys also know that poor defendants who come to trial from county jail wearing a prison jumpsuit, in handcuffs and leg irons, are deeply disadvantaged when they appear in court compared to the wealthier client who can afford bail and appears neat and respectable in a suit and tie. Even though the poor defendant from the county jail has come to court to prove his innocence, the jury "sees" a convicted felon. Competent defense counsel will therefore try hard to persuade a poor defendant to accept a plea bargain rather than risk conviction at trial, which inevitably carries a harsher punishment.

IS PLEA BARGAINING JUST?

The central argument for the existence of plea bargaining has always been expediency: if every case were to go through the trial process, the justice system would grind to a halt. Many people, including Supreme Court justices, believe there is no point in banning plea bargaining because it will simply reemerge surreptitiously in the back rooms and hallways as it has done for over a century. It is better, therefore, that the practice be conducted out in the open and be monitored to ensure fairness. Fairly executed, the practice of plea bargaining will increase efficiency and therefore the overall effectiveness of the justice system. Plea bargaining should be encouraged, since it enhances the capacity of the court to administer justice to a large volume of cases.

On the other side of the debate, plea bargaining has been criticized for seriously undermining the "justice" of our system, by creating an administrative structure that only appears to go through the motions of due process.[75] Quite simply, plea negotiations undermine the rule of law by permitting authorities to cut special deals for certain defendants. Plea bargaining increases the advantages of wealthy criminal defendants and multiplies the disadvantages of the poor. It denies Constitutional rights to thousands of defendants who are pressured to waive their rights, and it corrupts our system of justice beyond recognition. It also leads to excessive leniency for some and inconsistent or unfair outcomes for others.

asset forfeiture laws: statutes that authorize the confiscation of cash, vehicles, property, and other assets used in the commission of crime or purchased with criminal profits.

contingent plea agreement: agreement that the defendant forfeit specific assets prior to the start of plea negotiations.

The challenge to the practice of plea bargaining often comes from citizens such as victims groups or advocates for minorities and the poor, who do not share the organizational interests and pressures of the courtroom work group and who perceive this form of delivering justice as inherently unfair to defendants, victims, and the wider community. From the perspective of "insiders" or the courtroom work group, however, plea bargaining is a necessary accommodation to the overwhelming demands placed on the justice system. From the perspective of "outsiders," the citizens who come into the system as defendants, victims, witnesses, and bystanders, the informal process raises many doubts about the quality of the day-to-day justice we routinely practice in our courtrooms.

KEY TERMS

courtroom work group p. 221
adversarial system p. 221
judges p. 223
bench trial p. 223
Missouri merit selection plan p. 224
prosecutor p. 225
interests of justice p. 226
selective prosecution p. 227
nolle prosequi p. 227

defense counsel p. 228
elite private defense
    attorneys p. 228
indigent defense p. 229
assigned counsel systems p. 229
voluntary defender programs p. 229
public defender office p. 229
"dead bang case" p. 230
plea bargaining p. 230

going rate p. 230
straight plea p. 231
sentencing bargaining p. 231
charge bargaining p. 231
vertical overcharging p. 231
horizontal overcharging p. 231
asset forfeiture laws p. 233
contingent plea agreement p. 233

REVIEW AND STUDY QUESTIONS

1. What is the courtroom work group? Who are the "insiders" to the courtroom process and who are the "outsiders"?
2. Describe the role of the judge. What are the main methods of judicial selection?
3. Explain the formal role of the prosecutor. Identify key areas of discretion for the public prosecutor. What is the "interest of justice," and how does this define the unique role of the prosecutor?
4. Why does Justice Jackson refer to prosecutors as the "most powerful player" in the criminal justice process?
5. Describe the role and responsibilities of the defense attorney. How does the role of the defense attorney differ from that of the prosecutor? Why does Alan Dershowitz refer to the criminal defense attorney as the "last bastion of freedom"?

6. Identify the different segments of the criminal defense bar. Explain the three main systems of indigent defense.
7. What is plea bargaining? Define a straight plea, sentencing bargaining, and charge bargaining. How is plea bargaining different from a formal trial? How does this process change the roles of the defense, the prosecution, and the judge?
8. Identify some of the organizational pressures on prosecutors to participate in plea bargaining. Identify organizational pressures on defense attorneys to participate in plea bargaining.
9. List the strengths of plea bargaining. What are the advantages of negotiations over the formal adversarial process?
10. Identify the shortcomings in the use of plea negotiations instead of formal trials.

CHECK IT OUT

On the Web

Lawyer Joke Emporium, **www.nolo.com/humor/jokes.cfm**
Lawyers are the one profession everyone loves to rag on: even lawyers love to make fun of lawyers. Check out this Web site for all the lawyer jokes you could ever want!

American Judicature Society, **www.ajs.org**
The premier organization for judicial independence and ethics. Click on "Judicial Selection Methods" to find out how judges are appointed and selected in your state. Read about codes of ethics for judges and other useful information.

Prosecutors Directory, **www.prosecutor.info**
Go to this Web site and click on your state to see Web sites for state and federal offices in your county and state. Find out about local programs, victims' assistance and witness programs, community prosecutions, and much more in your local district attorney's office.

National District Attorney's Association, **www.ndaa.org**
Check out this site to find useful information about salaries for district attorneys nationwide; see results from the latest Department of Justice survey on state prosecutors. Click on the link to the National Center for Community Prosecution to find out about innovative programs across the country.

Mean Justice, **www.edwardhumes.com/links.htm# wrongful**
This informative site presents links about the issue of prosecutorial misconduct and cases of wrongful conviction by Pulitzer prize-winning journalist Edward Humes.

On Film
An Ordinary Crime (60 minutes)
A PBS documentary that chronicles a case in which the truth is corrupted and an innocent man is convicted through the process of plea bargaining and the zealous pursuit of the adversarial process by all the courtroom players. Available from **www.pbs.org**.

NOTES

1. *Commonwealth of Kentucky* v. *Paul Lewis Hayes,* 73-C-29, April 19, 1973.
2. Ibid., p. 103, April 20, 1973.
3. German Gutierrez, M. D., Court-ordered Psychiatric Evaluation, Paul Lewis Hayes, Eastern State Hospital, February 6, 1973.
4. Indictment No. 73-C-26, Indictment for Uttering a Forged Instrument, KRS 434.130, February 14, 1973.
5. Ibid.
6. KRS 431.190-434.130, February 14, 1973.
7. Gutierrez, Psychiatric Evaluation, Paul Lewis Hayes, February, 6, 1973.
8. Indictment No. 73-C-29, Count 1: Indictment for Uttering a Forged Instrument, KRS 434.130; Count 2: Indictment for Habitual Criminal, KRS 431.190, January 29, 1973.
9. *Commonwealth of Kentucky* v. *Paul Lewis Hayes,* 73-C-29, April 19, 1973, p. 156.
10. *Commonwealth of Kentucky* v. *Paul Lewis Hayes,* Instructions to the Jury, James J. Park, Jr., Presiding Judge, Fayette Circuit Court, April 19, 1973.
11. *Paul Lewis Hayes* v. *Henry Cowan,* United States District Court, Eastern District of Kentucky, No. 75–61, October 9, 1975.
12. Albert W. Alschuler, "Plea Bargaining and Its History," *Columbia Law Review 79* (1979), pp. 1–43.
13. Howard Abidinsky, *Law and Justice: An Introduction to the American Legal System* (Chicago: Nelson Hall, 1995), p. 349.
14. *Brady* v. *United States,* 397 U.S. 742,1970.
15. Rule 11(c), *Federal Rules of Criminal Procedure,* requires judges to determine that defendants understand the nature of the charges, voluntarily agree to waive their right to a jury trial, and accept the terms of the plea negotiation.
16. *Hayes* v. *Cowan,* 547 F2d 42 (1976).
17. Ibid., n. 2.
18. Ibid.
19. *Bordenkircher* v. *Hayes,* 434 U.S. 357 (1978).
20. *North Carolina* v. *Pearce,* 395 U.S. 711,725 (1969).
21. *Blackledge* v. *Perry,* 417 U.S. 21, 25 (1974).
22. C. Peter Erlinder and David C. Thomas, "Criminal Law: Prohibiting Prosecutorial Vindictiveness while Protecting Prosecutorial Discretion," *Journal of Criminal Law and Criminology 76* (1985), p. 341.
23. Justice Stewart, Majority, *Bordenkircher* v. *Hayes,* 434 U.S. 357 (1978).
24. *Rummell* v. *Estelle,* 445 U.S. 263 100 St.Ct. (1980).
25. Jodi M. Brown and Patrick A. Langan, *State Court Sentencing of Convicted Felons, 1994* (Washington, DC: U.S. Department of Justice, 1998).
26. U.S. Department of Justice, Bureau of Justice Statistics, *The Prosecution of Felony Arrests* (Washington, DC: U.S. Government Printing Office, 1990).
27. Peter F. Nardulli, *The Courtroom Elite* (Cambridge, MA: Ballinger, 1978)
28. Arthur Rossett and Donald R. Cressay, *Justice by Consent: Plea Bargains in the American Courts* (Philadelphia: Lippincott, 1976); Roy B. Fleming, Peter F. Nardulli, and James Eisenstein, *The Craft of Justice* (Philadelphia: University of Pennsylvania Press, 1992).
29. Donald Newman, *Conviction: The Determination of Guilt or Innocence without Trial* (Boston: Little, Brown, 1966).
30. Abraham S. Blumberg, "The Practice of Law as a Confidence Game: Organizational Cooptation of a Profession," *Law and Society Review 1* (1967), pp. 15–39.
31. Abidinsky, *Law and Justice,* pp. 89–104.
32. Lawrence M. Friedman, *A History of American Law* (New York: Simon & Schuster, 1973).
33. Jocelyn M. Pollock and Barbara Ramirez, "Women in the Legal Profession," in Alida V. Merlo and Joycelyn M. Pollock, eds., *Women, Law and Social Control* (Boston: Allyn & Bacon, 1995), p. 83.
34. *Bradwell* v. *Illinois,* 83 U.S. 130,140 (1873).
35. Pollock and Ramirez, "Women in the Legal Profession," p. 80.
36. U.S. Bureau of the Census, *Statistical Abstract of the United States, 2000* (Washington, DC: U.S. Government Printing Office, 2000), p. 179.
37. Pollock and Ramirez, "Women in the Legal Profession," p. 91.
38. Ibid.
39. U.S. Bureau of the Census, *Statistical Abstract of the United States, 1998* (Washington, DC: U.S. Government Printing Office, 1998).

40. B. L. Graham, "Judicial Recruitment and Racial Diversity on State Courts," in G. Larry Mays and Peter R. Gregware, eds., *Courts and Justice* (Prospect Heights, IL: Waveland Press, 1995), p. 219.

41. Stephen R. Bing and S. Stephen Rosenfeld, "The Quality of Justice in the Lower Criminal Courts in Metropolitan Boston," in John Robertson, ed., *Rough Justice: Perspectives on Lower Criminal Courts* (Boston: Little, Brown, 1974), pp. 259–285.

42. John A. Jenkins, "The Lobster Shift: One Night in the Nation's Busiest Court," *American Bar Association Journal 72* (1986), p. 56.

43. Maureen Mileski, "Courtroom Encounters: An Observation of a Lower Criminal Court," *Law And Society Review 5* (1971), pp. 473–533.

44. Henry R. Glick, *Courts, Politics and Justice* (New York: McGraw-Hill, 1993), pp. 112–155.

45. Ibid., p. 117.

46. Carol J. DeFrancis and Greg W. Steadman, "Prosecutors in State Courts, 1996," *BJS Bulletin,* (Washington, DC: National Institute of Justice, 1998).

47. Bureau of Justice Statistics, "Prosecutors in State Court, 1992," *BJS Bulletin* (Washington, DC: National Institute of Justice, 1993), pp. 1–8.

48. *American Bar Association General Standards* (Chicago: American Bar Association, 1999).

49. Kenneth Culp Davis, *Discretionary Justice* (Baton Rouge: Louisiana State University Press, 1969), p. 190.

50. William. F. McDonald, "The Prosecutor's Domain," in W. F. McDonald, ed., *The Prosecutor* (Beverly Hills, CA: Sage, 1979), pp. 15–59.

51. Abidinsky, Law and Justice, p. 209.

52. Kathleen B. Brosi, *A Cross-City Comparison of Felony Case Processing* (Washington, DC: U.S. Government Printing Office, 1979).

53. Susan Estrich, *Real Rape* (Cambridge, MA: Harvard University Press, 1987).

54. Alan Dershowitz, *The Best Defense,* (New York: Random House, 1982).

55. *Miranda* v. *Arizona,* 384 U.S. 436 (1966).

56. Glick, *Courts, Politics, and Justice,* p. 212.

57. American Bar Foundation, *Lawyer Statistic Report: The U.S. Legal Profession in the 1990s* (Chicago: American Bar Association, 1994).

58. Paul B. Wice, *Criminal Lawyers: An Endangered Species* (Beverly Hills, CA: Sage, 1978).

59. Ibid., p. 111.

60. Bureau of Justice Statistics, "Indigent Defense," *BJS Selected Findings* (Washington, DC: National Institute of Justice, 1996), pp. 1–4.

61. Ronald Smothers, "Court-Appointed Defense Offers the Poor a Lawyer, but the Cost May Be High." *The New York Times,* February 14, 1994, p. A9.

62. Lisa McIntyre, *The Public Defender: The Practice of Law in the Shadows of Repute* (Chicago: University of Chicago Press, 1987).

63. Andy Court, "Is There a Crisis?" *The American Lawyer,* January/February 1993, p. 46.

64. Jonathan Casper, *Criminal Courts: The Defendants Perspective* (Washington, DC: U.S. Government Printing Office, 1978).

65. Joseph Sanborn, "A Historical Sketch of Plea Bargaining," *Justice Quarterly 3* (1986), pp. 111–138; Lawrence Friedman, "Plea Bargaining in Historical Perspective," *Law and Society Review 7* (1979), pp. 247–259.

66. National Advisory Commission on Criminal Justice Standards and Goals, *Courts, Standard 3.1* (Washington, DC: U.S. Government Printing Office, 1973), p. 46.

67. Michael Rubinstein, Stevens H. Clarke, and Teresa J. White, *Alaska Bans Plea Bargaining* (Washington, DC: U.S. Government Printing Office, 1980).

68. *Santobello* v. *New York,* 92 S.Ct. 495, 273n, 354 (1971).

69. Milton Heumann, "Thinking about Plea Bargaining," in Peter F. Nardulli, ed., *The Study of the Criminal Courts* (Cambridge, MA: Ballinger, 1979), pp. 208–210.

70. Thomas Uhlman and N. Darlene Walker, "He Takes Some of My Time and I Take Some of His," *Law and Society Review 14* (1980), pp. 323–341.

71. Brown and Lanagan, *State Court Sentencing of Convicted Felons, 1994.*

72. Peter F. Nardulli, James Eisenstein, & Roy B. Flemming, *The Tenor of Justice: Criminal Courts and the Guilty Plea* (Urbana IL: University of Illinois Press, 1988); Herbert S. Miller, William F. McDonald, and James A. Cramer, *Plea Bargaining in the United States* (Washington, DC: National Institute of Law Enforcement and Criminal Justice, 1978).

73. Henry N. Pontell, *A Capacity to Punish* (Bloomington, IN: Indiana University Press, 1984).

74. Malcolm Feeley, *The Process Is the Punishment: Handling Cases in a Lower Court* (New York: Russell Sage Foundation, 1979).

75. George P. Fletcher, *With Justice for Some: Victims' Rights in Criminal Trials* (Reading, MA: Addison-Wesley, 1995).

C A S E   12

Judging Justice:
The Case of Reginald Denny

THE INTERSECTION OF TOTAL MADNESS

The night of April 29, 1992, is infamous as the start of one of the deadliest urban riots in U.S. history. Although the verdicts in the Rodney King trial (see Chapter 8) had been announced earlier that day, most of the residents of Los Angeles were unaware of the rising tide of destruction erupting among the crowds of young black men amassing on the city streets. Reginald Oliver Denny, 36, was certainly not thinking about the verdicts as he loaded his eighteen-wheel rig with 27 tons of sand and headed across the city toward the intersection of Florence and Normandie at 5:39 in the evening. Rarely listening to the news, Denny expected nothing out of the ordinary as he took his usual shortcut across Florence Avenue toward the plant in Inglewood. As always, he had his radio tuned to country music.[1]

As he drove into the intersection at Florence and Normandie, the scene was "total madness." People were everywhere, cars were going the wrong way, and the sound of breaking glass filled the air. Ahead of him, Denny could see a white medical supply truck blocking the intersection. He could see that the truck ahead was being looted, but he figured there was little in his rig full of sand of interest to looters. It never occurred to him that he was in any danger; he just wanted to get through the intersection and be on his way. While Denny concentrated on maneuvering his massive eighteen-wheeler through the crowd, he didn't see the white driver of the truck ahead, Larry Tarvin, being dragged out of his cab by a crowd of young men who were beating him to the cheers from the crowd proclaiming, "No pity for the white man."[2]

Later Denny testified that he could hear people shouting at him to stop, but before he could under-stand what they were saying or why, a volley of rocks came through his window and a hand reached in to pull him into the street.[3] The hand was that of Antoine Miller (19), helped by Henry Watson, who held Denny down on the ground with a foot planted on his neck while another man kicked him in the belly and yet another, Damien Williams, picked up a huge slab of loose concrete and smashed it on Denny's head, knocking him unconscious. Mercifully, Denny would never remember anything beyond the moment he saw rocks coming through his windshield.

As Denny lay in a pool of blood, Williams danced a victory jig over his body, imitating a football receiver who had just caught a touchdown pass.[4] Williams flashed some gang signs, pointed to the body, and waved at the television helicopter hovering overhead transmitting the scene live to millions of stunned citizens of Los Angeles County. Like the King beating, the horrifying brutality would be broadcast on the evening news and within hours flashed around the world. Damien walked away from Denny's limp body, leaving him on the street for others to come and rifle through his pockets while still others threw stones and bottles at the lifeless body.

Denny's life was saved by four African Americans who were watching TV in the safety of their own living room.[5] How could this be happening, they asked each other? Why wasn't anyone doing anything? Where were the ambulances? Where were the police? Rather than sit there and passively witness the death of a fellow human being, these four friends got into their car and drove to the intersection fifteen minutes away. When they arrived they lifted Denny back into his truck and drove him three miles to the nearest hospital. Suffering massive head injuries, Denny began having convulsions. Close to death, emergency room specialists and trauma specialists began to operate with only minutes to spare.

Reginald Denny nearly died that night. His skull was fractured in ninety-one places. He suffered neurological damage and became permanently susceptible to seizures. A visible crater remained on the right side of his head.[6] Another victim at that intersection, a Latino man, Fidel Lopez, was also pulled from a car and beaten senseless by Damien Williams, who stripped the unconscious man and spray-painted his torso and genitals with black spray paint, gleefully proclaiming him "black."[7] Lopez's life was saved by an ex-con, Bennie Newton, who threw his own body over Lopez, challenging the crowd to kill him first if they wanted to kill Lopez. The mob backed off and Newton drove Lopez to the hospital.

THE ARREST AND INDICTMENT

Fifty-four people lost their lives in the four-day riot, and many more were victims of vicious assaults. The victims were mostly Asian, Latino, or white; the perpetrators, mostly young African American men. Like the King beating, some of these scenes of violence were broadcast for the world to see. With the help of the videotapes, the Los Angeles Police Department (LAPD) had little trouble finding the men responsible for assaulting Denny at that first terrible scene of violence. On May 12, a squad of LAPD officers and FBI agents led by LAPD Chief Daryl Gates burst into the apartments of Damien Williams, Henry Watson, and Antoine Miller in the predawn hours to arrest them for the assault of Reginald Denny and others at the intersection.[8]

On May 13, at a press conference, District Attorney Ira Reiner announced the filing of state charges against Williams, Watson, and Miller. Damien Williams and Henry Keith Watson were charged with attempting to murder Denny. By May 28, additional charges had been brought against the defendants, involving six separate victims at the intersection that night. Williams was also charged with aggravated mayhem—intentionally causing permanent disability or disfigurement of Reginald Denny.[9]

"JUST US" JUSTICE?

The riots were sparked by the widespread belief that the LAPD treated black citizens unfairly and targeted African Americans for its harshest punishments. For many in the black community, the trial of the four black men charged with assaulting white citizens was going to be another instance of "just us" justice: aggressive and selective prosecution of black violence against whites (Damien Williams against Reginald Denny), while white violence against blacks (the LAPD officers against Rodney King) was seen as both legal and justified.

Almost immediately a defense committee was formed to raise funds for legal fees. The fact that Williams and his co-defendants were being held on bail of more than half a million dollars while the four police officers had been immediately released on bail of merely $5,000 fed the perception that this trial would be yet another travesty of justice for the black community. While the four white officers remained in the community awaiting trial, Williams and Watson each spent eighteen months in jail awaiting trial.[10] Many in the black community felt that the district attorney's office was grossly overcharging the defendants on the charges of torture and attempted murder. When the prosecution requested removing the judge assigned to the trial, who happened to be the only African American judge in the Superior Criminal Trial Division, there was a widespread feeling that if the outcome of this trial led to convictions of the defendants on the serious charges brought against them, there would be yet another outbreak of rage and violence, which, this time, would "burn the city down."[11]

FINDING OBJECTIVE JURORS?

The process of impaneling a jury is the real beginning of the trial process. From the pool of prospective jurors, the attorneys must agree on twelve individuals and six alternate jurors who will hear the evidence and decide the verdict of the trial. Who those eighteen people are is the most important element in the entire process. The purpose of the *voir dire* is to eliminate those potential jurors who come to the trial already prejudiced or who are unfit to serve for reasons of incompetence. Attorneys may petition the judge to remove a juror "for cause," such as a stated opinion of bias or previous experience as a victim of a similar crime. Additionally, each attorney is permitted a set number of "peremptory challenges," which allow striking potential jurors for reasons that need not be explained or justified to the court.

In highly publicized trials, jury selection presents a particularly difficult challenge. In theory, jurors are supposed to enter into the trial without prior opinions and prejudices about the case. But when the crime itself has been captured on videotape, as was the case in both the King beating and the Denny beating, and analyzed and dissected over and over again in the media, it is nearly impossible to find jurors who are free of preconceived opinions.

In the Denny trial, the process of jury selection was also complicated by the sequence of events prior to the trial. The verdict in the trial of the LAPD officers, the riots themselves, and the ongoing federal trials of the officers shaped citizens' beliefs about the justice and injustice of this case even before they walked into the courtroom. The Denny trial began the day after the sentences were announced in the federal trial of the four police officers in the King case. The conviction of Koon and Powell was celebrated by the black community, but neither side was satisfied by the sentence handed down by federal Judge Davis. To blacks, thirty months was a slap in the face; to the officers of the LAPD and their supporters, any jail time was outrageous for police officers who were just trying to do their job.

Potential jurors in the Denny trial were aware of the intense and conflicted feelings in the community about the upcoming Denny trial and were acutely aware that the verdict in this trial could be the spark of yet another siege of unrestrained violence. Both the federal trial of the white police officers and the state trial of the black defendants were held in the Criminal Court building in downtown Los Angeles. Jurors in all three trials at some point expressed fear for their own safety and the safety of their families.

THE JURY POOL

The prosecuting attorneys in the first King trial and the Denny trial faced the same obstacle: most of the jurors in the jury pool were predisposed with attitudes favorable to the defense. Attitudes among the Simi Valley jury were pro-police, while prospective jurors in the Denny trial held predominantly negative attitudes toward the police.[12] In the cities and neighborhoods of Simi Valley, people's life experi-

ences gave them a positive view of law enforcement. In South Central LA, people's life experience often included rude, disrespectful, violent, or unfair treatment by police at some point in their lives. In the King trial, most potential jurors thought the police were ethical and trying to do a fair and good job regardless of the race of the citizens; in the Denny trial most potential jurors believed that the criminal justice system was stacked in favor of the police and against blacks.

Thus, like the Simi Valley trial, the venue of the Denny trial gave an enormous advantage to the attorneys hired to defend the four young men. In the Simi Valley trial, the change of venue effectively eliminated the possibility of impaneling black jurors. There simply were not enough blacks in the jury pool drawn from predominantly white Ventura County. In the King trial, the jury pool of 260 people contained only six African Americans, and five of these wanted nothing to do with this explosive trial.

In the Denny trial, the jury pool was drawn from precisely those neighborhoods that had been hit hard by the riots.[13] Jury summonses were mailed to 1,200 people; only 153 showed up to serve, and many of these were reluctant to serve on this particular jury. Jurors may ask to be excused from duty by claiming hardships of various kinds. It is up to the judge to accept the reason as legitimate. In this trial, the judge excused all who asked, even when the hardship was a vague sense that they were "sick and tired of crime" and couldn't be objective in this case. Just as blacks were reluctant to serve on the Simi Valley trial, whites tried to avoid serving on this jury at all costs.

THE ART AND SCIENCE OF JURY SELECTION

The significance of jury selection is never underestimated by the attorneys, who give this process as much care and attention as they give to preparation of the evidence and arguments during the trial. These will be the people who will hear the argument and either find it persuasive or reject it. Ultimately, the truth will be what this particular jury believes. Both sides, if they can afford it, use the services of professional jury consultants, who offer guidance in the science and art of jury selection.

Jo-Ellan Demetris, the jury consultant who was retained to aid the defense of the four police officers, was also hired by Edie Faal, the defense attorney for the four defendants in the Denny trial.[14] The process of jury selection begins with an elaborate questionnaire designed by the attorneys with the aid of the consultant. These questionnaires explore the background, religious views, past experiences with crime and the justice system, hobbies, attitudes toward politics, police, and crime, views on the case, and any other topic the attorneys believe will help them select a juror.

Consultants use the "science" of research, which shows that men are more likely to vote one way than women; married people make different decisions than unmarried people; people who drive Ford pickup trucks and join bowling leagues react differently from those who drive Volvos and belong to country clubs. If the jury consultant tells an attorney that a person's opinion on chewing gum is relevant to predicting how he might assess evidence in the case, a question about chewing gum might appear on the questionnaire. They also use the "art" of intuition and human experience, offering their insights into the human character to the attorneys. The goal is to predict the reactions and responses of different kinds of people to the evidence and arguments that will be presented in the trial.

The attorneys also try to predict how the jurors will interact with each other in the deliberation process. Who will emerge as a leader with the ability to shape the views of others? Who among the jurors has the strength of character or independence of mind to be a lone "holdout," refusing to go along with the predominant opinion? Given the requirement of a unanimous verdict, a single determined juror can derail the entire process and lead to a mistrial. All the defense attorney needs is one juror who will stubbornly stick to his or her decision and the case can be won.

The questionnaires are pored over and analyzed by the attorneys and their consultants before the voir dire officially begins. Voir dire means literally "to see and to speak." With the questionnaires in mind and their own rankings, the attorneys then question each juror individually before the judge to plumb his or her attitudes and personalities. On the basis of the questionnaires and the voir dire, the attorneys rank the jurors in terms of whom they believe are most attractive and whom they most want to keep off the jury. In a complex game of strategy, each side must reserve their precious peremptory challenges to eliminate those jurors who are potentially most damaging. The other side, of course, is likely to try and seat those very same jurors.

No one needed a jury consultant in this case to explain that the race of the potential jurors mattered. Most prosecutors who have tried cases involving police brutality are aware that black jurors are more skeptical of police as witnesses in the courtroom. For African Americans, there is a strong presumption that police are willing to perjure themselves in a court of law in order to get a conviction or protect their fellow officers. This negative view of po-

lice honesty, by contrast, is rare among whites, who are far more likely to give the benefit of the doubt to the law enforcement officer on the stand. In the Simi Valley trial, the attorneys for the defense wanted to seat white jurors with positive attitudes and experiences with law enforcement, while attorneys for the prosecution were seeking jurors who were black or members of other minorities and therefore more open to the idea that police were capable of excessive force against citizens.

Although legally, attorneys are not permitted to use their peremptory challenges to remove jurors for reasons of race or gender, the practice is common. The lone potential black juror in the Simi Valley trial was removed by a peremptory challenge from Stone, defense attorney for Lawrence Powell. In the Denny trial, the preferences were reversed: the prosecution sought black jurors while the defense wanted to seat white jurors.

PERSUADING THE JURY DURING THE VOIR DIRE

During the voir dire process, attorneys have already begun to make their case to the jury, attempting to frame the arguments, hinting at the evidence that will come later, testing the waters to see their reactions. In both the Simi Valley trial and the Denny trial, the videotapes played a crucial role in jury selection process. Potential jurors in both trials had, of course, seen the images of the four officers beating Rodney King and of Williams and others beating Reginald Denny. Most had seen it played many times over.

In both trials, the fact that everyone had already seen the videotape allowed defense attorneys to screen out people who were convinced by the prosecution's central piece of evidence. During the voir dire, the defense was able to ask questions such as, "What did you think when you saw the tape?" "Are you able to believe there is another explanation for what you saw?" With these questions, the defense was already raising doubt about the tape and able to find jurors who doubted the tape told the whole story or who said they wanted to know what "really happened." The prosecution, on the other hand, tried to seat people who were horrified and shocked by what they saw. The "mock trial" before the real trial thus removed people who were most affected by the prosecution's evidence and included only people who were highly skeptical about its depicting the real "truth" of the matter.

After a solid month of voir dire, the jury in the Simi Valley trial included four members of the National Rifle Association, three jurors who had served in the military, two who were currently involved in police-related work, and two who had immediate family members who were police officers. The jury was entirely white except for one Asian American juror. The jury in the Denny trial consisted of five whites, three Latinos, three African Americans, and one Asian American. Nine of the twelve jurors were women. Six alternates were also chosen to serve in the event that one of the twelve was unable to continue to serve through the entire trial. Ultimately, the jury that participated in the deliberations consisted of four African Americans, four Latinos, two Asian Americans, and two whites. Except for one black and one Latino, all were women.

THE TRIAL OF WILLIAMS, WATSON, AND MILLER

The prosecution presented its case first by asking the jury to believe its own eyes. Like the King trial, the videotape was the center of the prosecution's case against the four young men. The tape shows the defendants engaged in the alleged acts and provided a literal demonstration of the crime itself. According to the prosecution, what was depicted on the videotape was an act of brutal violence against defenseless victims, plain and simple. Yet what we "see" is always open to interpretation. What jurors brought to the viewing of the tape in terms of their life experiences and assumptions proved to be more important than what was actually shown on the tape itself.

In addition to the videotape, the prosecution showed color slides of the injuries suffered by Denny and other victims at the intersection. Aware of the racial sensitivity of the case, the prosecution was careful to praise the actions of African American citizens who ultimately put their own lives on the line to rescue Denny and Lopez. These were the "good and decent citizens" of South Central LA, while the Watsons, Williamses, and Millers were thugs who preyed on innocent and helpless people. The prosecution continued to present its case by calling eyewitnesses who testified as to the brutality, racism, and intentional viciousness of the defendants against those who were targeted for no reason other than the color of their skin. They showed the callousness of Williams when he did a dance over the body of Denny, and his hate-inspired cruelty when he spray-painted the body of the unconscious Lopez, yelling, "Now he is black too!"

One of the challenges for the prosecution was the need to establish a specific intent to kill, required to support the charge of attempted murder. Intent is often difficult to prove in a court, but the videotape showed Williams smashing the hunk of concrete directly into Denny's skull. Under many circumstances, juries are satisfied that perpetrators know that such violence will probably cause lethal harm and therefore believe they had intent to inflict that harm.

The defense strategy countered the prosecution's arguments about the intent to commit murder. Edie Faal argued that if Damien Williams intended to kill Reginald Denny he surely would have done so, since there was nothing to stop him from doing so. The defense argued that there were no such thought process in the minds of Williams, Watson, or Miller. Williams simply moved on to the next act of random violence. The young men, according to their defense attorney, were caught up in a rage of contagion, a kind of mob mentality. The violence was thoughtless and random, not intentional or deliberate. None of the men had a criminal history of prior assaultive behavior. Character witnesses, especially for Henry Watson, testified that such behavior was abnormal for their personalities and that they were caught up in the angry passions of an extraordinary event.

In the Denny trial, the defense also called expert witnesses about the psychology of mob violence and group contagion to support this theory, while the prosecution countered with experts who denounced such theories. The crucial issue turned on which expert the jury found most persuasive. As one juror later remarked to the New York Times, "They seemed just like anyone, just like you and I. I see them just as two human beings. They just got caught up in the riot. I guess maybe they were in the wrong place at the wrong time."[15]

Just as the defense attorneys had done in the Simi Valley trial, Faal artfully tapped into the racial tensions and attitudes jurors brought with them into the courtroom based on their life experiences. Michael Stone, the defense attorney for Lawrence Powell, had raised the specter of the "thin blue line," which resonates with suburban white fear of the violence of inner-city blacks. He tapped into those unspoken sentiments when he talked about the "difficult job" that officers must do so that the rest of "us" are free to raise our families in safety and security. That closing statement was full of coded references in which the "us" were white middle-class families living in the homogenous suburbs of Simi Valley and the "them" were the dangerous blacks of South Central LA.

In the Denny trial, Edie Faal similarly tapped into the reservoir of racial beliefs and biases of jurors who believed the system was systematically biased against African Americans. Here was a white judge and a white prosecutor trying black defendants who had been arrested in a SWAT-style raid by Daryl Gates himself, the emblem of white police power over the black community. Faal deliberately used courtroom tactics that gave jurors the sense this was still a white criminal justice system gearing up to lynch black criminals who dared to harm whites even while it managed to find all kinds of legal reasoning to excuse white violence against blacks. During the trial, Faal and other defense attorneys raised objection after objection, knowing that many of them would be overruled by the judge. The tactic was not to win the legal point with the judge but to score a different kind of victory with the jury, who saw a white judge overruling black attorneys time and time again.[16]

Every trial attorney knows that the truth is what the jury feels and believes. The process of persuasion begins with the first encounter between potential jurors and the opposing attorneys. The battle is for the hearts and minds of the jury: every tactic is fair game. As part of the defense, Faal challenged the identity of the defendants even though they were ultimately positively identified by a series of witnesses as well as by the videotape. The purpose of this strategy was not to claim that this was a case of mistaken identification, because clearly it was not. The purpose was to humanize the young men for the jury. Rather than the monsters on the videotape, the jury saw two young men, they saw them smile as they stood for the jury, sheepishly show birthmarks or tatoos, and generally behave as human beings rather than the vicious angry men depicted on the videotape.

The most dramatic moment of the trial came after Reginald Denny, the victim, finished testifying. As he returned to his seat he embraced Georgiana Williams, mother of Damien Williams, and remained sitting with her and Henry Watson's mother for the remainder of the trial. Denny held no anger toward the men who had beaten him. He did not believe they intended to do him harm but had just been caught up in the violence of the mob.

THE DELIBERATIONS

Once each side rested its case, the judges offered legal instructions to the jury. These instructions explained the relevant law and offered the jury crucial guidance in their deliberation. In this case, and in the federal trial, the jurors faced the unspoken pressure that the verdict might lead to another social catastrophe. The whole world was watching and waiting to see if violence would erupt when the verdict was announced.

The judge's instructions tried to limit the influence of these external events on the jury. The jury was told by Judge Ouderkirk, "You must not be influenced by public opinion or public feeling. Apply the law regardless of the consequences." The judge repeated those instructions at several points during the deliberation process, especially when one of the Asian American jurors told the judge that she feared for her life and her family's safety. The judge assembled the jury and urged them to "make the right decision for the right reasons and have the courage to do that so when you look back on what you've done you will feel good about it."[17]

The first task for any jury is to elect a foreperson, whose job it is to manage the deliberations and to communicate questions or concerns to the judge. The job of the foreperson is to help the jury come to consensus. The jury consultant who assisted the prosecution in both the Simi Valley trial and the Denny trial predicted accurately who would be chosen to serve in this position. Both times the consultant identified strong women with clear opinions who were likely to emerge as leaders; both times, the consultant was right in predicting who had the personality for the job. In the Denny trial, the forewoman chosen by her fellow jurors was a 28-year-old legal secretary and single mother.

During deliberations, five of the original jury were replaced by alternates as the judge struggled to avoid a mistrial. Two were dismissed for health reasons, one for talking about the case to others,[18] a white man was dismissed for personal reasons, and a black woman because she was in intense personal conflict with the others, preventing deliberations from taking place.[19] The jury had to restart its deliberation three times as jurors were removed and alternates joined the jury. The final jury deliberated for two-and-a-half days before returning the final verdict.

Tensions often run high during jury deliberations, but in high-profile trials such as this one, the pressure on the jurors can lead to emotional stress and conflict. One juror erupted during deliberations, running down the hotel hallway screaming, "I can't take it anymore!"[20] Other jurors complained that she was willing to create a hung jury just to be able to go home. Jurors also insisted that one juror be removed whom they believed was mentally incompetent, while that juror insisted that she was being removed because she disagreed with the majority.

In their verdict, the jury agreed with the defense that the three men had been caught up in the mob violence of the riots, acting without premeditation in committing the violence seen on the tapes. They did not believe the prosecution had produced evidence of specific intent to harm, disfigure, or murder the victims. If Williams and Watson had wanted to kill Denny, they surely would have hit him more than once. All of the jurors resented the charge of robbery against Watson and Williams, since there was no factual evidence that they had tried to take anything from the victims. A fourth person, Gary Williams, was shown on the tape picking Denny's pocket but not beating him. He pleaded guilty to charges of grand theft and assault and was serving a three-year sentence.

The jurors did believe that the men were guilty of assault with a deadly weapon, known as a lesser and included offense in California, but the defense had the option of permitting no lesser verdict on the attempted murder charge. The jury was forced into an all-or-nothing choice on the attempted murder charge and chose to acquit rather than convict.

In the final hours of deliberation, all of the jurors except one agreed with Faal that the prosecutors had overcharged Williams and Watson with the attempted murder charge. The lone dissenting juror, the female Asian American juror who had complained to the judge that she was in fear of her life, held out for two days before finally changing her vote to acquit Williams on the attempted murder charge.[21]

Williams was acquitted of attempted murder, aggravated mayhem, and causing great bodily injury to Denny. He was convicted of simple mayhem, a felony offense, and misdemeanor assault against Lopez and other victims. Watson was found not guilty on the charges of attempted murder, aggravated mayhem, assault with a deadly weapon, and robbery, and was found guilty of one count of assaulting Denny. When the verdicts were announced, the judge reduced the bail on the third defendant, Antoine Miller, facing the least charges, and urged the attorneys to negotiate a plea bargain.

PEACE OR JUSTICE?

District Attorney Gil Garcetti denounced the verdicts, claiming that the jurors had opted for peace at the expense of justice. In the end, the prosecution admitted that what they were really up against was the community perception that the justice system is not fair to African Americans. The trial began a day after the sentence for Powell and Koon was handed down, a sentence the black community deeply believed was too lenient for their crime. According to Gil Garcetti, "The jury has returned a verdict of peace, not necessarily a verdict of justice."[22]

In the black community, the jury verdict was seen as just. According to Edie Faal, no one deserved to be beaten like Reginald Denny, nor did Rodney King deserve his treatment at the hands of the police. Both perpetrators deserve to be punished under the law for their actions. "But when the system comes in to administer justice, it should do so in an evenhanded manner. The difference in the way the system is treating the two sets of defendants is what's causing this uproar in the community."[23] Williams, Watson, and Miller should not be scapegoated as a symbol of the system's ability to restore law and order. They were duly punished for the crimes they committed.

Victim Reginald Denny embraced his perpetrators at the trial and afterward. He did not feel anger toward them, believing that they were confused in being violent toward him. When the verdicts were announced, Denny declared that he was satisfied and simply said to reporters, "Let's get on with life."[24] Fidel Lopez, another victim of the violence that took place at the intersection of Normandie and Florence, also had no anger at his attackers and expressed satisfaction at the verdicts. According to his 19-year-old daughter Melissa, if the verdict was unfair to her father, it is also a reminder that "this verdict is the kind of injustice black people always get."[25] Melissa and her father blamed the police who failed to protect them from the disorder and do their job on the streets of Los Angeles.[26] According to prosecutor Janet Moore, however, the remaining victims of the violence that night were not satisfied that justice had been done.

SENTENCING WILLIAMS: JUSTICE OR "JUST US"?

On December 7, 1993, Judge Ouderkirk sentenced Damien Williams to the maximum ten-year sentence, announcing "It's intolerable in this society to attack and maim people because of their race."[27] The judge played the videotape in the courtroom as a reminder of the violence of the act and to justify his sentence. Williams would receive credit for the two-and-a-half years he had already served while awaiting trial and would be eligible for parole in four years. Henry Watson was sentenced to probation and 320 hours of community service. Watson too had already served two-and-a-half years while awaiting trial.

To some black leaders in the community, the judge's decision was another example of injustice. When the sentence was announced a man in the courtroom yelled, "What about the Rodney King verdicts?" Koon and Powell had been sentenced to two-and-a-half years in jail, substantially below the federal guidelines for the crimes of which they were convicted. The judge justified his sentence for the officers by pointing out that the men had already suffered the loss of their careers, reputations, and financial security. He also remarked that "Putting a cop in prison for three years is different than putting anyone else in prison."[28] Yet, in the case of sentencing a young black male, Judge Ouderkirk elected to apply the maximum penalty. To many in the black community, this disparity between the two sentences seemed evidence of a continuing racial double standard in the administration of justice.

For the majority of citizens, both black and white, the overwhelming sentiment in the wake of the verdicts and sentences was relief. Community safety and community peace were seen as more important than the right verdict, and it was recognized that there was little agreement in the community as to what that right verdict would have been. Given all the complexity of issues in this case, most agreed that peace was desirable even at the expense of justice.

Case adapted from Lou Cannon, *Official Negligence: How Rodney King and the Riots Changed Los Angeles and the LAPD* (Boulder, Colorado: Westview Press, 1999); John Riley, "Beating Victim Denny 'Relieved'; Trucker Wants Healing for L.A.," *Newsday*, October 19, 1993; Edward J. Boyes and Ashley Dunn, "Williams, Watson Mean to Kill Denny, Prosecutor Says," *Los Angeles Times*, September 29, 1993; Jim Newton and Henry Weinstein, "Three Suspects Seized in Beating of Truck Driver during Riot," *Los Angeles Times*, May 13, 1992; John Riley, "Unease as Trial Progresses in Los Angeles," *Newsday*, September 19, 1993; Edward J. Boyer, "Attorney Depicts Williams as Scapegoat for Riots," *Los Angeles Times*, September 30, 1993; John Riley, "The Jury from Hell," *Newsday*, October 17, 1993; "Denny Judge: Do the Right Thing," *St. Petersburg Times*, October 20, 1993; "Denny Trial Deliberations Start Anew as Judge Removes Another Juror," *Minnesota Star Tribune*, October 1993, p. 1A; Ashley Dunn, "Removal of Denny Juror Not without Precedent," *Chicago Sun Times*, October 17, 1993; Haya El Nasser "Juror vs. Juror in Denny Trial," *USA Today*, October 15, 1993, p. 3A; John Riley, "It's Over at Denny Trial," *Newsday*, October 21, 1993; William Hamilton, "The Man Who Turned the Denny Case Around: Edi Faal and a Matter of Justice," *Washington Post*, October 23, 1993; Seth Mydans, "An Acquittal in Los Angeles," *The Houston Chronicle*, October 21, 1993; Jane Gross, "L.A. Riots Broke His Body, Not His spirit to Survive," *Star Tribune*, October 23, 1993; "Man Who Beat truck Driver in LA Gets 10 Years," *St. Louis Post-Dispatch*, December 8, 1993.

THINKING CRITICALLY ABOUT THIS CASE

1. Gil Garcetti, district attorney for Los Angeles County, remarked, "The jury returned verdicts that we find perhaps a bit incomprehensible, but that's the jury system."[29] Do you believe the decision of the jury is "incomprehensible"? Why or why not? How would you explain it? Should the justice system accept a jury verdict that is "incomprehensible"? Why or why not?

2. According to some observers, the trial of these four defendants was a form of selective prosecution: hundreds of people rioted that night in response to the King verdicts. The defense argued successfully that the defendants were swept up in mob mentality that undermined the degree of criminal intent behind their actions. Others argue that the context did not excuse or reduce their liability for their actions. Do you believe that juries should take into consideration the entire context of a criminal act? Why or why not? Is it possible to ignore the context and still make a just decision?

3. Many on the jury expressed fear for their own or their family's safety. Many citizens refused to serve on this particularly high-profile trial. Should the trial have been moved to another venue? Why or why not?

4. According to Jerome Skolnick, the jury should be applauded for its work in this trial. The system of justice is designed to prevent conviction of the innocent. The jury did its job, protecting the principle that the burden of proof rests on the prosecution to provide evidence beyond a reasonable doubt. The prosecution simply could not prove, beyond a reasonable doubt, that Damien Williams or Henry Watson specifically intended to kill or permanently disfigure Reginald Denny. Do you agree? Why or why not?

5. Both Reginald Denny and Fidel Lopez were sympathetic to the men who attacked them. Should this information be known to the jury? Should this information influence the jury? Why or why not?

6. If you were called to serve on the jury on this case, would you agree to serve? If you were on the jury, what would you decide?

CHECK OUT THIS CASE

On the Web

Read an eyewitness account of the 1992 riots by news reporters on the scene at **www.citivu.com/ktla/sc-ch1.html** and EmergencyNet News Service reports submitted during the three days of rioting at **www.emergency.com/la-riots.htm**.

Trials and Juries

LEARNING OBJECTIVES

After reading this chapter, the student should be able to:

- Identify and define pretrial motions; types of evidence and witnesses presented at trial; and describe the key steps of the trial process

- Understand the origins of the jury system and the purpose of the jury in the justice system

- Understand the role of the grand jury and the petit jury

- Under the process of jury selection and the issue of discrimination raised by the use of peremptory challenges

- Understand the concept of jury nullification; explain the historical significance of jury nullification and discuss the current status of jury nullification

Trial by jury is one of the central pillars of the ideal of democracy. The Sixth Amendment, in the Bill of Rights, affords all citizens the right to a public trial before a jury of their peers. An essential element of fairness is the presentation of evidence for both sides by zealous advocates in a public forum, where the ultimate judgment lies with the common wisdom of one's fellow citizens. In a jury trial, it is the collection of ordinary folk who are the "fact finders" of the case: they must decide whether evidence is credible and what "really" happened. And as long as the judicial procedure has conformed to the standards of due process, the "truth" is what the jury decides.

However, the jury has a broader function than determining the facts. Out there at the intersection of Florence and Normandie, there was little dispute about what happened. The videotapes clearly showed who did what to whom. In the King trials and the Denny trial, the responsibility of the jury was to determine the legal truth of the case. Did the facts fit the definition of attempted murder or simple mayhem? What was the motive of the defendants and their state of mind? Why did they act this way toward the victim? Juries may determine "truth" about the facts, but they are also given the responsibility to fit those facts to the law and determine the "justice" of the case.

This chapter examines the process of the trial and the institution of the jury as the key decision-making body at a public trial. The trial is about "truth" according to the rules of due process. As we have seen, the spectacle of the trial is the exception, not the rule in the adjudication process. Even so, the trial remains one of the central institutions where "justice" is seen to be done in our society. With television, the courtroom as an arena for the delivery of justice has become even more central in the public imagination, with celebrated trials witnessed by millions of American citizens.

In this chapter, we also take a careful and critical look at the institution of the jury itself. The jury system takes a collection of total strangers, throws them together for a relatively brief period of time while giving them no training in law or any real background about the defendants, victims, and their lives, and then asks them to make an impartial and objective determination of "truth" and "justice." Is this a realistic expectation? Many countries have no jury system at all; Japan

pretrial motions: written or oral requests to a judge, by the prosecution or defense, before the trial begins.

change of venue: written request to the judge to change the jurisdiction from the location where the crime was committed to a different jurisdiction.

motion to suppress: pretrial motion that requests the judge to deny the introduction of certain evidence in a trial.

motion for discovery: written or oral request to the opposing side to inform their opponent about evidence that will be produced during the trial.

motion for continuance: written or oral request to the judge by the defense or prosecution to delay trial proceedings.

motion to dismiss: written or oral request to the judge to dismiss the charges against the accused.

trial by jury: examination of the facts and law in a court before a jury authorized to give a verdict according to the evidence as to the guilt or innocence of the accused.

impaneling the jury: members of the jury pool are sworn in as potential jurors.

instituted one in the 1920s and then abolished it twenty years later; and although the jury system exists in both England and France, it is rarely used.

The jury verdict in the King trial led to massive riots. The jury verdict in the Reginald Denny case generated a great deal of public skepticism about the objectivity and neutrality of the jury. The juries in the Scottsboro trial and the Peairs trial made decisions that many felt were unjust. Many people doubt that juries are above the prejudices and passions that govern society. Is it really possible or even desirable that juries rise above the everyday opinions of ordinary citizens? How do we guarantee a "jury of one's peers" in a diverse society? How do we guarantee that juries are "objective," and what does this mean? Why do we have a jury system today? Are there alternatives that might be more satisfying to the determination of justice?

THE TRIAL PROCESS

Sometimes what takes place before the trial is more important than what happens at the trial. **Pretrial motions** are written or oral requests by attorneys to the judge before the actual trial begins. A request for a **change of venue** alters the jury pool and therefore the composition of the jury for a trial, which can have a significant impact on the outcome of the trial itself. Other common pretrial motions concern the investigatory process and the strength of the evidence against the defendant. A **motion to suppress** evidence asks that certain evidence not be allowed in court; a **motion for discovery** is a request by defense counsel to see the evidence, including the list of witnesses, that the prosecution intends to present at trial; a **motion for continuance** is a request for more time before the start of the trial; and a **motion to dismiss** requests the judge to dismiss the case, usually for lack of probable cause or because a plea agreement of some kind has been reached between the parties.

A formal **trial by jury** begins with the **impaneling of the jury.** Although the formal presentation of the evidence is supposed to begin at opening statements, attorneys begin to present their case to prospective jurors long before the bailiff calls the court to order, during the process of questioning potential jurors about the case.

The judge begins the formal presentations by the attorneys by signaling the prosecution to make its **opening statement,** followed by the opening statement of the defense. This is one of two times that each side has the opportunity to address the jury directly, without interruption from the opposing side. The opening statement presents the jury with an "overview" of the evidence and arguments that will come in the hours and days to follow. Like the jury selection process itself, the opening statement is an important moment to gain the sympathy and support of the jury.

The presentation of the evidence begins first with the prosecution. There are several different types of evidence, but it is necessary that all evidence offered in the trial be relevant to the material elements of the case. **Direct evidence** refers to the testimonial of eyewitnesses who actually saw or heard the crime. **Circumstantial evidence** requires a jury to make some inferences from the facts: if a person is coming out of a building where a robbery occurred, the jury must infer about the actions that took place inside the building.

Demonstrative evidence refers to physical objects such as a bloody glove or a photo of Denny's head or, in this case, videotapes of the crime that can actually be shown to the jury at the trial. The jury relies on its own eyes and ears to evaluate this evidence. **Testimonial evidence** refers to statements offered under oath in depositions outside the courtroom or by testifying in court as to what witnesses saw or heard. The jury must evaluate the credibility of the witnesses (are they telling the truth?), or the quality of what they say they saw (could they really see inside the windows of the pool hall?) in order to evaluate the evidence. **Hearsay evidence,** in which a person testifies as to what another person saw or said, is generally not permissible as evidence in criminal trials except in cases of a **dying declaration,** when the last words of a deceased witness may be relayed in court by a third party.

In addition to eyewitnesses who testify about what they themselves saw and heard, each side may hire **expert witnesses,** who offer their opinion about the evidence based on expert knowledge. Criminal defendants who are poor and represented by public defenders are often at a disadvantage because they lack funds to hire expert witnesses. One of the reasons for raising money to defend Williams and his friends was to have sufficient funds to hire an experienced private attorney like Edie Faal and to enable the attorney to hire expert witnesses about the theory of mob contagion. As we saw from all of the King trials and the Williams trial, expert witnesses are often very persuasive to juries.

Character witnesses know the defendant and offer information about the defendant as a person, beyond their actions in the crime itself. According to the rules of evidence, if one side calls either a character or expert witness, the other side is permitted to also call expert and character witnesses who present opposing opinions. It is the prerogative of the defense to offer character witnesses, which is often seen as a risky choice since it offers the prosecution the opportunity to introduce negative character witnesses and evidence of misconduct in the defendant's past. This type of witness generally benefits higher-status defendants, who may have many people able to come forward with glowing tales about their character.

When an attorney questions his or her own witness, the questioning is referred to as **direct examination.** On direct examination, attorneys are required to ask open-ended questions such as, "Tell the jury what you saw at the intersection of Florence and Normandie." When examining their own witnesses, attorneys are prohibited from "leading" the witness with question such as, "Isn't it true, that on the night of April 29, you saw Williams hit Denny with a hunk of concrete?"

After each direct examination, however, the opposing attorney is given an opportunity to cross-examine the witness. On **cross-examination,** leading questions are permissible and generally necessary to undermine the testimony supporting the opposing side. A skillful trial lawyer will use his or her own words to force "yes" or "no" questions from the witness that will raise some degree of doubt in the mind of the jury about their previous testimony. On cross-examination, witnesses are generally not permitted to explain their answers and are subject to manipulative questions from the attorney, who is seeking to recast their testimony in a light that is favorable to his or her client.

Once the prosecution and the defense have presented their cases and had the opportunity to challenge each other's evidence, each side offers a **closing statement** before the jury. Like the opening statement, this is a chance to address the jury directly, without interruption. Closing statements can run for many hours and often do, depending on the style and rhetorical skill of the attorney. Even more than opening statements, closing statements are the chance to tie the case together for the jury, to pull all the pieces of evidence presented in the trial and put all the facts together for the jury to see and accept. Although the closing statement is highly charged and emotional, attorneys may not make statements that extend beyond the evidence or make inferences based on that evidence. They may not hint to the jury that other evidence still exists out there or make reference to the refusal of a defendant to testify as evidence of guilt. In many jurisdictions, although not California, the defense presents closing arguments first and the prosecution is given the privilege of the last word before the jury.

Before they go out to make their deliberations, the jury is subject to **instructions from the judge.** The judge actually has the last word on the legal criteria relevant to the case. It is the job of the judge to explain to the jury the type of evidence needed to support the charges and the possible alternative verdicts they may choose from.

Jury deliberations may take anywhere from a few minutes to many weeks to come to a decision. Most jurisdictions require a unanimous verdict for felony convictions. If the jury is unable to reach a verdict, it is called a **hung jury.** The judge may require the jury to continue deliberating but may not continue this indefinitely. The lone holdout

opening statements: introduction to the jury by the prosecution and the defense of the evidence and arguments that will be presented in the trial.

direct evidence: eyewitness accounts of relevant facts of the case.

circumstantial evidence: evidence that requires a jury or judge to infer a fact about the case.

demonstrative evidence: evidence, such as a photograph or physical object, which demonstrates a fact about the case for the judge or jury.

testimonial evidence: statements offered under oath as to what a witness saw or heard.

hearsay evidence: testimonial regarding what another person saw or heard, which is generally not permissible as a criminal evidence.

dying declaration: the last words of a dying witness, which may be entered as hearsay evidence in a criminal trial.

expert witness: a person with specialized education, training, or qualifications in a particular field, who testifies on behalf of the prosecution or defense.

character witness: a person who offers testimony regarding the defendant that is unrelated to the facts of the case.

is important to the defense, because a conviction cannot occur without a unanimous verdict. If there is a hung jury, the judge must declare a **mistrial.** A mistrial is different from an acquittal. An acquittal is a finding of not guilty. The Constitutional prohibition against double jeopardy prevents the state from prosecuting the defendant again on the same charges. The defendant is free of all further prosecutions. With a mistrial, the prosecution may decide to try the defendant all over again with a new jury. In the first King trial, the jury deadlocked on one of the charges against Lawrence Powell. If the federal trial had not followed, it is likely that prosecutors would have retried Powell to seek a conviction on that charge. This is not a case of double jeopardy because a verdict was not reached in the first trial.

THE JURY

There are two kinds of juries, which serve two different functions. The grand jury is a body of sixteen to twenty-three citizens who serve as a protection against excessive prosecution by the government. The purpose of the grand jury is to hand down criminal indictments. The government must present evidence to the grand jury and show probable cause that the accused is guilty as charged. Prosecutor Janet Moore went before a grand jury to seek indictments of attempted murder, torture, aggravated mayhem, and robbery against Damien Williams.

The **petit jury** is composed of twelve or six citizens who hear evidence in the trial itself. In theory, the role of the jury is to determine the "facts" of the case and then apply the law as explained by the judge. Juries listen to witnesses, examine the evidence, view the videotapes, hear the experts on both sides, and ultimately decide who is

direct examination:
when counsel questions its own witnesses during the trial.

cross-examination:
when counsel questions witnesses called by the opposing side.

closing statement:
summary statement made by each attorney to the judge and the jury, reviewing the main arguments and facts of the case.

judge's instructions to the jury: the judicial responsibility to lay out the law that the jury should follow in making its verdict.

hung jury: a jury that is unable to come to a unanimous decision on a legal verdict.

mistrial: judicial ruling that the trial was invalid because it was terminated without a verdict or because of substantial error in due process proceedings.

petit jury: a panel of twelve or six citizens charged with determining the defendant's guilt or innocence in a trial.

The responsibility of the jury is to come to a unanimous decision regarding the evidence and the application of the law to those facts. The purpose of the jury has been to provide a role for the citizenry in the justice process and uphold the constitutional right of every citizen to be judged by his or her peers.

telling the truth, which evidence is more believable, and what inferences are more likely than others.

In practice, the distinction between the "facts" of the case and the application of the "law" is far from crystal clear. The job of the jury is far more complex than simply evaluating evidence. In the Williams and King cases, the jury was grappling with the issue of intent: what was in the mind of Powell when he was beating King, and what was in the mind of Williams when he hurled the object at Denny's head? Were they "justified" in being fearful or angry? Which laws apply to their actions, and where does justice lie in these matters?

The jury is also a deliberative body. This means that the twelve or six persons on the jury must discuss, debate, argue, cajole, and eventually come to a unanimous decision. Unlike legislatures, which rely on majority voting, the jury is unique in its requirement that these twelve or six individuals come to an agreement with each other about what is just. In 1972 the U.S. Supreme Court ruled it Constitutional for states to permit juries to split by 10–2 or 9–3 in noncapital cases, but only two states, Louisiana and Oregon, authorize nonunanimous verdicts.[30]

The deliberative process requires people to come to a consensus. It also creates the possibility that a single holdout may derail the entire process. A hung jury does not reach consensus and therefore is unable to deliver a verdict. The result is a mistrial: the prosecution must begin all over again with a new trial or the case must be dismissed. Judges try hard to avoid a mistrial, because it is a waste of resources expended in the trial. In the Denny trial, the judge sent the jury back numerous times with the order to continue to deliberate to overcome their internal differences. The lone holdout changed her mind and voted to acquit Williams of murder along with the rest of the jury.

Why Does the Jury Exist?

Historically, the role of the petit jury has been understood to be about judging the justice of the law itself and ensuring that it remains true to the conscience of the community. The purpose of the jury system is to protect the rights of the accused against governmental tyranny. In the Magna Carta of 1215, Britain's King John promised that "no free man shall be taken or imprisoned or in any way destroyed except by the lawful judgment of his peers." In the Bill of Rights, the Sixth Amendment guarantees citizens the right to a public trial before a jury of their peers. Who constitutes one's "peers," how those individuals are chosen, and what their responsibilities are, has evolved historically and continues to be a central concern in the justice system.

At the time of the Constitution, colonists were concerned about the power of the British monarchy to impose unjust laws on the people.[31] Mindful of the many times that colonists had been sent back to England to be tried before British juries who knew nothing of life in the colonies, the founding fathers explicitly formulated the jury as an institution of local justice. The U.S. jury system was intentionally designed so that local people—neighbors, friends, and relatives of the accused—were the ones to sit in judgment at trial. The jury was to be a pillar of democracy because ordinary citizens were to rely on their own consciences rather than the letter of the law. The jury was the means to ensure that the law accurately reflected the morals, values, and common sense of the people being asked to obey the law.

An amusing story illustrates the ideal of common-sense justice. Back in the wilder days of the West, a woman was on trial for pistol-whipping her neighbor.[32] She had done this in retaliation for his act of sewing up her horse's mouth, which he had done because the horse was eating his hay. After hearing all the facts, the judge clearly and firmly instructed the jury that no matter what the justification, it was illegal to take the law into one's own hand. He sternly told the jury that it was their duty to uphold the law and determine only if she was guilty of the fact of striking a man with a pistol. The jury politely listened to the judge and his explanation of their responsibilities and then proceeded to find the woman not guilty of a crime she had clearly committed. The foreman explained, "The judge trusted us to do justice. . . . That judge knew we wouldn't go along with all that legal horseshit as he was readin us."[33]

The power of **jury nullification** refers to the right of a jury to ignore the formal requirements of the law and rely on their conscience and values to acquit the defendant. In 1735, John Peter Zenger was put on trial for violating the laws against seditious libel when he published criticisms about the royal governor.[34] The law of the land prohibited the publication of any negative information about any public figures, whether or not the information was true. According to the letter of the law, Zenger was guilty. All the jury needed to do was to determine whether Zenger had, in fact, written and published the newsletter.

Andrew Hamilton, Zenger's lawyer, appealed to the conscience of the jury. He urged them to disobey the judge's instructions, telling them they had the duty and the power to determine the law as well as the facts. Hamilton told the jury "to see with their own eyes, to hear with their own ears, and to make use of their consciences and understanding in judging of the lives, liberties or estate of their fellow subjects."[35] The jury responded and acquitted Zenger.

Time and again in our history, juries have used the power of jury nullification to oppose unjust laws. The Fugitive Slave Law of 1850 was passed by Congress to stem the flow of fugitives from slave states to free states.[36] People who aided the slaves were subject to prosecution and punishment. Time and again, however, Northern juries acquitted defendants based on their rejection of the law itself, rather than on the facts of the case. They relied on a higher sense of justice, which they found to be in conflict with the law, and by their actions they declared the law null and void.

The dark side of the power of jury nullification can be seen in the willingness of all-white Southern juries to excuse white violence against blacks. The letter of the law declares all citizens equal regardless of race, but community norms of the South upheld vigilante justice against blacks who violated the racial codes of white supremacy. As late as the 1960s, the power of nullification allowed all-white juries in the South to acquit whites who used violence to "punish" blacks for crossing the color line.[37] One of the most infamous examples was the acquittal of two men who shot 14-year-old Emmet Till through the head for the "crime" of "talking fresh" to the wife of one of the men. Despite eyewitnesses who saw the men kidnap Till the night of the murder, an all-white jury took only one hour and seven minutes to acquit the defendants.[38]

The Ideal of Objectivity

The purpose of a jury composed of local citizens who know the accused and the victims also serves another purpose. As in the case of the pistol-whipping woman, local juries bring to the courtroom their knowledge about a person's character, history, and relationships in the community. Rather than having total strangers pass judgment on a given case, the definition of "peers" was conceived in terms of "those near him . . . who are well acquainted with his character and situation in life."[39] Local juries will be aware of the case, know the facts surrounding it and the circumstances that led up to it. In the eighteenth and nineteenth centuries, it was likely to be one's neighbor who was on the jury, not a complete stranger.

Our contemporary vision of the impartial and objective juror is very different from this earlier notion of neighbor as juror. In the nineteenth century, the ideal vision of the jury shifted from one that relied on local and specific knowledge about the defendant and the victim to an ideal in which jurors were total strangers with no prior knowledge or connection to anyone involved. The ideal shifted toward the stranger rather than the neighbor. Today, jurors will be removed if they have any personal connection to any of the parties in the case.

jury nullification: a jury verdict that is made without regard to the evidence or the law.

The ideal of the impartial juror can be seen in our attempts to find potential jurors in the highly publicized trials who are unfamiliar with the facts of the case. Typically, people who have read about a case or have heard about it are routinely excluded from the jury in the search for the "perfect stranger" who will come to the trial as a blank slate with no prior knowledge about the case. Mark Twain remarked in the nineteenth century that the search for the impartial juror often leads us to seat the ignorant juror, who doesn't read or talk with others in the community. "The jury system puts a ban upon intelligence and honesty and a premium upon ignorance, stupidity and perjury."[40] Are these the individuals we should be trusting to deliver "justice," Twain wonders? In the media-saturated world of today, people who are disconnected from the media often lead atypical or strange lives: does this ensure impartiality, or does it ensure ignorance?

The Issue of Representation

Along with the ideal of impartiality is the ideal that the jury should represent a cross section of the community. Like so many of our democratic institutions, the jury of the eighteenth, nineteenth, and twentieth centuries systematically excluded many of our citizens from participation. Blacks, women, non-property owners, and ethnic minorities were seen as intellectually, morally, and emotionally unfit to serve on a jury. In the colonies, only white males were eligible to serve. No black person sat on a jury until 1860.[41] Before the Civil War the only state to permit blacks to serve on juries was Massachusetts.[42] The first state law ever struck down as unconstitutional by the U.S. Supreme Court concerned the racial composition of the jury. In the 1880 decision of *Strauder* v. *West Virginia*,[43] the court ruled that a West Virginia statute limiting jury service to white males violated the equal protection clause of the Fourteenth Amendment and was therefore unconstitutional.

The first state to permit women to serve on juries was Utah in 1898, but it was not until the 1940s that a majority of states made women eligible to be jurors.[44] As we saw in the Scottsboro case (Chapter 2), blacks were systemically excluded from jury rolls on the assumption that they were unqualified to serve as intelligent or educated jurors. No blacks could be called for jury duty because they were not included on the master lists created by jury commissioners. The **key man system,** which was still operating in some jurisdictions until the 1970s, gave the power to a prominent man or group of men in the community to choose the pool of jurors. In theory, the key man system was to ensure the inclusion of community values in the justice process; in reality this system ensured that only the values of privileged white males were carried into the courtroom.

The goal of having juries that reflect a true cross section of the community has centered on the way to construct jury rolls that are inclusive of all members of the community. In 1968, in the Jury Selection and Service Act, Congress specified the use of voter registration lists as a source for prospective juror names for the selection of federal juries. Yet voter registration lists leave out many potential jurors.[45] African Americans, Hispanics, younger citizens, and the poor are far less likely to be registered to vote than white, middle-class Americans. In North Dakota, for instance, only 17 percent of eligible Native Americans are registered to vote.[46] Not surprisingly, therefore, only a handful of Native Americans appear on the jury rolls, despite the fact that Native Americans constitute 2 percent of the population of the entire state. Today, in the effort to construct a truly representative jury pool, most states supplement voter registration lists with other sources such as driver's license lists, telephone directories, tax rolls, and utility customers lists.

But should the jury pool be "representative" of the ethnic diversity of the community, or should the specific jury reflect the ethnicity of the defendant and the victim? How important is the gender, class, and racial composition of the jury to render verdicts that are fair, impartial, and just? This is a key question facing the institution of the jury.

key man system: eligibility for serving on a jury is based on recommendations from "key" persons of high character and reputation in the community.

In the 1940s, Gunnar Myrdal noted that the institution of the jury as a form of local democracy works only when people are judging others who are like themselves.[47] People are able to be fair when the victim and defendant are similar to themselves in terms of race, class, and gender. However, when an all-white jury is asked to judge a black defendant accused of harming a white victim, the jury becomes an institution of oppression. Similarly, we have seen juries composed entirely of men who are unable to empathize with women as victims in rape or domestic violence cases. The absence of women on the jury undermines the ability of all-male juries to be impartial: data show that all-male juries in the 1950s and 1960s failed to convict males accused of rape and acquitted them even when the evidence against them was strong.[48] "Mock jury" studies demonstrate that all-white juries are more likely to convict black defendants than white defendants.[49]

Jury Selection

In England, there is typically no *voir dire* or jury selection process: at the start of the trial, twelve citizens are chosen at random from the jury pool and that is the jury.[50] Attorneys rarely try to unseat any particular juror. In England, the trial is said to begin after jury selection takes place; in the United States, the trial is said to be over after jury selection has taken place.[51] As we have seen, the process of impaneling a particular jury for a given trial in the United States involves an elaborate process of jury selection in which the opposing attorneys attempt to seat a jury predisposed to their side. Attorneys may **challenge for cause** any potential juror who expresses attitudes and opinions prejudicial to their case. If attorneys are successful in seating a jury favorable to their case, they may have effectively won the trial before it has begun.

The defense in both the King trial and the Denny trial hired jury consultant Jo-Ellan Demetris to assist in the jury selection process. According to jury consultants, a trial is like a play: whether it is a hit will depend on how receptive the audience is. Juries are seen as passive bystanders to the drama of justice staged by the two opposing attorneys. Scientific jury selection became popular in the 1970s and has become a routine part of trial preparation for well-funded clients. The jury consultant uses standard social science techniques such as opinion surveys and focus groups to assess views that are correlated or associated with various demographic attributes. They will construct an ideal juror for the attorney according to age, occupation, hobbies, marital status, religion, race, political views, and social attitudes. They devise the questions that attorneys should ask on the questionnaire and during the *voir dire* and analyze the answers to rank the prospective jurors. In addition, consultants are looking for people who will be able to either persuade others to come over to their point of view or hold out against the viewpoint of others on the jury.

The use of **peremptory challenges** to influence the gender or racial composition of the jury is a long-established practice among attorneys. Attorneys have not needed highly paid jury consultants to get the message that the race and gender of the jury will influence their response to the defendant. Because peremptory challenges require no reason, attorneys have long used these to strike minorities from the jury. This strategy is easily successful because the number of minorities in any jury pool is usually small, even in those pools that are cross-sectional representations of the community. Removing all blacks or Hispanics from the panel is possible when there are only a handful to begin with.

In 1986, in *Batson* v. *Kentucky*,[52] the Supreme Court ruled that attorneys could not legitimately use the peremptory challenge to strike jurors solely because of their group membership. While the Court ruled that a black defendant did not have the right to a jury that reflected his race, the jury selection process could also not systematically exclude blacks either from the pool or from the individual jury. Since 1986, if there is a racial pattern in the use of peremptory challenges, the attorneys must offer a nondis-

voir dire: process by which lawyers and the judge question potential jurors for a given case.

challenge for cause: removal of jurors for stated reasons.

peremptory challenges: removal of a certain number of jurors by counsel for each side without reason.

criminatory reason for the dismissals. In 1994 the Supreme Court extended this rule to the use of peremptory challenges to exclude jurors on the basis of gender.

Although it is laudable that the Supreme Court has banned race- and gender-based peremptory challenges, it is also the case that attorneys are adept at coming up with legitimate reasons when challenged. In the Simi Valley trial, the defense had fourteen peremptory challenges. Aware that they could not legally strike for reasons of race alone, they grilled potential black jurors for attitudes, opinions, or connections that would constitute cause for dismissal. Most people agree that if attorneys look hard enough, it is always possible to find some legitimate reason to excuse a candidate.

JURY NULLIFICATION TODAY

The power of jury nullification has existed in the United States since colonial times.[53] At times it has played a noble role in upholding the conscience of the community against unjust laws, and at other times it has played an ignoble part in maintaining oppression and inequality within the wider society. The courts have upheld the ultimate power of the jury to acquit defendants by recognizing that it is a power that cannot be taken away from juries. "We recognize the undisputed power of the jury to acquit even if its verdict is contrary to the law as given by the judge and contrary to the evidence."[54]

Yet the courts have decided that juries should not be fully informed of this power, either in the judge's instructions or by statements of defense counsel. Although it is recognized that the "court cannot search the minds of jurors"[55] and prevent them from relying on their conscience when they decide a verdict, to tell jurors that they may nullify the law would be to invite anarchy. Thus, the courts have generally refused to permit defense attorneys to tell juries that they may disregard the law in making their decision: "By clearly stating to the jury that they may disregard the law . . . we would indeed be negating the rule of law in favor of the rule of lawlessness."[56]

The Fully Informed Jury Association is promoting legislation that would require the courts to instruct juries of their power to vote their conscience. Supporters range from members of the National Rifle Association to pro-life groups, groups in favor of legalization of marijuana, militia groups, abortion rights supporters, and gun control advocates. This organization advocates the passage of the "Fully Informed Jury Act," which would require judges to instruct jurors that they can determine both facts and law. Others believe that the promotion of jury nullification would create anarchy by encouraging juries to decide cases based on their own perceptions and beliefs rather than the requirements of the law.

Today, the power of jury nullification technically continues to exists. Judges do not tell juries, however, that they literally hold the legitimate power to question or overrule the law itself. But some observers argue that juries in recent decades have become more inclined to nullify the law. The enactment of three-strikes laws and mandatory sentencing, the widespread perception of racial inequities in the administration of justice, and the increasing recognition of complex factors that contribute to criminal conduct, such as battered women's syndrome, have led juries to return decisions based on a broader view of justice than simply applying the strict interpretation of the law to the facts of the case.

Did the Williams jury "nullify" the law when they acquitted Damien Williams of attempted murder? Was this jury attempting to come up with a fair decision by taking into account the King trial, the riots, and the history of racial tension between the LAPD and the young black men in South Central LA? Or was this verdict simply the fair application of legal principles, in which the jury legitimately found reasonable doubt in the prosecution's case?

Professor Paul Butler, associate professor of law at George Washington University Law School, argues that African American jurors should nullify the law and acquit black defendants who are guilty of nonviolent crimes in order to stop the flow of black men into the prison system.[57] Butler and others observe that juries are increasingly unwilling to convict clearly guilty defendants under harsh mandatory sentencing laws that they view as excessive or unjust. The power of jury nullification may serve to act as a check on governmental oppression of minorities through the power of the jury to say "no" to unjust laws.[58] On the other hand, jurists such as Supreme Court Justice Clarence Thomas take the position that nullification is a danger to the rule of the law.

The next case and chapter turns to a closer examination of the sentencing and the impact of mandatory sentencing laws, particularly for drug crimes, on the minority community. What is the justification for harsh drug laws? What purpose does it serve? And who has the power to decide the appropriate sentence for a given crime?

KEY TERMS

pretrial motions p. 246
change of venue p. 246
motion to suppress p. 246
motion for discovery p. 246
motion for continuance p. 246
motion to dismiss p. 246
trial by jury p. 246
impaneling the jury p. 246
opening statements p. 247
direct evidence p. 247

circumstantial evidence p. 247
demonstrative evidence p. 247
testimonial evidence p. 247
hearsay evidence p. 247
dying declaration p. 247
expert witness p. 247
character witness p. 247
direct examination p. 248
cross-examination p. 248
closing statement p. 248

judge's instructions to the
  jury p. 248
hung jury p. 248
mistrial p. 248
petit jury p. 248
jury nullification p. 250
key man system p. 251
voir dire p. 252
challenge for cause p. 252
peremptory challenges p. 252

REVIEW AND STUDY QUESTIONS

1. What is a pretrial motion? Give examples of the motions made before a trial.

2. Describe the different types of evidence admissible at a criminal trial. What is the difference between an eyewitness, a character witness, and an expert witness? What is hearsay, and under what special circumstances is it permissible in court? What is the difference between the processes of examination and cross-examination?

3. What is the purpose of the jury in our justice system? How has the jury acted as the "conscience of the community" in U.S. history?

4. What is the specific function of the grand jury? What is the specific function of the petit jury?

5. Describe the process of impaneling the jury. What is the *voir dire?* What are challenges for cause and peremptory challenges, and how do each of these function in the process of jury selection?

6. What does it mean to say that the jury is a deliberative institution? Why is the process of deliberation important to the jury? What is a hung jury and why does it lead to a mistrial?

7. What is the ideal of objectivity? What is the ideal of representation? What are the processes in place to create an impartial jury of peers for a defendant?

8. What are the mechanisms by which African Americans and women have been excluded from the jury? What did the Supreme Court rule in *Batson* v. *Kentucky?* Does this ruling prevent the systematic exclusion of minorities and women from the jury? Why or why not?

9. What is the power of jury nullification? What is the position of the courts on the right of a jury to effectively nullify the law by acquitting a defendant despite the facts and the law? What is the position of the Fully Informed Jury Association?

10. State the positions for and against the power of jury nullification. Why does Butler believe that African Americans should use the power of jury nullification for nonviolent offenses committed by blacks? Why does Supreme Court Justice Clarence Thomas oppose this power?

CHECK IT OUT

On the Web

Anatomy of a Murder!, www.thinkquest.org
Go to this Web site to take a fictional but legally accurate tour through a criminal murder trial. See actual documents filed at all stages of the criminal justice process. Follow the strategy of the defense and the prosecution and see all the steps that are never shown on TV.

On-line Resource Guide to the American Jury, www.crfc.org/americanjury/
Rich and informative Web site on the jury, sponsored by the Constitutional Rights Foundation of Chicago, the National Endowment for the Humanities, and the Chicago Historical Society. Has resources and information on the history of the jury, trial juries, grand juries, jury nullification, and rights of the accused. Explores a host of issues, including
media and juries and the future of juries. Many links to relevant sites on juries.

On Film

Inside the Jury (46 minutes)
This film covers the jury from the voir dire *through the deliberations in a case involving a defendant charged with armed robbery. See what happens after the attorneys rest their case. Available from Films for the Humanities and Sciences,* www.films.com.

12 Angry Men (96 minutes)
Classic 1957 film starring Henry Fonda as the lone holdout and honest juror in the deliberations for a murder trial, dedicated to the pursuit of the facts while prejudices and weaknesses cloud the judgment of the other eleven men.

NOTES

1. John Riley, "Beating Victim Denny 'Relieved'; Trucker Wants Healing for L. A.," *Newsday*, October 19, 1993, p. 19.
2. Lou Cannon, *Official Negligence: How Rodney King and the Riots Changed Los Angeles and the LAPD* (Boulder, CO: Westview, 1999), p. 304.
3. Ibid., p. 305.
4. Edward J. Boyes and Ashley Dunn, "Williams, Watson Mean to Kill Denny, Prosecutor Says," *Los Angeles Times*, September 29, 1993, p. A-1.
5. Jim Newton and Henry Weinstein, "Three Suspects Seized in Beating of Truck Driver during Riot," *Los Angeles Times*, May 13, 1992, p. A-1.
6. Riley, "Beating Victim Denny 'Relieved,'" p. 19.
7. John Riley, "Unease as Trial Progresses in Los Angeles," *Newsday*, September 19, 1993, p. 7.
8. Newton and Weinstein, "Three Suspects Seized," p. A-1.
9. Edward J. Boyer, "Attorney Depicts Williams as Scapegoat for Riots," *Los Angeles Times*, September 30, 1993, p. A-1.
10. John Riley, "The Jury From Hell," *Newsday*, October 17, 1993, p. 3.
11. Cannon, *Official Negligence*, p. 384.
12. Ibid., pp. 187–192.
13. Ibid., pp. 499–500.
14. Ibid., p. 500.
15. Ibid., p. 512.
16. Ibid., p. 506.
17. "Denny Judge: Do the Right Thing," *St. Petersburg (Florida) Times*, October 20, 1993, p. A1.
18. Boyer, "Attorney Depicts Williams as Scapegoat," p. A-1.
19. "Denny Trial Deliberations Start Anew as Judge Removes Another Juror," *Minnesota Star Tribune*, October 19, 1993, p. 1A; Ashley Dunn, "Removal of Denny Juror Not without Precedent," *Chicago Sun Times*, October 17, 1993, p. 24.
20. Haya El Nasser, "Juror vs. Juror in Denny Trial," *USA Today*, October 15, 1993, p. A.
21. John Riley, "Its over at Denny Trial," *Newsday*, October 21, 1993, p. 3.
22. John Riley, "It's Over at Denny Trial: 2nd Suspect Acquitted of Attempted Murder," *Newsday*, October 21, 1993, p. 3.
23. William Hamilton, "The Man Who Turned the Denny Case Around: Edie Faal and a Matter of Justice," *Washington Post*, October 23, 1993, p. D1.
24. Seth Mydans, "An Acquittal in Los Angeles," *The Houston Chronicle*, October 21, 1993, p. A1.
25. Jane Gross, "L.A. Riots Broke His Body, Not His Spirit to Survive," *Star Tribune* (Minneapolis), October 23, 1993, p. A4.
26. Ibid.
27. "Man Who Beat Truck Driver in LA Gets 10 Years," *St. Louis Post-Dispatch*, December 8, 1993, p. A1.
28. Cannon, *Official Negligence*, p. 524.
29. John Riley, "It's Over at Denny Trial," p. 3.
30. Jeffrey Abramson, *We, the Jury: The Jury System and the Ideal of Democracy* (New York: Basic Books, 1994), pp. 180–181.
31. Ibid., p. 28.
32. Stephen J. Adler, *The Jury: Disorder in the Court* (New York: Doubleday, 1994), p. 3.
33. Ibid., p. 3.
34. Abramson, *We, the Jury*, pp. 73–75.
35. Ibid., p. 74.
36. Ibid., pp. 80–82.
37. Randall Kennedy, *Race, Crime and the Law* (New York: Vintage, 1997), p. 65.
38. Abramson, *We, the Jury*, pp. 111–112.
39. Ibid. p. 18.
40. Mark Twain, *Roughing It* (New York: Harper and Brothers, 1913), pp. 55–58.

41. David Cole, *No Equal Justice* (New York: The Free Press, 1997), p. 105.

42. Kennedy, *Race, Crime and the Law,* p. 169.

43. *Strauder* v. *West Virginia,* 100 U.S. 303(1880).

44. Abramson, *We, the Jury,* pp. 112–113.

45. Hiroshi Fukurai, Edgar Butler, and Richard Krooth, "Where Did Black Jurors Go," in David Baker, ed., *Reading Racism and the Criminal Justice System* (Toronto, Canada: Canadians Scholars Press, 1994), p. 88.

46. Abramson, *We, the Jury,* p. 129.

47. Gunnar Myrdal, *An American Dilemma: The Negro Problem and Modern Democracy* (New York: Harper, 1944), pp. 552–553.

48. Abramson, *We, the Jury,* p. 113.

49. Sherri Lynn Johnson, "Black Innocence and the White Jury," *University of Michigan Law Review 83* (1985), pp. 1611–1708.

50. James Q. Wilson, "Criminal Justice in England and America," *The Public Interest,* Winter 1997, pp. 3–14.

51. Abramson, *We, the Jury,* p. 145.

52. *Batson* v. *Kentucky,* 476 U.S. 79 (1986).

53. Lawrence W. Crispo, Jill M. Slansky, and Geanene M. Yriate, "Jury Nullification: Law versus Anarchy," *Loyola of Los Angeles Law Review 31* (1997), pp. 1–61.

54. *Horning* v. *District of Columbia,* 254 U.S. 135, 138 (1920) 1006.

55. Ibid.

56. Ibid.

57. Paul Butler, "Racially Based Jury Nullification: Black Power in the Criminal Justice System," *Yale Law Journal 105* (1995), pp. 677–725.

58. Alan W. Scheflin, "Jury Nullification: The Right to Say No," *Southern California Law Review 45* (1972), pp. 168–226.

CASE 13

The Crime of Punishment:
The Story of Kemba Smith

In October 1994, Kemba Smith, a 24-year-old woman, seven months pregnant, pleaded guilty in federal court to charges of conspiracy to distribute cocaine, lying to federal authorities, and conspiracy to launder drug money.[1] For over three years Kemba was the girlfriend of Peter Michael Hall, an alleged drug dealer under federal indictment for running a cocaine distribution ring. During this time, Kemba carried and concealed illegal weapons for Peter; rode in a van carrying drugs from New York to North Carolina; carried drug money strapped to her body for him; purchased a vehicle and rented apartments for him in her name; and denied any knowledge of Peter's whereabouts on at least two occasions when questioned by federal agents. Kemba Smith admitted guilt and responsibility for these actions and was held in jail without bail until sentencing.[2]

At the sentencing hearing, federal U.S. District Judge Richard B. Kellam announced the sentence to a packed courtroom: 294 months on the drug conspiracy charge, 60 months for lying to authorities, and 60 months on the money laundering charge—the latter two sentences to run concurrently with the first. A stunned hush filled the courtroom as the reality sank in that 24-year-old Kemba Smith had been sentenced to 24 years in prison—one year for each year of her life—with no chance for parole.[3] Four months earlier, Kemba had given birth to a son, who was immediately taken from her. She was allowed to breast-feed him only once and to see him for only two days after he was born.

FROM DEBUTANTE TO MULE

Kemba Smith grew up the cherished only child of a professional middle-class couple in a comfortable suburb of Richmond, Virginia.[4] Born in 1971, she spent her

childhood attending Brownie and Girl Scout meetings and going to gymnastics, piano, and ballet lessons. Her dad, an accountant, and her Mom, a business education teacher, were college sweethearts who gave their only daughter all they felt she needed to follow in their footsteps. In high school she played flute in the marching band, while her father volunteered as the club treasurer to fund out-of-town trips. She was active in clubs such as Students Against Drunk Driving and belonged to the Future Homemakers of America, just as her mother had during her high school years. At age 16 she came out as a debutante dressed in white organza and pearls at the Alpha Kappa Alpha sorority ball.

By any standards, Kemba had a loving but sheltered upbringing. Her parents had been raised by strict parents, and they imposed similar rules for Kemba during her high school years. She had to obey a curfew, dress conservatively, and be responsible in her school work. Although Kemba admits that she sometimes snuck out without her parents' knowledge, she did not really start to date until her senior year in high school. By the time Kemba was entering college, she had little experience and exposure to the world beyond that created by her parents and childhood friends.

The decision to attend Hampton College, 73 miles away from home, was the first independent decision Kemba ever made. Her parents were against the idea of her being so far away and preferred her to attend a local college in Virginia which was predominantly attended by whites. But Kemba wanted to go to a historically black college such as Spellman, Howard, or Hampton. In her childhood, Kemba had been the minority in her middle-class community, with largely white friends. Now she wanted the "black experience" and chose Hampton despite her parents' desire to keep her close to home. In the fall of 1989, her mother and father helped her move into the dormitory, setting up a microwave and television to make the room feel just like home.

Like many young people living away from home for the first time in her life, Kemba had difficulty adjusting to the new social scene at Hampton.[5] In her world at home, she had always felt attractive and popular; here she was a little fish lost in a big sea. She felt awkward and unappealing and worried about being hip. She wanted a boyfriend badly, so she could feel like she fit in and belonged.

The turmoil in her social life was quickly reflected in her academic performance. The B grade-point average Kemba had maintained before college plummeted, and by the end of her first semester she had failed two of her five classes. She started smoking marijuana, which was always around the dorms. Her parents, alarmed by her failing grades, asked Kemba to see a counselor in Richmond, but Kemba believed her parents were overreacting and treating her like a little girl. She refused to see the psychologist beyond a few sessions and continued to cultivate her newfound image as a party girl on campus.

Girls like Kemba are easy targets for men like Peter Michael Hall. She met him at a party. Eight years older, with a lilting Jamaican accent, he was not a student but seemed to know all the college kids in her crowd. There was much about him to impress the young Kemba: he had money and spent it lavishly on expensive cars, clothes, restaurants, and apartments filled with high-tech equipment and luxurious furniture. He had style, charm, and personality, holding the spotlight at any gathering, usually surrounded

by the prettiest and most popular girls. Kemba was surprised and flattered when one spring night in her sophomore year of college, Peter called her and asked her to meet him. That night he took her, blindfolded, to his apartment for an overnight stay, and thus began their stormy three-year relationship.

BATTERED WOMEN: STANDING BY HER MAN

It was naive of Kemba to believe that she was Peter's "main girl," but she did. Shortly after their affair began, Peter demonstrated his "love" for her when he saw her hold hands briefly with another man. In a jealous rage, he beat her, choked her, and hit her so badly she wore shades the next day to hide her swollen eyes. He did this, he claimed, because she had betrayed him and he needed to teach her a lesson. In the aftermath of the violence, he cried and apologized, promised never to hurt her again, told her he loved her and needed her. Kemba shouldn't have believed him, but she did. He asked for forgiveness and she gave it.[6]

By summer she had moved in with Peter, spending almost all her time with him and losing contact with most of her former friends at Hampton. Their life together steadily went downhill over the next two years, and gradually, Kemba became aware of the extent of Peter's illegal drug activities. Once he was arrested and jailed for four months on state drug and fake ID charges. Peter's brother called Kemba and gave her money to give to a lawyer to get Peter out of jail. She did as she was told, not realizing that the money was from the cocaine business or that Peter's brother was also wanted by the federal authorities as his co-conspirator in the drug business. She believed Peter when he said this was mainly about immigration problems; she believed him when he said he was going to change his lifestyle.

Kemba's parents met Peter shortly after he was released from jail on bail. They lied to her parents and told them the lockup had been for reasons of immigration, a mistake that had finally been cleared up. He put on a good performance for Gus and Odessa Smith, and they were pleased their daughter was dating such a well-mannered young man. But that good impression was fleeting. Shortly afterward, federal agents in search of Peter Hall contacted the Smith home looking for Kemba. Gus called the Drug Enforcement Administration (DEA) to find out why they wanted to talk with his daughter.

As agents circled around Kemba and her parents asking questions about Peter and all those who worked for him, Peter began to beat Kemba again, this time with a belt and a brush, accusing her of ratting on him and lying to him. Like so many battered women, Kemba protested that she was loyal but cowered and suffered his humiliations and tortures. And like so many other battered women, Kemba comforted him when he wept afterward, believed his promises, excuses, and apologies, and forgave him yet again. Whatever he asked her to do, she did. She felt trapped. She was both afraid of losing him and afraid of him.

Their life together went from bad to worse as Peter began to run from the federal authorities. Again Peter was caught and arrested, this time in New York in February 1993, on state drug possession charges of carrying 10 ounces of crack in a taxicab. This time, a different friend contacted Kemba and asked her to help Peter get out of jail, and again she dutifully did as she was asked, coming to New York to deliver an envelope to a man in Brooklyn, rescuing her man yet again.

Peter was released from jail for a large sum of cash. Again he skipped town before trial, returning to Virginia with Kemba, whom he accused of not caring about him at all. Kemba almost left him this time, when one of his beatings caused a miscarriage in her first pregnancy. She called her father to wire her a bus ticket so she could come home, but Peter followed her onto the Greyhound bus, begging forgiveness, weeping with despair and love. She called her father and told him she was staying with Peter.

A few months later, one of the many associates hanging around Peter was found dead from bullet wounds to the neck and head. Peter had gone to Atlanta, and he phoned Kemba to join him there. When she arrived, he told her he had killed Derrick, a street dealer he said was ratting on him and on her to the federal government. Kemba thought that if he would kill Derrick for betraying him, there was little doubt what he would do to her if she did the same.

Finally, in the summer, after an investigation that had begun the year Kemba had finished high school, federal agents filed a sixteen-count indictment against Peter Michael Hall and his brother. Added to the charge of running a drug ring that had moved as much as $4 million worth of cocaine and crack cocaine between New York and Virginia was a murder warrant for the death of Derrick Taylor. Federal agents believed that Peter ran the operations in Virginia and that his modus operandus was to recruit college students, males to sell drugs and young women like Kemba, loyal girlfriends who were willing to act as "mules" for the transport of drugs, money, and weapons.

Kemba may have believed that she was Peter's "main girl," but he had several such girlfriends in different cities, performing a variety of services out of a sad mixture of love, fear, and devotion. Not all of them were as loyal or as fearful as Kemba.[7] Several of them had turned state's evidence and provided information that led to the jailing of members of the drug ring. In exchange for this information, most were released from jail without charges, including one girlfriend originally charged with being an accomplice in the murder of Derrick Taylor, who was subsequently placed in a federal witness protection program.[8]

When Kemba returned home from school that summer she was apprehended by federal agents in the middle of the night. Held on $50,000 bail, Kemba was asked to give information about Peter's whereabouts and his operation. Kemba's lawyer urged her to cooperate, warning her that they could put her away for a long time if she refused. Kemba talked, but it was all lies. She remembered the warnings Peter had given her about telling things to the police; she remembered his rage when he suspected he was betrayed, and she remembered what had happened to Derrick Taylor. Claiming that she did not know where Peter was, Kemba was released and sent home.

After she was released, her parents begged her to stay away from Peter, but Kemba felt her place was with her man. She joined him in hiding in Atlanta, but he feared that the authorities would find him through her and he sent her home. For a few months, Kemba lived at home and began to return to the life she had always known. She enrolled in a local college, got a job, and began to lead the kind of life she had known before Peter. But Peter still needed her, especially now that he no longer had access to cash from his drug operation. She sent him what he asked for, cleaning out a joint account she held with her mother. Rather than face her mother and explain the missing money, Kemba left home suddenly one day after lunch to join Peter on the run again.

THE TRUTH: TOO LITTLE TOO LATE

This time Kemba and Peter were truly down and out. Kemba found herself pregnant again and penniless. They reached the West Coast living on the streets, sleeping in bus stations, pawning whatever possessions they still had from the high-living days. Kemba was afraid to go back home, fearful her parents would be too angry to take her back. At last Kemba returned home, afraid for her unborn child and unable to live on the streets anymore. She was welcomed with open arms by her desperately worried parents and on September 1, 1993, with her father beside her, she turned herself in to federal authorities.

Still Kemba would not give Peter up. Was it loyalty or fear that kept her from revealing his whereabouts? Kemba says it was both. She still loved him but she was also scared—for what he might do to her, to her parents, or her child if she betrayed him to the police.

While she was still in jail trying to decide if she should turn in her lover, Seattle police reported that they found Peter Michael Hall dead of a gunshot wound to the head. No one knows who killed Peter. His death remains an open case for the Seattle police. Now Kemba had no reason not to be truthful with the federal authorities, and she immediately told everything she knew. On advice of her lawyers she pleaded guilty to all the federal charges against her.

THE CONSPIRACY

Although the government acknowledged that Kemba had never touched, used, or sold cocaine, nor did she ever personally benefit from the proceeds of the drug ring, they claimed that she knowingly and willingly aided and abetted the activities of the organization. For this she deserved the full punishment of the mandatory drug sentence. Although Kemba confessed to transporting approximately $15,000 between New York and Charlotte, North Carolina, four times, she was ultimately sentenced for trafficking more than 560 pounds, worth $4 million. Kemba was held responsible for the entire amount of drugs distributed by the operation from 1989 to 1993.[9]

Kemba's lawyers argued for the judge to show mercy in sentencing Kemba for her crimes. While Kemba admitted all the conduct that had brought her here, her attorneys argued that she was acting under the influence of coercion and duress. They believed that these psychological pressures merited a reduction in the mandatory sentencing guidelines, which set the penalties for people involved in the sale and distribution of illegal controlled substances. Under these circumstances, the sentencing guidelines permit a judge to reduce the mandatory sentence on conviction.

The government argued that it was because of Kemba's actions that drugs plague the streets and endanger the lives of innocent citizens. Because of the evil effect of the drug trade on society, Kemba Smith needed to be punished without mercy. Fernado Groene, Assistant U.S. Attorney handling the drug ring cases, declared in court, "Judge, the real tragedy of this case is that this is a drug case and that the distribution of drugs by the people who the defendant assisted, those lives are also ruined. She hasn't expressed remorse for the lives that those drugs have destroyed. . . . She turned her back on her parents, on the laws, on society, on the people who were being threatened . . . people who were being killed . . . and the only possible explanation is she did it willingly for the love of Mr. Hall, not because she was afraid of him."[10]

Despite a massive show of public support for Kemba and her family, requests for leniency from prominent Richmond citizens including the former mayor and former director of corrections for the state of Virginia, and despite testimony at the trial about her emotional state as a battered woman, the federal judge stated, "The law is the law" and "I think there isn't a soul alive that can understand how any woman or girl would permit some man to beat on her and then continue to live with him and to love him."[11] He also said, "I am just of the opinion I am not willing to say that her actions and conduct were controlled by her love for Peter Hall or her fear of Peter Hall. It went on too long a period to time for that to have existed."[12] In the judge's opinion, Kemba Smith knew what she was doing when she lied. While he recognized that Kemba was not a danger to society nor was she likely ever to pursue these activities again, the purpose of locking Kemba up for almost twenty-five years was to send a message to others like her not to get mixed up with the other Peter Halls out there.

According to Judge Kellam, "Putting the defendant in incarceration will certainly not benefit her tremendously. I think that the purpose of it is, and the only purpose of it, is a deterrent to others, so that everyone knows that if they violate the law, they must pay the penalty."[13] According to the sentence, Kemba Smith would be released from federal prison at the age of forty-eight; her son would be twenty-four.

FIGHTING FOR AN APPEAL

Gus and Odessa Smith spent their entire savings and took out a second mortgage on their home to pay for legal expenses to challenge Kemba's severe sentence. By the time Kemba was sentenced they had spent more than $25,000 in legal fees. After twenty-two years with his company, Gus lost his job as chief financial officer because of the public notoriety about his daughter. Within two years, the couple filed for federal bankruptcy protection to avoid being thrown out onto the street with their young grandson.[14] Gus and Odessa were forced to use public assistance of $131 dollars per month to support him.[15]

When an article about Kemba was featured in a popular news magazine about black America, the response was overwhelming. The magazine was flooded with letters about Kemba. A high school in Dayton, Ohio, began a "Free Kemba" campaign, first writing to Kemba Smith and then to black legislators, Oprah Winfrey, the NAACP, even President Clinton, to advocate for a reduction in her sentence. The youth strongly identified with Kemba, realizing that they too could make a similar mistake. The students formed a club that raised money to support a protest on the steps of the nation's capitol with signs reading "Let the punishment fit the crime," and "24.5 Years, too Harsh."

The students also joined forces with groups mobilized to oppose harsh mandatory sentencing and its impact on young blacks in the United States. Family Against Mandatory Minimums (FAMM) was formed in 1988 by Julie Stewart, sister of a man sentenced to five years in federal prison for growing marijuana plants. Says Julie, "I had enormous outrage at the system. Judges who had been on the bench twenty-five years had been told they were not able to make a judgment because Congress had already issued a sentence."[16] Membership in FAMM now exceeds 36,000 family members and others who have been affected by harsh prison sentences. Particularly vulnerable are young people between the ages of 18 and 25, who constitute over half of those convicted of federal drug trafficking.

In April 1997, the NAACP legal defense asked the federal appeals court in Richmond to vacate, set aside, or correct Kemba's sentence, claiming that the judge had never correctly received expert testimony about her status as a battered women. Judge Kellam declared that in his opinion, he simply did not believe that Kemba was afraid of Peter Hall. Yet traditional notions about self-defense do not always apply to the threatening relationship between a woman and her batterer, which transcends distance and time. Battered women often believe their batterer will hunt them down wherever they hide and are powerful enough to hurt them despite protection from the courts. Sadly, these women are often correct in these perceptions. Males who are unaware of the psychological impact of battering often do not understand the nature of the fear women in this position experience.

The NAACP also maintained there had been legal errors, including a failure by the attorneys for Kemba to adequately inform her of the implications of entering a guilty plea to the drug conspiracy. But a federal district court judge rejected the petition on a technicality even while he stated that, in his own personal opinion, he had a hard time finding this particular application of the law fair.[17] Judge Robert Doumar wrote, "The court is indeed sympathetic to the plight of petitioner Smith. She is the recipient of a truly heavy sentence—an occurrence that has become standard practice under the Sentencing Guidelines. . . . In the opinion of the undersigned, the Guidelines represent a prime example

of how Congress is sometimes unaware of the unintended consequences of its legislation."[18] Yet Judge Doumar refused to grant her a new hearing or reduce her sentence. A federal appeals court upheld the district court ruling, ending the legal avenues within the courts.[19]

ONE LAST HOPE

Kemba's last and final hope was a Presidential pardon from Bill Clinton. The NAACP submitted the petition, and a coalition of more than 650 clergy appealed to him to commute the sentences of Kemba and several others serving lengthy sentences for minor roles in the drug trade. Kemba's supporters included Congresswoman Maxine Waters, who advocated on her behalf by pointing out that before mandatory minimums for crack cocaine went into effect the racial disparity between white and black drug offenders in federal prisons was about 11 percent. After Congress passed stiffer mandatory sentences specifically for crack cocaine, the number of African Americans serving hard time in federal prison soared 49 percent higher than whites.[20] Waters and others kept steady pressure on President Clinton to grant Kemba clemency as one of his last Presidential acts. In his last hours in office, Clinton added Kemba to the 238 federal prisoners granted Presidential pardons. After six-and-a-half years in federal prison, Kemba was reunited with her parents and her 6-year-old son.

Gus and Odessa Smith have been at the heart of this activism. Their anger and despair had been channeled into the hope that one day the sentence would be overturned and the draconian laws would be repealed. On her release, Kemba pledged to apologize publicly for what she had put her parents through and to make them proud of her once more.[21] Kemba Smith is now a student in law school, and spends her time speaking to high school and college students about the dangers of getting involved with drugs.

Case adapted from Reginald Stuart, "Kemba's Nightmare," *Emerge* 7(7) May 1996, pp. 28–48; Libby Copeland, "Kemba Smith's Hard Time," *The Washington Post*, February 13, 2000; Mark Morris, "Pardoned Woman Backs Drug Law Change," *The Kansas City Star*, April 20, 2001; Anthony Lewis, "Abroad at Home: A Christmas Carol," *The New York Time*, December 23, 2000; Reginald Stuart, "Kemba's Nightmare II: Justice Denied," *Emerge* 9(7) May 1998; Betsy Peoples, "Advocates Fight a War on Drug Sentencing," *Emerge* 9 (7) May 1998; Rhonda Chriss Lokeman, "When Smart Women Make Foolish Choices," *Kansas City Star*, April 22, 2001; E. R. Shipp, "Gone Too Far for Too Long," *Daily News*, January 28, 2001.

THINKING CRITICALLY ABOUT THIS CASE

1. Does this punishment fit the crime? Why or why not? Outline the position of the prosecutor and the position of the defense attorney on a just sentence. Which do you agree with and why?

2. If you were given the power to create an alternative sentence, what sentence do you believe would be appropriate and why?

3. Should a judge take into consideration elements of Kemba's past, such as her upbringing, education, the support of her parents, and the community? Why or why not? Should the judge consider her status as a new mother? Why or why not?

4. Should the psychological state of Kemba during her years with Peter be a factor in the sentencing process? Why or why not?

5. If President Clinton had not pardoned Kemba, she would still be in federal prison in Danbury, Connecticut. Write an imaginary letter from Kemba to her son at age 13, explaining the reasons for her incarceration, hoping to guide him in his own future behavior.

6. If you were parents of a college-age student involved with a drug-dealing crowd, would you counsel your child to turn himself or herself in to the authorities as Gus and Odesssa Smith did? Why or why not?

7. Is drug trafficking a "victimless crime" in your opinion? Why or why not? Who are the victims of the drug trade, and who are the offenders?

CHECK OUT THIS CASE

On the Web

Kemba Smith Justice Page, **www.geocities.com/ CapitolHill/Lobby/8899/indexksj.html**
Read more about Kemba Smith.

Families against Mandatory Minimums, **www.famm. org/home.htm**
Check out this Web site to learn about others convicted under mandatory drug sentences and about legislation to restore judicial discretion in sentencing.

On Film

Drug Mules: Women Who Take the "Rap" (30 minutes)
This film exposes the plight of poor uneducated women who are victimized by both drug dealers and the criminal justice system into serving hard time for carrying drugs into the United States. Available from Oz Films, **www.filmakers.com.**

CHAPTER 13

Sentencing and Justice

If the trial is the symbolic center of the criminal justice process where "justice" may be seen and heard, the most dramatic moment comes with pronouncement of the sentence. The question of how to respond to offenders after they have been convicted is the most controversial and troubling decision point for the justice system. Recall the debates about Leona Helmsley's sentence for tax evasion in Chapter 4. Did Leona "deserve" four years in jail? Should she have been imprisoned at all? What is the societal purpose of locking up an old lady? Would it have been better to require her to provide some benefit for society with her vast wealth? Or was the purpose of the sentence to teach her a lesson and send a message to others considering a similar violation of the law? Consider the life sentence given to Paul Lewis Hayes (Chapter 11). What purpose does his lifetime in jail serve for society? Safer streets? Deterring crime? Retribution?

This chapter begins our examination of the fifth stage of the criminal justice process: corrections and punishment. When someone violates a common code of conduct, all societies feel it is important to respond in some fashion. We resent the harmful conduct of drug dealers like Peter Michael Hall and women like Kemba Smith who support and protect them. Our sense of justice leads us to desire some kind of societal reaction toward a person who acts unjustly toward others. And we usually want the response to reflect the seriousness of the crime and the degree of harm it brings to the wider community. In the sentencing of Kemba Smith and Paul Lewis Hayes, we see the awesome power of the criminal justice system to respond to crime by depriving citizens of their liberty for years, sometimes their entire lifetime, and in the case of capital punishment, even life itself.

Yet how we respond to those who have violated our criminal laws is also a reflection of who we are and what we value as a society. Winston Churchill observed that "The mood and temper of the public in regard to the treatment of crime and criminals is one of the most unfailing tests of the civilization of any country . . . the treatment of crime and criminal mark and measure the stored-up strength of a nation, and are a sign and proof of the living virtue in it."[22] At the time of the Salem witch trials (Chapter 1), an acceptable punishment was to hang people in public or crush them beneath giant rocks. Today we no longer permit such painful methods of punishment, and even attempt to put people to death in a "humane" and painless way through lethal injection. The use of incarceration has replaced corporal punishment and restitution as the main response to crime. Is this more "humane" than earlier modes of punishment? Why have we invested so much scarce public resources to warehouse millions of Americans who have committed crimes?

This chapter examines the history of criminal sentencing, shifting sensibilities about forms of punishment, and the varying rationales used to justify different responses to crime.[23] What is the purpose of criminal sentencing? Are we hoping to rehabilitate the offender? Avenge society? Deter others from crime? Teach our children a lesson? Heal the victim? Repair the damage caused by crime? Prevent future crime? Often there is more than a single aim of sentencing, but usually one or two have priority over others.

This chapter also looks at who in the justice system is charged with the responsibility of handing down a just sentence. Who determines the appropriate sentence for a given individual who has been convicted of a crime? Is it the judge, jury, prosecutor, probation officer, prison warden, parole board, psychiatrist, politician, victim, or community? Who should play this crucial role? Should the victim have a significant voice in the sentencing process? What about the community? And what about the case of drug crimes such as Kemba's? Who are the "victims" in the crime of drug trafficking?

We close the chapter by looking carefully at the specific rationale for the punishment of Kemba Smith. Kemba was a casualty in the war on drugs. By voluntarily engaging in the drug trade with her boyfriend, Kemba Smith made herself a target of the tactics the government uses to fight that war. The purpose of her punishment was deterrence: stiff sentences for people who aid and abet drug dealers will deter people from engaging in the drug trade. We will take a careful look at our current societal response to the crime of illegal drug trafficking and assess the impact of the current "war on drugs" on minority citizens and communities.

FIVE GOALS OF SENTENCING

There are five recognized philosophies of punishment that guide our response to criminal conduct: retribution, incapacitation, deterrence, rehabilitation, and restitution. Common everyday expressions with which we are all familiar capture some of the widely held sentiments about how offenders should be treated and why. To a certain extent, the modern criminal justice system embraces all of these goals. Yet these goals also compete with one another, and throughout history the justice system has generally embraced one or two above the rest. Let us examine each one in turn.

Retribution

retribution: sentencing philosophy that prioritizes punishment commensurate to the seriousness of the offense.

"You do the crime, you do the time" expresses a philosophy of "just deserts."[24] The infliction of some type of suffering or pain on an offender is a just and legitimate response, provided it is proportionate to the degree of suffering he or she chose to inflict on a victim. A crime violates our sense of "justice." A criminal act imposes some kind of injury on a victim and on the rest of the community. This injury evokes feelings of anger and outrage. In most of us, to some degree, an unjust action provokes the desire for vengeance. We feel that some equivalent action must be taken toward the individual in order to correct the imbalance created by the wrongdoing, and even more important, we feel entitled to inflict suffering upon that purpose. In fact, we feel we are in the right and it is our obligation to impose that kind of suffering. This is the essence of the goal of retribution: the retaliatory infliction of harm back upon the offender. We punish in order to avenge the harm suffered by the victim.

Biblical passages from the Old Testament are often cited in support of the goal of retribution. *Leviticus* (24:17–22) states, "When one man strikes another and kills him, he shall be put to death," and *Exodus* (21:23–24) states, "Whosoever sheds blood shall have his blood be shed. A life for life; eye for an eye; tooth for tooth; hand for hand, foot for foot, burning for burning, wound for wound." Under Mosaic law, the punishment that should fall on the offender is what was done to his or her neighbor.

The principle of an "eye for an eye" expresses a retributive goal in response to wrongdoing, but it also calls for proportionality and moderation in claiming revenge. The Biblical passage recognizes that the human desire for vengeance can itself become unjust. When punishment goes too far, it is no longer just. We need only to look at our own history to know that the emotion of vengeance often leads to a cycle of violence or blood feud when the victim exacts excessive revenge which spurs the "victim" to retaliate in turn. Most wars are fought in the name of "justice" for both sides.

Retribution through legal punishment is justified only in equal measure to the crime. The Biblical passage tells us that if an eye has been lost, it is only an eye that one is entitled to claim, not the life of the offender. If it is a life, it is only one life in response and not the death and destruction of an entire family or village. In ancient times, the principle of retribution was an important principle of regulation, designed to prevent war between families or clans if one member committed a crime against another.

In modern times the legitimate act of retribution may only be performed by the state, in part to prevent vigilante violence on the part of private citizens. Committing harm against a person, even in response to an illegal act, is illegal. Only the state holds the legitimate right to punish. Under the modern system of administration, the state imposes proportionate retributive punishment on the offender in the name of the victim and in the name of society as well. Due process protections exist to ensure that the process of accusation and conviction is fair and truthful, and only then is the state justified in inflicting harm in proportion to the harm of the crime.

The judge who imposes sentencing under a retributive philosophy seeks to create "just" punishment proportionate to the crime, the culpability of the offender, and the extent of the harmfulness of the criminal behavior. Victim impact statements are submitted to the judge at the time of sentencing to describe the suffering endured by the victims and their families and to assist the judge in determining the extent of punishment under a retributive philosophy. The goal of the sentence is to do unto the offenders in equal measure what they have done unto others.

Incapacitation

"Lock 'em up and throw away the key" suggests that society needs to be protected from persons who are dangerous to others. The goal of incapacitation seeks to protect society by physically restraining wrongdoers so they are unable to commit offenses again. We might lock an offender up in order to make it impossible for him to repeat his behavior, or we might physically disable the offender in some way that will make it impossible for him to repeat his behavior in the future—through chemical castration, for example. Or we might place an electronic bracelet on his ankle that monitors his every movement twenty-four hours a day and signals an alarm if he leaves a designated restricted area. All of these sanctions are designed to keep the public safe from that offender by literally taking away his capacity to commit crime.

The death penalty is the ultimate form of incapacitation. We might justify the use of capital punishment on the grounds that it achieves this goal: once we have put anyone to death, we can be certain the person will never hurt anyone again. It is one clearly recognized benefit of capital punishment over life in prison, which still holds open the possibility of harm inflicted by the offender on fellow prisoners.

Today, our predominant means of incapacitation is through imprisonment.[25] When we talk about "getting people off the streets," we acknowledge that our goal is to protect

incapacitation: elimination of the capacity to commit future crimes in society, usually through incarceration.

society. Habitual offenders, like Paul Lewis Hayes, are locked up for life on the theory that they have demonstrated that they cannot or will not stop their criminal conduct. Protection of the community from dangerous offenders is a key criterion for locking people in prison, particularly in institutions where little attempt is made to provide any treatment, counseling, or education inside the facility. The warehousing of prisoners, at the very least, incapacitates offenders by preventing them from committing more crimes against members of the community during the time they are locked up in prison.

Deterrence

"Next time they will think twice," or "We need to teach them a lesson," expresses the belief that a penal sentence will prevent or deter a person from repeating the same behavior in the future.[26] Under the goal of deterrence, we hope to influence the future conduct of a person who is tempted to commit crime. The goal of deterrence is to prevent future wrongdoing, not through physical restraint, but by influencing the mind of the offender and other potential offenders. This is, along with retribution, the most widely held justification for punishment today. We believe that by imposing some kind of punishment on a person who commits a wrongful act, we will influence that person's choices in the future. When the next opportunity to do crime arises, we expect the person will recall the punishment and choose to refrain from committing the crime.

Specific deterrence refers to the effect of the sanction on the particular individual who committed the crime. When we punish an individual in the expectation that next time he or she will behave differently, we are attempting to attain the goal of specific deterrent. **General deterrence** is the effect we hope the punishment will have on others who have yet to commit the crime. We use the expression "send a message" to refer to the goal of general deterrence. The goal of general deterrence is that we punish offenders to prevent others from committing crimes. By making the "costs" of crime (in the form of punishment) greater than the "benefits" or rewards from violating the law, we hope to enjoy an overall effect of reducing the amount of crime in the wider society. The person who is punished is made an "example" to others of what will happen if they choose to commit crime.

The goal of deterrence was first articulated in the eighteenth century, as the image of man as a rational actor began to gain dominance among intellectuals and policy makers.[27] Crime was no longer seen as an act of sin brought on by the devil or the result of innate evil on the part of the criminal, but a calculated act designed to bring about maximum reward. By this logic, Enlightenment philosophers reasoned that it made sense to raise the cost of crime above its rewards. Once people experienced the reality that "crime does not pay," they would stop committing it. The goal of deterrence is to reduce the overall amount of crime in society by raising the stakes for doing the crime.

Rehabilitation

"They're sick, they need help . . . " implies that the purpose of sentencing is to address the psychological, sociological, or personal problems that led to the crime. The goal of rehabilitation seeks to reform the offender through the interventions provided by the "correctional" system.[28] Like deterrence, the goal of rehabilitation has its eye on the future behavior of the convicted offender. By offering to the offender some form of treatment, training, counseling, or education, it is believed that whatever led the person to commit crime in the first place can be altered. The goal of rehabilitation is to improve the offender, to transform him or her and correct the flaw that led him down the path to criminal conduct. Most states call their agencies responsible for operating prisons and criminal sanctions *correctional departments*, reflecting one of the key underlying philosophies of modern punishment.

The discipline of corrections is closely allied to a medical model of criminal offending. Rooted in the nineteenth-century science of positivism, in which it was be-

deterrence: imposition of punishment in order to discourage the commission of future crimes by the offender and others.

specific deterrence: imposition of punishment to discourage an individual from committing crimes in the future. Also known as special or individual deterrence.

general deterrence: imposition of punishment in order to set an example to others contemplating crime.

rehabilitation: the process of changing the attitudes and behavior of offenders through training, education, treatment, or vocational programming to produce law-abiding conduct in the future.

lieved that all effects have a cause we can understand through science, all human behavior including criminal conduct is believed to be the result of environmental, psychological, or biological forces acting on the offender.[29] Just as disease has a cause in bacteria or viruses, so too does social deviance have a cause in "pathologies" of social life. These pathologies include negative nuclear families, dysfunctional communities, lack of education, poor diet and nutrition, brain injuries, fetal alcohol syndrome, child abuse, and so forth. While the causes vary and may differ from individual to individual, the goal of criminal justice sanctioning should be to correct the "root causes" in order to return the offender to society able to lead a productive and law-abiding life.

Restitution

"Make amends and say you are sorry" focuses on the victim and on the need for the offender to restore what was lost—financially, emotionally, or symbolically—directly to those who suffered the loss. The principle of restitution is as fundamental to the human experience as the emotion of revenge. When something has been broken or taken away, the goal of restitution demands that it be fixed or returned. The money should be paid back, the broken window repaired, the graffiti on the fence wiped clean, the stolen property returned.

Today, the state collects **fines** from offenders and dispenses a tiny portion of this to victim compensation funds. In the "golden age of the victim," before the rise of state systems of justice, criminal sentences centered around compensatory punishments that focused attention on restoration of the victim.[30] In addition to some degree of entitlement to express revenge against the offender, victims were offered restitution for their losses. The community required offenders, as well as their extended family, to pay victims back. Early legal systems spelled out the precise amount to redress different types of wrongs. In Roman law, for example, thieves were required to pay victims double restitution unless the property was found inside their house, in which case they had to pay triple damages.

The principle of restitution in early law operated in violent crimes as well as property crimes. Under Mosaic law, if two men were involved in a fight with the result that one person was badly injured but did not die, the perpetrator was required to pay for the loss of the injured man's time and support his family until he was thoroughly healed.[31] Some legal codes spelled out the precise compensation for different types of injuries: in the laws of eighth- and ninth-century Anglo-Saxons, if a man knocked out the front teeth of another man he had to pay 8 shillings; if it was an eye tooth, he had to only pay 4 shillings; but if he knocked out a molar, which is far more valuable for chewing, he owed 15 shillings.[32]

The payment of a death fine was found in many pre-Western and non-Western codes of law, requiring the murderer and his kin to compensate the victim's family for the loss of the murdered relative. Among the ancient Germans, homicide was atoned for by compensation in cattle and sheep to assuage the family and prevent the start of a dangerous spiral of retaliatory violence. In Anglo-Saxon times, the law stated that if anyone slayed a man he is subject to vengeance unless he compensated the family within twelve months the full worth of the man's estate; the amount of compensation depended on the age, rank, gender, and prestige of the injured party.[33]

Restitution is not only about the material loss suffered by the victim but also includes various forms of emotional and psychological restitution. Recall the Elaine Serrell Myer's family desire for justice in Chapter 6. They knew there was no way the offender could bring Elaine back to life. Yet they wanted the offender to take positive actions in her life that would, to some degree, give them the emotional satisfaction that their loved one was honored and had not died in vain. Recall the sentiments of the Hattori family (Chapter 5). Above all else, they desired an honest act of taking moral responsibility and expression of genuine remorse from Peairs. The emotional acts of

restitution: obligation on the part of an offender to repay the victim or the community with money, services, or symbolic gestures commensurate with the harm caused.

fine: penalty imposed by a court requiring the offender to pay a specified sum of money to the court.

repentance, remorse, and apology that restore a victim's faith in humanity are a significant element of the goal of restitution.

RANGE OF MODERN SENTENCES

The modern criminal justice system is an offender-focused system that relies on the state to formulate criminal laws, specify sentences, and administer sanctions. The victim is no longer central to that process. Nor are many of the premodern forms of penalties in use today: offenders cannot be paraded down the main square, tarred and feathered, or hoisted on a scaffold to be stoned by the community. At the time of the Salem witch trials there was a host of penal sanctions, such as whipping posts, ducking stools, branding, and stoning, which are no longer a part of our justice system.[34] Nor can a judge order an offender to care for a victim's family for the rest of his or her life. The range of penalties available to criminal justice practitioners is established by legal codes that reflect shifting social norms about the nature of legitimate criminal justice sanctioning.

Modern sanctions range from the imposition of death through incarceration in various forms and of various lengths, to a host of community-based sanctions and financial sanctions.[35] Thirty-seven states and the federal government administer capital punishment for specific offenses. Between 1930, when the federal government began to collect data on executions, and the end of 1998, 4,359 people had been legally executed. Sixty-seven percent of these executions took place in six Southern states: Texas, Florida, Virginia, Louisiana, Georgia, and South Carolina.[36]

The use of incarceration as a form of punishment is largely a nineteenth-century invention. To an extent, the shift toward incarceration as the predominant form of punishment was the result of a change in the attitudes of society toward physical violence.[37] Over the course of centuries, modern societies abandoned corporal punishments of whipping, beatings, branding, mutilation, and torture in favor of imprisonment.[38] The "spectacle of suffering" was no longer socially tolerable in public, and punishment began to disappear from public spaces to behind the prison wall.

In the past twenty years, the United States has seen an explosive growth in the use of incarceration as a form of punishment. The number of people in prison and jail increased sixfold from about 330,000 in 1970 to more than 2 million by the end of 2000.[39] The prison population quadrupled just between 1980 and 1997.[40] As a whole, the United States has an incarceration rate of about 699 inmates per 100,000 residents, the highest rate of incarceration in the entire world.[41] This rate is between five to eight times higher than in Canada or Europe. Texas was the state with the highest rate of incarceration in 1996, reaching a staggering 717 people behind bars for every 100,000 residents in that state.[42]

Offenders may also be given split sentences that combine periods of incarceration followed by periods of community-based supervision on probation or parole, or intermittent sentences that combine periods of freedom, for instance, during the work week, with periods of confinement over the weekend. Boot camps for juveniles and other less serious offenders became an alternative form of incarceration in the 1980s, combining a shorter period of incarceration with intensive military discipline and correctional treatment.[43]

A sentence of probation keeps an offender in the community but may carry a wide range of conditions. House arrest accompanied by some form of electronic surveillance maintains an individual within his or her own housing but severely restricts his or her movements beyond the home. Conditions of probation or parole may include hours of community work service, mandatory drug treatment, mandatory counseling, anger management or drunk driving classes. In addition, offenders may be ordered to pay a fine to the court or pay restitution to a victim compensation fund or directly to an individual victim.

WHO DECIDES?

The parties who determine a criminal sanction range from legislatures that write the criminal laws to judges, prosecutors, parole boards, juries, probation officers, victims, and communities.[44] There are three key sentencing models which emphasize discretion of different players in the criminal justice system.

The **judicial model of sentencing** relies on the wisdom and experience of the judge to craft a sentence that fits a given offender within the parameters set by the statutory code. When legislatures craft a criminal statute, the principle of legality requires that the punishment for violating the code be specified in the statute. But the scope of legal sanctions for a given offense may be extremely broad, ranging from probation to many years in prison. Statutes vary widely on the latitude of sanctions for a given crime, but in this model, it is the judge who has the legal responsibility to set a specific sentence for a given offender.

It is the responsibility of probation officers in most jurisdictions to prepare **presentencing reports** based on interviews with offenders and their families.[45] The purpose of the **presentence investigation (PSI)** is to help the judge select an appropriate sentence within the statutory framework. In some jurisdictions, a PSI is mandatory for all felonies; in others it may be done at the request of the judge. Presentencing investigations are rarely conducted for misdemeanor offenses and are generally required in cases where probation is being considered as a sanction.

The quality of reports varies: in some jurisdictions the report is highly detailed, including extensive information about the offender's past history, including facts about his or her childhood, current family life, extended family, work relationships, and so forth; in other jurisdictions the facts in the report do not extend much beyond what is known about the offender by his prior record and details of the current offense. PSIs have been known to contain subjective impressions and opinions about the offender, which are sometimes based on racial stereotypes, baseless rumors, or unsupported inferences about the offender's personality and future criminality.

The PSI also contains a recommendation for sentencing based on the information gathered in the investigation. In theory, this recommendation and background information is intended as a guide to the judge to assist him or her in making the sentencing decision. In practice, studies have found a high correspondence between the recommendation in the PSI and the judicial sentence.[46] In one study in California, researchers found that judges accepted 86 percent of the recommendations made by probation officers in PSIs.[47] Thus, in the judicial model of sentencing, probation officers play a substantial role in the sentencing decision.

The **administrative model of sentencing** depends on parole boards, prison wardens, and other administrators of the correctional system to determine when an offender has completed his or her sentence. An offender may be sentenced by a judge to a term in prison bounded by a minimum and a maximum length of time. The actual period served is "indeterminate," with the release date determined by the professionals in the correctional system. Offenders enter the prison system not knowing when they will be released. Their release date will depend on their behavior in the correctional system and their ability to demonstrate that they have been rehabilitated.

The **legislative model of sentencing** fixes specific sentences through mandatory sentences for specific crimes. As we have seen with habitual offenders acts, these statutes require a precise sentence if the person is convicted. The judge plays little or no role in the sentencing process. Mandatory minimum sentencing statutes did not eliminate or even reduce discretion in the criminal justice system. These laws may tie the hands of judges in determining sentences for convicted offenders, but they increase the discretionary power of prosecutors, who may choose to charge an individual under the mandatory statutes or not. In the investigation and conviction of drug offenses, prosecutors

judicial model of sentencing: sentencing decisions that rely on the broad discretion of the judge to craft the individual sentence within parameters set by statute.

presentence investigation/ report: an investigation and summary report of the background of a convicted offender, prepared to help the judge decide on an appropriate sentence for the individual.

administrative model of sentencing: use of parole boards, prison wardens, and other correctional officials to determine when an offender is to be granted conditional release from incarceration.

legislative model of sentencing: the setting of mandatory sentences for specific crimes established in the criminal statutes passed by legislative bodies.

often reduce charges if the suspect is willing to cooperate by becoming an informant or is able to forfeit substantial property assets to the justice department.

In addition to these three sources of sentencing authority, there is also the power of governors and Presidents to alter or negate sentences of convicted criminals through the **executive clemency** power to pardon or forgive or commute a sentence to a reduced form. President Clinton, as we saw, commuted Kemba's sentence to time already served. Executive authority is usually one of the last resorts for inmates on death row seeking to commute their death sentence to life imprisonment.

The simple fact is that we cannot eliminate discretionary decision making from the criminal justice system. The decision making of criminal justice personnel is an essential and necessary element of the justice system. We can change how and when in the justice process discretionary decisions are made, and we can change who has discretion over a given part of the process, but we cannot eliminate human decision making and judgment from the justice system.

Sentencing Models and the Goals of Punishment

The predominance of one of these models in the U.S. criminal justice system corresponds with the prevalence of one of the five goals of sentencing. When the primary goal of sentencing is retribution, there is an emphasis on determinate sentencing handed down by either judges or legislatures. **Determinate sentencing systems** specify a precise sentence for the crime, whether it is set by legislatures or judges at the time of sentence, hence the saying, "you do the crime, you do the time." Adhering to the goal of retribution and deterrence, determinate sentencing is calibrated to fit the crime as retribution, and it is believed to offer a predictable consequence for wrongdoing. According to the theory of deterrence, when punishment is swift, certain, and proportionate to the crime, rational human beings respond by refraining from crime.

Indeterminate sentencing systems function differently. A judge will set a maximum amount of time to be served as well as a minimum, but the actual amount of time served will depend on the individual's conduct and reformation within the correctional system. From the end of the nineteenth century until the late 1970s, most state criminal justice systems operated on an indeterminate sentencing structure. Indeterminate sentencing is compatible with the goal of rehabilitation: the sentence is individualized to fit the criminal rather than the crime.

The theory of rehabilitation suggests that if correctional systems are able to "correct" or cure the offender, it is best left up to the practitioners of the correctional system to determine which individuals have been reformed and can be safely paroled to the community and which ones need to remain behind bars. Prisoners are able to earn early release from prison for earned and statutory "good time" conduct inside the facility. Indeterminate sentencing has sometimes been called "bark and bite sentencing": the bark is the threat of the maximum, the bite is the minimum. No one in the system expects the maximum to be served or even believes it is in society's best interest. The threat of a long sentence hanging over inmates is seen as a powerful motivational tool, inducing them to cooperate with the prison regime and to participate in correctional treatment and programing. Only the worst inmates, those who are so angry, out of control, hostile, or unmanageable, are retained to serve their full sentence. The carrot of early release is seen as a key motivational and management tool for correctional systems.

The return to determinate sentencing, largely through a rise in mandatory sentencing statutes, the abolition of parole in some jurisdictions, and the passage of "truth in sentencing laws" in the past twenty years, has been driven by discontent with the judicial model, which resulted in wide **sentencing disparities** for similar offenses.[48] The era of judicial discretion, which allowed one judge to give an offender convicted of a rape twenty-five years in prison, and a different judge to give an offender convicted under the same statute only two years' probation, led to a growing political movement to

executive clemency: the power to pardon (forgive) a criminal conviction or commute a sentence, held by the chief executive officer.

determinate sentencing: imposition of a fixed or set amount of time in prison.

indeterminate sentencing: imposition of an unspecified amount of time in prison somewhere between a statutory minimum and maximum term.

sentencing disparities: imposition of widely different sentences for offenders convicted of the same offense.

reduce judicial discretion in sentencing. Critics argued that unbridled judicial discretion led to excessive leniency for some and excessive harshness for others. Critics similarly complained that parole boards operated in a discriminatory and inconsistent manner. Whites were more likely to make parole than blacks and other minorities when they faced largely white parole boards.

One means of reducing discretion is fixed-term or flat sentences, which became increasingly common in the 1970s.[49] One form of these sentences is the **mandatory minimum** sentence, which establishes a required minimum length of time an offender must serve in prison. These statutes have been common for armed, violent, repeat, or drug offenders for decades, but have now become common for property offenses as well. For example, in Illinois, the burglary of a residence carries with it a mandatory minimum of four years' incarceration.

The Habitual Criminal Act of Kentucky is similar to what we are now referring to as **"three strikes"** laws. Although some states enacted these types of laws decades ago, state legislatures passed a wave of these forms of laws during the 1990s. Between 1994 and 1995, twenty-four states adopted some kind of "three strikes" law, although there is a wide spectrum of offenses that qualify as "strikes" and some of these statutes actually require only two strikes while others specify four.[50]

Truth in sentencing laws are another means to limit the discretion of judges and parole boards. "Good behavior" time allowances and overcrowding of institutions have led to the release of many offenders before the termination of their sentence. Driven by statistics that show the average felon actually serves less than half of his or her sentence, these laws mandate that convicted offenders must serve most or all of their sentence before being released.

Sentencing guidelines were developed by specialized sentencing commissions to rein in the discretion of judges and provide some consistency to the sentencing process.[51] Sentencing guidelines create a standardized set of penalty options, specifying legitimate criteria based on the severity of the offense and the offender's past criminal history for varying the sentence. They are developed through an examination of the sentencing norms of the judges themselves. Judges are able to compute a score for an offense, add or deduct set points for mitigating or aggravating circumstances, prior criminal offenses, and specified features of the offender's current home life. Out of this mathematical accounting the judge comes up with a specific penalty according to a prearranged formula. The formula provides a **presumptive sentence,** which is the expected sentence for this crime and this offender. If the judge wishes to depart from the presumptive sentence in a given case, then he or she must provide written reasons for being more lenient or more harsh in sentencing.

DECIDING DEATH: THE ISSUE OF CAPITAL PUNISHMENT

At the time of the Salem witch trials, the execution of offenders was a public affair for all to witness as the victim suffered a torturous demise. By 1845 most states had outlawed public hangings and replaced them with discreet hangings behind prison walls. Today, the execution is a sanitized bureaucratic procedure carried out in the middle of the night in the deepest recesses of the penal system. Clinical, dispassionate, and efficient, the modern execution, in its effort to hide the cruelty, may intensify it.

The use of capital punishment has declined as part of the overall modern shift away from brutal and violent forms of punishment. Many nations have abolished the death penalty altogether, although it persists in about ninety-five countries around the world. The United States is the only advanced democratic nation among the list of nations to sanction the use of death as punishment for ordinary crimes.[52] The list includes China, Cuba, Iran, Iraq, Libya, and Russia.

mandatory minimum: the minimum penalty that must be imposed and carried out for all offenders convicted of a given offense.

"three strikes" laws: statutes that mandate life in prison for offenders convicted for a third time.

truth in sentencing laws: statutes that require that most or all of the sentence actually be served.

sentencing guidelines: standardized set of penalty options based on key characteristics of the offense and offender.

presumptive sentence: the expected sentence for a given crime and a given offender prescribed by the sentencing guidelines.

capital punishment: death by legal execution.

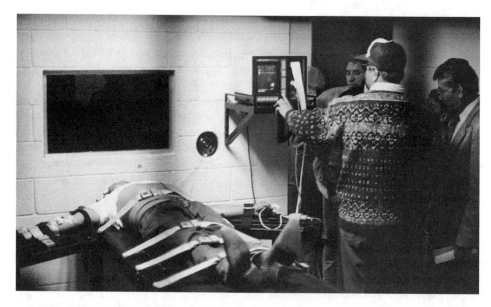

Corrections officials test equipment and rehearse procedure for a modern execution. Capital punishment in contemporary America is a clinical and dispassionate act carried out by correctional personnel who seek to execute the condemned in a manner that is professional, efficient, and painless.

In 1972, the Supreme Court ruling in *Furman* v. *Georgia*[53] called a halt to executions in this country by declaring that capital punishment as it was then applied violated the Eighth Amendment prohibition against cruel and unusual punishment. In a 5–4 decision, the Court did not declare the death penalty itself unconstitutional, but declared the absence of clear standards a violation of the Eighth Amendment. Without standards for juries and judges to guide them in deciding when the death penalty is appropriate, punishment by death was tantamount to being "struck by lightning." The justices also found that the lack of clear guidelines resulted in blatant discrimination against minorities, who were more likely to be given the death penalty than nonminorities.

In 1976, in *Greggs* v. *Georgia*,[54] the Supreme Court effectively reinstated the use of capital punishment by approving a state statute that addressed the concerns expressed in the *Furman* decision. In the wake of *Furman*, new death penalty laws were passed by thirty-five states. States that enacted a mandatory death penalty for a particularly heinous crime were seen as meeting the Constitutional standard for fairness and consistency, although a mandatory statute for the crime of rape was later struck down. Also deemed Constitutional were statutes that offered a **bifurcated trial** process and **guided discretion** statutes.

The bifurcated process established a two-part proceeding in which a separate sentencing hearing was held after the trial to establish guilt. The jury would then hear arguments from the prosecution and the defense as to the specific reasons why this particular crime deserved or did not merit a sentence of death. Guided discretion statutes are laws that specify the aggravating or mitigating circumstances that juries and judges should consider in making their decision. As long as the jury or judge focuses on the particular circumstances of the crime, there no longer is a wanton use of the death penalty and its use meets Constitutional standards. The first execution under the new rules took place in 1977. Twenty years later, 358 executions had occurred, over 100 of them in the state of Texas.[55] Over three thousand inmates are sitting on "death row" in various states.

The justification for the death penalty is often deterrence. The argument is that the death penalty saves lives because it deters the crime of homicide. Research shows no ev-

bifurcated trial: Constitutional requirement that the imposition of the death penalty be subject to a separate hearing after the adjudication of guilt or innocence has taken place.

guided discretion statutes: capital statutes that specify the mitigating and aggravating circumstances juries should consider in the penalty phase of a capital trial.

idence that there is a deterrent effect to the imposition of capital punishment. Indeed, on the contrary, some argue that the use of the death penalty by the state has a **brutalization effect,** increasing the incidence of homicide rather than lowering it.[56]

Other justifications include incapacitation and retribution. A person who is executed is incapable of ever harming another person, even behind the walls of a prison. Life imprisonment still leaves open the possibility of escape or inside violence, so the most secure form of protection is execution. The retributive rationale rests on the simple proposition that the taking of life in a heinous manner requires an equal and proportionate response. By embracing the use of capital punishment, society acknowledges the sanctity of life.

Opponents to the death penalty reject the belief that the way to show respect for life is to sanction state murder. Opponents, sometimes including family members of murder victims, believe that their personal or religious values prohibit the taking of a human life except in self-defense. Members of Murder Victims Families for Reconciliation, an anti-death penalty group of family members, asks the state not to execute people in their name. Critics of the death penalty point out that the death sentence is the ultimate rejection of the belief in redemption or rehabilitation.

The use of the death penalty has long been criticized for being discriminatory, and the evidence strongly suggests that this remains as true today as it was in the past. There are few women and few middle-class people sitting on death row. Since 1988, over 40 percent of those under the sentence of death were black, and nearly all the people on death row are too poor to pay for private counsel.[57] Many on death row were represented by poorly prepared defense counsel who failed to adequately present mitigating factors to the jury or who failed to investigate witnesses and gather evidence that might have acquitted their clients. Nowhere is the inequality in legal representation more important than when a person is facing death.

Data clearly show the continued influence of racism in the use of the death penalty. It appears that the race of the victim as well as of the offender strongly affects whether the death penalty is imposed. Statistically, black offenders who kill white victims are more likely to be executed than any other offender–victim combination. Historically in the United States, of more than 16,000 documented executions, only thirty have involved a white person sentenced to death for killing a black person. In recent times, the NAACP confirmed a similar pattern: between 1977 and 1995, of the 289 executions that took place, 4 involved white offenders who killed black victims, while 94 involved black offenders who killed white victims.[58]

One of the key arguments marshaled against the death penalty is the irreversibility of the sentence. The criminal justice system is notorious for making errors. Even a perfect system cannot be infallible. Mistakes will be made. The justice system fails to offer equal protection of due process to those who are poor, minority, or otherwise marginal to society. Eyewitnesses lie, prosecutors withhold evidence, informers misinform, and juries make mistakes. But once the death penalty has been carried out, nothing can be done to redress a wrongful conviction.

In 2000, the pro–death penalty Republican governor of Illinois became the first governor to declare a moratorium on the use of the death penalty, after thirteen people on death row in his state were found to be innocent.[59] The science of **DNA testing** has begun to offer reliable evidence to exonerate a growing number of convicted individuals serving prison sentences, including a number who are on death row. A nationwide study found over four hundred wrongful convictions in death penalty cases since 1992.[60] Currently only seven states give inmates the right to have their DNA tested, and in four states it is only in cases where the offender is facing the death penalty or life imprisonment.[61]

Proponents of the death penalty often decry the lengthy proceedings and appeals for death row inmates, because they believe that executions must be swift to have a true deterrent effect. The average death row inmate may sit on death row for as long as ten

brutalization effect: the theory that capital punishment contributes to greater violence in society, by increasing the tolerance for violence in society.

DNA testing: the forensic use of DNA (deoxyribonucleic acid), the genetic blueprint unique to each living organism.

years. The time spent on death row is far more dehumanizing and alienating than the worst experiences of the general inmate. Inmates on death row are isolated from the rest of the prison and from each other. They are rarely allowed to participate in any programs or engage in many recreational activities. Their time is spent alone with the knowledge of their future walk down that "green mile." In the words of Albert Camus,

> Many laws consider a pre-meditated crime more serious than a crime of pure violence. . . . For there to be equivalence, the death penalty would have to punish a criminal who had warned his victim of the date at which he would inflict a horrible death on him and who, from that moment onward, had confined him at his mercy for months. Such a monster is not encountered in private life.[62]

How do Americans feel about the death penalty? Public opinion polls show that today nearly 80 percent of Americans favor the death penalty, as compared to 59 percent in 1973 and only 42 percent in 1966.[63] According to these polls, lawmakers and judges infer that the conscience of our society finds the imposition of death by the state morally justifiable and acceptable.

But what does public support in opinion polls really mean? Would Americans be willing to witness the imposition of death as people did in the eighteenth century? Would the majority of citizens themselves choose the death penalty for a given offender if they were sitting on a jury? Sister Helen Prejean, who serves as a spiritual advisor to death row inmates and who has witnessed many executions, believes that most Americans would "vomit" if they were forced to witness an execution.[64] In her view, we carry out the executions at the darkest hour of midnight in the deepest bowels of the prison system because we, as a society, are not comfortable with the sight of killing a person "in cold blood." Some opinion polls and research show that support for the death penalty diminishes substantially when people are offered an alternative of life imprisonment without parole and required restitution to the victim's family.[65] Justice Thurgood Marshall believed that public opinion about capital punishment was a reliable indicator of public opinion only if the public was well informed about alternatives.

THE JUSTIFICATION FOR KEMBA'S SENTENCE

Kemba's sentence of twenty-four-and-a-half years with no eligibility for parole shocked her parents and other members of the community unfamiliar with the shift in sentencing structures toward determinate forms of sentencing. The human and social price of this sentence is astounding.[66] In addition to the estimated cost of about $30,000 per year to keep Kemba in prison, there are the many hidden financial costs. Who would raise her little boy? Kemba would earn nothing during those years in prison to help contribute to the cost of raising her son or for her own future. Nor would she contribute to the tax base as a productive member of society. When she was released at age 48, her earning capacity would be severely diminished by her lengthy period of incarceration and her status as an ex-con.

For the wider community, there is both the financial loss of a constructive taxpaying member of the workforce during her prime earning years between 24 and 48 and the added cost of her incarceration as she sits in forced idleness behind bars. Gus and Odessa, two productive and contributing citizens within the community, would now have to raise their grandson. They were forced to declare bankruptcy to pay for legal fees, and Gus lost his job because of the negative publicity. Studies estimate that for each person incarcerated, $12,000 worth of economic activity is removed from the local economy. Kemba's incarceration not only hurt her immediate family but also the neighborhood where she would buy her morning coffee, groceries, have her hair done, hire babysitters, or have her clothes cleaned.[67]

The financial costs are high, but we should not neglect to account for the human cost of this sentence, which affected not only Kemba but also her young son, who would grow up with a mother in prison. What would he tell his friends and teachers about his mother as he went to school and people asked questions? How would he maintain a relationship with her over the long years of separation? Gus and Odessa could look forward to twenty-four years of depressing visits to the federal prison as they struggled to raise their grandson and keep him connected to his incarcerated mother. Like so many parents of incarcerated men and women, Gus and Odessa would not enjoy the sympathy and support of the wider community: having an incarcerated daughter would be a hidden shame they would most likely keep to themselves.

Given all these costs to the taxpayer, to the community, to Kemba's family, and to Kemba herself, what was the justification for this sentence? What did society gain by imposing a sentence of this magnitude for a crime of this nature? What was the rationale that led the federal government to imprison a young woman for a quarter of a century for playing a small part in the criminal activity of her faithless boyfriend?

The reasoning behind the judge's sentence of Kemba was clearly articulated and rooted in the "deterrence" philosophy that has dominated sentencing in the past twenty years. The judge stated that the sole benefit of her incarceration was to send a message to other young girls not to trust men like Peter Michael Hall. The prosecutor, in asking for the sentence, had a different rationale: drug dealing was bad and the source of much harm and suffering in the community. Kemba chose to support the man she loved despite knowledge of his activities. She chose to lie to federal investigators on several occasions. The sentence was a pure act of retribution: you do the crime, you do the time.

Getting Tough on Drug Crimes

The mid-1970s saw a shift away from rehabilitation as a justification for punishment and toward the "just deserts" philosophy of punishment, which prioritized the twin goals of retribution and deterrence over the previously dominant philosophy of rehabilitation. In the next chapter, on prisons, we will examine why there is such a strong association between rehabilitation and prisons, but for most of the twentieth century the goal of rehabilitation was an ideal for correctional professionals and systems. In the late 1970s, a growing sentiment emerged that "rehabilitation was dead." An article written by Robert Martinson entitled "What Works? Questions and Answers about Prison Reform" signaled a growing conviction among politicians that "nothing worked" to reform criminals.[68] Although Martinson along with others published a book-length survey of correctional treatment only a year later and tried to publish yet another article highlighting those interventions that did work as well as those that did not,[69] the message that reached the public and legislators was that rehabilitation was a lost cause.

Ironically, one of the major impulses for the reforms of the 1970s came from civil rights activists with urgent concerns about racial and class disparities resulting from the broad discretion of judges and parole boards under the guise of rehabilitation. These activists lobbied heavily for a shift toward the determinate sentence to help dismantle the discretion that had opened the door to unfair race and class privilege in the justice process. The American Friends Service Committee published a study that called for an end to the indeterminate sentence, a system of sentencing they dubbed the "never knowing" system, because offenders and their families never knew exactly how long the offender would actually spend in jail.[70]

In addition to liberal critics, conservatives also lobbied for an end to indeterminate sentencing, which they viewed as being responsible for leniency toward many offenders.[71] Indeterminate sentencing worked something like this: the minimum sentence was usually about one-third of the maximum. Typically, an inmate could reduce both the maximum and the minimum by a third by earning time off for good behavior. The parole board could then release the person for serving a duration of time even less than the minimum. Everyone in the system understood how this worked and intended it to work that way. The judge did not intend the person to serve the maximum, or even the minimum, hoping that he or she would earn the good time by participating in programming. The threat of the lengthy sentence served as a powerful incentive to go to programming and cooperate with the correctional regime.[72]

The political problem was that the public did not understand the system: they saw an offender being released after serving only a fraction of the original sentence, which they thought was the intended punishment. In their perception, the offender "got off." Conservative critics argued that the system was being "soft on criminals" and that a deterrent effect was impossible under the indeterminate system of sentencing.[73]

The first mandatory drug sentences designed to enhance a deterrent effect were the New York Rockefeller drug laws of the 1970s, which mandated harsh prison terms and forbade plea bargaining for drug offenses. During the 1980s, Congress revised many of the drug laws to require lengthy mandatory prison terms. The federal government eliminated parole release, enacting many mandatory penalties and instituting sentencing guidelines to restrict judicial discretion. By the year 2000, there were more than half a million people in prison for drug offenses alone, which is about 100,000 more than there are prisoners for all offenses in all twelve nations of the European Union. Even worse, there are an estimated 600,000 children in the United States who have a parent in prison for drug offenses.[74]

Many of these laws are based on the theory that drug trafficking is a criminal conspiracy. In a criminal conspiracy, any form of involvement is considered equivalent to complete involvement. The reasoning behind these laws is the need to attack the organized crime network as a whole. If everyone is subject to the full punishment of the law, then even the low-level lookouts and couriers will be discouraged from participating in the elaborate operation needed to run an illegal drug business. The theory is that these punishments will cripple the drug trade, because low-level participants like Kemba will realize that a small amount of money is not worth ten years in prison.

This tactic in the battle to eradicate the illegal drug trade has had enormous consequences for women, who are typically used by men to perform risky jobs such as carrying money, mailing packages, transporting drugs, driving cars, or concealing weapons. Women like Rosa Montoya de Hernandez (see Chapter 7) and Kemba Smith have little to do with the actual business and usually have no knowledge about the operation. As low-level participants they may be paid a small fee for their involvement or, as in Kemba's case, they may perform these jobs out of love, loyalty, or fear. Because they have nothing to exchange in a plea agreement with the prosecution, these women end up serving lengthy sentences under the theory of the criminal conspiracy. From the 1970s to the mid-1990s, the percentage of women prisoners rose from 2.9 percent to almost 6 percent.[75] Between 1980 and 1997, the number of women in prison increased by 573 percent.[76] This astonishing rise in the number of women in prison is almost exclusively the result of tougher drug laws and mandatory sentencing policies. Drug offenses account for a full 49 percent of the increase in female incarceration. In New York State, 91 percent of female inmates are serving time for drug offenses.[77]

The federal Sentencing Reform Act of 1984 established sentencing guidelines for federal judges.[78] In an attempt to rein in judicial discretion, which might favor middle-class defendants over poor defendants by formally counting as mitigating circumstances features about a person's life such as employment, stable family, and education, the U.S. Sentencing Commission specifically forbade the use of those mitigating factors. Even though Kemba came from a stable home, was educated, and was likely to be a positive member of society, the judge was not allowed to take those factors into account.

Ironically, it is in the plea bargaining process that defendants are most able to avoid mandatory sentences. The other young women who provided information to the investigators were guilty of the same criminal conduct as Kemba, but they exchanged information about the drug ring leaders for immunity from prosecution. Because Kemba initially refused to cooperate and pleaded guilty once Peter Hall was dead, she no longer

The vast majority of women in prison are serving sentences for the crimes of prostitution, drug use, and drug trafficking. The rate of incarceration for women, especially women of color, has been the fastest growing segment of the prison population within the past decade. Most women in prison are mothers who are the primary caretakers of their children.

had anything to exchange through plea negotiations and was forced to face the full brunt of the law.

Minorities and the War on Drugs

The war on drugs is a collection of policies that utilizes proactive tactics by police and the courts to rigorously detect and punish illegal drug use and drug trafficking. As we have seen in the chapters on policing, police focus their tactical surveillance resources for drug offenses on disadvantaged minority neighborhoods. The routine infringements on civil liberties through the frisk and search is a common experience for blacks walking on streets, driving on the highway, or flying into the county. Sweeps of urban apartment houses or street corners is a common tactic in these neighborhoods. The result is that black drug criminality is more likely to be detected than white drug criminality.

The racial proportions in arrest rates therefore do not reflect the racial proportion of drug use. Although blacks constitute 12 percent of the overall population, they make up more than 40 percent of the arrests, even though there is no evidence that they use drugs more than any other ethnic group.[79] In 1990, 41 percent of those arrested for cocaine drug offenses were black, while only 10 percent of blacks report ever using the drug, a percentage similar to whites.

Research also indicates the existence of racial disparities in sentencing of drug offenders. The federal sentencing guidelines and various states' mandatory drug sentences impose harsher penalties for those involved in the use and sale of crack cocaine than powder cocaine. Under the federal sentencing guidelines, a person caught selling 5 grams of crack receives the same sentence as a dealer selling 500 grams of powder. Fifty grams of crack cocaine results in a ten-year sentence, while it takes an intent to distribute 5,000 grams of powder to earn a mandatory minimum of ten years. Crack cocaine is the only drug that results in a mandatory sentence of five years for a first offense of simple possession.[80] The differential in punishment for crack and cocaine, known as the

100:1 ratio, is justified by the argument that crack is a more potent delivery system for cocaine, is more physically addictive, and is associated with higher levels of violence. Although it has been estimated that 65 percent of crack users are actually white or Hispanic, the vast majority of those convicted for crimes involving crack are black.[81] In 1992, 92.6 percent of the defendants convicted for crack offenses nationally were black, as compared to only 4.7 percent who were white. By contrast, 45.2 percent of those convicted of powder cocaine offenses were white and only 20.7 percent were black.[82]

Altogether, these disproportionate rates of surveillance, arrest, conviction, and punishment for nonwhites are reflected in the growing numbers of minorities inside our nation's prisons. Since the mid-1980s, the growth in federal and state prison populations has been substantially fueled by incarcerations for drug offenses. In 1990, 1,860 of every 100,000 African Americans were behind bars, compared to only 289 out of every 100,000 whites.[83] By 2000, one in ten black males between the ages of 25 and 29 was either in jail or prison, compared to one in thirty-four Hispanic males and one in a hundred white males of the same age.[84]

Collateral Damage in the War on Drugs

Let us return to the question of the purpose of punishment. Kemba Smith was imprisoned so that others would learn from her mistake. We feel morally justified in using her life in this way because she voluntarily chose to break the law and harm others through her conduct. To an extent, therefore, she "deserved" to suffer. There was no need to incapacitate Kemba—no one believes that she would resume involvement in the drug business, because her involvement depended on the romantic link to her boyfriend. There is no public safety rationale for locking her up.

If we were to prioritize one of the other five goals of sentencing, it is easy to imagine a different kind of sentence for Kemba Smith. The goal of rehabilitation would stress the need to understand what drove Kemba to this kind of behavior. Many of the women who find themselves in positions like Kemba are drug addicted. An alternative sentence based on the goal of rehabilitation would be to offer them treatment for their addiction. In Kemba's case, she did receive counseling inside of prison to address issues of low-self esteem and gender inequality, which contributed to her willingness to remain in an abusive relationship. Since her release, Kemba has devoted herself to speaking out to young women about the dangers of "standing by" men who are violent and abusive.

If we shift our attention to the goal of restitution, we need to ask many serious questions about the genuine victims of the crime of drug trafficking. According to the prosecution, the real victims in this case were the people in the neighborhoods where drug use is rampant. They are the ones whose children became addicted, whose streets were riddled with violence, whose homes were robbed by addicts and whose parks were littered with discarded needles.

But was the community served by the punishment of Kemba Smith? In the "war on drugs," the "collateral" damage falls heavily on the victims themselves. These are also communities whose sons and daughters are going to jail for long periods of time, leaving young children in the care of grandparents and draining the community of its valuable human resources. By the year 2000, one in every fourteen black children in the United States had a parent serving time in either state or federal prison.[85]

If the community is the genuine victim, can we imagine alternative sentences under which Kemba could be required to serve the community and help to undo some of the harm she had a part in creating? In the final chapter of this text we will return to an examination of alternative sentencing and the use of innovations such as drug courts, which are beginning to slow down the rate of incarceration, particularly for drug offenses. Before we look at these community-based responses to crime, we must first take a closer look at the institution of the prison and try to gain some understanding of the place Kemba nearly spent twenty-four years of her life.

KEY TERMS

retribution p. 264
incapacitation p. 265
deterrence p. 266
specific deterrence p. 266
general deterrence p. 266
rehabilitation p. 266
restitution p. 267
fine p. 267
judicial model of
  sentencing p. 269

presentence investigation/
  report p. 269
administrative model of
  sentencing p. 269
legislative model of
  sentencing p. 269
executive clemency p. 270
determinate sentencing p. 270
indeterminate sentencing p. 270
sentencing disparities p. 270

mandatory minimum p. 271
"three strikes" laws p. 271
truth in sentencing laws p. 271
sentencing guidelines p. 271
presumptive sentence p. 271
capital punishment p. 271
bifurcated trial p. 272
guided discretion statutes p. 272
brutalization effect p. 273
DNA testing p. 273

REVIEW AND STUDY QUESTIONS

1. Identify and describe the five goals of sentencing. What is the common phrase that expresses each goal of sentencing?

2. Explain the difference between general and specific deterrence. How does the goal of restitution differ from the goal of rehabilitation?

3. Describe the three central models of sentencing. Identify which goal of sentencing is associated with each model. Identify who holds discretionary power in each model.

4. Contrast determinate sentencing and indeterminate sentencing. Which goals are associated with each form of sentencing and why?

5. What is sentencing disparity? Explain liberal and conservative positions against indeterminate sentencing.

6. Identify at least three ways that judicial discretion has been limited through sentencing reforms. How does each reform limit judicial discretion?

7. What were the effects of *Furman* v. *Georgia* and *Greggs* v. *Georgia* on the constitutionality of capital punishment? Define the bifurcated trial and guided discretion statutes.

8. Identify changes in the rate and use of incarceration from 1970 to 2000. How have these changes affected African American and Hispanic males?

9. Explain the change in U.S. sentencing policy for drug offenses within the past twenty years. What is the 100:1 ratio? How have these changes affected minorities and women?

10. Explain the rationale for Kemba Smith's sentence under the federal sentencing guidelines. Describe the collateral damages of this form of justice on the minority community.

CHECK IT OUT

On the Web
Cocaine and Federal Sentencing Policy, **www.ussc.gov/ crack/exec.htm**
Click here to read the 1995 report by the U.S. Sentencing Commission comparing the federal penalties for powder and crack cocaine and recommending elimination of these disparities in sentencing for the two. Download the 1997 report in PDF form at **http://www.ussc.gov/newcrack.pdf**.

State Sentencing Commissions, **www.ussc.gov/states/ nascaddr.htm**
Check out the sentencing commission Web site in your own state and access the sentencing guidelines for your state.

The Sentencing Project, **www.sentencingproject.org/**
Check out this Web site to access statistics on sentencing and race; and to learn about alternative sentencing programs across the nation.

Gallup Poll, **www.pollingreport.com**
Check out the latest public opinion polls on the public's views on the death penalty, drug policy, and mandatory sentencing. Find out what the American public feels today and how opinions toward sentencing and punishment are changing.

Death Penalty Information Center (DPIC), **www. deathpenaltyinfo.org**
This is an award-winning site that provides a wealth of information on the death penalty, including up-to-date statistics on executions state by state, including those that are scheduled to take place; the history of the death penalty; issues of race; public opinion; women and mental retardation. Click on the DPIC Quiz and test your own knowledge about the facts of the death penalty.

On Film

Drugs and Punishment: Are America's Drug Policies Fair? (BBC, 53 minutes)

This BBC production relates the history of U.S. drug policy and examines the impact and the pros and cons of the drug laws instituted under the Reagan administration. William Bennett is featured defending mandatory sentencing and conspiracy laws. Available from Films for the Humanities and Sciences, www.films.com.

Snitch (90 minutes)

This PBS documentary by Ofra Bikel takes a hard look at the issue of drug informers, who are able to reduce harsh mandatory sentences by informing on others, leading to harsh sentences for minor participants in the drug trade. Available online at www.pbs.com.

Crime Seen: Advances in DNA Testing (26 minutes)

After being identified in a lineup, Edward Honaker was convicted and sent to prison for rape. Ten years later, he was exonerated through advances in DNA analysis. This video spotlights the advances in DNA testing and explores the issue of wrongful convictions based on eyewitness identification. Available from Films for the Humanities and Sciences, www.films.com.

Judgment at Midnight (46 minutes)

ABC takes the viewer inside death row and the mind of the condemned and his executioners as the film follows the final preparation and execution of convicted murderer Antonio James. The film chronicles the experiences and feelings of his victims as well as of his family and explores the feelings of the warden responsible for carrying out the task of execution. Available from Films for the Humanities and Sciences, www.films.com.

NOTES

1. Reginald Stuart, "Kemba's Nightmare," *Emerge* 7(7) (May 1996), pp. 28–48; Libby Copeland, "Kemba Smith's Hard Time," *The Washington Post*, February 13, 2000, p. F-1.
2. Stuart, "Kemba's Nightmare," p. 45.
3. Ibid., p. 48.
4. Ibid., p. 32.
5. Ibid., pp. 34–35.
6. Ibid., p. 38.
7. Ibid., p. 42.
8. Copeland, "Kemba Smith's Hard Time," p. F-10.
9. Mark Morris, "Pardoned Woman Backs Drug Law Change," *The Kansas City Star*, April 20, 2001, p. B2.
10. Stuart, "Kemba's Nightmare," p. 46.
11. Anthony Lewis, "Abroad at Home; A Christmas Carol," *The New York Times*, December 23, 2000, p. A-19.
12. Stuart, "Kemba's Nightmare," p. 48
13. Ibid., p. 46.
14. Reginald Stuart, "Kemba's Nightmare II: Justice Denied," *Emerge*, 9(7) (May 1998), p. 43.
15. Ibid., p. 46.
16. Betsy Peoples, "Advocates Fight a War on Drug Sentencing," *Emerge*, 9(7) (May 1998), p. 50.
17. Stuart, "Kemba's Nightmare II: Justice Denied," p. 48.
18. Copeland, "Kemba Smith's Hard Time," p. F-1.
19. Tom Campbell, "Kemba Smith's Appeal Dismissed," Richmond *Times-Dispatch*, August 18, 1999, p. B1.
20. Rhonda Chriss Lokeman, "When Smart Women Make Foolish Choices," *The Kansas City Star*, April 22, 2001, p. B9.
21. E. R. Shipp, "Gone Too Far for Too Long," *Daily News*, January 28, 2001, p. 33.
22. Robert James, ed., *Winston S. Churchill: His Complete Speeches, 1897–1903* (New York: Chelsea House, 1974), p. 1598.
23. David Garland, *Punishment and Modern Society: A Study in Social Theory* (Chicago: University of Chicago Press, 1990).
24. Andrew von Hirsch, *Doing Justice: The Choice of Punishments* (New York: Hill & Wang, 1976).
25. Jacqueline Cohen, "Incapacitation as a Strategy for Crime Control: Possibilities and Pitfalls," in Michael Tonry and Norval Morris, eds., *Crime and Justice: An Annual Review of Research, Vol. 5* (Chicago: University of Chicago Press, 1983), pp. 1–84.
26. Hugo Adam Bedau, "Retributivism and the Theory of Punishment," *Journal of Philosophy* 75 (1978), pp. 601–620.
27. Cesare Beccaria, trans. Edward D. Ingraham, *On Crimes and Punishment* (Philadelphia: Philip N. Nicklin, 1819); Jeremy Bentham, *An Introduction to the Principles of Morals and Legislation* (New York: Hafner, 1948).
28. Karl Menninger, *The Crime of Punishment* (New York: Viking Press 1968).
29. David Garland, *Punishment and Welfare: A History of Penal Strategies* (Burlington, VT: Ashgate, 1985).
30. Stephen Schafter, *Victimology: The Victim and His Criminal* (Reston VA: Reston 1977), pp. 5–15.
31. Ibid., p. 8.
32. Ibid., p. 12
33. Daniel W. Van Ness, *Crime and Its Victims* (Downers Grove, IL: InterVarsity Press, 1986), pp. 64–66.
34. William Andrews, *Old Time Punishments* (London: Tabard Press, 1890).
35. Joan Petersilia, *Expanding Options for Criminal Sentencing* (Santa Monica, CA: Rand, 1987).
36. Tracy L. Snell, "Capital Punishment 1997," *BJS Bulletin* (Washington, DC: U.S. Department of Justice, 1998).
37. Michael Ignatieff, *A Just Measure of Pain: The Penitentiary in the Industrial Revolution* (London: Pantheon, 1978).

38. Pieter Spierenburg, *The Spectacle of Suffering* (Cambridge, U. K.: Cambridge University Press, 1984).

39. The Sentencing Project, *Facts about Prisons and Prisoners* (Washington, DC: The Sentencing Project, 2000).

40. Darrell K. Gilliard and Allen J. Beck, "Prisoners in 1997," *BJS Bulletin* (Washington, DC: Bureau of Justice Statistics, 1998).

41. The Sentencing Project, Facts about Prisons and Prisoners.

42. Gilliard and Beck, "Prisoners in 1997."

43. Doris Layton Mackenzie and Eugene E. Hebert, eds., *Correctional Boot Camps: A Tough Intermediate Sanction* (Washington, DC: U.S. Department of Justice, 1996).

44. Michael H. Tonry, "Sentencing," in Sanford Kadish, ed., *Encyclopedia of Crime and Justice* (New York: Free Press, 1983), pp. 1432–1440.

45. Anthony Walsh, "The Role of the Probation Officer in the Sentencing Process: Independent Professional or Judicial Hack?" *Criminal Justice and Behavior 12* (1985), pp. 289–303.

46. Charles E. Frazier and E. Wilbur Bock, "Effects of Court Officials on Sentence Severity," *Criminology 20* (1982), pp. 257–272.

47. Robert M. Carter and Leslie T. Wilkins, "Some Factors in Sentencing Policy," *Journal of Criminal Law, Criminology and Police Science 58* (1967), pp. 503–514.

48. Sandra Shane Du-Bow, Alice P. Brown, and Erik Olsen, *Sentencing Reform in the United States: History, Content, and Effect* (Washington, DC: National Institute of Justice, 1985).

49. Andrew von Hirsch and Kathleen Hanarahan, "Determinate Penalty Systems in America: An Overview," *Crime and Delinquency 27* (1981), pp. 289–316.

50. John Clark, James Austin, and D. Alan Henry, "'Three Strikes and You're Out': A Review of State Legislation," *NIJ Research in Brief* (Washington, DC: U.S. Department of Justice, 1997).

51. Bureau of Justice Assistance, *National Assessment of Structured Sentencing* (Washington, DC: U.S. Department of Justice, 1996).

52. Amnesty International, "The Death Penalty: List of Abolitionist and Retentionist Countries," February, 1999. *http://www.amnesty.org/ailib/intcam/dp/abrelist.htm.*

53. *Furman v. Georgia,* 408 U.S. 238 (1972).

54. *Greggs v. Georgia,* 96 S.Ct. 2726 (1976).

55. Amnesty International, "The Death Penalty: List of Abolitionist and Retentionist Countries."

56. William J. Bowers, "The Effect of Executions Is Brutalization, Not Deterrence," in Kenneth C. Hess and James A. Inciardi, eds., *Capital Punishment: Legal and Social Science Approaches* (Newbury Park, CA: Sage, 1988).

57. NAACP Legal Defense, *Death Row, USA* (New York: National Association for the Advancement of Colored People, 1988).

58. Ibid.

59. Henry Weinstein, "Death Penalty Moratorium Attracting Unlikely Adherents," *Los Angeles Times,* October 17, 2000, p. A-5.

60. Michael L. Radelet, Hugo Adam Bedau, and Constance E. Putnam, *In Spite of Innocence: Erroneous Convictions in Capital Cases* (Boston: Northeastern University Press, 1992).

61. Robert Tanner, "States Are Slow to Grant DNA Testing to People Seeking to Prove Innocence," *St. Louis Post-Dispatch,* June 22, 2000, p. A10.

62. Albert Camus, trans. Justin O'Brien, *Resistance, Rebellion and Death* (New York: Vintage Books, 1974), p. 199.

63. Hugo Adam Bedau, *The Death Penalty in America* (New York: Oxford University Press, 1982).

64. Sister Helen Prejean, *Dead Man Walking: An Eyewitness Account of the Death Penalty in the United States* (New York: Vintage Books, 1994).

65. William J. Bowers, "Capital Punishment and Contemporary Values: People's Misgivings and the Court's Misperceptions," *Law and Society Review 27,* (1993), p. 1.

66. Dina Rose and Todd Clear, "Incarceration, Social Capital and Crime: Implications for Social Disorganization Theory," *Criminology 36*(3), (1998) pp. 441–480.

67. Mercer Sullivan, *Getting Paid: Youth, Crime, and Work in the Inner City* (Ithaca, NY: Cornell University Press, 1989).

68. Robert Martinson, "What Works? Questions and Answers about Prison Reform," *Public Interest 35* (Spring 1974). pp. 22–54.

69. Douglas R. Lipton, Robert Martinson, and Judith Wilks, *The Effectiveness of Correctional Treatment: A Survey of Treatment Evaluation Studies* (New York: Praeger, 1975).

70. American Friends Service Committee, *Struggle for Justice: A Report on Crime and Punishment in America* (New York: Hill & Wang, 1971).

71. James Q. Wilson, *Thinking about Crime,* (New York: Basic Books, 1975).

72. Michael Tonry, *Malign Neglect: Race, Crime and Punishment in America* (New York: Oxford University Press, 1995), p. 166.

73. Franklin E. Zimring, "Making the Punishment Fit the Crime: A Consumer's Guide to Sentencing Reform," *Hastings Center Report 6*(6), 1976, pp. 13–21.

74. Judy Mann, "Mr. President, Show Mercy and Good Sense," *The Washington Post,* December 15, 2000, p. C-9.

75. Marc Mauer, *Young Black Americans and the Criminal Justice System: Five Years Later* (Washington, DC: The Sentencing Project, 2000).

76. Marc Mauer, Cathy Potler, and Richard Wolf, *Gender and Justice: Women, Drugs and Sentencing Policy* (Washington, DC: The Sentencing Project, 1999).

77. Ibid., p. 1.

78. Tonry, *Malign Neglect,* pp. 169–170.

79. Ibid., pp. 110–111.

80. Randall Kennedy, *Race, Crime and the Law* (New York: Vintage Books, 1997), p. 364.

81. Criminal Justice Brief Sheets, *Crack Cocaine Sentencing Policy: Unjustified and Unreasonable* (Washington, DC: The Sentencing Project, 1999).

82. David Cole, *No Equal Justice: Race and Class in the American Justice System* (New York: New Press, 1999), p. 142.

83. Samuel Walker, Cassia Spohn, and Miriam DeLone, *The Color of Justice: Race, Ethnicity and Crime in America* (Belmont, CA: Wadsworth, 1996), p. 156.

84. Criminal Justice Brief Sheets, *Facts about Prisons and Prisoners.*

85. Jenni Gainsborough and Marc Mauer, *Diminishing Returns: Crime and Incarceration in the 1990s* (Washington, DC: The Sentencing Project, 2000), p. 25.

CASE 14

Surviving Time: The Case of Rubin "Hurricane" Carter

Rubin "Hurricane" Carter spent almost twenty years of his life serving time for a crime he did not commit. In 1967 he was found guilty of a triple homicide. The conviction was overturned in 1976, but he was retried and convicted again in 1977. The second conviction was overturned by the federal courts in 1988, when Rubin Carter was finally released from the New Jersey state prison system.[1]

A YOUNG FIGHTER IS BORN

As a young boy, Rubin Carter was no angel. A severe speech impediment, which impaired his ability to communicate, led Carter to use his fists to do his talking. By the age of 11, Rubin had been booted out of school and sent to a disciplinary school, where his fellow schoolmates placed high value on his willingness to fight.[2]

Rubin Carter's trouble with the law also began at an early age while he was running with a gang of youth controlling their precious few blocks of neighborhood from other gangs just like themselves. Responding to a dare, Carter led a parade of young thieves on a swooping raid on an outdoor clothing vendor. Swift of feet, Carter would never have been caught if it weren't for the stern reaction of his God-fearing and law-abiding father, who found the stolen clothes, beat Rubin soundly, and hauled him down to the local police station. This was the first time Carter was alone in an interrogation room with white police officers. Carter, as usual, was silent, and for this he received a beating from a tough white cop who would have it in for him for the rest of his life.[3]

Carter was sentenced to probation for the theft, but the justice system was not so lenient the second time he came before a judge, this time on a charge of assaulting and cutting a prominent white man who

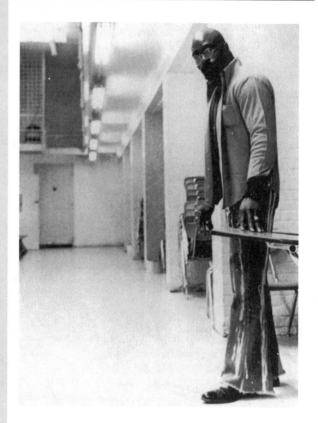

had the habit of preying on young boys deep in the woods. The judge spared no words in his disgust for Carter: "I only wish you were older so I could send you to State Prison . . . where they have cages for animals like you."[4] At the age of 11, Rubin Carter was sentenced to Jamesburg State Home for Boys until he turned 21.

THE WORLD OF THE REFORMATORY[5]

The Jamesburg State Home for Boys was nestled in the rural landscape of southern New Jersey, far from the dense city streets of Paterson and Newark. It resembled a tranquil college campus with its three-story red brick buildings arranged around a bucolic green parade ground. Each residential "cottage," eight in all, housed fifty to sixty boys who slept in a dormitory on the second floor; the basement housed the recreation room and showers, while the third floor was reserved for the couple known as the cottage "mother" and "father." The Jamesburg Home for Boys had been built in the era of the reformatory, when the hope was to provide a wholesome and family-like environment for wayward delinquents. The "cottage" system, with its homey architecture, reflected this lofty aspiration. But when young Carter arrived, he soon discovered the reality behind the red-brick facade of the Jamesburg State Home for Boys.

The juvenile system lumped all kinds of juvenile offenders together: some were there for truancy, while others had robbed, raped, or killed. Whites and blacks were segregated into separate cottages, with boys as young as age 8 thrown in with maturing young men of 17, 18, and older. The "reformatory" operated on a mixture of military-style discipline and delegated authority, under which the older boys in the cottage controlled the younger boys through sheer brutality and perverse forms of enslavement and domination. The cottage "father" and "mother" had little to do with the discipline inside the cottage. They were local white residents who despised their urban charges and kept them in line through the liberal use of blackjacks.

However, the staff preferred not to discipline the boys at all. Instead, they appointed two "line sergeants" chosen from among the inmates—generally the toughest and most malicious among the inmates—to keep discipline among the boys. These head boys, in turn, appointed their own lieutenants, relying on fear, humiliation, and violence to keep others in line. It was a pecking order of the most vicious kind. At the bottom were the youngest and the most vulnerable, who were forced to serve as "wives" or sexual servants on a relentless nightly tour of routinized gang rape.

The reformatory made little attempt to "reform" inmates. The inmates cleaned their own cottages, performed chores for the institution, and were contracted out as cheap labor to local farmers. The line sergeants in each cottage put the other boys to work—watching as they scrubbed the floors or cleaned the toilets. If someone faltered, brutal violence kept him at the task. Fear ran the social system of the cottage as it ran the wider institution. And when someone really stepped out of line, there was always "the hole": a small, isolated building deep in the woods, containing sixteen cells with nothing inside but a hard cement floor. Carter, whose explosive temper and willingness to fight soon made him top dog in the world of the cottage, also led him into many confrontations with the white staff. Carter

spent many days and nights alone in those stinking isolation cells.

ESCAPING THE SYSTEM

At the age of 17, the warden made Carter a sudden and surprising offer. With three years left until his twenty-first birthday, the warden offered to reduce his time at Jamesburg to three short months, provided Carter stayed completely out of trouble during that period.[6] If he got a single disciplinary report, even for failing to tie his shoelaces properly, he would be shipped out to a harsher institution, Annandale, whose reputation was even worse than Jamesburg's. "Why would you do this?" Carter asked. The reason, the warden explained, was that he could see Carter was getting too used to the violent world of the reformatory. Soon it would be too late for Carter. This was his one last chance to be free from the kind of "reform" that really took place for wayward boys in the state system.

Carter completed his three months with a perfect record, but on the last day of the third month, while the warden was away for the day, his second in command, who disapproved of the warden's decision to release Carter, issued a disciplinary report for Carter's use of bad language to a cottage supervisor.[7] The report wasn't true but it wouldn't matter: the power was all in the hands of the system. Carter was helpless.

He decided the only thing in his power was to run. At the age of 17, Carter escaped from the Jamesburg State Home and ran home to Paterson, New Jersey, where his family hid him from the police. They shipped him off to Philadelphia, where he enlisted in the Army and was sent to Fort Jackson to train for combat in the Korean War. It was in the military that Carter discovered a constructive use for his pugilistic gifts. By the time he was discharged from the Army in 1956, he had won the European Welterweight Champion title and returned to Paterson a prizefighter and a champion.[8]

BACK INSIDE

Carter's dreams of launching a professional boxing career were put on hold when he was immediately arrested for the escape from Jamesburg and sentenced to Annandale Reformatory for ten months as punishment.[9] Annandale made Jamesburg look like Sunday school.[10] This was where they sent the really tough juveniles. Annandale functioned more like a penitentiary than Jamesburg. On the first day, Rubin, a proud ex-seviceman and prizefighter, at age 21, had his head shaved, was told to strip and put on prison garb which consisted of short pants. In Rubin's memoir he said, "These [short pants], like the shave they gave your head when you entered the place, were designed to strip away your manhood and make you feel like a kid again, to wipe out whatever remained of your personal identity."[11] Rubin tried to resist wearing those clothes and landed in the Graveyard, the prison that exists within all prisons where the difficult prisoners go.

Ten months later Carter was released from Annandale.

> Finally my day came—that bright, beautiful morning when it was time for me to go home. A brutal, ugly year of wasted energy had gone out of my life. Ten long worthless months of bitter frustration had blown everything I had achieved, and had tickled my old animosity back to life. On that Tuesday morning when Annandale set me free, they might not have known it . . . but they had just unleashed a walking, ticking, short-fused time bomb set to explode on contact with an unsuspecting public. A society which fooled itself into believing that this miniature penitentiary sitting in the hills of its community was really an honest-to-God rehabilitation center.[12]

Within five weeks of his release, Carter, in an act of pure aggression, snatched the purse of an elderly black woman passing by him early one evening.[13] Not for money, just for fun. He ran down the street laughing, assaulted another man, and then another, both of them black. The crimes didn't make any sense: Carter had a good job working for a plastics manufacturer, plenty of money in his pockets, and he had his freedom. He hated whites and the justice system that had just locked him up, but he had nothing against these innocent black folks just minding their own business. Carter's actions were irrational.

It was only a matter of time before the Paterson police arrested Carter for the crimes, which had been witnessed by many who knew Carter. In the eyes of the police, these crimes confirmed what they had believed about Carter since he was 11 years old: Rubin Carter was a good-for-nothing "nigger punk," who was destined, sooner or later, to be locked up for the rest of his life. Carter plead guilty to the charges of assault and robbery. This time he was spared the niceties of the youth reformatory system and sent straight to Trenton State Prison.

UP TO THE BIG HOUSE

Trenton State Prison was built in 1836 by the famed British architect John Haviland, who adorned the facades with pink limestone and Egyptian symbols.[14] The Quaker vision for the penitentiary was a place of redemption and monklike prayer and industry. The cells were designed for prisoners to live in contemplative isolation alone with their Bible and individual piecework. In the oldest part of the Trenton prison, the original cells had oak doors purposely set low, so that on entering the cell each prisoner was forced to bow his head in penance. Inside the cell, the Quakers believed that genuine reform would take place as each prisoner was kept away from the corrupting influences of temptation and was able to commune with God and his own soul.

But the dream was an illusion. Oak doors quickly gave way to iron cages built in rows or tiers so a few guards could keep watch on the hundreds of imprisoned bodies.[15] The prison was organized around a huge and dusty yard surrounded by towers with armed guards looking down and ringed by razor wire. The vision that had inspired the Quakers had little in common with the giant maze of human warehouses.

In one corner of the yard, right next to the hospital, was the Death House, a one-story cement block building that held the electric chair and all those sentenced to end their life there.[16] Designed to hold nineteen men, two tiers of cells ran along one side of the building. The "last mile" to the dark green door led to the execution chamber itself: a windowless room with three or four wooden benches for spectators to witness the act. A waist-high barrier separated onlookers from the chair itself, sitting in the middle of the room elevated on a platform in all its grisly splendor.

A constant cacophony of sound surrounded life inside the prison: shrill bells, cell counts, whistles, the clanking of steel gates, the plumbing of hundreds of sinks and toilets flushing; the noisy locking contraptions of steel grating on steel. The ancient building of stone and brick heated up like an oven in the summer: the smallest cells were only 7½ feet long, and 4 or 4½ feet wide, and 7 feet high. The largest cells were less than twice that size and held up to four occupants.[17]

According to the Handbook for Inmates, inmates were required to walk in line as they moved at the sound of the bell from the mess hall to the industrial shop. They were to "maintain good posture with their face held forward."[18] Stepping out of line was a violation of the rules and grounds for a disciplinary report. The prison routine was regulated by bells: six o'clock sharp was the morning bell; another bell told inmates to be at their jobs making license plates or sewing clothes or lying idle in their cells; there was another bell to be back for a count.

Working in the tag shop making license plates, an inmate could earn about 11 cents a day. In a month's time, he might earn enough money to buy some candy, cigarettes, razor blades, or bars of soap from the commissary. These items were the currency of life inside prison. Traded and labored for, these luxuries acquired value of enormous proportion among the inmates. Cigarettes, soap, toilet paper, books, lights, food, newspapers, visits—the minutiae of life outside the prison—become the all-important focus of everyday life inside. And the all-powerful prison authorities held the absolute prerogative to take away these amenities for any reason at any time.

The dark economy of prison life operated through a violent sexual hierarchy among the inmates. The real currency of the prison involved the trade of petty privileges, toiletries, personal grudges, and sexual favors. The prison administration relied on this system to control the inmates, allowing the tough to prey on the weak because at least it kept the men occupied. The shower house was an open building with fifty stalls. Inside the cell, inmates were given a bucket for washing themselves and herded into the shower house every few days. There the guard on duty would calmly smoke a cigarette, willfully oblivious to the violence happening among the men. "Everyday . . . some poor unsuspecting fool would get ripped off in the dense clouds of concealing steam. He would be stabbed in his back, then humped in his backside while the shower cop had his smoke, butt pressed against the wall and his senses shut off from the anguished cries."[19]

During this period in prison, Carter made a decision about his life. Fighting was all he knew how to do and all he was good at. He didn't want to die in prison like so many around him. He knew his temper and rage would lead him back to prison, like so many of the boys he had grown up with. Already, familiar faces from the gangs of his youth were showing up at Trenton State Prison, and a few of Carter's old pals from Jamesburg were already entombed in the Death House waiting to be executed. Carter made a decision to focus all his energies on building the physical and mental capacity to get out of prison and become a professional prizefighter.

A DREAM PURSUED AND LOST

In September 1961, after four years and two months, Rubin Carter was released from prison ready to make good on his dream to join the world of boxing. Within a year he had acquired the nickname "Hurricane": an unstoppable force of nature in the ring. By the end of 1963 Carter was a contender for the U.S. middleweight championship. A successful Carter married, bought a house in Paterson, and began a family.[20]

On the night of June 17, 1966, two armed black men had entered an all-white barroom and opened fire on the patrons, killing three and wounding another. The shooting was believed to have been in retaliation for the earlier shooting death of a black bar owner by a white gunman. When "Hurricane" Carter was picked up for questioning late that same night, he was a celebrity earning $100,000 a year. But to the Paterson police officers who arrested him and interrogated him in the same windowless room in which he had sat at age 11, Rubin Carter was the punk they had sent off to prison three times before. Carter's nemesis, Lieutenant DeSimone, was placed in charge of the investigation.

Released after questioning, Carter went off to fight a match in Argentina. When he returned, he was arrested and charged with murder. Two eyewitnesses had come forward to testify that it was Carter and a young man with him in the car, John Arlis, who had walked into the bar and opened fire on three white patrons. At the trial, the testimony of these eyewitnesses, obtained through a plea agreement engineered by DeSimone, convicted Carter and the 20-year-old Arlis. Later, the veracity of these eyewitnesses, their motives for deciding to come forward, and the shady role played by the police investigators would be grounds for appeal.[21] The judge, noting Carter's "anti-social history," sentenced him to three life sentences.[22]

RESISTING PRISON

The first stop in any prison is the moment of transition, when the prisoner is forced to let go of his possessions and clothing and adopt the status and identity of an inmate. A person gives the prison guard his name, age, crime, and sentence, and in exchange, is assigned a number, in Carter's case, number 45472, meaning he was the 45,472nd prisoner to be interred behind the thick stone walls of Trenton State Prison. Carter watched as the man ahead of him went through the drill.[23] The man removed all his clothing, watch, and jewelry, placing these belongings into a cardboard box to be carted away. Next he was handed his drinking cup, spoon, blanket, and prison-issue khaki uniform stamped with NJSP on the back. The trousers had thick black stripes about the same width as the bar cells.

When it came Carter's turn, he suddenly balked. On previous occasions he had cooperated, but Carter knew the loss of self-respect that accompanied this stripping away of his outside self. Carter understood prison life and what it did to the spirit of the men there. No matter what the cost, Carter refused to become what the prison told him he was. He refused to remove his suit. On his first day, Rubin "Hurricane" Carter was sent to the hole still wearing his expensive gray suit, diamond ring, gold watch, and black patent leather shoes.

At Trenton, the "hole" was literally cut into the wall itself.[24] About thirty-five cells ran along the deepest tier. The cells were deeper than graves. There were no sinks, no faucets, no toilets. A concrete slab and a bucket were the only "furnishings." There was no light, no books, no contact with other inmates or guards. Inmates were fed through an opening at the bottom of the door: one cup of water three times a day and four slices of bread. After several months in the deepest level of Trenton's system of solitary confinement, Rubin Carter was still unwilling to change into prison clothing.

Every fifteen days Carter, still wearing his own clothes, was allowed out to take a shower, and every thirty days he received a medical inspection. One of these inspections landed Carter in the prison hospital for an operation that would eventually take his right eye: with the loss of that eye went Carter's hopes of ever returning to professional boxing. Still refusing to wear the same prison outfits as others, Carter proposed a compromise he could live with. If the warden permitted him to wear the white scrubs of the hospital, he would be willing to take off his now ragged and tattered clothing. The administration agreed, and on his release from the hospital, Carter was sent to 7 Wing, the cellblock reserved for "incorrigibles" like himself who refused to go along with the internal prison regime.

Refusal continued to be Rubin Carter's main weapon of psychological survival in prison. He took his punishments in solitary rather than submit to the degradation of the routine of prison life. Carter understood that the psychological harm of incarceration was far more damaging to him than any of the physical threats. He was prepared to die rather than lose his sense of himself as a human being. He refused to be interviewed by prison psychologists or to meet with a parole officer to discuss his participation in his own "rehabilitation." Carter felt disdainful of his fellow inmates, who seemed to accept the degradation of their lives and did all they could to live up to the prison's view of them as animals. Drugs and booze flowed freely inside the walls: a steady supply of dope and prison-made hooch, a kind of sugary, foul-tasting wine, meant that many continued the destructive life that had brought them to prison in the first place.

Carter remained aloof from the prison scene—working on his appeals, studying the law, writing an autobiography that was published to much acclaim in 1974. Although Carter had ended his formal schooling at the eighth grade, he educated himself as a jailhouse lawyer, learning the law and moving on to tackle erudite reading material such as Freud, Jung, Malcolm X, Nelson Mandela, and many others.

STANDING UP FOR PRISONERS' RIGHTS AT RAHWAY STATE PRISON

Prison administrators rarely give reasons to prisoners when they move them, and they move them often. In 1971 Carter was transferred to Rahway State Prison.[25] Originally built in 1896 as a youth reformatory, the physical layout at Rahway resembled the less oppressive architecture of the Jamesburg institution. But the social structure of the prison was the same as at Trenton and other institutions.

In the 1970s, tensions among inmates were running high. A growing political consciousness was infecting black and other minority prisoners. Black Muslims and other militant prisoners were growing incensed by the indeterminate sentencing system, which relied on the parole system for release and seemed to favor white inmates over black inmates. The inmate population at both Trenton State Prison and Rahway was 80 percent black, 5 percent Hispanic, and 15 percent white. With the exception of a few black guards, the entire prison administration was white.

Attica, a maximum security prison in upstate New York, exploded in violence in 1971 when inmates rebelled against the inhumane conditions of their confinement. Forty-three people were killed before the New York National Guard fought to take the prison away from inmate control. Shortly afterward, Rahway State Prison too erupted in violence, for many of the same reasons. Conditions were abysmal, with overcrowding, brutality, poor food, unsanitary conditions, and few programs.

In the midst of the tensions, Rubin Carter found himself in a leadership role, counseling his fellow prisoners to avoid violence and try to make their demands through peaceful channels. When a riot erupted at Rahway, Carter led a group of inmates to wait it out in a separate wing of the prison. The riot lasted twenty-seven hours, with seven guards including the warden beaten and held hostage by about two hundred inmates.

After the riots, Carter became active in a growing movement among the inmates to organize peacefully for their rights.[26] He joined the Rahway Inmate Committee, which expressed demands about medical conditions, overcrowding, recreation, telephone privileges, and the right to wear civilian clothing. He was elected chairman of the Rahway Inmate Committee, which he renamed the Rahway People's Council. Within the prison different ethnic groups formed various factions: the blacks were the largest, but there were also the Hispanics, Italians, and Muslims. Carter sought support from the toughest leader in each group, promising to improve conditions and expand their rights.

The more outspoken Carter became, the more the prison administration sought ways to limit his power. Carter was brought before a prison tribunal composed of prison staff and was told that he was being punished for inciting a riot and holding an illegal meeting. As punishment Carter was transferred to the Vroom Readjustment Unit (VRU), the institution of the New Jersey corrections system for the criminally insane and other incorrigibles.[27] The Vroom building was more than one hundred years old and had been designed entirely for isolation. Inmates rarely left their cells except for a brief trip to the yard every few days. Meals were served in the cells, and the cells were designed to prevent communication between adjacent inmates.

Carter, by now well educated and connected to a growing network of writers, reporters, lawyers, activists, and celebrities, who believed he had been unjustly convicted, filed a suit in federal court alleging he had been illegally transferred to the VRU. A federal district court judge ordered Carter to be released from the VRU on the grounds that his due process rights had been violated and that "inciting" was not a recognizable offense under the disciplinary rules of the prison.[28] After ninety-two days in the VRU, Carter was transferred away from Rahway and back to Trenton State Prison.

A TASTE OF FREEDOM

By the time Carter's appeal was heard for the first time he was a national celebrity. His autobiography was a bestseller. Bob Dylan came to the prison to meet Carter and wrote a song about his plight, which further enhanced his growing support among liberal activists and radical reformers. The NAACP and other organizations became involved as it became clear that Carter had been framed by the two eyewitnesses, who had lied to protect themselves from criminal prosecution on other charges. Muhammed Ali and many other celebrities joined the bandwagon to free Hurricane Carter.[29]

On March 17, 1976, the convictions of Carter and John Arlis were overturned by the New Jersey Supreme Court in a 7–0 decision.[30] The Supreme Court agreed that the men had been denied a fair trial. The case was remanded back to state court on the grounds that the prosecution had failed to inform the defense and the jury of the plea agreement it had made with the two key eyewitnesses in exchange for their testimony. Even more significant was the fact that both of

the eyewitnesses, now in prison, were saying they had lied in order to avoid going to prison and in response to serious pressure from the investigators.[31]

The prosecution began immediate proceedings for a new trial against Carter and Arlis. Both men were released from jail on bond, posted by heavyweight champion Muhammed Ali. Now 38, Carter had spent about half of his life, eighteen years, locked up in prison. With the vision in his right eye gone, Carter would never return to professional boxing.

In a trial watched by the world, Arlis and Carter were convicted a second time by a second jury. One of the key witnesses took the stand again, recanted the statements he had made about lying, and repeated his original testimony.[32] Despite information given to the jury about the plea agreement, the all-white jury believed the two white men when they testified they were telling the truth.

Race was an important factor in this trial.[33] The white victims drinking in an all-white part of town had been gunned down by two black men in an act thought to be in retaliation for the shooting of a local black bar owner by a white man. All the witnesses, victims, and jury in the courtroom were white. Although Carter was only a passing acquaintance of the bar owner's son, and did not personally know any of the people who were killed, the prosecutor nonetheless argued that the motive for the killing was racial revenge. The prosecutor put forth the theory that Carter and Arlis, out of deep-seated black rage, were willing to kill four innocent strangers on behalf of a black man they barely knew, in front of many witnesses, for the simple reason that they were consumed with a desire for revenge against white society. According to the prosecution, it also made sense that Arlis and Carter would then drive around the neighborhood all night, making no effort to run or hide. The prosecution presented no particular evidence that either Arlis or Carter held negative feelings toward whites or had even acted or expressed any desire to seek revenge against whites. The theory was based on racist assumptions about black criminality and black rage, and the all-white jury bought it.

REFORMATION ON THE INSIDE

After nine short months of freedom, Rubin Carter was sent back to Trenton State Prison. This time the anger and hope that had sustained him in his struggle to clear his name was gone. He divorced his wife and cut off ties with the outside world. This time Carter would have to find a different way to survive.

Now Carter retreated to the inner life of his spirit and his mind. He read a book about a concentration camp survivor who had come to the realization that prisons could control you physically but not spiritually. Carter looked around him and saw so many men whose spirit had been broken and destroyed by the prison system. Indeed, the entire system was designed to do just that. But true freedom, he came to understand, was about the inner life and here, even in prison with all the suffering it imposed, was the opportunity for growth and even freedom.[34]

Carter began to study classics in philosophy, religion, the civil rights movement, and the theory of nonviolence. Carter came to the understanding that his moral system, based on "giving as good as you got," was the equivalent of the corrupt moral system of the prison itself. Carter wrote in his journal: "A real revelation is not 'an eye for an eye' or 'do as others do, just do it first,' but a revelation is to change worse to better; hate to love; war to peace; it means turning things around; a total change from the opposite of what it is now."[35]

Carter's language changed, as did his demeanor. He continued to oppose the prison's assault on his dignity and selfhood, and he took the punishment that was doled out rather than give in to being a mere number warehoused like so much junk to be thrown away. The system locked him in the hole, kept him in administrative segregation, and sent him back to the dreaded Vroom at least once more before his final release. But Carter nourished his soul with his new understandings about the world and the human condition. Locked away in the deepest and darkest prisons, Carter liberated himself to a level of freedom he had never experienced before in his life.

SEEKING PHYSICAL FREEDOM ONE LAST TIME

At this point, Carter might have disappeared inside the system forever as he attempted to lead the ascetic life of a monk inside the bowels of the system. Forgotten by the outside world and cut off from everyone, Carter could have simply disappeared along with the many thousands, now millions of Americans who are locked away. But a twist of fate created a tie between Carter and the outside world. A young black man from Brooklyn, Lester Martin, had been adopted by an unconventional group of liberal Canadians.[36] Lester read Carter's book and wrote to him. For some reason, the young man touched something in Carter, and he wrote Lester back. Soon afterward, Lester came down to Trenton for Carter's first visit with someone from the outside world in many years. Thus began a friendship with Lester and the group of young adults who were raising him, which would ultimately lead to the release of Arlis and Carter.

It took nine years. If it weren't for the passionate dedication of these Canadians who revived the legal battle for Carter's appeals, Rubin probably would have remained behind bars for the rest of his life. Their enthusiasm and energy renewed his own commitment to try again to fight for his physical freedom. This time, the Canadians and Carter's lawyers abandoned the New Jersey state court system and filed an appeal in federal court. The brief argued that the prosecutor had illegally appealed to racist beliefs without presenting any specific evidence that either Carter or Arlis was personally vengeful toward whites and that the prosecution and the police had illegally concealed evidence of a failed polygraph by the key eyewitness in the case.

The moment of victory came suddenly and completely when a federal court overturned the conviction and ordered their immediate release from prison. Judge H. Lee Sarokin stated that, "To not throw out these convictions would be to commit a crime as heinous as those for which they were unjustly convicted. . . . I cannot, in the face of the conclusions reached in my opinion and the injustices found, permit Mr. Carter to spend another day or even an hour in prison, particularly considering that he has spent almost twenty years in confinement based upon a conviction which I have found to be constitutionally faulty."[37] After losing an appeal, the district attorney's office decided to forego a third trial for Carter and Arlis.

Together the two men had collectively served thirty-four years in prison. Carter lost nineteen years of his life, his boxing career, his wife, and his two children. Neither the state of New Jersey nor the attorney general's office ever offered Carter, Arlis, or their families an apology or compensation of any kind for their loss. At a press conference two years after his release, at the age of 50, Carter talked about what he had felt and learned from his tragic experience:

> The State of NJ has just now seen fit to dismiss the charges and the indictment—the same indictment that they used 22 years ago to take my life by seeking the death penalty. But they failed to get the death penalty . . . instead they sentenced me to a life of living death—and there is no other way to describe the nature of prison. Prison destroys everything that is valuable in a human being. It destroys families—it destroyed mine. It destroys one's dignity and self-respect in too many ways to even mention here. It got to me and I knew I was innocent. It gets to everybody. I was locked away in an iron cage for not one but three of my lifetimes. I was a prisoner, a number, a thing to be guarded with a maximum of security and a minimum of compassion. Not a person. Not a human being. But a body to be counted fifteen or twenty times a day. . . . After all that has been said and done—the fact that the most productive years

of my life between the ages of twenty nine and fifty have been stolen; the fact that I was deprived of seeing my children grow up—wouldn't you think I have the right to be bitter? Wouldn't anyone under those circumstances have a right to be bitter. . . . If I have learned nothing else in life, I've learned that bitterness only consumes the vessel that contains it. And for me to permit bitterness to control or infect my life in any way whatsoever, would be to allow those who imprisoned me to take even more than the twenty two years they've already taken . . . that would make me an accomplice to their crime. . . ."[38]

Carter went to live in Canada as he readjusted to life on the outside. After a few years, he returned to the United States and became executive director of an organization, Association in Defense of the Wrongly Convicted, to assist prisoners and death row inmates in their struggle for justice.

Case adapted from Paul B. Wice, *Rubin "Hurricane" Carter and the American Justice System* (New Brunswick: Rutgers University Press, 2000); Rubin "Hurricane" Carter, *The Sixteenth Round* (New York: Viking Press, 1974); James S. Hirsch, *Hurricane: The Miraculous Journey of Rubin Carter* (Boston: Houghton Mifflin Co, 2000).

THINKING CRITICALLY ABOUT THIS CASE

1. Why did Rubin Carter refuse to wear the prison uniform? Does his refusal make "sense" to you? Why or why not?
2. Is the prison a place for rehabilitation? Why or why not? What would need to change for prisons to genuinely reform inmates?
3. Rubin Carter learned violence on the street, but he learned it even better behind the walls, first in juvenile reformatory and then in prison. Why are prisons such violent environments? Are prisons violent because they hold violent inmates, or are the inmates violent because they are in prison?
4. What should conditions be like inside a prison? Should prisoners have access to education including college? Why or why not? Should prisoners have access to recreation? Why or why not? Treatment? Why or why not?
5. Should prisoners enjoy a degree of civil rights inside the prison? Why or why not? Do you support the prisoner's right to vote? Why or why not?
6. The absence of contact with the opposite sex is a major deprivation for incarcerated men and women. Would you support the implementation of conjugal visits in which married partners or couples are permitted to have overnight visits at the prison facility? Why or why not?
7. Carter once observed that released prisoners who have been inside for a long time "have so much anger that they have to swallow that the first person who looks at them the wrong way, they lose it. There comes a point where the prison should never set you free." What are the implications of this observation? What needs to change so that prisoners can be safely released back into the community?
8. Carter used to tell his fellow inmates, "Don't leave your manhood at the front gates and expect to pick it up on your way out." What is the meaning of this statement?

CHECK OUT THIS CASE

On The Web

www.lawbuzz.com/justice/hurricane/hurricane.htm
Find out more about the trials and the legal issues involved in the Rubin Carter case.

On Film

Hurricane (145 minutes)
Academy Award–winning film by Norman Jewison starring Denzel Washington as Rubin "Hurricane" Carter.

Inside the Prison World

At the heart of the correctional system that supervises more than 6.5 million Americans is a vast network of jails and prisons housing more than 2 million convicted adults, juveniles, and defendants awaiting trial. For most Americans, the daily lives of these imprisoned persons is both out of sight and out of mind. Unlike the trial, which takes place in a public setting and may even be broadcast on television, the process of punishment takes place behind thick fortress-like walls far from the centers of everyday life. Whereas colonial Americans doled out punishment in the bright light of day for all to see, the process of punishment for Kemba Smith (Chapter 13) and Rubin Carter, day after day and year after year, is not witnessed by the general public. It is easy for the public to believe that prisons are like "country clubs," offering inmates free room and board, weight-lifting rooms, and color television. The reality is far different.

The thirty-year odyssey of Rubin Carter through the penal institutions of the state of New Jersey offers us an insider's view of the prison world. Like layers in geological rock, we can detect traces of penal history preserved in prison practices such as the wearing of striped uniforms, the chain gang, lock-step marching, individual cells, shaved heads, the use of bells and enforced silence, solitary confinement, the ubiquitous inmate hierarchy of violence and sexual assault, the sheer idleness and boredom, racial tensions among the inmates, riots, prisoners' rights, and the ever-present hostility between the guards and inmates. All these features tell us something about the hopes, intentions, and failures of the prison system in our society.

Imprisonment is a costly response to crime. A society must have substantial resources to be able to create specialized institutions whose sole function is to deprive people of their liberty. The institution must provide for all the necessities to maintain them by housing, feeding, and clothing those held within their walls. Even higher is the cost of guarding them to prevent escape, rioting, or fighting back. Incarceration is an act of state coercion that must be continually maintained in order to keep people inside. The most costly item on the bill is the custodial staff and technology to maintain constant surveillance and vigilance over those who are imprisoned.

But we expect something more from our prison system than merely locking people away from society. The goal of rehabilitation is one key founding aspiration of the prison system. In Carter's view, "Prison destroys everything that is valuable in a human being." The pains of imprisonment described by Rubin Carter suggest that incarceration is more destructive than rehabilitative—less about correction and more about retribution. Is that what we intend? Are prisons intended to be destructive institutions that destroy human beings and their families? Why, then, do we call them "correctional systems"?

In this chapter, we continue our exploration of the goals of sentencing by looking at the purposes incarceration serves in our search for justice. What is the purpose of the prison, and why have we, as a society, come to rely on imprisonment as the dominant response to crime? Prisons exact a heavy price on inmates, their families, and communities, but they also take a huge toll on the "keepers" as well. What is the work of corrections like today? And what does the future hold?

ORIGINS OF THE PRISON: ENLIGHTENMENT AND REFORM

Before the nineteenth century, jails and prisons were typically used to hold the accused awaiting trial and the convicted awaiting punishment. The accused and convicted "witches" of the seventeenth century languished in jail while they waited for trials or the scaffold. Their confinement itself was not conceived as punishment. In the teeming jails and dungeons of Europe, men, women, and children were thrown together in huge stockades or pits. In the seventeenth and eighteenth centuries, transportation and banishment to the vast wild spaces was a cost-effective means of dealing with the growing number of petty thieves, pickpockets, and prostitutes overwhelming cities such as London and Paris.[39] The only other use of incarceration was debtors' prison, which confined people until they could pay their debts, usually through their extended family or some other benefactor. Apart from keeping the iron gates locked, little attention was given to what went on inside among the prisoners.

By the end of the eighteenth century, one of the problems with the system of punishment was its heavy reliance on the threat of the gallows for almost all felony offenses.[40] In England, the nobles of Parliament passed a series of statutes that punished the crimes of poaching, petty theft, pickpocketing, and setting fires in the forest with death by hanging. Under what was known as the infamous **"bloody codes,"** Parliament passed nearly two hundred capital offenses. However, the imposition of hanging for these crimes was both too extreme and too erratic to serve as a rational deterrent. The sight of a servant swinging from the gallows for the theft of silver from his master's kitchen angered the crowd, who had far more sympathy for the servant than for his master. Yet letting people go with a pardon of mercy undermined the rule of law that protected private property.

The same logic that gave birth to the institution of the modern police force also led to the founding ideals of the modern prison.[41] The concept of deterrence, as we have seen, relies on the belief that all people are rational and that the decision to commit crime is a calculated decision based on weighing costs and benefits. According to Enlightenment thinkers, the solution to crime was to devise a rational form of punishment that would be both certain and proportionate to the crime. A system based on fines and deprivation of one's liberty through incarceration seemed a logical and rational alternative to the messy gallows.

Another contributing factor to the rise of prisons was the decline in the use of **corporal punishment.** Whipping, branding, mutilation, dunking, public humiliation, stoning, and banishment all focused on the body of the offender. These public punishments took place before raucous crowds, who witnessed the punishment with a mixture of vengeful satisfaction and gleeful relief. By the nineteenth century, the growing

"bloody codes": a system of laws in eighteenth-century England that permitted capital punishment for a wide range of property and minor offenses.

corporal punishment: punishment inflicted on the body through whipping, branding, mutilation, or torture.

Before the shift to incarceration, most punishments involved the imposition of physical pain on the body of the offender within the public setting of the town market square. Whippings, brandings, and executions were public spectacles attended by members of the community.

THE WHIPPING-POST AND PILLORY AT NEW CASTLE, DELAWARE.—[SKETCHED BY EARL SHINN.]—[SEE PAGE 394.]

bourgeois middle class no longer approved of the violent spectacle of punishment in the city streets. There was a shift in sensibilities away from the brutality of corporal punishment, and more value was placed on impersonal and bureaucratic forms of governance and social control.[42]

Penitentiary: Redemption and Reform

The use of incarceration as a form of punishment was a nineteenth-century innovation. It was the golden age of the asylum.[43] Large-scale institutions for the poor, orphans, the mentally ill, the criminal, and juvenile delinquents were invented to care for dependent and troublesome populations. The modern penitentiary is a peculiarly American invention, owing as much to the religious philosophy and understanding of the Quakers as to the rationality of European classicists. Observers from Europe flocked to the New World to study these new penal innovations.[44]

The ideal of rehabilitation, originally conceived as a form of religious redemption through monastic silence, contemplation, and hard labor, was at the heart of the American vision of the penitentiary. Quakers believed that everyone had God within him or her and everyone could be redeemed. Prisoners had been corrupted by the evil influences of alcohol, the city, and sin. But they could be reformed as acceptable members of society through the contemplative power of the penitentiary.

The **Walnut Street Jail** in Philadelphia, opened in 1790, was the first American **penitentiary** and the first penal institution to adopt the monastic structure of individual cells for solitary confinement of inmates.[45] Less serious offenders were held in larger cells, where they worked together at various trades. The solitary system developed at the Walnut Street Jail was adopted by the first major large-scale U.S. institutions, the Eastern and Western Penitentiaries, built in 1826 and 1829 in different parts of Pennsylvania. The architecture of these vast and hugely expensive institutions was based on the concept that prisoners needed complete isolation from their corrupting environment in the city and from the influence of their fellow prisoners.

In the **separate system,** individual cells were built with individual exercise yards attached to them. The prisoner washed, ate, worked, and slept in his cell, seeing no one

Walnut Street Jail: the first American penitentiary, opened in Philadelphia in 1790.

penitentiary: an institution intended to isolate prisoners from society and from one another so they could reflect on their past, repent, and emerge as reformed sinners.

separate system: complete solitary confinement in an individual cell, to encourage redemption and prevent social contamination via association with others in the prison; first used in the Walnut Street Jail in Philadelphia.

other than the guard who brought meals but who was forbidden to speak. Europeans flocked to the United States to see and praise this innovative new design, described in glowing terms as allowing prisoners to gain peace and serenity through religious contemplation and meditation. Others, however, noted the intense cruelty of this form of imprisonment, by which a man could be confined in a twelve-by-eight cell, with no human contact, for three, ten, or even twenty years. According to Charles Dickens, who visited Eastern Penitentiary in 1842, "Very few men are capable of estimating the immense amount of torture and agony which this dreadful punishment, prolonged for years, inflicts upon the sufferers."[46]

The separate system was soon supplanted by a different model that was far more economical to administer. The **congregate system** was developed in the Auburn Prison in upstate New York in 1823. Also known as the *silent system*, the Auburn Prison held prisoners at night in individual cells, but put them together in large work groups during the day to perform manual labor. The use of group labor supported the institution financially, but prisoners were supposedly shielded from corruption by the strict enforcement of silence. Auburn invented the "hole," or the use of **punitive solitary confinement** for those who violated the rules of silence, the **lockstep,** a peculiar form of marching for prisoners, and the wearing of **striped uniforms** to degrade inmates and make it more difficult for them to escape.

The penitentiary was considered a noble experiment in human reform. The use of solitary confinement as a form of punishment was a humane and civilized alternative to whipping, beatings, and other forms of corporal punishments. Each prisoner, in theory, was a soul who could be saved. But the reality of the prison never came close to the dreams of the reformers. Institutions in the northern states became dumping grounds for poor immigrants who flooded the cities during the nineteenth century. What characterized most of the inmates was not a perverse degradation of the soul but economic dislocation and poverty. Enforced silence, isolation, and the "hole" were perhaps even more inhumane than the previous system of whipping and beatings for crimes of property. And despite the intentions of the reformers, brutality by guards flourished behind the walls without the watchful eye of the public crowd to keep it in check.

On a practical level, prisons were expensive to operate. The economic need to run the institution itself led to the efficient use of convict labor. For much of the nineteenth century, Auburn-style prisons operated like factories or "industrial prisons," making use of the unskilled labor force for work in industries such as textile mills and turning handsome profits for the institution.[47] In some states, cheap inmate labor was leased out to private businesses under the **contract system.** Private employers bid for control of the labor force, at the same time generating profits for the warden. In agricultural regions, prison labor was used for farming on plantation prisons, generating revenue and resources for the warden to support the institution.[48]

The Reformatory Movement

By the close of the nineteenth century, penitentiaries had become a national scandal, sparking a wave of prison reform. Far from the contemplative vision of the founders, these institutions were brutal environments with heavy emphasis on forced labor and custody. Beginning in 1870, a treatment philosophy began to supplant the religious ideals of the earlier prison regimes.[49] Treatment professionals, social workers, psychologists, and probation officers became the new personnel to try to reform the criminals held in institutions. The reformatory movement advocated the use of vocational preparation, treatment interventions, education, and an internal system of privileges or rewards to motivate offenders to earn their way toward rehabilitation and release back to society as productive members of that society.

At the heart of the reformatory model was the indeterminate sentence: confinement should not be for a set period of time but should be based on the inmate's behavior in

congregate system: penitentiary system developed in Auburn, New York, in which inmates were held in solitary confinement at night but worked with fellow prisoners during the day under a rule of complete silence.

punitive solitary confinement: use of solitary confinement under conditions of extreme deprivation as a punishment for disciplinary infractions.

lockstep: peculiar form of marching for prisoners, in which they were required to move in unison with their hands on each others' shoulders.

striped uniform: specialized uniform designed to reduce escapes and to impose humiliation on the convict.

contract system: form of prison industry in which the labor of inmates was leased to an outside contractor or business for a fee.

reformatory movement: nineteenth-century prison reform movement generally reserved for youth and women, which focused on rehabilitation, reform, and the use of indeterminate sentencing.

the system. The concept of parole or conditional release was developed in Ireland in the 1850s in one of the first reformatory systems; prisoners were able to earn early release or could have their privileges taken away if their conduct failed to meet specified criteria.[50]

The first U.S. reformatory opened in 1876 in Elmira, New York, primarily for youth and first-time offenders.[51] The reformatory movement coincided with the establishment of a juvenile justice system, and the philosophy was the dominant ideal adopted by the juvenile correctional authorities.[52] When Rubin Carter was sent to Jamesburg State Home for Boys, the institution was authorized to hold him until his twenty-first birthday, but at their discretion they could release him at any time. The warden who offered Rubin a release almost three years before his twenty-first birthday held complete discretion in these matters. Under the administrative model of sentencing, prison officials held enormous power over the actual length of a prisoner's sentence. They used this release authority as a carrot to induce cooperation on the part of the prisoners.

The reformatories were designed primarily for the young first-time offender or for females whose primary crimes were prostitution or promiscuity beyond the bounds of marriage.[53] Until 1870, most women prisoners were housed in left-over rooms in prisons built for men. However, between 1860 to 1935, twenty-one institutions for women were built in the United States. These reformatories were designed and built specifically for women, reflecting the belief that women were in need of a gentler, more homelike environment. These institutions sought to prepare women for domestic life as wives or servants. Women's reformatories largely served minor offenders, often young white working-class women, while black women continued to be shunted off to custodial-type institutions.

Before long, these institutions, for males or females, devolved to the pure custodial model, relying primarily on constant surveillance, brutality, and solitary confinement to contain the inmates.[54] The inmate population was mostly poor immigrants. Middle-class reformers treated their charges harshly and with far more discipline than love. There was nothing "homelike" in the cottages with their tidy brick facades and deceptively tranquil green lawns. The problem of inmates constantly escaping from the institutions increased reliance on force, physical restraint, and punishment. As we can see in Jamesburg State Home for Boys, there was little in that experience that would "reform" young boys like Rubin Carter into law-abiding citizens. Reformatories became the proverbial "schools for crime" and the first step toward doing time in the penitentiary.

The Big House

The penitentiary and reformatory designed by passionate and educated reformers to transform "criminals" into model citizens did not survive beyond the early years of enthusiastic experimentation and reform. The physical buildings remained with their thick walls and hundreds of individual cells, and practices such as solitary confinement, marching in formation, and the wearing of the prison stripes persisted, but the goals of redemption and rehabilitation were rapidly subordinated to the practical agenda of confinement for thousands upon thousands of young, poor, uneducated European immigrants and Southern blacks.

The term **"Big House"** referred to the maximum security prison, noted for its harshness and reserved for the really tough criminals.[55] The prison regime that survived into the twentieth century had less idealistic reform and more sheer boredom for the inmate. The profitable use of prison labor diminished in the twentieth century because of opposition from labor unions, who fought for laws that prevented unfair labor competition from cheap inmate workers. Many states passed **state-use laws,** which forbade the use of prison labor for market goods and mandating that convict labor be utilized only for prison needs or state needs such as making license plates.

Work became less productive and more a tool for punishment. The image of the Big House, where convicts are forced to break up rocks for no apparent purpose other than

"Big House": slang for maximum security prisons infamous for harsh conditions and tough inmate populations.

state-use laws: laws requiring prison industry to produce goods solely for use by state institutions.

to maintain order and to impose misery, was the prototype for the early-twentieth-century maximum security prison. In the South, plantation prisons with hard field labor and chain gangs were commonplace for both black men and black women. Prisoners spent their time sitting in their cells, engaged in some kind of menial work such as prison laundry, breaking rocks, or making licence plates, or milling about the yard. As Carter noted, boredom is the "inmate's worst enemy."[56]

Modern Correctional Systems

By the late twentieth century, most states had a centralized department of corrections to oversee all the penal institutions in the state, with the Federal Bureau of Prisons responsible for the federal penal system. Many states prefer the term "correctional institution" instead of prison, penitentiary, or reform school. Prisons today are a growth industry: in 1981, state governments spent about $3.2 billion operating prisons and jails and another $500 million on new prison construction. Thirteen years later, in 1993, states were still spending about $500 million a year to build new facilities, but the cost of operating existing facilities had escalated to almost $16 billion a year; by 1996, states spent over $25 billion to operate, maintain, and build new prison cells.[57] In 1995, for the first time in history, the state of California spent more money on building prisons than it did on financing the state college system.[58] Employment in the field of corrections is also booming. Among Fortune 500 companies, only General Motors employs more people than the U.S. correctional system.[59]

Today institutions are distinguished by the level of custody associated with the facility.[60] **Maximum security prisons** are designed to hold the most dangerous, aggressive, and incorrigible inmates. They are typically surrounded by massive walls, supplemented by armed guard towers and layers of razor wire. The prison regime in a maximum security facility is heavily focused on custody and control. Inmates may be locked down in their cells much of the time, and movement is heavily restricted and monitored.

Medium security prisons are less fortress-like and inmates have more mobility within the facility, although there is generally a maximum security wing for inmates who violate the rules. **Minimum security prisons** have the least internal restrictions on inmates, dormitory living is common, and the external structure of the building may be surrounded by a simple high fence.

Most correctional systems have all three types of facilities as well as an array of supplemental correctional facilities such as boot camps, forestry camps, prison farms, halfway houses, or ranches, which function more as open institutions with greater interaction with the life outside the facility than prisons, which operate as closed total institutions. We will look at some of these alternatives to prison when we examine community corrections.

A third wave of prison building has occurred in recent decades, with a fourth style of prison design known as the **super-max prison** or maxi-maxi prison. Designed to address the rampant violence in the maximum security prison, the super-max aims to achieve order and control through technology and design as well as correctional supervision. The first super-max was the Federal Penitentiary in Marion, Illinois. Other institutions have copied its high tech super-controlled regime, giving rise to the term "marionization" to refer to super-maximum security facilities in which inmate movement is severely restricted.[61]

In most modern correctional systems there is a complex process of **classification,** which determines the type of institution in which inmates will serve their time. The idea of classification is to determine the security level, educational, vocational, and treatment needs of the offender. The classification may depend on the offense, the prior history of the offender, psychological or educational needs, and behavioral record in the system. System-wide classification determines where a particular inmate will serve and classification within the institution determines which wing or cellblock the

maximum security prison: facility designed to impose maximal restriction on inmates in order to contain the most incorrigible and violent offenders.

medium security prison: prison designed to impose less restrictive conditions on inmates, allowing more visitation, programming, and recreation for inmates.

minimum security prison: institution designed to permit the least dangerous inmates relative freedom of movement within the confines of a locked perimeter.

super-max prison: a new generation of maximum security facility, which relies on technology and high levels of supervision and restriction of inmate movement.

classification: process through which the custodial, educational, and treatment needs of the offender are assessed in order to ascertain placement in the correctional system.

The contemporary maximum and medium security facility is composed of many tiers of cells stacked one on top of the other to facilitate efficient surveillance by correctional personnel. These cells resemble cages for human beings warehoused as punishment for their crime. Approximately two million Americans are locked inside our nation's prisons and jails.

inmate will be assigned to. Prisoners typically are continually reclassified as they move around the system.

Rubin Carter refused to cooperate in the classification process when he declined to be interviewed by staff social workers or psychologists. Despite the custodial regime of Trenton State Prison, the facility nonetheless maintained a treatment staff to offer some rehabilitation or correctional programming for qualified inmates. In most correctional settings there is constant tension between the custodial staff, which includes the correctional officers or guards, and the treatment staff of social workers, psychologists, and medical workers. This tension between those who view the prisoners as objects of punishment and those who view them as recipients of services reflects the contradictory aims of the system itself.

In recent decades, there has been substantial growth in the use of private correctional facilities such as Corrections Corporation of America, the largest private company, Wackenhut, and Esmor Corporation. In 1983, there were no privately operated facilities; by 1994, private beds were up to about 45,000 across the nation, by 1997 the number had reached 62,000 beds.[62] The pressure from overcrowding has led many states to contract out their prisoners to private facilities or in some cases to send prisoners to other states. In addition, private companies contract with state prison systems to provide goods such as furniture, clothing, and security systems, and services such as medical care or food service.

As private companies, these are for-profit businesses that claim to offer correctional facilities to states at competitive prices, thus saving taxpayers millions of dollars.[63] To critics, however, profit-making on our incarcerated population is highly problematic: companies are likely to cut corners wherever possible and to avoid costly state unions to control costs. For-profit prisons also have an incentive to keep people locked up: release of an inmate is loss of revenue. The economic incentive for the prison business is to run a full-occupancy institution. Critics are also concerned about the absence of oversight and regulation of private prisons and the serious possibility for abuse of the highly vulnerable and neglected criminal population.

In addition to state and federal prisons, there are also networks of **jails** operated by local authorities, usually counties. Jails serve a distinct purpose from prison. Jails are designed as short-term detention facilities for defendants awaiting trial or for short-term

jail: facility authorized to hold persons awaiting trial and those sentenced for misdemeanors and minor felony offenses.

stays of incarceration on minor offenses. Jails range in size from small-town lockups that can house only a few occupants at a time to modern facilities that house thousands of inmates for periods of up to five years or more.

Jails have a notorious history of being neglected, vermin-ridden, decrepit places, where inmates are housed in large cagelike rooms containing a number of offenders ranging from the drunk who needs to sleep it off to the shoplifter to the dangerous predator.[64] Sanitary facilities are often very poor, facilities are old, and staffing is minimal. Many jails lack any recreational or educational facilities, so inmates remain idle and in their cells for most of their stay. On the other hand, some jail facilities are run according to the best of modern standards in both physical and correctional programming.[65]

The Structure of Correctional Management Today   The management of modern correctional facilities is a highly specialized professional occupation requiring skills not dissimilar to the management of other large organizations. Historically, the warden was an autocratic figure appointed through political connections to the governor, with the power to run the institution according to his or her own rules. After World War II, most states established departments of correction, run by commissioners and supported by an executive bureaucracy, that set policy for the correctional system as a whole. These policies are carried out by superintendents or wardens, who, in turn, are supported by numerous layers of deputies or middle managers responsible for key administrative functions within the institution. Since the 1960s, there has also been a large support staff in most institutions: doctors, nurses, chaplains, psychologists, teachers, counselors, clerks, and secretaries, with specific jobs associated with the needs of the incarcerated population.

The most difficult job and the one with the greatest degree of direct contact with the inmates is that of the correctional officer. The job of the modern correctional officers is largely focused on the custodial function of maintaining security, order, and discipline among the inmate population. In the jargon of prison culture, correctional officers are referred to as "hacks," "pigs," or "screws": there is little about the job of the line officer that deals with treatment or rehabilitation.

While they are not always in direct conflict with each other, the nature of the prison system means that there is constant tension between guards and inmates, which can erupt into violence at any time. Like police officers, prison guards face a constant challenge to their authority among those who are constantly seeking to undermine it. Similar to the war model of policing, in which police come to view citizens as "enemies," prison guards are structured to view inmates as dangerous, threatening, and less than human.

These are social conditions highly conducive to abuse of authority through violence on the part of a minority of guards who choose to use violence to exert control over inmates. In a classic social psychological experiment, researcher Phillip Zombardo of Stanford University set up a mock prison environment with college students randomly assigned to play the roles of guards and inmates.[66] The experiment elicited substantial aggressive and sadistic behavior on the part of a few of the "guards," as well as disturbing signs of psychological deterioration on the part of those assigned to play "inmates." It had to be called off after only a few days to protect the participants. This experiment illustrates the power of the "structured conflict" to bring out negative behaviors in people who occupy those roles.

There are some ironic similarities between the working environment of the correctional guard and conditions of life for the inmate. Guards are subject to the constant threat of danger, and experience tremendous isolation, boredom, loneliness, and anxiety in an environment in which no one can be trusted. Correctional staff are isolated from management and often feel disrespected in their status as guards. They are also vulnerable to informants or prison snitches who might relay any rule violations or infractions to their superiors. Many guards refer to themselves as the "other inmates" and refer to their job as "doing life" on the installment plan.

INSIDE THE PRISON WORLD

Regardless of the prevailing philosophy or the type of facility where a person is incarcerated, prisons and jails are coercive institutions that maintain complete control over the inmate's existence. Segregated from society, the entire life of the inmate is regulated by the institution: inmates live, eat, work, sleep, wash, and recreate in one environment totally controlled by their "keepers." Erving Goffman, a sociologist who studied concentration camps, mental asylums, and prisons, coined the term **total institution** to describe the social structure of these types of organizations.[67] A total institution is one that maintains complete control over the lives of the inmates.

Most of us in modern society occupy a wide range of social roles: we are simultaneously sons and daughters, classmates, baseball players, lovers, spouses, customers, employees, students, friends, siblings, and parents. We possess not one social identity but many. The complexity of modern society and the separation of different parts of life allow us, as social actors, to have considerable control over the presentation of ourselves to others in order to "manage" the image we project. We use clothing, hairstyle, jewelry, speech, cars, and demeanor to control how we want others to see us. The process of "impression management" is a natural part of how we maintain a sense of our own identity in any given social setting.

The total institution stands in sharp contrast to outside society. Within the world of the "total institution" there are only two social roles: that of the "keeper" or prison staff, and that of the "kept" or inmate. The inmate is forced to occupy a single social role, that of a convict, twenty-four hours a day. The relationship between the guard and the inmate is one of **structured conflict**: inmates are locked up against their will and are subordinate to the domination of the institution; guards are the personnel who represent that authority and must enforce it as part of their job.[68]

The process of entering the institution involves a deliberate "stripping away" of all the markers of a person's outside identities. Goffman called this a **status degradation ceremony** because it marks a downward social transition into the lowly status of an inmate. People's heads are shaved; rings, necklaces, earrings, and watches are taken away; their naked bodies are searched, often brutally and in a dehumanizing fashion; they may be required to stand naked while they are washed down, examined, or deloused. Literally stripped of all that represented their former identity, the prisoners are now handed the markings of their new all-encompassing social status as inmates.

Recall the clothing used in the congregate system: the striped pajamas were intentionally designed to identify incarcerated persons as convicts and to humiliate them. The short pants put on the men at Annandale symbolically marked them as inferior beings, like children, dependent on the institution for their every need, big and small. The final insult of all is the taking away of one's name and its replacement with a number. The institutional ritual told Carter that he was no longer Mr. Rubin Carter but now inmate 45,472.

Rubin Carter resisted the status degradation ceremony when he entered Trenton State Prison for the second time. He had experienced it before when he had been incarcerated, and he knew the psychological pain of being stripped of his identity and his dignity. Although he paid dearly for his resistance, he refused to submit to this assault on his sense of self.

What Carter feared most was the possibility that he might become socialized to his status as an inmate and come to accept his position as so many around him did. Donald Clemmer used the term **prisonization** to refer to the process of assimilation whereby inmates became accustomed to their life as inmates.[69] Prisonization is the taking on of the folkways, mores, customs, and general culture of the penitentiary. The longer they are in the institution, the more inmates become "prisonized" to the rules of the institution and the values of the inmate subculture. Clemmer believed that at some

total institution: term coined by Erving Goffman to refer to institutions organized so that those who work in the institution exercise total control over every aspect of the lives of those who are inmates of the institution.

structured conflict: relationship between inmates and guards within the institution, in which inmates are confined against their will and guards are charged with the responsibility of enforcing their detention.

status degradation ceremony: ritual that marks the transition from a citizen to the lower status of inmate.

prisonization: process whereby a new inmate becomes socialized to the inmate subculture and adapts to prison life.

point a person internalizes these values and they become a permanent part of his or her value system. Others argue that inmates adopt the values during their period in prison but return to the norms of the outside world when they are released.

Pains of Imprisonment

In 1958, sociologist Gresham Sykes studied the Trenton State Prison where Rubin Carter later spent so many years of his life.[70] Sykes argued that the prison experience is shaped by deprivations of a profound and deeply shameful nature, which he called the **pains of imprisonment.** The deprivation of liberty does not even begin to describe what is really taken away from the person who is incarcerated. Sykes describes the utter dependence on the institution for all the goods and services of daily life. If the prison does not provide a place to relieve oneself, the inmate is utterly powerless to maintain even basic personal hygiene. Humans are reduced to the status of animals. In the hole, Carter lived with only a bucket for his bodily needs. The prison controlled toilet paper, soap, clothing, food, water, light, even air to breathe. An adult is forced to become completely dependent on guards and prison management for every last detail of his or her basic physical needs, reducing grown men and women to the state of infantile dependency.

Inmates are deprived of heterosexual interactions. This is far more significant than merely the absence of sexual contact. Gender identity represents a significant part of one's personal sense of self: being masculine or feminine is a social role that depends on the presence of the opposite sex. Just as it is impossible to be a parent without a child or a teacher without a student, it is psychologically difficult to maintain an identity as masculine without the presence of women. According to Sykes, the perverse nature of homosexual sex in prison, in which weak inmates are forced to take on the feminine roles of "wives" or "ladies" is the result of this deprivation.

The form of sexual intimidation and violent sexual assault that Carter witnessed in all of the institutions in which he was confined is ubiquitous in most maximum and medium security prisons and jails. The hidden secret of the prison system is that some unknown number of men are systematically and continually subjected to rape. There is little available data on this topic, given its sensitive nature. Some believe prison rape to be ubiquitous, while others believe it is relatively rare. Most agree that prison rape, like rape in the outside culture, is more about violence and control than it is about sexual relationships or bonding. Older inmates, often called "wolves," offer protection to young inmates, "punks," who trade sex for security and goods from the commissary. The punks are treated like sexual slaves who are owned and may be lent or traded to other inmates. Only the men who have been forced to be "ladies" are seen as homosexuals and are generally despised for it. The "wolves" are seen as real men who rely on their toughness and willingness to use violence to protect their status.

The prison also deprives inmates of their autonomy. Every decision is made for them by the institution. As Rubin Carter observed, along with the absence of women, the other most difficult pain of imprisonment is the complete absence of control.

> Two of the hardest things about being in jail are, first that you can never make a decision for yourself—every one, from the time to eat or sleep, walk, talk or even breathe, is already made up for you; the only thing that is yours to decide which requires no deep concentration, is whether or not to stand up or sit down in your cell. . . . The other . . . is the unreasonable absence of women.[71]

Inmates are told when to eat, when to shower, when to walk, where to stand, when to sleep and when to wake, lights go out at a certain time and they must wake at a certain time. They are often moved around from cell to cell or institution to institution like so many boxes in a giant storehouse. They have no control over what happens to them.

Finally, the prison deprives inmates of security over their own personal safety. Men in prison exist in a constant state of fear of assault from fellow inmates. It is impossible

pains of imprisonment: deprivations of prison life, including absence of goods, autonomy, heterosexual interaction, and security.

to let one's guard down, so everyone wears the "mask" of toughness as a form of protection. As long-time prisoner Jack Abbott wrote, "Everyone is afraid. It is not an emotional, psychological fear. It is a practical matter. If you do not threaten someone at the very least someone will threaten you."[72] The ability to protect oneself by locking one's doors or moving away from dangerous people is not an option for a person held under these conditions. The prison deprives inmates of the peace of mind that comes from being safe.

The impact of these deprivations is difficult for people outside of prison to truly comprehend. The pains of imprisonment are assaults on one's sense of self-respect, dignity, and self-esteem. Animals might be quite content to be warehoused if they are adequately fed and exercised. But human beings are not animals, and the indignities, humiliations, and frustrations of prison life generate enormous rage and attack the very spirit of the inmates. Carter believed that the real danger of prison life was its impact on his own psychological well-being, and he resisted taking on the inmate role as much as he could. He was willing to endure physical suffering over this kind of social death. When Carter refused to enter a cell in the VRU unit that was littered with rat droppings, his words of resistance were very telling: "My name is Rubin, not Fido."[73]

Prison Subculture: Importation versus Deprivation

The inmate social system was heavily studied between the 1940s and 1960s describing many different "roles" in the subculture of the inmates. A common thread in all the different descriptions is the predominance of violence, the value placed on physical strength, the aggressive pattern of sexual activity, and the proscription against "snitching" to the guards or prison administration. Sykes and others believe the psychological harms of deprivation are responsible for much of the violence and pathology of the prison subculture. The frustration and degradation generate a continual atmosphere of violence, which then erupts between inmates over petty issues. Lives may be lost over a pack of cigarettes, a second dessert, a sexual favor, an offhand comment, or a careless glance.

The **importation theory** of prison violence argues that the inmate culture is the result of values and norms imported from street culture. In their classic research, Irwin and Creesey found many of the same "social types" inside prisons as on the outside.[74] The current dominance of gangs in prisons provides strong support for the idea that much of what takes place in prisons has strong connections to patterns of interaction in the outside world. Patterns of race relations in prison mirror and intensify existing historical patterns of segregation and hostility in the wider society.

Beginning in the 1960s, the influence of racially or ethnically homogenous gangs operating in prisons has grown in significance in the internal dynamics of the prison.[75] Opposing gangs, segregated by racial and ethnic affiliation, compete for dominance within the inmate population. Sexual assault and gang rape is often committed across racial lines to assert dominance of blacks over whites in an intentional form of racial revenge for historical oppression in the outside world.[76]

Some researchers argue that gang activity is the result of the breakdown in earlier authoritarian systems of control, in which powerful white inmates were delegated substantial power and control by autocratic administrations. Known in southern prisons as the **building tender system,** this type of management system is similar to the structure at Jamesburg, where the administration appointed certain inmates to keep order in their own units. This system was dismantled during the era of increased civil rights for prisoners to a secure environment. The **paradox of reform,** some believe, is that the prisoners' rights movement, legal mandates, and shifts in management philosophies that were intended to improve prison conditions have actually unleashed even more virulent forms of violence than during the repressive days of the "Big House."[77] On the other hand, others believe that the source of violence and risk of assault has merely shifted from the building tenders and guards of the old-style regime to the violent gangs and aggressive inmates of today.[78]

importation theory: theory that inmate subculture is brought into the institution from criminal subcultures in the outside society.

deprivation theory: theory that the inmate subculture is formed as an adaptation to and reaction to the deprivations of prison life.

building tender system: system of inmate control whereby the most violent and intimidating inmates were chosen as "building tenders" by guards to control their fellow inmates by violence and coercion.

paradox of reform: theory that legal interventions designed to improve the conditions of incarceration may have contributed to more serious violent conditions in prisons.

There is also a great deal of drug and alcohol use and abuse behind the walls. In fact, some believe that it is as easy to obtain drugs in prison as it is to get them outside. Drugs are smuggled into the institution partly by visitors but principally through prison staff who are blackmailed or enticed by financial reward. Gangs control the terrain of the prison in the same way they control parts of the city streets, claiming a portion of the yard or a particular recreation room. They also control the drug trade and a sex trade that operate on the inside as they do on the outside.[79]

Both the importation theory of prison violence and the deprivation theory of prison violence point to important casual factors of prison violence. In prisons where the pains of imprisonment are lessened through a more enlightened or genuinely rehabilitative regime, there is significantly less violence among the inmates. A brutal and punitive prison administration, on the other hand, stokes tension and rage among the inmates and allows the worst abuses to occur unchecked. On the other hand, the racial tensions in the institution and the impact of gangs is clearly a factor beyond the control of prison authorities. These dynamics originate in the wider society and are brought into the prison.

The Prisoners' Rights Movement

When Rubin Carter was disciplined for refusing to take a prison job and transferred to the VRU as punishment, he knew he had rights within the prison system even though he was an inmate. After nearly ten years behind walls, Carter had educated himself in the laws governing his conditions of confinement. Not only was Carter able to understand the law as it pertained to his own circumstances, he also knew that the courts had ruled that as a **jailhouse lawyer,** he was permitted to advise other inmates on their own legal issues.

The recognition that prisoners retain some degree of civil rights did not occur until the 1960s and 1970s. In 1871, in *Ruffin* v. *Commonwealth*,[80] the Virginia courts ruled that a convicted felon "has as a consequence of his crime, not only forfeited his liberty but all his personal rights. . . . He is for the time being a slave of the state." The Ruffin doctrine declared that prisoners, while they were behind bars, were, in the eyes of the law, "civilly dead."

Although this legal theory was amended in the twentieth century, so that prisoners retained some rights while incarcerated, the courts maintained a **hands-off doctrine,** deferring to prison administrators and preferring to leave matters of correctional policy in the hands of legislators and the executive branch of government. Courts also feared an avalanche of prisoner litigation if they set the precedent of interfering with the prerogatives of the penal authority. However, in 1964, in *Cooper* v. *Pate*,[81] the U.S. Supreme Court ruled that inmates could file lawsuits under the federal Civil Rights Act, Section 1983, against public officials for alleged violations of the prisoners' civil rights. This case involved the First Amendment rights of Black Muslims to practice their religion by having access to the Koran.

The prisoners' rights movement coincided with increased political consciousness within the prison system and the wider society.[82] Black and Hispanic prisoners became increasingly militant and angry over the injustices of the indeterminate sentencing system. Rubin Carter lived through this period while in Rahway State Prison. The civil rights movement and the Black Power movement laid the groundwork for a growing political consciousness among inmates, especially inmates of color.

On September 9, 1971, a riot broke out in the prison at Attica in upstate New York.[83] The riot lasted for four days. Prisoners led by militant Black Muslims took over large portions of the prison and presented the administration with a list of demands, largely for more due process in discipline and grievance, better food, and more treatment programs. Negotiations began with outside civil rights attorneys and journalist observers. But Governor Nelson Rockefeller decided not to cooperate and ordered the prison to be stormed by state police and correctional guards. Of the forty-three individuals who were killed, thirty-nine were killed by state officers in the retaking of the prison. In the aftermath, prisoners were brutally and violently beaten by guards.

jailhouse lawyer:
a prisoner who gives legal advice and assistance to other prisoners.

hands-off doctrine:
refusal of the courts to hear inmates' cases regarding conditions of confinement and Constitutional deprivations within institutions.

In 1974, the Supreme Court ruled in *Wolff* v. *McDonald*[84] that there was "no iron curtain drawn between the Constitution and the prisons of this country," signaling an end to the hands-off doctrine on the part of the courts. Since *Cooper* there is a recognition that prisoners retain some civil rights inside prison, although not equal to a free citizen. The role of the court is to strike a balance between the security needs of the administration and the civil rights of the inmates.

During the 1970s, the federal courts became willing to assert and defend the Constitutional rights of prisoners more actively. The entire prison system of several states—Arkansas, Alabama, Rhode Island, and Mississippi—were declared to be unconstitutional. By 1980, one of every five cases filed in federal court was on behalf of prisoners. Most of the issues concerned the details of everyday life in prison. The key issues concerned overcrowding, brutality, poor medical care, inadequate or unhygienic living conditions, access to lawyers, access to mail, religious freedom particularly led by Black Muslims, and due process in disciplinary transfers and good time forfeiture. By 1988, thirty-five states were under court order to improve their conditions of confinement. In the 1990s, however, the courts to an extent returned to a reliance on the hands-off doctrine, ruling against a number of due process protections for inmates in disciplinary matters and signaling a reluctance on the part of the courts to interfere with the discretion of state administrators.[85]

CONTEMPORARY PRISONS ISSUES

Women in Prison

Women constitute about 6 percent of the prison population, and women's institutions have both been neglected by administrators and ignored by researchers for most of the twentieth century. Although men vastly outnumber women in the prison system, the number of women being sent to prison accelerated faster during the 1980s and 1990s than it did among men.[86] Between 1980 and 1997, the number of women in prison increased by 573 percent.[87] Since the 1960s, prison litigation on behalf of women has focused on the inferiority of programming for women, the absence of different levels of incarceration as exist for men, resulting in the overclassification of many women into secure facilities, and the right to have equal treatment to that available to men.[88]

Life behind the walls for Kemba Smith most likely was very different than it was for Rubin Carter. Research has found that the women's inmate subculture differs from the male subculture, although in some respects there are similarities. Giallombardo found that women inmates tended to form pseudo-families with extended kin roles to provide support, protection, emotional sustenance, and shared resources.[89] While homosexuality was prohibited within these families, women also formed stable and consensual relationships in prison based on consensual sex. The pattern of exploitation and assault typical of male prisons is not commonly found in women's institutions. Gang activity in women's prisons is also different from that in men's prisons. Although younger women are joining gangs today, there is little evidence of substantial gang activity in women's prisons. Women's prisons are less violent, so there is less need for group protection and the pseudo-families serve this function to some extent.

Kemba Smith is, in some respects, very typical of the female prison population. The average female inmate is black or Hispanic, between the ages of 25 and 35, and is a single parent with one to three children.[90] She is typically serving time for a drug offense or for nonviolent property crime. Most incarcerated women leave children behind and were the primary caregivers for those children. When women are put behind bars, there is a profound loss for their children, who are punished by the loss of their mother. When a father is incarcerated, the care for the children is usually assumed by the mother; but when a mother goes to prison, her children have usually lost their sole caregiver. The separation from their children and the attempt to maintain contact with their children while they are behind the wall is a key issue for women. Children generally are dependent on relatives or foster care.

Many women enter into the system already pregnant. Women generally are allowed to deliver their babies in an outside hospital, although they will be separated from the infant within days of the birth. In the Bedford Hills Correctional Center in New York state, where nearly 80 percent of the inmates have children, there is a prison nursery on a floor of the prison hospital where mother and baby share a room for the first year of the child's life. Older children are permitted to come for longer stays, and there is even a camp near the facility for inmates' children. According to Sister Elaine, "The kids have done nothing wrong to cause this painful separation. We need to do all we can to strengthen bonds so the kids don't come back to prison later in a different way."[91]

Overcrowding, Race, and Violence

The modern correctional administrator faces an enormous number of challenges, and overcrowding is often at the top of the list.[92] Sentencing policies of the previous three decades have led to huge increases in the number of inmates. The judicial process continues to funnel people to prison despite the limited capacity of institutions to house them adequately. Double and triple bunking of inmates in cells designed for single occupancy heightens stress, increases vulnerability to assaults, and raises tensions between inmates and guards. Studies show a strong relationship between overcrowding and inmate rule violations.[93] In addition, the density of housing adds to the spread of infectious diseases within the institution as well as adding to a range of stress-related illnesses such as high blood pressure.

As noted earlier, violence in prison, inmate-on-inmate violence as well as inmate assault of guards, has increased significantly in the post-rights era.[94] The largest single contributor to the increase in prison populations is drug sentencing, which has fallen

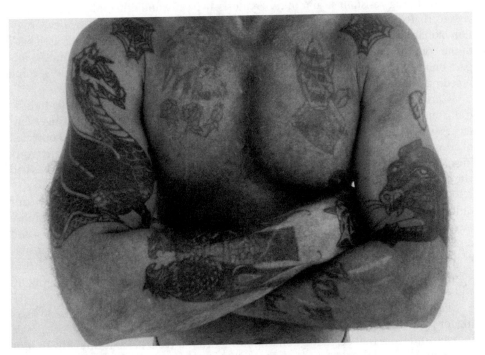

Prison culture today is dominated by racially segregated gangs with strong ties and associations to gangs on the outside. Violence, drugs, rape, intimidation, and extortion are common inside many of our nation's prison facilities. Overcrowding has exacerbated many of the negative features of prison life, making it difficult for authorities to control and manage the population.

disproportionately on minorities. The disparity in sentencing of racial minorities has increased racial hostility as minority gangs assert power and control over whites within the institution. Race has become the key feature of the inmate subculture. Even in women's prisons, where racial dynamics have been less prominent, the recent influx of new female prisoners has been predominantly African American, and there are signs of increasing racial tensions.

Overcrowding exacerbates the problem by both increasing the incidence of violence and making violence harder to control. The condition of overcrowding, in turn, leads to a heavier reliance on solitary confinement and punitive disciplinary segregation to maintain order. Inmates come to prison from violent subcultures on the street and are maintained in an environment that also relies on violence as a means of survival. It is not surprising, therefore, that many prisoners who are initially arrested for nonviolent offenses are later arrested for violent offenses.[95]

Health Care and Special Needs Inmates

Another major challenge facing prison administrators today concerns the growing crisis of long-term health problems among prisoners with AIDS, drug-resistant tuberculosis, age-related illnesses, and mental illness. The rate of confirmed AIDS among prisoners is estimated to be at least six times higher than that among the general population.[96] Even by 1995, one-third of all inmate deaths in state prisons across the nation were due to AIDS.[97] The number of inmates who are HIV positive is unknown but can be presumed to be substantially higher. Many of the inmates entering prison are intravenous drug users and are entering the institution already infected. Among inmates, the rate of transmission is not known, given the hidden nature of prison sexual activity, but by all estimates there is a growing epidemic inside our nation's prisons which will be felt in the near future as the incubation period ends and more inmates with HIV need medical attention.

Other infectious diseases are also spreading rapidly in modern prisons. The transmission of drug-resistant strains of tuberculosis, hepatitis, and other infectious diseases is exacerbated by conditions of overcrowding and the lack of adequate medical attention in many institutions. Given that approximately 10 million persons are released back to the community each year after spending some time in either jail or prison, the impact on the public health of the wider society is also in jeopardy as prisons become breeding grounds for serious disease.[98]

Caring for elderly inmates is the third looming crisis facing correctional administrators in the twenty-first century. A natural consequence of the shift toward longer sentences is the aging of the inmate population: although few elderly people are convicted of crime, changes in sentencing practices have meant that many more inmates are growing old behind bars. In the state of California alone, the number of geriatric inmates will rise from 5,000 in 1994 to about 126,400 in the year 2020.[99]

As inmates age, their health needs skyrocket, compounded by the unhealthy conditions of confinement. A need for special geriatric wards is emerging, requiring more intensive health care and the purchase of equipment such as wheelchairs, walkers, and replacing stairs with ramps. While the cost of incarceration for the average inmate hovers between $20,000 and $30,000 per year, the cost of confining elderly inmates soars to $69,000 per year.[100] As the inmate population ages, the need to care for these inmates will continue to stress the resources of state budgets and prison systems.

Further compounding the management of inmate populations is the crisis of caring for mentally ill inmates. Researchers estimate that approximately 9 percent of male inmates and twice that percentage among women, about 18.5 percent, suffer from serious mental illness.[101] Rollbacks in state mental health systems in the 1970s led to a corresponding rise in the number of mentally ill persons in the prison system. The mentally ill are often homeless and end up in the penal system for lack of an alternative system of care. Some estimate that 40 percent of all seriously mentally ill people in the United

States are currently behind bars. In most states, jails and prisons function as the largest mental health provider in the state.

The delivery of psychiatric services is extremely difficult inside of the prison system. Prisons are intended to deliver punishment through custodial confinement, not psychiatric treatment. Inmates on medication are not monitored to ensure that they are taking their medication to prevent psychotic outbreaks, and frequent transfers between institutions leads to disruptions in the provision of medication. Inmates with serious mental illnesses are difficult to manage behaviorally. Correctional officers are not trained to distinguish between psychotic behavior and outward signs of disobedience, and so they usually respond punitively. Psychotic inmates are routinely placed in disciplinary solitary confinement or administrative segregation, which tends to make their mental condition deteriorate even further.

WHAT ABOUT REHABILITATION?

In 1974, Robert Martinson asked the question "What works?" in prison rehabilitation programs. Martinson reported that "With few and isolated exceptions, the rehabilitative efforts that have been reported so far have no appreciable effects on recidivism."[102] This answer led many people to declare that the ideal of rehabilitation was dead. Since prisons had never been successful at changing people from criminals to model citizens, the purpose of prisons is punishment, nothing more.

There are, however, many advocates of the belief that "some things do work some of the time" within the field of correctional treatment and programming. Ted Palmer, Paul Gendreau, Robert Ross, and many others believe the evidence clearly shows that some programs work when they are appropriately matched with the right offender.[103]

The fact remains, however, that the correctional treatment model has problems that prevent the kind of optimistic results researchers often claim they can produce. First, most criminal conduct is not the result of some kind of sickness or personal flaw in the offender that can simply be "cured" or "corrected." The commission of crime is a socially embedded activity involving a whole set of social relationships. Many offenders return to friends and a criminal lifestyle, and despite what they may have learned while in prison, they find it easier to go back to old habits and patterns of behavior.

Programming in prisons remains a vital element of the prison world, regardless of its long-term impact on recidivism or future criminal activity of inmates. Work programs relieve the stress of boredom and sometimes help build a person's work skills; religious programs offer inmates access to services for various denominations, mentor programs, and spiritual guidance and counseling. Recreational programs focus on physical activity, which relieves the stress of incarceration. Basketball, softball, and weightlifting are often criticized by people offended by the concept of inmates enjoying themselves. But correctional administrators value these programs because they assist them in managing the inmate population on a day-to-day basis, providing a healthy alternative to using drugs or making trouble.

The single exception to the disappointing effect of prison programs on recidivism is the impact on future criminal behavior of earning a college education behind the walls. Research has found that college-level education significantly lowers inmate recidivism.[104] Yet college programs are increasingly rare in prison, partly because few inmates have completed high school and many have serious learning problems, but also because of political pressure from those opposed to offering a free college education to people who have committed crime.

Drug treatment is one of the most common treatment programs behind the wall. The most prevalent systems are self-help groups such as AA and NA, which offer mutual support for people suffering from addiction. Inmates can continue to participate in these programs once they leave the prison, because every town and community has AA groups that are free and open to anyone who wishes to attend. Other common treatment programs behind the wall include anger management, parenting classes, life skills groups, individual and group counseling, and specialized treatment for sex offenders.

Can prison change a person? Here the answer from the evidence is probably negative. Prison treatment programs cannot *make* people change how they think and how they act in the future. We can ask the question differently: can prison programs help people change who want to lead a different life when they leave the institution? Here the answer is a most definite yes. Rubin Carter found that personal change and growth was possible even in the worst possible circumstances. Carter made constructive use of his time in prison to educate himself, shift his values, attitudes, and ultimately, his behavior. The prison did not assist Carter in making these changes; just the opposite, the prison did everything possible to make it hard for Carter to develop constructive attitudes and ideas. Rubin Carter was able to find peace despite the prison, not because of it.

It is possible, however, for prisons to offer those who want to change the opportunity to use their time behind the walls constructively to build new lives for themselves and their families. Ninety-five percent of people in prison will return to the community at some point. This is often cited as a compelling reason to emphasize vocational, educational, and treatment programs in prison. But there is another reason to be concerned about penal institutions that do nothing more than warehouse human beings in conditions of indignity and violence. As Winston Churchill remarked, how we treat criminals tells us a great deal about who we are as a society and as a nation. In the words of Victor Hassein, a lifer in the Pennsylvania prison system:

> Today in prison I find myself longing for any glimpse of an attempt to rehabilitate, not because I believe in rehabilitation but because I worry about a society that no longer bothers to consider its possibility.[105]

KEY TERMS

"bloody codes" p. 291
corporal punishment p. 291
Walnut Street Jail p. 292
penitentiary p. 292
separate system p. 292
congregate system p. 293
punitive solitary
    confinement p. 293
lockstep p. 293
striped uniform p. 293
contract system p. 293

reformatory movement p. 293
"Big House" p. 294
state-use laws p. 294
maximum security prison p. 295
medium security prison p. 295
minimum security prison p. 295
super-max prison p. 295
classification p. 295
jail p. 296
total institution p. 298
structured conflict p. 298

status degradation
    ceremony p. 298
prisonization p. 298
pains of imprisonment p. 299
importation theory p. 300
deprivation theory p. 300
building tender system p. 300
paradox of reform p. 300
jailhouse lawyer p. 301
hands-off doctrine p. 301

REVIEW AND STUDY QUESTIONS

1. Describe the intentions of the reformers who invented penitentiaries. How did the use of penitentiaries differ from previous forms of punishment?
2. Define and describe the separate and congregate systems of confinement. Where was each practiced?

What were the significant differences between them? Which one was ultimately successful and why?
3. Describe the reformatory model of incarceration. What form of sentencing is associated with this era of penal reform?

4. Identify and describe the different types of institutions found in most state correctional systems.
5. What is a "total institution"? Define and illustrate the concept of a status degradation ceremony within the prison setting.
6. Describe the four key deprivations associated with imprisonment. Why does Sykes refer to these as the "pains" of imprisonment? Define the concept of prisonization.
7. Explain the importation theory of prison culture. Contrast this theory with the deprivation theory.
8. To what extent do prisoners have Constitutional rights? Explain the "paradox of reform."
9. Explain the relationship between overcrowding, race, and violence in prisons.
10. What health care challenges are facing the modern prison?

CHECK IT OUT

On the Web

National Criminal Justice Reference Service, **vrlib.ncjrs. org/corrections.asp**
Excellent Web site with access to full text of publications on matters related to corrections. Read recent NIJ research reports on AIDS-HIV, health care, inmate programs, jail, women in prison, and lots more.

Federal Bureau of Prisons, **www.bop.gov/bopmain.html**
Check out this Web site and click on Public Information to access Quick Facts on inmates in the federal prison system. See the latest figures on gender, race, age, and offense for federal prisoners.

Prison Law and Prisoner Rights Overview, **www.law. cornell.edu/topics/prisoners_rights/html**
Excellent Web site for learning more about prisoners' rights.

Family and Corrections Network, **www.fcnetwork.org**
Browse this Web site dedicated to the children and family members of prisoners. Check out the reading room and see what is being done to help inmates and their families.

Stop Prison Rape, **www.spr.org/**
This nonprofit human rights organization is dedicated to ending sexual violence committed against men, women, and youth in all forms of detention. Founded by survivors of prison rape twenty years ago, this Web site offers real-life stories of rape and survival in our nation's prisons.

Prisoners Dictionary of Slang, **dictionary.prisonwall.org**
An interesting compendium of prison terms found across the United States and around the world.

On Film

Let the Doors Be Made of Iron: 19th Century Prison Reform (23 minutes)
Academy Award-nominated documentary using dramatic reenactments, photographs, and lithographs to trace the story of the Eastern State Penitentiary. Brings the hopes and reality of the so-called humane experiment to life. Available from Films for the Humanities and Sciences, www.films.com.

Quiet Rage: The Stanford Prison Experiment (50 minutes)
This video documents the classic landmark study of a mock prison, which demonstrates the effect of the roles of the prison environment on the psyches of the subjects and their treatment of fellow human beings. Classic black-and-white footage from the original experiment is interspersed with a current group of college students on a tour of the mock prison. Available from Insight Media, www.insight-media.com.

Women Doing Time (48 minutes)
A 48 Hours video that goes inside New York's Bedford Hills Correctional Facility, one of the oldest prisons for women, to examine what it means for women to be serving time. Available from Insight Media, www.insight-media.com.

Attica Riot: Chaos behind Bars (50 minutes, abridged)
This video tells the story of the Attica riot, offering footage of the uprising and commentary from both correctional officers and prisoners. Available from Insight Media, www.insight-media.com.

Supermax, a Prison within a Prison (40 minutes)
ABC news anchor Ted Koppel takes us inside the world of solitary confinement in today's super-max security prisons and the effect of this confinement on the inmates and the correctional officers as well. Part One of a two-part series. Available from Films for the Humanities and Sciences, www.films.com.

Prison Gangs and Racism Behind Bars (40 minutes)
Ted Koppel explores racist hatred in the prison between ethnic and white supremacist gangs. He interviews those who are put in solitary confinement because of their gang affliations, spends a night in a cell, and explores the impact of this confinement on the psychological and emotional health of inmates who will one day return to the public streets. Part Two of a two-part series. Available from Films for the Humanities and Sciences, www.films.com.

NOTES

1. Paul B. Wice, *Rubin "Hurricane" Carter and the American Justice System* (New Brunswick, NJ: Rutgers University Press, 2000).
2. Rubin "Hurricane" Carter, *The Sixteenth Round* (New York: Viking Press, 1974).
3. Ibid., p. 25.
4. Ibid., p. 41.
5. Ibid., pp. 43–76.
6. Ibid., p. 82.
7. Ibid., p. 87.
8. James S. Hirsch, *Hurricane: The Miraculous Journey of Rubin Carter* (Boston: Houghton Mifflin Co, 2000), p. 75.
9. Wice, *Rubin "Hurricane" Carter*, p. 30.
10. Carter, p. 139.
11. Ibid., p. 141.
12. Ibid., p. 156.
13. Hirsch *Hurricane*, p. 76.
14. Ibid., p. 4.
15. Ibid., p. 88.
16. Carter, *The Sixteenth Round*, pp. 180–181.
17. Ibid., p. 88.
18. Ibid., p. 89.
19. Ibid., p. 162.
20. Hirsch, *Hurricane*, pp. 19–20.
21. Wice, *Rubin "Hurricane" Carter*, p. 67.
22. Carter, *The Sixteenth Round*, p. 307.
23. Ibid., pp. 89–91.
24. Hirsch, *Hurricane*, pp. 91–92.
25. Ibid., p. 98.
26. Ibid., pp. 102–104.
27. Ibid., pp. 105–106
28. Ibid., p. 107.
29. Ibid., pp. 114–132.
30. Ibid., p. 132.
31. Wice, *Rubin "Hurricane" Carter*, p. 80.
32. Ibid., pp. 115–118.
33. Ibid., pp. 129–130.
34. Hirsch, *Hurricane*, p. 169.
35. Ibid., p. 171.
36. Ibid., pp. 189–197.
37. Wice, *Rubin "Hurricane" Carter*, pp. 184–185.
38. Ibid., pp. 190–191.
39. Thorstein Sellin, *Slavery and the Penal System* (New York: Elsevier, 1976).
40. Georg Rusche and Otto Kirchheimer, *Punishment and Social Structure* (New York: Russell and Russell, 1939).
41. Michael Ignatieff, *A Just Measure of Pain* (New York: Pantheon, 1978).
42. Pieter C. Spierenburg, *The Spectacle of Suffering* (Cambridge, U.K.: Cambridge University Press, 1985).
43. David Rothman, *The Discovery of the Asylum* (Boston: Little, Brown, 1971).
44. Gustave de Beaumone and Alexis de Toqueville, *On the Penitentiary System of the United States and Its Application in France* (Philadelphia: Carey, Lea and Blanchard, 1833).
45. Paul Takagi, "The Walnut Street Jail: A Penal Reform to Centralize the Powers of the State," *Federal Probation 39*, December 1975, pp. 18–26.
46. Charles Dickens, *American Notes*, Vol. 1 (London: Chapman & Hall, 1842), p. 238.
47. Dario Melossi and Massimo Pavarini, *The Prison and the Factory: Origins of the Penitentiary System* (London: Macmillan, 1981).
48. Sellin, *Slavery and the Penal System.* (New York: Elsevier, 1976).
49. David J. Rothman, *Conscience and Convenience: The Asylum and Its Alternatives in Progressive America* (Boston: Little, Brown, 1980).
50. Elizabeth Eileen Dooley, "Sir Walter Crofton and the Irish or Intermediate System of Prison Discipline," *New England Journal of Prison Law 575* Winter 1981, pp. 72–96.
51. Zebulon Brockway, *Fifty Years of Prison Service* (Montclair, NJ: Patterson Smith, 1969).
52. Anthony Platt, *The Child-Savers: The Invention of Delinquency* (Chicago: University of Chicago Press, 1970).
53. Estelle B. Freedman, *Their Sisters' Keepers: Women's Prison Reform in America, 1830–1930* (Ann Arbor: University of Michigan Press, 1981); Nicole Hahn Rafter, "Chastizing the Unchaste: Social Control Functions of a Women's Reformatory, 1894–1931," in Stanley Cohen and Andrew Scull, eds., *Social Control and the State* (Oxford, U.K.: Martin Robertson, 1983), pp. 288–310.
54. Rothman, *Conscience and Convenience.*
55. John Irwin, *Prisons in Turmoil* (Boston: Little, Brown, 1980).
56. Carter, *The Sixteenth Round*, p. 165.
57. Ann L. Pastore and Kathleen Maguire, eds. *Sourcebook of Criminal Justice Statistics 1999* (Washington, DC: U.S.Government Printing Office, 2000), p. 11.
58. Elizabeth Alexander, "The Care and Feeding of the Correctional-Industrial Complex" in John P. May and Kahalid R. Pitts, eds., *Building Violence: How America's Rush to Incarcerate Creates More Violence* (Thousand Oaks, CA: Sage, 2000), p. 53.
59. Ibid., p. 52.
60. Richard G. Singer, "Prisons: Typologies and Classifications," in Sanford Kadish, ed. *Encyclopedia of Crime and Justice* (New York: Free Press, 1983).
61. Raymond Holt, "Marion: Separating Fact from Fiction," *Federal Prisons Journal 2* (1991), pp. 33–34.
62. Ken Silverstein, "America's Private Gulag," in Daniel Burton-Rose, ed., *The Celling of America: An Inside Look at the U.S. Prison Industry* (Monroe, ME: Common Courage Press, 1998), pp. 156–163.
63. Charles H. Logan, *Private Prisons: Cons and Pros* (New York: Oxford University Press, 1990).
64. Ronald Goldfarb, *Jails: The Ultimate Ghetto* (New York: Archer Press, 1975).
65. Stephen H. Gettinger, *New Generation Jails: An Innovative Approach to an Age-Old Problem* (Washington, DC: National Institute of Corrections, 1984).

66. Philip G. Zimbardo, "The Pathology of Imprisonment," *Society 9* (1972), pp. 4–8.

67. Erving Goffman, *Asylums* (New York: Bantam, 1987).

68. James Jacob and Lawrence Kraft, "Integrating the Keepers: A Comparison of Black and White Prison Guards in Illinois," *Social Problems 25* (1978), pp. 304–318.

69. Donald Clemmer, *The Prison Community* (New York: Holt, Rinehart & Winston, 1940).

70. Gresham M. Sykes, *The Society of Captives: A Study of a Maximum Security Prison* (Princeton, NJ: Princeton University Press, 1958).

71. Carter, *The Sixteenth Round*, p. 170.

72. Jack Abbott, *In the Belly of the Beast: Letters from Prison* (New York: Random House, 1981), p. 121.

73. Hirsch, *Hurricane*, p. 210.

74. John Irwin and Donald R. Cressey, "Thieves, Convicts and the Inmate Culture," *Social Problems 10* (1962), pp. 142–155.

75. Leo Carrol, *Hacks, Blacks and Cons: Race Relations in a Maximum Security Prison* (Princeton, NJ: Princeton University Press, 1974).

76. James B. Jacobs, "Race Relations and the Prisoner Subculture," in Norval Morris and Michael Tonry, eds., *Crime and Justice: An Annual Review of Research* (Chicago: University of Chicago Press, 1979), pp. 1–27.

77. Robert Johnson, *Hard Time: Understanding and Reforming the Prison* (Belmont, CA: Wadsworth, 1996).

78. Ben M. Crouch and James W. Marquart, "Resolving the Paradox of Reform: Litigation, Prisoner Violence and the Perceptions of Risk," *Justice Quarterly 7* (1990), pp. 103–122.

79. Paige H. Ralph, "From Self-Preservation to Organized Crime: The Evolution of Inmates Gangs" in James W. Marquart and Jonathan R. Sorensen, eds., *Correctional Contexts* (Los Angeles, CA: Roxbury, 1997), pp. 182–186.

80. *Ruffin v. Commonwealth*, 62 Va. 790, (1871), 88, 341.

81. *Cooper v. Pate*, 378 U.S. 546 (1964), 343.

82. James B. Jacobs, *New Perspectives on Prisons and Imprisonment* (Ithaca, NY: Cornell University Press, 1983).

83. Burt Useem and Peter Kimball, *States of Siege: U.S. Prison Riots, 1971–1986* (New York: Oxford University Press, 1989).

84. *Wolff v. McDonald*, 94 S. Ct. 2963 (1974).

85. John McLaren, "Prisoners' Rights: The Pendulum Swings," in Joycelyn M. Pollack, ed., *Prisons Today and Tomorrow* (Gaithersburg, MD: Aspen, 1997), p. 377.

86. U.S. Bureau of Justice Statistics, *Women in Prison* (Washington, DC: U.S. Department of Justice, 1994.)

87. Marc Mauer, Cathy Potler, and Richard Wolf, *Gender and Justice: Women, Drugs and Sentencing Policy* (Washington, DC: The Sentencing Project, 1999).

88. Lawrence Bershad, "Discriminatory Treatment of the Female Offenders in the Criminal Justice System," *Boston College Law Review 26* (1985), pp. 389–438.

89. Rose Giallombardo, *Society of Women: A Study of a Women's Prison* (New York: Wiley, 1966).

90. American Correctional Association, *The Female Offender: What Does the Future Hold?* (Washington, DC: St. Mary's Press, 1990).

91. Todd R. Clear and George F. Cole, *American Corrections* (Belmont, CA: Wadsworth, 1994), p. 284.

92. Alida V. Merlo, "The Crisis and Consequences of Prison Overcrowding," in Pollack, ed., *Prisons: Today and Tomorrow*, pp. 52–74.

93. Ibid., p. 65.

94. Johnson, *Hard Time*.

95. John P. May, "Feeding a Public Health Epidemic," in May and Pitts, eds., *Building Violence*, p. 134.

96. Laura Maruschak, "HIV in Prisons and Jail, 1995," *BJS Bulletin* (Washington, DC: Department of Justice, Bureau of Justice Statistics, 1997), pp. 1–12.

97. Ibid.p. 10.

98. May, "Feeding a Public Health Epidemic," p. 134.

99. Stephen R. Donzinger, ed., *The Real War on Crime: The Report of the National Criminal Justice Commission* (New York: HarperCollins, 1996), p. 54.

100. May, "Feeding a Public Health Epidemic."

101. Andrea Wiseman, "Mental Illness Behind Bars," in May and Pitts, eds., *Building Violence*, pp. 105–109.

102. Robert Martinson, "What Works?—Questions and Answers about Prison Reform," *The Public Interest 35* (1974), p. 54.

103. Daniel Antonowicz and Robert Ross, "Essential Components of Successful Rehabilitation Programs for Offenders," *International Journal of Offender Therapy and Comparative Criminology 38* (1994), pp. 97–104; Paul Gendreau and Robert Ross, "Revivification of Rehabilitation: Evidence for the 1980s," *Justice Quarterly 4* (1987), pp. 349–407; Ted Palmer, *A Profile of Correctional Effectiveness and New Directions for Research* (Albany, NY: SUNY Press, 1994).

104. David Clark, *Analysis of Return Rates of Inmate College Program Participants* (Albany, NY: New York State Department of Correctional Services, 1991).

105. Victor Hassine, *Life without Parole: Living in Prison Today* (Los Angeles: Roxbury, 1996), p. 84.

C A S E 15

Circles of Hope: Community Justice in South St. Paul

A SHATTERED HOME

Darrol Bussler was tired at the end of a long day in April 1994 when he opened the kitchen door to his suburban home in South St. Paul, Minnesota.[1] He reached for the kitchen light only to discover it had been smashed, along with all the light fixtures and nearly every mirror, picture, appliance, piece of china, and glass in his two-story home. The VCR, television, and stereo were gone. Later, the insurance company would estimate the damage at over $16,000.

The dollar figure could not express the anguish Darrol felt as he stared at a mound of flour, eggs, mayonnaise, and chocolate dumped in the middle of his kitchen floor. Nor could it reflect the true value of the shattered bedroom mirror that had belonged to his parents or the treasured stereo bought as a gift by a group of his devoted students.[2] Irreplaceable mementos, objects, pictures, and family heirlooms lay broken in heaps everywhere in the house.

CRIME AS SYMPTOM

That night Darrol lay awake trying to answer two questions: who would do this to him? And why? Darrol soon realized that something more valuable than material things had been damaged that night. Darrol had lived in that house for nearly twenty years. He worked hard at treating others well; he believed there was no one who looked upon him as an enemy. What had happened to the world he thought he knew? Not just possessions, but Darrol's sense of

security and trust in his neighbors, community, and fellow human beings were shaken to the core.

Darrol could remember a time when block parties on his street were an annual affair. He himself had hosted an open house at Christmas time when he first moved into the neighborhood. That, he realized with a shock, had been 1977. As the years went by, he had become so busy with his job and his own social life that he barely had casual conversations with his neighbors, much less dinner parties. People had died or moved away; Darrol no longer knew his neighbors and their children.

As Bussler sat in his bedroom staring at the broken mirror on his parents' dresser, he realized, "I hadn't talked to my neighbors in years.... We had all become strangers to one another.... I felt a need to reconnect, to restore authentic relationships in my neighborhood."[3] Something had gone terribly wrong in his community, and he vowed he was going to take some positive steps to make things better. "This vandalism was a symptom of something gone wrong in my neighborhood, our community and our society. By the time the police called the next morning, informing me that they had identified the offenders, I had already made a decision: I will work with whoever did this."[4]

Two teens from the neighborhood were charged with the crime. Darrol didn't know either of them or their parents. Both pleaded guilty to robbing Darrol and to committing a series of other burglaries in the neighborhood as well. Darrol realized that whatever he was feeling was probably experienced by others in the neighborhood who, directly or indirectly, had been robbed of a sense of security and trust in their own home, neighborhood, and community.

Darrol wrote a letter to the district attorney's office asking for an opportunity to meet with the boys and talk about restitution for himself and the neighborhood. Darrol had very specific ideas about what he thought would make a difference. But there was no response from the system. After several months, Darrol phoned the district attorney's office to inquire about the status of his case and whether he might be able to participate in the process. He was rebuffed: "The court is not interested in creativity. The court is interested in consistency," he was told.[5] Disappointed, Darrol's feelings turned to anger as he wondered why he wasn't allowed to be part of the process. He believed he had something valuable to offer and was frustrated with a justice system that denied him, the victim, the chance to be involved.

A COMMUNITY RESTORED

Luckily for Darrol, someone in the prosecutor's office was listening. His letter was forwarded to a local victim–offender mediation program, which contacted Darrol to explore the option of meeting with the two offenders. Along with their mothers and two mediators, Darrol met with the young men in his own home, seated around the damaged dining table. Darrol wanted to meet the boys there, at the scene of the crime, so he could show these young men how he personally had been affected by their actions.

At the mediation meeting, Darrol shared with the boys the loss of trust he had suffered because of their actions and discussed what could be done to help restore a sense of community. Darrol was not interested in simply replacing the objects that had been broken or destroyed. When he saw the destruction of his home, Darrol realized that something less visible but even more important had been taken away when these young men acted with such disregard for himself and others. Darrol wanted restitution for the material damage the boys had caused, but he

also wanted them to help restore the frayed bonds in the community.

As part of the restitution agreement, the two boys agreed to help Darrol host a neighborhood dinner. Darrol would buy the food and the boys would help prepare and serve it. They would hand deliver an invitation to each neighbor's door, introducing themselves and extending the invitation personally. In addition, Darrol asked each boy to deliver a written apology to the homeowners they had vandalized and to deliver these letters in person. The restitution agreement reflected Darrol's belief that what was broken was more than just a mirror: it was the network of personal relationships that had sustained his community. The crime was a symptom of a community that had lost connection. Darrol was determined that this crime would be the start of something positive for the community, that the two boys would help make that happen, and, in the process, hopefully, realize that they too were part of the community.

The neighborhood event was a huge success. Thirty people attended the dinner and subsequently decided to form a neighborhood club and reestablish the tradition of annual block parties. The experience for the boys was also positive. Both were surprised by Darrol's request and by the acceptance they felt from the neighborhood. For at least one of the boys, the event was a turning point, shifting his future away from the path of crime. "One of the boys asked me, "Why are you doing this?" He didn't understand. Someone caring was foreign to his world. But he finally got it. This boy would turn his life around."[6]

CONTINUING THE JOURNEY

For Darrol and his immediate neighborhood, the work with the boys was an enormous success. Trust was restored in the neighborhood, and people felt relieved and reassured about the future. But Darrol wondered about future crimes. Could something like this be set up for victims and offenders so that those affected by crime, along with the community, could play an active role in the justice process? What about other neighborhoods? Could something like this be available for all victims in the city? Darrol began meeting with community volunteers and representatives from the schools, city, corrections, courts, and churches to explore the possibility of forming a permanent partnership between the community and the justice system to respond to harm, so that the people most affected by crime—victims and offenders and their community—were invited to be active participants in the process.

FINDING PARTNERS IN THE SYSTEM

Darrol soon discovered that he was not alone in his quest to create a partnership between the justice system and the community. Mark Carey, Director of Community Corrections in the Dakota County Department of Corrections, had worked as a probation and parole officer his entire career. Like many in this line of work, Carey increasingly felt as if he worked in a bizarre human factory tending a "conveyer belt of justice."[7] In Dakota County, on any given day, about eight thousand offenders were "supervised" by a probation or parole officer. For the individual probation or parole officer, the reality of the job had become a steady stream of faces, constant demands of paperwork, and ceaseless processing of case after case.

Under these conditions, the ideal of working individually with offenders, getting to know them and their families and genuinely helping them turn their lives around, seemed impossible. With caseloads averaging 140 for high-risk adult offenders and fifty for high-risk juvenile offenders, probation officers were lucky if they spent more than half an hour a month on any given case. For the majority of offenders, supervision on probation was practically nonexistent, leading one high-ranking official to refer to probation in the state of Minnesota as a "fraud."[8]

Like many justice professionals in the courts, policing, and corrections, Mark Carey was searching for a way to create stronger partnerships with the community to enhance positive outcomes for offenders, victims, and the community. Mark Carey could recall a time when probation officers worked with fewer offenders, reaching out to the community to ascertain the unique challenges and strengths for each individual. When Darrol contacted Carey he had already begun working with his own staff to develop a vision and mission for his agency based on the principles of restorative justice. For a correctional agency this was a significant change, as the staff began to define their primary clientele to include victims and communities as well as offenders.

Mark Carey was not the only justice professional seeking a different solution to the problem of probation. Two judges in the city of Minneapolis had decided they wanted to see more involvement from communities in the sentencing and probation process.[9] They had heard of a judge in Canada who used Native American circle processes to develop sentencing recommendations with input from families and the wider community. They were eager to try a similar process in their own community and to refer appropriate cases to a community-justice process alternative. They too were very interested in what Darrol had to say.

The third system to respond positively to Darrol's ideas about community justice was the local school system in South St. Paul. The superintendent of schools realized that a victim–offender–community process of mediation was a positive alternative to the juvenile justice system for some youth. The schools were also interested in exploring the use of restorative justice for learning, behavioral issues, and conflict resolution in the schools. The school board offered to provide funds to bring the Canadian judge down from the Yukon to offer training in peacemaking circles for the project.

A COMMUNITY JUSTICE INITIATIVE

The South St. Paul Restorative Justice Council emerged from collaboration among the community, community corrections, the courts, and the schools. The mission of the council is "to develop and sustain restorative processes in our community to promote healing, increase accountability and provide support."[10] The council is a partnership among the public schools, city police, corrections, the courts, and community volunteers.

Within three years, the South St. Paul Restorative Justice Council implemented a range of innovations for people under community corrections: crime repair crews to help victims in the immediate aftermath of the crime; mentoring programs based in churches for high-risk juveniles; a repeat drunk-driving-program; expanded victim–offender mediation; family group conferencing; and, most important, a circle sentencing process modeled after the Canadian program. All of these programs are informed by the goals of restorative justice: healing the victim, involving the community, and repairing the bonds between the offender and those he or she has violated.

CIRCLES IN THE UNITED STATES

In 1997, the South St. Paul council implemented one of the first non-Native uses of circle sentencing in the United States.[11] The peacemaking circle comes from Native American and aboriginal forms of conflict resolution. In the circle sentencing process, the victim, offender, their families, community members, and justice professionals meet face to face in an elaborate process designed to hear all voices and to respectfully devise a program of supervision for the offender that will meet the needs of the victim for restitution and healing, the offender for accountability, and the community for wholeness. In the circle process, the most active participants are those who are directly affected by the crime; justice professionals play a supportive and guiding role.

Over a three-year period, the South St. Paul Restorative Justice Council actively accepted thirty-five cases referred from the police, district attorney, schools, and courts. Over two-thirds were referred by the police as precharge diversion for juveniles. According to the police, "the typical referral is a first time offender.... It may be a case where the victim needs some assurance and answers to such questions of why he/she was targeted. Or it may be that a victim is interested in finding some way of helping the kids so they won't violate again. We may refer a case because it will be good for the community to learn about the factors of the case and be involved in setting limits."[12] Rather than refer these cases to the district attorney for charging, the police use their discretion in the belief that this will be a more constructive outcome for this particular crime.

Most adult cases are referred to the circle by judges. Offenses range from possession of controlled substances to drug trafficking, to theft, to assault with a knife. Over a three-year period, eleven of these cases were sent back to court because the victim or the offender was unwilling to participate. Of the twenty-one cases that completed the entire process, seven were felony offenses and fourteen were misdemeanors. In total, the council worked directly with thirty-six victims, fifty-six offenders, and involved a total of sixty community members. The median number of circles per case is two, but for more complicated cases, many more circles were held. There are application circles, support circles, healing circles, agreement circles, and follow-up circles to see that the agreements are being met by all.

THE CIRCLE PROCESS: ACCOUNTABILITY AND HEALING

One of the first cases confronting the South St. Paul Restorative Circle illustrates the unique goals of community-based restorative justice.[13] A woman pleaded guilty to a charge of drug trafficking; a large amount of marijuana had been found stored in her home. The defendant was a knowing but minor player in a large drug operation, involved because of her relationship with her boyfriend, who violently abused her. The prosecution wanted her to go to jail for her crime; the defense requested the judge to consider the mitigating circumstances of her victimization and asked that she be sentenced to probation. The judge, after much consideration, referred the case to the circle process and ordered a stay of adjudication to allow the community to hear the case.

The aim of the circle process is to heal the wounds created by crime and to promote accountability for the future health and well-being of the community. One of the first priorities is to help offenders take responsibility for their crime and to understand the harm caused by their actions. Community members in the circle discovered that in this case the offender recognized that her actions were illegal but did not genuinely understand the evil of drug use or realize the harm brought to the community through drug trafficking. To help her realize the serious impact of her conduct, an accountability circle was held so the offender could hear from young people who had suffered through serious chemical dependencies.

At the same time, the council also formed a circle of support for the offender to help her deal with her own victimization from domestic violence. This circle included survivors of battering, who provided guidance and positive assistance for the offender in creating a better future for herself so as to avoid repetitions of this behavior in the future.

Lastly, there was a sentencing circle to consider the offender's obligations to the community. The prosecutor expressed a strong desire to see her serve time behind bars, but the community members in the circle disagreed. They saw no point in sending her to jail. They believed it would be far more beneficial for the community if the offender were required to work for the community. The ultimate sentencing agreement contained a series of community service commitments, including speaking to high school students, especially young women, about the dangers of drugs and involvement in the drug trade. The community council was responsible for follow-up circles that monitored the fulfillment of the contract.

LOOKING TO THE FUTURE

The work of the South St. Paul Restorative Justice Council continues. The system is cautious: defense attorneys worry about the rights of offenders, judges are concerned about equity, and many professionals feel uneasy about the potential for the community to act as vigilantes or to become dominated by one or two powerful sets of interests. Despite the doubts, however, acceptance of the use of community-based circles is growing. Three more communities in the St. Paul area have started their own councils and circle projects working with justice professionals.

Case adapted from Kay Harvey, "One Victim's 'Wakeup Call' Produces Reconciliation," *Saint Paul Press*, October 29, 1995; Darrol Bussler and Mark E. Carey with William DuBois, "Coming Full Circle: A County-Community Restorative Justice Partnership," in William DuBois and R. Dean Wright, eds., *Applying Sociology: Making a Better World* (Boston: Allyn and Bacon, 2001); Robert B. Coates, Mark Umbreit, and Betty Vos, "Restorative Justice Circles in South St. Paul Minnesota," *Research Monograph* (Minneapolis, MN: Center for Resortative Justice and Peacemaking, University of Minnesota, 2000).

THINKING CRITICALLY ABOUT THIS CASE

1. How would you feel if your own home was vandalized by neighborhood teenagers? Would you want to meet the persons who destroyed your home face to face? Why or why not? What forms of restitution would be important to you?

2. Why did Darrol Bussler want to participate in the justice process? What could Darrol offer that the justice system could not? How does his perspective differ from that of the justice system?

3. Why did Darrol Bussler see the vandalism as a "symptom" of the decline of community? How is crime linked to the tightness of social bonds and stability in the community? Do you agree with Darrol's analysis that strengthening the bonds in the community would prevent future crimes?

4. Mark Carey had a vision of what the job of the probation officer should be. What was that vision? Do you agree with this ideal of the job of the probation officer? What do you believe is the central function of probation?

5. The restorative justice approach to crime asks the justice system to balance the needs of victims and the community with the needs of offenders in the wake of crime. In your view, who are the "clients" of the justice system? Whose needs should the system address?

6. Many professionals in the justice system have been working to increase community participation in the justice process. Why does the justice system need to partner with the community to respond effectively to crime? Why does the community need to partner with the justice system?

7. What are the potential dangers in a community justice project such as the one in South St. Paul? Are there dangers for offenders? For victims? For the public? Would you volunteer to participate in such a project in your own community? Why or why not?

CHECK OUT THIS CASE

On the Web

Minnesota Restorative and Community Justice, **www.corr.state.mn.us/organization/commjuv/restorativejustice.htm**
Go to this Web site to learn lots more about restorative justice and community partnerships and projects including the South St. Paul project.

University of Saskatchewan **http://www.usask.ca/nativelaw/jah_circle.html**
Find out more about sentencing circles used in North America at this Web site.

On Film

Circles (58 minutes)
*This video offers an inside look at the Native American sentencing circle used in the first North American partnership between the justice system and the community. Available from Insight Media, **www.insight-media.com.***

CHAPTER 15

Community and Corrections

LEARNING OBJECTIVES

After reading this chapter, the student should be able to:

- Identify the historical origins of probation and parole

- Describe the functions of probation and parole today

- Identify the three periods of community corrections, identify the goals and philosophy of each period, and identify specific programs developed during each period

- Define the concept of "net widening" and show how it undermines goals of community corrections

In Chapter 14 we learned that over 2 million Americans are serving a criminal sentence behind the bars of a locked correctional facility. But even more Americans are serving a criminal sentence while they are living and working within the community. Alongside the sharp rise in imprisonment has been a parallel growth in the numbers of persons living under the supervision of the justice system. In 1999, approximately 4.6 million people were under the supervision of state or federal probation and parole authorities.[14] Most Americans are surprised to discover that the vast majority of people under correctional supervision live in the community.

This final chapter takes a careful look at the system of community corrections. For many, the sentence of probation is the proverbial "slap on the wrist." In Dakota County, where Mark Carey worked, even high-risk adult offenders received an average of only thirty-five minutes of probation supervision time per month. The minimal nature of this "supervision" angers the public, who are concerned about public safety and feel that offenders placed on probation have not been punished adequately for their crimes.

Many justice professionals, however, believe that community-based corrections has enormous potential for enhancing public safety, satisfying victims, and holding offenders accountable for their crimes. The use of alternatives to incarceration has a history that dates back to the nineteenth century, when the first experiments in community supervision began in the city of Boston, Massachusetts. In the 1960s and 1970s there was an explosion of community-based alternatives to incarceration; in the 1980s and 1990s, technology such as drug testing and electronic monitoring greatly enhanced the ability of the system to "supervise" offenders and control their movements within the wider community.

Yet questions remain concerning the effectiveness of community corrections, the impact on public safety, and the role of the community in the process. Can offenders be safely monitored while living in the community? What services and resources are available for people on probation and parole? Do these improve the likelihood of offender rehabilitation and reform? What about victims? Should community correction deal with the needs of victims? And what about the community? Should the community be involved in the process of supervising, sentencing, sanctioning, or helping offenders?

The term *community justice* is increasingly used to refer to criminal justice innovations that seek to involve the community, including community policing, community courts, and community corrections.[15] For the most part, traditional community corrections programs have been physically located within the community but have not actually involved the community in the supervision or rehabilitation of offenders. Darrol Bussler's quest to play an active role in the disposition of his case was breaking new ground for the criminal justice system A question for the future is whether community corrections will move in the direction of the South St. Paul experiment to include victims and the community in a broader understanding encompassed by the concepts of community justice and restorative justice.

THE ORIGINS OF PROBATION AND PAROLE

The founding ideals of both probation and parole are to provide individualized justice to those offenders who are ready and willing to reform. The term **probation** comes from the Latin word *probare*, which means "to test or to prove." Probationers are given a second chance to "prove" they are able to conform to societal laws. Offenders placed on probation are usually at the "front end" of the system, placed there at the time of sentencing by the courts. These offenders tend to be first-time, juvenile, or low-level criminals.

Parole is the practice of permitting the final portion of a criminal sentence to be served in the community under the supervision of the parole authority. The word *parole* derives from the French for "word of honor," signifying the pledge to behave as a law-abiding citizen. Parole occurs at the "back end" of the justice process: offenders have already served a significant portion of their sentence in the prison system. Parolees, therefore, have usually been convicted of more serious offenses, are older, and have been inside the prison system and are coping with readjustment and reintegration back into the community after a period of time behind bars.

Probation and parole have their roots in the discretionary decision-making power of the justice system to respond to individual offenders with leniency in recognition of their willingness to reform. The capacity of courts to exercise a degree of mercy for individual offenders reaches back to the thirteenth century in England, when convicted criminals were permitted to plead for leniency by reading the text of the Fifty-First Psalm in court.[16] Called the **benefit of clergy,** this practice gave the judge the option of saving the convicted person from the gallows. Similarly, the practice of **judicial reprieve** allowed judges to suspend imposition of punishment on a convicted criminal indefinitely, provided he or she continued to refrain from crime. The power of judicial reprieve was declared unconstitutional in the United States in 1916,[17] but the concept of court supervision under a suspended sentence has continued under the authority of the probation service, which formalized court supervision of convicted offenders.

The first person to conceive of a formal function of court supervision and the first volunteer probation officer himself was a wealthy philanthropist named John Augustus.[18] A Boston bootmaker by trade, Augustus had considerable financial resources and chose to devote himself to the humanitarian goal of assisting those who had fallen on hard times through the evils of alcohol. The invention of probation began with his plea to the Boston Police court in 1841, when he posted bail for a man charged with being a common drunkard. The judge granted bail and was willing to defer sentencing for three weeks under the condition that the man be released into the custody of Augustus. Augustus took on the task of assisting the man in taking positive steps toward his own reform, and reappeared with him before the judge at the appointed time as a testimonial of his good efforts at sobriety.

Thus began Augustus's lifework, which ultimately led him to bail out 1,152 men and 794 women, most charged with violation of temperance laws in the Boston courts. Au-

probation: a sentence the offender serves in the community under correctional supervision.

parole: conditional release of an inmate from incarceration under supervision after a portion of the prison sentence has been served.

benefit of clergy: medieval privilege that allowed clergy and other offenders to avoid the gallows at the judge's discretion.

judicial reprieve: postponement of the execution of a sentence by a judge.

gustus was selective in whom he chose to assist, screening them for good character and positive influences in their lives. He accompanied them to court, posted bail, paid their fines, assisted them in finding lodging and employment, worked with their families, and helped them find confidence in themselves to live responsibly and soberly.

Augustus offered his services to the courts on a volunteer basis. But as judges grew more familiar with Augustus, they were eager to have an alternative sentence for individual offenders who were ripe for rehabilitation. The practice coincided with the emerging dominant ideology of rehabilitation and reform of the Progressive era: individual criminals who could be "saved" from a life of crime should be treated differently by the correctional system and given the chance for reform. The first official probation officer was Edward Savage, who resigned his post as chief of police in the city of Boston in 1878.[19] By 1891 Massachusetts had a legislated state-wide probation system under the formal authority of the courts.

The institutionalization of parole was a key component to the reformatory movement in penal reform. The "father of parole" is Captain Alexander Maconochie, of Norfolk Island in the United Kingdom who created a system whereby inmates could earn early release, known as a **ticket of leave,** through hard work and good behavior.[20] The practice of parole was then adopted in the Irish penal system by Sir Walter Crafton, who implemented it as part of a complete system of graduated confinements including spending time in a kind of halfway house before finally earning a ticket of leave.

In the United States, **good time laws** were first passed in 1817 to enable prison wardens to reward compliant inmates and to offer incentives for working hard in prison industries and outside contract labor sites. With the reformatory movement and the growing popularity of indeterminate sentencing laws, conditional release through parole became more closely tied to the goal of rehabilitation. By the end of the nineteenth century, more than half the states had some kind of parole authority to make the release decision for individual inmates and to supervise them to some extent during the remainder of their legal sentence.[21] The U.S. Board of Parole for the federal system was created by Congress in 1930; by 1932, forty-four states and the federal system relied on parole as the key system of release from prison.[22]

PROBATION TODAY

Probation is the most common sentence given to offenders in the United States. In most jurisdictions, probation is a statutory alternative to imprisonment for the majority of felony convictions, although offenders convicted of very serious crimes such as murder, rape, or robbery are generally ineligible for probation in most state penal codes. Of the 5.5 million offenders living in the community under the legal supervision of the correctional system in 1997, 3.8 million or almost 70 percent are on probation.[23] About 32 percent of felons convicted in state court are sentenced to "straight probation."[24]

Although probation originated in the judicial branch of government, in some jurisdictions it is under the executive branch as a part of the correctional agency of state government. In some states it is unified as one central agency across the state, while in others it is highly decentralized and operates independently at the county or local level. Those who argue that probation should remain a judicial function feel that probation officers should work closely with sentencing judges, extending the authority of the judge to exercise discretion and supervise offenders in the community. Others argue that the human service function of probation is best administered by correctional agencies. Many states combine probation and parole into a single agency, arguing that the professionalization of community supervision is best served by a unification. In the federal system, probation is administered by the federal district courts.

ticket of leave: system of conditional release from prison.

good time laws: first passed in 1817, these authorize wardens to release inmates before full completion of their sentence as a reward for good behavior.

The Job of the Probation Officer

Probation is a sentence, but it is also a job. The two primary functions of the probation officer are investigation and recommendation through the **presentence investigation report** (PSI) and the actual supervision of the offender until the legal sentence is terminated. The presentence investigation process includes a more or less thorough examination of the offender, his history including past crimes, employment, education, his family and close associates, his mental and physical health, and any history of drug abuse. In some jurisdictions, PSI reports are very thorough and detailed; in others they provide only a brief sketch of the basic facts. The purpose of the PSI is to assist the judge in the formulation of the sentence. The PSI generally includes a sentencing recommendation that details specific conditions of probation for the offender and how intensive the supervision should be.

The second function of the probation officer is the job of supervision itself. Probation is a sentence of conditional release into the community. The **conditions of probation** vary, but the basic concept is that for the duration of the original sentence the offender is neither entirely free nor is locked up. Rather, probationers' status in the community is conditional: they may remain out of jail as long as they abide by certain rules and conditions. Failure to comply with the conditions of the probation order are grounds for revocation of this conditional freedom and imposition of the jail sentence. It is the legal responsibility of the probation officer to ensure that the conditions of probation are being met by the probationer.

Thus, one of the central duties of probation is the protection of public safety and enforcement of the rules. Probation officers may be required to visit probationers in their homes; administer daily urine screens for drug use; or they may use electronic monitoring technology such as electronic bracelets or other tracking devices to monitor offenders. Violating the conditions of probation by committing new crimes or breaking the technical rules of probation may be grounds for revocation of probation and imprisonment of the offender.

Standard conditions of probation are fairly common across all the states. These conditions require the probationer to: refrain from any further violations of the law; hold down regular employment or course of study; participate in any specified treatment plan; support any dependents; remain within the geographical jurisdiction of the court; and maintain regular contact with the probation officer. In addition to these standard conditions, judges may add any special conditions that are relevant to the particular offender. These special conditions may include payment of restitution to the victim or a victim compensation fund; performance of community service work; mandatory treatment for alcohol or drug abuse; anger management counseling; completion of a GED; abstention from the use of alcohol; even participation in religious services for the period of probation. As long as the condition is related to the offense, the courts have upheld novel requirements of probation devised by the courts. More than half the states exact a fee from probationers to help defray the cost of supervision.

The issue of heavy caseloads is one of the key factors that negatively impacts the quality of the probation supervision. As we saw in Minnesota, caseloads often run high, reaching as many as three hundred cases per officer in some jurisdictions. Under these conditions, the job of maintaining supervision and helping offenders is a highly perfunctory bureaucratic task that may mean little more than simply receiving a postcard or making a phone call once a month.

Conflicting Philosophies of Probation

Inherent in the job of the modern probation officer is a tension between the two basic components of the probation supervision function.[25] On the one hand, probation has its origins in the humanitarian desire to assist convicted persons in rehabilitation. In this

presentence investigation and report: collection of information by a probation officer about an offender's character, family life, work habits, and prior record to assist and guide the judge in sentencing.

conditions of probation: court-ordered conditions that must be met by probationers and are enforced by probation officers.

sense, the work of probation has much in common with the job of social work: helping offenders get counseling and treatment, offering vocational and employment assistance, providing constant guidance and support for the individuals and their families. But the job of the probation officer also involves supervision of the offender, a function that has more in common with law enforcement, in which offenders must be monitored to assure they do not commit additional crimes and to protect public safety.

These two functions are often incompatible and lead to **role strain** for probation officers, who find themselves torn between conflicting goals. The social worker function may require a probation officer to offer sympathetic support to offenders who have violated technical conditions of their probation or even committed minor crimes. The social worker function prioritizes the desire to offer repeated chances to offenders. The supervisory function leads to a more hard-line attitude toward probationers who violate the terms of the agreement. Some probation officers see enforcement of legal rules as the prime component of their job and believe their central obligation is to protect public safety by ensuring that probationers comply with the legal requirements of the court order; others prioritize the social worker function.

The tension between these two philosophical positions often erupts most acutely around the issue of **revocation of probation** for rule violations. The "law enforcer" prioritizes the rules. From this perspective, the issue of revocation is straightforward: if the rules are violated, the individual should be brought back to court for resentencing. For the probation officer whose central priority is to assist an offender toward rehabilitation, revoking probation status, particularly for technical violations of the rules such as breaking curfew, is seen as undermining the more important goal of rehabilitation. Being in an enforcement role undermines trust, which reduces the ability of the probation officer to genuinely help the offender deal effectively with his or her problems. As we will see, in some programs these roles are divided between two different probation officers to help each perform his or her functions more effectively, without inherent conflict.

PAROLE TODAY

Like probation, parole is a form of conditional release from incarceration. Persons on parole are neither free nor behind bars: rather, they remain in the legal custody of the state and must conform to specified conditions in order to remain in the community. Failure to comply with the rules leads to revocation of parole and return to imprisonment. Unlike probation, which is generally a judicial function, parole is an administrative function located in an independent state agency or operates as part of the correctional system.

Parole Boards

Parole refers both to the decision to release people before their complete sentence has been served and a period of community-based supervision. Under indeterminate sentencing systems, the release decision is made by a **parole board,** which may be part of the department of corrections or an autonomous body whose members are appointed by the governor.[26] The parole board considers a host of factors in determining parole release for individual offenders, including their own record of performance within the institution, their prospects for work and noncriminal lifestyle upon release, victims' preferences, needs of the institution for available beds, and the wider politics of the community.

Parole eligibility, defined by various statutes, is the earliest date at which an inmate may be considered for conditional release. Offenders do not apply for parole but are

role strain: tension between two facets of the job of probation and parole: rule enforcement and rehabilitation.

revocation of probation: return of an offender to court for sentencing for failure to meet conditions of probation.

parole board: administrative agency charged with the authority to grant conditional release for prisoners eligible for parole.

parole eligibility: determined by statute and the amount of time an inmate has served.

automatically considered for parole when they become eligible. Nearly all jurisdictions have **statutory good time** laws, which automatically reduce an inmate's sentence by a specified number of days for each month of time served without disciplinary problems. These range from more than thirty days for every month of "good time" served to as few as five days for each "good time" month served in the federal prison system. In addition to statutory good time, there may also be **earned good time** statutes, which credit inmates with time off their full sentence for participation in work, educational, or treatment programs. Accumulation of good time credits (statutory and earned) may result in **unconditional mandatory release** from prison without parole supervision.

Parole release is a reduction in the sentence in addition to good time reductions. The parole board reviews the inmate's record, interviews the inmate, solicits recommendations from the prosecutor's office, and hears testimony from victims, family members, and other witnesses to assist them in making their decision. Criticism of the discretionary parole decision was a key factor in the political movement to end indeterminate sentencing. Parole boards hold broad discretion, and offenders believed they were often treated arbitrarily, with substantial discrimination based on race and class of the offender. When Rubin Carter was in Rahway State Prison (see Chapter 14), one of the demands of the 1972 riot was the abolition of parole. Inmates were demoralized by never knowing when they would be released and felt it unfair to rely on the judgment of a group of strangers who held such power over their lives.

Since 1975, most states' legislative codes have shifted toward determinate sentencing, reducing reliance on parole release. In the early 1970s, more than 70 percent of prisoners were released from jail through decisions made by parole boards; by 1997, only 36 percent of conditional release decisions were made by parole authorities.[27] Under determinate sentencing systems, parole serves as a mandatory period of community supervision structured as part of the sentence itself. Once the offender has served the required portion of the sentence behind bars, the offender is released to a period of community supervision. In 1997, 22 percent of prisoners were released from prison unconditionally; the remaining 88 percent were released under some kind of community correctional supervision.[28]

In jurisdictions where parole decision making still exists, parole hearings have become more formalized. In about half these states, offenders are permitted to have counsel present and to call witnesses, and a transcript of the proceedings is maintained. Today, most parole authorities provide a written and oral explanation of their decision, although the courts have refused to concede equivalent due process rights to the offender in a parole hearing as are granted to a defendant in court proceedings.[29]

Parole Supervision

The job of the parole officer is similar to that of the probation officer. Parolees constitute about 11 percent of the population under correctional supervision.[30] Similar to probation officers, the job of parole officers is to monitor compliance of parolees with the conditions of parole. Standard conditions of parole include the same requirements to maintain contact with the parole officer, continue employment or education, and refrain from any further criminal activity or associations. Parolees must contact their parole officer if they change jobs, residence, or marital status. In addition, parolee contracts may include individualized conditions tailored to the particular circumstances. Failure to comply with the conditions of parole may lead to the **revocation of parole,** resulting in a return to incarceration for the offender.

Parole officers are charged with assisting parolees in adjusting to community life and continuing to pursue a noncriminal lifestyle. Officers make referrals to community agencies and employment agencies, and work with the family of the offender to assist in the transition to life outside prison. Like probation, however, the job of parole is heavily weighted toward supervision and policing. This is more acute in parole than it is in probation because the offenses of parolees are generally more serious than those of peo-

statutory good time: number of days deducted from a sentence determined by statute for a time served without disciplinary reports.

earned good time: number of days deducted from a sentence for participation in specified programs while in prison.

unconditional mandatory release: release from prison required by statute when a criminal has served his or her full sentence minus statutory and earned good time.

revocation of parole: administrative removal of an offender from parole status for failure to comply with parole conditions, usually requiring the return of the offender to incarceration.

ple who are sentenced to probation. Parole officers, therefore, stress the law enforcement aspect of their work more than probation officers, and in many states they are armed peace officers. Like probation, however, individual officers appear to emphasize different aspects of the job according to their personal preferences for control versus assistance, as well as the overall philosophy of the agency.[31]

HISTORY OF COMMUNITY CORRECTIONS

For decades, community corrections was synonymous with probation or parole. Beginning in the 1960s, three distinct periods of expansion and development in community corrections took place. The first began with the community corrections movement of the 1960s, which centered around the concept of diversion; the second, started in the 1980s, focused on the provision of a continuum of graduated intermediate sanctions and closer supervision within the community; and the third arose in the 1990s with the concept of community/restorative justice and the growing inclusion of victims and the community as stakeholders in the justice process.

    Each of these periods impacted the work of probation and parole creating new programs, techniques and approaches within the field. Like many criminal justice policies, different periods of community corrections overlap with one another and many programs share features in common. Although each period of growth within community corrections has been based on a distinctive philosophy, each has also built upon the innovations of earlier periods.[32]

THE DIVERSION MOVEMENT OF THE 1960S AND 1970S

In 1967, the President's Crime Commission endorsed the concept of formal diversion programs designed to rehabilitate and treat offenders in order to reduce the negative impact of incarceration and to reduce reliance on costly incarceration.[33] Incarcerating less serious offenders with violent or chronic offenders was seen as likely to socialize offenders to hardened criminal lifestyles rather than prevent future crimes. The federal government urged states to seek the "least restrictive" option for first-time or young offenders and to set up social service programs for referrals from the justice system to deal with the underlying problems driving crime.

    The concept of diversion refers to the decision to remove a particular offender from the formal mechanics of the system at some stage in criminal justice processing. Informal diversionary practices are inherent in the discretionary authority of police, prosecutors, and judges, whereas formal diversion requires an offender to attend a particular type of alternative program such as drug treatment or job training. During the 1960s community corrections was driven by the goal of keeping people out of the formal system and providing rehabilitative community-based interventions as an alternative to incarceration.

    During the 1970s, an estimated 1,200 diversion programs were established throughout the nation to provide treatment and services as an alternative to traditional criminal justice processing.[34] These might include diversion to an employment training program, drug treatment, education, or counseling program. The hope was that these programs would reduce recidivism at the same time as they reduced the costs of correctional supervision.

    A key criticism of the expanding diversion programs of the 1960s and 1970s was the problem known as **net widening.**[35] The traditional forms of diversion, often referred to as "old" or **"true" diversion,** literally kept people out of the criminal justice system altogether. When a police officer drives a teenaged shoplifter home to his parents rather

diversion: removal of offenders from the criminal justice process at any stage prior to criminal conviction.

formal diversion: removal of eligible offenders from the routine criminal justice process to an alternative program.

net widening: increase in the correctional population by the diversion of less serious offenders into programs intended for more serious offenders, thus expanding the overall correctional population.

"true" diversion: discretionary decision by criminal justice personnel to release offenders at any stage in the process prior to conviction.

than bringing him to the station house for booking and arrest, or a prosecutor enters a *nolle pros* for a minor theft, these justice professionals are informally "diverting" particular low-level offenders away from the formal sequence of events. Informally, diversion may take place any time before a person is convicted. Individuals seen as low-risk offenders and therefore likely to cease from all future criminal conduct are determined not to need any criminal justice supervision at all.

But once formal diversion programs became established, criminal justice professionals tended to refer these kinds of cases to formal diversion programs rather than simply letting low-risk offenders go. Individuals previously dropped from the system were now assigned to programs, thus increasing the overall numbers of people under correctional supervision and driving up costs rather than saving money. Although the **recidivism** rate of many diversion programs initially appeared low compared to the recidivism rates among those going to jail, researchers discovered that their success was due to "widening the net" to include low-risk participants who were unlikely to commit crimes in the future even without the benefit of a program.[36]

Diversion programs, many of which still exist today in many jurisdictions, particularly for juveniles, were seen as a panacea for the criminal justice system during the 1960s and 1970s. The hope was that these programs would effectively rehabilitate offenders at the same time that they would be considerably cheaper than prison. The expectations were so high that the results were bound to be disappointing: diversion did not reduce the overall size of the prison population or reduce costs because of net widening, and many diversion programs failed to demonstrate high rates of success with more serious offenders.[37]

THE INTERMEDIATE SANCTIONS MOVEMENT

Motivation for the second wave of expansion of community-based corrections in the 1980s shared much in common with the diversion movement. State systems struggled with prison overcrowding and the need to lower the high cost of imprisonment. As prisons came under legal pressure to reduce overcrowding, state judicial systems began seeking alternative punishments less extreme than incarceration but more punitive than traditional probation. During the 1980s and 1990s, the intermediate sanctions movement led to a wide array of alterative sentences, ranging from shock incarceration to intensive probation, house arrest, electronic monitoring, and more. The goal has been to create a continuum of graduated sanctions between probation and prison tailored to the seriousness of the crime.

The general disillusionment with the rehabilitative promise of diversion programs coincided with the demand for greater surveillance for offenders on probation and a tougher approach to probation as a form of punishment at the same time the pressure to control costs of imprisonment became even more acute. In the mid-1980s there was serious effort to control the skyrocketing costs of imprisonment in several states. Intervention by the courts, which ordered states to reduce overcrowding, left states with one of two choices: build more prison beds at a hefty price tag or find less expensive alternatives. The alternative sanctions movement was an effort to increase the correctional supervision of probation while avoiding the full-scale costs of incarceration. Judges were searching for a wider range of punishment options between the leniency of probation and the extreme deprivation of incarceration. State correctional systems began to explore a more extensive use of community service, restitution, fines, and intensive supervision similar to programs in some European countries.[38]

During the 1980s and 1990s, several key types of community-based correctional programs emerged: intensive supervision probation or intensive probation supervision (ISP or IPS), boot camps or shock incarceration; house arrest or degrees of confinement with the use of electronic monitoring; and day reporting centers combined with drug

recidivism: repetition of criminal conduct.

intermediate sanctions: a variety of punishments that are more restrictive than traditional probation but less extreme than incarceration.

testing, treatment, and intensive supervision. These programs were often combined or overlapped with one another, but the common denominator among them was enhanced close supervision by the correctional system. During this period, every major probation and parole agency in the nation experimented with the establishment of programs of intensive surveillance using enhanced probation supervision through reduced caseloads, electronic monitoring, house arrest, drug testing, day reporting centers, and boot camps. By 1998, all states were operating some kind of ISP programs; all states reported use of some electronic monitoring; about thirty-five states were operating boot camps; and across the nation there are about 125 operating day reporting centers.[39] An estimated 10 percent of probationers across the nation were assigned to these forms of community-based correctional supervision by the end of the 1990s.

Intensive Supervised Probation

Intensive supervised probation (ISP) programs, sometimes called intensive supervision programs or intensive surveillance programs and also known as intensive probation supervision, flourished between 1985 and 1995. Hundreds of programs emerged to correct the looseness of probation and enable more serious offenders to be sentenced within the community.[40] ISP programs offer much greater supervision than traditional probation. They typically involve daily face-to-face contact five times a week, mandatory alcohol and drug testing, mandatory curfews, and other special conditions designed to provide close supervision and enhanced levels of treatment for more serious offenders. Caseloads for officers in these programs are reduced to facilitate tighter control.

The first program was instituted in Georgia in 1985 in response to overcrowding in the prisons and the need to control costs by diverting some offenders from a prison cell to the more cost-effective supervision in the community.[41] Twenty-five offenders are assigned to two probation officers, one officer serving as the surveillance officer while the other officer provides counseling and support. The probationer is required to meet with an officer face to face five times a week, be working full time or enrolled in an educational program, perform mandatory community service, and pay a supervision fee to the courts to defray the costs of the program.

Day Reporting Centers

A **day reporting center** (DRC) is a nonresidential program providing intensive supervision for offenders who would otherwise be incarcerated.[42] The first center opened in Massachusetts in 1986 and was modeled after "probation centers" in England and Wales. DRCs may be used at the front end as an alternative to imprisonment or they may be used at the back end for offenders on parole. The purpose of the center is to provide high levels of structure and supervision without twenty-four-hour-a-day incarceration. Offenders live in their own homes but are required to report to the center seven days a week and provide an itinerary of their movements with the case manager for the entire twenty-four hours of the day.

Centers vary in the degree and nature of the supervision. Random drug testing is generally utilized to monitor offenders, and case managers use telephone contact and home visits to maintain surveillance over offenders. Offenders are required to be either employed or in school; to participate in treatment programs offered at the center; and may be required to perform community service.

Monitoring through Technology

The use of electronic technology to extend the reach of correctional surveillance emerged through the application of defense industry technology to the problem of community supervision in the mid-1980s.[43] These technologies enable the enforcement of **house arrest** using the home as a detention center during specified hours of the day.

intensive supervision probation: a program of closer surveillance and more intensive programming for higher-risk juvenile and adult offenders.

day reporting centers: program of community-based supervision to which offenders must report daily and where their activities are monitored and structured throughout most of the day.

house arrest: sentence requiring the convicted offender to remain in his or her house during specified periods.

There are two major types of systems of **electronic monitoring.** One is based on a computer-programmed telephone system that contacts the offender at random intervals at home. The verification that the offender is at home is achieved through various methods including video images, voice verification systems, or electronic devices or "keys" strapped to the offender. The alternative method of electronic surveillance uses an electronic bracelet locked onto the offender, which emits radio frequencies monitored by a telephone unit connected to a computer. Drive-by systems enable probation officers to confirm a person's presence at home by passing by in an automobile.[44] The basic objective of all of these systems is to enforce home detention through the ability to detect failure to comply with the court order for house arrest.

Shock Incarceration and Boot Camps

A key innovation of the 1980s was the use of intensified periods of confinement known as **shock incarceration.**[45] Although these are institutionally based, the innovation is part of the impulse to provide an alternative to lengthy periods of imprisonment for relatively serious offenders and to include short but intense periods of incarceration as part of a graduated continuum of sanctions.[46] According to the underlying theory of shock incarceration, shorter but more intense experiences of incarceration have a greater impact on the offender at the same time that shorter periods reduce the costs of incarceration. These programs typically rely on the military model of **boot camp** to impose a rigorous routine of mandatory physical exercise, drill, and hard labor on youthful offenders. In most programs, the day is highly structured, beginning before sunrise and requiring almost constant activity until lights out sixteen hours later. These forms of confinement are a stark contrast to the enforced idleness of the typical prison routine.

Boot camp programs vary in the degree to which they also offer treatment, educational, and other type of programming in addition to military-style discipline and routine. They also vary in the extent to which they supervise offenders in the community after the program and the intensity of that supervision. The popularity of boot camps with the public derives from the sense that discipline and rigor are helpful structures for offenders, although there does not appear to be sufficient evidence that the boot camp experience changes offenders' behavior once they are back living in the community. The concept of shorter but more intense forms of incarceration relies on the research finding that the period of time when inmates are most willing to embark on personal rehabilitation programs is relatively early in their incarceration, usually within the first three months, when the stress of incarceration and adjusting to the pains of imprisonment are felt most acutely by the inmate. It is at this time that inmates express the greatest willingness to participate in programming. Over time, as inmates adjust to the daily routine of prison life, they lose the motivation to engage in rehabilitative programming to change their lives.

Like all intermediate punishments, one of the key criteria for the success of boot camps is to reduce prison populations and control costs. Yet research shows that the net-widening effect remains an obstacle for boot camps: there is only a cost-saving outcome if the offenders sent to boot camps are those who would have been sentenced to longer prison terms.[47] If those sentenced to boot camp would have been sentenced to probation, then boot camps actually increase rather than decrease state costs, because boot camps cost more to operate than probation or even traditional prison systems.

THE RESTORATIVE AND COMMUNITY JUSTICE MOVEMENTS

The new wave of community corrections variously referred to as **restorative justice** or **community justice** focuses on a new set of objectives beyond offender rehabilitation or supervision. As a victim, Darrol Bussler wanted his unique needs met by the correc-

electronic monitoring: use of monitoring technology to trigger alarms if an offender moves beyond prescribed physical locations.

shock incarceration: use of shorter but more intense periods of incarceration, designed to have a deeper impact on the offender.

boot camp: short-term incarceration that relies on intensive military style drill, physical exercise, and correctional treatment.

restorative justice: a response to crime that seeks to restore the well-being of victims and the larger community while promoting responsible and productive behavior in offenders.

community justice: criminal justice activities that explicitly include the community and include prevention and enhancement of the quality of life and health of the community as part of their goals.

tional system; he wanted to play a role in the justice process and to interact directly with those who had violated him. The opportunity for Bussler to meet with the two boys and plan their community event would not have occurred under a traditional community corrections program. Diversion and intermediate sanctions programs prioritize the rehabilitation and close supervision of the offender exclusively by justice professionals. The primary goal is to rehabilitate or effectively punish the offender within a community setting. Much of the innovation is focused on finding the right combination of programs, services, and intensive supervision that will "work" with a given offender. These community corrections programs do not rely on actual involvement of the community and none of these programs aims to meet the needs of victims of crime.

Community restorative justice, by contrast, is not merely community based, it is victim centered and community involved. Restorative justice is a philosophical approach to justice that seeks to promote maximum involvement of the victim, the offender, and the community in the justice process. The goal of sentencing in restorative justice is to provide restitution for victims, promote accountability for offenders, and facilitate reintegration and reconciliation of offenders into positive relationships with the community. Emerging from the victims' movement, restorative innovations in community corrections have emphasized direct encounters between victims and offenders through mediation, family group conferences, and Native American circles. Programs have attempted to develop genuine partnerships between the community and the justice system, with direct accountability of offenders to the community and victims through community service and restitution. The South St. Paul Restorative Justice Council represents a third wave of community corrections, which expands the focus of the justice system beyond the offender to include victims and the community.

Community Service

Community service work is a court-ordered sanction that requires the offender to perform unpaid labor in the community. The use of unpaid labor as a form of criminal sanction has a long history in the prison system and includes chain gangs, picking up trash on the highway, and breaking rocks. Community-based service orders first appeared in this country in the 1960s and became more common during the 1980s as either a condition of probation or a stand-alone form of intermediate sanction. Unpaid work was an attractive alternative to the imposition of fines for offenders too poor to pay fines, as a mild form of restitution for "respectable" white-collar offenders, and as a cost-effective alternative to incarceration that provides value to the community. One of the drawbacks to the use of community service, however, has been the perception that it is a lenient sanction. Recall the outrage that many in the public felt at the suggestion that Leona Helmsley be sentenced to perform community service work rather than serve time behind bars for tax evasion (see Chapter 4). The public has generally viewed community work service as a lenient response to crime.

In the 1990s, the use of community service as a means of providing reparation directly to those who have been vandalized or victimized emerged with new vigor in the restorative justice model.[48] Rather than pay a fine to the court or sit in jail at the taxpayers' expense, the restorative paradigm calls for direct accountability between offenders, in this case, the two young men who broke into his home, and the people they have harmed. When Darrol Bussler realized he was not the only victim, he was articulating a key insight of the restorative justice paradigm: crime is a violation of persons and relationships. Many people are affected by crime, including people in the community. Darrol was the primary victim, but secondary victims included the people in the neighborhood who no longer felt safe.

By requiring the boys to host a party, the community service order was directly restoring what had been damaged by the crime. Rather than using community service orders merely to impose punishment, community service orders in a restorative approach require offenders to give back to the victim and the community, promoting reconciliation between the offenders and the community. People convicted of DUI may be

community service: performance of unpaid work for the community as compensation for injury or harm done to the community.

required to speak about drunk driving to high school audiences or work at a trauma center for accident victims. Dennis Maloney refers to community work service as "earned redemption" for offenders: by doing good for the community, they are able literally to "pay back" those they have harmed. By working to do something positive for those they have hurt in the past, the social bonds between victim and the offender are sometimes repaired. In Darrol's case, both boys expressed surprise that so many in the neighborhood were willing to give them a second chance.

Community Courts

The shift toward community-based justice has also brought innovation in the courts, which are seeking greater involvement of the community and victims. The Midtown Community Court in Manhattan was launched in 1991 to bring the community and the courts closer together and to deal with the thousands of misdemeanors, property, and drug offenses that were undermining the quality of life in the city.[49] The key principle of the community court is to act in partnership with the community and at the same time bring together all the resources of the system to help address the problem of crime constructively. A community advisory committee provides input from the community; police regularly hold community meetings at the court; and mediation, counseling, education, and treatment are all available under one roof, monitored by frequent interaction with the judge. The community court prioritizes the goal of restoration and helping offenders and the community address the problems that cause crime. The Manhattan Midtown Community Court relies on community service as the primary punishment.

The drug court is another example of a problem-solving community court. As of March 1997, there were 161 drug courts operating across the nation.[50] The first drug court was launched in 1989 in Dade County (Miami) Florida. The purpose of the drug court is to provide addicts with direct access to treatment closely monitored by the court. These courts partner with a wide range of community agencies to provide comprehensive services to address underlying issues such as unemployment, illiteracy, and lack of adequate housing. The drug court judge is personally involved in monitoring offenders' progress through the treatment program; failure to cooperate results in short jail stays, but there is a willingness to give participants a second, third, or fourth chance as they struggle to overcome addiction. The primary goal of these courts is to help drug users rather than to punish them.

Victim–Offender Mediation, Conferencing, Boards, and Circles

In traditional justice processes, decisions are made by justice professionals: judges, probation officers, police, or parole authorities. In restorative processes, decision making is shared between justice professionals and the parties most directly affected by the crime: victims, offenders, their families, and others who are affected by the event are included in the decision-making process.

Darrol Bussler was first contacted by a **victim–offender mediation** program. Victim–offender mediation programs offer the victim a direct voice in the criminal justice process: victims and offenders negotiate a restitution agreement that is perceived as fair by both sides. Many mediation programs today include family members in the mediation and resemble a conferencing model.

Communities have also set up **reparative boards** and community accountability panels staffed by community volunteers to provide supervision for offenders on probation and for offenders returning to the community from incarceration, similar to traditional parole supervision. Reparative boards originated in Vermont in the mid-1990s and are used for supervision of both juveniles and adults on probation. The boards work with victims and offenders to examine the harm of the offense, develop a restitution agreement, and monitor the behavior of the offender in the completion of that agree-

victim–offender mediation: face-to-face facilitated meetings between victims and offenders to promote victim healing, restitution, and offender accountability.

reparative boards: community volunteer boards supervised by the justice system that provide supervision and support for juveniles and adults on probation and for those reintegrating into the community from prison or jail.

ment. These community boards are assisted by probation officers, who provide administrative support, training, and input from the justice system. The commissioner of corrections for the state of Vermont has committed to transforming Vermont's correctional system from one that simply executes "retributive court-imposed sanctions" to a system that focuses on forming partnerships with the community through reparative boards to "restore victims, offenders and communities."[51]

In **family group conference** and **circle programs,** an even wider circle of participants participates in the partnership with the justice system. In the restorative justice circles of South St. Paul, the circle process is used as a structured form of dialogue among many participants. The council itself is staffed by community members who are responsible for accepting a referral into the program and for facilitating the process. Participants include offenders and their support systems, victims and their support systems, other individuals who have been affected by the crime such as secondary or indirect victims, and wider community members with an interest in positive resolution of the case. In addition to the direct parties, an array of justice professionals may be present at a circle process. These include justice professionals such as probation officers, the judge, prosecuting and defense counsel, arresting police officers, and professionals such as teachers, guidance counselors, or social service agents.

The process used in South St. Paul can be quite complex: some of the circles are dedicated to healing of the victim; others may focus on the offender and the problems that led to the behavior; still others focus on preventative changes in the community that will help to reduce the occurrence of the problem. In some programs, circles are held as part of the preparation process for release of an offender back into the community. Victims are given an opportunity to meet with offenders to talk about the effects of the crime on their life, ask questions, and gain reassurance about the future of living in the community with the offender. Offenders and their families are offered support for living a crime-free lifestyle in the community.

THE ROLE OF THE COMMUNITY

These latest forms of community justice create new roles for the community, victims, and offenders. Ironically, the earliest form of community corrections, the efforts of John Augustus, relied on the volunteer efforts of a member of the community willing to supervise wayward members of the community as they struggled to get sober and reform their bad behaviors. In the twentieth century, however, most community corrections programs have been operated by justice professionals, with little involvement of the community in the process.

The dilemma of modern probation and parole systems is the enormous burden of caseloads, which precludes adequate relationship building between overburdened justice professionals and any given offender. Offenders are unsupervised and therefore less accountable for meeting the conditions of probation. They are also unable to receive the kind of services they need. Victims are given even less attention. Many probation and parole officers point out that meeting the needs of victims stretches their limited resources even further.

In community and restorative justice, the natural capacity of people in the community to provide supervision and support for both victims and offenders is an untapped resource for the justice system. The benefit of the community involvement such as in the case study at the beginning of this chapter is to lighten the load for probation by bringing the resources of the community into the supervision and counseling process. Included in the circle are probation officers, but there are many other individuals as well—guidance counselors, grandmas, neighbors, ministers—who might have much to offer the probationer. These additional community members also serve a supervisory function, as in when they see a probationer walking the streets whom they know should

family group conferencing: form of restorative justice that originated in New Zealand, in which offenders, victims, and their families meet under the authority of the justice system to discuss the impact of the harm and negotiate accountability by the offender to the victim and the community.

circle program: alternative process involving victims, offenders, the community, and the justice system, derived from aboriginal forms of justice used to promote victim healing, offender accountability, and rehabilitation and alternative forms of sentencing with input from all stakeholders.

be in school or at work. More people are aware of the conditions of probation and it is far more difficult for the probationer to avoid detection than when on traditional probation.

PROBLEM SOLVING IN COMMUNITY AND RESTORATIVE JUSTICE

The criminal justice system is a reactive system: once a crime has occurred, steps are taken to respond to the offender and victim. For the most part, the criminal justice system does not engage in a proactive problem-solving approach to crime. Rather than address the underlying causes of crime in the community, the criminal justice system reacts to individual offenders and victims.

Darrol's response to his victimization was to try to correct what he perceived to be the source of the criminal conduct in his own community: connections had been lost, young people no longer cared about hurting those they didn't even know; people had stopped looking out for one another and being responsible for the quality of life past their own front yard. By taking steps to strengthen the relationships in the community, Darrol sought a problem-solving approach to crime.

Community-based restorative justice attempts to address the problems that give rise to crime by engaging the community in a partnership with the justice system. For those who are committed to this new wave of community-based justice programs, the ability to improve public safety is greatly improved when the justice system joins forces with the community. Community policing, community courts, and community corrections are all part of a growing effort in the criminal justice system to act in concert with the community to respond to crime and to engage in problem solving about the underlying issues that lead to crime. According to Kay Pranis, the Restorative Justice Planner for the Department of Corrections in Minnesota, the creation of genuinely safe communities requires active citizen involvement.[52]

LOOKING TOWARD THE FUTURE

The future of community and restorative justice is uncertain. For some, community-based restorative justice is the most constructive option for the future. With 2 million Americans sitting idly behind bars and another 4½ million under the supervision of probation or parole authorities, many believe the justice system must seek to engage the community in a problem-solving approach to crime with the aim of creating healthier communities. Community policing, community courts, and community corrections may be the building blocks for a coming era of community-based restorative justice.

Winston Churchill believed that the treatment of the criminal by a society was a measure of the strength and virtue of that society.[53] The U.S. criminal justice system rests on values that are fundamental to our legal system and the highest ideals of American culture. Equality before the law, rules of fundamental fairness, standards of dignity, and the hope of rehabilitation and reform are enduring principles that have guided efforts to create a system that truly delivers "justice for all." In this text, we have seen many efforts to bring the daily reality of the criminal justice system into alignment with these high ideals: the struggle for equal enforcement and protection of the law for minorities, the criminalization of violence against women, the inclusion of minorities and women as justice professionals, and the attainment of rights for victims to be treated with dignity and respect. Social movements of the twenty-first century will extend efforts of the past and new movements will arise to seek transformation of the justice system. The one prediction we can make for certain is that the criminal justice system will continue to change. As citizens and future justice professionals, every reader of this text can choose to participate in defining what justice will mean for future generations.

KEY TERMS

probation p. 316
parole p. 316
benefit of clergy p. 316
judicial reprieve p. 316
ticket of leave p. 317
good time laws p. 317
presentence investigation
   and report p. 318
conditions of probation p. 318
role strain p. 319
revocation of probation p. 319
parole board p. 319
parole eligibility p. 319

statutory good time p. 320
earned good time p. 320
unconditional mandatory
   release p. 320
revocation of parole p. 320
diversion p. 321
formal diversion p. 321
net widening p. 321
"true" diversion p. 321
recidivism p. 322
intermediate sanctions p. 322
intensive supervision
   probation p. 323

day reporting centers p. 323
house arrest p. 323
electronic monitoring p. 324
shock incarceration p. 324
boot camp p. 324
restorative justice p. 324
community justice p. 324
community service p. 325
victim–offender mediation p. 326
reparative boards p. 326
family group conferencing p. 327
circle programs p. 327

REVIEW AND STUDY QUESTIONS

1. Describe the origins of the probation function. From what Latin term does the word "probation" come, and what does it mean? Identify the primary goal of the founder of the probation function.

2. Describe the origins of the parole function. From what French term does the word derive? Explain the "ticket of leave" practice.

3. Describe the two key functions of the probation officer's job. Define the concept of role strain and explain why there is an inherent conflict in the probation officer's job. Describe the key functions of the parole officer today. What is the job of the parole board?

4. Define standard conditions of probation and parole. What does revocation of parole or probation mean?

5. Identify the three distinct periods of expansion and development in community corrections. Identify the key goals for community corrections in each period.

6. What is diversion? What is the difference between "true" diversion and formal diversion? Explain the

concept of net widening. Explain why net widening undermines achievement of the goals of community corrections.

7. What are intermediate sanctions? Describe the practices of ISP, boot camps, and day reporting centers. How do these sanctions differ from traditional probation or traditional incarceration?

8. Explain the distinctive goals of community and restorative justice programs compared to the intermediate sanctions movement and the diversion movement. What is community service, and how is it related to the philosophy of restorative justice?

9. What is a community court? Demonstrate how the community court takes a problem-solving approach to crime.

10. Describe the key practices of restorative justice: victim–offender mediation, family group conferencing, boards, and circles. Explain how these practices involve victims and the community in the justice process.

CHECK IT OUT

On the Web

American Probation and Parole Association, **www. appa-net.org**
A very useful Web site with access to free publications, information about best practices in probation and parole, and lots of great links for practitioners.

Community Justice Exchange, **www.comunityjustice.org**
The Community Justice Exchange provides information and assistance to help bring together criminal justice agencies and ordinary citizens to make communities

safer. Click on "Community Courts" to learn more about problem-solving and community courts.

Center for Restorative Justice and Mediation, **ssw.che. umn.edu**
This Web site offers access to a wide range of information about restorative justice and victim–offender mediation, including recent evaluation and research on programs across the country and around the world. There are also many links to other good restorative justice and community justice Web sites.

Real Justice, **www.realjustice.org**
This nonprofit organization is devoted to the promotion of the conferencing method of restorative justice in North America. A wealth of information about the origins of family group conferencing and its uses in the criminal justice and other settings is provided.

On Film

Life after Prison: Success on the Outside (42 minutes)
Award-winning program that talks to parolees about success and failure after prison and examines the specific steps needed to transition successfully to life on the outside.

High Risk Offender (58 minutes)
A powerful look at the relationship between six offenders and their parole officer and therapists as they struggle to

remain on the right side of the law. Offenders range from white-collar offenders to armed robbers to murderers, who provide a tough look at the unique problems and situations of the parole officer and his clients. Winner of Gold Apple Award. Available from First Run-Icarus Films, **www.frif.com.**

Exploring Alternatives to Prison and Probation (22 minutes)
A look at the range of innovative solutions being tried around the country, including community service, house arrest with electronic monitoring, boot camp, and intensive supervised probation. Available from Filmakers Library, **www.filmakers.com.**

NOTES

1. Kay Harvey, "One Victim's 'Wakeup Call' Produces Reconciliation," *Saint Paul (Minnesota) Pioneer Press,* October 29, 1995, p. 11-A.
2. Darrol Bussler and Mark E. Carey, with William DuBois, "Coming Full Circle: A County-Community Restorative Justice Partnership," in William DuBois and R. Dean Wright, eds., *Applying Sociology: Making a Better World,* (Boston: Allyn & Bacon, 2001), p. 140.
3. Ibid., p. 141.
4. Ibid.
5. Ibid.
6. Ibid.
7. Ibid., p. 142.
8. Ibid.
9. Robert B. Coates, Mark Umbreit, and Betty Vos, *Restorative Justice Circles in South St. Paul, Minnesota,* Research Monograph (Minneapolis, MN: Center for Restorative Justice and Peacemaking, University of Minnesota, August 2000), p. 15.
10. Bussler and Carey, "Coming Full Circle," p. 146.
11. Ibid.
12. Coates et al., *Restorative Justice Circles,* p. 24.
13. with Kay Pranis, Restorative Justice Planner, Department of Corrections, Minnesota, personal interview, February, 11, 2002.
14. Bureau of Justice Statistics, *Probation and Parole in 1999* (Washington, DC: U.S. Department of Justice, 2000), p. 3.
15. Todd R. Clear and David R. Karp, *The Community Justice Ideal: Preventing Crime and Achieving Justice* (Boulder, CO: Westview, 1999), p. 21.
16. Todd R. Clear and George F. Cole, *American Corrections,* 3rd ed. (Belmont, CA: Wadsworth, 1994), pp. 173–175.
17. Ex parte United States, 242 U.S. (1916).
18. Samuel Walker, *Popular Justice: A History of American Criminal Justice* (New York: Oxford University Press, 1980), pp. 87–89.
19. Ibid., p. 88.
20. Ibid., p. 95.
21. Lawrence M. Friedman, *Crime and Punishment in American History* (New York: Basic Books, 1993), pp. 161–162.
22. Clear and Cole, *American Corrections,* p. 407.
23. Bureau of Justice Statistics, *Probation and Parole in 1999,* p. 3.
24. Bureau of Justice Statistics, *Felony Sentences in State Courts, 1996,* Bulletin NCJ-173939 (Washington, DC: U.S. Department of Justice, May 1999), p. 2.
25. Carl B. Klockars, Jr., "A Theory of Probation Supervision," *The Journal of Criminal Law, Criminology and Police Science* 63 (1972), pp. 550–557.
26. Clear and Cole, *American Corrections,* p. 417–422.
27. Ann L. Pastore and Kathleen Maguire, eds., *Sourcebook on Criminal Justice Statistics, 1999* (Washington, DC: U.S. Government Printing Office, 2000), p. 534.
28. Ibid.
29. *Greenholtz v. Inmates of Nebraska Penal and Correctional Complex,* 422 U.S. 1 (1979).
30. Pastore and Maguire, eds., *Sourcebook on Criminal Justice Statistics, 1999,* p. 484.
31. Todd R. Clear and Edward J. Latessa, "Surveillance v. Control: Probation Officers Roles in Intensive Supesrvision," *Justice Quarterly* 10 (1993), pp. 441–462.
32. Coates et al., *Restorative Justice Circles,* p. 3.
33. President's Crime Commission, *The Challenge of Crime in a Free Society* (Washington, DC: U.S. Government Printing Office, 1967).
34. Samuel Walker, *Sense and Nonsense about Crime and Drugs* (Belmont, CA: Wadsworth, 1998), p. 207.
35. Stanley Cohen, *Visions of Social Control,* (Cambridge, UK,: Polity Press, 1985), pp. 50–56.
36. Thomas G. Blomberg, "Widening the Net: An Anomaly in the Evaluation of Diversion Programs," in Malcom Klein and K. S. Teilman, eds., *Handbook of Criminal Justice Evaluation* (Beverly Hills, CA: Sage, 1980), pp. 571–592.
37. Andrew Scull, "Community Corrections: Panacea, Progress or Pretence?," in David Garland and Peter Young, eds., *The Power to Punish* (London: Heinemann, 1983).

38. Norval Morris and Michael Tonry, *Between Prison and Probation: Intermediate Punishments in a Rational Sentencing System* (New York: Oxford University Press, 1990).

39. Ibid., p. 6.

40. Joan Petersilia, "A Decade of Experimenting with Intermediate Sanctions: What Have We Learned?," *Federal Probation 62* (1998), pp. 3–9.

41. Joan Petersilia, Susan Turner, James Kahan, and Joyce Peterson, *Granting Felons Probation* (Santa Monica, CA: Rand, 1985).

42. John F. Larivee, "Day-Reporting in Massachusetts," in Michael Tonry and Kate Hamilton, eds., *Intermediate Sanctions in Overcrowded Times* (Boston: Northeastern University Press, 1995), pp. 128–130.

43. Terry L. Baumer and Michael G. Maxfield, "Electronically Monitored Home Detention," in Tonry and Hamilton, eds., *Intermediate Sanctions in Overcrowded Times*, pp. 104–108.

44. J. Robert Lilly, "Electronic Monitoring in the U.S.," in Tonry and Hamilton, eds., *Intermediate Sanctions in Overcrowded Times*, pp. 113–114.

45. Doris Layton MacKenzie and Claire Souryal, *Multisite Evaluation of Shock Incarceration, National Institute of Justice Research Report* (Washington, DC: U.S. Government Printing Office, 1994).

46. "Partial and Short-Term Confinement: Introduction," in Tonry and Hamilton, eds., *Intermediate Sanctions in Overcrowded Times*, p. 121.

47. Dale G. Parent, "Boot Camps Failing to Achieve Goals," in Tonry and Hamilton, eds., *Intermediate Sanctions in Overcrowded Times*, pp. 139–147.

48. Gordon Bazemore and Dennis Malony, "Rehabilitating Community Service: Toward Restorative Service Sanctions in a Balanced Justice System," *Federal Probation 58* (1999), pp. 24–35.

49. John Feinblatt and Michele Sviridoff, "The Midtown Community Court Experiment," in Robert P. McNamara, ed., *Sex, Scams and Street Life: The Sociology of New York City's Times Square* (Westport, CT: Praeger, 1995), pp. 83–96.

50. Clear and Karp, *The Community Justice Ideals*, p. 167.

51. Michael E. Smith, "What Future for 'Public Safety' and 'Restorative Justice' in Community Corrections?," *Sentencing and Corrections: Issues for the 21st Century 11* (2001), pp. 1–7.

52. Kay Pranis, "Getting Started: Community Organizing for Criminal Justice Circles," (Minneapolis, MN: Minnesota Department of Corrections, 1999), P. 1.

53. Robert James, ed, *Winston S. Churchill: His Complete Speeches, 1897–1903* (New York: Chelsea House, 1974) p. 1598.

APPENDIX A

THE BILL OF RIGHTS

The First Ten Amendments to the U.S. Constitution

Amendment I

Congress shall make no law respecting an establishment of religion, or prohibiting the free exercise thereof; or abridging the freedom of speech, or of the press; or the right of the people peaceably to assemble, and to petition the government for a redress of grievances.

Amendment II

A well regulated militia, being necessary to the security of a free state, the right of the people to keep and bear arms, shall not be infringed.

Amendment III

No soldier shall, in time of peace be quartered in any house, without the consent of the owner, nor in time of war, but in a manner to be prescribed by law.

Amendment IV

The right of the people to be secure in their persons, houses, papers, and effects, against unreasonable searches and seizures, shall not be violated, and no warrants shall issue, but upon probable cause, supported by oath or affirmation, and particularly describing the place to be searched, and the persons or things to be seized.

Amendment V

No person shall be held to answer for a capital, or otherwise infamous crime, unless on a presentment or indictment of a grand jury, except in cases arising in the land or naval forces, or in the militia, when in actual service in time of war or public danger; nor shall any person be subject for the same offense to be twice put in jeopardy of life or limb; nor shall be compelled in any criminal case to be a witness against himself, nor be deprived of life, liberty, or property, without due process of law; nor shall private property be taken for public use, without just compensation.

Amendment VI

In all criminal prosecutions, the accused shall enjoy the right to a speedy and public trial, by an impartial jury of the state and district wherein the crime shall have been committed, which district shall have been previously ascertained by law, and to be informed of the nature and cause of the accusation; to be confronted with the witnesses against him; to have compulsory process for obtaining witnesses in his favor, and to have the assistance of counsel for his defense.

Amendment VII

In suits at common law, where the value in controversy shall exceed twenty dollars, the right of trial by jury shall be preserved, and no fact tried by a jury, shall be otherwise reexamined in any court of the United States, than according to the rules of the common law.

Amendment VIII
Excessive bail shall not be required, nor excessive fines imposed, nor cruel and unusual punishments inflicted.

Amendment IX
The enumeration in the Constitution, of certain rights, shall not be construed to deny or disparage others retained by the people.

Amendment X
The powers not delegated to the United States by the Constitution, nor prohibited by it to the states, are reserved to the states respectively, or to the people.

APPENDIX B

AMENDMENT XIV TO THE U.S. CONSTITUTION

Section 1.   All persons born or naturalized in the United States, and subject to the jurisdiction thereof, are citizens of the United States and of the state wherein they reside. No state shall make or enforce any law which shall abridge the privileges or immunities of citizens of the United States; nor shall any state deprive any person of life, liberty, or property, without due process of law; nor deny to any person within its jurisdiction the equal protection of the laws.

Section 2.   Representatives shall be apportioned among the several states according to their respective numbers, counting the whole number of persons in each state, excluding Indians not taxed. But when the right to vote at any election for the choice of electors for President and Vice President of the United States, Representatives in Congress, the executive and judicial officers of a state, or the members of the legislature thereof, is denied to any of the male inhabitants of such state, being twenty-one years of age, and citizens of the United States, or in any way abridged, except for participation in rebellion, or other crime, the basis of representation therein shall be reduced in the proportion which the number of such male citizens shall bear to the whole number of male citizens twenty-one years of age in such state.

Section 3.   No person shall be a Senator or Representative in Congress, or elector of President and Vice President, or hold any office, civil or military, under the United States, or under any state, who, having previously taken an oath, as a member of Congress, or as an officer of the United States, or as a member of any state legislature, or as an executive or judicial officer of any state, to support the Constitution of the United States, shall have engaged in insurrection or rebellion against the same, or given aid or comfort to the enemies thereof. But Congress may by a vote of two-thirds of each House, remove such disability.

Section 4.   The validity of the public debt of the United States, authorized by law, including debts incurred for payment of pensions and bounties for services in suppressing insurrection or rebellion, shall not be questioned. But neither the United States nor any state shall assume or pay any debt or obligation incurred in aid of insurrection or rebellion against the United States, or any claim for the loss or emancipation of any slave; but all such debts, obligations and claims shall be held illegal and void.

Section 5.   The Congress shall have power to enforce, by appropriate legislation, the provisions of this article.

APPENDIX C

VICTIM'S BILL OF RIGHTS

A 1986 amendment to the Rhode Island Constitution guarantees the rights of crime victims. It requires that victims be treated with dignity and respect during the criminal justice process, that victims be entitled to compensation for injury or loss, and that a victim shall have the right to address the court before sentencing.

The Victim's Bill of Rights, which became law in 1983, guarantees certain rights to the victim of a crime who makes a timely report and who cooperates with law enforcement authorities in the investigation and prosecution of the case, as well as the immediate family of a person who has died or who has become incapacitated as the result of a crime.

A Victim's Rights Are

- to be notified of the status of the investigation, to be notified of a defendant's arraignment and release.
- to be protected from harm and threats of harm because of cooperation in the prosecution of a case.
- to be notified of all court proceedings where the victim's presence is required . . . and to be notified of the cancellation of proceedings.
- to be informed about the procedure to follow to receive a witness fee.
- to have efforts made on the victim's behalf so that loss of pay because of court appearances is minimized.
- to be provided, when possible, with a secure waiting area during court proceedings.
- to have personal property promptly returned when it is no longer needed as evidence.
- to be informed of financial assistance and other social services available and to be informed of the Crime Victim Compensation Program and how to apply.
- to have a victim impact statement inserted in the case file and presented to the court for review before a plea agreement is accepted.
- to address the court about the impact of the crime before a plea agreement is accepted or before a sentence is imposed after a trial.
- to be consulted by probation and parole officials in preparation of a pre-sentence report.
- to be informed of the disposition of the case.
- to be notified when the inmate responsible for the crime is to appear before the parole board so the victim can address the parole board.
- to be notified when a defendant is released from custody at the Adult Correctional Institution.
- to be informed of the right to request restitution.

Source: Rhode Island Department of Attorney General, *http://www.riag.state.ri.us/victim/vbor.html* (February 21, 2002).

AUTHOR INDEX

SUBJECT INDEX

PHOTO CREDITS